한국의 토익 수험자 여러분께,

토익 시험은 세계적인 직무 영어능력 평가 시험으로, 지난 40여 년간 비즈니스 현장에서 필요한 영어능력 평가의 기준을 제시해 왔습니다. 토익 시험 및 토익스피킹, 토익라이팅 시험은 세계에서 가장 널리 통용되는 영어능력 검증 시험으로, 160여 개국 14,000여 기관이 토익 성적을 의사결정에 활용하고 있습니다.

YBM은 한국의 토익 시험을 주관하는 ETS 독점 계약사입니다.

ETS는 한국 수험자들의 효과적인 토익 학습을 돕고자 YBM을 통하여 'ETS 토익 공식 교재'를 독점 출간하고 있습니다. 또한 'ETS 토익 공식 교재' 시리즈에 기출문항을 제공해 한국의 다른 교재들에 수록된 기출을 복제하거나 변형한 문항으로 인하여 발생할 수 있는 수험자들의 혼동을 방지하고 있습니다.

복제 및 변형 문항들은 토익 시험의 출제의도를 벗어날 수 있기 때문에 기출문항을 수록한 'ETS 토익 공식 교재'만큼 시험에 잘 대비할 수 없습니다.

'ETS 토익 공식 교재'를 통하여 수험자 여러분의 영어 소통을 위한 노력에 큰 성취가 있기를 바랍니다.

감사합니다.

Dear TOEIC Test Takers in Korea,

The TOEIC program is the global leader in English-language assessment for the workplace. It has set the standard for assessing English-language skills needed in the workplace for more than 40 years. The TOEIC tests are the most widely used English language assessments around the world, with 14,000+ organizations across more than 160 countries trusting TOEIC scores to make decisions.

YBM is the ETS Country Master Distributor for the TOEIC program in Korea and so is the exclusive distributor for TOEIC Korea.

To support effective learning for TOEIC test-takers in Korea, ETS has authorized YBM to publish the only Official TOEIC prep books in Korea. These books contain actual TOEIC items to help prevent confusion among Korean test-takers that might be caused by other prep book publishers' use of reproduced or paraphrased items.

Reproduced or paraphrased items may fail to reflect the intent of actual TOEIC items and so will not prepare test-takers as well as the actual items contained in the ETS TOEIC Official prep books published by YBM.

We hope that these ETS TOEIC Official prep books enable you, as test-takers, to achieve great success in your efforts to communicate effectively in English.

Thank you.

입문부터 실전까지 수준별 학습을 통해 최단기 목표점수 달성!

ETS TOEIC® 공식수험서 스마트 학습 지원

www.ybmbooks.com에서도 무료 MP3를 다운로드 받을 수 있습니다.

ETS 토익 모바일 학습 플랫폼!
ETS 토익기출 수험서 앱

구글플레이　앱스토어

교재 학습 지원
- LC 음원 MP3
- 교재 해설 동영상 강의
- 교재/부록 모의고사 채점 분석
- 단어 암기장

부가 서비스
- 데일리 학습(토익 기출문제 풀이)
- 토익 최신 경향 무료 특강
- 토익 타이머

모의고사 결과 분석
- 파트별/문항별 정답률
- 파트별/유형별 취약점 리포트
- 전체 응시자 점수 분포도

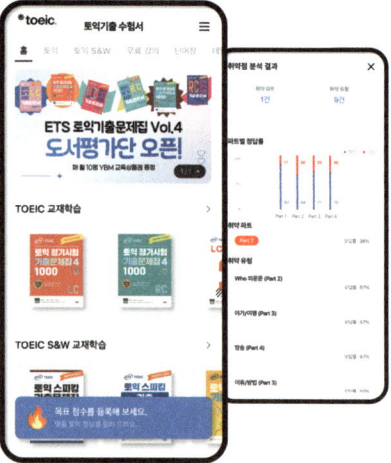

ETS 토익 학습 전용 온라인 커뮤니티!
ETS TOEIC® Book 공식카페

etstoeicbook.co.kr

강사진의 학습 지원	토익 대표강사들의 학습 지원과 멘토링
교재 학습관 운영	교재별 학습게시판을 통해 무료 동영상 강의 등 학습 지원
학습 콘텐츠 제공	토익 학습 콘텐츠와 정기시험 예비특강 업데이트

*toeic.

ETS 토익 정기시험
기출문제집 5
1000　LC

발행인	허문호
발행처	YBM

편집	이태경, 정유상, 김유나
디자인	김현경
마케팅	고영노, 김동진, 박찬경, 하재희, 문근호, 고은

초판발행	2025년 12월 15일
2쇄 발행	2025년 12월 26일

신고일자	1964년 3월 28일
신고번호	제 1964-000003호
주소	서울시 종로구 종로 104
전화	(02) 2000-0515 [구입문의] / (02) 2000-0304 [내용문의]
팩스	(02) 2285-1523
홈페이지	www.ybmbooks.com
ISBN	978-89-17-24379-6

ETS, TOEIC and 토익 are registered trademarks of Educational Testing Service, Princeton, New Jersey, U.S.A., used in the Republic of Korea under license. Copyright © 2025 by Educational Testing Service, Princeton, New Jersey, U.S.A. All rights reserved. Reproduced under license for limited use by YBM. These materials are protected by United States Laws, International Copyright Laws and International Treaties. In the event of any discrepancy between this translation and official ETS materials, the terms of the official ETS materials will prevail. All items were created or reviewed by ETS. All item annotations and test-taking tips were reviewed by ETS.

서면에 의한 저자와 출판사의 허락 없이 내용의 일부 혹은 전부를 인용 및 복제하거나 발췌하는 것을 금합니다.
낙장 및 파본은 교환해 드립니다.
구입철회는 구매처 규정에 따라 교환 및 환불처리 됩니다.

ETS 토익 정기시험
기출문제집 5
1000 LC

PREFACE

Dear test taker,

English-language proficiency has become a vital tool for success. It can help you excel in business, travel the world, and communicate effectively with friends and colleagues. The TOEIC® test measures your ability to function effectively in English in these types of situations. Because TOEIC scores are recognized around the world as evidence of your English-language proficiency, you will be able to confidently demonstrate your English skills to employers and begin your journey to success.

The test developers at ETS are excited to help you achieve your personal and professional goals through the use of the ETS TOEIC® 정기시험 기출문제집 1000 Vol. 5. This book contains test questions taken from actual, official TOEIC tests. These questions will help you become familiar with the content and the format of the TOEIC test. This book also contains detailed explanations of the question types and language points contained in the TOEIC test. These test questions and explanations have all been prepared by the same test specialists who develop the actual TOEIC test, so you can be confident that you will receive an authentic test-preparation experience.

Features of the ETS TOEIC® 정기시험 기출문제집 1000 Vol. 5 include the following.

- Ten full-length test forms all accompanied by answer keys and official scripts
- Specific and easy to understand explanations for learners
- The very same ETS voice actors that you will hear in an official TOEIC test

By using the ETS TOEIC® 정기시험 기출문제집 1000 Vol. 5 to prepare for the TOEIC test, you can be assured that you have a professionally prepared resource that will provide you with accurate guidance so that you are more familiar with the tasks, content, and format of the test and that will help you maximize your TOEIC test score. With your official TOEIC score certificate, you will be ready to show the world what you know!

We are delighted to assist you on your TOEIC journey with the ETS TOEIC® 정기시험 기출문제집 1000 Vol. 5 and wish you the best of success.

최신 기출문제 전격 공개!

유일무이 **출제기관이 독점 제공한 기출문제가 담긴 유일한 교재!**
이 책에는 정기시험 기출문제 10세트가 수록되어 있다. 시험에 나온 최신 기출문제로 실전 감각을 키워 시험에 확실하게 대비하자!

국내최고 **정기시험 성우 음성으로 실전 대비!**
이 책에 수록된 10세트의 LC 음원은 모두 실제 시험에서 나온 정기시험 성우의 음원이다. 시험장에서 듣게 될 음성으로 공부하면 까다로운 영국·호주 발음도 걱정 없다.

독점제공 **ETS 제공 표준점수 환산표로 실력 진단!**
출제기관 ETS가 독점 제공하는 표준점수 환산표를 수록했다. 채점 후 환산표를 통해 자신의 실력이 어느 정도인지 가늠해 보자!

스마트 학습 **동영상 강의, 기출어휘 단어장, 채점서비스 무료 제공!**
ETS 토익기출 수험서 앱 다운로드 및 실행 ▶ 토익 ▶ 실전서 ▶ ETS 토익 정기시험 기출문제집 1000 Vol. 5 LC를 클릭해 무료 제공하는 자료로 스마트하게 학습하자!

* ybmbooks.com에서도 단어장 MP3파일, 단어장 PDF, 정답 PDF, 토익 연습용 답안지 PDF 제공

TOEIC 소개

TOEIC Test of English for International Communication(국제적 의사소통을 위한 영어 시험)의 약자로, 영어가 모국어가 아닌 사람들이 일상생활 또는 비즈니스 현장에서 꼭 필요한 실용적 영어 구사 능력을 갖추었는가를 평가하는 시험이다.

시험 구성

구성	PART	유형		문항 수	시간	배점
Listening	Part 1	사진 묘사		6	45분	495점
	Part 2	질의 응답		25		
	Part 3	짧은 대화		39		
	Part 4	짧은 담화		30		
Reading	Part 5	단문 빈칸 채우기		30	75분	495점
	Part 6	장문 빈칸 채우기		16		
	Part 7	독해	단일 지문	29		
			이중 지문	10		
			삼중 지문	15		
Total	7 Parts			200문항	120분	990점

평가 항목

LC	RC
단문을 듣고 이해하는 능력	읽은 글을 통해 추론해 생각할 수 있는 능력
짧은 대화체 문장을 듣고 이해하는 능력	장문에서 특정한 정보를 찾을 수 있는 능력
비교적 긴 대화체에서 주고받은 내용을 파악할 수 있는 능력	글의 목적, 주제, 의도 등을 파악하는 능력
장문에서 핵심이 되는 정보를 파악할 수 있는 능력	뜻이 유사한 단어들의 정확한 용례를 파악하는 능력
구나 문장에서 화자의 목적이나 함축된 의미를 이해하는 능력	문장 구조를 제대로 파악하는지, 문장에서 필요한 품사, 어구 등을 찾는 능력

※ 성적표에는 전체 수험자의 평균과 해당 수험자가 받은 성적이 백분율로 표기되어 있다.

수험 정보

시험 접수

시험 약 2개월 전부터 아래와 같은 방법으로 접수할 수 있다.
인터넷 접수: TOEIC위원회 공식 홈페이지(https://exam.toeic.co.kr)를 통해 접수
모바일 접수: TOEIC위원회 공식 애플리케이션 또는 모바일 웹사이트
　　　　　　(https://m.exam.toeic.co.kr)를 통해 접수

시험장 준비물

신분증	규정 신분증만 가능 (주민등록증, 운전면허증, 기간 만료 전의 여권, 공무원증 등)
필기구	연필, 지우개 (볼펜이나 사인펜은 사용 금지)

시험 진행 시간

09:20	입실 (9:50 이후 입실 불가)
09:30 ~ 09:45	답안지 작성에 관한 오리엔테이션
09:45 ~ 09:50	휴식
09:50 ~ 10:05	신분증 확인
10:05 ~ 10:10	문제지 배부 및 파본 확인
10:10 ~ 10:55	듣기 평가 (LISTENING TEST)
10:55 ~ 12:10	독해 평가 (READING TEST)

성적 확인

성적은 TOEIC 홈페이지에 안내된 성적 발표일에 인터넷 홈페이지, 애플리케이션을 통해 확인 가능하다. 최초 성적표 발급은 우편 또는 온라인을 통해 수령 가능하며, 재발급은 성적 유효기간(시험 시행일로부터 2년) 내에만 가능하다. 단, 유효기간은 공공기관에 한하여 2023년 4월부터 5년으로 연장되었다.

토익 점수

TOEIC 점수는 듣기 영역(LC) 점수와 읽기 영역(RC) 점수, 그리고 두 영역을 합계한 전체 점수로 구성된다. 각 영역의 점수는 5점 단위로 5점에서 495점까지 주어지고, 두 영역을 합계한 전체 점수는 10점에서 990점까지 주어진다. TOEIC 성적은 각 문제 유형의 난이도에 따른 점수 환산표에 의해 결정된다.

토익 경향 분석

PART 1 사진 묘사 Photographs

총 6문제

1인 등장 사진
주어는 He/She, A man/woman 등이며 주로 앞부분에 나온다.

2인 이상 등장 사진
주어는 They, Some men/women/people, One of the men/women 등이며 주로 중간 부분에 나온다.

사물/배경 사진
주어는 A car, Some chairs 등이며 주로 뒷부분에 나온다.

사람 또는 사물 중심 사진
주어가 일부는 사람, 일부는 사물이며 주로 뒷부분에 나온다.

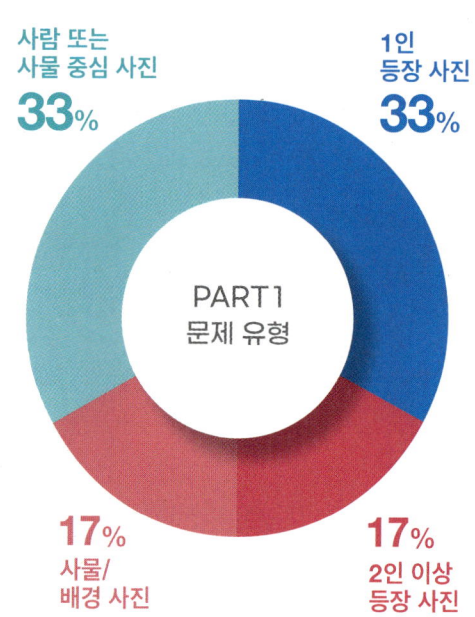

PART 1 문제 유형
- 1인 등장 사진 33%
- 2인 이상 등장 사진 17%
- 사물/배경 사진 17%
- 사람 또는 사물 중심 사진 33%

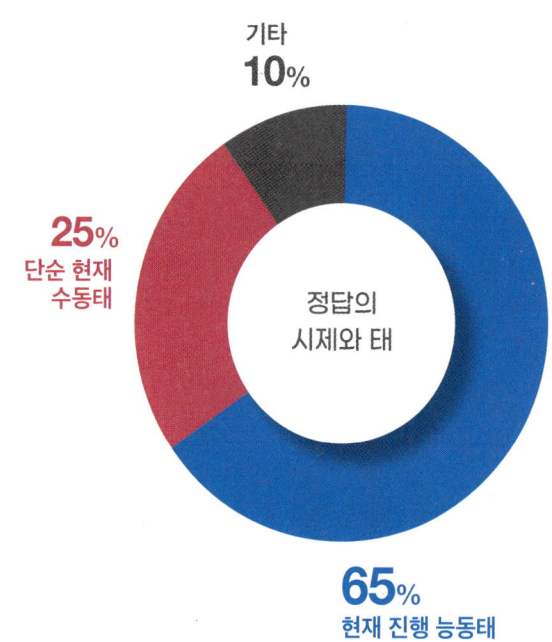

정답의 시제와 태
- 현재 진행 능동태 65%
- 단순 현재 수동태 25%
- 기타 10%

현재 진행 능동태
<is/are + 현재분사> 형태이며 주로 사람이 주어이다.

단순 현재 수동태
<is/are + 과거분사> 형태이며 주로 사물이 주어이다.

기타
<is/are + being + 과거분사> 형태의 현재 진행 수동태, <has/have + been + 과거분사> 형태의 현재 완료 수동태, '타동사 + 목적어' 형태의 단순 현재 능동태, There is/are와 같은 단순 현재도 나온다.

PART 2 질의 응답 Question-Response

총 25문제

평서문
질문이 아니라 객관적인 사실이나 화자의 의견 등을 나타내는 문장이다.

의문사 의문문
각 의문사마다 1~2개씩 나온다. 의문사가 단독으로 나오기도 하지만 What time ~?, How long ~?, Which room ~? 등과 같이 다른 명사나 형용사와 같이 나오기도 한다.

명령문
동사원형이나 Please 등으로 시작한다.

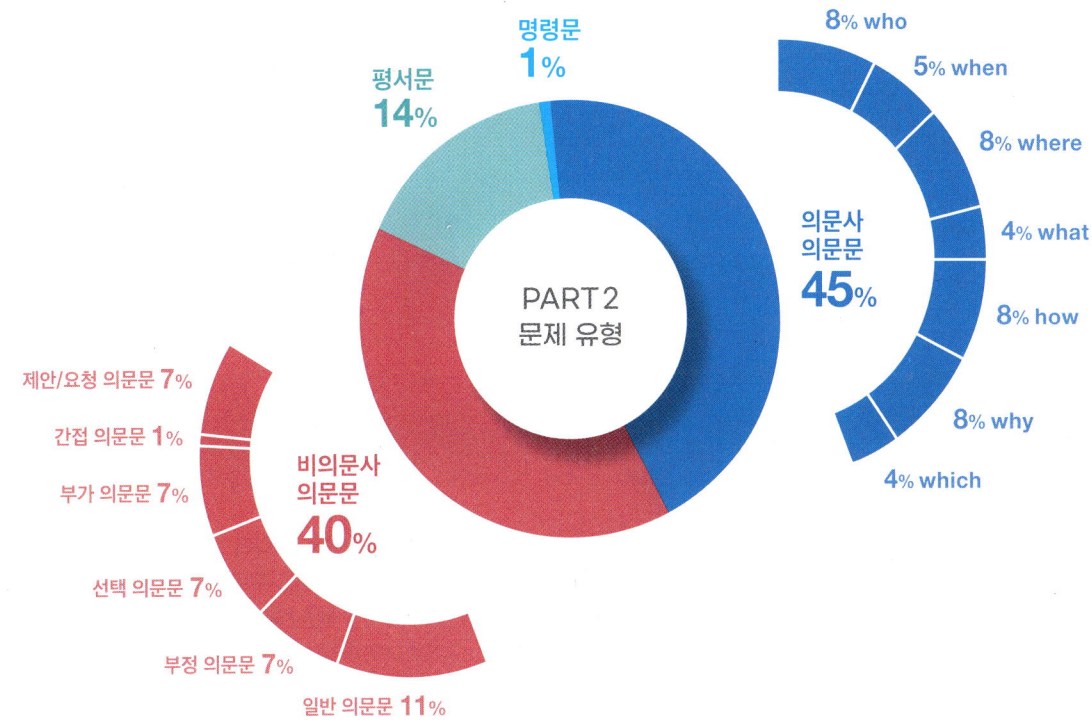

비의문사 의문문
일반 의문문 적게 나올 때는 1~2개, 많이 나올 때는 3~4개씩 나오는 편이다.
부정 의문문 Don't you ~?, Isn't he ~? 등으로 시작하는 문장이며 일반 긍정 의문문보다는 약간 더 적게 나온다.
선택 의문문 A or B 형태로 나오며 A와 B의 형태가 단어, 구, 절일 수 있다.
부가 의문문 ~ don't you?, ~ isn't he? 등으로 끝나는 문장이며, 일반 부정 의문문과 비슷하다고 볼 수 있다.
간접 의문문 의문사가 문장 앞이 아니라 문장 중간에 들어 있다.
제안/요청 의문문 정보를 얻기보다는 상대방의 도움이나 동의 등을 얻기 위한 목적이 일반적이다.

토익 경향 분석

PART 3 짧은 대화 Short Conversations

총 13대화문 39문제 (지문당 3문제)

- 3인 대화의 경우 남자 화자 두 명과 여자 화자 한 명 또는 남자 화자 한 명과 여자 화자 두 명이 나온다. 따라서 문제에서는 2인 대화에서와 달리 the man이나 the woman이 아니라 the men이나 the women 또는 특정한 이름이 언급될 수 있다.

- 대화 & 시각 정보는 항상 파트의 뒷부분에 나온다.

- 시각 정보의 유형으로는 chart, map, floor plan, schedule, table, weather forecast, directory, list, invoice, receipt, sign, packing slip 등 다양한 자료가 골고루 나온다.

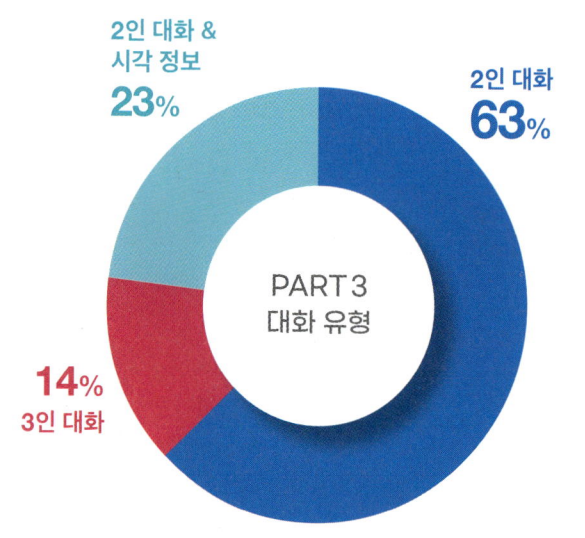

PART 3 대화 유형
- 2인 대화 63%
- 2인 대화 & 시각 정보 23%
- 3인 대화 14%

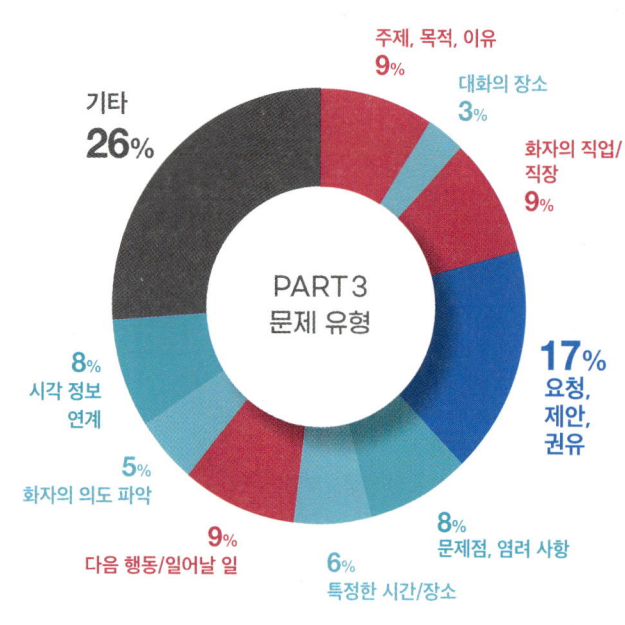

PART 3 문제 유형
- 요청, 제안, 권유 17%
- 기타 26%
- 주제, 목적, 이유 9%
- 대화의 장소 3%
- 화자의 직업/직장 9%
- 문제점, 염려 사항 8%
- 특정한 시간/장소 6%
- 다음 행동/일어날 일 9%
- 화자의 의도 파악 5%
- 시각 정보 연계 8%

- 주제, 목적, 이유, 대화의 장소, 화자의 직업/직장 등과 관련된 문제는 주로 대화의 첫 번째 문제로 나오며 다음 행동/일어날 일 등과 관련된 문제는 주로 대화의 세 번째 문제로 나온다.

- 화자의 의도 파악 문제는 주로 2인 대화에 나오지만, 가끔 3인 대화에 나오기도 한다. 시각 정보 연계 대화에는 나오지 않고 있다.

- Part 3에서 화자의 의도 파악 문제는 2개가 나오고 시각 정보 연계 문제는 3개가 나온다.

PART 4 짧은 담화 Short Talks

총 10담화문 30문제 (지문당 3문제)

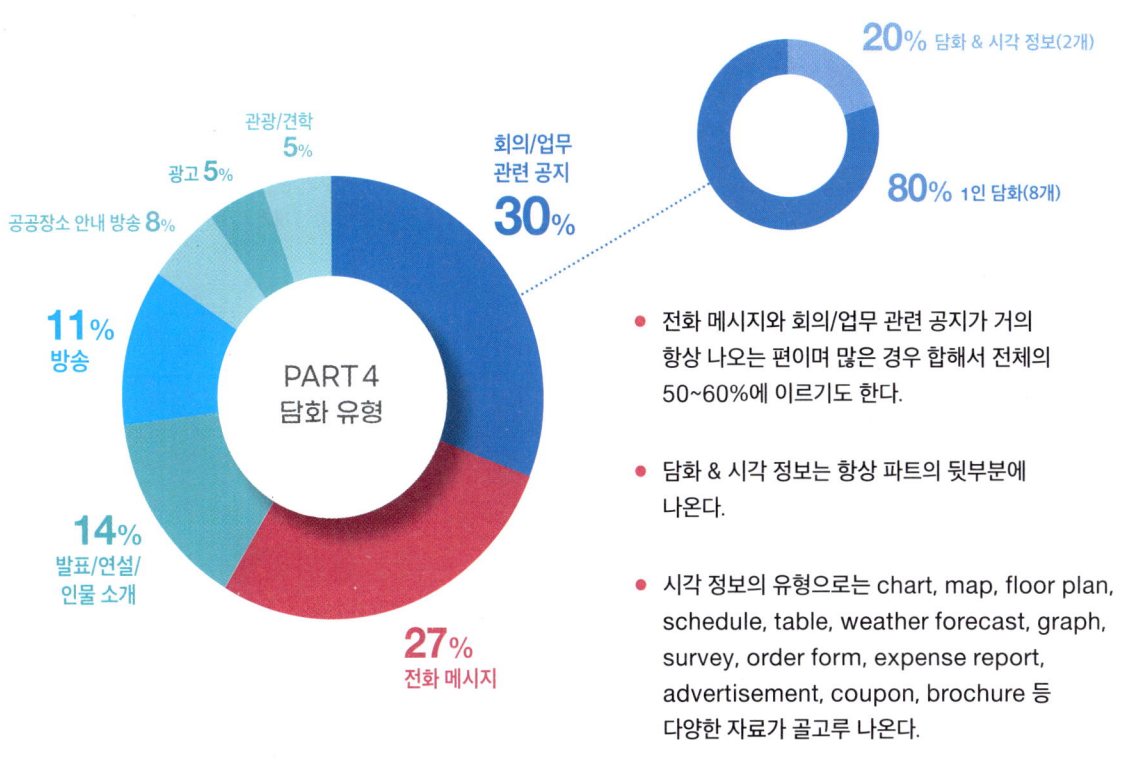

- 전화 메시지와 회의/업무 관련 공지가 거의 항상 나오는 편이며 많은 경우 합해서 전체의 50~60%에 이르기도 한다.

- 담화 & 시각 정보는 항상 파트의 뒷부분에 나온다.

- 시각 정보의 유형으로는 chart, map, floor plan, schedule, table, weather forecast, graph, survey, order form, expense report, advertisement, coupon, brochure 등 다양한 자료가 골고루 나온다.

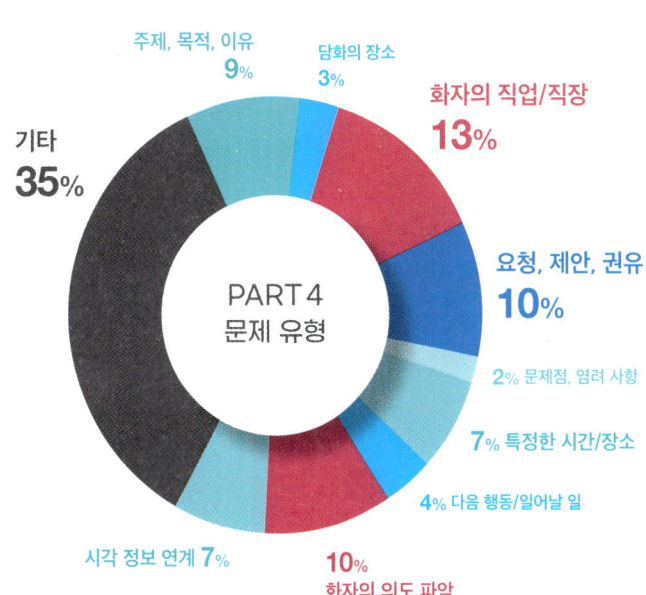

- 문제 유형은 기본적으로 Part 3과 거의 비슷하다.

- 주제, 목적, 이유, 담화의 장소, 화자의 직업/직장 등과 관련된 문제는 주로 담화의 첫 번째 문제로 나오며 다음 행동/일어날 일 등과 관련된 문제는 주로 담화의 세 번째 문제로 나온다.

- Part 4에서 화자의 의도 파악 문제는 3개가 나오고 시각 정보 연계 문제는 2개가 나온다.

토익 경향 분석

PART 5 단문 빈칸 채우기 Incomplete Sentences 총 30문제

문법 문제
시제와 대명사와 관련된 문법 문제가 2개씩, 한정사와 분사와 관련된 문법 문제가 1개씩 나온다. 시제 문제의 경우 능동태/수동태나 수의 일치와 연계되기도 한다. 그 밖에 한정사, 능동태/수동태, 부정사, 동명사 등과 관련된 문법 문제가 나온다.

어휘 문제
동사, 명사, 형용사, 부사와 관련된 어휘 문제가 각각 2~3개씩 골고루 나온다. 전치사 어휘 문제는 3개씩 꾸준히 나오지만, 접속사나 어구와 관련된 어휘 문제는 나오지 않을 때도 있고 3개가 나올 때도 있다.

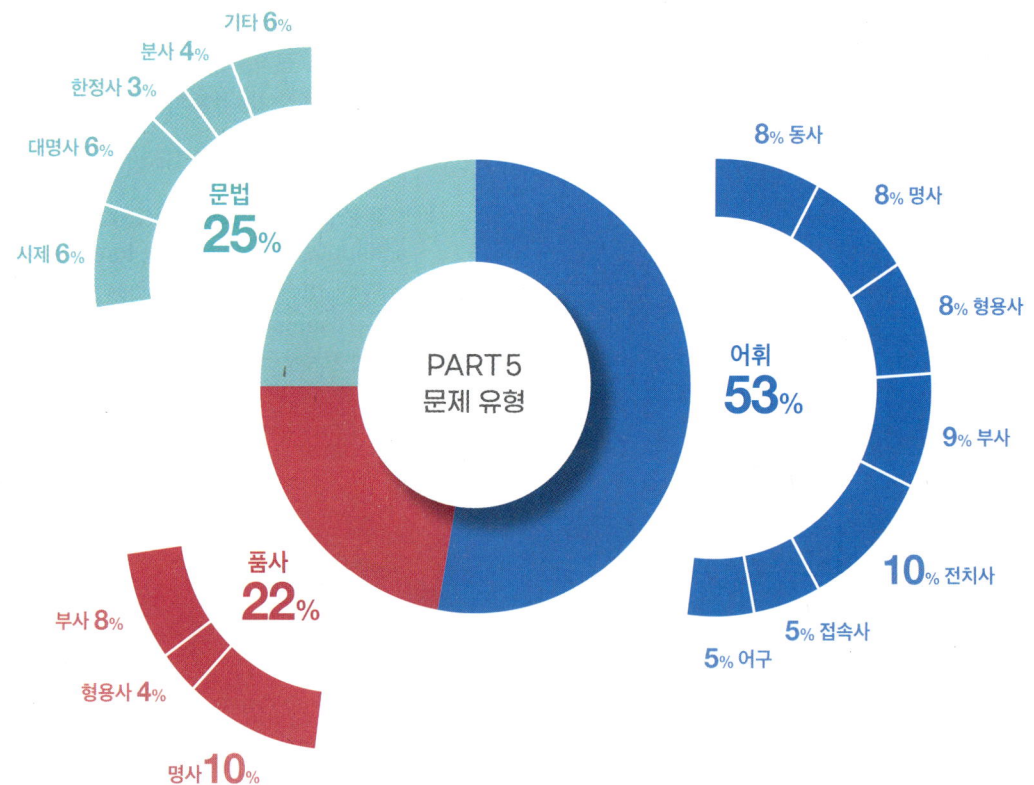

PART 5 문제 유형

문법 25%
- 기타 6%
- 분사 4%
- 한정사 3%
- 대명사 6%
- 시제 6%

어휘 53%
- 8% 동사
- 8% 명사
- 8% 형용사
- 9% 부사
- 10% 전치사
- 5% 접속사
- 5% 어구

품사 22%
- 부사 8%
- 형용사 4%
- 명사 10%

품사 문제
명사와 부사와 관련된 품사 문제가 2~3개씩 나오며, 형용사와 관련된 품사 문제가 상대적으로 적은 편이다.

PART 6 장문 빈칸 채우기 Text Completion

총 4지문 16문제 (지문당 4문제)

한 지문에 4문제가 나오며 평균적으로 어휘 문제가 2개, 품사나 문법 문제가 1개, 문맥에 맞는 문장 고르기 문제가 1개 들어간다. 문맥에 맞는 문장 고르기 문제를 제외하면 문제 유형은 기본적으로 파트 5와 거의 비슷하다.

문맥에 맞는 문장 고르기
문맥에 맞는 문장 고르기 문제는 지문당 한 문제씩 나오는데, 나오는 위치의 확률은 4문제 중 두 번째 문제, 세 번째 문제, 네 번째 문제, 첫 번째 문제 순으로 높다.

어휘 문제
동사, 명사, 부사, 어구와 관련된 어휘 문제는 매번 1~2개씩 나온다. 부사 어휘 문제의 경우 therefore(그러므로)나 however(하지만)처럼 문맥의 흐름을 자연스럽게 연결해 주는 부사가 자주 나온다.

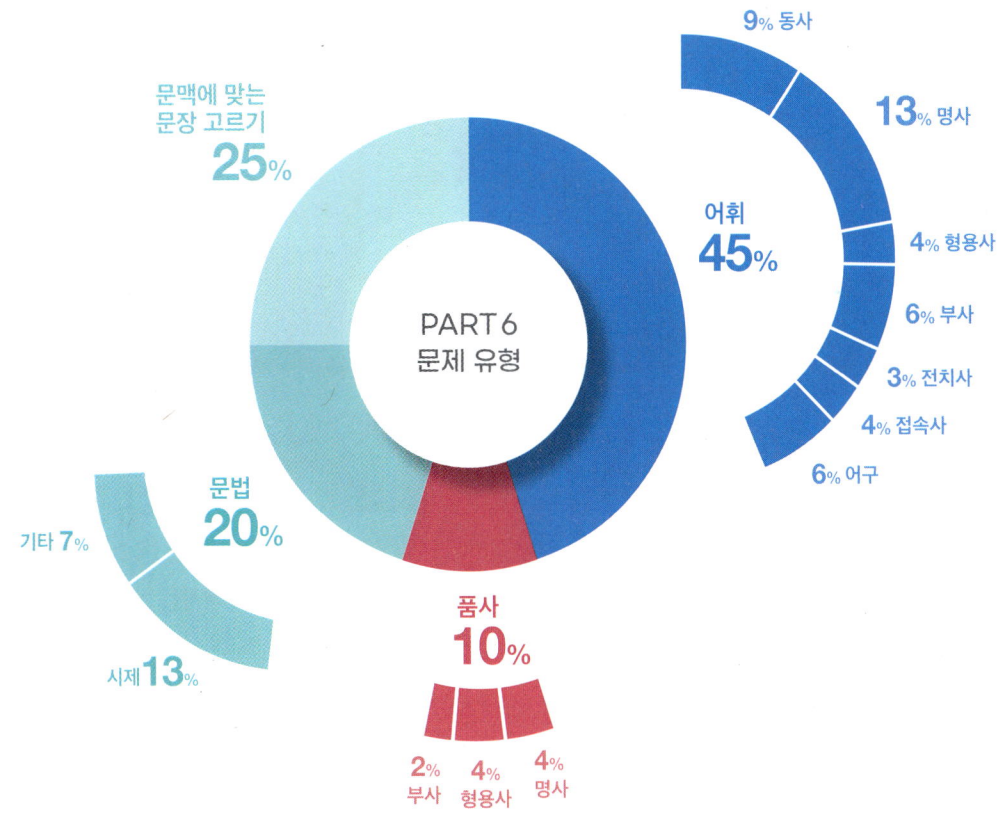

문법 문제
문맥의 흐름과 밀접하게 관련되어 있는 시제 문제가 2개 정도 나오며, 태나 수의 일치와 연계되기도 한다. 그 밖에 대명사, 능동태/수동태, 부정사, 접속사/전치사 등과 관련된 문법 문제가 나온다.

품사 문제
명사나 형용사 문제가 부사 문제보다 좀 더 자주 나온다.

토익 경향 분석

PART 7 독해 Reading Comprehension

지문 유형	지문당 문제 수	지문 개수	비중 %
단일 지문	2문항	4개	약 15%
	3문항	3개	약 16%
	4문항	3개	약 22%
이중 지문	5문항	2개	약 19%
삼중 지문	5문항	3개	약 28%

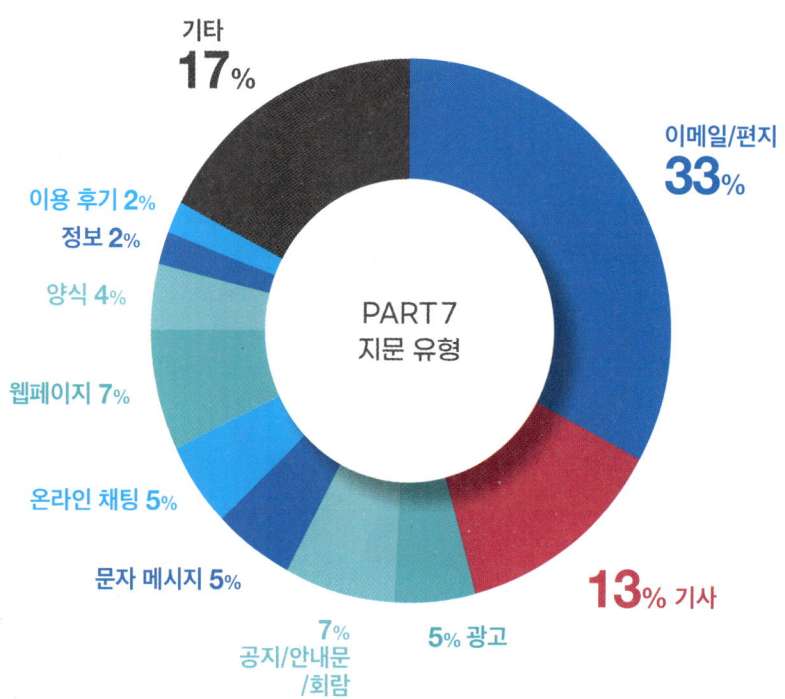

기타 17%
이용 후기 2%
정보 2%
양식 4%
웹페이지 7%
온라인 채팅 5%
문자 메시지 5%
공지/안내문/회람 7%
광고 5%
기사 13%
이메일/편지 33%

PART 7 지문 유형

- 이메일/편지, 기사 유형 지문은 거의 항상 나오는 편이며 많은 경우 합해서 전체의 50~60%에 이르기도 한다.

- 기타 지문 유형으로 agenda, brochure, comment card, coupon, flyer, instructions, invitation, invoice, list, menu, page from a catalog, policy statement, report, schedule, survey, voucher 등 다양한 자료가 골고루 나온다.

(이중 지문과 삼중 지문 속의 지문들을 모두 낱개로 계산함 - 총 23지문)

총 15지문 54문제 (지문당 2~5문제)

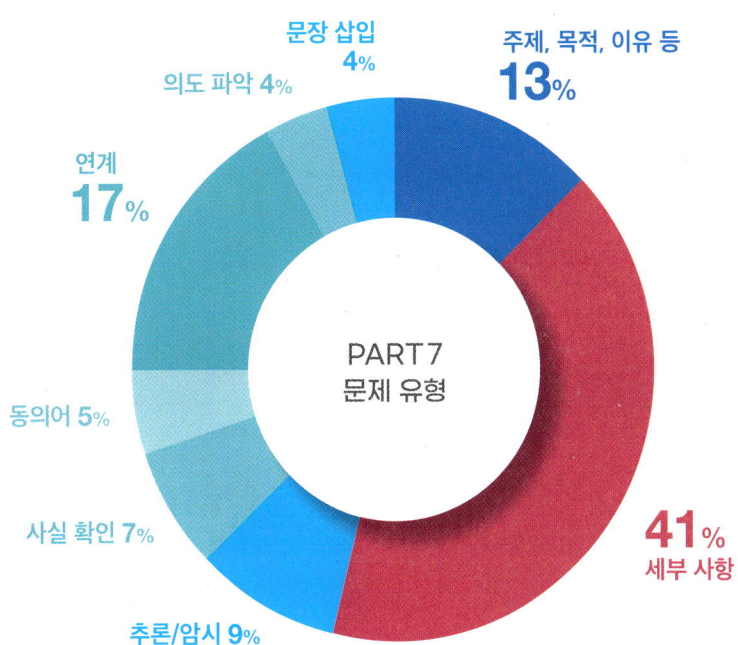

- 동의어 문제는 주로 이중 지문이나 삼중 지문에 나온다.
- 연계 문제는 일반적으로 이중 지문에서 한 문제, 삼중 지문에서 두 문제가 나온다.
- 의도 파악 문제는 문자 메시지(text-message chain)나 온라인 채팅(online chat discussion) 지문에서 출제되며 두 문제가 나온다.
- 문장 삽입 문제는 주로 기사, 이메일, 편지, 회람 지문에서 출제되며 두 문제가 나온다.

점수 환산표 및 산출법

점수 환산표 이 책에 수록된 각 TEST를 풀고 난 후, 맞은 개수를 세어 점수를 환산해 보자.

LISTENING Raw Score (맞은 개수)	LISTENING Scaled Score (환산 점수)	READING Raw Score (맞은 개수)	READING Scaled Score (환산 점수)
96-100	475-495	96-100	460-495
91-95	435-495	91-95	425-490
86-90	405-470	86-90	400-465
81-85	370-450	81-85	375-440
76-80	345-420	76-80	340-415
71-75	320-390	71-75	310-390
66-70	290-360	66-70	285-370
61-65	265-335	61-65	255-340
56-60	240-310	56-60	230-310
51-55	215-280	51-55	200-275
46-50	190-255	46-50	170-245
41-45	160-230	41-45	140-215
36-40	130-205	36-40	115-180
31-35	105-175	31-35	95-150
26-30	85-145	26-30	75-120
21-25	60-115	21-25	60-95
16-20	30-90	16-20	45-75
11-15	5-70	11-15	30-55
6-10	5-60	6-10	10-40
1-5	5-50	1-5	5-30
0	5-35	0	5-15

점수 산출 방법 아래의 방식으로 점수를 산출할 수 있다.

STEP 1

자신의 답안을 수록된 정답과 대조하여 채점한다. 각 Section의 맞은 개수가 본인의 Section별 '실제 점수(통계 처리하기 전의 점수, raw score)'이다. Listening Test와 Reading Test의 정답 수를 세어, 자신의 실제 점수를 아래의 해당란에 기록한다.

	맞은 개수	환산 점수대
LISTENING		
READING		
총점		

Section별 실제 점수가 그대로 Section별 TOEIC 점수가 되는 것은 아니다. TOEIC은 시행할 때마다 별도로 특정한 통계 처리 방법을 사용하며 이러한 실제 점수를 환산 점수(converted[scaled] score)로 전환하게 된다. 이렇게 전환함으로써, 매번 시행될 때마다 문제는 달라지지만 그 점수가 갖는 의미는 같아지게 된다. 예를 들어, 어느 한 시험에서 총점 550점의 성적을 받는 실력이라면 다른 시험에서도 거의 550점대의 성적을 받게 되는 것이다.

STEP 2

실제 점수를 위 표에 기록한 후 왼쪽 페이지의 점수 환산표를 보도록 한다. TOEIC이 시행될 때마다 대개 이와 비슷한 형태의 표가 작성되는데, 여기 제시된 환산표는 본 교재에 수록된 Test용으로 개발된 것이다. 이 표를 사용하여 자신의 실제 점수를 환산 점수로 전환하도록 한다. 즉, 예를 들어 Listening Test의 실제 정답 수가 61~65개이면 환산 점수는 265점에서 335점 사이가 된다. 여기서 실제 정답 수가 61개이면 환산 점수가 265점이고, 65개이면 환산 점수가 335점 임을 의미하는 것은 아니다. 본 책의 Test를 위해 작성된 이 점수 환산표가 자신의 영어 실력이 어느 정도인지 대략적으로 파악하는 데 도움이 되긴 하지만, 이 표가 실제 TOEIC 성적 산출에 그대로 사용된 적은 없다는 사실을 밝혀 둔다.

ETS 토익 정기시험 기출문제집 5
1000 LC

TEST 01
무료 동영상 강의

저자와 출판사의 사전 허락 없이 내용의 일부 혹은 전부를 인용 및 복제하거나 발췌하여 사용할 수 없습니다.

LC
기출 TEST 01

LISTENING TEST

In the Listening test, you will be asked to demonstrate how well you understand spoken English. The entire Listening test will last approximately 45 minutes. There are four parts, and directions are given for each part. You must mark your answers on the separate answer sheet. Do not write your answers in your test book.

PART 1

Directions: For each question in this part, you will hear four statements about a picture in your test book. When you hear the statements, you must select the one statement that best describes what you see in the picture. Then find the number of the question on your answer sheet and mark your answer. The statements will not be printed in your test book and will be spoken only one time.

Statement (C), "They're sitting at a table," is the best description of the picture, so you should select answer (C) and mark it on your answer sheet.

1.

2.

3.

4.

5.

6.

PART 2

Directions: You will hear a question or statement and three responses spoken in English. They will not be printed in your test book and will be spoken only one time. Select the best response to the question or statement and mark the letter (A), (B), or (C) on your answer sheet.

7. Mark your answer on your answer sheet.
8. Mark your answer on your answer sheet.
9. Mark your answer on your answer sheet.
10. Mark your answer on your answer sheet.
11. Mark your answer on your answer sheet.
12. Mark your answer on your answer sheet.
13. Mark your answer on your answer sheet.
14. Mark your answer on your answer sheet.
15. Mark your answer on your answer sheet.
16. Mark your answer on your answer sheet.
17. Mark your answer on your answer sheet.
18. Mark your answer on your answer sheet.
19. Mark your answer on your answer sheet.
20. Mark your answer on your answer sheet.
21. Mark your answer on your answer sheet.
22. Mark your answer on your answer sheet.
23. Mark your answer on your answer sheet.
24. Mark your answer on your answer sheet.
25. Mark your answer on your answer sheet.
26. Mark your answer on your answer sheet.
27. Mark your answer on your answer sheet.
28. Mark your answer on your answer sheet.
29. Mark your answer on your answer sheet.
30. Mark your answer on your answer sheet.
31. Mark your answer on your answer sheet.

PART 3

Directions: You will hear some conversations between two or more people. You will be asked to answer three questions about what the speakers say in each conversation. Select the best response to each question and mark the letter (A), (B), (C), or (D) on your answer sheet. The conversations will not be printed in your test book and will be spoken only one time.

32. What type of food product does the speakers' company sell?
    (A) Candy
    (B) Cheese
    (C) Bread
    (D) Pasta

33. What does the man suggest?
    (A) Lowering prices
    (B) Hiring more workers
    (C) Publishing a recipe
    (D) Offering additional options

34. What does the woman say she will do?
    (A) Send a schedule update
    (B) Contact a production manager
    (C) Visit the company headquarters
    (D) Plan an advertising campaign

35. Why is the man calling?
    (A) To sign up for lessons
    (B) To enter a competition
    (C) To buy tickets to an event
    (D) To ask about branded merchandise

36. What did Ife Rotimi do last month?
    (A) She won a regional tournament.
    (B) She gave a television interview.
    (C) She started an institute.
    (D) She hired a new coach.

37. What does the woman say is required?
    (A) A parking permit
    (B) A photo ID
    (C) Contact information
    (D) Advance payment

38. What event are the speakers planning?
    (A) A fund-raising dinner
    (B) An art gallery opening
    (C) An awards ceremony
    (D) A children's book fair

39. What task does the woman ask the man to help with?
    (A) Arranging a shuttle service
    (B) Choosing a catering firm
    (C) Preparing a speech
    (D) Sending out invitations

40. What does the woman say she will do?
    (A) E-mail a list
    (B) Speak with a colleague
    (C) Provide a password
    (D) Post a job opening

41. What event are the speakers preparing for?
    (A) A new-employee orientation
    (B) A grand opening
    (C) A community festival
    (D) A trade show

42. What is mentioned about some pens?
    (A) They are available in multiple colors.
    (B) They use permanent ink.
    (C) They are preferred by book authors.
    (D) They are made from paper.

43. What does the woman offer to do?
    (A) Reserve a booth
    (B) Place an order
    (C) Organize a focus group
    (D) Revise a budget

GO ON TO THE NEXT PAGE

44. Where does the woman work?

    (A) At a delivery service
    (B) At an electronics store
    (C) At a recycling facility
    (D) At a real estate agency

45. What does the man want to dispose of?

    (A) Yard waste
    (B) Used furniture
    (C) Electronics
    (D) Books

46. What does the woman say can be found on a Web site?

    (A) A list of companies
    (B) Hours of operation
    (C) A permit application
    (D) Directions to a site

47. How do the speakers know each other?

    (A) They took a class together.
    (B) They used to work for the same company.
    (C) They grew up in the same neighborhood.
    (D) They met on a train.

48. What type of business does the man most likely own?

    (A) A fitness center
    (B) A real estate agency
    (C) A culinary school
    (D) A bakery

49. What advantage does the woman point out about a rental space?

    (A) Its price
    (B) Its size
    (C) Its location
    (D) Its design

50. Who most likely are the speakers?

    (A) Film actors
    (B) Museum directors
    (C) Video game developers
    (D) Investigative journalists

51. What did the man recently do?

    (A) He secured some funding.
    (B) He tested a product.
    (C) He read a script.
    (D) He conducted an interview.

52. What does the woman suggest?

    (A) Consulting a colleague
    (B) Planning an event
    (C) Negotiating a contract
    (D) Giving a client an update

53. Who most likely is the man?

    (A) A delivery driver
    (B) A security guard
    (C) A maintenance worker
    (D) A customer service representative

54. What problem does the woman describe?

    (A) A device is malfunctioning.
    (B) A key is missing.
    (C) A parking area is unavailable.
    (D) A package was not received.

55. What does the woman mean when she says, "it's supposed to be below freezing tonight"?

    (A) She is surprised by the weather forecast.
    (B) She wants a service to be completed sooner.
    (C) She will move some items indoors.
    (D) She would prefer to park near her apartment.

56. Why do the men want to speak to the woman?

    (A) To review a building design
    (B) To discuss a loan
    (C) To develop an advertising plan
    (D) To purchase some supplies

57. What type of business do the men own?

    (A) A sports equipment store
    (B) A winter apparel store
    (C) An automobile dealership
    (D) A hotel chain

58. According to the men, what has changed recently?

    (A) Roads have become more accessible.
    (B) Costs have decreased.
    (C) Tourism has increased.
    (D) Weather patterns have shifted.

59. What does the man want to do?

    (A) Provide training opportunities
    (B) Upgrade machinery
    (C) Hire additional employees
    (D) Reorganize the factory layout

60. What is the woman concerned about?

    (A) Increasing expenses
    (B) Introducing errors
    (C) Reducing productivity
    (D) Causing confusion

61. What does the man mean when he says, "High-quality video can be recorded and edited with a smartphone"?

    (A) A new policy should be established.
    (B) An idea is easy to implement.
    (C) Data security is a concern.
    (D) Some information should be verified.

Day	Time	Activity
Tuesday	Noon	Facility tour
Wednesday	8:00 A.M.	Meeting with Chicago staff
Thursday	2:00 P.M.	Shareholder presentation
Friday	4:45 P.M.	Return flight

62. Where is the woman?

    (A) At a restaurant
    (B) At a travel agency
    (C) At an airport
    (D) At a warehouse

63. Look at the graphic. When does the woman prefer to meet with an investor?

    (A) On Monday
    (B) On Tuesday
    (C) On Wednesday
    (D) On Thursday

64. What good news does the man share?

    (A) A colleague received a promotion.
    (B) A conference proposal was accepted.
    (C) An airline ticket has been upgraded.
    (D) A company won an award.

Web Site Outline

Page 1   About Us

Page 2   Admission Tickets

Page 3   General Rules

Page 4   Exhibitions and Special Events

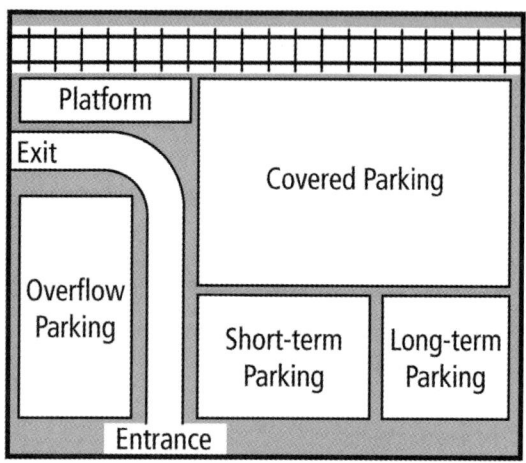

65. Where do the speakers work?
    (A) At an amusement park
    (B) At an art museum
    (C) At a concert hall
    (D) At a botanical garden

66. Look at the graphic. Which page on the Web site does the man want to change?
    (A) Page 1
    (B) Page 2
    (C) Page 3
    (D) Page 4

67. Why does the woman say she cannot complete a task until Monday?
    (A) She requires approval from a manager.
    (B) She is attending a workshop.
    (C) Some software is being updated.
    (D) Some clients will be arriving soon.

68. What news does the man share?
    (A) A station road will be closed for repair.
    (B) A project has been approved.
    (C) A parking area has been expanded.
    (D) An office will relocate.

69. Look at the graphic. Where do the speakers decide to install some bicycle racks?
    (A) Near the covered parking area
    (B) Near the long-term parking area
    (C) Near the short-term parking area
    (D) Near the overflow parking area

70. Why does the woman say she will contact some companies?
    (A) To arrange a loan
    (B) To apply for a permit
    (C) To ask for estimates
    (D) To create a proposal

PART 4

Directions: You will hear some talks given by a single speaker. You will be asked to answer three questions about what the speaker says in each talk. Select the best response to each question and mark the letter (A), (B), (C), or (D) on your answer sheet. The talks will not be printed in your test book and will be spoken only one time.

71. What type of products does the business repair?
    (A) Computers
    (B) Vehicles
    (C) Light fixtures
    (D) Kitchen appliances

72. What special benefit does the speaker mention?
    (A) Free pickup
    (B) Online scheduling
    (C) Extended warranties
    (D) A membership loyalty program

73. Why will a business close on Friday?
    (A) For an inventory count
    (B) For employee training
    (C) For a company celebration
    (D) For equipment installation

74. Who most likely is the speaker?
    (A) A facilities manager
    (B) A human resources representative
    (C) A security officer
    (D) A corporate executive

75. According to the speaker, what will the listeners find in a binder?
    (A) A map of the building
    (B) An employment contract
    (C) An identification badge
    (D) Log-in credentials

76. What does the speaker say about department files?
    (A) They are only accessible from company computers.
    (B) They must be password protected.
    (C) They must follow a specific naming convention.
    (D) They must be archived annually.

77. Where does the speaker work?
    (A) At a laundry facility
    (B) At an amusement park
    (C) At a sports stadium
    (D) At a fitness center

78. What does the speaker say about an item she ordered a month ago?
    (A) It arrived later than expected.
    (B) It was damaged during delivery.
    (C) She needs help assembling it.
    (D) She is pleased with it.

79. What does the speaker ask the listener to confirm?
    (A) Whether a new product will be available soon
    (B) When a replacement part will be shipped
    (C) How long a warranty lasts
    (D) Who to contact about future orders

80. What type of product does the speaker's company make?
    (A) Furniture
    (B) Luggage
    (C) Bedding
    (D) Clothing

81. What does the speaker recommend doing?
    (A) Manufacturing some products locally
    (B) Offering free shipping
    (C) Participating in a trade show
    (D) Developing a new product line

82. What will happen at the next meeting?
    (A) A vote will take place.
    (B) A consultant will give a presentation.
    (C) Some contracts will be updated.
    (D) Safety procedures will be reviewed.

GO ON TO THE NEXT PAGE

83. What is the announcement mainly about?
    (A) A promotional event
    (B) A vacation package
    (C) A building renovation
    (D) A travel delay

84. Why does the speaker say, "A bus will be departing for that destination in fifteen minutes"?
    (A) To suggest an alternative arrangement
    (B) To explain an extended wait time
    (C) To recommend changing the travel date
    (D) To inform customers about a new destination

85. What does the speaker remind the listeners about?
    (A) How to download a mobile application
    (B) Where a waiting area is located
    (C) How to reserve tickets
    (D) Where to buy food

86. Where does the speaker most likely work?
    (A) At a graphic design company
    (B) At a law firm
    (C) At a photography studio
    (D) At a museum

87. What did the listener receive by e-mail?
    (A) A newsletter
    (B) Some images
    (C) An invoice
    (D) Some contracts

88. Why is the speaker unavailable next week?
    (A) She will be working at another branch.
    (B) She will be with other clients.
    (C) She will be on vacation.
    (D) She will be at an industry conference.

89. Who most likely are the listeners?
    (A) Investors
    (B) Government officials
    (C) Engineers
    (D) Journalists

90. What does the speaker mean when she says, "All of ours are at least ten years old"?
    (A) An event needs to be relocated.
    (B) An upgrade is not feasible.
    (C) A project team has a lot of experience.
    (D) Some company policies are outdated.

91. According to the speaker, what can be requested by e-mail?
    (A) Some presentation slides
    (B) Some product samples
    (C) A report summary
    (D) A discounted ticket

92. What does the speaker want to do?
    (A) Increase online sales
    (B) Upgrade a payment system
    (C) Create a new product line
    (D) Add store locations

93. According to the speaker, what is the customers' main complaint?
    (A) Long lines
    (B) High prices
    (C) Unavailable items
    (D) Unfriendly staff

94. Why does the speaker say, "that's our busiest location"?
    (A) To request some feedback
    (B) To compliment some staff
    (C) To express frustration
    (D) To justify a choice

Tenant	Floors
Burger Incorporated	1–5
Aegis Technologies	6–10
Barnum Financial Services	11–14
Heinkel Media Group	15–17

Location	Grams per Ton
Site 1	150
Site 2	270
Site 3	390
Site 4	410

95. According to the speaker, what is special about the Reston Office Tower?

    (A) It features an indoor garden.
    (B) It exhibits work from local artists.
    (C) It runs on solar power.
    (D) It has won many awards.

96. Look at the graphic. Which floors will be occupied in January?

    (A) Floors 1–5
    (B) Floors 6–10
    (C) Floors 11–14
    (D) Floors 15–17

97. What does the speaker say is available on a Web site?

    (A) Some photographs
    (B) An event schedule
    (C) A floor layout
    (D) A recorded interview

98. Who most likely are the listeners?

    (A) Safety engineers
    (B) Laboratory technicians
    (C) Legal consultants
    (D) Business investors

99. Look at the graphic. Where will a new mine be built?

    (A) At site 1
    (B) At site 2
    (C) At site 3
    (D) At site 4

100. What does the speaker say is the next step?

    (A) Applying for permits
    (B) Installing equipment
    (C) Hiring additional staff
    (D) Updating a manual

This is the end of the Listening test.

TEST 02
무료 동영상 강의

LC

기출 TEST 02

LISTENING TEST

In the Listening test, you will be asked to demonstrate how well you understand spoken English. The entire Listening test will last approximately 45 minutes. There are four parts, and directions are given for each part. You must mark your answers on the separate answer sheet. Do not write your answers in your test book.

PART 1

Directions: For each question in this part, you will hear four statements about a picture in your test book. When you hear the statements, you must select the one statement that best describes what you see in the picture. Then find the number of the question on your answer sheet and mark your answer. The statements will not be printed in your test book and will be spoken only one time.

Statement (C), "They're sitting at a table," is the best description of the picture, so you should select answer (C) and mark it on your answer sheet.

1.

2.

3.

4.

5.

6.

PART 2

Directions: You will hear a question or statement and three responses spoken in English. They will not be printed in your test book and will be spoken only one time. Select the best response to the question or statement and mark the letter (A), (B), or (C) on your answer sheet.

7. Mark your answer on your answer sheet.
8. Mark your answer on your answer sheet.
9. Mark your answer on your answer sheet.
10. Mark your answer on your answer sheet.
11. Mark your answer on your answer sheet.
12. Mark your answer on your answer sheet.
13. Mark your answer on your answer sheet.
14. Mark your answer on your answer sheet.
15. Mark your answer on your answer sheet.
16. Mark your answer on your answer sheet.
17. Mark your answer on your answer sheet.
18. Mark your answer on your answer sheet.
19. Mark your answer on your answer sheet.
20. Mark your answer on your answer sheet.
21. Mark your answer on your answer sheet.
22. Mark your answer on your answer sheet.
23. Mark your answer on your answer sheet.
24. Mark your answer on your answer sheet.
25. Mark your answer on your answer sheet.
26. Mark your answer on your answer sheet.
27. Mark your answer on your answer sheet.
28. Mark your answer on your answer sheet.
29. Mark your answer on your answer sheet.
30. Mark your answer on your answer sheet.
31. Mark your answer on your answer sheet.

PART 3

Directions: You will hear some conversations between two or more people. You will be asked to answer three questions about what the speakers say in each conversation. Select the best response to each question and mark the letter (A), (B), (C), or (D) on your answer sheet. The conversations will not be printed in your test book and will be spoken only one time.

32. What kind of work does the man do?
    (A) He is a tour guide.
    (B) He is a landlord.
    (C) He repairs appliances.
    (D) He delivers food.

33. What has caused problems for the speakers' business?
    (A) Road construction
    (B) Cold weather
    (C) An expired permit
    (D) A broken intercom

34. What will the woman update on a mobile application?
    (A) Instructions
    (B) Prices
    (C) Photographs
    (D) Hours of operation

35. What industry do the speakers most likely work in?
    (A) Fitness
    (B) Entertainment
    (C) Landscaping
    (D) Travel

36. What does the man suggest?
    (A) Providing online access to videos
    (B) Creating volunteer opportunities
    (C) Offering free transportation
    (D) Adding additional time slots

37. Why do the speakers need to wait?
    (A) Promotional items have not been ordered.
    (B) A facility is not available.
    (C) A budget is too small.
    (D) A program has not been approved.

38. Who is the woman?
    (A) A store owner
    (B) A television celebrity
    (C) A business consultant
    (D) An event sponsor

39. What does the woman say about online shopping?
    (A) It is cheaper than buying in person.
    (B) It makes shopping a social experience.
    (C) It is reducing traffic problems in the city.
    (D) It is affecting specialty shops.

40. What does the woman suggest doing?
    (A) Offering clearance sales
    (B) Holding live events
    (C) Meeting with store owners
    (D) Retraining store staff

41. Why have a company's sales increased?
    (A) A rebate program was started.
    (B) A competitor went out of business.
    (C) A celebrity endorsed the company.
    (D) A product won an award.

42. What industry do the speakers most likely work in?
    (A) Banking
    (B) Telecommunications
    (C) Solar energy
    (D) Music

43. What does the man say he is planning to do?
    (A) Hire new employees
    (B) Provide additional training
    (C) Upgrade some equipment
    (D) Open another location

44. What upcoming event are the speakers discussing?
    (A) A trade show
    (B) A client meeting
    (C) An awards ceremony
    (D) A press conference

45. What product has the speakers' company recently developed?
    (A) A video game
    (B) A mobile phone
    (C) A lawn mower
    (D) A vacuum cleaner

46. Why does the woman recommend Kavi?
    (A) He is a good communicator.
    (B) He enjoys traveling.
    (C) He leads a product development team.
    (D) He lives near the event venue.

47. Where do the speakers most likely work?
    (A) At a publishing house
    (B) At a dental clinic
    (C) At a financial firm
    (D) At a real estate agency

48. What does the man tell the woman about?
    (A) A new product
    (B) A schedule change
    (C) A policy update
    (D) A job candidate

49. Why will the man most likely contact Kelly Graham?
    (A) To plan an office celebration
    (B) To arrange a training session
    (C) To request a document
    (D) To order some supplies

50. What industry do the men work in?
    (A) Travel
    (B) Manufacturing
    (C) Video production
    (D) Construction

51. How did the men learn about the woman?
    (A) From her Web site
    (B) From a trade publication
    (C) From a colleague
    (D) From a recruitment agency

52. What does the woman want to do next week?
    (A) Attend an orientation session
    (B) Visit some facilities
    (C) Interview some applicants
    (D) Finalize a contract

53. What type of business do the speakers work for?
    (A) A law firm
    (B) An advertising agency
    (C) An engineering firm
    (D) An event-planning company

54. Why does the man say, "that can take a lot of time"?
    (A) To reject a suggestion
    (B) To express sympathy
    (C) To request additional pay
    (D) To offer assistance

55. What does the woman suggest?
    (A) Contacting some former clients
    (B) Making reservations early
    (C) Staying at affordable hotels
    (D) Consulting with an expert

56. What industry do the men most likely work in?
    (A) Fashion
    (B) Cosmetics
    (C) Advertising
    (D) Technology

57. Why did the men request a meeting?
    (A) To negotiate a merger
    (B) To ask for funding
    (C) To discuss a product design
    (D) To suggest a marketing strategy

58. What will the speakers most likely do next?
    (A) Set a release date
    (B) Sign a contract
    (C) Collect customer feedback
    (D) Review some drawings

59. What type of business does the woman work in?
    (A) A hair salon
    (B) A real estate agency
    (C) An interior design firm
    (D) A car rental company

60. Why does the woman say, "our current carpeting is a light color"?
    (A) To suggest an expense was not justified
    (B) To express surprise about a decision
    (C) To describe a problem with an order
    (D) To indicate the need to make a change

61. What does the man's business offer?
    (A) A bulk discount
    (B) Same-day delivery
    (C) Free cleaning services
    (D) Monthly inspections

62. What did the man's client request?
    (A) A large shipment
    (B) A shortened timeline
    (C) A change in design
    (D) A more expensive material

63. Look at the graphic. How much does the man's coffee cost?
    (A) $2.00
    (B) $3.25
    (C) $3.75
    (D) $4.25

64. What does the woman say about David?
    (A) He is retiring.
    (B) He is organizing a party.
    (C) He is on vacation.
    (D) He accepted another position.

Bradley's Schedule	
Tuesday	Inspector's visit (2–5 P.M.)
Wednesday	Bank loan meeting (1–4 P.M.)
Thursday	Dental cleaning (2–4 P.M.)
Friday	Café project (1–4 P.M.)

65. What does the man most likely do?

(A) Install windows
(B) Repair roofs
(C) Remove trees
(D) Plant gardens

66. What does the woman provide?

(A) A floor layout
(B) An address
(C) A form of payment
(D) Proof of insurance

67. Look at the graphic. Which appointment will the man try to reschedule?

(A) The inspector's visit
(B) The bank loan meeting
(C) The dental cleaning
(D) The café project

Professional Introduction Tips	
...	Tip 1: Explain your current role
:)	Tip 2: Be upbeat and friendly
⏱	Tip 3: Be brief
💳	Tip 4: Provide a business card

68. What industry do the speakers most likely work in?

(A) Legal
(B) Construction
(C) Agriculture
(D) Robotics

69. Why does the woman want the man to attend a conference?

(A) To learn more about the latest industry trends
(B) To accept a reward on behalf of the company
(C) To host a panel discussion
(D) To screen job candidates

70. Look at the graphic. Which tip does the woman point out?

(A) Tip 1
(B) Tip 2
(C) Tip 3
(D) Tip 4

PART 4

Directions: You will hear some talks given by a single speaker. You will be asked to answer three questions about what the speaker says in each talk. Select the best response to each question and mark the letter (A), (B), (C), or (D) on your answer sheet. The talks will not be printed in your test book and will be spoken only one time.

71. Where do the listeners most likely work?
    (A) At a taxi service
    (B) At a car repair shop
    (C) At a shipping company
    (D) At a driving school

72. What problem does the speaker mention?
    (A) A training manual should be updated.
    (B) An invoice was incorrect.
    (C) Frequent maintenance is required.
    (D) Some supplies are missing.

73. What should the listeners remind customers about?
    (A) Some schedule changes
    (B) An online survey
    (C) A promotional offer
    (D) A safety policy

74. What does the company sell?
    (A) Office furniture
    (B) Kitchen appliances
    (C) Garden tools
    (D) Tablet computers

75. What does the speaker say will happen in December?
    (A) A promotional sale will begin.
    (B) Special equipment will be delivered.
    (C) Some temporary staff will be hired.
    (D) Some profits will be donated to a charity.

76. According to the speaker, what can the listeners find on a social media site?
    (A) A manual
    (B) A video
    (C) Some photographs
    (D) A price list

77. What is the episode mainly about?
    (A) Hiring
    (B) Accounting
    (C) Fund-raising
    (D) Publishing

78. What does the speaker mean when he says, "these things are constantly changing"?
    (A) He recommends professional development courses.
    (B) He questions the value of an investment.
    (C) Some information will be excluded.
    (D) Using technology is important.

79. What does the speaker say is important for organizations to do?
    (A) Be leaders in their industries
    (B) Establish successful advertising methods
    (C) Collect community feedback
    (D) Use familiar and current strategies

80. What does the speaker say the company sells?
    (A) Home appliances
    (B) Office supplies
    (C) Sporting goods
    (D) Entertainment systems

81. What will the listeners discuss with their supervisors?
    (A) A new sales goal
    (B) Training opportunities
    (C) A financial bonus
    (D) Increasing efficiency

82. How will the company offer more flexibility?
    (A) By introducing shared workspaces
    (B) By allowing employees to switch assignments
    (C) By permitting remote work
    (D) By increasing vacation time

GO ON TO THE NEXT PAGE

83. What is the purpose of the meeting?
    (A) To evaluate vendor contracts
    (B) To review hiring policies
    (C) To revise budget proposals
    (D) To assess editing software

84. What did the speaker ask the listeners to bring to the meeting?
    (A) A list of concerns
    (B) A completed survey
    (C) A project timeline
    (D) A laptop computer

85. Why might some of the listeners look for Sumit?
    (A) To get a document
    (B) To ask additional questions
    (C) To volunteer for an event
    (D) To check the status of a request

86. What did the speaker recently receive?
    (A) Sales results
    (B) Production schedules
    (C) An inspection report
    (D) An advertising proposal

87. What does the speaker mean when he says, "We have a lot of work to do"?
    (A) Extra shifts will be scheduled.
    (B) A job opening will be posted soon.
    (C) Customer orders have increased.
    (D) A change is necessary.

88. What will the speaker do next?
    (A) Distribute some manuals
    (B) Give a demonstration
    (C) Answer some questions
    (D) Show a video

89. Where does the speaker work?
    (A) At a museum
    (B) At a park
    (C) At a library
    (D) At a theater

90. What will happen in March?
    (A) A new facility will open.
    (B) An exhibition will be held.
    (C) Renovations will take place.
    (D) Operating hours will be extended.

91. What does the speaker say can be found online?
    (A) Volunteer information
    (B) A calendar of upcoming events
    (C) Ticket prices
    (D) An area map

92. Who are today's guests on the podcast?
    (A) Government officials
    (B) Business owners
    (C) Real estate developers
    (D) Cooking-school instructors

93. Why does the speaker say, "The Salazar family has kept the operation small"?
    (A) To indicate why a product is only sold online
    (B) To justify the high price of a product
    (C) To suggest that a company is having financial difficulties
    (D) To explain why a product is not well-known

94. What will the listeners be able to do after the podcast?
    (A) Request some product samples
    (B) Subscribe to a newsletter
    (C) Enter a contest
    (D) Sign up for a class

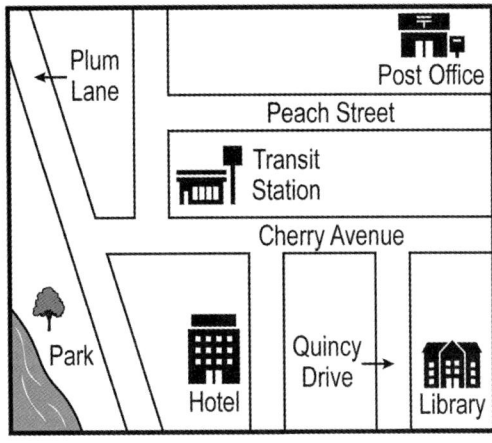

Workshop (February)	Days
Podcasting	Mondays
Entrepreneurship for Beginners	Tuesdays
Introduction to Coding	Wednesdays
Accounting for Small Businesses	Thursdays

98. Where does the speaker work?

    (A) At a restaurant
    (B) At a public library
    (C) At a community center
    (D) At a hospital

99. Look at the graphic. Which workshop will be offered on Fridays starting in March?

    (A) Podcasting
    (B) Entrepreneurship for Beginners
    (C) Introduction to Coding
    (D) Accounting for Small Businesses

100. What will Bianca do next week?

    (A) Request feedback from participants
    (B) Order office supplies
    (C) Update registration information
    (D) Contact some vendors

95. According to the speaker, why was a transit route changed?

    (A) Some streets are being resurfaced.
    (B) Some roads are closed for a bicycle race.
    (C) A group of residents is hosting a fund-raising concert.
    (D) A local politician will be speaking in a park.

96. Look at the graphic. Where will the listeners find a new bus stop?

    (A) On Plum Lane
    (B) On Peach Street
    (C) On Cherry Avenue
    (D) On Quincy Drive

97. Why should the listeners check a mobile phone application?

    (A) To apply for a job
    (B) To scan a promotional code
    (C) To view bus schedule updates
    (D) To purchase bus tickets

This is the end of the Listening test.

**ETS 토익 정기시험
기출문제집 5
1000 LC**

TEST 03
무료 동영상 강의

저자와 출판사의 사전 허락 없이 내용의 일부 혹은 전부를 인용 및 복제하거나 발췌하여 사용할 수 없습니다.

LC

기출 TEST 03

LISTENING TEST

In the Listening test, you will be asked to demonstrate how well you understand spoken English. The entire Listening test will last approximately 45 minutes. There are four parts, and directions are given for each part. You must mark your answers on the separate answer sheet. Do not write your answers in your test book.

PART 1

Directions: For each question in this part, you will hear four statements about a picture in your test book. When you hear the statements, you must select the one statement that best describes what you see in the picture. Then find the number of the question on your answer sheet and mark your answer. The statements will not be printed in your test book and will be spoken only one time.

Statement (C), "They're sitting at a table," is the best description of the picture, so you should select answer (C) and mark it on your answer sheet.

1.

2.

3.

4.

5.

6.

PART 2

Directions: You will hear a question or statement and three responses spoken in English. They will not be printed in your test book and will be spoken only one time. Select the best response to the question or statement and mark the letter (A), (B), or (C) on your answer sheet.

7. Mark your answer on your answer sheet.
8. Mark your answer on your answer sheet.
9. Mark your answer on your answer sheet.
10. Mark your answer on your answer sheet.
11. Mark your answer on your answer sheet.
12. Mark your answer on your answer sheet.
13. Mark your answer on your answer sheet.
14. Mark your answer on your answer sheet.
15. Mark your answer on your answer sheet.
16. Mark your answer on your answer sheet.
17. Mark your answer on your answer sheet.
18. Mark your answer on your answer sheet.
19. Mark your answer on your answer sheet.
20. Mark your answer on your answer sheet.
21. Mark your answer on your answer sheet.
22. Mark your answer on your answer sheet.
23. Mark your answer on your answer sheet.
24. Mark your answer on your answer sheet.
25. Mark your answer on your answer sheet.
26. Mark your answer on your answer sheet.
27. Mark your answer on your answer sheet.
28. Mark your answer on your answer sheet.
29. Mark your answer on your answer sheet.
30. Mark your answer on your answer sheet.
31. Mark your answer on your answer sheet.

PART 3

Directions: You will hear some conversations between two or more people. You will be asked to answer three questions about what the speakers say in each conversation. Select the best response to each question and mark the letter (A), (B), (C), or (D) on your answer sheet. The conversations will not be printed in your test book and will be spoken only one time.

32. Where do the speakers most likely work?
    (A) At a shipping company
    (B) At a restaurant
    (C) At a gift shop
    (D) At a farm

33. What does the man suggest considering?
    (A) An advertising strategy
    (B) An online menu
    (C) The price of an item
    (D) The results of a survey

34. What does the woman say she will do?
    (A) Pay a deposit
    (B) Contact a supplier
    (C) Reschedule a delivery
    (D) Arrange some merchandise

35. Where is the conversation most likely taking place?
    (A) At a fitness center
    (B) At a hotel
    (C) At a train station
    (D) At a corporate office

36. What type of event will the men attend this evening?
    (A) A company gala
    (B) An opera
    (C) A sports match
    (D) A lecture

37. What did Sergey forget to bring?
    (A) Gloves
    (B) Sunglasses
    (C) A hat
    (D) An umbrella

38. What has Mr. Hoffman decided to do?
    (A) Extend store hours
    (B) Start a delivery service
    (C) Offer a rewards program
    (D) Stop selling certain products

39. What business do the speakers most likely work for?
    (A) A bakery
    (B) A flower shop
    (C) A grocery store
    (D) A pharmacy

40. What does the woman ask the man to help her do?
    (A) Mail some packages
    (B) Take inventory
    (C) Create a job posting
    (D) Help some customers

41. What problem does the woman mention?
    (A) A product is faulty.
    (B) A company's sales are decreasing.
    (C) Some materials are damaged.
    (D) A sales department is understaffed.

42. Where do the speakers most likely work?
    (A) At a publishing firm
    (B) At a sporting goods company
    (C) At a travel agency
    (D) At a state park

43. What does the man say he will do this afternoon?
    (A) Sign a document
    (B) Ship an order
    (C) Review customer feedback
    (D) Send a list

GO ON TO THE NEXT PAGE

44. Why is the woman calling?
    (A) To verify some facts
    (B) To confirm a deadline
    (C) To inquire about an article
    (D) To apply for a position

45. What does the man offer to do?
    (A) Search a database
    (B) Renew a subscription
    (C) Consult with colleagues
    (D) Send an updated schedule

46. Why does the man congratulate the woman?
    (A) She appeared on television.
    (B) She was nominated for an award.
    (C) She is publishing a book.
    (D) She is starting her own business.

47. Where does the conversation most likely take place?
    (A) At a furniture store
    (B) At an electronics store
    (C) At a sporting goods store
    (D) At a building supply store

48. Why does the man want a refund?
    (A) He found a less expensive option.
    (B) He bought the wrong size.
    (C) He does not like the color of an item.
    (D) He noticed an item is damaged.

49. What does the woman imply when she says, "Let me find the manager"?
    (A) She needs to attend to other customers.
    (B) She does not have the authority to complete a request.
    (C) A transaction was not processed correctly.
    (D) A quality complaint needs to be documented.

50. What most likely is the man's job?
    (A) Plumber
    (B) Auto mechanic
    (C) Food delivery person
    (D) Computer technician

51. What did the woman do while the man was gone?
    (A) She created an advertisement.
    (B) She finalized a contract.
    (C) She addressed a customer complaint.
    (D) She had new software installed.

52. What does the woman say has recently changed?
    (A) Costs have been reduced.
    (B) A competitor has opened a location nearby.
    (C) The number of customers has increased.
    (D) Safety regulations have been introduced.

53. What type of company do the speakers work for?
    (A) An investment firm
    (B) An advertising agency
    (C) A staffing service
    (D) A construction company

54. What has HMD Incorporated recently done?
    (A) It has built a new headquarters.
    (B) It has donated to a charity.
    (C) It has developed a new line of products.
    (D) It has won an industry award.

55. What does the man say he will do?
    (A) Update his team's goals
    (B) Conduct some research
    (C) Apply for a permit
    (D) Arrange for a meeting

56. What did the man perform a maintenance check on?

    (A) A motorcycle
    (B) A car
    (C) A bus
    (D) An airplane

57. What news does Camille share?

    (A) A delivery will be delayed.
    (B) An expense will increase.
    (C) A staff member is unavailable.
    (D) A rainstorm is predicted.

58. Why is the customer traveling to Toronto?

    (A) To participate in a competition
    (B) To present at a conference
    (C) To attend a wedding
    (D) To sign a contract

59. What type of business does the man work for?

    (A) An electric company
    (B) An Internet provider
    (C) A landscaping service
    (D) A water supplier

60. What does the woman imply when she says, "my company has asked me to relocate to Spain"?

    (A) She enjoys traveling for business.
    (B) She was surprised by a job transfer.
    (C) She has no complaints about a service.
    (D) She would like paperwork sent to a different address.

61. What does the woman agree to do?

    (A) Pay a bill
    (B) Read a policy
    (C) Return a call
    (D) Complete a survey

62. Look at the graphic. Which dollar amount will the man change?

    (A) $2.37
    (B) $4.55
    (C) $7.86
    (D) $2.91

63. What will be added at the front of the store?

    (A) An additional checkout stand
    (B) A holiday display
    (C) A special food section
    (D) A seating area

64. According to the man, why did a shipment arrive late?

    (A) He forgot to place an order.
    (B) It was delivered to the wrong address.
    (C) Some supplies were unavailable.
    (D) Weather conditions were poor.

Hours of Operation	
Monday	9 A.M. - 5 P.M.
Tuesday	8 A.M. - 4 P.M.
Wednesday	10 A.M. - 6 P.M.
Thursday	8 A.M. - 5 P.M.
Friday	9 A.M. - Noon

65. What does the man say he needs to have done?

(A) He needs to schedule a job interview.
(B) He needs to cancel a doctor's appointment.
(C) He needs to have his photograph taken.
(D) He needs to renew his driver's license.

66. What does the woman ask the man to bring to an appointment?

(A) An application form
(B) Some references
(C) A study guide
(D) A payment receipt

67. Look at the graphic. Which day will the man request an appointment for?

(A) Monday
(B) Tuesday
(C) Wednesday
(D) Thursday

Transportation Reimbursement Form

Section 1: Full name

Section 2: Transportation type

Section 3: Payment method

Section 4: Department code

Section 5: Amount to be reimbursed

68. What event did the woman attend last week?

(A) A professional conference
(B) A training workshop
(C) A car auction
(D) A product demonstration

69. What will the man do with the documents the woman provides?

(A) Process a request
(B) Postpone a reservation
(C) Make a schedule
(D) Finalize a report

70. Look at the graphic. Which section does the woman ask about?

(A) Section 2
(B) Section 3
(C) Section 4
(D) Section 5

PART 4

Directions: You will hear some talks given by a single speaker. You will be asked to answer three questions about what the speaker says in each talk. Select the best response to each question and mark the letter (A), (B), (C), or (D) on your answer sheet. The talks will not be printed in your test book and will be spoken only one time.

71. Which event is being planned?
    (A) A holiday parade
    (B) A music festival
    (C) A sports competition
    (D) A company picnic

72. What problem does the speaker mention?
    (A) A stage needs to be repainted.
    (B) Some participants have canceled.
    (C) There is not enough fencing.
    (D) A parking area cannot be used.

73. What will Eniola most likely do today?
    (A) Select a caterer
    (B) Hire a maintenance worker
    (C) Confirm a start time
    (D) Check a budget

74. What type of event are the listeners most likely attending?
    (A) A trade show
    (B) A press conference
    (C) A charity auction
    (D) A grand opening ceremony

75. What does the speaker emphasize about a machine?
    (A) Its durability
    (B) Its ease of use
    (C) Its speed
    (D) Its energy efficiency

76. What does the speaker offer the listeners?
    (A) A free sample
    (B) A product discount
    (C) A meal voucher
    (D) A training brochure

77. What industry does the speaker work in?
    (A) Food manufacturing
    (B) Building construction
    (C) Computer technology
    (D) Entertainment

78. Why is the company making a change?
    (A) To create employment opportunities
    (B) To reduce manufacturing costs
    (C) To comply with a government policy
    (D) To increase control over quality

79. What will be sent out later in the morning?
    (A) Work assignments
    (B) Calendar invitations
    (C) A press release
    (D) Product specifications

80. What is the focus of the podcast?
    (A) Technology
    (B) Agriculture
    (C) Finance
    (D) Cooking

81. Why does the speaker apologize?
    (A) For having some audio problems
    (B) For delaying some Web site updates
    (C) For forgetting to thank a sponsor
    (D) For providing an incorrect date

82. Who is Junko Adachi?
    (A) The director of a nonprofit organization
    (B) The president of a national bank
    (C) A successful inventor
    (D) A well-known author

GO ON TO THE NEXT PAGE

83. What industry does the speaker work in?

    (A) Real estate
    (B) Construction
    (C) Technology
    (D) Manufacturing

84. According to the speaker, what has caused a problem?

    (A) Bad weather
    (B) An employee absence
    (C) A supply shortage
    (D) The age of a building

85. Why does the speaker say, "I'll be available for the next couple of hours"?

    (A) To inform the listener of new business hours
    (B) To confirm the listener's appointment
    (C) To remind the listener to submit a payment
    (D) To encourage the listener to call back soon

86. Who most likely is the speaker?

    (A) A marketing consultant
    (B) A bank manager
    (C) A hospital director
    (D) A factory owner

87. According to the speaker, what were some auditors impressed with?

    (A) Customer service
    (B) Employee satisfaction
    (C) Community outreach
    (D) Worker safety

88. What does the speaker ask supervisors to do?

    (A) Reward staff for their efficiency
    (B) Review marketing strategies with their teams
    (C) Schedule team-building exercises
    (D) Recommend staff for promotions

89. Why does the speaker call employees in early?

    (A) He wants to pass out some gifts.
    (B) He expects a busy night.
    (C) The owner will give a speech.
    (D) New uniforms have arrived.

90. What should be retrieved from storage?

    (A) Promotional signs
    (B) Heat lamps
    (C) Extra tables
    (D) Storage containers

91. What does the speaker mean when he says, "Management will be watching closely"?

    (A) A decision about an item will be made soon.
    (B) A client may not renew a contract.
    (C) A large profit is expected.
    (D) More people might be hired.

92. What type of news is the broadcast about?

    (A) Travel
    (B) Art
    (C) Financial
    (D) Sports

93. Why does the speaker say, "That technology is now widely available"?

    (A) To praise a marketing plan
    (B) To recommend a computer application
    (C) To explain the growth of a trend
    (D) To correct some wrong information

94. What did Professor Yun Hang do last month?

    (A) He spoke at a conference.
    (B) He published a book.
    (C) He started a business.
    (D) He won an award.

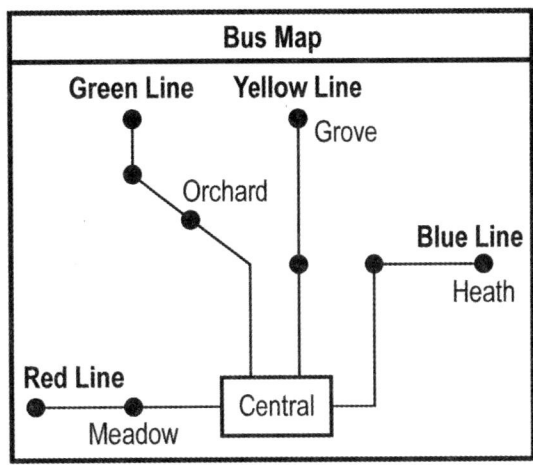

95. Why is the speaker calling?
    (A) To file a complaint
    (B) To purchase some tickets
    (C) To revise an order
    (D) To promote a product

96. What did the speaker find out yesterday?
    (A) A printer was replaced.
    (B) An application was approved.
    (C) A sales event was announced.
    (D) A lease was extended.

97. Look at the graphic. Which number does the speaker want to change?
    (A) 2005
    (B) 25
    (C) 2
    (D) 6

98. Who most likely is the listener?
    (A) An actor
    (B) A photographer
    (C) A writer
    (D) An athlete

99. According to the speaker, what should the listener do to prepare?
    (A) Update a résumé
    (B) Review some videos
    (C) Contact a colleague
    (D) Make a recording

100. Look at the graphic. Which bus stop does the speaker recommend getting off at?
    (A) Orchard
    (B) Heath
    (C) Grove
    (D) Meadow

This is the end of the Listening test.

ETS 토익 정기시험 기출문제집 5
1000 LC

TEST 04
무료 동영상 강의

저자와 출판사의 사전 허락 없이 내용의 일부 혹은 전부를 인용 및 복제하거나 발췌하여 사용할 수 없습니다.

LC
기출 TEST 04

LISTENING TEST

In the Listening test, you will be asked to demonstrate how well you understand spoken English. The entire Listening test will last approximately 45 minutes. There are four parts, and directions are given for each part. You must mark your answers on the separate answer sheet. Do not write your answers in your test book.

PART 1

Directions: For each question in this part, you will hear four statements about a picture in your test book. When you hear the statements, you must select the one statement that best describes what you see in the picture. Then find the number of the question on your answer sheet and mark your answer. The statements will not be printed in your test book and will be spoken only one time.

Statement (C), "They're sitting at a table," is the best description of the picture, so you should select answer (C) and mark it on your answer sheet.

1.

2.

3.

4.

5.

6.

PART 2

Directions: You will hear a question or statement and three responses spoken in English. They will not be printed in your test book and will be spoken only one time. Select the best response to the question or statement and mark the letter (A), (B), or (C) on your answer sheet.

7. Mark your answer on your answer sheet.
8. Mark your answer on your answer sheet.
9. Mark your answer on your answer sheet.
10. Mark your answer on your answer sheet.
11. Mark your answer on your answer sheet.
12. Mark your answer on your answer sheet.
13. Mark your answer on your answer sheet.
14. Mark your answer on your answer sheet.
15. Mark your answer on your answer sheet.
16. Mark your answer on your answer sheet.
17. Mark your answer on your answer sheet.
18. Mark your answer on your answer sheet.
19. Mark your answer on your answer sheet.
20. Mark your answer on your answer sheet.
21. Mark your answer on your answer sheet.
22. Mark your answer on your answer sheet.
23. Mark your answer on your answer sheet.
24. Mark your answer on your answer sheet.
25. Mark your answer on your answer sheet.
26. Mark your answer on your answer sheet.
27. Mark your answer on your answer sheet.
28. Mark your answer on your answer sheet.
29. Mark your answer on your answer sheet.
30. Mark your answer on your answer sheet.
31. Mark your answer on your answer sheet.

PART 3

Directions: You will hear some conversations between two or more people. You will be asked to answer three questions about what the speakers say in each conversation. Select the best response to each question and mark the letter (A), (B), (C), or (D) on your answer sheet. The conversations will not be printed in your test book and will be spoken only one time.

32. Who most likely is the woman?
    (A) A landscape architect
    (B) An interior designer
    (C) A real estate agent
    (D) A building inspector

33. What is the man looking forward to?
    (A) Living in a particular area
    (B) Walking to work
    (C) Going on vacation
    (D) Saving money for a house

34. What does the woman ask for?
    (A) Some references
    (B) Some identification
    (C) A signature
    (D) A payment

35. What most likely is the man's job?
    (A) Boat crew member
    (B) Restaurant owner
    (C) Seafood inspector
    (D) Delivery truck driver

36. Why is the woman concerned?
    (A) A road has been temporarily closed.
    (B) A permit has expired.
    (C) Traffic may cause a delay.
    (D) Some supplies are no longer available.

37. What does the man say he will check?
    (A) Some webcams
    (B) A list of ingredients
    (C) An address
    (D) Some maps

38. According to the man, what does Pelican produce?
    (A) Household cleaners
    (B) Cosmetics
    (C) Industrial textiles
    (D) Pharmaceuticals

39. What does the woman say she is concerned about?
    (A) Hiring skilled workers
    (B) Securing a bank loan
    (C) Finding transportation
    (D) Making enough product

40. Why does the man recommend reading an e-mail?
    (A) To consider a business proposal
    (B) To prepare for a client meeting
    (C) To view some construction plans
    (D) To learn the details of a complaint

41. What will the woman do next month?
    (A) Reorganize a department
    (B) Attend a conference
    (C) Relocate to an overseas office
    (D) Take a vacation

42. What does the man want the woman to do?
    (A) Help with some contracts
    (B) Prepare a project timeline
    (C) Update some software
    (D) Call a sales representative

43. What does the woman ask the man for?
    (A) Some employee names
    (B) Some credit card information
    (C) A file password
    (D) A telephone number

44. Why is the woman calling?
    (A) To negotiate a payment
    (B) To reschedule an appearance
    (C) To book a venue
    (D) To ask about security

45. Who most likely is Giovanni Marino?
    (A) An actor
    (B) A politician
    (C) A writer
    (D) A photographer

46. What will the man send in an e-mail?
    (A) A revised contract
    (B) A reimbursement form
    (C) An invitation to a video conference
    (D) Directions to a location

47. What are the speakers discussing?
    (A) A conference schedule
    (B) A company policy
    (C) A catering menu
    (D) A supply order

48. What do the men want to do?
    (A) Rent a car
    (B) Go to a restaurant
    (C) Speak with a manager
    (D) Change some flight reservations

49. What does the woman say she needs to do now?
    (A) Work on a report
    (B) Meet with a client
    (C) Print some materials
    (D) Check her e-mails

50. Who most likely is the woman?
    (A) A journalist
    (B) A librarian
    (C) A musician
    (D) A software developer

51. What does the woman recommend that the man do?
    (A) Consult a manual
    (B) Sign up for a class
    (C) Listen to some music
    (D) Use a particular mobile app

52. What does the man say happens each month?
    (A) He publishes a blog post.
    (B) He meets with a social group.
    (C) He travels for work.
    (D) He volunteers for a community event.

53. What does the woman want the man to look at?
    (A) A marketing plan
    (B) A conference calendar
    (C) Schedule changes
    (D) Survey results

54. What does the man imply when he says, "the company's certainly had other priorities"?
    (A) His workload has decreased.
    (B) He is not responsible for some results.
    (C) Some criticism is accurate.
    (D) Some decisions led to a successful outcome.

55. What has the woman suggested in the past?
    (A) Rewarding staff performance
    (B) Extending business hours
    (C) Encouraging professional development
    (D) Organizing team-building events

56. What type of business do the women own?
    (A) A hair salon
    (B) A recording studio
    (C) A clothing company
    (D) A fitness center

57. What does the man say regarding television?
    (A) It is an industry he once worked in.
    (B) It reaches more people than magazines.
    (C) It needs more programs about sports.
    (D) It is not the only advertising platform available.

58. According to the man, why would Saskia Hoffman be a good choice?
    (A) She recently won an award.
    (B) She lives nearby.
    (C) She charges affordable rates.
    (D) She is well known in her field.

59. What does the speakers' company manufacture?
    (A) Art supplies
    (B) Puzzles
    (C) Shipping materials
    (D) Power tools

60. What does the woman imply when she says, "A week is not a long time"?
    (A) Some prices will likely increase.
    (B) Some temporary employees have been hired.
    (C) A colleague's work is excellent.
    (D) An order may not be filled.

61. What will the woman do next?
    (A) Review a contract
    (B) Print out an invoice
    (C) Share some illustrations
    (D) Confirm a client meeting

Axiom Bank
Billing Statement

Name: Lola Rossi

Transaction Date	Amount
May 3	$203.00
May 15	$350.00
May 18	$75.50
May 29	$83.15

62. Where does the man most likely work?
    (A) At an airport
    (B) At a bank
    (C) At a real estate agency
    (D) At a department store

63. Look at the graphic. Which amount does the woman ask about?
    (A) $203.00
    (B) $350.00
    (C) $75.50
    (D) $83.15

64. What does the man give the woman?
    (A) An updated statement
    (B) A list of fees
    (C) A discount card
    (D) A brochure

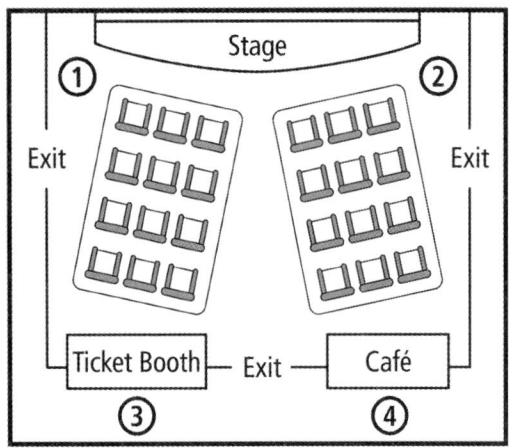

May	Growing roses
June	Natural pest remedies
July	Composting
August	Drought-tolerant plants

65. What does the man thank the woman for doing?

   (A) Printing programs
   (B) Setting up lighting
   (C) Reserving a venue
   (D) Paying a performer

66. What does the man say he is worried about?

   (A) Reviews from critics
   (B) Ticket sales
   (C) A performance schedule
   (D) The cost of merchandise

67. Look at the graphic. Where will a table be set up?

   (A) At location 1
   (B) At location 2
   (C) At location 3
   (D) At location 4

68. Why is the woman at the garden center?

   (A) To enroll in a course
   (B) To join a gardening club
   (C) To buy some supplies
   (D) To return a purchase

69. Look at the graphic. Which month's post will the woman most likely read?

   (A) May's post
   (B) June's post
   (C) July's post
   (D) August's post

70. What kind of products will the man show to the woman?

   (A) Indoor plants
   (B) Plant fertilizers
   (C) Gardening tools
   (D) Irrigation systems

PART 4

Directions: You will hear some talks given by a single speaker. You will be asked to answer three questions about what the speaker says in each talk. Select the best response to each question and mark the letter (A), (B), (C), or (D) on your answer sheet. The talks will not be printed in your test book and will be spoken only one time.

71. What field does the speaker most likely work in?
    (A) Finance
    (B) Transportation
    (C) Construction
    (D) Robotics

72. What does the speaker say the listeners can receive notifications about?
    (A) Route changes
    (B) Mobile app updates
    (C) New products
    (D) Schedule delays

73. According to the speaker, how can the listeners reduce a cost?
    (A) By purchasing a digital ticket
    (B) By reserving multiple permits
    (C) By traveling at less busy hours
    (D) By joining a loyalty program

74. What is the purpose of the meeting?
    (A) To explain a restoration project
    (B) To prepare for a public event
    (C) To train some new tour guides
    (D) To recruit some volunteers

75. According to the speaker, why will a task be challenging?
    (A) Funding has not been secured.
    (B) Unfavorable weather is predicted.
    (C) Some permits have been delayed.
    (D) Some important information is missing.

76. Who is Vivek Hazarika?
    (A) An architect
    (B) A gardener
    (C) A salesperson
    (D) An archaeologist

77. What is the purpose of the session?
    (A) To discuss customer feedback
    (B) To explain an attendance policy
    (C) To discourage mobile phone use
    (D) To train new sales staff

78. What will be on a list that the listeners will receive?
    (A) Potential clients to contact
    (B) Employees who have exceeded sales goals
    (C) Products offered by the company
    (D) Departments within the company

79. What will the listeners do next?
    (A) Memorize prepared scripts
    (B) Listen to recorded calls
    (C) Take a brief survey
    (D) Brainstorm conversational topics

80. What does the speaker's company sell?
    (A) Sound systems
    (B) Light fixtures
    (C) Umbrellas
    (D) Refrigerators

81. Why does the speaker say, "we do use outside suppliers for parts"?
    (A) To recommend a different company
    (B) To justify an increased price
    (C) To explain the source of a problem
    (D) To decline a proposal

82. What does the speaker say he will do today?
    (A) Interview some applicants
    (B) Send a shipment
    (C) Train some staff
    (D) Update a spreadsheet

GO ON TO THE NEXT PAGE

83. What type of business is being advertised?
    (A) An event planning company
    (B) A financial advising service
    (C) An attorney's office
    (D) A staffing agency

84. What aspect of a business does the speaker emphasize?
    (A) Its large size
    (B) Its reasonable prices
    (C) Its business hours
    (D) Its long history

85. How can the listeners receive a discount?
    (A) By mentioning an advertisement
    (B) By referring friends
    (C) By paying with a credit card
    (D) By using a coupon

86. What does the speaker mean when he says, "this is an important opportunity"?
    (A) A new client has an urgent problem.
    (B) Some information is needed from the listeners.
    (C) Some deadlines are flexible.
    (D) The listeners have done a good job.

87. What will the speaker's business do next year?
    (A) Redesign advertising materials
    (B) Open new locations
    (C) Hire a new vendor
    (D) Implement a security policy

88. What will Thilo do next?
    (A) Practice his conference presentation
    (B) Provide a construction update
    (C) Summarize some financial data
    (D) Contact a supply vendor

89. What does the speaker say is new about this year's event?
    (A) It takes place outdoors.
    (B) It is sponsored by a major publication.
    (C) It has been sold out for months.
    (D) It is being streamed live.

90. Why is Ms. Alabi being recognized?
    (A) She is a talented songwriter.
    (B) She invented a musical instrument.
    (C) She started a major record label.
    (D) She supports several charities.

91. According to the speaker, what will happen after Ms. Alabi receives her award?
    (A) Photographs will be taken.
    (B) Dinner will be served.
    (C) Some musicians will perform.
    (D) Some interviews will be held.

92. Which department does the speaker most likely work in?
    (A) Sales
    (B) Accounting
    (C) Human resources
    (D) Information technology

93. Why does the speaker say, "those have been popular lately"?
    (A) To express disbelief
    (B) To explain a shortage
    (C) To agree with a proposal
    (D) To make a correction

94. What will the listeners do next?
    (A) Take a lunch break
    (B) Ask questions about a policy
    (C) Read a report
    (D) View a demonstration

Monday	18°C	☀☁
Tuesday	24°C	☀
Wednesday	21°C	🌧
Thursday	22°C	☀

95. Where are the listeners?
    (A) At a farm
    (B) At a factory
    (C) At a museum
    (D) At a stadium

96. Look at the graphic. When is the tour taking place?
    (A) On Monday
    (B) On Tuesday
    (C) On Wednesday
    (D) On Thursday

97. What will happen at the end of the tour?
    (A) Pictures will be taken.
    (B) Food will be served.
    (C) Gifts will be given out.
    (D) A shuttle bus will arrive.

Name	Assignment
Ji-Soo	Organizing the food-serving station
Amanda	Hanging decorations
Sandrine	Creating flower arrangements
Murat	Setting up tables and chairs

98. What type of event is being held tonight?
    (A) A grand opening
    (B) A company anniversary
    (C) A retirement party
    (D) A wedding celebration

99. Look at the graphic. Which assignment will Kota be responsible for?
    (A) Organizing the food-serving station
    (B) Hanging decorations
    (C) Creating flower arrangements
    (D) Setting up tables and chairs

100. What does the speaker say she has to do at noon?
    (A) Go to the airport
    (B) Pick up some tablecloths
    (C) Cook a meal
    (D) Attend a meeting

This is the end of the Listening test.

ETS 토익 정기시험 기출문제집 5
1000 LC

TEST 05
무료 동영상 강의

저자와 출판사의 사전 허락 없이 내용의 일부 혹은 전부를 인용 및 복제하거나 발췌하여 사용할 수 없습니다.

LC

기출 TEST 05

LISTENING TEST

In the Listening test, you will be asked to demonstrate how well you understand spoken English. The entire Listening test will last approximately 45 minutes. There are four parts, and directions are given for each part. You must mark your answers on the separate answer sheet. Do not write your answers in your test book.

PART 1

Directions: For each question in this part, you will hear four statements about a picture in your test book. When you hear the statements, you must select the one statement that best describes what you see in the picture. Then find the number of the question on your answer sheet and mark your answer. The statements will not be printed in your test book and will be spoken only one time.

Statement (C), "They're sitting at a table," is the best description of the picture, so you should select answer (C) and mark it on your answer sheet.

1.

2.

3.

4.

5.

6.

PART 2

Directions: You will hear a question or statement and three responses spoken in English. They will not be printed in your test book and will be spoken only one time. Select the best response to the question or statement and mark the letter (A), (B), or (C) on your answer sheet.

7. Mark your answer on your answer sheet.
8. Mark your answer on your answer sheet.
9. Mark your answer on your answer sheet.
10. Mark your answer on your answer sheet.
11. Mark your answer on your answer sheet.
12. Mark your answer on your answer sheet.
13. Mark your answer on your answer sheet.
14. Mark your answer on your answer sheet.
15. Mark your answer on your answer sheet.
16. Mark your answer on your answer sheet.
17. Mark your answer on your answer sheet.
18. Mark your answer on your answer sheet.
19. Mark your answer on your answer sheet.
20. Mark your answer on your answer sheet.
21. Mark your answer on your answer sheet.
22. Mark your answer on your answer sheet.
23. Mark your answer on your answer sheet.
24. Mark your answer on your answer sheet.
25. Mark your answer on your answer sheet.
26. Mark your answer on your answer sheet.
27. Mark your answer on your answer sheet.
28. Mark your answer on your answer sheet.
29. Mark your answer on your answer sheet.
30. Mark your answer on your answer sheet.
31. Mark your answer on your answer sheet.

PART 3

Directions: You will hear some conversations between two or more people. You will be asked to answer three questions about what the speakers say in each conversation. Select the best response to each question and mark the letter (A), (B), (C), or (D) on your answer sheet. The conversations will not be printed in your test book and will be spoken only one time.

32. What does the woman ask the man to do for her?
    (A) Greet a client in the lobby
    (B) Present a product pitch
    (C) Organize some binders
    (D) Make some photocopies

33. What does the man say about some equipment?
    (A) It is operating smoothly.
    (B) It was purchased recently.
    (C) It needs to be plugged in.
    (D) It has not yet been updated.

34. Where is the man?
    (A) At the office
    (B) At a train station
    (C) At a store
    (D) At a client's headquarters

35. Where does the woman most likely work?
    (A) At a furniture store
    (B) At a moving company
    (C) At a post office
    (D) At an office supply store

36. Why will a representative visit the man's company tomorrow?
    (A) To provide an estimate
    (B) To sign a contract
    (C) To give a presentation
    (D) To place an order

37. What information will the man most likely provide next?
    (A) A company's operating hours
    (B) An account number
    (C) A street address
    (D) A telephone number

38. What department does the man work in?
    (A) Legal
    (B) Accounting
    (C) Human resources
    (D) Public relations

39. What kind of work has the woman been hired to do?
    (A) Scientific research
    (B) Book editing
    (C) Office management
    (D) Legal advising

40. What will the man send the woman this afternoon?
    (A) A password
    (B) A travel reimbursement
    (C) A security badge
    (D) A contract

41. What recently happened at the business?
    (A) Its monthly rent increased.
    (B) It received many orders.
    (C) It was featured in a magazine.
    (D) It passed an inspection.

42. According to the man, what will help the business?
    (A) Purchasing updated equipment
    (B) Offering different products
    (C) Extending store hours
    (D) Hiring more employees

43. Who does Rebecca say she will call today?
    (A) A packaging designer
    (B) An Internet service provider
    (C) A delivery service
    (D) A bank

GO ON TO THE NEXT PAGE

44. What do the speakers manufacture?
    (A) Shoes
    (B) Luggage
    (C) Furniture
    (D) Sports equipment

45. Who does the man suggest contacting?
    (A) A leather supplier
    (B) A delivery driver
    (C) An interior designer
    (D) A machine technician

46. Why is the woman opposed to making a change?
    (A) She has contracts with clients.
    (B) She is concerned about quality.
    (C) Overhead expenses will increase.
    (D) A license will expire soon.

47. What are the speakers meeting to discuss?
    (A) Safety regulations
    (B) Equipment upgrades
    (C) Budget cuts
    (D) Consultant recommendations

48. What does the man mean when he says, "it takes a lot of effort to develop and launch new styles"?
    (A) He is excited about a challenge.
    (B) He is surprised at a competitor's choices.
    (C) He is doubtful about a suggestion.
    (D) He thinks more employees should be hired.

49. Who most likely is Junko?
    (A) A focus group leader
    (B) A clothing designer
    (C) A sales associate
    (D) An accountant

50. Why did the man miss a meeting?
    (A) He was stuck in traffic.
    (B) He had a medical appointment.
    (C) He was speaking with a client.
    (D) He was away on vacation.

51. Which sport does the speakers' organization promote?
    (A) Tennis
    (B) Volleyball
    (C) Swimming
    (D) Gymnastics

52. Why were T-shirts ordered early?
    (A) To avoid potential delays
    (B) To get free delivery
    (C) To receive a discount
    (D) To meet heavy demand

53. What industry do the speakers most likely work in?
    (A) Energy
    (B) Finance
    (C) Construction
    (D) Manufacturing

54. What is the reason a company did not get a contract?
    (A) Some costs were too high.
    (B) A facility failed an inspection.
    (C) Some paperwork was submitted late.
    (D) A competitor can complete a project faster.

55. What does the woman ask the men to do?
    (A) Visit a facility
    (B) Conduct some research
    (C) Rewrite a proposal
    (D) Contact some vendors

56. What did the company do last month?

    (A) It opened a second location.
    (B) It merged with another business.
    (C) It launched a new product.
    (D) It conducted an employee survey.

57. Why does the man say, "we do have money available in the budget"?

    (A) To request another budget analysis
    (B) To suggest hiring additional employees
    (C) To agree with a proposed renovation
    (D) To recommend an increase in advertising

58. What does the man say he has to do this afternoon?

    (A) Have his car repaired
    (B) Give a presentation
    (C) Go to a dentist appointment
    (D) Attend a reception

59. Where does the woman work?

    (A) At a recycling company
    (B) At an appliance store
    (C) At a manufacturing company
    (D) At an architectural firm

60. What does the man ask the woman to do?

    (A) Revise a contract
    (B) Match a competitor's offer
    (C) Refund a delivery fee
    (D) Sign in at a security desk

61. What does the man say he will do this afternoon?

    (A) Conduct an inspection
    (B) Sign a document
    (C) Deliver some materials
    (D) Update a Web site

Train Tunnel Construction Project	
Phase 1	Assemble drill machine
Phase 2	Drill through rock
Phase 3	Install support columns
Phase 4	Lay down electrical cables

62. Look at the graphic. Which project phase was just completed?

    (A) Phase 1
    (B) Phase 2
    (C) Phase 3
    (D) Phase 4

63. What does the woman ask the man to do?

    (A) Request an earlier delivery date
    (B) Consult with a safety inspector
    (C) Post some construction plans
    (D) Forward an invoice

64. What does the woman intend to do next?

    (A) Review some data
    (B) Move a vehicle
    (C) Increase the size of a crew
    (D) Contact the management team

GO ON TO THE NEXT PAGE

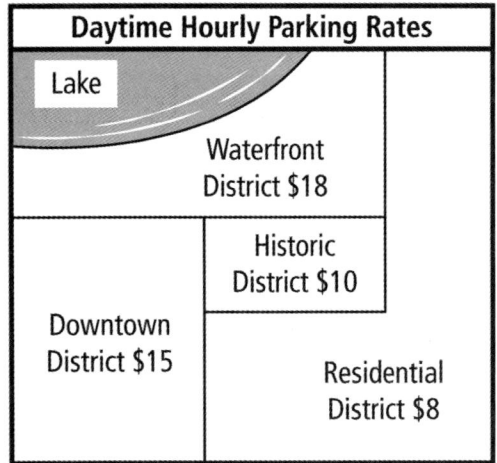

65. What type of business do the speakers work for?
    (A) A restaurant
    (B) A law firm
    (C) An office-supply store
    (D) A flower shop

66. Look at the graphic. In which area of the city does the business make most of its deliveries?
    (A) The waterfront district
    (B) The historic district
    (C) The residential district
    (D) The downtown district

67. How does the man propose lowering business expenses?
    (A) By reducing packaging waste
    (B) By introducing bicycle delivery
    (C) By switching to a new supplier
    (D) By moving to a smaller building

68. Who most likely is the woman?
    (A) A hotel manager
    (B) An interior designer
    (C) A construction worker
    (D) A real estate agent

69. Look at the graphic. Which step does the man ask about?
    (A) Step 1
    (B) Step 2
    (C) Step 3
    (D) Step 4

70. What will the man most likely do next?
    (A) Send a contract
    (B) Go to the lobby
    (C) Look at some photographs
    (D) Review a cost estimate

PART 4

Directions: You will hear some talks given by a single speaker. You will be asked to answer three questions about what the speaker says in each talk. Select the best response to each question and mark the letter (A), (B), (C), or (D) on your answer sheet. The talks will not be printed in your test book and will be spoken only one time.

71. Who most likely is the speaker?
    (A) A department manager
    (B) A news reporter
    (C) A marketing consultant
    (D) A computer programmer

72. Why does the speaker congratulate a team?
    (A) For keeping expenses low
    (B) For creating a useful tool
    (C) For meeting a tight deadline
    (D) For achieving the most sales

73. What are the listeners required to do?
    (A) Register for some training
    (B) Review a floor plan
    (C) Participate in a mentoring program
    (D) Provide copies of certifications

74. What are the listeners invited to do?
    (A) Download a calendar
    (B) Reserve tickets
    (C) Submit a picture
    (D) Share a story

75. What guideline does the speaker emphasize?
    (A) Recordings must be kept short.
    (B) Electronic devices must be turned off.
    (C) Professional references must be provided.
    (D) Vehicles must be parked in a designated area.

76. According to the speaker, what may cause a delay?
    (A) Bad weather
    (B) Holidays
    (C) A construction project
    (D) Staff changes

77. What is the focus of a tour?
    (A) Food
    (B) Architecture
    (C) Nature
    (D) Art

78. What does the speaker imply when she says, "we have such a large group today"?
    (A) She is happy about the popularity of a tour.
    (B) She will need to use a microphone.
    (C) An additional tour guide is needed.
    (D) A shop is not big enough for everyone.

79. What will a ticket allow the listeners to do?
    (A) Attend a performance
    (B) Visit a museum
    (C) Participate in a class
    (D) Enter a contest

80. What industry was the Novikov Award created for?
    (A) Aviation
    (B) Chemical engineering
    (C) Medical research
    (D) Television production

81. Why was this year's award recipient selected?
    (A) For launching a unique advertising campaign
    (B) For developing a successful training program
    (C) For maintaining a perfect safety record
    (D) For making a scientific discovery

82. What does the speaker ask the listeners to do?
    (A) Get ready to watch a video
    (B) Applaud the winner
    (C) Share copies of a handout
    (D) Read a set of directions

GO ON TO THE NEXT PAGE

83. Who is the speaker presenting to?
    (A) Loan officers
    (B) Construction workers
    (C) City council members
    (D) Bus drivers

84. What does the speaker say about some existing structures?
    (A) They are in disrepair.
    (B) They are very small.
    (C) They were not assembled correctly.
    (D) They were installed last year.

85. Why does the speaker say, "its models include a display for advertisements"?
    (A) To respond to a request for information
    (B) To justify a cost
    (C) To express surprise
    (D) To suggest adding to a product line

86. What does the speaker's company sell?
    (A) Clothing
    (B) Flowers
    (C) Toys
    (D) Wallpaper

87. Why does the speaker praise the listener's team?
    (A) They stayed under budget.
    (B) They won an award.
    (C) They showed creativity.
    (D) They completed some work on schedule.

88. Why does the speaker say, "we have a full supply of those in stock"?
    (A) To report that inventory has been completed
    (B) To offer to share some supplies with another store
    (C) To explain that some designs are not needed
    (D) To confirm that a customer's order can be filled

89. According to the speaker, what will be opening soon?
    (A) A restaurant
    (B) A sports arena
    (C) A performing arts center
    (D) A train station

90. Why did the building's designer win an award?
    (A) For using solar power
    (B) For creating a rooftop garden
    (C) For installing a moving light display
    (D) For employing sound-absorbing walls

91. What does the speaker emphasize about upcoming events?
    (A) Many of them are sold out.
    (B) Some of them will be affected by the weather.
    (C) Public transportation will be free.
    (D) Discounts are available for large groups.

92. Who is Mona Alamri?
    (A) A local official
    (B) A ship captain
    (C) A marine scientist
    (D) An engineer

93. What is the focus of today's podcast episode?
    (A) Coastal mapping
    (B) Offshore wind farms
    (C) Electric ships
    (D) Bridge construction

94. What does the speaker alert the listeners to?
    (A) A schedule change
    (B) A volunteer opportunity
    (C) An updated Web site
    (D) A project start date

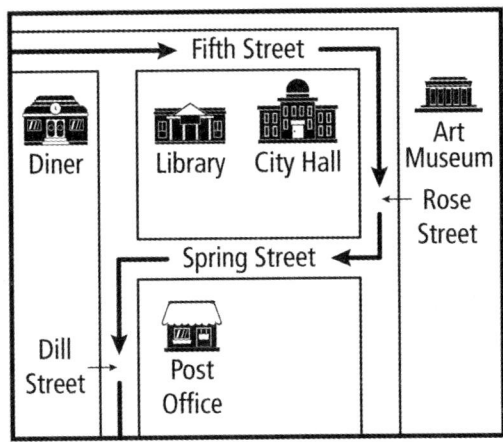

Market Research Stage Chart

Stage 1	Analyze Target Population
Stage 2	Design Application
Stage 3	Develop Application
Stage 4	Launch Pilot Software

95. Where are the listeners?
    (A) At a bicycle race
    (B) At a marathon
    (C) At a parade
    (D) At a festival

96. What will proceeds from the event support?
    (A) Creating an athletic field
    (B) Renovating a city library
    (C) Repairing a bridge
    (D) Building a new playground

97. Look at the graphic. On which street does the speaker say the listeners can find a beverage stand?
    (A) Fifth Street
    (B) Rose Street
    (C) Spring Street
    (D) Dill Street

98. What industry is the mobile app intended for?
    (A) Entertainment
    (B) Travel
    (C) Education
    (D) Finance

99. Look at the graphic. Which stage of market research will Sarai talk about?
    (A) Stage 1
    (B) Stage 2
    (C) Stage 3
    (D) Stage 4

100. What will begin next Friday?
    (A) A seasonal work schedule
    (B) A business conference
    (C) A construction project
    (D) A contract negotiation

This is the end of the Listening test.

ETS 토익 정기시험 기출문제집 5 1000 LC

TEST 06
무료 동영상 강의

저자와 출판사의 사전 허락 없이 내용의 일부 혹은 전부를 인용 및 복제하거나 발췌하여 사용할 수 없습니다.

LC

기출 TEST 06

LISTENING TEST

In the Listening test, you will be asked to demonstrate how well you understand spoken English. The entire Listening test will last approximately 45 minutes. There are four parts, and directions are given for each part. You must mark your answers on the separate answer sheet. Do not write your answers in your test book.

PART 1

Directions: For each question in this part, you will hear four statements about a picture in your test book. When you hear the statements, you must select the one statement that best describes what you see in the picture. Then find the number of the question on your answer sheet and mark your answer. The statements will not be printed in your test book and will be spoken only one time.

Statement (C), "They're sitting at a table," is the best description of the picture, so you should select answer (C) and mark it on your answer sheet.

1.

2.

3.

4.

5.

6.

PART 2

Directions: You will hear a question or statement and three responses spoken in English. They will not be printed in your test book and will be spoken only one time. Select the best response to the question or statement and mark the letter (A), (B), or (C) on your answer sheet.

7. Mark your answer on your answer sheet.
8. Mark your answer on your answer sheet.
9. Mark your answer on your answer sheet.
10. Mark your answer on your answer sheet.
11. Mark your answer on your answer sheet.
12. Mark your answer on your answer sheet.
13. Mark your answer on your answer sheet.
14. Mark your answer on your answer sheet.
15. Mark your answer on your answer sheet.
16. Mark your answer on your answer sheet.
17. Mark your answer on your answer sheet.
18. Mark your answer on your answer sheet.
19. Mark your answer on your answer sheet.
20. Mark your answer on your answer sheet.
21. Mark your answer on your answer sheet.
22. Mark your answer on your answer sheet.
23. Mark your answer on your answer sheet.
24. Mark your answer on your answer sheet.
25. Mark your answer on your answer sheet.
26. Mark your answer on your answer sheet.
27. Mark your answer on your answer sheet.
28. Mark your answer on your answer sheet.
29. Mark your answer on your answer sheet.
30. Mark your answer on your answer sheet.
31. Mark your answer on your answer sheet.

PART 3

Directions: You will hear some conversations between two or more people. You will be asked to answer three questions about what the speakers say in each conversation. Select the best response to each question and mark the letter (A), (B), (C), or (D) on your answer sheet. The conversations will not be printed in your test book and will be spoken only one time.

32. According to the woman, what happened last week?
    (A) A new product was launched.
    (B) A new location opened.
    (C) An advertising campaign started.
    (D) A budget was approved.

33. What industry do the speakers work in?
    (A) Finance
    (B) Retail
    (C) Energy
    (D) Tourism

34. What does the man say he will check on?
    (A) Transportation
    (B) Tickets
    (C) Some prices
    (D) Some contracts

35. Where do the speakers most likely work?
    (A) At a hotel
    (B) At a beauty salon
    (C) At a gym
    (D) At a shopping mall

36. How does the man plan to address a problem?
    (A) By resending a confirmation e-mail
    (B) By giving a verbal reminder
    (C) By extending hours of operation
    (D) By discounting the price of a service

37. Why will landscapers come next week?
    (A) To install a water fountain
    (B) To cut down some tree branches
    (C) To plant some flowers
    (D) To cut the grass

38. What is the woman's job?
    (A) School administrator
    (B) Reporter
    (C) Laboratory technician
    (D) Nurse

39. What does the man ask the woman to help with?
    (A) Updating training materials
    (B) Recording an interview
    (C) Ordering some supplies
    (D) Designing a Web page

40. What will take place next week?
    (A) A press conference
    (B) An awards ceremony
    (C) A facility inspection
    (D) A board meeting

41. Where most likely are the speakers?
    (A) At a café
    (B) At a museum
    (C) At a public library
    (D) At a community center

42. Why is the woman unable to help?
    (A) She is new to the job.
    (B) She is busy with another task.
    (C) She needs to attend a workshop.
    (D) She will be leaving for the day.

43. Why is an item unavailable?
    (A) It is sold out.
    (B) It has not been unpacked yet.
    (C) A shipment has been lost.
    (D) A repair has not been made yet.

GO ON TO THE NEXT PAGE

44. Who most likely are the speakers?

    (A) Repair technicians
    (B) News reporters
    (C) Business owners
    (D) Construction engineers

45. What project is being proposed?

    (A) A wind farm
    (B) A road expansion
    (C) A tourism initiative
    (D) A building expansion

46. What does the woman plan to inquire about?

    (A) Architectural specifications
    (B) Staffing arrangements
    (C) A funding source
    (D) A project timeline

47. Why did the man miss a meeting?

    (A) His train was late.
    (B) His car was being repaired.
    (C) He had a medical appointment.
    (D) He was meeting with some clients.

48. What good news does the woman mention?

    (A) More employees will be hired.
    (B) A facility will be remodeled.
    (C) Some equipment will be upgraded.
    (D) A permit has been approved.

49. What does the man say he will do?

    (A) Speak to a manager
    (B) Present at a conference
    (C) Read an article
    (D) Sign up for a training course

50. What are the speakers planning?

    (A) A company retreat
    (B) An industry conference
    (C) A retirement party
    (D) A grand opening celebration

51. What are the women excited about?

    (A) Traveling to a new city
    (B) Giving a product demonstration
    (C) Meeting a guest speaker
    (D) Attending a workshop

52. What will the man research?

    (A) Driving directions
    (B) Weather conditions
    (C) Equipment rentals
    (D) Dining options

53. Who most likely is the man?

    (A) A service technician
    (B) A salesperson
    (C) A delivery driver
    (D) A real estate agent

54. Why does the woman say, "There's a lot of traffic right now"?

    (A) To request time off work
    (B) To explain a delay
    (C) To disagree with a plan
    (D) To recommend another route

55. What will the man most likely do next?

    (A) Listen to a news report
    (B) Go to another client's home
    (C) Cancel an Internet subscription
    (D) Consult a handbook

56. What did the man do last month?
   (A) He managed a trade show booth.
   (B) He attended a company picnic.
   (C) He participated in a research project.
   (D) He met with overseas clients.

57. Why will the woman be joining the man next month?
   (A) Her job title has changed.
   (B) Her colleague is unavailable.
   (C) She has more experience than the man.
   (D) She will be needed to translate documents.

58. What will the man send the woman a link to?
   (A) An itinerary
   (B) A magazine article
   (C) An online store
   (D) A list of hotels

59. What type of product are the speakers discussing?
   (A) T-shirts
   (B) Stickers
   (C) Water bottles
   (D) Tote bags

60. What does the woman propose offering to some employees?
   (A) A gym membership
   (B) A restaurant voucher
   (C) A salary bonus
   (D) An extra vacation day

61. What does the woman mean when she says, "Great Fitness orders from us all the time"?
   (A) An invoice contains an error.
   (B) More staff should be hired.
   (C) Great Fitness's order is the priority.
   (D) Great Fitness has complained about a delivery.

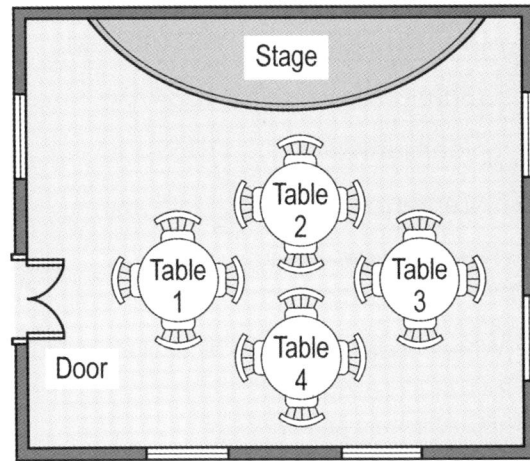

62. Why is the company hosting a banquet?
   (A) To open a new facility
   (B) To celebrate an anniversary
   (C) To announce a merger
   (D) To honor a retiring colleague

63. What does the man say should be included in a presentation?
   (A) A summary of a company's profits
   (B) A preview of a company's new product
   (C) Some survey results
   (D) Some photographs

64. Look at the graphic. Where will the woman be seated?
   (A) Table 1
   (B) Table 2
   (C) Table 3
   (D) Table 4

DESTINATION	DEPARTURE TIME
• Springdale	10:34 A.M.
• Johnsonville	10:57 A.M.
• Centerton	11:15 A.M.
• Belton City	11:41 A.M.

65. Where does the woman most likely work?

    (A) At a bus station
    (B) At a train station
    (C) At a ferry terminal
    (D) At an airport

66. Look at the graphic. What is the man's new departure time?

    (A) 10:34 A.M.
    (B) 10:57 A.M.
    (C) 11:15 A.M.
    (D) 11:41 A.M.

67. What does the woman ask the man for?

    (A) His date of travel
    (B) His seat preference
    (C) A form of payment
    (D) A confirmation number

Electrical Switch Type	Cost
60 amp	$25
80 amp	$30
100 amp	$38
125 amp	$46

68. What has the woman recently purchased?

    (A) A dishwasher
    (B) A toaster oven
    (C) A refrigerator
    (D) A clothes dryer

69. What does the man ask the woman to do?

    (A) Check a warranty
    (B) Visit a Web site
    (C) Examine some equipment
    (D) Take some photographs

70. Look at the graphic. How much will the woman probably pay for an electrical switch?

    (A) $25
    (B) $30
    (C) $38
    (D) $46

PART 4

Directions: You will hear some talks given by a single speaker. You will be asked to answer three questions about what the speaker says in each talk. Select the best response to each question and mark the letter (A), (B), (C), or (D) on your answer sheet. The talks will not be printed in your test book and will be spoken only one time.

71. Where most likely is the announcement being made?
    (A) At an art gallery
    (B) At a trade show
    (C) At a shopping mall
    (D) At a sporting event

72. What does the speaker say has changed?
    (A) Opening hours
    (B) A location
    (C) An entry fee
    (D) A policy

73. What does the speaker say is available at the information desk?
    (A) A discount coupon
    (B) A parking pass
    (C) A lost item
    (D) A map

74. Who most likely are the listeners?
    (A) Students
    (B) Professional athletes
    (C) Business investors
    (D) News reporters

75. Why does the speaker say, "I've been a computer programmer for seven years"?
    (A) To indicate that she is well qualified for a role
    (B) To express appreciation for her employer
    (C) To correct some inaccurate information
    (D) To give a reason for a change in profession

76. According to the speaker, why should the listeners raise their hands?
    (A) To make a suggestion
    (B) To request a booklet
    (C) To provide a definition
    (D) To ask a question

77. What industry does the speaker work in?
    (A) Technology
    (B) Travel
    (C) Agriculture
    (D) Food service

78. According to the speaker, what would be useful?
    (A) Knowledge of specialized software
    (B) An understanding of consumer trends
    (C) Customer-service training
    (D) Team-building skills

79. What does the speaker imply when he says, "I hope you haven't accepted any offers yet"?
    (A) He thinks the listener deserves a promotion.
    (B) He would like to hire the listener.
    (C) A company would not be good to work for.
    (D) A salary offer is too low.

80. What is the news segment about?
    (A) The restoration of historic ships
    (B) The distribution of goods
    (C) A shortage of city housing
    (D) The construction of a new port

81. What problem does the speaker mention?
    (A) Storage space is not affordable.
    (B) Trained workers are difficult to find.
    (C) There is a shortage of supplies.
    (D) Poor road conditions are causing delays.

82. Who is Pablo Alvarez?
    (A) A real estate agent
    (B) A city official
    (C) A business owner
    (D) An accountant

GO ON TO THE NEXT PAGE

83. What is the focus of the workshop?
    (A) Flower arranging
    (B) Photography
    (C) Painting
    (D) Creative writing

84. What does the speaker say is included in a workshop fee?
    (A) A museum membership
    (B) A potted plant
    (C) Some supplies
    (D) A meal

85. What will most likely happen next?
    (A) The listeners will sign some forms.
    (B) The listeners will introduce themselves.
    (C) The speaker will give a demonstration.
    (D) The speaker will lead a tour.

86. What service does the company provide?
    (A) Legal
    (B) Architectural
    (C) Graphic design
    (D) Artificial intelligence

87. What does the speaker say about Friday?
    (A) A client will visit.
    (B) Interviews will be conducted.
    (C) An office will close early.
    (D) Bonuses will be announced.

88. What does the speaker imply when she says, "making a good impression is important"?
    (A) She will be providing her business card.
    (B) She does not want employees to be late.
    (C) She expects workstations to be clean.
    (D) She is unsatisfied with some potential job candidates.

89. Where do the listeners most likely work?
    (A) At a hospital
    (B) At a factory
    (C) At a bank
    (D) At an auto repair shop

90. Who visited the business yesterday?
    (A) A journalist
    (B) A safety inspector
    (C) A politician
    (D) A repair person

91. Why are the listeners asked to start working right away?
    (A) A large order was placed.
    (B) Several employees are on vacation.
    (C) A task will take longer than usual.
    (D) An inspection will be conducted in the afternoon.

92. Why is the speaker calling?
    (A) To ask the listener to donate to a charity
    (B) To offer the listener a job
    (C) To explain a publishing delay
    (D) To request an interview for an article

93. How did the speaker first learn about the listener?
    (A) She read one of his books.
    (B) She attended a workshop he led.
    (C) She saw his comment on a social media post.
    (D) She watched a documentary about his work.

94. What will the speaker most likely do next?
    (A) Print and sign a contract
    (B) Send some information
    (C) Reserve a meeting room
    (D) Contact a talent agent

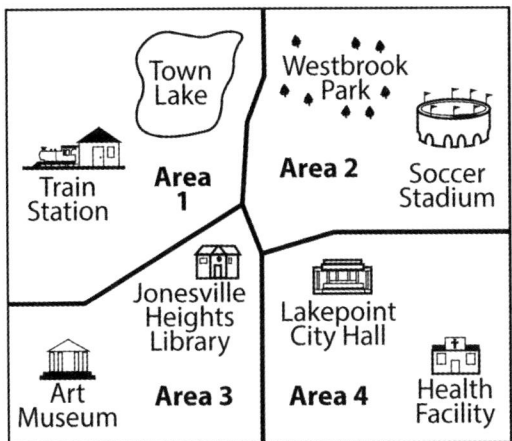
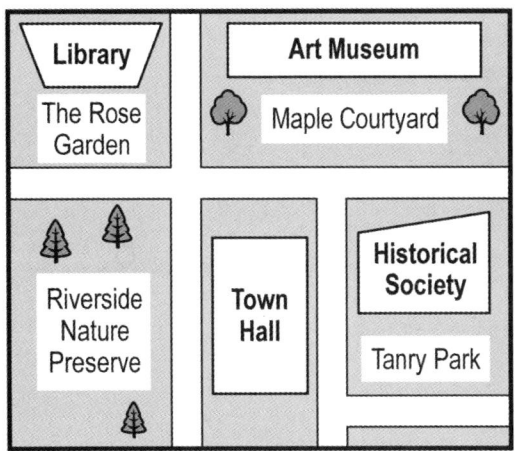

95. What type of service is being advertised?
 (A) Recycling
 (B) Transportation
 (C) Grocery delivery
 (D) Exercise classes

96. According to the speaker, how can the listeners use a new service?
 (A) By entering payment information
 (B) By placing a phone call
 (C) By visiting a community center
 (D) By using a mobile application

97. Look at the graphic. Which area was recently added?
 (A) Area 1
 (B) Area 2
 (C) Area 3
 (D) Area 4

98. What event is the speaker mainly discussing?
 (A) An archaeology festival
 (B) A museum opening
 (C) A gardening fair
 (D) An outdoor concert

99. Look at the graphic. Where will a workshop take place?
 (A) In The Rose Garden
 (B) In Maple Courtyard
 (C) In Tanry Park
 (D) In Riverside Nature Preserve

100. What does the speaker recommend?
 (A) Arriving early
 (B) Walking
 (C) Volunteering
 (D) Bringing a jacket

This is the end of the Listening test.

ETS 토익 정기시험
기출문제집 5
1000 LC

TEST 07
무료 동영상 강의

LC
기출 TEST 07

LISTENING TEST

In the Listening test, you will be asked to demonstrate how well you understand spoken English. The entire Listening test will last approximately 45 minutes. There are four parts, and directions are given for each part. You must mark your answers on the separate answer sheet. Do not write your answers in your test book.

PART 1

Directions: For each question in this part, you will hear four statements about a picture in your test book. When you hear the statements, you must select the one statement that best describes what you see in the picture. Then find the number of the question on your answer sheet and mark your answer. The statements will not be printed in your test book and will be spoken only one time.

Statement (C), "They're sitting at a table," is the best description of the picture, so you should select answer (C) and mark it on your answer sheet.

1.

2.

3.

4.

5.

6.

PART 2

Directions: You will hear a question or statement and three responses spoken in English. They will not be printed in your test book and will be spoken only one time. Select the best response to the question or statement and mark the letter (A), (B), or (C) on your answer sheet.

7. Mark your answer on your answer sheet.
8. Mark your answer on your answer sheet.
9. Mark your answer on your answer sheet.
10. Mark your answer on your answer sheet.
11. Mark your answer on your answer sheet.
12. Mark your answer on your answer sheet.
13. Mark your answer on your answer sheet.
14. Mark your answer on your answer sheet.
15. Mark your answer on your answer sheet.
16. Mark your answer on your answer sheet.
17. Mark your answer on your answer sheet.
18. Mark your answer on your answer sheet.
19. Mark your answer on your answer sheet.
20. Mark your answer on your answer sheet.
21. Mark your answer on your answer sheet.
22. Mark your answer on your answer sheet.
23. Mark your answer on your answer sheet.
24. Mark your answer on your answer sheet.
25. Mark your answer on your answer sheet.
26. Mark your answer on your answer sheet.
27. Mark your answer on your answer sheet.
28. Mark your answer on your answer sheet.
29. Mark your answer on your answer sheet.
30. Mark your answer on your answer sheet.
31. Mark your answer on your answer sheet.

PART 3

Directions: You will hear some conversations between two or more people. You will be asked to answer three questions about what the speakers say in each conversation. Select the best response to each question and mark the letter (A), (B), (C), or (D) on your answer sheet. The conversations will not be printed in your test book and will be spoken only one time.

32. What complaint does the man make?
    (A) A room is too small.
    (B) A noise is distracting.
    (C) Some software is slow.
    (D) A printer is broken.

33. What does the woman say she will do?
    (A) Change her chair
    (B) Borrow a computer laptop
    (C) Contact the help desk
    (D) Work from home

34. What does the man remind the woman about?
    (A) A team lunch
    (B) A training session
    (C) A project deadline
    (D) A policy change

35. What most likely is the man's occupation?
    (A) Server
    (B) Chef
    (C) Farmer
    (D) Food critic

36. What does the woman say she likes?
    (A) The design of a menu
    (B) The business hours of a restaurant
    (C) The flavor of a dish
    (D) The color of some tablecloths

37. Why is the man going to make a phone call?
    (A) To inquire about a job
    (B) To consult a colleague
    (C) To change a delivery date
    (D) To ask about a cost

38. Where do the speakers most likely work?
    (A) At a hospital
    (B) At a law firm
    (C) At an accounting company
    (D) At a publishing headquarters

39. What does the woman request?
    (A) A newsletter subscription
    (B) A parking pass
    (C) Budget data
    (D) Staff biographies

40. What does the woman suggest the man do?
    (A) Call a coworker
    (B) Ask for an extension
    (C) Send out a survey
    (D) Request overtime hours

41. What type of business is the man calling?
    (A) A shoe company
    (B) A marketing agency
    (C) A shipping company
    (D) A tailor shop

42. What does the man decide to do?
    (A) Contact a different business
    (B) Exchange some merchandise
    (C) Write an online review
    (D) Download a catalog

43. What will the woman send by e-mail?
    (A) Some design images
    (B) A sales receipt
    (C) Some delivery options
    (D) A Web site link

GO ON TO THE NEXT PAGE

44. What is the woman's area of expertise?

    (A) Music
    (B) Biology
    (C) History
    (D) Mathematics

45. What is the woman's current job?

    (A) A recruiter for universities
    (B) A curator for museums
    (C) A consultant for film studios
    (D) An editor for publishing companies

46. What will the woman do next week?

    (A) Promote her new book
    (B) Audition for a movie
    (C) Teach a seminar
    (D) Visit another country

47. What are the speakers preparing for in June?

    (A) A company merger
    (B) A fund-raising event
    (C) An industry convention
    (D) A product launch

48. Why is the woman pleased?

    (A) She has been promoted to manager.
    (B) She will have networking opportunities.
    (C) An advertising campaign was successful.
    (D) An article about the company is positive.

49. What does the man remind the woman about?

    (A) Bringing business cards
    (B) Compiling a guest list
    (C) Reviewing a contract
    (D) Submitting receipts

50. Who most likely are the speakers?

    (A) Tour guides
    (B) Hotel managers
    (C) Marine biologists
    (D) Business owners

51. What is Minoru asked to do?

    (A) Confirm a reservation
    (B) Create a logo
    (C) Print some documents
    (D) Review some résumés

52. What event is taking place next month?

    (A) A seasonal sale
    (B) A trade show
    (C) A community fair
    (D) A company picnic

53. Where is the conversation taking place?

    (A) At a bus station
    (B) At a city museum
    (C) At a state park
    (D) At a sports stadium

54. Why does the woman say she is concerned?

    (A) She is late for an appointment.
    (B) She does not have a credit card.
    (C) She did not reserve tickets.
    (D) She is unfamiliar with a location.

55. Why does the man say, "The visitor center is about 400 meters up the road"?

    (A) To correct some information
    (B) To offer a possible solution
    (C) To suggest a payment option
    (D) To point out a place to park

56. What are the speakers attending?

    (A) A property inspection
    (B) A contract signing
    (C) A building demolition
    (D) A grand opening

57. What does the woman say she is pleased about?

    (A) Using the latest technology
    (B) Improving safety policies
    (C) Keeping expenses within budget
    (D) Investing in a community

58. What does the woman suggest doing?

    (A) Distributing some handouts
    (B) Posing for a photograph
    (C) Enlarging some drawings
    (D) Scheduling an interview with a reporter

59. Where does the man most likely work?

    (A) At a garden center
    (B) At a restaurant
    (C) At a furniture store
    (D) At a hardware store

60. What motivated the woman to visit the business?

    (A) She read about it in the newspaper.
    (B) She heard an announcement on the radio.
    (C) She received a coupon in the mail.
    (D) She saw an advertisement on TV.

61. Why does the woman say, "it's a covered patio"?

    (A) To offer reassurance
    (B) To make a complaint
    (C) To explain a decision
    (D) To correct a misunderstanding

Professor Kwon's Schedule

Monday	Order equipment
Tuesday	Collect sample
Wednesday	Treat samples
Thursday	Analyze data

62. Who are the speakers?

    (A) Interns
    (B) Researchers
    (C) Maintenance staff
    (D) Inspectors

63. Why should the woman check a manual?

    (A) To review waste disposal instructions
    (B) To learn how to clean some equipment
    (C) To check which chemicals to use
    (D) To determine which protective clothing to wear

64. Look at the graphic. What day does the conversation take place?

    (A) On Monday
    (B) On Tuesday
    (C) On Wednesday
    (D) On Thursday

	Planting Calendar			
	Spring	Early Summer	Late Summer	Fall
Beets			✓	
Cabbage	✓			
Celery		✓		
Garlic				✓

65. Why does the man want to make a decision quickly?

  (A) A busy season is approaching.
  (B) A team is starting another project.
  (C) A client has changed a deadline.
  (D) A permit must be renewed.

66. Look at the graphic. Which logo design does the man prefer?

  (A) Design 1
  (B) Design 2
  (C) Design 3
  (D) Design 4

67. What is scheduled for next week?

  (A) A trade show
  (B) A focus group
  (C) A store opening
  (D) A safety inspection

68. What does the woman ask about?

  (A) Leasing some land
  (B) Offering workshops
  (C) Opening a farm stand
  (D) Replacing some equipment

69. Look at the graphic. When is the most popular crop planted?

  (A) Spring
  (B) Early summer
  (C) Late summer
  (D) Fall

70. What does the man offer to do?

  (A) Check an inventory
  (B) Select some seeds
  (C) Get an estimate
  (D) Reach out to customers

PART 4

Directions: You will hear some talks given by a single speaker. You will be asked to answer three questions about what the speaker says in each talk. Select the best response to each question and mark the letter (A), (B), (C), or (D) on your answer sheet. The talks will not be printed in your test book and will be spoken only one time.

71. Why does the speaker thank the listeners?
 (A) For responding to an employee survey
 (B) For arriving early for a shift
 (C) For agreeing to work overtime
 (D) For planning a holiday party

72. Where do the listeners most likely work?
 (A) At an appliance store
 (B) At a hotel
 (C) At a factory
 (D) At a hospital

73. What will the speaker do next?
 (A) Give a demonstration
 (B) Distribute some documents
 (C) Authorize a purchase
 (D) Conduct some interviews

74. What does the speaker compliment the listeners on?
 (A) Decorating an auditorium
 (B) Learning new dance steps
 (C) Selling tickets for a performance
 (D) Winning a competition

75. What does the speaker recommend doing?
 (A) Getting some rest
 (B) Drinking lots of water
 (C) Opening a window
 (D) Scheduling an additional performance

76. What is Erina responsible for?
 (A) Payroll
 (B) Marketing
 (C) Lighting
 (D) Costumes

77. Who most likely are the listeners?
 (A) Musicians
 (B) Actors
 (C) A television production team
 (D) Software technicians

78. What does the speaker say happened last week?
 (A) An article was published.
 (B) A renovation was completed.
 (C) A budget was approved.
 (D) Some equipment was replaced.

79. What will the listeners do next?
 (A) Pose for photographs
 (B) Tune some instruments
 (C) Interview a celebrity
 (D) Take a break

80. What is the purpose of the talk?
 (A) To welcome new employees
 (B) To explain a new policy
 (C) To celebrate a team's achievements
 (D) To share customer feedback

81. What will the listeners do after lunch?
 (A) Sign a document
 (B) Watch a video
 (C) Meet with some customers
 (D) Plan an event

82. Why does the speaker say, "That certainly wasn't on her résumé"?
 (A) To express surprise
 (B) To offer a recommendation
 (C) To make an excuse
 (D) To show disappointment

GO ON TO THE NEXT PAGE

83. What does the speaker say Bruxton is known for?
    (A) Its architectural landmarks
    (B) Its archaeological significance
    (C) Its connections to a renowned artist
    (D) Its collection of botanical gardens

84. According to the speaker, what should some passengers in the last car do?
    (A) Present their tickets to the conductor
    (B) Move to a car ahead of theirs
    (C) Store heavy luggage in another car
    (D) Refrain from talking on mobile phones

85. According to the speaker, why will there be a delay?
    (A) A staff change will take place.
    (B) An express train needs to pass.
    (C) Maintenance work is being done.
    (D) Weather conditions require caution.

86. What industry does the speaker most likely work in?
    (A) Landscape design
    (B) Architecture
    (C) Agriculture
    (D) Corporate catering

87. What does the speaker mean when she says, "grass does require a lot of water"?
    (A) She agrees with a choice.
    (B) She needs volunteers to help.
    (C) Water costs have increased.
    (D) A design plan should be changed.

88. What does the speaker ask the listeners to send her?
    (A) Supply lists
    (B) Photographs
    (C) Vacation dates
    (D) Travel recommendations

89. What is the broadcast mainly about?
    (A) A new company owner
    (B) A business partnership
    (C) Some store closings
    (D) A product rebranding

90. What goal does the speaker mention?
    (A) Introducing a new product line
    (B) Becoming more environmentally friendly
    (C) Launching a social media campaign
    (D) Expanding a customer base

91. What does the Willoughby store chain plan to do in July?
    (A) Renovate some of its stores
    (B) Display beachwear
    (C) Host a grand opening event
    (D) Distribute a customer survey

92. What is the purpose of the meeting?
    (A) To propose increasing an advertising budget
    (B) To announce a company merger
    (C) To discuss ways to improve a business
    (D) To recommend developing new products

93. Why does the speaker say, "Let's not forget that the Business Council's yearly ratings will be published soon"?
    (A) To offer to form a committee
    (B) To support a proposal
    (C) To congratulate award winners
    (D) To suggest joining an organization

94. What does the speaker suggest doing next month?
    (A) Advertising on social media
    (B) Hiring additional employees
    (C) Finalizing a production schedule
    (D) Offering a discount to new customers

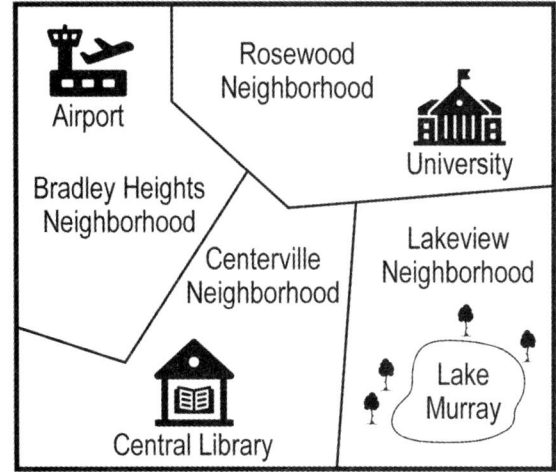

Variety	Price ($)
Tulips	10 dozen
Fringed tulips	295.00
Triumph tulips	280.00
Double early tulips	240.00
Parrot tulips	275.00

95. What happened last fall?
    (A) An electric train line was added.
    (B) A construction project was interrupted.
    (C) Some computer systems were upgraded.
    (D) Some city funding was approved.

96. What department does the speaker most likely work in?
    (A) Permits
    (B) Transportation
    (C) Parks
    (D) Housing

97. Look at the graphic. Which neighborhood will be served first?
    (A) Bradley Heights
    (B) Rosewood
    (C) Centerville
    (D) Lakeview

98. What does the speaker say she enjoyed seeing while she was in Boston?
    (A) An art exhibit
    (B) A sports event
    (C) A holiday parade
    (D) A rock concert

99. Who most likely is the speaker?
    (A) An interior decorator
    (B) A shop owner
    (C) A journalist
    (D) A painter

100. Look at the graphic. What type of tulips will the speaker most likely order?
    (A) Fringed tulips
    (B) Triumph tulips
    (C) Double early tulips
    (D) Parrot tulips

This is the end of the Listening test.

ETS 토익 정기시험 기출문제집 5
1000 LC

TEST 08
무료 동영상 강의

저자와 출판사의 사전 허락 없이 내용의 일부 혹은 전부를 인용 및 복제하거나 발췌하여 사용할 수 없습니다.

LC

기출 TEST 08

LISTENING TEST

In the Listening test, you will be asked to demonstrate how well you understand spoken English. The entire Listening test will last approximately 45 minutes. There are four parts, and directions are given for each part. You must mark your answers on the separate answer sheet. Do not write your answers in your test book.

PART 1

Directions: For each question in this part, you will hear four statements about a picture in your test book. When you hear the statements, you must select the one statement that best describes what you see in the picture. Then find the number of the question on your answer sheet and mark your answer. The statements will not be printed in your test book and will be spoken only one time.

Statement (C), "They're sitting at a table," is the best description of the picture, so you should select answer (C) and mark it on your answer sheet.

1.

2.

3.

4.

5.

6.

PART 2

Directions: You will hear a question or statement and three responses spoken in English. They will not be printed in your test book and will be spoken only one time. Select the best response to the question or statement and mark the letter (A), (B), or (C) on your answer sheet.

7. Mark your answer on your answer sheet.
8. Mark your answer on your answer sheet.
9. Mark your answer on your answer sheet.
10. Mark your answer on your answer sheet.
11. Mark your answer on your answer sheet.
12. Mark your answer on your answer sheet.
13. Mark your answer on your answer sheet.
14. Mark your answer on your answer sheet.
15. Mark your answer on your answer sheet.
16. Mark your answer on your answer sheet.
17. Mark your answer on your answer sheet.
18. Mark your answer on your answer sheet.
19. Mark your answer on your answer sheet.
20. Mark your answer on your answer sheet.
21. Mark your answer on your answer sheet.
22. Mark your answer on your answer sheet.
23. Mark your answer on your answer sheet.
24. Mark your answer on your answer sheet.
25. Mark your answer on your answer sheet.
26. Mark your answer on your answer sheet.
27. Mark your answer on your answer sheet.
28. Mark your answer on your answer sheet.
29. Mark your answer on your answer sheet.
30. Mark your answer on your answer sheet.
31. Mark your answer on your answer sheet.

PART 3

Directions: You will hear some conversations between two or more people. You will be asked to answer three questions about what the speakers say in each conversation. Select the best response to each question and mark the letter (A), (B), (C), or (D) on your answer sheet. The conversations will not be printed in your test book and will be spoken only one time.

32. Who most likely are the speakers?
    (A) Electricians
    (B) Real estate agents
    (C) House painters
    (D) Decorators

33. What do the speakers agree to do?
    (A) Come back on another day
    (B) Replace an item
    (C) Apply a discount
    (D) Try a new technique

34. What will the woman do next?
    (A) Go to her truck
    (B) Call her manager
    (C) Calculate a bill
    (D) Revise a schedule

35. Where do the speakers work?
    (A) At a laboratory
    (B) At a cafeteria
    (C) At a grocery store
    (D) At a hotel

36. What problem does the man mention?
    (A) Some data are incomplete.
    (B) A deadline was missed.
    (C) Funding may be insufficient.
    (D) Equipment might be faulty.

37. What does the man say he will do?
    (A) Monitor a situation
    (B) Place an order
    (C) Make a phone call
    (D) Compile test results

38. What are the speakers mainly discussing?
    (A) Starting a book club
    (B) Digitizing some books
    (C) Partnering with another business
    (D) Opening a new library location

39. What does the man like about a project?
    (A) Costs will be reduced.
    (B) A process will be faster.
    (C) An organization will receive publicity.
    (D) Access to some materials will be expanded.

40. What does the man suggest doing?
    (A) Attending a workshop
    (B) Hiring additional employees
    (C) Investing in new equipment
    (D) Changing a program design

41. Who most likely are the speakers?
    (A) Information technology specialists
    (B) Artists
    (C) Architects
    (D) Newspaper journalists

42. What will take place next week?
    (A) A meeting with a government official
    (B) A tour of a construction site
    (C) A community celebration
    (D) A trade show

43. What does the man want to do?
    (A) Review a contract
    (B) Create a model
    (C) Reserve a meeting room
    (D) Update a Web site

GO ON TO THE NEXT PAGE

44. Where does the man most likely work?
    (A) At a university library
    (B) At a government facility
    (C) At a home improvement store
    (D) At a county park

45. What does the woman want to do in the spring?
    (A) Write a book
    (B) Apply for a job
    (C) Take a course
    (D) Plant a garden

46. What does the man ask the woman to do?
    (A) Make a payment
    (B) Visit a Web site
    (C) Provide contact information
    (D) Wait for a supervisor

47. What are the speakers working on?
    (A) A piece of music
    (B) A television cartoon
    (C) A theater production
    (D) An advertisement

48. What does the woman say she will do?
    (A) Pick up some lunch
    (B) Set up an interview
    (C) Buy some art supplies
    (D) Turn on some equipment

49. What does the man suggest that they do later?
    (A) Download some software
    (B) Review some expenses
    (C) Contact a performer
    (D) Read a script

50. What does Ms. Stewart like about a restaurant?
    (A) Its varied menu
    (B) Its positive reviews
    (C) Its convenient location
    (D) Its outdoor seating

51. What problem does Sakura mention?
    (A) A kitchen appliance is broken.
    (B) A space may not be available.
    (C) A daily special is no longer offered.
    (D) A delivery may be delayed.

52. What will the man do next?
    (A) Provide a menu
    (B) Speak to a chef
    (C) Prepare a dining area
    (D) Order restaurant supplies

53. Where are the speakers?
    (A) At a trade show
    (B) At a press conference
    (C) At a job fair
    (D) At a factory opening

54. Why does the man say, "It handles 10,000 plants in an hour"?
    (A) To express amazement
    (B) To justify an expense
    (C) To correct an error
    (D) To recommend caution

55. What will the speakers do next?
    (A) Exchange business cards
    (B) Watch a product demonstration
    (C) Review financing options
    (D) Contact an event organizer

56. Where is the conversation taking place?

    (A) At an airport
    (B) At a travel agency
    (C) At a bus station
    (D) At a train station

57. Why are the men traveling to Toronto?

    (A) To attend a sports event
    (B) To meet with a client
    (C) To tour a factory
    (D) To present at a conference

58. What does the woman offer to do?

    (A) Rebook a trip
    (B) Restart a computer system
    (C) Provide some vouchers
    (D) Call a hotel

59. What has the man been doing?

    (A) Repairing a vehicle
    (B) Painting a fence
    (C) Training an assistant
    (D) Cleaning out a shed

60. Why does the woman say, "It was Hamdy Equipment that sold it to us"?

    (A) To complain about a decision
    (B) To correct some misinformation
    (C) To make a suggestion
    (D) To give a compliment

61. What will the man check next?

    (A) An invoice
    (B) A manual
    (C) Some cattle
    (D) Some vegetables

Tire Model	Price per Tire
City Cruiser	$75
Snow King	$98
High Summit	$120
Sport Plus	$133

62. Who most likely is the woman?

    (A) A mechanic
    (B) A customer
    (C) An auto parts supplier
    (D) A social media coordinator

63. Look at the graphic. Which tire model should have been listed on an invoice?

    (A) City Cruiser
    (B) Snow King
    (C) High Summit
    (D) Sport Plus

64. What does the man invite the woman to share?

    (A) Some consultant names
    (B) Some feedback
    (C) An e-mail address
    (D) A collection of photographs

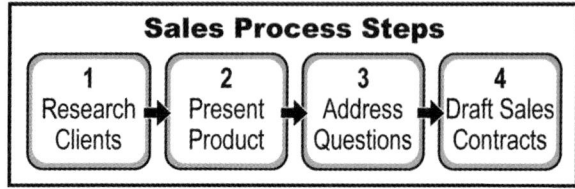

65. Why does the woman want to buy a new pillow?
    (A) Her pillow is old.
    (B) Her pillow is too small.
    (C) She heard about a new model.
    (D) She developed a pain in her neck.

66. Look at the graphic. How much is the pillow that the man recommends?
    (A) $20
    (B) $25
    (C) $30
    (D) $45

67. What does the woman ask about?
    (A) A product warranty
    (B) A promotional discount
    (C) The store's business hours
    (D) The materials used in a product

68. What is the man's area of expertise?
    (A) Packaging new products
    (B) Developing software
    (C) Designing fitness equipment
    (D) Training employees

69. According to the man, what did he recently do?
    (A) Reserve a conference room
    (B) Complete some paperwork
    (C) Meet with a supervisor
    (D) Fix some equipment

70. Look at the graphic. Which step of the sales process does the woman especially enjoy?
    (A) Step 1
    (B) Step 2
    (C) Step 3
    (D) Step 4

PART 4

Directions: You will hear some talks given by a single speaker. You will be asked to answer three questions about what the speaker says in each talk. Select the best response to each question and mark the letter (A), (B), (C), or (D) on your answer sheet. The talks will not be printed in your test book and will be spoken only one time.

71. Who most likely is the speaker?
    (A) A geologist
    (B) A boat captain
    (C) A maintenance supervisor
    (D) A city official

72. What is the speaker mainly discussing?
    (A) Conducting a safety inspection
    (B) Buying some new equipment
    (C) Building a new facility
    (D) Recruiting qualified staff

73. What will happen next?
    (A) A survey will be administered.
    (B) A video will be shown.
    (C) An expert will speak.
    (D) A process will be demonstrated.

74. What type of industry does the speaker most likely work in?
    (A) Transportation
    (B) Hospitality
    (C) Construction
    (D) Pharmaceutical

75. What will be Alka Raj's job responsibility?
    (A) Ensuring compliance with safety practices
    (B) Creating product development schedules
    (C) Ordering new equipment
    (D) Hiring and training staff

76. Why does the speaker say he is thrilled?
    (A) An employee will be promoted.
    (B) Some deadlines will be met.
    (C) Product sales have increased.
    (D) A trip abroad has been approved.

77. What problem does the speaker mention?
    (A) Some clients are unhappy.
    (B) Some offices are too cold.
    (C) Some construction is too noisy.
    (D) Some colleagues are sick.

78. What are the listeners temporarily allowed to do?
    (A) Use their personal e-mail accounts
    (B) Work from a conference room
    (C) Go home early
    (D) Close some windows

79. Who most likely is Marion?
    (A) A cafeteria employee
    (B) A parking garage attendant
    (C) A product supplier
    (D) A building manager

80. Where is the meeting taking place?
    (A) At a pharmacy
    (B) At a hospital
    (C) At a car dealership
    (D) At a jewelry store

81. What is the speaker mainly discussing?
    (A) Business travel
    (B) Company policies
    (C) Parking
    (D) Vacation

82. Why does the speaker say, "the break room is open 24 hours a day"?
    (A) To disagree with an idea
    (B) To ask for assistance
    (C) To explain a schedule
    (D) To suggest an alternative

GO ON TO THE NEXT PAGE

83. Who is the advertisement intended for?
    (A) Store owners
    (B) Tour guides
    (C) Interior designers
    (D) Paper manufacturers

84. How can the listeners receive a discount?
    (A) By entering a code
    (B) By writing a review
    (C) By using a special link
    (D) By ordering large quantities

85. What does the speaker emphasize about a product?
    (A) Shipping costs are included.
    (B) It is available in many sizes.
    (C) There are several framing options.
    (D) Licensed images are available.

86. What is the announcement mostly about?
    (A) A renovated station
    (B) A frequent-traveler program
    (C) Services on a train
    (D) Some new train destinations

87. According to the speaker, what can be found on a ticket?
    (A) An access code
    (B) A discount coupon
    (C) An assistance telephone number
    (D) A layout of the train

88. What does the speaker mean when he says, "there's significant maintenance work on the track ahead"?
    (A) The listeners cannot visit a specific station.
    (B) The listeners should anticipate some delays.
    (C) The listeners may need to plan alternate routes.
    (D) The listeners will receive a ticket refund.

89. Who is the speaker?
    (A) A plumber
    (B) A city employee
    (C) A bank supervisor
    (D) A swimming pool cleaner

90. Why is the woman calling?
    (A) To request a price quote
    (B) To cancel an order
    (C) To report a malfunction
    (D) To respond to an inquiry

91. What does the speaker say about Lihong Hao?
    (A) She has a professional certification.
    (B) She is an environmental expert.
    (C) She will be available next week.
    (D) She has recently been promoted.

92. What industry does the speaker most likely work in?
    (A) Construction
    (B) Transportation
    (C) Marketing
    (D) Shipping

93. Why does the speaker say, "I only use the highest-quality materials in my work"?
    (A) To recommend a product
    (B) To justify a price
    (C) To refuse an offer
    (D) To request a promotion

94. What does the speaker say could happen in April?
    (A) An employee could retire.
    (B) An invoice could arrive.
    (C) A project could begin.
    (D) A price could increase.

Inventory Report	
Refrigerator Model	**Quantity in Stock**
JH-883	265
JK-966	400
LH-655	380
LK-303	410

Wilson Park - Tuesday Tour Schedule	
10:00 A.M.	Cave Exploration
12:30 P.M.	Boat Tour
1:45 P.M.	Mountain Bike Ride
3:30 P.M.	Bird-Watching

95. What is the talk mainly about?

    (A) Merging with another company
    (B) Revising an inspection process
    (C) Building a new manufacturing plant
    (D) Selling products internationally

96. Look at the graphic. What is the company's top-selling refrigerator model?

    (A) JH-883
    (B) JK-966
    (C) LH-655
    (D) LK-303

97. What does the speaker say he will do?

    (A) Put together a team
    (B) Visit a business partner
    (C) Sign a contract
    (D) Prepare a presentation

98. What does the speaker encourage the listeners to do?

    (A) Visit a gift shop
    (B) Buy an annual membership
    (C) Use public transportation
    (D) Make a reservation online

99. Look at the graphic. When can the listeners book a tour today?

    (A) At 10:00 A.M.
    (B) At 12:30 P.M.
    (C) At 1:45 P.M.
    (D) At 3:30 P.M.

100. What does the speaker say about some brochures?

    (A) They contain trail maps.
    (B) They contain discount coupons.
    (C) They list a schedule of holidays.
    (D) They list volunteer opportunities.

This is the end of the Listening test.

TEST 09
무료 동영상 강의

저자와 출판사의 사전 허락 없이 내용의 일부 혹은 전부를 인용 및 복제하거나 발췌하여 사용할 수 없습니다.

LC

기출 TEST 09

LISTENING TEST

In the Listening test, you will be asked to demonstrate how well you understand spoken English. The entire Listening test will last approximately 45 minutes. There are four parts, and directions are given for each part. You must mark your answers on the separate answer sheet. Do not write your answers in your test book.

PART 1

Directions: For each question in this part, you will hear four statements about a picture in your test book. When you hear the statements, you must select the one statement that best describes what you see in the picture. Then find the number of the question on your answer sheet and mark your answer. The statements will not be printed in your test book and will be spoken only one time.

Statement (C), "They're sitting at a table," is the best description of the picture, so you should select answer (C) and mark it on your answer sheet.

1.

2.

3.

4.

5.

6.

PART 2

Directions: You will hear a question or statement and three responses spoken in English. They will not be printed in your test book and will be spoken only one time. Select the best response to the question or statement and mark the letter (A), (B), or (C) on your answer sheet.

7. Mark your answer on your answer sheet.
8. Mark your answer on your answer sheet.
9. Mark your answer on your answer sheet.
10. Mark your answer on your answer sheet.
11. Mark your answer on your answer sheet.
12. Mark your answer on your answer sheet.
13. Mark your answer on your answer sheet.
14. Mark your answer on your answer sheet.
15. Mark your answer on your answer sheet.
16. Mark your answer on your answer sheet.
17. Mark your answer on your answer sheet.
18. Mark your answer on your answer sheet.
19. Mark your answer on your answer sheet.
20. Mark your answer on your answer sheet.
21. Mark your answer on your answer sheet.
22. Mark your answer on your answer sheet.
23. Mark your answer on your answer sheet.
24. Mark your answer on your answer sheet.
25. Mark your answer on your answer sheet.
26. Mark your answer on your answer sheet.
27. Mark your answer on your answer sheet.
28. Mark your answer on your answer sheet.
29. Mark your answer on your answer sheet.
30. Mark your answer on your answer sheet.
31. Mark your answer on your answer sheet.

PART 3

Directions: You will hear some conversations between two or more people. You will be asked to answer three questions about what the speakers say in each conversation. Select the best response to each question and mark the letter (A), (B), (C), or (D) on your answer sheet. The conversations will not be printed in your test book and will be spoken only one time.

32. What is the purpose of the man's call?
    (A) To question a charge on a bill
    (B) To inquire about a job opening
    (C) To purchase a membership
    (D) To cancel a reservation

33. According to the woman, what additional service does the business offer?
    (A) Equipment rentals
    (B) Spa treatments
    (C) Personalized training sessions
    (D) Nutrition consultations

34. What does the woman ask the man to provide?
    (A) Some referral letters
    (B) Some contact information
    (C) A copy of a receipt
    (D) A discount code

35. Who most likely is the man?
    (A) A business client
    (B) A board member
    (C) A potential investor
    (D) A new employee

36. What does the man say he learned from another factory?
    (A) Assembly-line schedules
    (B) Budgeting strategies
    (C) Manufacturing regulations
    (D) Sourcing considerations

37. What is done at the start of each shift?
    (A) A database review
    (B) A cleanliness test
    (C) An attendance check
    (D) A uniform inspection

38. According to the man, what is the human resources department concerned about?
    (A) Lack of interest in a newsletter
    (B) Employee compliance with a policy
    (C) A shortage of qualified applicants
    (D) Inadequate training materials

39. Which department does the woman most likely work in?
    (A) Sales
    (B) Shipping
    (C) Legal
    (D) Graphic design

40. What does the man say he will do?
    (A) Reassign a task
    (B) Publish a news report
    (C) Move a project deadline
    (D) Repair a link on a Web site

41. What are the speakers mainly discussing?
    (A) A future business trip
    (B) An upcoming workshop
    (C) A job opportunity
    (D) A new employee's progress

42. What is the woman concerned about?
    (A) Difficulty speaking in public
    (B) Missing an appointment
    (C) A lack of experience
    (D) A negative performance review

43. What does the woman say she will do?
    (A) Update her résumé
    (B) Speak to a colleague
    (C) Review a budget
    (D) Register for a training program

GO ON TO THE NEXT PAGE

44. What have the speakers been working on?
    (A) An advertising campaign
    (B) A software update
    (C) An office renovation
    (D) A training course

45. Why does the woman say, "The café is just down the street"?
    (A) To praise a planning decision
    (B) To give directions
    (C) To reject an offer
    (D) To show concern about parking

46. What does the woman offer to show the man?
    (A) A schedule
    (B) A photograph
    (C) A map
    (D) A menu

47. Who most likely is the man?
    (A) A salesperson
    (B) A journalist
    (C) A company intern
    (D) A safety inspector

48. What does the woman say her company's goal is?
    (A) To decrease material waste
    (B) To open additional facilities
    (C) To improve employee morale
    (D) To acquire international contracts

49. What does the woman hope will happen?
    (A) Some funding will become available.
    (B) A fashion line will be popular.
    (C) A process will be widely adopted.
    (D) Export fees will be reduced.

50. Which department are the speakers most likely hiring for?
    (A) Product Development
    (B) Technical Support
    (C) Public Relations
    (D) Graphic Design

51. Why is the woman unsure about a candidate?
    (A) He lives too far from headquarters.
    (B) He might have limited availability.
    (C) He cannot provide any references.
    (D) He does not have relevant experience.

52. What does the woman suggest doing?
    (A) Scheduling a press conference
    (B) Canceling a training session
    (C) Making a lunch reservation
    (D) Postponing a phone call

53. What is the conversation mainly about?
    (A) A holiday gathering
    (B) A community festival
    (C) An art gallery opening
    (D) A fashion design show

54. Why does the woman say, "I have many options for you to consider"?
    (A) To recommend budgeting carefully
    (B) To offer reassurance
    (C) To praise the work her team did
    (D) To question a decision

55. What will the woman do next?
    (A) Contact a colleague
    (B) Drive to a bank
    (C) Retrieve items from a vehicle
    (D) Take the man to an event venue

56. What is unique about the woman's cookbook recipes?

    (A) They are inspired by the woman's university friends.
    (B) They are intended for large holiday celebrations.
    (C) They are collected from places the woman has traveled to.
    (D) They add unusual ingredients to traditional dishes.

57. What did the woman most likely study at university?

    (A) Accounting
    (B) Biology
    (C) History
    (D) Computer science

58. According to the man, what will some of the readers appreciate about the recipes?

    (A) They appear in multiple languages.
    (B) They explain how to measure ingredients.
    (C) They list alternative cooking methods.
    (D) They include color photographs.

59. Which industry do the speakers work in?

    (A) Pharmaceuticals
    (B) Technology
    (C) Construction
    (D) Agriculture

60. What will the men be doing?

    (A) Planning a hiring process
    (B) Leading a discussion
    (C) Conducting a tour
    (D) Inspecting a renovation project

61. What will the woman most likely do next?

    (A) Write a review
    (B) Download a mobile application
    (C) Consult a manager
    (D) Print some documents

Waterville Water Park Special Offers	
Day	Offer
Monday	Free parking
Tuesday	Discounted menu items
Wednesday	Discounted admission
Thursday	Free arcade tickets

62. What problem does the woman mention?

    (A) Low attendance
    (B) High maintenance costs
    (C) Few trained staff
    (D) Poor customer service

63. Look at the graphic. Which day does the woman want to change the special offer for?

    (A) Monday
    (B) Tuesday
    (C) Wednesday
    (D) Thursday

64. What does the man say he wants to confirm?

    (A) Some posters have been distributed.
    (B) A schedule has been printed.
    (C) Some repairs have been completed.
    (D) A park map has been updated.

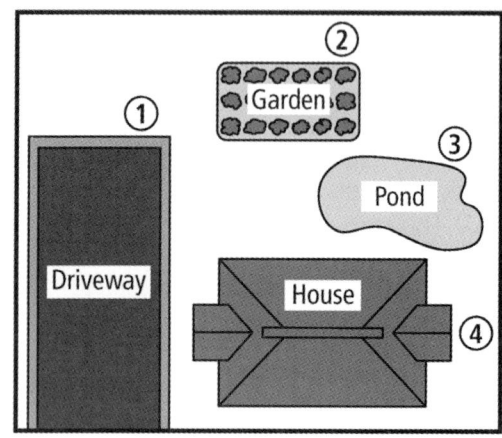

65. Where most likely is the gift shop?

    (A) At an airport
    (B) At a sports stadium
    (C) At a museum
    (D) At a concert hall

66. Look at the graphic. How much will the woman pay for an item?

    (A) $35
    (B) $18
    (C) $25
    (D) $12

67. What does the man suggest doing?

    (A) Visiting a Web site
    (B) Registering for a class
    (C) Printing some tickets
    (D) Becoming a member

68. Look at the graphic. Where does the woman want to install a fence?

    (A) In location 1
    (B) In location 2
    (C) In location 3
    (D) In location 4

69. How can the woman receive a discount?

    (A) By posting a review on social media
    (B) By paying half the cost in advance
    (C) By enrolling in a loyalty program
    (D) By referring a friend

70. Why will the man visit the property on Saturday?

    (A) To obtain a signature
    (B) To deliver some materials
    (C) To take some photographs
    (D) To take some measurements

PART 4

Directions: You will hear some talks given by a single speaker. You will be asked to answer three questions about what the speaker says in each talk. Select the best response to each question and mark the letter (A), (B), (C), or (D) on your answer sheet. The talks will not be printed in your test book and will be spoken only one time.

71. What is the focus of the tour?
    (A) Rock formations
    (B) Wildlife species
    (C) Bridges
    (D) Buildings

72. What does the speaker say is available on board the boat?
    (A) Personalized merchandise
    (B) Professional photography
    (C) Meals made to order
    (D) Recorded audio guides

73. What will the listeners most likely do next?
    (A) Go to their seats
    (B) Present their tickets
    (C) Put on their name tags
    (D) Store their belongings

74. According to the speaker, what is the business launching?
    (A) A rewards program
    (B) A recycling program
    (C) A new logo
    (D) A delivery service

75. What should the listeners be prepared to show?
    (A) A coupon
    (B) A receipt
    (C) A piece of identification
    (D) A signed enrollment form

76. Why will the business be closed tomorrow?
    (A) For some floor repairs
    (B) For a national holiday
    (C) For a training exercise
    (D) For an equipment installation

77. What is the speaker reporting on?
    (A) A store opening
    (B) A celebrity visit
    (C) A traffic delay
    (D) A sports tournament

78. What is causing a problem?
    (A) A fallen tree
    (B) A broken piece of equipment
    (C) A permitting process
    (D) A parking lot closure

79. Who is Mr. Wei?
    (A) A landscaper
    (B) A photographer
    (C) An athlete
    (D) A road maintenance worker

80. Where does the speaker work?
    (A) At a print shop
    (B) At a social media company
    (C) At an electronics store
    (D) At a community center

81. What does the speaker imply when he says, "I was just about to post it"?
    (A) He misunderstood the timeline for a task.
    (B) Some technical assistance is needed.
    (C) It is too late to make a change.
    (D) An immediate answer is required.

82. What does the speaker say will happen at one o'clock?
    (A) A client will visit.
    (B) An interview will take place.
    (C) A shipment will arrive.
    (D) A staff meeting will be held.

GO ON TO THE NEXT PAGE

83. What is the focus of a project?
    (A) Analyzing survey results
    (B) Documenting operating procedures
    (C) Reducing technology expenses
    (D) Recruiting qualified staff

84. Which industry does the speaker most likely work in?
    (A) Aviation
    (B) Forestry management
    (C) Real estate
    (D) Health care

85. What will the listeners see on their screens?
    (A) Workplace policies
    (B) Budget proposals
    (C) Definitions of technical terms
    (D) Work assignments

86. What does the speaker's company develop?
    (A) Recipes
    (B) Medical devices
    (C) Educational software
    (D) Web sites

87. Why will the speaker meet with some of the listeners?
    (A) To finalize some relocation plans
    (B) To go over professional certifications
    (C) To confirm project deadlines
    (D) To prepare for some product demonstrations

88. Why does the speaker say, "a new restaurant has opened close by"?
    (A) To complain about some noise
    (B) To suggest an alternative
    (C) To highlight an accomplishment
    (D) To clarify a misunderstanding

89. What kind of service is being advertised?
    (A) Career training
    (B) Financial planning
    (C) Language translation
    (D) Home inspection

90. According to the speaker, what is unique about the business?
    (A) Its employees work remotely.
    (B) Its services are free of charge.
    (C) Its services are guaranteed.
    (D) It operates worldwide.

91. Why should the listeners visit a Web site?
    (A) To download a brochure
    (B) To complete a survey
    (C) To find a nearby location
    (D) To schedule an appointment

92. Who are the listeners?
    (A) Shareholders
    (B) Customers
    (C) Employees
    (D) Journalists

93. According to the speaker, what happened six months ago?
    (A) A corporate office was relocated.
    (B) An advertising campaign was launched.
    (C) A business partnership was formed.
    (D) A new executive director was hired.

94. Why does the speaker say, "total sales revenues are still being calculated"?
    (A) To express disappointment
    (B) To warn against reaching a conclusion too soon
    (C) To offer an excuse for missing an important deadline
    (D) To suggest that a budget be revised

City Parking Garage Rates	
Monday–Thursday	$22
Friday	$24
Saturday	$10
Sunday	Free

95. Who most likely is the speaker?
    (A) A news reporter
    (B) A garage attendant
    (C) An engineer
    (D) A city official

96. Look at the graphic. Which parking rate has been changed?
    (A) $22
    (B) $24
    (C) $10
    (D) Free

97. What will be presented next month?
    (A) A marketing proposal
    (B) A revenue report
    (C) Survey results
    (D) Some construction plans

Flight Number	Destination	Gate
BK107	Austin	A5
AU354	Los Angeles	D8
MX262	Detroit	C3
YT418	New Orleans	B2

98. Look at the graphic. What is the destination of the affected flight?
    (A) Austin
    (B) Los Angeles
    (C) Detroit
    (D) New Orleans

99. According to the announcement, what will Claudia provide at the counter?
    (A) Seat assignments
    (B) Airport maps
    (C) Food vouchers
    (D) Hotel recommendations

100. What does the speaker remind the listeners about?
    (A) Complimentary Internet access
    (B) Boarding procedures
    (C) Automatic text notifications
    (D) Luggage size restrictions

This is the end of the Listening test.

ETS 토익 정기시험
기출문제집 5
1000 LC

TEST 10
무료 동영상 강의

저자와 출판사의 사전 허락 없이 내용의 일부 혹은 전부를 인용 및 복제하거나 발췌하여 사용할 수 없습니다.

LC
기출 TEST 10

LISTENING TEST

In the Listening test, you will be asked to demonstrate how well you understand spoken English. The entire Listening test will last approximately 45 minutes. There are four parts, and directions are given for each part. You must mark your answers on the separate answer sheet. Do not write your answers in your test book.

PART 1

Directions: For each question in this part, you will hear four statements about a picture in your test book. When you hear the statements, you must select the one statement that best describes what you see in the picture. Then find the number of the question on your answer sheet and mark your answer. The statements will not be printed in your test book and will be spoken only one time.

Statement (C), "They're sitting at a table," is the best description of the picture, so you should select answer (C) and mark it on your answer sheet.

1.

2.

3.

4.

5.

6.

PART 2

Directions: You will hear a question or statement and three responses spoken in English. They will not be printed in your test book and will be spoken only one time. Select the best response to the question or statement and mark the letter (A), (B), or (C) on your answer sheet.

7. Mark your answer on your answer sheet.
8. Mark your answer on your answer sheet.
9. Mark your answer on your answer sheet.
10. Mark your answer on your answer sheet.
11. Mark your answer on your answer sheet.
12. Mark your answer on your answer sheet.
13. Mark your answer on your answer sheet.
14. Mark your answer on your answer sheet.
15. Mark your answer on your answer sheet.
16. Mark your answer on your answer sheet.
17. Mark your answer on your answer sheet.
18. Mark your answer on your answer sheet.
19. Mark your answer on your answer sheet.
20. Mark your answer on your answer sheet.
21. Mark your answer on your answer sheet.
22. Mark your answer on your answer sheet.
23. Mark your answer on your answer sheet.
24. Mark your answer on your answer sheet.
25. Mark your answer on your answer sheet.
26. Mark your answer on your answer sheet.
27. Mark your answer on your answer sheet.
28. Mark your answer on your answer sheet.
29. Mark your answer on your answer sheet.
30. Mark your answer on your answer sheet.
31. Mark your answer on your answer sheet.

PART 3

Directions: You will hear some conversations between two or more people. You will be asked to answer three questions about what the speakers say in each conversation. Select the best response to each question and mark the letter (A), (B), (C), or (D) on your answer sheet. The conversations will not be printed in your test book and will be spoken only one time.

32. What is the speakers' business planning to do in June?
    (A) Expand a space
    (B) Take product inventory
    (C) Plan an annual sale
    (D) Change a window display

33. Where do the speakers most likely work?
    (A) At a dance studio
    (B) At a culinary school
    (C) At a music shop
    (D) At an arts and crafts store

34. What does the man say he would like to do by the end of the year?
    (A) Advertise a contest
    (B) Offer private lessons
    (C) Increase operating hours
    (D) Provide repair services

35. What type of project is the man working on?
    (A) Restoring a piece of art
    (B) Designing a logo
    (C) Renovating a lobby
    (D) Developing a hair dye

36. Why does the woman recommend avoiding the color red?
    (A) It is expensive to produce.
    (B) It fades quickly.
    (C) It is too bright.
    (D) It is very popular.

37. What does the woman ask the man to do?
    (A) Pay a deposit
    (B) Send a picture
    (C) Test a product
    (D) Schedule a consultation

38. What is the man trying to do?
    (A) Join a tour group
    (B) Pick up some luggage
    (C) Call a taxi
    (D) Buy some gifts

39. What does the woman ask to see?
    (A) Photo identification
    (B) A valid visa
    (C) A customs declaration
    (D) A boarding pass

40. Why does the woman say, "That area is past security"?
    (A) To clarify a policy
    (B) To express surprise
    (C) To reject a request
    (D) To describe a floor plan

41. Where do the speakers most likely work?
    (A) At a bookstore
    (B) At a marketing firm
    (C) At an electronics manufacturer
    (D) At a dental office

42. What does the woman say she is familiar with?
    (A) A university course
    (B) A software program
    (C) An industry conference
    (D) A safety procedure

43. What does the man remind the woman about?
    (A) A lunch break
    (B) A dress code
    (C) A parking policy
    (D) A benefits program

GO ON TO THE NEXT PAGE

44. What is the man concerned about?
 (A) A staff shortage
 (B) A design budget
 (C) A project timeline
 (D) A weather forecast

45. What is Camille working on?
 (A) Durability testing
 (B) Contract negotiations
 (C) A marketing presentation
 (D) A product manual

46. What would the man like assistance with?
 (A) Interviewing a job candidate
 (B) Making a video
 (C) Booking a venue
 (D) Packing some materials

47. What most likely is the man's job?
 (A) Gift shop worker
 (B) Flight attendant
 (C) Security guard
 (D) Rideshare driver

48. How does the woman recommend getting to terminal A?
 (A) By taking a shuttle bus
 (B) By riding an escalator
 (C) By using a bridge
 (D) By crossing a street

49. What does the woman say is by the rental-car lot?
 (A) A department store
 (B) A bank
 (C) A restaurant
 (D) A fuel station

50. Where are the speakers?
 (A) On a bus
 (B) On a boat
 (C) At a car dealership
 (D) At a train station

51. Why does the man say, "I heard the Day Street Bridge is being worked on"?
 (A) To confirm some information
 (B) To make a correction
 (C) To explain a delay
 (D) To recommend leaving early

52. What does the woman say she will do tomorrow?
 (A) Purchase a monthly pass
 (B) Download a map
 (C) Check a schedule
 (D) Use alternate transportation

53. What product is the man calling about?
 (A) A portable game system
 (B) A printer
 (C) A camera
 (D) A tablet computer

54. Why will the man go to a store?
 (A) To purchase an extended warranty
 (B) To resolve a problem
 (C) To receive a refund
 (D) To pick up some accessories

55. Who will the woman most likely give a note to?
 (A) A parking attendant
 (B) A product designer
 (C) A customer
 (D) A colleague

56. Where do the women most likely work?

    (A) At a medical clinic
    (B) At a department store
    (C) At a hotel
    (D) At a manufacturing plant

57. What does the man request?

    (A) A schedule
    (B) A list of employees
    (C) A facility tour
    (D) A signature

58. What will the women most likely do next?

    (A) Attend a staff meeting
    (B) Check some reports
    (C) Take a lunch break
    (D) Move some boxes

59. Why is the woman calling?

    (A) To inquire about a service
    (B) To arrange an interview
    (C) To request a refund
    (D) To make a reservation

60. What does the man say about his company?

    (A) It ensures customer satisfaction.
    (B) It has been in business for three years.
    (C) It operates 24 hours a day.
    (D) It is family owned.

61. According to the man, what will his company provide?

    (A) Directions to a facility
    (B) Pickup and delivery
    (C) A member discount
    (D) An updated receipt

DONATION FORM

Prize	Donation
Bicycle	$50
Theater tickets	$75
Camera	$100
Weekend getaway	$150

Name _____

62. Where is the conversation taking place?

    (A) At a department store
    (B) At a fitness center
    (C) At a library
    (D) At a restaurant

63. Look at the graphic. Which prize could the woman win?

    (A) A bicycle
    (B) Theater tickets
    (C) A camera
    (D) A weekend getaway

64. How will winners be notified?

    (A) By telephone
    (B) By text message
    (C) By e-mail
    (D) By letter

Name of Flower Arrangement	Price
Sunshine	$45
Rainbow	$60
Harmony	$75
Bright Day	$110

65. Why does the woman want to purchase flowers?

    (A) To decorate a building lobby
    (B) To observe a company anniversary
    (C) To mark the completion of a work project
    (D) To celebrate a coworker's promotion

66. Look at the graphic. How much will the woman pay for the flower arrangement?

    (A) $45
    (B) $60
    (C) $75
    (D) $110

67. What additional item do the speakers discuss?

    (A) A chocolate bar
    (B) A greeting card
    (C) A bunch of balloons
    (D) A decorative bow

Jebreen Farms Grain Bins	
Bin 1	Barley
Bin 2	Wheat
Bin 3	Corn
Bin 4	Oats

68. Who most likely is the man?

    (A) A new employee
    (B) An investor
    (C) A university professor
    (D) A business owner

69. Look at the graphic. Where will the upcoming harvest be stored?

    (A) Bin 1
    (B) Bin 2
    (C) Bin 3
    (D) Bin 4

70. What does the man ask about?

    (A) When some work will begin
    (B) How long a process will take
    (C) Who will buy a product
    (D) When a delivery will arrive

PART 4

Directions: You will hear some talks given by a single speaker. You will be asked to answer three questions about what the speaker says in each talk. Select the best response to each question and mark the letter (A), (B), (C), or (D) on your answer sheet. The talks will not be printed in your test book and will be spoken only one time.

71. What does Schneider Technology produce?
    (A) Automobile engines
    (B) Audio equipment
    (C) Navigation devices
    (D) Medical equipment

72. Who will the listeners meet with at ten o'clock?
    (A) An important client
    (B) The company president
    (C) The head of security
    (D) A government official

73. What will the listeners do next?
    (A) Set up their computer accounts
    (B) Receive their security badges
    (C) Tour a facility
    (D) Watch a demonstration

74. Where does the announcement most likely take place?
    (A) On a train
    (B) On a ship
    (C) On an airplane
    (D) On a bus

75. What is causing a delay?
    (A) Weather conditions
    (B) Heavy traffic
    (C) Malfunctioning equipment
    (D) A staff shortage

76. What does the speaker remind the listeners to do?
    (A) Store luggage in overhead compartments
    (B) Show tickets to an attendant
    (C) Avoid eating and drinking
    (D) Keep children in their seats

77. What project does the speaker mention?
    (A) The addition of traffic lights
    (B) The renovation of a museum
    (C) The expansion of a sports stadium
    (D) The construction of a bridge

78. What does the speaker imply when he says, "the workers arrive in six weeks"?
    (A) The listeners should attend a welcome reception.
    (B) Some training will be offered soon.
    (C) The listeners have a limited amount of time.
    (D) A hiring need has already been fulfilled.

79. What does the speaker assure the listeners of?
    (A) Videos will be available online.
    (B) Prices will not increase.
    (C) Roads will remain open.
    (D) A schedule will not change.

80. What does the company make?
    (A) Clothing
    (B) Jewelry
    (C) Eyeglass frames
    (D) Ceramic vases

81. How is the company different from its competitors?
    (A) It uses eco-friendly materials.
    (B) It offers online consultations.
    (C) It promises one-week delivery.
    (D) It provides product prototypes.

82. Why should the listeners visit a Web site?
    (A) To enter a contest
    (B) To receive a discount code
    (C) To start an order
    (D) To view some photographs

GO ON TO THE NEXT PAGE

83. What is the focus of the podcast?
    (A) Real estate
    (B) Food services
    (C) Graphic design
    (D) Tourism

84. What does the speaker say Rebecca Taylor is known for?
    (A) Organizing workshops
    (B) Providing technology support
    (C) Promoting products
    (D) Predicting market trends

85. According to the speaker, what will Ms. Taylor do in Chicago?
    (A) Release a book
    (B) Speak at a conference
    (C) Appear on television
    (D) Announce an award winner

86. What is the main topic of the workshop?
    (A) Creating new advertisements
    (B) Designing Web sites
    (C) Giving effective presentations
    (D) Writing for business communication

87. Why does the speaker say, "we don't want to offend our clients"?
    (A) To stress the importance of some guidelines
    (B) To announce a change
    (C) To request feedback
    (D) To propose that a meeting be rescheduled

88. What are the listeners asked to do?
    (A) Update some contact information
    (B) Rewrite some e-mails
    (C) Do an online search
    (D) Download some software

89. Why is Clementine Stores in the news report?
    (A) It filed a complaint.
    (B) It closed some factories.
    (C) It merged with another company.
    (D) It started an internship program.

90. According to the report, what do the companies have in common?
    (A) They have international clients.
    (B) They are family-owned businesses.
    (C) They sell athletic clothing.
    (D) They have similar logos.

91. Who is Friedrich Weber?
    (A) A news reporter
    (B) A public relations associate
    (C) A corporate attorney
    (D) A graphic designer

92. Where does the speaker most likely work?
    (A) At a café
    (B) At an appliance store
    (C) At a food manufacturing plant
    (D) At a repair shop

93. What is the speaker concerned about?
    (A) Package labeling
    (B) Increased temperature readings
    (C) Product costs
    (D) Limited business hours

94. Why does the speaker say, "customers often take a while to make their selection"?
    (A) To recommend rearranging a display
    (B) To encourage staff to be attentive
    (C) To emphasize a problem
    (D) To remind staff of a policy

Workshop Registration
1. Name
   [First] [Last]
2. Street Address
3. Telephone Number
4. E-mail

PARKING RATES	
1 hour or less	$3.00
1–3 hours	$5.00
3–5 hours	$7.00
5–8 hours	$9.00

95. How does the speaker begin the meeting?
    (A) By announcing contest winners
    (B) By reading a new policy
    (C) By distributing a sign-up sheet
    (D) By introducing new employees

96. Look at the graphic. Which section does the speaker say the listeners should leave blank?
    (A) Section 1
    (B) Section 2
    (C) Section 3
    (D) Section 4

97. What does the speaker say will happen next week?
    (A) A cafeteria will be closed.
    (B) Free snacks will be provided.
    (C) Certificates will be distributed.
    (D) New ID badges will be issued.

98. Where does the speaker work?
    (A) At a hair salon
    (B) At a doctor's office
    (C) At a talent agency
    (D) At a photographer's studio

99. What does the speaker ask the listener to do?
    (A) Write an online review
    (B) Confirm an appointment
    (C) Submit a form
    (D) Download an application

100. Look at the graphic. How much will the listener most likely pay for parking?
     (A) $3.00
     (B) $5.00
     (C) $7.00
     (D) $9.00

This is the end of the Listening test.

LC
ANSWERS

TEST 1
TEST 2
TEST 3
TEST 4
TEST 5
TEST 6
TEST 7
TEST 8
TEST 9
TEST 10

기출 TEST 1

1 (B)	2 (D)	3 (C)	4 (A)	5 (A)
6 (C)	7 (B)	8 (C)	9 (B)	10 (A)
11 (B)	12 (B)	13 (C)	14 (C)	15 (A)
16 (B)	17 (B)	18 (A)	19 (B)	20 (C)
21 (A)	22 (C)	23 (A)	24 (A)	25 (A)
26 (B)	27 (B)	28 (A)	29 (C)	30 (C)
31 (C)	32 (B)	33 (D)	34 (B)	35 (C)
36 (A)	37 (D)	38 (A)	39 (D)	40 (A)
41 (C)	42 (D)	43 (B)	44 (C)	45 (C)
46 (A)	47 (A)	48 (D)	49 (C)	50 (C)
51 (B)	52 (A)	53 (C)	54 (A)	55 (B)
56 (B)	57 (A)	58 (C)	59 (A)	60 (C)
61 (B)	62 (C)	63 (C)	64 (D)	65 (D)
66 (A)	67 (C)	68 (B)	69 (A)	70 (C)
71 (B)	72 (C)	73 (A)	74 (B)	75 (D)
76 (A)	77 (B)	78 (D)	79 (A)	80 (D)
81 (A)	82 (B)	83 (D)	84 (A)	85 (D)
86 (A)	87 (B)	88 (C)	89 (D)	90 (B)
91 (C)	92 (B)	93 (A)	94 (D)	95 (A)
96 (C)	97 (D)	98 (D)	99 (C)	100 (A)

기출 TEST 2

1 (B)	2 (D)	3 (B)	4 (A)	5 (C)
6 (A)	7 (A)	8 (B)	9 (C)	10 (A)
11 (C)	12 (C)	13 (A)	14 (A)	15 (B)
16 (C)	17 (A)	18 (B)	19 (C)	20 (C)
21 (B)	22 (C)	23 (A)	24 (A)	25 (B)
26 (B)	27 (B)	28 (A)	29 (B)	30 (C)
31 (C)	32 (D)	33 (D)	34 (A)	35 (B)
36 (B)	37 (D)	38 (C)	39 (D)	40 (C)
41 (A)	42 (C)	43 (A)	44 (A)	45 (D)
46 (A)	47 (B)	48 (D)	49 (C)	50 (C)
51 (B)	52 (C)	53 (C)	54 (C)	55 (C)
56 (D)	57 (C)	58 (D)	59 (A)	60 (C)
61 (C)	62 (B)	63 (C)	64 (A)	65 (A)
66 (B)	67 (A)	68 (D)	69 (A)	70 (D)
71 (B)	72 (D)	73 (C)	74 (D)	75 (D)
76 (B)	77 (C)	78 (C)	79 (D)	80 (A)
81 (C)	82 (C)	83 (B)	84 (D)	85 (A)
86 (B)	87 (D)	88 (B)	89 (B)	90 (C)
91 (A)	92 (B)	93 (D)	94 (D)	95 (A)
96 (B)	97 (C)	98 (C)	99 (A)	100 (D)

기출 TEST 3

1 (D)	2 (A)	3 (D)	4 (B)	5 (C)
6 (A)	7 (A)	8 (B)	9 (B)	10 (B)
11 (A)	12 (A)	13 (C)	14 (C)	15 (C)
16 (B)	17 (C)	18 (B)	19 (C)	20 (C)
21 (C)	22 (B)	23 (C)	24 (A)	25 (B)
26 (B)	27 (A)	28 (A)	29 (C)	30 (C)
31 (C)	32 (B)	33 (C)	34 (B)	35 (C)
36 (A)	37 (D)	38 (B)	39 (D)	40 (C)
41 (B)	42 (B)	43 (D)	44 (C)	45 (A)
46 (D)	47 (D)	48 (B)	49 (B)	50 (C)
51 (D)	52 (C)	53 (B)	54 (C)	55 (D)
56 (D)	57 (A)	58 (C)	59 (B)	60 (C)
61 (D)	62 (A)	63 (C)	64 (D)	65 (C)
66 (A)	67 (C)	68 (A)	69 (A)	70 (C)
71 (B)	72 (C)	73 (D)	74 (A)	75 (C)
76 (B)	77 (C)	78 (D)	79 (A)	80 (B)
81 (D)	82 (A)	83 (B)	84 (D)	85 (D)
86 (B)	87 (A)	88 (B)	89 (B)	90 (C)
91 (A)	92 (C)	93 (C)	94 (A)	95 (C)
96 (B)	97 (C)	98 (A)	99 (B)	100 (C)

기출 TEST 4

1 (C)	2 (D)	3 (A)	4 (B)	5 (A)
6 (B)	7 (C)	8 (C)	9 (C)	10 (B)
11 (C)	12 (A)	13 (A)	14 (B)	15 (C)
16 (A)	17 (A)	18 (B)	19 (A)	20 (C)
21 (B)	22 (A)	23 (B)	24 (C)	25 (B)
26 (A)	27 (A)	28 (A)	29 (B)	30 (C)
31 (B)	32 (C)	33 (A)	34 (C)	35 (D)
36 (C)	37 (A)	38 (B)	39 (D)	40 (A)
41 (C)	42 (A)	43 (C)	44 (B)	45 (C)
46 (A)	47 (B)	48 (C)	49 (A)	50 (B)
51 (D)	52 (C)	53 (D)	54 (C)	55 (A)
56 (C)	57 (D)	58 (C)	59 (B)	60 (D)
61 (C)	62 (B)	63 (A)	64 (B)	65 (C)
66 (B)	67 (D)	68 (C)	69 (A)	70 (B)
71 (B)	72 (D)	73 (A)	74 (A)	75 (D)
76 (B)	77 (D)	78 (A)	79 (B)	80 (C)
81 (C)	82 (B)	83 (D)	84 (A)	85 (A)
86 (C)	87 (B)	88 (B)	89 (D)	90 (C)
91 (C)	92 (A)	93 (C)	94 (D)	95 (C)
96 (A)	97 (D)	98 (C)	99 (B)	100 (D)

기출 TEST 5

1 (C)	2 (B)	3 (A)	4 (D)	5 (B)
6 (B)	7 (B)	8 (B)	9 (B)	10 (C)
11 (B)	12 (C)	13 (C)	14 (B)	15 (B)
16 (C)	17 (C)	18 (A)	19 (B)	20 (B)
21 (C)	22 (C)	23 (C)	24 (C)	25 (B)
26 (B)	27 (A)	28 (C)	29 (C)	30 (B)
31 (A)	32 (D)	33 (B)	34 (B)	35 (B)
36 (A)	37 (C)	38 (C)	39 (A)	40 (D)
41 (B)	42 (D)	43 (C)	44 (C)	45 (A)
46 (B)	47 (D)	48 (C)	49 (B)	50 (D)
51 (A)	52 (C)	53 (C)	54 (D)	55 (B)
56 (D)	57 (C)	58 (C)	59 (A)	60 (B)
61 (C)	62 (B)	63 (A)	64 (D)	65 (A)
66 (D)	67 (B)	68 (B)	69 (A)	70 (D)
71 (A)	72 (B)	73 (A)	74 (D)	75 (A)
76 (B)	77 (A)	78 (D)	79 (B)	80 (A)
81 (B)	82 (A)	83 (C)	84 (A)	85 (B)
86 (D)	87 (C)	88 (C)	89 (C)	90 (D)
91 (A)	92 (D)	93 (C)	94 (A)	95 (A)
96 (C)	97 (B)	98 (D)	99 (A)	100 (A)

기출 TEST 6

1 (C)	2 (A)	3 (D)	4 (B)	5 (D)
6 (C)	7 (A)	8 (A)	9 (C)	10 (C)
11 (B)	12 (C)	13 (B)	14 (B)	15 (A)
16 (B)	17 (A)	18 (C)	19 (C)	20 (C)
21 (B)	22 (A)	23 (C)	24 (C)	25 (B)
26 (B)	27 (A)	28 (C)	29 (C)	30 (B)
31 (B)	32 (C)	33 (C)	34 (C)	35 (A)
36 (B)	37 (C)	38 (D)	39 (A)	40 (B)
41 (C)	42 (B)	43 (B)	44 (B)	45 (A)
46 (C)	47 (B)	48 (A)	49 (C)	50 (A)
51 (D)	52 (C)	53 (A)	54 (B)	55 (B)
56 (D)	57 (B)	58 (C)	59 (A)	60 (D)
61 (C)	62 (B)	63 (D)	64 (B)	65 (A)
66 (C)	67 (D)	68 (D)	69 (C)	70 (A)
71 (B)	72 (B)	73 (C)	74 (A)	75 (A)
76 (C)	77 (D)	78 (A)	79 (B)	80 (B)
81 (A)	82 (C)	83 (C)	84 (D)	85 (B)
86 (C)	87 (A)	88 (D)	89 (D)	90 (D)
91 (C)	92 (B)	93 (A)	94 (B)	95 (B)
96 (D)	97 (B)	98 (A)	99 (C)	100 (B)

기출 TEST 7

1 (B)	2 (A)	3 (A)	4 (C)	5 (A)
6 (D)	7 (B)	8 (B)	9 (A)	10 (B)
11 (C)	12 (B)	13 (B)	14 (C)	15 (A)
16 (B)	17 (A)	18 (B)	19 (C)	20 (B)
21 (C)	22 (C)	23 (B)	24 (B)	25 (B)
26 (C)	27 (B)	28 (C)	29 (B)	30 (A)
31 (B)	32 (B)	33 (A)	34 (A)	35 (B)
36 (C)	37 (D)	38 (A)	39 (A)	40 (C)
41 (A)	42 (B)	43 (D)	44 (C)	45 (C)
46 (D)	47 (C)	48 (B)	49 (A)	50 (D)
51 (B)	52 (C)	53 (C)	54 (D)	55 (B)
56 (C)	57 (D)	58 (B)	59 (A)	60 (C)
61 (D)	62 (A)	63 (B)	64 (D)	65 (A)
66 (D)	67 (B)	68 (A)	69 (B)	70 (C)
71 (B)	72 (C)	73 (A)	74 (B)	75 (A)
76 (D)	77 (C)	78 (D)	79 (D)	80 (A)
81 (B)	82 (A)	83 (C)	84 (B)	85 (A)
86 (A)	87 (A)	88 (C)	89 (B)	90 (D)
91 (A)	92 (C)	93 (B)	94 (D)	95 (D)
96 (B)	97 (B)	98 (A)	99 (B)	100 (C)

기출 TEST 8

1 (D)	2 (B)	3 (A)	4 (D)	5 (C)
6 (A)	7 (C)	8 (B)	9 (C)	10 (A)
11 (C)	12 (B)	13 (C)	14 (A)	15 (A)
16 (B)	17 (A)	18 (A)	19 (C)	20 (B)
21 (A)	22 (A)	23 (A)	24 (C)	25 (B)
26 (A)	27 (B)	28 (B)	29 (C)	30 (C)
31 (C)	32 (A)	33 (B)	34 (A)	35 (A)
36 (B)	37 (A)	38 (B)	39 (D)	40 (A)
41 (C)	42 (A)	43 (B)	44 (B)	45 (D)
46 (C)	47 (B)	48 (A)	49 (D)	50 (D)
51 (B)	52 (A)	53 (C)	54 (A)	55 (C)
56 (A)	57 (D)	58 (C)	59 (A)	60 (C)
61 (D)	62 (B)	63 (B)	64 (C)	65 (D)
66 (C)	67 (B)	68 (B)	69 (D)	70 (C)
71 (D)	72 (B)	73 (C)	74 (D)	75 (A)
76 (B)	77 (B)	78 (B)	79 (D)	80 (B)
81 (B)	82 (D)	83 (A)	84 (D)	85 (D)
86 (C)	87 (A)	88 (B)	89 (B)	90 (A)
91 (A)	92 (D)	93 (B)	94 (C)	95 (D)
96 (C)	97 (A)	98 (C)	99 (C)	100 (A)

기출 TEST 9

1 (D)	2 (A)	3 (C)	4 (B)	5 (C)
6 (C)	7 (C)	8 (A)	9 (B)	10 (B)
11 (B)	12 (C)	13 (A)	14 (B)	15 (B)
16 (A)	17 (A)	18 (B)	19 (C)	20 (A)
21 (C)	22 (C)	23 (B)	24 (B)	25 (C)
26 (B)	27 (B)	28 (A)	29 (C)	30 (A)
31 (A)	32 (C)	33 (A)	34 (B)	35 (D)
36 (C)	37 (B)	38 (A)	39 (D)	40 (A)
41 (C)	42 (C)	43 (B)	44 (A)	45 (C)
46 (D)	47 (B)	48 (A)	49 (C)	50 (C)
51 (B)	52 (D)	53 (C)	54 (B)	55 (C)
56 (D)	57 (C)	58 (A)	59 (A)	60 (B)
61 (B)	62 (A)	63 (D)	64 (C)	65 (C)
66 (A)	67 (D)	68 (B)	69 (B)	70 (D)
71 (D)	72 (B)	73 (A)	74 (A)	75 (C)
76 (B)	77 (C)	78 (A)	79 (B)	80 (B)
81 (C)	82 (D)	83 (B)	84 (A)	85 (D)
86 (C)	87 (D)	88 (B)	89 (A)	90 (B)
91 (C)	92 (C)	93 (C)	94 (B)	95 (D)
96 (C)	97 (B)	98 (B)	99 (A)	100 (D)

기출 TEST 10

1 (D)	2 (C)	3 (C)	4 (D)	5 (B)
6 (B)	7 (A)	8 (A)	9 (B)	10 (B)
11 (B)	12 (B)	13 (B)	14 (C)	15 (A)
16 (C)	17 (B)	18 (A)	19 (A)	20 (A)
21 (B)	22 (C)	23 (C)	24 (C)	25 (B)
26 (A)	27 (B)	28 (A)	29 (A)	30 (C)
31 (C)	32 (A)	33 (C)	34 (B)	35 (C)
36 (B)	37 (B)	38 (B)	39 (D)	40 (C)
41 (D)	42 (B)	43 (A)	44 (C)	45 (A)
46 (B)	47 (D)	48 (C)	49 (D)	50 (A)
51 (C)	52 (C)	53 (C)	54 (B)	55 (D)
56 (A)	57 (D)	58 (D)	59 (A)	60 (C)
61 (B)	62 (B)	63 (A)	64 (A)	65 (D)
66 (C)	67 (B)	68 (A)	69 (C)	70 (B)
71 (C)	72 (B)	73 (A)	74 (C)	75 (A)
76 (D)	77 (B)	78 (C)	79 (A)	80 (B)
81 (D)	82 (C)	83 (A)	84 (D)	85 (B)
86 (D)	87 (A)	88 (B)	89 (A)	90 (D)
91 (B)	92 (A)	93 (B)	94 (C)	95 (D)
96 (B)	97 (A)	98 (A)	99 (B)	100 (B)

ANSWER SHEET

ETS 토익® 정기시험 기출문제집

수험번호		성명	한글
응시일자 : 20 년 월 일			한자
			영자

Test 01 (Part 1~4)

(Answer bubbles for questions 1–100)

Test 02 (Part 1~4)

(Answer bubbles for questions 1–100)

ANSWER SHEET

ETS 토익 정기시험 기출문제집

성명 한글 / 한자 / 영자

수험번호

응시일자 : 20   년   월   일

Test 03 (Part 1~4)

Test 04 (Part 1~4)

ANSWER SHEET

ETS 토익 정기시험 기출문제집

성명 한글 / 한자 / 영자

수험번호

응시일자 : 20   년   월   일

Test 05 (Part 1~4)

Test 06 (Part 1~4)

ANSWER SHEET

ETS 토익 정기시험 기출문제집

수험번호

응시일자 : 20   년   월   일

성명
- 한글
- 한자
- 영자

Test 07 (Part 1~4)

Test 08 (Part 1~4)

ANSWER SHEET

ETS 토익 정기시험 기출문제집

수험번호

응시일자 : 20   년   월   일

성명 한글 / 한자 / 영자

Test 09 (Part 1~4)

Test 10 (Part 1~4)

*toeic.

ETS 토익 정기시험
기출문제집 5
1000 LC

정답 및 해설

기출 TEST 1

동영상 강의

1 (B)	2 (D)	3 (C)	4 (A)	5 (A)
6 (C)	7 (B)	8 (C)	9 (B)	10 (A)
11 (B)	12 (B)	13 (C)	14 (C)	15 (A)
16 (B)	17 (B)	18 (A)	19 (B)	20 (C)
21 (A)	22 (C)	23 (A)	24 (A)	25 (A)
26 (B)	27 (B)	28 (A)	29 (C)	30 (C)
31 (C)	32 (B)	33 (D)	34 (B)	35 (C)
36 (A)	37 (D)	38 (A)	39 (D)	40 (A)
41 (C)	42 (D)	43 (B)	44 (C)	45 (C)
46 (A)	47 (A)	48 (D)	49 (C)	50 (C)
51 (B)	52 (A)	53 (C)	54 (A)	55 (B)
56 (B)	57 (A)	58 (C)	59 (A)	60 (C)
61 (B)	62 (C)	63 (C)	64 (D)	65 (D)
66 (A)	67 (C)	68 (B)	69 (A)	70 (C)
71 (B)	72 (C)	73 (A)	74 (B)	75 (D)
76 (A)	77 (B)	78 (D)	79 (A)	80 (D)
81 (A)	82 (B)	83 (D)	84 (A)	85 (D)
86 (A)	87 (B)	88 (C)	89 (D)	90 (B)
91 (C)	92 (B)	93 (A)	94 (D)	95 (A)
96 (C)	97 (D)	98 (D)	99 (C)	100 (A)

PART 1

1

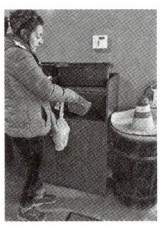

W-Br

(A) The woman is carrying a tray of food.
(B) The woman is wearing a jacket.
(C) The woman is tying up her hair.
(D) The woman is removing her hat.

(A) 여자가 음식이 담긴 쟁반을 나르고 있다.
(B) 여자가 재킷을 입고 있다.
(C) 여자가 머리를 묶고 있다.
(D) 여자가 모자를 벗고 있다.

어휘 carry 나르다, 휴대하다 tray 쟁반 tie up 묶다 remove 벗다

해설 1인 등장 사진 – 사람의 동작/상태 묘사
(A) 동사 오답. 여자가 음식이 담긴 쟁반을 나르고 있는(is carrying a tray of food) 모습이 아니므로 오답.
(B) 정답. 여자가 재킷을 입고 있는(is wearing a jacket) 모습이므로 정답. be wearing은 입고 있는 상태를 나타내는 표현이다.
(C) 동사 오답. 여자가 머리를 묶는(is tying up her hair) 모습이 아니므로 오답.
(D) 동사 오답. 여자가 모자를 벗는(is removing her hat) 모습이 아니므로 오답.

2

W-Am

(A) Some people are standing next to a filing cabinet.
(B) Some people are searching through a desk.
(C) Some people are watching a presentation.
(D) Some people are looking at a book.

(A) 사람들이 파일 캐비닛 옆에 서 있다.
(B) 사람들이 책상을 샅샅이 뒤지고 있다.
(C) 사람들이 발표를 보고 있다.
(D) 사람들이 책을 보고 있다.

어휘 search through ~을 샅샅이 뒤지다 presentation 발표(회)

해설 2인 이상 등장 사진 – 사람의 동작/상태 묘사
(A) 동사 오답. 파일 캐비닛 옆에 서 있는(are standing next to a filing cabinet) 사람들의 모습이 보이지 않으므로 오답.
(B) 동사 오답. 책상을 샅샅이 뒤지고 있는(are searching through a desk) 사람들의 모습이 보이지 않으므로 오답.
(C) 사진에 없는 명사를 이용한 오답. 사진에 발표(a presentation)를 하는 모습이 보이지 않으므로 오답.
(D) 정답. 책을 보고 있는(are looking at a book) 사람들의 모습이 보이므로 정답.

3

M-Au

(A) A woman is holding a phone up to her ear.
(B) A woman is pouring a beverage into a glass.
(C) Some light fixtures are hanging from the ceiling.
(D) Some tiles are being installed in a hallway.

(A) 여자가 전화기를 귀에 대고 있다.
(B) 여자가 음료를 유리잔에 따르고 있다.
(C) 조명들이 천장에 매달려 있다.
(D) 타일들이 복도에 설치되고 있다.

어휘 pour 따르다, 붓다 beverage 음료 light fixture 조명
hang from ~에 매달려 있다 ceiling 천장
install 설치하다 hallway 복도

해설 2인 이상 등장 사진 – 사람/사물/풍경 혼합 묘사
(A) 동사 오답. 여자가 전화기를 귀에 대고 있는(is holding a phone up to her ear) 모습이 아니므로 오답.

2

(B) 동사 오답. 여자가 음료를 유리잔에 따르고 있는(is pouring a beverage into a glass) 모습이 아니므로 오답.
(C) 정답. 조명들(Some light fixtures)이 천장에 매달려 있는 (are hanging from the ceiling) 모습이므로 정답.
(D) 동사 오답. 타일들(Some tiles)이 설치되고 있는(are being installed) 모습이 아니므로 오답.

4

W-Am

(A) A wooden crate is filled with vegetables.
(B) One of the men is putting vegetables into a shopping bag.
(C) A backpack has been set on the ground.
(D) One of the men is reaching into a bucket.

(A) 나무 상자가 채소로 가득 차 있다.
(B) 남자들 중 한 명이 채소를 쇼핑백에 넣고 있다.
(C) 배낭이 바닥에 놓여 있다.
(D) 남자들 중 한 명이 양동이 속에 손을 넣고 있다.

어휘 crate (운송용) 상자　be filled with ~로 가득 차 있다
reach into ~ 속에 손을 넣다　bucket 양동이

해설 2인 이상 등장 사진 – 사람/사물/풍경 혼합 묘사
(A) 정답. 나무 상자(A wooden crate)가 채소로 가득 차 있는 (is filled with vegetables) 모습이므로 정답.
(B) 동사 오답. 남자들 중 한 명이 채소를 쇼핑백에 넣고 있는(is putting vegetables into a shopping bag) 모습이 아니므로 오답.
(C) 동사 오답. 배낭(A backpack)이 바닥에 놓여 있는(has been set on the ground) 모습이 아니므로 오답.
(D) 동사 오답. 남자들 중 한 명이 양동이 속에 손을 넣고 있는(is reaching into a bucket) 모습이 아니므로 오답.

5

M-Cn

(A) Painting supplies have been laid out on the floor.
(B) He's laying a brush down on a windowsill.
(C) He's lifting a can of paint by its handle.
(D) Cans of paint have been placed on a step stool.

(A) 페인트용 물품들이 바닥에 펼쳐져 있다.
(B) 남자가 붓을 창틀에 내려놓고 있다.
(C) 남자가 손잡이를 이용해 페인트 통을 들어 올리고 있다.
(D) 페인트 통들이 계단식 발판에 놓여 있다.

어휘 supplies 용품, 물품　lay ~ out ~을 펼치다, ~을 배치하다
lay ~ down ~을 내려놓다　windowsill 창틀, 창턱
lift 들어 올리다　handle 손잡이　place 놓다, 두다
step stool 계단식 발판

해설 1인 등장 사진 – 사람/사물/풍경 혼합 묘사
(A) 정답. 페인트용 물품들(Painting supplies)이 바닥에 펼쳐져 있는(have been laid out on the floor) 모습이므로 정답.
(B) 동사 오답. 남자가 붓을 창틀에 내려놓고 있는(is laying a brush down on a windowsill) 모습이 아니므로 오답.
(C) 동사 오답. 남자가 페인트 통을 들어 올리고 있는(is lifting a can of paint) 모습이 아니므로 오답.
(D) 위치 오답. 페인트 통들(Cans of paint)이 계단식 발판에 놓여 있는(have been placed on a step stool) 모습이 아니므로 오답.

6

▶ 동영상 강의

M-Au

(A) A path is covered with fallen branches.
(B) A tree is lying across a grassy area.
(C) Some water has pooled on a path.
(D) Some cyclists are riding through a field.

(A) 길이 떨어진 나뭇가지들로 덮여 있다.
(B) 나무가 풀밭을 가로질러 놓여 있다.
(C) 길에 물이 고여 있다.
(D) 자전거 타는 사람들이 들판을 지나 달리고 있다.

어휘 path 길, 오솔길　be covered with ~로 덮여 있다
branch (나뭇)가지　lie 놓여 있다　grassy 풀밭의, 풀로 덮인
pool 고이다, 웅덩이를 이루다　ride 타다

해설 사물/풍경 사진 – 풍경 묘사
(A) 사진에 없는 명사를 이용한 오답. 사진에 떨어진 나뭇가지들 (fallen branches)의 모습이 보이지 않으므로 오답.
(B) 동사 오답. 나무(A tree)가 풀밭을 가로질러 놓여 있는(is lying across a grassy area) 모습이 아니므로 오답.
(C) 정답. 물(Some water)이 길에 고여 있는(has pooled on a path) 모습이므로 정답.
(D) 사진에 없는 명사를 이용한 오답. 사진에 자전거 타는 사람들 (Some cyclists)의 모습이 보이지 않으므로 오답.

PART 2

7　W-Am / M-Au

Where is the conference being held?
(A) A three-day vacation.
(B) At the Riverview Hotel.
(C) In the supply cabinet.

콘퍼런스가 어디에서 열리나요?
(A) 3일간의 휴가요.
(B) 리버뷰 호텔에서요.
(C) 물품 캐비닛에요.

어휘 vacation 휴가　supply 물품, 공급(품)

해설 콘퍼런스가 열리는 장소를 묻는 Where 의문문
(A) 질문과 상관없는 오답. How long 의문문에 대한 응답이므로 오답.
(B) 정답. 콘퍼런스가 열리는 장소를 묻는 질문에 리버뷰 호텔이라고 구체적인 장소로 응답하고 있으므로 정답.
(C) 질문과 상관없는 오답. Where 의문문과 어울리는 위치 표현이지만 행사가 열릴 만한 장소가 아니므로 오답.

8 M-Cn / W-Br

When does the warehouse manager arrive?
(A) Sure, no problem.
(B) About twelve shipping boxes.
(C) Not until this afternoon.

창고 관리자가 언제 도착하나요?
(A) 물론이죠, 문제없습니다.
(B) 약 12개의 배송용 상자들이요.
(C) 오늘 오후나 되어야 합니다.

어휘 warehouse 창고

해설 창고 관리자의 도착 시간을 묻는 When 의문문
(A) Yes/No 불가 오답. When 의문문에는 Yes/No 응답이 불가능한데, Sure도 일종의 Yes 응답이라고 볼 수 있으므로 오답.
(B) 질문과 상관없는 오답. How many 의문문에 대한 응답이므로 오답.
(C) 정답. 창고 관리자의 도착 시간을 묻는 질문에 오늘 오후나 되어야 한다고 대략적인 시간으로 응답하고 있으므로 정답.

9 M-Au / W-Am

There's a nice park nearby, right?
(A) Did you order paper for the copier?
(B) Yes—it's next to Greendale Lake.
(C) They're in the parking garage.

근처에 멋진 공원이 있죠, 그렇죠?
(A) 복사 용지를 주문했나요?
(B) 네, 그린데일 호수 옆에 있습니다.
(C) 그들은 주차장에 있습니다.

어휘 nearby 근처에　parking garage 주차장

해설 근처에 멋진 공원이 있는지 확인하는 부가 의문문
(A) 질문과 상관없는 오답.
(B) 정답. 근처에 멋진 공원이 있는지 확인하는 질문에 네(Yes)라고 대답한 뒤, 구체적인 위치를 덧붙이고 있으므로 정답.
(C) 유사 발음 오답. 질문의 park와 부분적으로 발음이 유사한 parking을 이용한 오답.

10 W-Br / M-Au

Who sent the meeting minutes to the accounting department?
(A) Our office assistant.
(B) They have a savings account.
(C) Cash and credit cards.

누가 회의록을 회계부에 보냈나요?
(A) 우리 사무 보조 직원이요.
(B) 그들은 저축 예금 계좌를 갖고 있어요.
(C) 현금과 신용카드요.

어휘 meeting minutes 회의록　accounting 회계
assistant 보조, 조수　account 계좌, 계정

해설 회의록을 회계부에 보낸 사람을 묻는 Who 의문문
(A) 정답. 회의록을 회계부에 보낸 사람을 묻는 질문에 사무 보조 직원이라고 구체적인 직책으로 응답하고 있으므로 정답.
(B) 유사 발음 오답. 질문의 accounting과 부분적으로 발음이 유사한 account를 이용한 오답.
(C) 연상 단어 오답. 질문의 accounting에서 연상 가능한 Cash와 credit cards를 이용한 오답.

11 W-Am / M-Cn

I'd like to know what you think of our new finance analyst.
(A) I've prepared the decorations for tomorrow.
(B) He seems very competent.
(C) It's finally stopped raining.

우리 신임 재무 분석가를 어떻게 생각하시는지 알고 싶어요.
(A) 제가 내일 사용할 장식들을 준비해 놨어요.
(B) 그분은 아주 유능하신 것 같아요.
(C) 드디어 비가 그쳤네요.

어휘 analyst 분석가　decoration 장식(물)　seem ~인 것 같다
competent 유능한, 능숙한

해설 부탁/요청의 평서문
(A) 평서문과 상관없는 오답.
(B) 정답. 신임 재무 분석가에 대한 의견을 구하는 평서문에 아주 유능한 것 같다는 의견을 제시하고 있으므로 정답.
(C) 유사 발음 오답. 평서문의 finance와 부분적으로 발음이 유사한 finally를 이용한 오답.

12 W-Br / W-Am

Let's go on the company retreat.
(A) Oh, did he?
(B) Yes, that's a good idea.
(C) He tried to solve that problem.

회사 야유회를 갑시다.
(A) 아, 그가 그랬나요?
(B) 네, 좋은 생각입니다.
(C) 그는 그 문제를 해결하려 했어요.

어휘 retreat 야유회, 짧은 여행　solve 해결하다

해설 제안/권유의 평서문
(A) 평서문과 상관없는 오답. 평서문에 3인칭 대명사 he로 지칭할 인물이 언급되지 않았으므로 오답.
(B) 정답. 회사 야유회를 가자고 제안하는 평서문에 네(Yes)라고 대답한 뒤, 좋은 생각이라고 동의하고 있으므로 정답.
(C) 평서문과 상관없는 오답. 평서문에 3인칭 대명사 He로 지칭할 인물이 언급되지 않았으므로 오답.

13 M-Cn / M-Au

What time can I pick up my glasses?
(A) No, it's not very heavy.
(B) About twenty meters.
(C) We close at six o'clock.

제 안경을 몇 시에 가져갈 수 있나요?
(A) 아니요, 그렇게 무겁지 않습니다.
(B) 약 20미터요.
(C) 저희는 6시에 문을 닫습니다.

어휘 pick up 가져가다, 가져오다

해설 안경을 가져갈 수 있는 시간을 묻는 What 의문문
(A) Yes/No 불가 오답. What 의문문에는 Yes/No 응답이 불가능하므로 오답.
(B) 질문과 상관없는 오답. How long 또는 How far 의문문에 대한 응답이므로 오답.
(C) 정답. 안경을 가져갈 수 있는 시간을 묻는 질문에 6시에 문을 닫는다며 그 전에 가져가야 함을 우회적으로 알리고 있으므로 정답.

14 M-Au / W-Am

The sales team knows how to use the tracking software, don't they?
(A) It's on the lower shelf.
(B) A twelve-thirty departure.
(C) I haven't seen them using it yet.

영업팀이 추적 소프트웨어 이용법을 알죠, 그렇지 않나요?
(A) 그건 아래쪽 선반에 있어요.
(B) 12시 30분 출발입니다.
(C) 그분들이 그걸 이용하는 걸 아직 본 적이 없어요.

어휘 tracking 추적, 파악 departure 출발, 떠남

해설 영업팀이 추적 소프트웨어 이용법을 아는지 확인하는 부가 의문문
(A) 질문과 상관없는 오답. Where 의문문에 대한 응답이므로 오답.
(B) 질문과 상관없는 오답. When 의문문에 대한 응답이므로 오답.
(C) 정답. 영업팀이 추적 소프트웨어 이용법을 아는지 확인하는 질문에 그들이 이용하는 것을 본 적이 없다는 말로 자신은 알지 못함을 우회적으로 알려 주고 있으므로 정답.

15 W-Br / M-Cn

Are you going to the hardware store on Mill Street?
(A) That store hasn't opened yet.
(B) The blue package you sent me.
(C) Some nails and a hammer.

밀 가에 있는 철물점에 가시는 건가요?
(A) 그 매장은 아직 열지 않았어요.
(B) 당신이 제게 보낸 파란색 소포요.
(C) 못 몇 개와 망치요.

어휘 hardware store 철물점 package 소포, 포장물 nail 못

해설 밀 가에 있는 철물점에 가는지 묻는 Be동사 의문문
(A) 정답. 밀 가에 있는 철물점에 가는지 묻는 질문에 그 매장은 아직 열지 않았다는 말로 그곳에 가고 있는 게 아님을 우회적으로 나타내고 있으므로 정답.
(B) 질문과 상관없는 오답.
(C) 연상 단어 오답. 질문의 hardware store에서 연상 가능한 nails and a hammer를 이용한 오답.

16 M-Cn / W-Am

Would you be able to write the introduction for the workshop?
(A) That was a great book.
(B) OK, I'd be happy to.
(C) He doesn't have any more.

워크숍 소개를 작성해 주실 수 있으신가요?
(A) 그건 훌륭한 책이었어요.
(B) 좋아요, 기꺼이 하겠습니다.
(C) 그는 더 이상 갖고 있지 않아요.

어휘 introduction 소개(글), 서문

해설 부탁/요청의 의문문
(A) 연상 단어 오답. 질문의 write에서 연상 가능한 book을 이용한 오답.
(B) 정답. 워크숍 소개 작성을 요청하는 말에 좋다(OK)고 수락하며 기꺼이 하겠다는 의사를 밝히고 있으므로 정답.
(C) 질문과 상관없는 오답. 질문에 3인칭 대명사 He로 지칭할 인물이 언급되지 않았으므로 오답.

17 W-Br / M-Au

I picked up some flowers for Tunji's retirement party.
(A) No, pick any day.
(B) That was thoughtful.
(C) A delivery driver.

제가 툰지의 은퇴 파티를 위해 꽃을 좀 사왔습니다.
(A) 아니요, 아무 날이나 고르세요.
(B) 사려 깊으시네요.
(C) 배송 기사님이요.

어휘 retirement 은퇴, 퇴직 pick 고르다, 뽑다
thoughtful 사려 깊은, 배려심 있는

해설 **정보 전달의 평서문**
(A) 파생어 오답. 평서문의 picked와 파생어 관계인 pick을 이용한 오답.
(B) 정답. 툰지의 은퇴 파티를 위해 꽃을 좀 사왔다고 알리는 평서문에 사려 깊다는 말로 칭찬하고 있으므로 정답.
(C) 평서문과 상관없는 오답.

18 W-Br / M-Cn

Which meeting room did you tell the interns to go to?
(A) The Jefferson Room.
(B) The meeting was fun, thanks.
(C) Yes, it's a conference call.

인턴들에게 어느 회의실로 가라고 얘기하셨나요?
(A) 제퍼슨 룸이요.
(B) 회의가 재미있었어요, 감사합니다.
(C) 네, 전화 회의입니다.

어휘 conference call 전화 회의

해설 인턴들에게 가라고 말한 회의실을 묻는 Which 의문문
(A) 정답. 인턴들에게 가라고 말한 회의실을 묻는 질문에 제퍼슨 룸이라고 특정 회의실로 응답하고 있으므로 정답.
(B) 단어 반복 오답. 질문의 meeting을 반복 이용한 오답.
(C) Yes/No 불가 오답. Which 의문문에는 Yes/No 응답이 불가능하므로 오답.

19 W-Am / M-Cn

Is your dental appointment next Tuesday?
(A) You can borrow mine.
(B) I'll have to check my calendar.
(C) Yes, it was a good meeting.

당신 치과 예약이 다음 주 화요일인가요?
(A) 제 것을 빌리셔도 됩니다.
(B) 제 일정표를 확인해 봐야 해요.
(C) 네, 좋은 회의였어요.

어휘 dental 치과의, 치아의 appointment 예약, 약속
borrow 빌리다

해설 치과 예약이 다음 주 화요일인지 묻는 Be동사 의문문
(A) 질문과 상관없는 오답.
(B) 정답. 치과 예약이 다음 주 화요일인지 묻는 질문에 일정표를 확인해야 한다며 자신도 알지 못함을 우회적으로 나타내고 있으므로 정답.
(C) 질문과 상관없는 오답.

20 M-Cn / M-Au

Why aren't there any brochures in the lobby?
(A) No, I haven't received my confirmation e-mail yet.
(B) My winter coat.
(C) Because someone just took the last one.

왜 로비에 안내 책자가 하나도 없는 거죠?
(A) 아니요, 저는 아직 확인 이메일을 받지 못했어요.
(B) 제 겨울 코트요.
(C) 누군가 방금 마지막 것을 가져갔기 때문입니다.

어휘 brochure 안내 책자 confirmation 확인(서)

해설 로비에 안내 책자가 하나도 없는 이유를 묻는 Why 의문문
(A) Yes/No 불가 오답. Why 의문문에는 Yes/No 응답이 불가능하므로 오답.
(B) 질문과 상관없는 오답.
(C) 정답. 로비에 안내 책자가 하나도 없는 이유를 묻는 질문에 누군가 방금 마지막 것을 가져갔기 때문이라며 이유를 알려 주고 있으므로 정답.

21 W-Br / W-Am

What's the process for submitting my expense report?
(A) You send it to the finance department.
(B) The end of the day.
(C) That's correct.

지출 보고서를 제출하는 절차가 어떻게 되죠?
(A) 재무팀에 보내세요.
(B) 하루 일과가 끝날 때요.
(C) 맞습니다.

어휘 process 절차, 과정 expense 지출 (비용), 경비
finance 재무, 재정 correct 맞는, 정확한

해설 지출 보고서 제출 절차를 묻는 What 의문문
(A) 정답. 지출 보고서 제출 절차를 묻는 질문에 재무팀에 보내라고 절차를 알려 주고 있으므로 정답.
(B) 질문과 상관없는 오답. When 의문문에 대한 응답이므로 오답.
(C) 질문과 상관없는 오답.

22 M-Cn / W-Am

Do you sell your products online or in stores?
(A) About twenty percent off.
(B) A product demonstration.
(C) Only online.

제품을 온라인으로 판매하시나요, 아니면 매장에서 판매하시나요?
(A) 약 20퍼센트 할인이요.
(B) 제품 시연회요.
(C) 온라인으로만요.

어휘 demonstration 시연(회), 시범

해설 제품 판매 방식을 묻는 선택 의문문
(A) 연상 단어 오답. 질문의 sell에서 연상 가능한 twenty percent off를 이용한 오답.
(B) 파생어 오답. 질문의 products와 파생어 관계인 product를 이용한 오답.
(C) 정답. 제품을 온라인으로 판매하는지, 아니면 매장에서 판매하는지 묻는 질문에 온라인에서만 판매한다며 둘 중 하나를 선택해 응답하고 있으므로 정답.

23 M-Au / M-Cn

How often do you charge this device?

(A) Whenever the light turns red.
(B) A wireless one.
(C) At the hardware store.

이 기기를 얼마나 자주 충전하세요?
(A) 표시등이 빨간색으로 바뀔 때마다요.
(B) 무선 제품이요.
(C) 철물점에서요.

어휘 charge 충전하다 device 기기 turn (상태 등이) 바뀌다, 변하다

해설 기기 충전 빈도를 묻는 How often 의문문
(A) 정답. 기기 충전 빈도를 묻는 질문에 표시등이 빨간색으로 바뀔 때마다라고 빈도로 응답하고 있으므로 정답.
(B) 연상 단어 오답. 질문의 device에서 연상 가능한 wireless를 이용한 오답.
(C) 질문과 상관없는 오답. Where 의문문에 대한 응답이므로 오답.

24 W-Br / M-Cn

The tickets to Friday night's concert cost ten dollars each.

(A) Actually, they're fifteen.
(B) No, I can't play the guitar.
(C) It's in aisle five.

금요일 밤 콘서트 입장권은 각각 10달러입니다.
(A) 실은, 15달러입니다.
(B) 아니요, 저는 기타 칠 줄 몰라요.
(C) 5번 통로에 있어요.

어휘 cost 비용이 들다 aisle 통로, 복도

해설 정보 전달의 평서문
(A) 정답. 금요일 밤 콘서트 입장권은 각각 10달러라는 평서문에 실제로는 15달러라고 정보를 정정해 주고 있으므로 정답.
(B) 연상 단어 오답. 평서문의 concert에서 연상 가능한 guitar를 이용한 오답.
(C) 연상 단어 오답. 평서문의 ten에서 연상 가능한 five를 이용한 오답.

25 M-Cn / W-Br ▶ 동영상 강의

Can't you update the database today?

(A) I did it yesterday.
(B) That's an interesting movie.
(C) No, just me.

오늘 데이터베이스를 업데이트할 수 없으신가요?
(A) 어제 했습니다.
(B) 흥미로운 영화네요.
(C) 아니요, 저만요.

해설 오늘 데이터베이스를 업데이트할 수 없는지 확인하는 부정 의문문
(A) 정답. 오늘 데이터베이스를 업데이트할 수 없는지 확인하는 질문에 어제 했다며 업데이트가 이미 완료되었음을 우회적으로 나타내고 있으므로 정답.
(B) 질문과 상관없는 오답.
(C) 질문과 상관없는 오답.

26 W-Am / M-Au ▶ 동영상 강의

How are we going to fit the extra supplies in that closet?

(A) I've already read them.
(B) Natalie's in charge of supplies.
(C) It's the door at the end of the hallway.

추가 물품을 저 수납장에 어떻게 넣을까요?
(A) 저는 이미 그것들을 읽었습니다.
(B) 나탈리가 물품을 담당해요.
(C) 복도 끝에 있는 문이요.

어휘 fit 맞추다, 맞게 하다 extra 추가의, 여분의 closet 벽장
in charge of ~을 책임지는

해설 추가 물품을 수납장에 넣을 방법을 묻는 How 의문문
(A) 질문과 상관없는 오답.
(B) 정답. 추가 물품을 수납장에 넣을 방법을 묻는 질문에 나탈리가 물품을 담당한다는 말로 담당자가 따로 있음을 알리고 있으므로 정답.
(C) 질문과 상관없는 오답. Where 의문문에 대한 응답이므로 오답.

27 W-Br / W-Am

Have all the new windows been installed?

(A) Sure, I'll close the blinds.
(B) The construction crew is almost finished.
(C) This isn't the tallest ladder available.

새 창문이 모두 설치되었나요?
(A) 물론이죠, 제가 블라인드를 닫을게요.
(B) 공사 작업팀이 일을 거의 끝마쳤습니다.
(C) 이것은 이용 가능한 가장 높은 사다리가 아닙니다.

어휘 install 설치하다 crew 작업팀, 조 ladder 사다리
available 이용 가능한

해설 새 창문이 모두 설치되었는지 묻는 조동사(Have) 의문문
(A) 연상 단어 오답. 질문의 windows에서 연상 가능한 blinds를 이용한 오답.
(B) 정답. 새 창문이 모두 설치되었는지 묻는 질문에 공사 작업팀이 일을 거의 끝마쳤다는 말로 곧 설치 작업이 완료된다는 뜻을 나타내고 있으므로 정답.
(C) 질문과 상관없는 오답.

28 W-Br / M-Cn

Would you rather go to lunch now or at noon?
(A) I'm taking a client to lunch.
(B) On the corner of Fourth and Main.
(C) The daily special is soup and a sandwich.

점심 식사를 하러 지금 가실 건가요, 아니면 정오에 가실 건가요?
(A) 저는 고객을 모시고 점심 식사를 할 거예요.
(B) 4번 가와 메인 가가 만나는 모퉁이에요.
(C) 오늘의 특선 요리는 수프와 샌드위치입니다.

해설 점심 식사를 하러 갈 시간을 묻는 선택 의문문
(A) 정답. 점심 식사를 하러 지금 가는지, 아니면 정오에 가는지 묻는 질문에 고객을 모시고 점심 식사를 할 거라며 점심 약속이 있음을 알려 주는 제3의 답변을 한 정답.
(B) 질문과 상관없는 오답. Where 의문문에 대한 응답이므로 오답.
(C) 연상 단어 오답. 질문의 lunch에서 연상 가능한 soup and a sandwich를 이용한 오답.

29 M-Cn / M-Au

You're taking the training in the afternoon, aren't you?
(A) The new head of the accounting department.
(B) No, I take my coffee black.
(C) Well, it depends on my schedule.

오후에 교육을 들으러 가시죠, 그렇지 않아요?
(A) 신임 회계부장님이요.
(B) 아니요, 저는 커피를 블랙으로 마셔요.
(C) 음, 제 일정에 달려 있어요.

어휘 accounting 회계 depend on ~에 따라 다르다, ~에 달려 있다

해설 오후에 교육을 들으러 가는지 확인하는 부가 의문문
(A) 질문과 상관없는 오답. Who 의문문에 대한 응답이므로 오답.
(B) 파생어 오답. 질문의 taking과 파생어 관계인 take를 이용한 오답.
(C) 정답. 오후에 교육을 들으러 가는지 확인하는 질문에 일정에 달려 있다는 말로 아직 알 수 없다는 뜻을 나타내고 있으므로 정답.

30 W-Br / M-Au

Shouldn't Ms. Ishida look over the financial projections?
(A) I just got this monitor.
(B) To the south entrance.
(C) I'm meeting with her at ten.

이시다 씨가 재무 계획을 살펴봐야 하지 않아요?
(A) 방금 이 모니터를 받았어요.
(B) 남쪽 입구로요.
(C) 제가 10시에 그분을 만날 거예요.

어휘 look over ~을 살펴보다 financial 재무의, 재정의 projection 계획, 예상

해설 이시다 씨가 재무 계획을 살펴봐야 하지 않는지 확인하는 부정 의문문
(A) 질문과 상관없는 오답.
(B) 질문과 상관없는 오답. Where 의문문에 대한 응답이므로 오답.
(C) 정답. 이시다 씨가 재무 계획을 살펴봐야 하지 않는지 확인하는 질문에 10시에 그 사람을 만날 것이라는 말로 만나서 확인해 보겠다는 의미를 우회적으로 전달하고 있으므로 정답.

31 W-Br / M-Cn

When are you going to choose a new project manager?
(A) The projector's not working correctly.
(B) Next to the front entrance.
(C) I'm really busy this week.

언제 신임 프로젝트 관리자를 선택하실 건가요?
(A) 프로젝터가 제대로 작동하지 않아요.
(B) 정문 옆이요.
(C) 제가 이번 주에 정말 바쁩니다.

어휘 correctly 제대로, 정확하게

해설 신임 프로젝트 관리자를 선택할 시점을 묻는 When 의문문
(A) 유사 발음 오답. 질문의 project와 부분적으로 발음이 유사한 projector를 이용한 오답.
(B) 질문과 상관없는 오답. Where 의문문에 대한 응답이므로 오답.
(C) 정답. 신임 프로젝트 관리자를 선택할 시점을 묻는 질문에 이번 주에 정말 바쁘다는 말로 그 이후에나 할 수 있다는 뜻을 우회적으로 나타내고 있으므로 정답.

PART 3

32-34 W-Am / M-Cn

W Hey, Oliver. Did you see the focus group results for **[32] our new spicy cheddar cheese?** Everyone really liked it.

M Yes. It should be a great addition to our company's line of cheeses.

W Several people mentioned that they'd like to use it in recipes—to add to sauces, for example.

M **[33] So maybe we should consider selling a shredded version that would melt easily when cooked.**

W I'm sure we could do that. **[34] I'll get in touch with the production manager with that request.**

여 안녕하세요, 올리버. **우리의 새 매운 체다 치즈**에 대한 포커스 그룹 결과를 보셨나요? 모든 분이 정말로 좋아하셨어요.

남 네. 우리 회사의 치즈 제품 라인에 훌륭한 추가 제품이 될 겁니다.

여 여러 사람들이 조리법에 사용하고 싶다고 언급하셨어요. 예를 들면, 소스에 추가하는 것이죠.
남 **그럼 조리 시에 쉽게 녹을 수 있는 잘게 조각난 버전을 판매하는 걸 고려해 보는 게 좋겠어요.**
여 분명 그렇게 할 수 있을 거예요. **제가 생산 관리자에게 연락해 그 요청 사항을 전달할게요.**

어휘 focus group 포커스 그룹(시장 조사 등을 위해 선정된 그룹) addition 추가(되는 것) recipe 조리법 consider 고려하다 shredded 잘게 조각난 melt 녹다, 녹이다 easily 쉽게 get in touch with ~에게 연락하다

32 What type of food product does the speakers' company sell?
(A) Candy
(B) Cheese
(C) Bread
(D) Pasta

화자들의 회사는 어떤 종류의 식품을 판매하는가?
(A) 사탕
(B) 치즈
(C) 빵
(D) 파스타

해설 전체 내용 관련 – 화자들의 회사가 판매하는 식품
여자가 첫 대사에서 우리의 새 매운 체다 치즈(our new spicy cheddar cheese)라고 말하고 있으므로 정답은 (B)이다.

33 What does the man suggest?
(A) Lowering prices
(B) Hiring more workers
(C) Publishing a recipe
(D) Offering additional options

남자는 무엇을 제안하는가?
(A) 가격 내리기
(B) 추가 직원 고용하기
(C) 조리법 출판하기
(D) 추가 옵션 제공하기

어휘 lower 내리다, 낮추다 hire 고용하다 publish 출판하다 additional 추가적인

해설 세부 사항 관련 – 남자의 제안 사항
남자가 두 번째 대사에서 조리 시에 쉽게 녹을 수 있는 잘게 조각난 버전을 판매하는 걸 고려해 보는 게 좋겠다(So maybe we should consider selling a shredded version that would melt easily when cooked)고 제안하고 있다. 이는 다른 옵션을 추가하자는 뜻이므로 정답은 (D)이다.

Paraphrasing
대화의 selling a shredded version
→ 정답의 Offering additional options

34 What does the woman say she will do?
(A) Send a schedule update
(B) Contact a production manager
(C) Visit the company headquarters
(D) Plan an advertising campaign

여자는 무엇을 할 것이라고 말하는가?
(A) 최신 일정 보내기
(B) 생산 관리자에게 연락하기
(C) 회사 본사 방문하기
(D) 광고 캠페인 계획하기

어휘 contact 연락하다 headquarters 본사 advertising 광고

해설 세부 사항 관련 – 여자가 할 일
여자가 마지막 대사에서 생산 관리자에게 연락해 그 요청 사항을 전달하겠다(I'll get in touch with the production manager with that request)고 했으므로 정답은 (B)이다.

Paraphrasing
대화의 get in touch with → 정답의 Contact

35-37 M-Au / W-Br

M Hi. **35 I'm calling to book three tickets for this Thursday's tennis match.** Are there any seats left?
W Just a few! Tickets for Thursday's match have been selling quickly.
M I'm not surprised! After all, **36 Ife Rotimi won the regional championship tournament last month.** Everyone wants to see her play after her incredible performance. What seats are available?
W Well, there's only one group of three seats together. **37 Advance payment is required to hold them.**

남 안녕하세요. **이번 주 목요일에 있을 테니스 경기 입장권을 세 매 예매하려고 전화했어요.** 좌석이 남아 있나요?
여 겨우 몇 개만 있어요! 목요일 경기 입장권이 빠르게 판매되고 있거든요.
남 놀랍지 않네요! 어쨌든, **이페 로티미가 지난달에 지역 선수권 대회에서 우승했잖아요.** 놀라운 성적을 거둔 후로 모두 그녀가 경기하는 것을 보고 싶어 하니까요. 어떤 좌석을 이용할 수 있나요?
여 흠, 세 개의 좌석이 붙어 있는 건 하나뿐이네요. **이 자리를 맡으시려면 사전 결제가 필요합니다.**

어휘 book 예약하다 after all 어쨌든, 결국 regional 지역의 incredible 믿을 수 없는 performance 성과, 실적, 공연 advance 사전의 payment 결제, 지불 required 필요한 hold 확보하다, 유지하다

35
Why is the man calling?
(A) To sign up for lessons
(B) To enter a competition
(C) To buy tickets to an event
(D) To ask about branded merchandise

남자는 왜 전화하는가?
(A) 레슨에 등록하려고
(B) 대회에 참가하려고
(C) 행사 입장권을 구입하려고
(D) 브랜드 상품에 관해 물어보려고

어휘 sign up for ~에 등록하다, ~을 신청하다   enter 참가하다
competition 대회   branded 브랜드화된, 유명 상표의
merchandise 상품

해설 전체 내용 관련 – 남자가 전화하는 목적
남자가 첫 대사에서 이번 주 목요일에 있을 테니스 경기 입장권을 세 매 예매하려고 전화했다(I'm calling to book three tickets for this Thursday's tennis match)고 했으므로 정답은 (C)이다.

Paraphrasing
대화의 book three tickets for this Thursday's tennis match
→ 정답의 buy tickets to an event

36
What did Ife Rotimi do last month?
(A) She won a regional tournament.
(B) She gave a television interview.
(C) She started an institute.
(D) She hired a new coach.

이페 로티미는 지난달에 무엇을 했는가?
(A) 지역 대회에서 우승했다.
(B) 텔레비전 인터뷰를 했다.
(C) 협회를 시작했다.
(D) 새 코치를 고용했다.

어휘 institute 협회, 기관

해설 세부 사항 관련 – 이페 로티미가 지난달에 한 일
남자가 두 번째 대사에서 이페 로티미가 지난달에 지역 선수권 대회에서 우승했다(~ Ife Rotimi won the regional championship tournament last month)고 했으므로 정답은 (A)이다.

37
What does the woman say is required?
(A) A parking permit
(B) A photo ID
(C) Contact information
(D) Advance payment

여자는 무엇이 필요하다고 말하는가?
(A) 주차 허가증
(B) 사진이 있는 신분증
(C) 연락처
(D) 사전 결제

어휘 permit 허가증

해설 세부 사항 관련 – 여자가 필요하다고 말하는 것
여자가 마지막 대사에서 자리를 맡으려면 사전 결제가 필요하다(Advance payment is required to hold them)고 했으므로 정답은 (D)이다.

38-40 W-Br / M-Cn

W **38 Thanks for agreeing to help me organize the library's annual fund-raising dinner, Klaus.** We hope the event brings in enough money to expand our children's book section.

M What task would you like me to start with?

W **39 Well, I could use some help sending out the invitations.**

M OK, I can take care of that. **40 Is there a list of attendees available?**

W It's in my computer files. **40 I'll e-mail it to you.**

여 도서관의 연례 기금 마련 만찬 준비를 도와주시기로 동의해 주셔서 감사합니다, 클라우스. 이 행사를 통해 아동 도서 섹션을 확장할 수 있는 충분한 돈이 마련되기를 바랍니다.
남 제가 어떤 일부터 시작하면 될까요?
여 음, 초대장 발송을 도와주시면 좋겠습니다.
남 알겠습니다, 제가 처리할 수 있습니다. 이용 가능한 참석자 명단이 있나요?
여 제 컴퓨터 파일에 있습니다. 이메일로 보내 드릴게요.

어휘 agree 동의하다, 합의하다   organize 준비하다, 조직하다
annual 연례적인, 해마다의   fund-raising 기금 마련
bring in ~을 가져오다   expand 확장하다, 확대하다
task 일, 업무   could use ~이 필요하다   invitation 초대(장)
take care of ~을 처리하다   attendee 참석자

38
What event are the speakers planning?
(A) A fund-raising dinner
(B) An art gallery opening
(C) An awards ceremony
(D) A children's book fair

화자들은 어떤 행사를 계획하고 있는가?
(A) 기금 마련 만찬
(B) 미술관 개관식
(C) 시상식
(D) 아동 도서 박람회

해설 전체 내용 관련 – 화자들이 계획하는 행사
여자가 첫 대사에서 남자에게 도서관의 연례 기금 마련 만찬 준비를 도와주기로 동의해 줘서 고맙다(Thanks for agreeing to help me organize the library's annual fund-raising dinner, Klaus)고 했으므로 정답은 (A)이다.

39 What task does the woman ask the man to help with?
(A) Arranging a shuttle service
(B) Choosing a catering firm
(C) Preparing a speech
(D) Sending out invitations

여자는 남자에게 어떤 일을 도와달라고 요청하는가?
(A) 셔틀버스 서비스 준비하기
(B) 출장 요리 업체 선택하기
(C) 연설 준비하기
(D) 초대장 발송하기

어휘 arrange 준비하다, 마련하다 catering 출장 요리 제공(업)

해설 세부 사항 관련 – 여자의 요청 사항
여자가 두 번째 대사에서 초대장 발송을 도와주면 좋겠다(Well, I could use some help sending out the invitations)고 했으므로 정답은 (D)이다.

40 What does the woman say she will do?
(A) E-mail a list
(B) Speak with a colleague
(C) Provide a password
(D) Post a job opening

여자는 무엇을 할 것이라고 말하는가?
(A) 명단을 이메일로 보내기
(B) 동료와 이야기하기
(C) 비밀번호 제공하기
(D) 채용 공고 게시하기

어휘 colleague 동료 post 게시하다 job opening 공석, 빈자리

해설 세부 사항 관련 – 여자가 할 일
남자가 두 번째 대사에서 이용 가능한 참석자 명단이 있는지(Is there a list of attendees available?) 묻자, 여자가 그것을 이메일로 보내 주겠다(I'll e-mail it to you)고 응답하고 있으므로 정답은 (A)이다.

41-43 3인 대화 W-Br / M-Au / M-Cn

W Hey, Brian and Matteo. **⁴¹I found some great pens to give away at the community festival to promote our business.**
M1 Great. Can we put our cleaning service logo on them?
W Yes, for no extra charge. And they're biodegradable. **⁴²They're made from paper.**
M2 So when we hand them out, we can mention that.
M1 As well as talk about the organic cleaning supplies our company uses.
W OK. **⁴³I'll go ahead and order several cases.**

여 안녕하세요, 브라이언, 마테오. **제가 지역 축제에서 업체 홍보용으로 나눠 주기 좋은 펜을 몇 개 발견했어요.**
남1 잘됐네요. 거기에 우리 청소 서비스 로고를 넣을 수 있나요?
여 네, 추가 요금 없이요. 그리고 생분해성입니다. **종이로 만들어지거든요.**
남2 그럼 우리가 그걸 나눠 줄 때, 그 부분을 언급할 수 있겠네요.
남1 우리 회사가 이용하는 유기농 청소 용품에 관해서도 이야기하고요.
여 좋습니다. 그럼 제가 바로 여러 케이스 주문할게요.

어휘 give away 나눠 주다, 증정하다 community 지역 사회 promote 홍보하다 extra 추가의 charge (청구) 요금 biodegradable 생분해성의, 자연 분해성의 hand ~ out ~을 나눠 주다 organic 유기농의

41 What event are the speakers preparing for?
(A) A new-employee orientation
(B) A grand opening
(C) A community festival
(D) A trade show

화자들은 어떤 행사를 준비하고 있는가?
(A) 신입 직원 오리엔테이션
(B) 개장식
(C) 지역 축제
(D) 무역 박람회

해설 전체 내용 관련 – 화자들이 준비하는 행사
여자가 첫 대사에서 지역 축제에서 업체 홍보용으로 나눠 주기 좋은 펜을 몇 개 발견했다(I found some great pens to give away at the community festival to promote our business)고 했으므로 정답은 (C)이다.

42 What is mentioned about some pens?
(A) They are available in multiple colors.
(B) They use permanent ink.
(C) They are preferred by book authors.
(D) They are made from paper.

펜과 관련해 언급되는 것은 무엇인가?
(A) 다양한 색상으로 구입할 수 있다.
(B) 영구적인 잉크를 이용한다.
(C) 도서 작가들이 선호한다.
(D) 종이로 만들어진다.

어휘 permanent 영구적인, 영속적인 author 작가, 저자

해설 세부 사항 관련 – 펜과 관련해 언급되는 것
여자가 두 번째 대사에서 펜들이 종이로 만들어진다(They're made from paper)고 했으므로 정답은 (D)이다.

43 What does the woman offer to do?
(A) Reserve a booth
(B) Place an order
(C) Organize a focus group
(D) Revise a budget

여자는 무엇을 하겠다고 제안하는가?
(A) 부스 예약하기
(B) 주문하기
(C) 포커스 그룹 조직하기
(D) 예산 수정하기

어휘 reserve 예약하다 booth 부스, 임시 칸막이 공간
revise 수정하다, 변경하다 budget 예산

해설 세부 사항 관련 – 여자의 제안 사항
여자가 마지막 대사에서 바로 여러 케이스 주문하겠다(I'll go ahead and order several cases)고 했으므로 정답은 (B)이다.

Paraphrasing
대화의 order several cases → 정답의 Place an order

44-46 W-Br / M-Au

W **44 Jamestown Recycling Facility.** How can I help you?

M Hi. I'm preparing to move soon, and **45 I have some electronics, such as televisions and computers, that I'd like to get rid of** before I put my house on the market. My friend mentioned you might take them.

W Yes, that's right. We'll take all electronics.

M Great. I just have one question. Do you provide a pickup service?

W No, unfortunately you'll have to bring everything here yourself. However, **46 on our Web site we list a number of companies that can remove and dispose of the items for you.**

여 제임스타운 재활용 시설입니다. 무엇을 도와드릴까요?
남 안녕하세요. 제가 곧 이사할 준비를 하고 있는데, 집을 내놓기 전에 치우고 싶은 텔레비전과 컴퓨터 같은 전자 제품들이 있습니다. 제 친구가 그쪽에서 가져갈지도 모른다고 말해 주었어요.
여 네, 그렇습니다. 저희는 모든 전자 제품을 받습니다.
남 잘됐네요. 질문이 하나 있습니다. 수거 서비스도 제공하시나요?
여 아니요, 유감스럽게도 모든 것을 이곳으로 직접 가져오셔야 합니다. 하지만 저희 웹사이트에 물품들을 대신 치우고 처리해 줄 수 있는 많은 회사들의 목록이 있습니다.

어휘 recycling 재활용 electronics 전자 제품
get rid of ~을 없애다 put ~ on the market ~을 시장에 내놓다
unfortunately 유감스럽게도, 안타깝게도 a number of 많은
remove 치우다, 없애다 dispose of ~을 처리하다

44 Where does the woman work?
(A) At a delivery service
(B) At an electronics store
(C) At a recycling facility
(D) At a real estate agency

여자는 어디에서 일하는가?
(A) 배송 서비스 회사
(B) 전자 제품 매장
(C) 재활용 시설
(D) 부동산 중개업체

해설 전체 내용 관련 – 여자의 근무 장소
여자가 첫 대사에서 제임스타운 재활용 시설(Jamestown Recycling Facility)이라고 자신이 근무하는 곳을 밝히고 있으므로 정답은 (C)이다.

45 What does the man want to dispose of?
(A) Yard waste
(B) Used furniture
(C) Electronics
(D) Books

남자는 무엇을 처리하고 싶어 하는가?
(A) 정원 쓰레기
(B) 중고 가구
(C) 전자 제품
(D) 책

해설 세부 사항 관련 – 남자가 처리하고 싶어 하는 것
남자가 첫 대사에서 집을 내놓기 전에 치우고 싶은 텔레비전과 컴퓨터 같은 전자 제품들이 있다(~ I have some electronics, such as televisions and computers, that I'd like to get rid of ~)고 했으므로 정답은 (C)이다.

46 What does the woman say can be found on a Web site?
(A) A list of companies
(B) Hours of operation
(C) A permit application
(D) Directions to a site

여자는 웹사이트에서 무엇을 찾을 수 있다고 말하는가?
(A) 회사 목록
(B) 운영 시간
(C) 허가 신청서
(D) 현장으로 가는 길 안내

어휘 operation 운영, 영업 application 신청(서), 지원(서) directions 길 안내 site 현장, 위치, 장소

해설 세부 사항 관련 – 웹사이트에서 찾을 수 있는 것
여자가 마지막 대사에서 웹사이트에 물품들을 대신 치우고 처리해 줄 수 있는 많은 회사들의 목록이 있다(~ on our Web site we list a number of companies that can remove and dispose of the items for you)고 했으므로 정답은 (A)이다.

Paraphrasing
대화의 list a number of companies
→ 정답의 A list of companies

47-49 M-Cn / W-Am

M Zaina! What a surprise! **47 I haven't seen you since we took that class for business owners together last year.** How are you?

W Great, thanks. I was just in the neighborhood and **48 thought I'd stop in for a cookie or a piece of cake. You have so many delicious baked goods here.**

M Thank you! It's been a good year for business. I'm even considering opening a second location.

W Really? Well, I noticed that Sunnyvale Restaurant went out of business, and the building's up for lease. **49 It's very close to the local university.** You'd probably get a lot of walk-in customers.

남 재이나! 놀랍네요! **작년에 업체 소유주들을 위한 수업을 함께 들은 이후로 만나지 못했잖아요.** 어떻게 지내세요?

여 잘 지내고 있어요, 감사합니다. 이 지역에 막 와서 **쿠키나 케이크 한 조각 먹으러 들러야겠다고 생각했거든요. 여기 맛있는 제과제품이 아주 많네요.**

남 감사합니다! 올해 사업이 잘되고 있어요. 심지어 2호점 개장을 고려하고 있습니다.

여 정말인가요? 음, 써니베일 레스토랑이 폐업해서 그 건물이 임대 매물로 나온 것을 봤어요. **지역 대학교와 아주 가까워요.** 아마 지나가다 들르는 고객이 많을 거예요.

어휘 owner 소유주, 주인 neighborhood 지역, 인근 stop in for ~을 위해 잠깐 들르다 baked goods 제과 제품 location 지점, 위치 notice (보거나 듣고) 알다, 알아채다 go out of business 폐업하다 up for lease 임대 매물로 나온 local 지역의, 현지의 walk-in 지나가다 들르는, 예약 없이 방문하는

47 How do the speakers know each other?
(A) They took a class together.
(B) They used to work for the same company.
(C) They grew up in the same neighborhood.
(D) They met on a train.

화자들은 서로 어떻게 알고 있는가?
(A) 수업을 함께 들었다.
(B) 전에 같은 회사에 근무했었다.
(C) 같은 지역에서 자랐다.
(D) 기차에서 만났다.

어휘 used to 전에 ~했다, ~하곤 했다 grow up 자라다, 성장하다

해설 세부 사항 관련 – 화자들이 서로 알게 된 계기
남자가 첫 대사에서 작년에 업체 소유주들을 위한 수업을 함께 들은 이후로 만나지 못했다(I haven't seen you since we took that class for business owners together last year)고 했으므로 정답은 (A)이다.

48 What type of business does the man most likely own?
(A) A fitness center
(B) A real estate agency
(C) A culinary school
(D) A bakery

남자는 어떤 종류의 업체를 소유하고 있을 것 같은가?
(A) 피트니스 센터
(B) 부동산 중개업체
(C) 요리 학원
(D) 제과점

해설 세부 사항 관련 – 남자가 소유한 업체
여자가 첫 대사에서 쿠키나 케이크를 한 조각 먹으러 들러야겠다고 생각했다는 말과 함께 남자의 업체에 맛있는 제과제품이 아주 많다(~ thought I'd stop in for a cookie or a piece of cake. You have so many delicious baked goods here)고 했으므로 정답은 (D)이다.

49 What advantage does the woman point out about a rental space?
(A) Its price
(B) Its size
(C) Its location
(D) Its design

여자는 임대 공간과 관련해 어떤 장점을 언급하는가?
(A) 가격
(B) 크기
(C) 위치
(D) 디자인

어휘 advantage 장점, 이점 point out 언급하다, 가리키다 rental 임대, 대여

해설 세부 사항 관련 – 여자가 언급하는 임대 공간의 장점
여자가 마지막 대사에서 임대 가능한 공간에 대해 이야기하면서 지역 대학교와 아주 가깝다(It's very close to the local university)고 했으므로 정답은 (C)이다.

50-52 W-Br / M-Au

W Hi, Koji. **⁵⁰I think our new video game is nearly ready to be released.** Are you aware of any improvements that need to be made before then?

M Actually, ⁵¹**I just finished testing the game this morning.** I found a problem in the third stage of the game. There were a few times when my character couldn't move.

W Oh, that's strange!

M I double-checked the problem using a different controller. The same issue came up.

W Oh. ⁵²**I think Pauline had a similar problem with a game she tested. Maybe you should ask her about it.**

여 안녕하세요, 코지. **우리 신작 비디오 게임 출시 준비가 거의 다 된 것 같아요.** 그 전에 개선되어야 할 점이 있는지 알고 계신 게 있을까요?

남 실은, 제가 오늘 아침에 막 그 게임 테스트 작업을 마쳤습니다. 게임의 세 번째 단계에서 문제를 하나 발견했어요. 제 캐릭터를 움직일 수 없었던 적이 여러 번 있었어요.

여 아, 그거 이상하네요!

남 제가 다른 조종기를 이용해서 이 문제를 이중으로 점검했습니다. 그런데 같은 문제가 발생했어요.

여 오. **폴린도 테스트했던 게임에서 유사한 문제를 겪었던 것 같아요. 그 부분에 대해 그녀에게 물어보는 게 좋겠어요.**

어휘 release 출시하다, 발매하다 be aware of ~을 알고 있다 improvement 개선, 향상 double-check 이중으로 점검하다 issue 문제, 사안 come up 발생하다 similar 유사한

50 Who most likely are the speakers?
(A) Film actors
(B) Museum directors
(C) Video game developers
(D) Investigative journalists

화자들은 누구인 것 같은가?
(A) 영화 배우
(B) 박물관 관장
(C) 비디오 게임 개발자
(D) 탐사 기자

어휘 investigative 조사의, 취조의

해설 전체 내용 관련 – 화자들의 직업
여자가 첫 대사에서 신작 비디오 게임 출시 준비가 거의 다 된 것 같다(I think our new video game is nearly ready to be released)고 했으므로 정답은 (C)이다.

51 What did the man recently do?
(A) He secured some funding.
(B) He tested a product.
(C) He read a script.
(D) He conducted an interview.

남자는 최근에 무엇을 했는가?
(A) 자금을 확보했다.
(B) 제품을 테스트했다.
(C) 원고를 읽었다.
(D) 인터뷰를 실시했다.

어휘 secure 확보하다, 얻다 funding 자금 (제공) script 원고, 대본 conduct 실시하다, 수행하다

해설 세부 사항 관련 – 남자가 최근에 한 일
남자가 첫 대사에서 오늘 아침에 막 그 게임 테스트 작업을 마쳤다(I just finished testing the game this morning)고 했으므로 정답은 (B)이다.

Paraphrasing
대화의 this morning → 질문의 recently
대화의 finished testing the game → 정답의 tested a product

52 What does the woman suggest?
(A) Consulting a colleague
(B) Planning an event
(C) Negotiating a contract
(D) Giving a client an update

여자는 무엇을 제안하는가?
(A) 동료와 상의하기
(B) 행사 계획하기
(C) 계약 협의하기
(D) 고객에게 최신 정보 제공하기

어휘 consult 상의하다, 상담하다 negotiate 협의하다, 협상하다 contract 계약(서)

해설 세부 사항 관련 – 여자의 제안 사항
여자가 마지막 대사에서 폴린도 테스트했던 게임에서 유사한 문제를 겪었던 것 같다며 그 부분에 대해 그녀에게 물어보는 게 좋겠다(I think Pauline had a similar problem with a game she tested. Maybe you should ask her about it)고 했으므로 정답은 (A)이다.

Paraphrasing
대화의 ask her about it → 정답의 Consulting a colleague

53-55 M-Au / W-Am

M: ⁵³**You've reached the maintenance office at Hillview Apartment Complex.**

W: Hi. This is Palavi Sen from unit 35B. ⁵⁴**I'm calling because the new thermostat in my apartment isn't working. It keeps shutting off and turning on randomly**, so my apartment is getting cold.

M: When did this issue start?

W: A few hours ago. The thermostat was just installed yesterday.

M: OK. ⁵⁵**I can come and take a look at it tomorrow morning.**

W: But it's supposed to be below freezing tonight!

남: 힐뷰 아파트 단지 관리소입니다.

여: 안녕하세요. 저는 35B호에 사는 팔라비 센입니다. 제 아파트의 새 온도 조절 장치가 작동하지 않아서 전화했어요. 계속 무작위로 꺼졌다 켜졌다 해서, 아파트가 추워지고 있어요.

남: 그 문제가 언제 시작되었나요?

여: 몇 시간 전에요. 온도 조절 장치는 어제 막 설치했어요.

남: 알겠습니다. 제가 내일 오전에 가서 봐 드릴 수 있습니다.

여: 하지만 오늘 밤에 영하로 떨어질 거예요!

어휘 reach 연락하다 maintenance 유지 관리 unit 호, 세대 thermostat 온도 조절 장치 shut off 꺼지다, 닫히다 turn on 켜지다 randomly 무작위로 take a look 보다 be supposed to ~하기로 되어 있다, ~해야 하다 below freezing 영하의

---

53 Who most likely is the man?
(A) A delivery driver
(B) A security guard
(C) A maintenance worker
(D) A customer service representative

남자는 누구인 것 같은가?
(A) 배송 기사
(B) 경비원
(C) 시설 관리 직원
(D) 고객 서비스 직원

어휘 representative 직원, 대표자

해설 전체 내용 관련 – 남자의 직업

남자가 첫 대사에서 힐뷰 아파트 단지 관리소(You've reached the maintenance office at Hillview Apartment Complex)라고 말한 것에서 관리소 직원임을 알 수 있으므로 정답은 (C)이다.

---

54 What problem does the woman describe?
(A) A device is malfunctioning.
(B) A key is missing.
(C) A parking area is unavailable.
(D) A package was not received.

여자는 어떤 문제를 설명하는가?
(A) 장치가 오작동하고 있다.
(B) 열쇠를 분실했다.
(C) 주차 구역을 이용할 수 없다.
(D) 배송품을 받지 못했다.

어휘 describe 설명하다, 묘사하다 device 장치, 기기 malfunction 오작동하다 unavailable 이용할 수 없는

해설 전체 내용 관련 – 여자가 설명하는 문제

여자가 첫 대사에서 아파트의 새 온도 조절 장치가 작동하지 않아서 전화했다며 계속 무작위로 꺼졌다가 켜진다(I'm calling because the new thermostat in my apartment isn't working. It keeps shutting off and turning on randomly ~)고 했으므로 정답은 (A)이다.

Paraphrasing
대화의 the new thermostat ~ isn't working
→ 정답의 A device is malfunctioning

---

55 What does the woman mean when she says, "it's supposed to be below freezing tonight"?
(A) She is surprised by the weather forecast.
(B) She wants a service to be completed sooner.
(C) She will move some items indoors.
(D) She would prefer to park near her apartment.

여자가 "오늘 밤에 영하로 떨어질 거예요"라고 말할 때 무엇을 의미하는가?
(A) 일기 예보에 놀랐다.
(B) 서비스가 더 빨리 완료되기를 원한다.
(C) 물건들을 실내로 옮길 것이다.
(D) 자신의 아파트 근처에 주차하고 싶어 한다.

어휘 complete 완료하다 indoors 실내로, 실내에

해설 화자의 의도 파악 – 오늘 밤에 영하로 떨어질 것이라는 말의 의미

남자가 세 번째 대사에서 자신이 내일 오전에 가서 봐 줄 수 있다(I can come and take a look at it tomorrow morning)고 말하자, 여자가 인용문을 언급하고 있다. 이는 오늘 밤에 날씨가 추우니 내일 아침보다 더 빨리 와서 봐 주길 원한다는 뜻이므로 정답은 (B)이다.

56-58 3인 대화 W-Br / M-Cn / M-Au

> W   Good morning! Welcome to Jasper Bank.
> M1   **56 Thanks for meeting with us to discuss a loan for our business.**
> W   Why don't you tell me more about your business? I understand it's a repair shop?
> M2   Well, ten years ago, we opened as a snowmobile repair shop, but after a few years, **57 we also started renting out snowmobiles and other sports equipment.**
> M1   Yes, and **58 because winter tourism has increased recently**, we'd like to expand our space so that we can carry more inventory.

> 여   안녕하세요! 재스퍼 은행에 오신 것을 환영합니다.
> 남1   사업 자금 대출을 논의하기 위해 만나 주셔서 감사합니다.
> 여   두 분의 업체에 대해 더 말씀해 주시겠어요? 수리점이라고 알고 있는데요?
> 남2   음, 10년 전에, 저희는 스노모빌 수리점으로 문을 열었는데, 몇 년 후에는, 스노모빌과 기타 스포츠 장비 대여도 시작했습니다.
> 남1   네, 그리고 최근 겨울철 관광 산업이 증가해서, 더 많은 재고를 취급할 수 있도록 공간을 확장하고자 합니다.

어휘 loan 대출 snowmobile 스노모빌 rent out 대여해 주다 equipment 장비 tourism 관광 산업 increase 증가하다 carry 취급하다 inventory 재고 (목록), 재고 조사

56 Why do the men want to speak to the woman?
(A) To review a building design
(B) To discuss a loan
(C) To develop an advertising plan
(D) To purchase some supplies

남자들은 왜 여자와 이야기하고 싶어 하는가?
(A) 건물 설계도를 검토하려고
(B) 대출을 논의하려고
(C) 광고 계획을 세우려고
(D) 용품을 구입하려고

어휘 review 살펴보다, 검토하다 develop a plan 계획을 세우다

해설 전체 내용 관련 – 남자들이 여자와 이야기하고 싶어 한 이유
첫 번째 남자가 첫 대사에서 사업 자금 대출을 논의하기 위해 만나 줘서 감사하다(Thanks for meeting with us to discuss a loan for our business)고 했으므로 정답은 (B)이다.

57 What type of business do the men own?
(A) A sports equipment store
(B) A winter apparel store
(C) An automobile dealership
(D) A hotel chain

남자들은 어떤 종류의 업체를 소유하고 있는가?
(A) 스포츠 장비 매장
(B) 겨울 의류 매장
(C) 자동차 대리점
(D) 호텔 체인

어휘 apparel 의류 dealership 대리점, 판매점

해설 전체 내용 관련 – 남자들의 업체
두 번째 남자가 첫 대사에서 자신들의 업체가 수리점이면서 스노모빌과 기타 스포츠 장비 대여도 시작했다(~ we also started renting out snowmobiles and other sports equipment)고 했으므로 정답은 (A)이다.

58 According to the men, what has changed recently?
(A) Roads have become more accessible.
(B) Costs have decreased.
(C) Tourism has increased.
(D) Weather patterns have shifted.

남자들에 따르면, 최근에 무엇이 바뀌었는가?
(A) 도로들이 더 접근하기 쉽게 되었다.
(B) 비용이 하락했다.
(C) 관광 산업이 증가했다.
(D) 날씨 패턴이 변했다.

어휘 accessible 접근 가능한, 이용 가능한 cost 비용 decrease 하락하다, 감소하다 shift 변하다, 바뀌다

해설 세부 사항 관련 – 최근에 바뀐 것
첫 번째 남자가 마지막 대사에서 최근 겨울철 관광 산업이 증가했다(~ winter tourism has increased recently ~)고 했으므로 정답은 (C)이다.

59-61 M-Au / W-Am   ▶동영상 강의

> M   Many of our factory workers have expressed interest in upgrading their skills. **59 I'd like to implement a peer-training program, where learners shadow more-experienced employees and observe how they do their jobs.**
> W   I'm afraid that might become a burden for our long-time employees. **60 They'll have to slow down their work to explain what they're doing.**
> M   **61 What if we videotaped experienced employees doing specific tasks? High-quality video can be recorded and edited with a smartphone.**
> W   I like that idea. It would allow us to capture our workers' expertise without slowing down the production line.

남 우리 공장 직원들 중 많은 분들이 자신의 능력을 업그레이드하는 데 관심을 보였습니다. **동료 교육 프로그램을 시행했으면 하는데, 배우는 사람들이 경험이 더 많은 직원들을 그림자처럼 따라다니면서 어떻게 일하는지 관찰하는 겁니다.**

여 저는 그게 오랫동안 근무한 직원들에게 부담이 될 수 있을 것 같아서 걱정이에요. **무엇을 하고 있는지 설명하기 위해 업무 속도를 늦춰야 할 겁니다.**

남 경험 많은 직원들이 특정 업무를 하는 모습을 영상으로 녹화하면 어떨까요? 스마트폰으로 고품질의 영상을 녹화하고 편집할 수 있어요.

여 그 아이디어가 좋네요. 생산 라인의 속도를 늦추지 않고 우리 직원들의 전문 기술을 담을 수 있을 거예요.

어휘 express 나타내다, 표현하다 interest in ~에 대한 관심 skill 기술, 기량 implement 시행하다 peer 동료, 또래 shadow 그림자처럼 따라다니다 experienced 경험 많은 observe 관찰하다 burden 부담(감) long-time 장기적인 slow down 속도를 늦추다 videotape 녹화하다 specific 특정한, 구체적인 capture 담다, 포착하다 expertise 전문 기술, 전문 지식

59 What does the man want to do?
(A) Provide training opportunities
(B) Upgrade machinery
(C) Hire additional employees
(D) Reorganize the factory layout

남자는 무엇을 하고 싶어 하는가?
(A) 교육 기회 제공하기
(B) 기계 업그레이드하기
(C) 추가 직원 고용하기
(D) 공장 구획 재편성하기

어휘 opportunity 기회 machinery 기계(류) reorganize 재편성하다, 개편하다 layout 구획, 배치(도)

해설 전체 내용 관련 – 남자가 하고 싶어 하는 것

남자가 첫 대사에서 동료 교육 프로그램을 시행하고 싶다며, 배우는 사람들이 경험이 더 많은 직원들을 따라다니면서 어떻게 일하는지 관찰하는 것(I'd like to implement a peer-training program, where learners shadow more-experienced employees and observe how they do their jobs)이라고 했으므로 정답은 (A)이다.

Paraphrasing
대화의 implement a peer-training program
→ 정답의 Provide training opportunities

60 What is the woman concerned about?
(A) Increasing expenses
(B) Introducing errors
(C) Reducing productivity
(D) Causing confusion

여자는 무엇을 걱정하는가?
(A) 비용 증가
(B) 오차 유발
(C) 생산성 감소
(D) 혼란 초래

어휘 introduce an error 오차를 유발하다 reduce 감소시키다 cause 초래하다 confusion 혼란, 혼동

해설 세부 사항 관련 – 여자가 걱정하는 것

여자가 첫 대사에서 장기 재직 직원들에게 부담이 될 수 있을 것 같아서 걱정이라며, 무엇을 하고 있는지 설명하기 위해 업무 속도를 늦춰야 할 것(They'll have to slow down their work to explain what they're doing)이라고 했다. 업무 속도를 늦추는 것은 생산성 감소에 해당하므로 정답은 (C)이다.

Paraphrasing
대화의 slow down their work
→ 정답의 Reducing productivity

61 What does the man mean when he says, "High-quality video can be recorded and edited with a smartphone"?
(A) A new policy should be established.
(B) An idea is easy to implement.
(C) Data security is a concern.
(D) Some information should be verified.

남자가 "스마트폰으로 고품질의 영상을 녹화하고 편집할 수 있어요"라고 말할 때 무엇을 의미하는가?
(A) 새로운 정책이 확립되어야 한다.
(B) 아이디어가 시행되기 쉽다.
(C) 데이터 보안이 걱정이다.
(D) 정보가 확인되어야 한다.

어휘 policy 정책, 방침 establish 확립하다, 설립하다 concern 우려, 걱정 verify 확인하다, 인증하다

해설 화자의 의도 파악 – 스마트폰으로 고품질의 영상을 녹화하고 편집할 수 있다는 말의 의미

남자가 두 번째 대사에서 경험 많은 직원들이 특정 업무를 하는 모습을 영상으로 녹화할 것(What if we videotaped experienced employees doing specific tasks?)을 제안하면서 인용문을 언급했다. 이는 스마트폰을 이용하면 쉽게 녹화할 수 있다는 의미이므로 정답은 (B)이다.

62-64 대화 + 일정표 W-Am / M-Cn ▶동영상 강의

W Hi, Suresh. **62 I'm at the airport waiting for my flight.** I want to meet with a potential investor while I'm in Chicago. Her name's Marta Gomez. I can send you her contact information.

M OK. **63 Which day would you prefer to meet with her?**

TEST 1 17

W ⁶³**How about right after my meeting with the Chicago staff?**

M OK. By the way, ⁶⁴**did you see that our company won an award for our contributions to the community?** It was just announced this morning.

여 안녕하세요, 수레쉬. **저는 공항에서 비행기를 기다리고 있어요.** 제가 시카고에 머무르는 동안 잠재 투자자를 만나길 원해요. 그분 성함이 마타 고메즈입니다. 그분의 연락처를 보내 드릴 수 있어요.

남 알겠습니다. 어느 요일에 그분과 만나고 싶으신가요?

여 **시카고 직원들과의 회의 직후가 어떨까요?**

남 좋습니다. 그건 그렇고, **우리 회사가 지역 사회에 기여한 공로를 인정받아 상을 받은 것을 보셨나요?** 오늘 아침에 막 발표되었어요.

어휘 potential 잠재적인, 가능성 있는 investor 투자자 contact information 연락처 win an award 상을 받다 contribution 기여, 공헌 shareholder 주주

Day	Time	Activity
Tuesday	Noon	Facility tour
⁶³**Wednesday**	8:00 A.M.	**Meeting with Chicago staff**
Thursday	2:00 P.M.	Shareholder presentation
Friday	4:45 P.M.	Return flight

요일	시간	활동
화요일	정오	시설 견학
수요일	오전 8시	시카고 직원들과의 회의
목요일	오후 2시	주주 발표
금요일	오후 4시 45분	복귀 항공편

62 Where is the woman?
(A) At a restaurant
(B) At a travel agency
(C) At an airport
(D) At a warehouse

여자는 어디에 있는가?
(A) 레스토랑
(B) 여행사
(C) 공항
(D) 창고

해설 전체 내용 관련 – 여자가 있는 곳
여자가 첫 대사에서 공항에서 비행기를 기다리고 있다(I'm at the airport waiting for my flight)고 했으므로 정답은 (C)이다.

63 Look at the graphic. When does the woman prefer to meet with an investor?
(A) On Monday
(B) On Tuesday
(C) On Wednesday
(D) On Thursday

시각 정보에 의하면, 여자는 투자자와 언제 만나기를 선호하는가?
(A) 월요일
(B) 화요일
(C) 수요일
(D) 목요일

해설 시각 정보 연계 – 여자가 투자자를 만나려는 요일
남자가 첫 대사에서 투자자를 어느 요일에 만나고 싶은지(Which day would you prefer to meet with her?) 묻자, 여자가 시카고 직원들과의 회의 직후(How about right after my meeting with the Chicago staff?)를 제안하고 있다. 일정표에서 시카고 직원들과의 회의가 수요일인 것을 알 수 있으므로 정답은 (C)이다.

64 What good news does the man share?
(A) A colleague received a promotion.
(B) A conference proposal was accepted.
(C) An airline ticket has been upgraded.
(D) A company won an award.

남자는 어떤 좋은 소식을 공유하는가?
(A) 동료가 승진했다.
(B) 콘퍼런스 제안이 받아들여졌다.
(C) 항공권이 업그레이드되었다.
(D) 회사가 상을 받았다.

어휘 share 공유하다 receive a promotion 승진되다 proposal 제안(서) accept 받아들이다, 수락하다

해설 세부 사항 관련 – 남자가 공유하는 좋은 소식
남자가 마지막 대사에서 여자에게 소속 회사가 지역 사회에 기여한 공로를 인정받아 상을 받은 것을 봤는지(~ did you see that our company won an award for our contributions to the community?) 물으며, 오늘 아침에 발표됐다고 했으므로 정답은 (D)이다.

65-67 대화 + 웹페이지 목록 M-Au / W-Br

M Marion, ⁶⁵**we keep getting calls from people who want to visit the botanical garden but can't find parking information.** Isn't it on our Web site?

W It is, but you have to click on the "About Us" page and scroll to the bottom of that page. Maybe people don't see it.

M Oh, ⁶⁶**I think we should move that information from the "About Us" page and make a**

separate page for directions and parking information. That way, people can find it more easily.

W I'd be happy to make that change. But ⁶⁷**we're in the middle of updating our software, so it'll have to wait until Monday.**

남 매리언, **식물원 방문을 원하지만 주차 정보를 찾지 못하는 사람들로부터 계속 전화를 받고 있어요.** 그게 우리 웹사이트에 있지 않나요?

여 있긴 한데, "소개" 페이지를 클릭한 다음, 그 페이지 맨 아래까지 스크롤해야 해요. 사람들이 못 찾는 것 같아요.

남 아, **그 정보를 "소개" 페이지에서 옮겨서 길 안내와 주차 정보를 위한 별도의 페이지를 만들어야 할 것 같아요.** 그러면 사람들이 더 쉽게 찾을 수 있을 거예요.

여 제가 그렇게 변경하겠습니다. 하지만 **소프트웨어를 업데이트하는 중이라, 월요일까지 기다려야 할 거예요.**

어휘 botanical garden 식물원 bottom 맨 아래, 바닥 separate 별도의, 분리된 directions 길 안내 (정보) in the middle of ~하는 과정에 있는 admission 입장(료) general 일반적인, 전반적인 exhibition 전시(회)

Web Site Outline

⁶⁶ Page 1 About Us

Page 2 Admission Tickets

Page 3 General Rules

Page 4 Exhibitions and Special Events

웹사이트 개요

1 페이지 소개

2 페이지 입장권

3 페이지 일반적인 규정

4 페이지 전시회 및 특별 행사

---

65 Where do the speakers work?
(A) At an amusement park
(B) At an art museum
(C) At a concert hall
(D) At a botanical garden

화자들은 어디에서 일하는가?
(A) 놀이공원
(B) 미술관
(C) 콘서트홀
(D) 식물원

해설 전체 내용 관련 – 화자들의 근무 장소
남자가 첫 대사에서 식물원 방문을 원하지만 주차 정보를 찾지 못하는 사람들로부터 계속 전화를 받고 있다(~ we keep getting calls from people who want to visit the botanical garden but can't find parking information)고 했으므로 정답은 (D)이다.

66 Look at the graphic. Which page on the Web site does the man want to change?
(A) Page 1
(B) Page 2
(C) Page 3
(D) Page 4

시각 정보에 의하면, 남자는 웹사이트의 어느 페이지를 변경하고 싶어 하는가?
(A) 1페이지
(B) 2페이지
(C) 3페이지
(D) 4페이지

해설 시각 정보 연계 – 남자가 변경하려는 페이지
남자가 두 번째 대사에서 그 정보를 "소개" 페이지에서 옮겨서 길 안내와 주차 정보를 위한 별도의 페이지를 만들 것(~ I think we should move that information from the "About Us" page and make a separate page for directions and parking information)을 제안하고 있다. 웹페이지 목록에서 소개 페이지는 1페이지이므로 정답은 (A)이다.

67 Why does the woman say she cannot complete a task until Monday?
(A) She requires approval from a manager.
(B) She is attending a workshop.
(C) Some software is being updated.
(D) Some clients will be arriving soon.

여자는 왜 월요일까지 일을 완료할 수 없다고 말하는가?
(A) 관리자의 승인이 필요하다.
(B) 워크숍에 참석하고 있다.
(C) 소프트웨어가 업데이트되고 있다.
(D) 고객들이 곧 도착할 것이다.

어휘 approval 승인

해설 세부 사항 관련 – 월요일까지 일을 완료할 수 없는 이유
여자가 마지막 대사에서 소프트웨어를 업데이트하는 중이라, 월요일까지 기다려야 할 것(~ we're in the middle of updating our software, so it'll have to wait until Monday)이라고 했으므로 정답은 (C)이다.

Paraphrasing
대화의 it'll have to wait until Monday
→ 질문의 cannot complete a task until Monday

68-70 대화 + 역 안내도 M-Au / W-Am

> M Good news! ⁶⁸**We have finally received the go-ahead for our department's project to install bicycle racks at the train station downtown.**
>
> W At last! So, now we need to decide where to place the racks. How about by the station entrance?
>
> M Hmm. If we asked riders, ⁶⁹**I bet they'd say that the most convenient spot is as close to the platform as possible.**
>
> W ⁶⁹**Let's do that.** ⁷⁰**I'll contact some companies for estimates.**

남 좋은 소식입니다! 시내 기차역에 자전거 거치대를 설치하는 우리 부서의 프로젝트가 드디어 승인을 받았습니다.
여 마침내 됐네요! 그럼, 이제 우리는 거치대를 어디에 놓을지 결정해야 합니다. 역 입구 옆은 어떤가요?
남 흠. 우리가 자전거 이용객들에게 묻는다면, 틀림없이 가능한 한 승강장과 가까운 곳이 가장 편리한 자리라고 말할 겁니다.
여 그렇게 합시다. 제가 견적을 위해 몇몇 회사에 연락할게요.

어휘 go-ahead 승인 rack 거치대, ~걸이 I bet 틀림없이 convenient 편리한 estimate 견적(서) covered 지붕으로 덮인 overflow 초과의 short-term 단기의 long-term 장기의

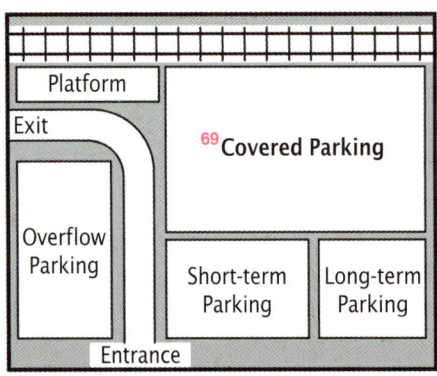

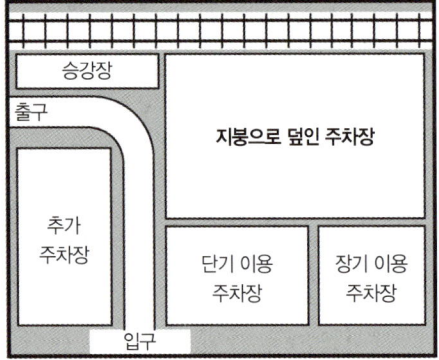

68 What news does the man share?
(A) A station road will be closed for repair.
(B) A project has been approved.
(C) A parking area has been expanded.
(D) An office will relocate.

남자는 어떤 소식을 공유하는가?
(A) 역 앞 도로가 수리를 위해 폐쇄될 것이다.
(B) 프로젝트가 승인되었다.
(C) 주차 구역이 확장되었다.
(D) 사무실이 이전할 것이다.

어휘 approve 승인하다 relocate 이전하다, 재배치되다

해설 세부 사항 관련 – 남자가 공유하는 소식
남자가 첫 대사에서 좋은 소식이라며, 시내 기차역에 자전거 거치대를 설치하는 우리 부서의 프로젝트가 드디어 승인을 받았다(We have finally received the go-ahead for our department's project to install bicycle racks at the train station downtown)는 소식을 공유하고 있으므로 정답은 (B)이다.

Paraphrasing
대화의 have finally received the go-ahead for our department's project
→ 정답의 A project has been approved

69 Look at the graphic. Where do the speakers decide to install some bicycle racks?
(A) Near the covered parking area
(B) Near the long-term parking area
(C) Near the short-term parking area
(D) Near the overflow parking area

시각 정보에 의하면, 화자들은 어디에 자전거 거치대를 설치하기로 결정하는가?
(A) 지붕으로 덮인 주차장 근처에
(B) 장기 이용 주차장 근처에
(C) 단기 이용 주차장 근처에
(D) 추가 주차장 근처에

어휘 decide 결정하다

해설 시각 정보 연계 – 자전거 거치대 설치 장소로 결정하는 곳
남자가 두 번째 대사에서 거치대 설치 위치와 관련해 틀림없이 가능한 한 승강장과 가까운 곳이 가장 편리한 자리라고 말할 것(~ I bet they'd say that the most convenient spot is as close to the platform as possible)이라고 하자, 여자도 그렇게 하자(Let's do that)고 했다. 역 안내도에서 상단에 위치한 승강장과 가장 가까운 곳은 지붕으로 덮인 주차장이므로 정답은 (A)이다.

70 Why does the woman say she will contact some companies?
(A) To arrange a loan
(B) To apply for a permit
(C) To ask for estimates
(D) To create a proposal

여자는 왜 몇몇 회사에 연락하겠다고 말하는가?
(A) 대출을 준비하기 위해
(B) 허가증을 신청하기 위해
(C) 견적을 요청하기 위해
(D) 제안서를 만들기 위해

어휘 loan 대출 apply for ~을 신청하다, ~에 지원하다
ask for ~을 요청하다 create 만들어 내다

해설 세부 사항 관련 – 여자가 몇몇 회사에 연락하는 목적
여자가 마지막 대사에서 견적을 위해 몇몇 회사에 연락하겠다(I'll contact some companies for estimates)고 했으므로 정답은 (C)이다.

PART 4

71-73 녹음 메시지

> W-Br You've reached Select Repair Service. **⁷¹We specialize in all makes and models of automobiles.** Our factory-trained specialists will keep your vehicle running in top condition. **⁷²As an added benefit, we offer extended warranties on all vehicles we service.** You can enjoy three extra years of worry-free driving. **⁷³Please note that Select Repair Service will be closing on Friday, June 30, so we can complete our quarterly inventory of supplies.** Thank you for your patience. A representative will be with you shortly.
>
> 셀렉트 리페어 서비스입니다. 저희는 모든 자동차 브랜드와 모델을 전문으로 다룹니다. 공장에서 교육을 받은 저희 전문가들이 여러분의 차량을 최상의 상태로 운행할 수 있도록 관리해 드릴 것입니다. 추가 혜택으로 저희가 정비해 드리는 모든 차량에 연장된 품질 보증 서비스를 제공해 드립니다. 추가로 3년 동안 걱정 없이 운전하실 수 있습니다. 저희 셀렉트 리페어 서비스가 분기별 재고 조사를 완료하기 위해, 6월 30일 금요일에 문을 닫을 예정임을 알려 드립니다. 기다려 주셔서 감사합니다. 곧 직원이 연결될 것입니다.
>
> 어휘 reach 연락하다 specialize in ~을 전문으로 하다 make 제품, ~제 automobile 자동차 vehicle 차량 benefit 혜택 extend 연장하다 warranty 품질 보증(서) worry-free 걱정 없는 note 유의하다 quarterly 분기별 patience 인내(심) shortly 곧, 머지않아

71 What type of products does the business repair?
(A) Computers
(B) Vehicles
(C) Light fixtures
(D) Kitchen appliances

업체는 어떤 종류의 제품을 수리하는가?
(A) 컴퓨터
(B) 차량
(C) 조명
(D) 주방 기기

어휘 appliance (가전) 기기

해설 전체 내용 관련 – 업체가 수리하는 제품
화자가 초반부에 모든 자동차 브랜드와 모델을 전문으로 다룬다(We specialize in all makes and models of automobiles)고 했으므로 정답은 (B)이다.

Paraphrasing
담화의 automobiles → 정답의 Vehicles

72 What special benefit does the speaker mention?
(A) Free pickup
(B) Online scheduling
(C) Extended warranties
(D) A membership loyalty program

화자는 어떤 특별 혜택을 언급하는가?
(A) 무료 수거
(B) 온라인 일정 관리
(C) 연장된 품질 보증 서비스
(D) 회원 보상 프로그램

어휘 loyalty program 고객 보상 프로그램

해설 세부 사항 관련 – 화자가 언급하는 특별 혜택
화자가 중반부에 추가 혜택으로 정비하는 모든 차량에 연장된 품질 보증 서비스를 제공한다(As an added benefit, we offer extended warranties on all vehicles we service)고 했으므로 정답은 (C)이다.

Paraphrasing
담화의 an added benefit → 질문의 special benefit

73 Why will a business close on Friday?
(A) For an inventory count
(B) For employee training
(C) For a company celebration
(D) For equipment installation

업체는 왜 금요일에 문을 닫을 것인가?
(A) 재고 조사 때문에
(B) 직원 교육 때문에
(C) 회사 기념 행사 때문에
(D) 장비 설치 때문에

어휘 count 계산, 셈 celebration 기념 행사, 축하 행사 installation 설치

해설 세부 사항 관련 – 금요일에 문을 닫는 이유

화자가 후반부에 분기별 재고 조사를 완료하기 위해 6월 30일 금요일에 문을 닫을 예정(Please note that Select Repair Service will be closing on Friday, June 30, so we can complete our quarterly inventory of supplies)이라고 했으므로 정답은 (A)이다.

Paraphrasing
담화의 our quarterly inventory of supplies
→ 정답의 an inventory count

74-76 담화

M-Au Welcome, new employees! My name is Diego, and **⁷⁴I facilitate all orientation sessions. Before we start today, you will need to set up your employee account.** ⁷⁵**If you look at the first page of your training binder, you'll see your username and a temporary password. Please open the laptops you were given this morning and log in using those credentials.** You will then be prompted to create your own password. Once that's complete, ⁷⁶**you'll have access to all your department's files. Please note that you can only access them from your company computer.**

환영합니다, 신입 사원 여러분! 제 이름은 디에고이며, 앞으로 모든 오리엔테이션을 진행하게 되었습니다. 오늘 시작하기에 앞서, 여러분은 직원 계정을 설정하셔야 할 것입니다. 교육용 바인더 첫 번째 페이지를 보시면, 사용자 이름과 임시 비밀번호가 보일 것입니다. 오늘 아침에 지급받으신 노트북 컴퓨터를 열어서 그 정보를 이용해 로그인하시기 바랍니다. 그 후에는 개인 비밀번호를 만들도록 안내를 받으실 것입니다. 그것이 완료되는 대로, 여러분 부서의 모든 파일에 접근하실 수 있을 것입니다. 오직 여러분의 회사 컴퓨터에서만 접근할 수 있다는 점에 유의하시기 바랍니다.

어휘 facilitate (원활히) 진행시키다, 용이하게 하다, 촉진하다 session (특정 활동을 하는) 시간 set up 설정하다, 설치하다 temporary 임시의, 일시적인 credentials (증명용) 정보 be prompted to ~하도록 안내를 받다 complete 완료된 have access to ~에 접근할 수 있다, ~을 이용할 수 있다 access 접근하다, 이용하다

74 Who most likely is the speaker?
(A) A facilities manager
(B) A human resources representative
(C) A security officer
(D) A corporate executive

화자는 누구인 것 같은가?
(A) 시설 관리자
(B) 인사부 직원
(C) 보안 직원
(D) 기업 임원

어휘 human resources 인사(부), 인적 자원 corporate 기업의 executive 임원, 이사

해설 전체 내용 관련 – 화자의 직업

화자가 초반부에 자신이 모든 오리엔테이션을 진행한다고 소개하면서 청자들의 직원 계정을 설정해야 한다(~ I facilitate all orientation sessions. Before we start today, you will need to set up your employee account)며 그 방법을 설명하고 있다. 이는 신입 사원들의 회사 적응을 돕는 일을 하는 인사부 직원의 업무에 해당하므로 정답은 (B)이다.

75 According to the speaker, what will the listeners find in a binder?
(A) A map of the building
(B) An employment contract
(C) An identification badge
(D) Log-in credentials

화자에 따르면, 청자들은 바인더에서 무엇을 찾을 수 있는가?
(A) 건물 안내도
(B) 고용 계약서
(C) 신분 확인 명찰
(D) 로그인 정보

어휘 employment 고용, 취업 identification 신분 증명(서)

해설 세부 사항 관련 – 청자들이 바인더에서 찾을 수 있는 것

화자가 중반부에 교육용 바인더 첫 번째 페이지에 사용자 이름과 임시 비밀번호가 있다며, 그 정보를 이용해 로그인하라(If you look at the first page of your training binder, you'll see your username and a temporary password. ~ log in using those credentials)고 했으므로 정답은 (D)이다.

76 What does the speaker say about department files?
(A) They are only accessible from company computers.
(B) They must be password protected.
(C) They must follow a specific naming convention.
(D) They must be archived annually.

화자는 부서 파일에 대해 무엇이라고 말하는가?
(A) 오직 회사 컴퓨터에서만 접근할 수 있다.
(B) 비밀번호로 보호되어야 한다.
(C) 특정 명명 규칙을 따라야 한다.
(D) 해마다 보관되어야 한다.

어휘 follow 따르다, 준수하다 naming convention 명명 규칙 archive 보관하다 annually 해마다, 연례적으로

해설　세부 사항 관련 – 화자가 부서 파일에 대해 하는 말
화자가 후반부에 부서 파일을 언급하면서 오직 회사 컴퓨터에서만 접근할 수 있다(~ you'll have access to all your department's files. Please note that you can only access them from your company computer)고 했으므로 정답은 (A)이다.

Paraphrasing
담화의 can only access → 정답의 are only accessible

77-79 전화 메시지

W-Br　Hello. **77 This is Heather Ross calling from Denville Amusement Park.** About a month ago, I ordered one of your new video-game machines, *Space Defenders*. **78 I'm really happy with my purchase**, since the game has been incredibly popular with our park guests! I'm considering buying some additional machines in the near future. **79 I heard you may be releasing a new game soon. Could you call me back and let me know if that's true?** Thanks!

안녕하세요. **덴빌 놀이공원의 헤더 로스입니다.** 약 한 달 전에, 귀사의 새 비디오 게임기 중 하나인 〈스페이스 디펜더스〉를 주문했어요. **구매한 것에 정말로 만족하고 있는데**, 이 게임이 저희 공원 손님들에게 믿을 수 없을 정도로 인기가 있기 때문입니다! 가까운 미래에 추가 기계를 몇 대 구입하는 것을 고려하고 있습니다. **귀사에서 곧 신작 게임을 출시할 수도 있다는 얘기를 들었습니다. 제게 다시 전화 주셔서 그게 사실인지 알려 주시겠습니까?** 감사합니다!

어휘　incredibly 믿을 수 없을 정도로　popular 인기 있는　release 출시하다, 발매하다

77 Where does the speaker work?
(A) At a laundry facility
(B) At an amusement park
(C) At a sports stadium
(D) At a fitness center

화자는 어디에서 일하는가?
(A) 세탁 시설
(B) 놀이공원
(C) 스포츠 경기장
(D) 피트니스 센터

어휘　laundry 세탁(물)

해설　전체 내용 관련 – 화자의 근무 장소
화자가 초반부에 자신을 덴빌 놀이공원의 헤더 로스(This is Heather Ross calling from Denville Amusement Park)라고 소개하고 있으므로 정답은 (B)이다.

78 What does the speaker say about an item she ordered a month ago?
(A) It arrived later than expected.
(B) It was damaged during delivery.
(C) She needs help assembling it.
(D) She is pleased with it.

화자는 한 달 전에 주문한 제품에 대해 무엇이라고 말하는가?
(A) 예상보다 늦게 도착했다.
(B) 배송 중에 손상되었다.
(C) 조립하는 데 도움이 필요하다.
(D) 만족하고 있다.

어휘　damaged 손상된, 피해를 입은　assemble 조립하다

해설　세부 사항 관련 – 화자가 주문품에 대해 하는 말
화자가 중반부에 약 한 달 전에 주문한 게임기를 언급하면서 정말로 만족하고 있다(I'm really happy with my purchase ~)고 했으므로 정답은 (D)이다.

Paraphrasing
담화의 am really happy with → 정답의 is pleased with

79 What does the speaker ask the listener to confirm?
(A) Whether a new product will be available soon
(B) When a replacement part will be shipped
(C) How long a warranty lasts
(D) Who to contact about future orders

화자는 청자에게 무엇을 확인해 달라고 요청하는가?
(A) 신제품이 곧 이용 가능할 것인지
(B) 언제 교체 부품이 배송될 것인지
(C) 얼마나 오래 품질 보증 서비스가 지속되는지
(D) 향후 주문과 관련해 누구에게 연락해야 하는지

어휘　confirm 확인해 주다　replacement 교체(품)　last 지속되다　contact 연락하다

해설　세부 사항 관련 – 화자의 요청 사항
화자가 후반부에 청자의 회사에서 곧 신작 게임을 출시할 수도 있다는 얘기를 들었다며 자신에게 다시 전화해서 그게 사실인지 알려 달라(I heard you may be releasing a new game soon. Could you call me back and let me know if that's true?)고 요청했으므로 정답은 (A)이다.

Paraphrasing
담화의 let me know if that's true → 질문의 confirm
담화의 be releasing a new game soon
→ 정답의 a new product will be available soon

80-82 회의 발췌

> **W-Am** The first agenda item for our board meeting is the annual sales report. We're all disappointed by the drop in **80 our clothing sales.** The decline is mostly due to distribution issues. Because our factories are all overseas, it takes too long for orders to reach customers. So **81 I'm recommending that we start manufacturing some clothing locally.** We'll be looking for a location to build a manufacturing facility. **82 I hired a consultant to put together a list of locations we could use. He'll be at our next board meeting to explain the pros and cons of each.**

> 우리 이사회 회의의 첫 번째 안건은 연 매출 보고서입니다. 우리는 모두 **의류 매출** 감소에 실망했습니다. 이러한 감소는 대부분 유통 문제로 인한 것입니다. 우리 공장이 모두 해외에 있기 때문에, 주문한 물건이 고객들께 도달하는 데 너무 오래 걸립니다. 따라서 **일부 의류를 이 지역에서 제조하기 시작할 것을 제안합니다.** 우리는 제조 시설을 지을 장소를 찾을 예정입니다. **우리가 이용할 수 있을 만한 장소들의 목록을 만들어 줄 컨설턴트를 고용했습니다. 이분께서 다음 이사회 회의에 오셔서 각각의 장단점을 설명해 주실 것입니다.**

> **어휘** agenda item 안건, 의제 board 이사회, 위원회 be disappointed by ~에 실망하다 drop 감소, 하락 decline 감소, 하락 distribution 유통, 분배 overseas 해외에 manufacture 제조하다 clothing 의류 locally 지역에서 look for ~을 찾다, ~을 구하다 put together 만들다, 준비하다 pros and cons 장단점

80 What type of product does the speaker's company make?
(A) Furniture
(B) Luggage
(C) Bedding
(D) Clothing

화자의 회사는 어떤 종류의 제품을 만드는가?
(A) 가구
(B) 여행 가방
(C) 침구류
(D) 의류

해설 전체 내용 관련 – 화자의 회사가 만드는 것

화자가 초반부에 회의 주제를 소개하면서 자사의 의류 매출(our clothing sales)을 언급했으므로 정답은 (D)이다.

81 What does the speaker recommend doing?
(A) Manufacturing some products locally
(B) Offering free shipping
(C) Participating in a trade show
(D) Developing a new product line

화자는 무엇을 할 것을 제안하는가?
(A) 일부 제품을 지역에서 제조하기
(B) 무료 배송 제공하기
(C) 무역 박람회 참가하기
(D) 신제품 라인 개발하기

어휘 participate in ~에 참가하다 trade show 무역 박람회

해설 세부 사항 관련 – 화자의 제안 사항

화자가 중반부에 일부 의류를 이 지역에서 제조하기 시작할 것을 제안한다(~ I'm recommending that we start manufacturing some clothing locally)고 했으므로 정답은 (A)이다.

Paraphrasing
담화의 clothing → 정답의 products

82 What will happen at the next meeting?
(A) A vote will take place.
(B) A consultant will give a presentation.
(C) Some contracts will be updated.
(D) Safety procedures will be reviewed.

다음 회의에서 무슨 일이 있을 것인가?
(A) 투표가 진행될 것이다.
(B) 컨설턴트가 발표할 것이다.
(C) 계약이 업데이트될 것이다.
(D) 안전 절차가 검토될 것이다.

어휘 vote 투표 take place 진행되다, 개최되다 give a presentation 발표하다 procedure 절차

해설 세부 사항 관련 – 다음 회의에서 있을 일

화자가 후반부에 컨설턴트를 고용했다며 그 사람이 다음 이사회 회의에 와서 장단점을 설명할 것(I hired a consultant ~ He'll be at our next board meeting to explain the pros and cons of each)이라고 했으므로 정답은 (B)이다.

Paraphrasing
담화의 explain the pros and cons of each
→ 정답의 give a presentation

83-85 공지

> **M-Cn** Attention, passengers. **83 All trains to Midway Station are delayed for track repairs.** Repair crews are working on a stretch of track just south of the town of Wheedon. They expect to complete the repair within the hour. We apologize for the delay. **84 We understand that many commuters need to get to Midway as soon as possible. A bus will be departing for that destination in fifteen minutes.** Also, **85 a reminder that the station café opens at eight A.M., and there are food kiosks on platform one.**

승객 여러분께 알립니다. **미드웨이 역으로 향하는 모든 열차가 철로 수리로 인해 지연되었습니다.** 수리팀이 위든 시의 바로 남쪽 철로 구간에서 작업을 하고 있습니다. 한 시간 내로 수리를 완료할 것으로 예상하고 있습니다. 지연에 대해 사과드립니다. **저희는 많은 통근자들께서 가능한 한 빨리 미드웨이로 가셔야 한다는 것을 알고 있습니다. 그 목적지로 가는 버스가 15분 뒤에 출발할 예정입니다.** 그리고 **역내 카페가 오전 8시에 문을 열며, 1번 승강장에 음식 주문용 단말기가 있다는 사실을 상기시켜 드립니다.**

어휘 delay 지연시키다; 지연, 지체   stretch (길게 뻗은) 구간   apologize for ~에 대해 사과하다   commuter 통근자   get to ~로 가다, ~에 도착하다   depart 출발하다, 떠나다   destination 목적지, 도착지   reminder 상기시키는 것   kiosk (주문용) 단말기, 가판대

83 What is the announcement mainly about?
(A) A promotional event
(B) A vacation package
(C) A building renovation
(D) A travel delay

공지는 주로 무엇에 관한 것인가?
(A) 홍보 행사
(B) 휴가 패키지
(C) 건물 보수
(D) 운행 지연

어휘 promotional 홍보의, 판촉의   renovation 개조, 보수

해설 전체 내용 관련 – 공지 주제
화자가 초반부에 미드웨이 역으로 향하는 모든 열차가 철로 수리로 인해 지연되었다(All trains to Midway Station are delayed for track repairs)고 언급한 뒤로, 그에 따른 조치를 설명하고 있으므로 정답은 (D)이다.

Paraphrasing
담화의 All trains to Midway Station are delayed
→ 정답의 A travel delay

84 Why does the speaker say, "A bus will be departing for that destination in fifteen minutes"?
(A) To suggest an alternative arrangement
(B) To explain an extended wait time
(C) To recommend changing the travel date
(D) To inform customers about a new destination

화자는 왜 "그 목적지로 가는 버스가 15분 뒤에 출발할 예정입니다"라고 말하는가?
(A) 대체 방안을 제안하기 위해
(B) 대기 시간 연장에 대해 설명하기 위해
(C) 여행 날짜 변경을 권하기 위해
(D) 고객들에게 새로운 목적지에 관해 알리기 위해

어휘 alternative 대체의, 대안의   arrangement 조치, 처리   extend 연장하다, 확장하다

해설 화자의 의도 파악 – 목적지로 가는 버스가 15분 뒤에 출발할 예정이라는 말의 의도
화자가 중반부에 많은 통근자들이 가능한 한 빨리 미드웨이로 가야 한다는 것을 알고 있다(We understand that many commuters need to get to Midway as soon as possible)고 밝히면서 인용문을 언급하고 있다. 이는 통근자들의 신속한 이동을 위해 대체 교통 수단을 제공한다는 뜻이므로 정답은 (A)이다.

85 What does the speaker remind the listeners about?
(A) How to download a mobile application
(B) Where a waiting area is located
(C) How to reserve tickets
(D) Where to buy food

화자는 청자들에게 무엇에 대해 상기시키는가?
(A) 모바일 애플리케이션을 다운로드하는 방법
(B) 대기 구역이 있는 곳
(C) 티켓을 예매하는 방법
(D) 음식을 구입하는 곳

어휘 remind 상기시키다   reserve 예약하다

해설 세부 사항 관련 – 화자가 상기시키는 것
화자가 후반부에 역내 카페가 오전 8시에 문을 열며, 1번 승강장에 음식 주문용 단말기가 있다는 사실을 상기시킨다(~ a reminder that the station café opens at eight A.M., and there are food kiosks on platform one)고 했으므로 정답은 (D)이다.

Paraphrasing
담화의 food kiosks on platform one
→ 정답의 Where to buy food

86-88 전화 메시지

W-Br   I'm calling about **86,87 the work my design team's doing to update your company logo. 87 I've just e-mailed two versions for you to review.** The first is a modern design with bold colors and simple lettering. The second image reflects the history of your brand and its logo. It's less trendy, but it doesn't depart much from the original, which you may prefer. Take your time to think about which one you'd like to choose. **88 I'll be on vacation all next week**, but if you call the office, my assistant will set up a meeting for when I get back.

저희 디자인팀이 귀사의 로고를 업데이트하기 위해 진행 중인 작업과 관련해 전화합니다. 제가 방금 검토해 보실 수 있도록 두 가지 버전을 이메일로 보내 드렸습니다. 첫 번째는 대담한 색상과 단순한 글자가 들어간 현대적인 디자인입니다. 두 번째 이미지는 귀사의 브랜드와 그

TEST 1   **25**

로고의 역사까지 반영합니다. 요즘 스타일은 아니지만, 원래의 것에서 크게 벗어나지 않으므로, 선호하실 수 있습니다. 어느 것을 선택하고 싶으신지 시간을 갖고 생각해 보시기 바랍니다. **저는 다음 주 내내 휴가 중이지만**, 사무실로 전화하시면, 제 비서가 제가 복귀하는 시점에 맞춰 회의 일정을 잡아 드릴 것입니다.

> **어휘** bold 대담한, 강렬한 lettering 글자(체) reflect 반영하다 trendy 유행하는, 인기 있는 depart from ~에서 벗어나다 original 원래의; 원본 choose 선택하다 assistant 비서, 조수 set up 일정을 잡다, 설정하다

86 Where does the speaker most likely work?
(A) At a graphic design company
(B) At a law firm
(C) At a photography studio
(D) At a museum

화자는 어디에서 일하는 것 같은가?
(A) 그래픽 디자인 회사
(B) 법률 회사
(C) 사진 촬영 스튜디오
(D) 박물관

해설 전체 내용 관련 – 화자의 근무 장소
화자가 초반부에 소속 디자인팀이 청자 회사의 로고를 업데이트하기 위해 진행 중인 작업(~ the work my design team's doing to update your company logo)을 언급하고 있으므로 정답은 (A)이다.

87 What did the listener receive by e-mail?
(A) A newsletter
(B) Some images
(C) An invoice
(D) Some contracts

청자는 이메일로 무엇을 받았는가?
(A) 소식지
(B) 이미지
(C) 거래 내역서
(D) 계약서

해설 세부 사항 관련 – 청자가 이메일로 받은 것
화자가 초반부에 청자 회사의 로고(your company logo)를 업데이트하는 작업을 언급하면서 검토를 위해 두 가지 버전을 이메일로 보냈다(I've just e-mailed two versions for you to review)고 했다. 따라서 로고 이미지를 보낸 것으로 볼 수 있으므로 정답은 (B)이다.

88 Why is the speaker unavailable next week?
(A) She will be working at another branch.
(B) She will be with other clients.
(C) She will be on vacation.
(D) She will be at an industry conference.

화자는 왜 다음 주에 시간을 낼 수 없는가?
(A) 다른 지점에서 근무할 예정이다.
(B) 다른 고객들과 함께 있을 것이다.
(C) 휴가 중일 것이다.
(D) 업계 콘퍼런스에 가 있을 것이다.

> **어휘** branch 지점, 지사 industry 업계, 산업

해설 세부 사항 관련 – 화자가 다음 주에 시간이 없는 이유
화자가 후반부에 다음 주 내내 휴가 중일 것(I'll be on vacation all next week ~)이라고 했으므로 정답은 (C)이다.

89-91 연설

> W-Am After the transportation agency released the draft of our improvement plan last week, members of the press asked if we're considering installing more fuel-efficient engines in our trains. **89 I've scheduled this press conference to officially respond to your inquiries.** Eighteen months ago, **90 we hired a firm to determine if this upgrade would be feasible for our trains.** It reported that the upgrade would be economical only for relatively new trains— that is, those less than five years old. All of ours are at least ten years old. I hope this addresses your questions. **91 If you're interested in more details, e-mail our media relations department to receive a summary of the findings.**

> 교통국에서 지난주에 개선 계획 초안을 공개한 후로, 기자들이 열차에 연비가 더 좋은 엔진을 설치하는 것을 고려하고 있는지 질문했습니다. 여러분의 문의에 공식적으로 답변해 드리기 위해 이 기자 회견 일정을 잡았습니다. 18개월 전에, 이 업그레이드를 실제로 열차에 적용할 수 있을지 알아보기 위해 업체를 고용했습니다. 그곳에서는 이 업그레이드가 오직 비교적 새 열차들, 다시 말해서, 연식이 5년 미만인 열차들에 대해서만 경제적일 것이라고 알려 주었습니다. 저희가 보유한 것들은 모두 최소 10년은 되었습니다. 이것으로 여러분의 궁금증이 해결되기를 바랍니다. 더 자세한 정보에 관심이 있으시면, 저희 언론 홍보팀에 이메일을 보내셔서 결과 요약본을 받아 보시기 바랍니다.

> **어휘** transportation agency 교통국 release 공개하다 draft 초안 improvement 개선, 향상 press 언론, 기자단 fuel-efficient 연비가 좋은 press conference 기자 회견 officially 공식적으로, 정식으로 respond 답변하다, 대응하다 inquiry 문의, 질문 determine 결정하다, 밝혀내다 feasible 실현 가능한 economical 경제적인, 절약이 되는 relatively 비교적, 상대적으로 address 해결하다, 처리하다 be interested in ~에 관심이 있다 details 상세 정보, 세부 사항 media relations department 언론 홍보팀 summary 요약(본) findings 결과물

89 Who most likely are the listeners?
(A) Investors
(B) Government officials
(C) Engineers
(D) Journalists

청자들은 누구인 것 같은가?
(A) 투자자
(B) 정부 공무원
(C) 엔지니어
(D) 기자

어휘 official 공무원

해설 전체 내용 관련 – 청자들의 직업
화자가 중반부에 청자들의 문의에 공식적으로 답변하기 위해 해당 기자 회견 일정을 잡았다(I've scheduled this press conference to officially respond to your inquiries)고 밝히고 있으므로 정답은 (D)이다.

90 What does the speaker mean when she says, "All of ours are at least ten years old"?
(A) An event needs to be relocated.
(B) An upgrade is not feasible.
(C) A project team has a lot of experience.
(D) Some company policies are outdated.

화자가 "저희가 보유한 것들은 모두 최소 10년은 되었습니다"라고 말할 때 무엇을 의미하는가?
(A) 행사 위치가 이전되어야 한다.
(B) 업그레이드를 실현하기 어렵다.
(C) 프로젝트 팀이 많은 경험을 지니고 있다.
(D) 몇몇 회사 정책이 구식이다.

어휘 relocate 이전하다, 재배치하다 outdated 구식인, 낡은

해설 화자의 의도 파악 – 보유한 것들이 모두 최소 10년은 되었다는 말의 의도
화자가 중반부에 업그레이드를 실제로 열차에 적용할 수 있을지 알아보기 위해 업체를 고용했는데, 그곳에서 업그레이드가 연식이 5년 미만인 열차들에 대해서만 경제적일 것이라고 알려 주었다(~ It reported that the upgrade would be economical only for relatively new trains—that is, those less than five years old)고 밝히면서 인용문을 언급하고 있다. 따라서 모두 최소 10년이 되었다는 말은 업그레이드를 하기에 경제적으로 효용성이 없어 실현하기 어려울 것이라는 뜻이므로 정답은 (B)이다.

91 According to the speaker, what can be requested by e-mail?
(A) Some presentation slides
(B) Some product samples
(C) A report summary
(D) A discounted ticket

화자에 따르면, 무엇이 이메일로 요청될 수 있는가?
(A) 발표 슬라이드
(B) 제품 샘플
(C) 보고서 요약본
(D) 할인 티켓

해설 세부 사항 관련 – 이메일로 요청할 수 있는 것
화자가 후반부에 더 자세한 정보에 관심이 있으면, 언론 홍보팀에 이메일을 보내 결과 요약본을 받아 보라(If you're interested in more details, e-mail our media relations department to receive a summary of the findings)고 했으므로 정답은 (C)이다.

Paraphrasing
담화의 a summary of the findings
→ 정답의 A report summary

92-94 회의 발췌

M-Cn As regional sales manager, **92 I want to explore the use of a more modernized payment system in our cosmetics stores.** This system would allow any sales associate to take customer payments from a tablet anywhere in the store. Why should we do this? **93 The main complaint about shopping at our stores is waiting in long lines to pay.** A lot of our stores could benefit from this, but **94 I've decided to conduct a trial run at our store in the Center City Mall.** By far, that's our busiest location.

지역 영업 관리자로서, **저는 화장품 매장에서 더욱 현대화된 결제 시스템을 사용하는 것을 검토하고자 합니다.** 이 시스템은 영업 사원이 매장 내 어디서나 태블릿을 통해 고객 결제를 처리할 수 있게 해 줄 것입니다. 우리가 왜 이렇게 해야 할까요? **우리 매장에서 쇼핑하는 것과 관련된 주된 불만은 결제하기 위해 줄을 길게 서서 대기하는 것입니다.** 많은 매장들이 이것으로 혜택을 볼 수 있겠지만, **저는 센터 시티 몰에 있는 매장에서 시범 운영을 하기로 결정했습니다.** 단연코, 그곳이 가장 바쁜 지점입니다.

어휘 regional 지역의 explore 탐구하다, 조사하다 modernized 현대화된 payment 결제, 지불 (금액) cosmetics 화장품 associate 직원, 동료 complaint 불만 benefit from ~로부터 혜택을 보다 conduct 실시하다, 수행하다 trial run 시범 운영 by far 단연코, 확실히

92 What does the speaker want to do?
(A) Increase online sales
(B) Upgrade a payment system
(C) Create a new product line
(D) Add store locations

화자는 무엇을 하고 싶어 하는가?
(A) 온라인 판매량 늘리기
(B) 결제 시스템 업그레이드하기
(C) 신제품 라인 만들기
(D) 매장 지점 추가하기

어휘 add 추가하다

해설 전체 내용 관련 – 화자가 하고 싶어 하는 것
화자가 초반부에 더욱 현대화된 결제 시스템을 사용하는 것을 검토하고 싶다(~ I want to explore the use of a more modernized payment system in our cosmetics stores)고 했으므로 정답은 (B)이다.

> **Paraphrasing**
> 담화의 use of a more modernized payment system
> → 정답의 Upgrade a payment system

93 According to the speaker, what is the customers' main complaint?
(A) Long lines
(B) High prices
(C) Unavailable items
(D) Unfriendly staff

화자에 따르면, 고객들의 주된 불만은 무엇인가?
(A) 긴 줄
(B) 높은 가격
(C) 구매 불가능한 제품
(D) 불친절한 직원

어휘 unfriendly 불친절한

해설 세부 사항 관련 – 고객들의 주된 불만
화자가 중반부에 매장에서 쇼핑하는 것과 관련된 주된 불만은 결제하기 위해 줄을 길게 서서 대기하는 것(The main complaint about shopping at our stores is waiting in long lines to pay)이라고 했으므로 정답은 (A)이다.

94 Why does the speaker say, "that's our busiest location"?
(A) To request some feedback
(B) To compliment some staff
(C) To express frustration
(D) To justify a choice

화자는 왜 "그곳이 가장 바쁜 지점입니다"라고 말하는가?
(A) 의견을 요청하기 위해
(B) 직원들을 칭찬하기 위해
(C) 불만을 표현하기 위해
(D) 선택을 정당화하기 위해

어휘 feedback 의견, 반응 compliment 칭찬하다; 칭찬 frustration 불만, 좌절(감) justify 정당화하다

해설 화자의 의도 파악 – 그곳이 가장 바쁜 지점이라는 말의 의도
화자가 후반부에 센터 시티 몰에 있는 매장에서 시범 운영을 하기로 결정했다(~ I've decided to conduct a trial run at our store in the Center City Mall)고 알리면서 인용문을 언급하고 있다. 이는 가장 바쁜 지점에서 시범 운영을 실시하는 것이 타당하다는 뜻이므로 정답은 (D)이다.

95-97 방송 + 표

> W-Br In local news, the downtown Reston Office Tower is completed. **95 The most extraordinary feature of the building is its beautiful garden, located in the lobby.** Reston's management office has confirmed the tenant list for the building. And **96 we interviewed the CEO of Barnum Financial Services about its new offices.** He said he and his team are excited to move in in January. **97 A recording of the full interview with the CEO is available on our Web site.**

> 지역 소식입니다. 시내 레스턴 오피스 타워가 완공되었습니다. 이 건물의 가장 놀라운 특징은 로비에 있는 아름다운 정원입니다. 레스턴의 관리소는 건물에 입주할 회사 명단을 확정했습니다. 그리고 저희는 바넘 파이낸셜 서비스의 새 사무실과 관련해 그곳의 CEO를 인터뷰했습니다. 그는 자신과 팀원들이 1월에 입주하게 되어 기쁘다고 말했습니다. 이 CEO와의 전체 인터뷰를 담은 녹화 영상은 저희 웹사이트에서 보실 수 있습니다.

어휘 extraordinary 놀라운, 예사롭지 않은 feature 특징 confirm 확정하다, 확인해 주다 tenant 세입자, 임차인 move in 입주하다

Tenant	Floors
Burger Incorporated	1-5
Aegis Technologies	6-10
96 Barnum Financial Services	**11-14**
Heinkel Media Group	15-17

세입자	층
버거 주식회사	1-5
이지스 테크놀로지	6-10
바넘 파이낸셜 서비스	**11-14**
하인켈 미디어 그룹	15-17

95 According to the speaker, what is special about the Reston Office Tower?
(A) It features an indoor garden.
(B) It exhibits work from local artists.
(C) It runs on solar power.
(D) It has won many awards.

화자에 따르면, 레스턴 오피스 타워는 무엇이 특별한가?
(A) 실내 정원이 특징이다.
(B) 지역 미술가들의 작품을 전시한다.
(C) 태양열 에너지로 운영된다.
(D) 많은 상을 받았다.

어휘 feature 특징으로 하다 exhibit 전시하다 run 운영되다

해설 세부 사항 관련 – 레스턴 오피스 타워의 특별한 점
화자가 초반부에 레스턴 오피스 타워를 언급하면서 이 건물의 가장 놀라운 특징이 로비에 있는 아름다운 정원(The most extraordinary feature of the building is its beautiful garden, located in the lobby)이라고 했으므로 정답은 (A)이다.

Paraphrasing
담화의 The most extraordinary feature → 질문의 special
담화의 its beautiful garden, located in the lobby
→ 정답의 an indoor garden

96 Look at the graphic. Which floors will be occupied in January?
(A) Floors 1–5
(B) Floors 6–10
(C) Floors 11–14
(D) Floors 15–17

시각 정보에 의하면, 1월에 어느 층이 입주할 것인가?
(A) 1–5층
(B) 6–10층
(C) 11–14층
(D) 15–17층

어휘 occupied 점유된, 사용 중인

해설 시각 정보 연계 – 1월에 입주하는 층
화자가 중반부에 바넘 파이낸셜 서비스의 CEO를 인터뷰했다며, 1월에 입주하게 되어 기쁘다고 말했다(~ we interviewed the CEO of Barnum Financial Services about its new offices. He said he and his team are excited to move in in January)고 했다. 표에 바넘 파이낸셜 서비스의 층이 11-14로 표기되어 있으므로 정답은 (C)이다.

97 What does the speaker say is available on a Web site?
(A) Some photographs
(B) An event schedule
(C) A floor layout
(D) A recorded interview

화자는 웹사이트에서 무엇을 이용할 수 있다고 말하는가?
(A) 사진들
(B) 행사 일정표
(C) 층별 배치도
(D) 인터뷰 녹화 영상

어휘 layout 배치(도), 구획

해설 세부 사항 관련 – 웹사이트에서 이용할 수 있는 것
화자가 후반부에 바넘 파이낸셜 서비스의 CEO와의 전체 인터뷰를 담은 녹화 영상을 웹사이트에서 볼 수 있다(A recording of the full interview with the CEO is available on our Web site)고 했으므로 정답은 (D)이다.

Paraphrasing
담화의 A recording of the full interview
→ 정답의 A recorded interview

98-100 회의 발췌 + 표

M-Au Good morning, and **⁹⁸thank you for attending this meeting for prospective investors.** ZZ Mining has been planning to expand our operations by opening an additional silver mine. Let me show you the laboratory analysis of our exploratory drilling. On the screen, you can see information about the ore extracted from different sites. The highest-grade site had 410 grams of silver per ton of ore. However, **⁹⁹the site with 390 grams per ton has a larger deposit, so that's where we'll build the new mine. ¹⁰⁰Our next step is to apply for the necessary permits.** We'll do that next week.

안녕하세요. **잠재 투자자들을 위한 회의에 참석해 주셔서 감사합니다**. ZZ 마이닝은 은광을 추가로 개발해 사업을 확대할 계획입니다. 저희 탐사 시추에 대한 실험실 분석 결과를 보여 드리겠습니다. 스크린에서, 여러 다른 부지에서 추출된 광석에 관한 정보를 보실 수 있습니다. 최고 등급의 부지는 광석 1톤당 410그램의 은이 있었습니다. 하지만 **1톤당 390그램이 있는 부지에 매장량이 더 많기 때문에, 저희는 그곳에 새로운 광산을 지을 것입니다. 다음 단계는 필수 허가를 신청하는 일입니다.** 저희는 이것을 다음 주에 할 것입니다.

어휘 prospective 잠재적인, 유망한 investor 투자자
operation 사업, 영업 mine 광산 laboratory 실험실
analysis 분석 exploratory 탐사의 drilling 시추, 구멍 뚫기
ore 광석 extract 추출하다 grade 등급 deposit 매장량
necessary 필수의, 필요한

Location	Grams per Ton
Site 1	150
Site 2	270
99 Site 3	**390**
Site 4	410

위치	톤당 그램
부지 1	150
부지 2	270
부지 3	**390**
부지 4	410

98 Who most likely are the listeners?
(A) Safety engineers
(B) Laboratory technicians
(C) Legal consultants
(D) Business investors

청자들은 누구인 것 같은가?
(A) 안전 관리 기술자
(B) 실험실 기술자
(C) 법률 자문
(D) 사업 투자자

어휘 legal 법률과 관련된, 법률의

해설 전체 내용 관련 – 청자들의 직업
화자가 초반부에 청자들에게 잠재 투자자들을 위한 회의에 참석한 것에 대해 감사하다(~ thank you for attending this meeting for prospective investors)고 했으므로 정답은 (D)이다.

99 Look at the graphic. Where will a new mine be built?
(A) At site 1
(B) At site 2
(C) At site 3
(D) At site 4

시각 정보에 의하면, 새로운 광산은 어디에 지어질 것인가?
(A) 부지 1
(B) 부지 2
(C) 부지 3
(D) 부지 4

해설 시각 정보 연계 – 새 광산이 지어질 곳
화자가 후반부에 1톤당 390그램이 있는 부지에 매장량이 더 많기 때문에 그곳에 새로운 광산을 지을 것(~ the site with 390 grams per ton has a larger deposit, so that's where we'll build the new mine)이라고 했다. 표에서 1톤당 390그램으로 표기된 곳은 부지 3이므로 정답은 (C)이다.

100 What does the speaker say is the next step?
(A) Applying for permits
(B) Installing equipment
(C) Hiring additional staff
(D) Updating a manual

화자는 다음 단계가 무엇이라고 말하는가?
(A) 허가 신청하기
(B) 장비 설치하기
(C) 추가 직원 고용하기
(D) 설명서 업데이트하기

어휘 manual (사용) 설명서, 안내서

해설 세부 사항 관련 – 화자가 다음 단계라고 말하는 것
화자가 후반부에 다음 단계는 필수 허가를 신청하는 일(Our next step is to apply for the necessary permits)이라고 했으므로 정답은 (A)이다.

기출 TEST 2

동영상 강의

1 (B)	2 (D)	3 (B)	4 (A)	5 (C)
6 (A)	7 (A)	8 (B)	9 (C)	10 (A)
11 (C)	12 (C)	13 (A)	14 (A)	15 (B)
16 (C)	17 (A)	18 (B)	19 (C)	20 (C)
21 (B)	22 (C)	23 (A)	24 (A)	25 (B)
26 (B)	27 (B)	28 (A)	29 (B)	30 (C)
31 (C)	32 (D)	33 (D)	34 (A)	35 (B)
36 (B)	37 (D)	38 (C)	39 (D)	40 (B)
41 (A)	42 (C)	43 (A)	44 (A)	45 (D)
46 (A)	47 (B)	48 (D)	49 (C)	50 (C)
51 (B)	52 (B)	53 (C)	54 (A)	55 (C)
56 (D)	57 (C)	58 (D)	59 (A)	60 (D)
61 (C)	62 (B)	63 (C)	64 (A)	65 (A)
66 (B)	67 (A)	68 (D)	69 (A)	70 (D)
71 (B)	72 (D)	73 (C)	74 (A)	75 (D)
76 (B)	77 (C)	78 (C)	79 (D)	80 (A)
81 (C)	82 (C)	83 (B)	84 (D)	85 (A)
86 (A)	87 (D)	88 (B)	89 (B)	90 (C)
91 (A)	92 (B)	93 (D)	94 (D)	95 (A)
96 (B)	97 (C)	98 (C)	99 (A)	100 (D)

PART 1

1

M-Au

(A) A man is closing a metal gate.
(B) **A man is walking down a stone path.**
(C) Some potted plants line a walkway.
(D) Some flags are hanging from balconies.

(A) 남자가 금속 문을 닫고 있다.
(B) 남자가 돌길을 따라 걷고 있다.
(C) 화분에 심은 식물들이 보도에 늘어서 있다.
(D) 깃발들이 발코니에 걸려 있다.

어휘 potted plant 화분에 심은 식물   line 늘어서 있다
hang 걸려 있다, 매달려 있다

해설 1인 등장 사진 – 사람/사물/풍경 혼합 묘사
(A) 동사 오답. 남자가 금속 문을 닫고 있는(is closing a metal gate) 모습이 아니므로 오답.
(B) 정답. 남자가 돌길을 따라 걷고 있는(is walking down a stone path) 모습이므로 정답.

(C) 사진에 없는 명사를 이용한 오답. 사진에 화분에 심은 식물들(Some potted plants)의 모습이 보이지 않으므로 오답.
(D) 사진에 없는 명사를 이용한 오답. 사진에 깃발들(Some flags)의 모습이 보이지 않으므로 오답.

2

W-Am

(A) Some shopping bags have been placed on a train platform.
(B) Some people are lined up to buy train tickets.
(C) A woman is pulling her luggage behind her.
(D) **A man is leaning against a railing.**

(A) 쇼핑백들이 기차 승강장에 놓여 있다.
(B) 사람들이 기차표를 구입하기 위해 줄지어 서 있다.
(C) 여자가 뒤에 짐을 끌고 있다.
(D) 남자가 난간에 기대고 있다.

어휘 luggage 짐, 수하물, 여행 가방   lean against ~에 기대다
railing 난간

해설 2인 이상 등장 사진 – 사람/사물/풍경 혼합 묘사
(A) 사진에 없는 명사를 이용한 오답. 사진에 쇼핑백들(Some shopping bags)의 모습이 보이지 않으므로 오답.
(B) 동사 오답. 기차표를 구입하기 위해 줄지어 서 있는(are lined up to buy train tickets) 사람들의 모습이 보이지 않으므로 오답.
(C) 동사 오답. 여자가 짐을 끌고 있는(is pulling her luggage) 모습이 아니므로 오답.
(D) 정답. 남자가 난간에 기대고 있는(is leaning against a railing) 모습이므로 정답.

3

M-Au

(A) Some wooden planks are leaning against a wall.
(B) **A vehicle is parked next to a building.**
(C) Some stones have been stacked on a pallet.
(D) A package has been left near a door.

(A) 목재 판자들이 벽에 기대어져 있다.
(B) 차량이 건물 옆에 주차되어 있다.
(C) 돌들이 화물 운반대에 쌓여 있다.
(D) 소포가 문 근처에 놓여 있다.

어휘 plank 판자, 널빤지   vehicle 차량   stack 쌓다
pallet 화물 운반대, 팔레트

해설 | 사물/풍경 사진 - 풍경 묘사
(A) 동사 오답. 목재 판자들(Some wooden planks)이 벽에 기대어져 있는(are leaning against a wall) 모습이 아니므로 오답.
(B) 정답. 차량(A vehicle)이 건물 옆에 주차되어 있는(is parked next to a building) 모습이므로 정답.
(C) 사진에 없는 명사를 이용한 오답. 사진에 화물 운반대(a pallet)의 모습이 보이지 않으므로 오답.
(D) 사진에 없는 명사를 이용한 오답. 사진에 소포(A package)의 모습이 보이지 않으므로 오답.

어휘 | tie 묶다 apron 앞치마 reach for ~을 향해 손을 뻗다 shelf 선반 counter 조리대 refrigerator 냉장고
해설 | 1인 등장 사진 - 사람의 동작/상태 묘사
(A) 동사 오답. 여자가 앞치마 뒷부분을 묶고 있는(is tying the back of her apron) 모습이 아니므로 오답.
(B) 동사 오답. 여자가 선반에 있는 음식을 향해 손을 뻗고 있는(is reaching for food on a shelf) 모습이 아니므로 오답.
(C) 정답. 여자가 조리대에서 일하고 있는(is working at a counter) 모습이므로 정답.
(D) 동사 오답. 여자가 음식을 냉장고에 넣고 있는(is putting food into a refrigerator) 모습이 아니므로 오답.

4
W-Br

(A) A man is holding up his phone.
(B) A man is pinning a note to a bulletin board.
(C) A man is dropping an item into a bin.
(D) A man is washing some windows.

(A) 남자가 전화기를 들고 있다.
(B) 남자가 메모를 게시판에 핀으로 고정하고 있다.
(C) 남자가 물건을 쓰레기통에 버리고 있다.
(D) 남자가 창문을 닦고 있다.

어휘 | pin 핀으로 고정하다 bulletin board 게시판 bin 쓰레기통
해설 | 1인 등장 사진 - 사람의 동작/상태 묘사
(A) 정답. 남자가 전화기를 들고 있는(is holding up his phone) 모습이므로 정답.
(B) 동사 오답. 남자가 메모를 게시판에 핀으로 고정하고 있는(is pinning a note to a bulletin board) 모습이 아니므로 오답.
(C) 동사 오답. 남자가 물건을 쓰레기통에 버리고 있는(is dropping an item into a bin) 모습이 아니므로 오답.
(D) 동사 오답. 남자가 창문을 닦고 있는(is washing some windows) 모습이 아니므로 오답.

6
W-Am

(A) He's setting up a buffet.
(B) He's putting plates on dining tables.
(C) He's watering some plants in a garden.
(D) He's carrying food up a stairway.

(A) 남자가 뷔페를 준비하고 있다.
(B) 남자가 식탁에 접시를 놓고 있다.
(C) 남자가 정원에서 식물에 물을 주고 있다.
(D) 남자가 계단 위로 음식을 나르고 있다.

어휘 | set up 준비하다, 설치하다 plate 접시 stairway 계단
해설 | 1인 등장 사진 - 사람의 동작/상태 묘사
(A) 정답. 남자가 뷔페를 준비하고 있는(is setting up a buffet) 모습이므로 정답.
(B) 동사 오답. 남자가 식탁에 접시를 놓고 있는(is putting plates on dining tables) 모습이 아니므로 오답.
(C) 동사 오답. 남자가 식물들에게 물을 주고 있는(is watering some plants) 모습이 아니므로 오답.
(D) 동사 오답. 남자가 계단 위로 음식을 나르고 있는(is carrying food up a stairway) 모습이 아니므로 오답.

5
M-Cn

(A) She's tying the back of her apron.
(B) She's reaching for food on a shelf.
(C) She's working at a counter.
(D) She's putting food into a refrigerator.

(A) 여자가 앞치마 뒷부분을 묶고 있다.
(B) 여자가 선반에 있는 음식을 향해 손을 뻗고 있다.
(C) 여자가 조리대에서 일하고 있다.
(D) 여자가 음식을 냉장고에 넣고 있다.

PART 2

7 M-Cn / W-Br

Will you order the pasta or the chicken?
(A) I'll have the pasta.
(B) Yes, I studied Italian.
(C) I think we should paint the kitchen.

파스타를 주문하시겠어요, 아니면 닭고기로 하시겠어요?
(A) 파스타로 할게요.
(B) 네, 이탈리아어를 공부했어요.
(C) 주방에 페인트칠을 해야 할 것 같아요.

| 해설 | 원하는 음식을 묻는 선택 의문문
(A) 정답. 파스타를 주문할지, 아니면 닭고기로 할지 묻는 질문에 파스타를 선택해 응답하고 있으므로 정답.
(B) 연상 단어 오답. 질문의 pasta에서 연상 가능한 Italian을 이용한 오답.
(C) 연상 단어 오답. 질문의 pasta와 chicken에서 연상 가능한 kitchen을 이용한 오답.

8 W-Am / W-Br

Who should I talk to about getting a ticket to Bangkok?

(A) How about after the conference?
(B) The agent at the ticket counter.
(C) In front of the theater.

방콕행 티켓 구입과 관련해서 누구에게 이야기해야 하나요?
(A) 콘퍼런스 후에는 어때요?
(B) 매표소에 있는 직원이요.
(C) 극장 앞에요.

| 어휘 | agent 직원, 대리인
| 해설 | 방콕행 티켓 구입 관련 문의 대상을 묻는 Who 의문문
(A) 질문과 상관없는 오답.
(B) 정답. 방콕행 티켓 구입 관련 문의 대상을 묻는 질문에 매표소에 있는 직원이라고 알려 주고 있으므로 정답.
(C) 연상 단어 오답. 질문의 ticket에서 연상 가능한 theater를 이용한 오답.

9 M-Au / W-Br

Would you like the report to be e-mailed or printed out?

(A) An electric heater.
(B) Page 25.
(C) Either way is fine.

보고서를 이메일로 받아 보시겠어요, 아니면 출력해 드릴까요?
(A) 전기 난로요.
(B) 25페이지요.
(C) 어느 쪽이든 좋습니다.

| 해설 | 보고서를 받을 방식을 묻는 선택 의문문
(A) 질문과 상관없는 오답.
(B) 연상 단어 오답. 질문의 report에서 연상 가능한 Page 25를 이용한 오답.
(C) 정답. 보고서를 이메일로 받을지, 아니면 출력한 것을 받을지 묻는 질문에 어느 쪽이든 좋다며 둘 다 상관없다는 의사를 표현하고 있으므로 정답.

10 W-Am / W-Br

Have you decided how much to charge for your concert tickets?

(A) Yes—fifteen dollars each.
(B) I've read about that.
(C) A jazz band.

콘서트 티켓을 얼마로 할지 정하셨나요?
(A) 네, 각각 15달러요.
(B) 그것에 대해 읽어 봤어요.
(C) 재즈 밴드요.

| 어휘 | charge 부과하다, 청구하다
| 해설 | 콘서트 티켓 가격을 결정했는지 묻는 조동사(Have) 의문문
(A) 정답. 콘서트 티켓 가격을 결정했는지 묻는 질문에 네(Yes)라고 대답한 뒤, 각각 15달러라고 구체적인 금액을 알려 주고 있으므로 정답.
(B) 질문과 상관없는 오답.
(C) 연상 단어 오답. 질문의 concert에서 연상 가능한 jazz band를 이용한 오답.

11 M-Au / W-Am

How often does the store offer a sales promotion?

(A) A discount on appliances.
(B) Sure, I can buy some.
(C) Every three months.

그 가게는 얼마나 자주 판촉 행사를 하나요?
(A) 가전 제품 할인이요.
(B) 물론이죠, 제가 구입할 수 있어요.
(C) 3개월마다요.

| 어휘 | sales promotion 판촉 행사 appliance 가전 제품
| 해설 | 판촉 행사 빈도를 묻는 How often 의문문
(A) 연상 단어 오답. 질문의 sales promotion에서 연상 가능한 discount를 이용한 오답.
(B) Yes/No 불가 오답. How 의문문에는 Yes/No 응답이 불가능한데, Sure도 일종의 Yes 응답이라고 볼 수 있으므로 오답.
(C) 정답. 판촉 행사 빈도를 묻는 질문에 3개월마다라고 구체적인 빈도를 제시하고 있으므로 정답.

12 W-Am / W-Br

The tour starts at noon today, doesn't it?

(A) Please start this washing machine.
(B) He's playing a folk tune.
(C) No—it's been postponed an hour.

투어가 오늘 정오에 시작하죠, 그렇지 않나요?
(A) 이 세탁기를 작동시켜 주세요.
(B) 그는 민속 음악을 연주하고 있어요.
(C) 아니요, 1시간 연기되었어요.

| 어휘 | fork tune 민속 음악 postpone 연기하다, 미루다
| 해설 | 투어가 정오에 시작하는지 확인하는 부가 의문문
(A) 파생어 오답. 질문의 starts와 파생어 관계인 start를 이용한 오답.
(B) 질문과 상관없는 오답. 질문에 3인칭 대명사 He로 지칭할 인물이 언급된 적이 없으므로 오답.
(C) 정답. 투어가 정오에 시작하는지 확인하는 질문에 아니요(No)라고 대답한 뒤, 1시간 연기되었다며 부정 답변과 일관된 내용을 덧붙이고 있으므로 정답.

13 W-Am / M-Au

Let's begin our meeting about the Taylor project.

(A) Good idea—we have a lot to get through.
(B) Some project proposals.
(C) No, in room 725.

테일러 프로젝트에 관한 회의를 시작합시다.
(A) 좋은 생각이에요. 우리가 해야 할 일이 아주 많아요.
(B) 프로젝트 제안서들이요.
(C) 아니요, 725호에요.

어휘 get through 해내다, 처리하다   proposal 제안(서)

해설 제안/권유의 평서문
(A) 정답. 테일러 프로젝트에 관한 회의를 시작하자고 제안하는 평서문에 좋은 생각이라고 동의한 뒤, 해야 할 일이 아주 많다고 덧붙이고 있으므로 정답.
(B) 단어 반복 오답. 평서문의 project를 반복 이용한 오답.
(C) 연상 단어 오답. 평서문의 meeting에서 연상 가능한 room을 이용한 오답.

14 M-Cn / W-Br

There's a dental clinic on Main Street, isn't there?

(A) Yes, it's very convenient.
(B) A toothbrush and toothpaste.
(C) I'll have the main dish, thanks.

메인 가에 치과가 있죠, 그렇지 않나요?
(A) 네, 아주 편리합니다.
(B) 칫솔과 치약이요.
(C) 저는 메인 요리로 할게요, 감사합니다.

어휘 dental clinic 치과   convenient 편리한

해설 메인 가에 치과가 있는지 확인하는 부가 의문문
(A) 정답. 메인 가에 치과가 있는지 확인하는 질문에 네(Yes)라고 대답한 뒤, 아주 편리하다며 긍정 답변과 일관된 내용을 덧붙이고 있으므로 정답.
(B) 연상 단어 오답. 질문의 dental clinic에서 연상 가능한 toothbrush and toothpaste를 이용한 오답.
(C) 단어 반복 오답. 질문의 Main을 반복 이용한 오답.

15 W-Am / M-Au

Where is the book reading going to take place?

(A) Sure—I can give you a tour later.
(B) At the library.
(C) It lasts a while.

도서 낭독회는 어디에서 열리나요?
(A) 물론이죠, 제가 나중에 견학시켜 드릴게요.
(B) 도서관에서요.
(C) 한동안 지속됩니다.

어휘 take place 열리다, 개최되다   last 지속되다

해설 도서 낭독회가 열리는 장소를 묻는 Where 의문문
(A) Yes/No 불가 오답. Where 의문문에는 Yes/No 응답이 불가능한데, Sure도 일종의 Yes 응답이라고 볼 수 있으므로 오답.
(B) 정답. 도서 낭독회가 열리는 장소를 묻는 질문에 도서관이라고 구체적인 장소로 응답하고 있으므로 정답.
(C) 질문과 상관없는 오답. How long 의문문에 대한 응답이므로 오답.

16 M-Cn / M-Au

When's the bus going to be here?

(A) A round-trip ticket.
(B) Let's break for lunch.
(C) At 3:30 P.M.

버스가 언제 이곳에 오나요?
(A) 왕복 티켓이요.
(B) 점심 식사를 위해 잠시 쉬겠습니다.
(C) 오후 3시 30분에요.

어휘 round-trip 왕복의

해설 버스가 오는 시간을 묻는 When 의문문
(A) 연상 단어 오답. 질문의 bus에서 연상 가능한 round-trip을 이용한 오답.
(B) 질문과 상관없는 오답.
(C) 정답. 버스가 오는 시간을 묻는 질문에 오후 3시 30분이라고 구체적인 시간으로 응답하고 있으므로 정답.

17 M-Cn / W-Am

The estimated price for this car insurance is higher than we expected.

(A) We'll check to see if there's a cheaper rate.
(B) There's another filling station nearby.
(C) The parking garage on the corner.

자동차 보험 견적이 저희가 예상한 것보다 높네요.
(A) 더 저렴한 요금이 있는지 한번 확인해 보겠습니다.
(B) 근처에 다른 주유소가 있어요.
(C) 모퉁이에 있는 주차장이요.

어휘 estimated price 견적, 예상 가격   insurance 보험
rate 요금   filling station 주유소   nearby 근처에

해설 정보 전달의 평서문
(A) 정답. 자동차 보험 견적이 예상한 것보다 높다는 평서문에 더 저렴한 요금이 있는지 알아보겠다며 문제에 대한 해결책을 제시하고 있으므로 정답.
(B) 연상 단어 오답. 평서문의 car에서 연상 가능한 filling station을 이용한 오답.
(C) 연상 단어 오답. 평서문의 car에서 연상 가능한 parking garage를 이용한 오답.

18 W-Am / M-Au

Why haven't the renovations been completed yet?

(A) It's on the top shelf.
(B) Because some materials were delayed.
(C) Some guests haven't received an invitation.

개조 공사가 왜 아직 완료되지 않았죠?

(A) 맨 위쪽 선반에 있어요.
(B) 일부 자재가 지연되어서요.
(C) 일부 손님들께서 초대장을 받지 못하셨어요.

어휘 renovation 개조, 보수   complete 완료하다   shelf 선반
material 자재, 재료   delay 지연시키다

해설 개조 공사가 아직 완료되지 않은 이유를 묻는 Why 의문문

(A) 질문과 상관없는 오답. Where 의문문에 대한 응답이므로 오답.
(B) 정답. 개조 공사가 아직 완료되지 않은 이유를 묻는 질문에 일부 자재가 지연되었기 때문이라는 이유를 제시하고 있으므로 정답.
(C) 질문과 상관없는 오답.

19 M-Au / W-Br

I'll give you my office number in case you have questions about the data.

(A) The theater is reserved for that date.
(B) The file cabinet needs to be moved.
(C) Thanks—I appreciate that.

데이터에 관한 질문이 있으실 경우에 대비해 제 사무실 번호를 알려 드릴게요.

(A) 극장은 그 날짜에 예약이 되어 있어요.
(B) 파일 캐비닛을 옮겨야 해요.
(C) 고마워요, 그렇게 해 주셔서 감사합니다.

어휘 reserve 예약하다   appreciate 감사하다

해설 제안/권유의 평서문

(A) 유사 발음 오답. 평서문의 data와 부분적으로 발음이 유사한 date를 이용한 오답.
(B) 연상 단어 오답. 평서문의 office에서 연상 가능한 file cabinet을 이용한 오답.
(C) 정답. 질문이 있을 경우에 대비해 자신의 사무실 번호를 알려 주겠다고 제안하는 평서문에 감사를 표현하고 있으므로 정답.

20 M-Au / M-Cn

Which parking area should we use?

(A) The fee is fifteen dollars.
(B) About a twenty-minute delay.
(C) The one by Smith's Pharmacy.

어느 주차 구역을 이용해야 하나요?

(A) 요금은 15달러입니다.
(B) 약 20분 정도 지연이요.
(C) 스미스 약국 옆에 있는 것이요.

어휘 fee 요금, 수수료   pharmacy 약국

해설 이용할 주차 구역을 묻는 Which 의문문

(A) 질문과 상관없는 오답. How much 의문문에 대한 응답이므로 오답.
(B) 질문과 상관없는 오답.
(C) 정답. 이용할 주차 구역을 묻는 질문에 parking area를 대명사 one으로 지칭해 스미스 약국 옆에 있는 것이라고 구체적으로 응답하고 있으므로 정답.

21 W-Am / W-Br

Let's take a taxi to the airport.

(A) My seats are in section 21.
(B) Sure, that will be the easiest.
(C) The café is a few blocks away.

공항까지 택시를 탑시다.

(A) 제 좌석은 21번 구역에 있어요.
(B) 좋아요, 그게 가장 쉬울 거예요.
(C) 그 카페는 몇 블록 떨어져 있어요.

해설 제안/권유의 평서문

(A) 평서문과 상관없는 오답. Where 의문문에 대한 응답이므로 오답.
(B) 정답. 공항까지 택시를 타고 가자고 제안하는 평서문에 좋다(Sure)고 대답한 뒤, 그게 가장 쉬울 것이라며 긍정 답변과 일관된 내용을 덧붙이고 있으므로 정답.
(C) 평서문과 상관없는 오답. Where 의문문에 대한 응답이므로 오답.

22 M-Au / M-Cn

Our team training session was well attended, wasn't it?

(A) They were delivered yesterday.
(B) No, just down the hall.
(C) Actually, not everyone was there.

우리 팀 교육에 참석자가 많았죠, 그렇지 않나요?

(A) 그것들은 어제 배송되었어요.
(B) 아니요, 바로 복도 저쪽에 있어요.
(C) 사실, 모두가 거기 온 건 아니었어요.

어휘 well attended 참석자가 많은

해설 팀 교육에 참석자가 많았는지 확인하는 부가 의문문

(A) 질문과 상관없는 오답. 질문에 3인칭 복수 대명사 They로 지칭할 사물이 언급된 적이 없으므로 오답.
(B) 질문과 상관없는 오답.
(C) 정답. 팀 교육에 참석자가 많았는지 확인하는 질문에 사실 모두가 온 것은 아니었다며 참석자가 그렇게 많지는 않았음을 우회적으로 알려 주고 있으므로 정답.

23 M-Cn / W-Am ▶동영상 강의

Why's the company discontinuing its newsletter?
(A) Only the print version.
(B) Two to three times per week.
(C) How far is the main office building?

회사에서 왜 소식지를 중단하는 건가요?
(A) 인쇄 버전만요.
(B) 일주일에 두세 번이요.
(C) 본관 건물은 얼마나 멀리 있나요?

어휘 discontinue 중단하다, 그만두다
해설 회사에서 소식지를 중단하는 이유를 묻는 Why 의문문
(A) 정답. 회사에서 소식지를 중단하는 이유를 묻는 질문에 인쇄 버전만 중단되는 것이라며 정보를 바로잡고 있으므로 정답.
(B) 질문과 상관없는 오답. How often 또는 How many times 의문문에 대한 응답이므로 오답.
(C) 연상 단어 오답. 질문의 company에서 연상 가능한 main office building을 이용한 오답.

24 M-Au / W-Am ▶동영상 강의

Weren't you planning to take the afternoon off?
(A) The clients wanted to meet today.
(B) I took it off the middle shelf.
(C) He created a great project plan.

오후에 휴가를 내실 계획 아니었나요?
(A) 고객들이 오늘 만나고 싶어 했어요.
(B) 가운데 선반에서 꺼냈어요.
(C) 그가 훌륭한 프로젝트 계획을 세웠어요.

해설 오후에 휴가를 낼 계획이 아니었는지 확인하는 부정 의문문
(A) 정답. 오후에 휴가를 낼 계획이 아니었는지 확인하는 질문에 고객들이 오늘 만나고 싶어 했다며 휴가를 내지 못한 이유를 알려 주고 있으므로 정답.
(B) 단어 반복 오답. 질문의 take ~ off를 반복 이용한 오답.
(C) 질문과 상관없는 오답. 질문에 3인칭 대명사 He로 지칭할 인물이 언급된 적이 없으므로 오답.

25 M-Cn / W-Am

Dr. Molina sees patients in her Middleville office.
(A) The instructor was so patient with the students.
(B) Oh, that's only two kilometers from my house.
(C) We have some digital thermometers in stock.

몰리나 선생님은 미들빌 사무실에서 환자를 진료하세요.
(A) 강사님은 수강생들을 정말 참을성 있게 대해 주셨어요.
(B) 아, 그곳은 저희 집에서 2킬로미터밖에 되지 않아요.
(C) 디지털 체온계 재고가 있어요.

어휘 patient 환자; 참을성 있는, 인내심 있는 instructor 강사 thermometer 체온계, 온도계 in stock 재고가 있는

해설 정보 전달의 평서문
(A) 파생어 오답. 평서문의 patients와 파생어 관계인 patient를 이용한 오답.
(B) 정답. 몰리나 선생님이 미들빌 사무소에서 환자를 진료한다는 평서문에 그곳이 자신의 집에서 2킬로미터밖에 떨어져 있지 않다며 관심을 표현하고 있으므로 정답.
(C) 연상 단어 오답. 평서문의 patients에서 연상 가능한 thermometers를 이용한 오답.

26 W-Am / W-Br

Who's going out for lunch?
(A) I enjoyed that book too.
(B) I'll be leaving work before then.
(C) What are you doing this weekend?

누가 점심 먹으러 나가나요?
(A) 저도 그 책을 즐겁게 읽었어요.
(B) 저는 그 전에 퇴근할 거예요.
(C) 이번 주말에 뭐 하세요?

해설 점심 먹으러 나가는 사람을 묻는 Who 의문문
(A) 질문과 상관없는 오답.
(B) 정답. 점심 먹으러 나가는 사람을 묻는 질문에 그 전에 퇴근할 것이라며 자신은 아니라는 뜻을 우회적으로 나타내고 있으므로 정답.
(C) 질문과 상관없는 오답.

27 W-Am / M-Au

Do the tickets go on sale this week or next?
(A) The cafeteria downstairs.
(B) They're already sold out.
(C) Sure, no problem.

티켓은 이번 주에 판매되나요, 아니면 다음 주인가요?
(A) 아래층에 있는 구내식당이요.
(B) 이미 매진되었어요.
(C) 물론이죠, 문제없습니다.

어휘 go on sale 판매되다 cafeteria 구내식당 downstairs 아래층에, 아래층으로 sold out 매진된, 품절된

해설 티켓을 판매하는 시점을 묻는 선택 의문문
(A) 질문과 상관없는 오답. Where 의문문에 대한 응답이므로 오답.
(B) 정답. 이번 주와 다음 주 중 티켓이 언제 판매되는지 묻는 질문에 이미 매진되었다며 벌써 판매가 완료되었음을 알려 주는 제3의 답변을 한 정답.
(C) 질문과 상관없는 오답. 요청 의문문에 대한 응답이므로 오답.

28 M-Au / M-Cn

When will you finish updating the sales data?
(A) I'm waiting for information from one more store.
(B) In the top drawer.
(C) Sales increased by five percent.

판매 데이터 업데이트는 언제 완료되나요?
(A) 한 군데 매장의 정보를 더 기다리고 있습니다.
(B) 맨 위쪽 서랍에요.
(C) 판매량이 5퍼센트 증가했어요.

어휘 drawer 서랍   increase 증가하다, 인상되다

해설 판매 데이터 업데이트가 완료되는 시점을 묻는 When 의문문
(A) 정답. 판매 데이터 업데이트가 완료되는 시점을 묻는 질문에 한 군데 매장의 정보를 더 기다리고 있다며 그 후에 마칠 수 있다는 뜻을 나타내고 있으므로 정답.
(B) 질문과 상관없는 오답. Where 의문문에 대한 응답이므로 오답.
(C) 단어 반복 오답. 질문의 sales를 반복 이용한 오답.

29   W-Am / M-Cn

Who's leading the planning session tomorrow?
(A) Leadership strategies.
(B) I'll be out of the office.
(C) Just a few hours.

누가 내일 기획 세션을 진행하나요?
(A) 리더십 전략이요.
(B) 저는 사무실에 없을 겁니다.
(C) 몇 시간 동안만요.

어휘 strategy 전략

해설 내일 기획 세션을 진행할 사람을 묻는 Who 의문문
(A) 유사 발음 오답. 질문의 leading과 부분적으로 발음이 유사한 Leadership을 이용한 오답.
(B) 정답. 내일 기획 세션을 진행할 사람을 묻는 질문에 사무실에 없을 것이라며 자신은 아니라는 뜻을 나타내고 있으므로 정답.
(C) 질문과 상관없는 오답. How long 의문문에 대한 응답이므로 오답.

30   M-Cn / W-Br   ▶동영상 강의

Aren't we meeting with the clients this evening?
(A) No, it's on the opposite side.
(B) The television was fixed.
(C) My flight to Japan leaves at six.

우리 오늘 저녁에 고객들과 만나는 거 아닌가요?
(A) 아니요, 그 반대편에 있어요.
(B) 텔레비전이 수리되었어요.
(C) 제 일본행 비행기가 6시에 떠나요.

어휘 opposite 반대편의, 맞은편의

해설 오늘 저녁에 고객들과 만나는지 확인하는 부정 의문문
(A) 질문과 상관없는 오답.
(B) 질문과 상관없는 오답.
(C) 정답. 오늘 저녁에 고객들과 만나는지 확인하는 질문에 자신의 일본행 비행기가 6시에 떠난다며 고객들을 만날 수 없다는 사실을 우회적으로 전달하고 있으므로 정답.

31   W-Am / M-Cn

They invited me to the opening, didn't they?
(A) I plan to submit my application.
(B) A membership fee.
(C) Check your inbox.

그분들이 저를 개업식에 초대했죠, 그렇지 않나요?
(A) 저는 지원서를 제출할 계획이에요.
(B) 회비요.
(C) 수신함을 확인해 보세요.

어휘 submit 제출하다   application 지원서, 신청서   inbox 수신함

해설 자신이 개업식에 초대되었는지 여부를 확인하는 부가 의문문
(A) 연상 단어 오답. 질문의 opening을 공석으로 잘못 이해했을 경우 연상 가능한 application을 이용한 오답.
(B) 질문과 상관없는 오답.
(C) 정답. 자신이 개업식에 초대되었는지 여부를 확인하는 질문에 수신함을 확인해 보라고 조언하고 있으므로 정답.

PART 3

32-34   W-Am / M-Cn

W **32 How were your deliveries?**

M Not bad, except at that new residential building on South Street. **32 I had to call them on my phone to come pick up their food.** At first, **33 I tried to call on the building intercom, but it's still broken.**

W You're not the first to say that. Last week, a customer called to complain that their food was cold by the time they found it.

M Maybe we just can't make deliveries there until the landlord fixes the intercom system.

W **34 I'm going to update the instructions on our mobile app** telling customers to meet us at the building's front door. Let's see if that helps.

여 배달은 어떠셨나요?

남 나쁘지 않았어요, 사우스 가에 있는 그 신축 주거 건물에서만 빼고요. **휴대폰으로 고객에게 전화해서 음식을 가지러 오시라고 해야 했거든요.** 처음에는, **건물 인터폰으로 시도해 봤는데, 아직도 고장 난 상태더라고요.**

여 그렇게 말하는 사람이 당신이 처음이 아니에요. 지난주에는, 한 고객이 전화해서 음식을 찾았을 때는 이미 식어 있었다며 불만을 제기했어요.

남 건물주가 인터폰 시스템을 고칠 때까지 그곳에는 배달을 하지 못할 수도 있겠어요.

여 고객들에게 건물 정문에서 우리와 만나도록 부탁하는 **안내문을 모바일 앱에 업데이트할게요.** 이게 도움이 되는지 두고 봅시다.

어휘 delivery 배달, 배송 except ~을 제외하고
residential 주거의 intercom 인터폰 broken 고장 난, 망가진
complain 불평하다, 항의하다 landlord 건물주, 집주인
instructions 안내문, 설명서

32 What kind of work does the man do?
(A) He is a tour guide.
(B) He is a landlord.
(C) He repairs appliances.
(D) He delivers food.

남자는 어떤 종류의 일을 하는가?
(A) 여행 가이드이다.
(B) 건물주이다.
(C) 가전 기기를 수리한다.
(D) 음식을 배달한다.

해설 전체 내용 관련 - 남자가 하는 일
여자가 첫 대사에서 배달은 어땠는지(How were your deliveries?) 묻자 남자가 휴대폰으로 고객에게 전화해서 음식을 가지러 오라고 해야 했다(I had to call them on my phone to come pick up their food)고 말하는 것으로 보아 남자는 음식을 배달한다는 것을 알 수 있다. 따라서 정답은 (D)이다.

33 What has caused problems for the speakers' business?
(A) Road construction
(B) Cold weather
(C) An expired permit
(D) A broken intercom

무엇이 화자들의 업체에 문제를 일으켰는가?
(A) 도로 공사
(B) 추운 날씨
(C) 만료된 허가증
(D) 고장 난 인터폰

어휘 expired 만료된 permit 허가증

해설 세부 사항 관련 - 문제의 원인
남자가 첫 대사에서 건물 인터폰으로 시도해 봤는데, 아직도 고장 난 상태(I tried to call on the building intercom, but it's still broken)라고 했으므로 정답은 (D)이다.

34 What will the woman update on a mobile application?
(A) Instructions
(B) Prices
(C) Photographs
(D) Hours of operation

여자는 모바일 애플리케이션에 무엇을 업데이트할 것인가?
(A) 안내문
(B) 가격
(C) 사진
(D) 운영 시간

해설 세부 사항 관련 - 여자가 업데이트할 것
여자가 마지막 대사에서 안내문을 모바일 앱에 업데이트하겠다(I'm going to update the instructions on our mobile app ~)고 했으므로 정답은 (A)이다.

35-37 W-Br / M-Au

W We're getting close to the time of year when ³⁵**we need to begin planning our Theater in the Park series for the summer. We have lots of decisions to make about shows, dates, and performers.**

M You're right. I'll set up a meeting for this month. You know, I had an idea. ³⁶**Why don't we invite community residents to volunteer to help with building sets, painting, and setting up the stage?**

W We could, but I don't know if we'll be able to use volunteers this year. ³⁷**We'll need approval to start that kind of program.** It'll take time. Let's check into that for next year.

여 **여름철 공원 속 극장 시리즈 준비를 시작해야** 할 시기가 다가오고 있어요. **공연과 날짜, 그리고 공연자들과 관련해서 결정해야 할 것들이 많아요.**

남 맞아요. 제가 이번 달에 회의를 잡을게요. 있잖아요, 제가 아이디어가 하나 있었어요. **지역 주민들에게 세트 제작, 페인팅, 무대 설치 등을 돕는 자원봉사를 요청해 보는 건 어떨까요?**

여 그럴 수도 있긴 한데, 올해 자원봉사자들을 활용할 수 있을지는 모르겠어요. **그런 프로그램을 시작하려면 승인이 필요할 거예요.** 시간이 걸릴 겁니다. 그 부분은 내년을 대비해서 검토해보죠.

어휘 theater 극장, 연극 resident 주민, 거주자
volunteer 자원봉사를 하다; 자원봉사자 approval 승인

35 What industry do the speakers most likely work in?
(A) Fitness
(B) Entertainment
(C) Landscaping
(D) Travel

화자들은 어떤 업계에서 일하는 것 같은가?
(A) 피트니스
(B) 연예
(C) 조경
(D) 여행

해설	전체 내용 관련 – 화자들의 근무 업계

여자가 첫 대사에서 여름철 공원 속 극장 시리즈 준비를 시작해야 한다(~ we need to begin planning our Theater in the Park series for the summer)며 공연과 날짜, 그리고 공연자들과 관련해서 결정해야 할 것들이 많다(We have lots of decisions to make about shows, dates, and performers)고 말하는 것으로 보아 화자들은 연예 업계에서 일한다는 것을 알 수 있다. 따라서 정답은 (B)이다.

Paraphrasing
대화의 shows → 정답의 Entertainment

36 What does the man suggest?
(A) Providing online access to videos
(B) Creating volunteer opportunities
(C) Offering free transportation
(D) Adding additional time slots

남자는 무엇을 제안하는가?
(A) 온라인 영상 이용 제공
(B) 자원봉사 기회 창출
(C) 무료 교통편 제공
(D) 추가 시간대 편성

어휘 access 이용, 접속 opportunity 기회 transportation 교통(편) additional 추가적인 time slot 시간대

해설 세부 사항 관련 – 남자의 제안 사항
남자가 첫 대사에서 지역 주민들에게 세트 제작, 페인팅, 무대 설치 등을 돕는 자원봉사를 요청해 보는 건 어떨지(Why don't we invite community residents to volunteer to help with building sets, painting, and setting up the stage?) 제안하고 있으므로 정답은 (B)이다.

Paraphrasing
대화의 invite community residents to volunteer to help → 정답의 Creating volunteer opportunities

37 Why do the speakers need to wait?
(A) Promotional items have not been ordered.
(B) A facility is not available.
(C) A budget is too small.
(D) A program has not been approved.

화자들은 왜 기다려야 하는가?
(A) 홍보용 물품이 주문되지 않았다.
(B) 시설을 이용할 수 없다.
(C) 예산이 너무 적다.
(D) 프로그램이 승인되지 않았다.

어휘 promotional 홍보의, 판촉의 facility 시설 budget 예산 approve 승인하다

해설 세부 사항 관련 – 화자들이 기다려야 하는 이유
여자가 마지막 대사에서 남자가 제안한 것과 같은 프로그램을 시작하려면 승인이 필요할 것(We'll need approval to start that kind of program)이라고 했으므로 정답은 (D)이다.

Paraphrasing
대화의 will need approval → 정답의 has not been approved

38-40 M-Cn / W-Am ▶동영상 강의

M Back to our podcast with special guest Kimberly Stuart, **38 who's currently advising our city on business development projects.** Before the break, we promised to address the decline of shopping downtown.

W Yes—and it's been the worst at **39 the kind of stores that sell unique items like antiques and jewelry. These items have always been purchased at brick-and-mortar stores but are now being purchased mostly online.**

M So, do those stores have a future?

W I think they do, **40 especially if we make a point of organizing live community activities downtown, such as concerts or festivals.** When people walk around town, they are likely to browse at stores—and make purchases.

남 다시 특별 초대 손님인 킴벌리 스튜어트와 함께하는 저희 팟캐스트로 돌아왔습니다. **이분께서는 현재 우리 시의 사업 개발 프로젝트에 자문을 해 주고 계시죠.** 광고 시간 전에, 저희가 도심 지역 쇼핑 감소 문제를 다루겠다고 약속드렸습니다.

여 네, 특히 **골동품이나 주얼리 같은 독특한 제품들을 판매하는 종류의 가게들이** 가장 심각했어요. 이런 물건들은 항상 오프라인 매장에서 구매되어 왔는데, 지금은 대부분 온라인에서 구매되고 있거든요.

남 그럼, 그런 가게들도 미래가 있을까요?

여 저는 그렇다고 생각해요. 특히 **우리가 도심에서 활발한 지역 사회 현장 활동들을 마련하는 것을 중요하게 생각한다면요. 콘서트나 축제처럼요.** 사람들이 시내를 걸어 다니다 보면, 가게들을 둘러보게 되고 구매도 하게 될 가능성이 크거든요.

어휘 currently 현재 development 개발, 발전 break (방송 등에서) 광고 시간, 휴식 address (문제 등을) 다루다 decline 감소, 하락, 축소 purchase 구매하다; 구매 antique 골동품 brick-and-mortar store 오프라인 매장 make a point of -ing ~을 중요하게 여기다, 반드시 ~하다 organize 준비하다, 개최하다 browse 둘러보다, 훑어보다

38 Who is the woman?
(A) A store owner
(B) A television celebrity
(C) A business consultant
(D) An event sponsor

여자는 누구인가?
(A) 매장 소유주
(B) 텔레비전 유명인
(C) 사업 컨설턴트
(D) 행사 후원자

어휘 celebrity 유명 인사 sponsor 후원자, 후원업체

해설 전체 내용 관련 – 여자의 직업

남자가 첫 대사에서 여자를 소개하면서 현재 우리 시의 사업 개발 프로젝트에 자문을 해 주고 있다(~ who's currently advising our city on business development projects)고 했으므로 정답은 (C)이다.

Paraphrasing
대화의 advising our city on business development projects
→ 정답의 A business consultant

39 What does the woman say about online shopping?
(A) It is cheaper than buying in person.
(B) It makes shopping a social experience.
(C) It is reducing traffic problems in the city.
(D) It is affecting specialty shops.

여자는 온라인 쇼핑에 대해 무엇이라고 말하는가?
(A) 직접 가서 구입하는 것보다 저렴하다.
(B) 쇼핑을 사회적 경험으로 만들어 준다.
(C) 도시 내의 교통 문제를 감소시켜 준다.
(D) 전문점들에 영향을 미치고 있다.

어휘 in person 직접 reduce 감소시키다 specialty 특제품

해설 세부 사항 관련 – 여자가 온라인 쇼핑에 대해 하는 말

여자가 첫 대사에서 골동품이나 주얼리 같은 독특한 제품들을 판매하는 가게들에 대해 언급하며 이런 물건들은 항상 오프라인 매장에서 구매되어 왔지만 지금은 대부분 온라인에서 구매되고 있다(~ the kind of stores that sell unique items like antiques and jewelry. These items have always been purchased at brick-and-mortar stores but are now being purchased mostly online)고 말하는 것으로 보아 온라인 쇼핑이 골동품 및 보석 전문점들에 영향을 미쳤음을 알 수 있다. 따라서 정답은 (D)이다.

Paraphrasing
대화의 stores that sell unique items
→ 정답의 specialty shops

40 What does the woman suggest doing?
(A) Offering clearance sales
(B) Holding live events
(C) Meeting with store owners
(D) Retraining store staff

여자는 무엇을 하자고 제안하는가?
(A) 재고 정리 세일 행사 열기
(B) 현장 행사 개최하기
(C) 매장 소유주들과 만나기
(D) 매장 직원 재교육하기

어휘 clearance sale 재고 정리 세일 retrain 재교육하다

해설 세부 사항 관련 – 여자의 제안 사항

여자가 마지막 대사에서 특히 콘서트나 축제처럼 도심에서 활발한 지역 사회 활동들을 마련하는 것을 중요하게 생각한다면(~ especially if we make a point of organizing live community activities downtown, such as concerts or festivals)이라며 도심 지역 쇼핑을 활성화하는 방법을 제안하고 있으므로 정답은 (B)이다.

Paraphrasing
대화의 organizing live community activities
→ 정답의 Holding live events

41-43 M-Au / W-Br

M **41 Our company has seen a huge spike in sales ever since it launched the rebate program for customers.** With the rebate, customers get money back. And they're telling their friends, increasing our sales.

W Yes. The rebate's been great for our company **42 because now more homeowners have an incentive to install solar panels on their properties**, since they're rewarded for the electricity their solar panels produce. But our technicians can't keep up with the high demand.

M You're right. **43 I'm planning to hire more technicians.** I've already received some résumés from potential candidates.

남 **우리 회사는 고객 대상 환급 프로그램을 시작한 이후로 매출이 크게 급증했어요.** 환급 프로그램 덕분에, 고객들은 돈을 돌려받죠. 그리고 친구들에게 알리면서 우리 판매량을 증가시키고 있습니다.

여 네. 환급 프로그램이 우리 회사에 큰 도움이 됐어요. **이제 더 많은 주택 소유자들이 자신의 건물에 태양광 패널을 설치할 유인을 갖게 됐거든요.** 자신의 태양광 패널이 생산한 전기에 대해 보상을 받으니까요. 하지만 우리 기술자들이 높은 수요를 따라가지 못하고 있어요.

남 맞아요. **기술자들을 더 고용할 계획이에요.** 이미 잠재적인 후보자들로부터 이력서를 받아 두었습니다.

어휘 spike 급증, 급등 rebate 환급 incentive 유인, 장려책
solar panel 태양광 패널 property 건물, 부동산
reward 보상하다, 사례하다 keep up with ~을 따라잡다
demand 수요, 요구 résumé 이력서 potential 잠재적인
candidate 후보자, 지원자

41 Why have a company's sales increased?
(A) A rebate program was started.
(B) A competitor went out of business.
(C) A celebrity endorsed the company.
(D) A product won an award.

회사의 매출은 왜 증가했는가?
(A) 환급 프로그램이 시작되었다.
(B) 경쟁사가 폐업했다.
(C) 유명인이 회사를 홍보했다.
(D) 제품이 상을 받았다.

어휘 competitor 경쟁사, 경쟁자 go out of business 폐업하다
endorse (유명인이 광고에서) 홍보하다

해설 세부 사항 관련 – 판매량이 증가한 이유
남자가 첫 대사에서 회사가 고객 대상 환급 프로그램을 시작한 이후로 매출이 크게 급증했다(Our company has seen a huge spike in sales ever since it launched the rebate program for customers)고 했으므로 정답은 (A)이다.

Paraphrasing
대화의 a huge spike → 질문의 have increased
대화의 launched the rebate program
→ 정답의 A rebate program was started

42 What industry do the speakers most likely work in?
(A) Banking
(B) Telecommunications
(C) Solar energy
(D) Music

화자들은 어떤 업계에서 일하는 것 같은가?
(A) 금융
(B) 통신
(C) 태양열 에너지
(D) 음악

해설 전체 내용 관련 – 화자들의 근무 업계
여자가 첫 대사에서 환급 프로그램이 회사에 도움이 된 것이 고객인 주택 소유자들이 자신들의 건물에 태양광 패널을 설치할 유인을 갖게 되었기 때문(~ because now more homeowners have an incentive to install solar panels on their properties ~)이라고 말하는 것으로 보아 화자들은 태양열 에너지와 관련된 분야에서 일한다는 것을 알 수 있다. 따라서 정답은 (C)이다.

43 What does the man say he is planning to do?
(A) Hire new employees
(B) Provide additional training
(C) Upgrade some equipment
(D) Open another location

남자는 무엇을 계획하고 있다고 말하는가?
(A) 신입 직원 고용하기
(B) 추가 교육 제공하기
(C) 장비 업그레이드하기
(D) 다른 지점 개장하기

어휘 additional 추가적인 training 교육, 훈련 equipment 장비
location 지점, 위치

해설 세부 사항 관련 – 남자가 계획하는 것
남자가 마지막 대사에서 기술자들을 더 고용할 계획(I'm planning to hire more technicians)이라고 했으므로 정답은 (A)이다.

Paraphrasing
대화의 hire more technicians → 정답의 Hire new employees

44-46 M-Cn / W-Br

M Fernanda, I was just looking at the company calendar, and **44 I noticed that the national electronics trade show is coming up soon.**

W Oh, that's right! It'll be a great opportunity for us to showcase **45 the product that we've been developing—our new robotic vacuum cleaner.**

M We'll need to decide who we want to send to represent our company at the trade show.

W Well, I know just the right person—Kavi. **46 Kavi does a good job of clearly explaining highly technical concepts in a way that everyone can understand.**

남 페르난다, 방금 회사 일정표를 보고 있었는데, **전국 가전 무역 박람회가 곧 열린다는 걸 알게 됐어요.**

여 아, 맞아요! 우리가 개발해 온 제품, 새 로봇 진공청소기를 선보일 아주 좋은 기회가 될 거예요.

남 무역 박람회에 우리 회사 대표로 누구를 보낼지 정해야겠네요.

여 음, 제가 딱 맞는 사람을 알고 있어요. 카비요. 카비는 아주 **기술적인 개념도 누구나 이해할 수 있는 방식으로 명확하게 설명하거든요.**

어휘 calendar 일정표 notice 알게 되다, 알아차리다
electronics 가전 (기기) trade show 무역 박람회
showcase 선보이다, 전시하다 develop 개발하다, 발전시키다
vacuum cleaner 진공청소기 represent 대표하다
clearly 명확히 highly 아주, 매우 concept 개념, 발상

44 What upcoming event are the speakers discussing?
(A) A trade show
(B) A client meeting
(C) An awards ceremony
(D) A press conference

화자들은 다가오는 어떤 행사에 대해 이야기하고 있는가?
(A) 무역 박람회
(B) 고객 회의
(C) 시상식
(D) 기자 회견

해설 전체 내용 관련 – 화자들이 논의 중인 행사
남자가 첫 대사에서 전국 가전 무역 박람회가 곧 열린다는 걸 알게 됐다(~ I noticed that the national electronics trade show is coming up soon)고 말한 뒤 이 행사 참가에 대한 이야기를 이어 가고 있으므로 정답은 (A)이다.

Paraphrasing
대화의 is coming up → 질문의 upcoming

45 What product has the speakers' company recently developed?
(A) A video game
(B) A mobile phone
(C) A lawn mower
(D) A vacuum cleaner

화자들의 회사는 최근 어떤 제품을 개발했는가?
(A) 비디오 게임
(B) 휴대전화
(C) 잔디 깎는 기계
(D) 진공청소기

해설 세부 사항 관련 – 화자들의 회사가 개발한 것
여자가 첫 대사에서 자신들이 개발해 온 제품인 새 로봇 진공청소기(~ the product that we've been developing—our new robotic vacuum cleaner)를 언급하고 있으므로 정답은 (D)이다.

46 Why does the woman recommend Kavi?
(A) He is a good communicator.
(B) He enjoys traveling.
(C) He leads a product development team.
(D) He lives near the event venue.

여자는 왜 카비를 추천하는가?
(A) 의사소통 능력이 뛰어나다.
(B) 여행을 즐긴다.
(C) 제품 개발팀을 이끌고 있다.
(D) 행사 장소 근처에 살고 있다.

어휘 communicator 전달자 lead 이끌다, 진행하다 venue 개최 장소, 행사장

해설 세부 사항 관련 – 카비를 추천하는 이유
여자가 마지막 대사에서 카비가 아주 기술적인 개념도 누구나 이해할 수 있는 방식으로 명확하게 설명한다(Kavi does a good job of clearly explaining highly technical concepts in a way that everyone can understand)고 말하는 것으로 보아 의사소통 능력이 뛰어나다는 의미임을 알 수 있다. 따라서 정답은 (A)이다.

Paraphrasing
대화의 does a good job of clearly explaining ~ in a way that everyone can understand
→ 정답의 a good communicator

47-49 M-Au / W-Br

M Dr. Fuentes, sorry to interrupt. Do you have a minute?
W Yes. **47 My nine o'clock dental cleaning patient just canceled.**
M **48 I know you're looking for a new receptionist. I'd like to recommend someone for the position.**
W Oh. Who do you have in mind?
M Well, a former colleague of mine has just moved back to town. Her name's Kelly Graham, and she has several years of experience.
W OK. **49 Could you tell Kelly to send me her résumé?** I'd be happy to look it over.

남 푸엔테스 선생님, 방해해서 죄송합니다. 잠깐 시간 괜찮으세요?
여 네. 9시에 예정되어 있던 스케일링 환자가 방금 취소했거든요.
남 선생님께서 새 접수 담당자를 찾고 계시는 걸로 알고 있습니다. 그 자리에 추천해 드리고 싶은 사람이 있어요.
여 아. 누구를 염두에 두고 계신 건가요?
남 음, 제 예전 직장 동료가 최근에 이 동네로 다시 이사 왔어요. 이름은 켈리 그레이엄이고, 몇 년간 일한 경험이 있어요.
여 알겠어요. 켈리에게 저한테 이력서를 보내라고 전해 주시겠어요? 기꺼이 검토해 볼게요.

어휘 interrupt 방해하다 dental cleaning 스케일링 patient 환자 receptionist 접수 담당자, 안내 담당자 position 일자리 have ~ in mind ~을 염두에 두다 former 이전의, 전직의 résumé 이력서

47 Where do the speakers most likely work?
(A) At a publishing house
(B) At a dental clinic
(C) At a financial firm
(D) At a real estate agency

화자들은 어디에서 일하는 것 같은가?
(A) 출판사
(B) 치과
(C) 금융 회사
(D) 부동산 중개업체

해설 전체 내용 관련 – 화자들의 근무 장소
여자가 첫 대사에서 9시에 예정되어 있던 스케일링 환자가 방금 취소했다(My nine o'clock dental cleaning patient just canceled)고 말하는 것으로 보아 화자들은 치과에서 근무하고 있다는 것을 알 수 있다. 따라서 정답은 (B)이다.

48 What does the man tell the woman about?
(A) A new product
(B) A schedule change
(C) A policy update
(D) A job candidate

남자는 여자에게 무엇에 대해 이야기하는가?
(A) 신제품
(B) 일정 변경
(C) 정책 업데이트
(D) 입사 지원자

어휘 policy 정책, 방침   candidate 지원자, 후보자

해설 세부 사항 관련 – 남자가 여자에게 이야기하는 것
남자가 두 번째 대사에서 여자가 새 접수 담당자를 찾고 있는 걸로 알고 있다(I know you're looking for a new receptionist)며 그 자리에 추천하고 싶은 사람이 있다(I'd like to recommend someone for the position)고 말하는 것으로 보아 입사 지원자를 추천하고 있음을 알 수 있다. 따라서 정답은 (D)이다.

Paraphrasing
대화의 someone for the position → 정답의 A job candidate

49 Why will the man most likely contact Kelly Graham?
(A) To plan an office celebration
(B) To arrange a training session
(C) To request a document
(D) To order some supplies

남자는 왜 켈리 그레이엄에게 연락할 것 같은가?
(A) 사무실 축하 행사를 계획하기 위해
(B) 교육 일정을 잡기 위해
(C) 서류를 요청하기 위해
(D) 용품을 주문하기 위해

어휘 celebration 축하 행사, 기념 행사   arrange 마련하다, 정리하다   supplies 용품, 물품

해설 세부 사항 관련 – 남자가 켈리 그레이엄에게 연락하는 이유
여자가 마지막 대사에서 켈리에게 자신에게 이력서를 보내라고 전해달라(Could you tell Kelly to send me her résumé?)고 했으므로 정답은 (C)이다.

Paraphrasing
대화의 her résumé → 정답의 a document

50-52 3인 대화 M-Cn / W-Br / M-Au

M1 Ms. Gao? I'm Hector, and this is my colleague Sergey. Thanks for meeting with us.

W It's a pleasure to meet you both. How can I help you?

M2 **50 We're making some training videos for our client, FiveStar Industries.**

M1 **51 We found your advertisement in a trade publication.** We need someone to choose appropriate filming sites at FiveStar's factories, and it said you have lots of experience scouting for industrial locations.

W Sure. **52 I'd want to start by touring their factories. Can you schedule a time for me to do that next week?**

M2 Yes, I'll call them today to arrange it.

남1 가오 씨? 저는 헥터이고, 이쪽은 제 동료 세르게이입니다. 저희와 만나 주셔서 감사합니다.
여 두 분 모두 만나서 반갑습니다. 무엇을 도와드릴까요?
남2 저희가 고객인 파이브스타 인더스트리를 위한 교육용 동영상을 제작하고 있는데요.
남1 업계 간행물에서 귀하의 광고를 봤습니다. 파이브스타의 공장에서 적합한 촬영 장소를 선정해 줄 분이 필요한데, 그 광고에 산업 시설 관련 촬영지 섭외 경험이 많으시다고 나와 있더라고요.
여 물론입니다. 그곳 공장들을 둘러보는 것부터 시작하고 싶어요. 제가 그렇게 할 수 있도록 다음 주에 시간을 잡아 주실 수 있나요?
남2 네, 제가 오늘 그쪽에 연락해서 일정을 조율하겠습니다.

어휘 colleague 동료   advertisement 광고   trade publication 업계 간행물   appropriate 적합한, 알맞은   filming 촬영   site 장소, 현장   scout 물색하다, 찾아다니다   location 촬영지, 지점, 위치   arrange 조율하다, 마련하다

50 What industry do the men work in?
(A) Travel
(B) Manufacturing
(C) Video production
(D) Construction

남자들은 어떤 업계에서 일하는가?
(A) 여행
(B) 제조
(C) 동영상 제작
(D) 건설

TEST 2   43

해설 전체 내용 관련 – 남자들의 근무 업계
두 번째 남자가 첫 대사에서 고객사인 파이브스타 인더스트리를 위한 교육용 동영상을 제작하고 있다(We're making some training videos for our client, FiveStar Industries)고 했으므로 정답은 (C)이다.

51 How did the men learn about the woman?
(A) From her Web site
(B) From a trade publication
(C) From a colleague
(D) From a recruitment agency

남자들은 여자에 대해 어떻게 알았는가?
(A) 여자의 웹사이트를 통해
(B) 업계 간행물을 통해
(C) 동료 직원을 통해
(D) 채용 대행사를 통해

어휘 recruitment 채용 agency 대행사, 대리점

해설 세부 사항 관련 – 남자들이 여자를 알게 된 경로
첫 번째 남자가 두 번째 대사에서 업계 간행물에서 여자의 광고를 봤다(We found your advertisement in a trade publication)고 했으므로 정답은 (B)이다.

52 What does the woman want to do next week?
(A) Attend an orientation session
(B) Visit some facilities
(C) Interview some applicants
(D) Finalize a contract

여자는 다음 주에 무엇을 하고 싶어 하는가?
(A) 오리엔테이션에 참석하기
(B) 시설 방문하기
(C) 지원자 면접 보기
(D) 계약 최종 확정하기

어휘 finalize 최종 확정하다, 마무리하다 contract 계약(서)

해설 세부 사항 관련 – 여자가 다음 주에 하고 싶어 하는 것
여자가 마지막 대사에서 공장들을 둘러보는 것부터 시작하고 싶다(I'd want to start by touring their factories)며 그렇게 할 수 있도록 다음 주에 시간을 잡아 달라(Can you schedule a time for me to do that next week?)고 요청하고 있으므로 정답은 (B)이다.

Paraphrasing
대화의 touring their factories → 정답의 Visit some facilities

53-55 M-Au / W-Br

M **53 Our engineering firm** has been asked to cut the corporate travel budget by twenty percent, but it won't be easy. The engineering consultants have to travel to meet with clients.

W Right, and they often travel on short notice. Flight arrangements made at the last minute are expensive, especially for nonstop flights. **54 It would be cheaper if they took connecting flights.**

M Yes, but that can take a lot of time.

W True. **55 Maybe we can make up for the cost of the flights by economizing on hotels.** Let's look into that.

남 우리 엔지니어링 회사가 출장 예산을 20퍼센트 절감하라는 요청을 받았는데, 쉽지는 않을 것 같아요. 엔지니어링 컨설턴트들은 고객들과 만나기 위해 출장을 가야만 해요.

여 그렇죠, 그리고 보통 촉박하게 출장을 가잖아요. 항공편을 임박해서 예약하면 비싸요. 특히 직항은 더 그렇고요. **환승 항공편을 이용하면 더 저렴할 텐데요.**

남 네, 하지만 그건 시간이 많이 걸릴 수 있어요.

여 맞아요. **아마 호텔 비용을 절약해서 항공편 비용을 만회할 수 있을 거예요.** 그 부분을 알아봅시다.

어휘 corporate 기업의 budget 예산, 비용
on short notice 촉박하게 arrangement 조치, 준비
at the last minute 임박해서, 마지막 순간에 nonstop 직항의
connecting flight 환승 항공편 make up for ~을 만회하다
economize 비용을 절약하다

53 What type of business do the speakers work for?
(A) A law firm
(B) An advertising agency
(C) An engineering firm
(D) An event-planning company

화자들은 어떤 종류의 업체에서 일하는가?
(A) 법률 회사
(B) 광고 대행사
(C) 엔지니어링 회사
(D) 행사 기획사

해설 전체 내용 관련 – 화자들의 근무 업체
남자가 첫 대사에서 우리 엔지니어링 회사(Our engineering firm)라고 했으므로 정답은 (C)이다.

54 Why does the man say, "that can take a lot of time"?
(A) To reject a suggestion
(B) To express sympathy
(C) To request additional pay
(D) To offer assistance

남자는 왜 "그건 시간이 많이 걸릴 수 있어요"라고 말하는가?
(A) 제안을 거절하기 위해
(B) 공감을 표현하기 위해
(C) 추가 수당을 요청하기 위해
(D) 도움을 제공하기 위해

어휘 reject 거절하다, 거부하다 suggestion 제안, 의견
sympathy 공감, 동정(심) additional pay 추가 수당
assistance 도움, 지원

해설 화자의 의도 파악 – 시간이 많이 걸릴 수 있다는 말의 의도

여자가 첫 대사에서 환승 항공편을 이용하면 더 저렴할 것(It would be cheaper if they took connecting flights)이라고 말하자 남자가 인용문을 언급하고 있다. 이는 환승 항공편을 이용하는 것이 좋은 방법이 아니라는 뜻으로, 여자의 제안을 거절하려는 의도로 한 말임을 알 수 있다. 따라서 정답은 (A)이다.

55 What does the woman suggest?
(A) Contacting some former clients
(B) Making reservations early
(C) Staying at affordable hotels
(D) Consulting with an expert

여자는 무엇을 제안하는가?
(A) 예전 고객들에게 연락하기
(B) 일찍 예약하기
(C) 저렴한 호텔에서 숙박하기
(D) 전문가에게 상담하기

어휘 make a reservation 예약하다 affordable 저렴한
consult 상담하다

해설 세부 사항 관련 – 여자의 제안 사항

여자가 마지막 대사에서 아마 호텔 비용을 절약해서 항공편 비용을 만회할 수 있을 것(Maybe we can make up for the cost of the flights by economizing on hotels)이라고 말하는 것은 저렴한 호텔을 이용하자 제안하는 것이므로 정답은 (C)이다.

Paraphrasing
대화의 economizing on hotels
→ 정답의 Staying at affordable hotels

56-58 3인 대화 M-Cn / M-Au / W-Br

M1 Thanks for meeting with us, Ms. Azuma. This is Scott Ajibade, one of our senior project managers.

M2 I admire your work, Ms. Azuma.

W Thank you. I was surprised by your invitation. I typically design jewelry, but ⁵⁶**your company's known for making computers and mobile phones.**

M1 Scott's team is currently working on a smartwatch. But there's a lot of competition, as you know.

M2 ⁵⁷**We're hoping you can create a fresh design that will help our product stand out.**

W ⁵⁸**Do you already have an idea of what the watch should look like, or are we starting from scratch?**

M2 ⁵⁸**I have some preliminary sketches we can look at**, but none of them seem quite right.

남1 저희와 만나 주셔서 감사합니다, 아주마 씨. 이쪽은 스캇 아지바데이고, 저희 수석 프로젝트 관리자들 중 한 분이세요.
남2 작품이 인상적입니다, 아주마 씨.
여 감사합니다. 초대를 받아서 놀랐어요. 저는 보통 주얼리를 디자인하는데, **귀사는 컴퓨터와 휴대폰을 만드는 것으로 알려져 있잖아요.**
남1 스캇의 팀이 현재 스마트워치 관련 작업을 하고 있어요. 하지만 아시다시피 경쟁이 치열하죠.
남2 **저희 제품이 돋보일 수 있도록 새로운 디자인을 만들어 주셨으면 해요.**
여 **시계가 어떤 모습이어야 한다는 아이디어가 이미 있으신가요, 아니면 완전히 처음부터 시작하는 건가요?**
남2 **살펴볼 만한 초기 스케치가 좀 있긴 한데**, 그중에 딱 이거다 싶은 건 없어요.

어휘 admire 감탄하다, 존경하다 invitation 초대(장)
typically 보통, 일반적으로 competition 경쟁, 경연 대회
stand out 돋보이다, 두드러지다 from scratch 맨 처음부터
preliminary 예비 단계의, 사전의

56 What industry do the men most likely work in?
(A) Fashion
(B) Cosmetics
(C) Advertising
(D) Technology

남자들은 어떤 업계에서 일하는 것 같은가?
(A) 패션
(B) 화장품
(C) 광고
(D) 기술

해설 　전체 내용 관련 – 남자들의 근무 업계
여자가 첫 대사에서 남자들의 회사에 대해 컴퓨터와 휴대폰을 만드는 것으로 알려져 있다(~ your company's known for making computers and mobile phones)고 언급하고 있으므로 정답은 (D)이다.

Paraphrasing
대화의 computers and mobile phones
→ 정답의 Technology

57 Why did the men request a meeting?
(A) To negotiate a merger
(B) To ask for funding
(C) To discuss a product design
(D) To suggest a marketing strategy

남자들은 왜 회의를 요청했는가?
(A) 합병을 협의하려고
(B) 자금을 요청하려고
(C) 제품 디자인을 논의하려고
(D) 마케팅 전략을 제안하려고

어휘 　negotiate 협의하다, 협상하다　merger 합병, 통합
funding 자금　strategy 전략

해설 　세부 사항 관련 – 남자들이 회의를 요청한 이유
두 번째 남자가 두 번째 대사에서 자사의 제품이 돋보일 수 있도록 새로운 디자인을 만들어 주었으면 한다(We're hoping you can create a fresh design that will help our product stand out)고 했으므로 정답은 (C)이다.

Paraphrasing
대화의 a fresh design that will help our product stand out
→ 정답의 a product design

58 What will the speakers most likely do next?
(A) Set a release date
(B) Sign a contract
(C) Collect customer feedback
(D) Review some drawings

화자들은 다음에 무엇을 할 것 같은가?
(A) 발매 날짜 정하기
(B) 계약서에 서명하기
(C) 고객 의견 수집하기
(D) 그림 검토하기

어휘 　release 발매, 출시　collect 수집하다, 모으다
feedback 의견　review 검토하다

해설 　세부 사항 관련 – 화자들이 다음에 할 일
대화 후반부에 여자가 시계가 어떤 모습이어야 한다는 아이디어가 이미 있는지, 아니면 완전히 처음부터 시작하는 것인지(Do you already have an idea of what the watch should look like, or are we starting from scratch?) 묻자, 두 번째 남자가 살펴볼 만한 초기 스케치가 좀 있다(I have some preliminary sketches we can look at, ~)고 응답하는 것으로 보아 화자들은 그 그림들을 함께 검토할 것임을 추론할 수 있다. 따라서 정답은 (D)이다.

Paraphrasing
대화의 have some preliminary sketches we can look at
→ 정답의 Review some drawings

59-61 W-Am / M-Cn

W　Hi. I'd like to purchase some new carpeting. It's for the waiting room at ⁵⁹**my hair salon.**
M　We have many different styles. ⁶⁰**Are you looking for something different?**
W　⁶⁰**Well, we get a lot of customers walking through,** and our current carpeting is a light color.
M　No matter what color you get, all our carpets are durable and can take high amounts of foot traffic. For businesses like yours, I recommend placing a protective mat near the door.
W　That's a good idea.
M　Also, ⁶¹**I offer free cleaning services for a year for all purchases.**

여　안녕하세요. 새 카펫을 좀 구매하려고 합니다. **제 미용실의** 대기실에 쓸 거예요.
남　저희는 다양한 스타일을 보유하고 있어요. **뭔가 다른 것을 찾고 계신가요?**
여　음, 저희 가게에는 오고 가는 손님들이 많은데, 현재 카펫이 밝은 색상이에요.
남　어떤 색상을 선택하시든, 저희 카펫은 모두 내구성이 뛰어나고 많은 발길에도 견딜 수 있습니다. 귀사와 같은 사업장에는, 출입문 근처에 보호용 매트를 깔아 두실 것을 권해 드려요.
여　좋은 아이디어네요.
남　그리고, 모든 구매에 대해 1년간 무료 세척 서비스도 제공해 드립니다.

어휘 　carpeting 카펫(류)　current 현재의
durable 내구성이 뛰어난　foot traffic 발길, 보행자 왕래
place 놓다, 두다　protective 보호용의, 보호하는

59 What type of business does the woman work in?
(A) A hair salon
(B) A real estate agency
(C) An interior design firm
(D) A car rental company

여자는 어떤 종류의 업체에서 일하는가?
(A) 미용실
(B) 부동산 중개업체
(C) 인테리어 디자인 회사
(D) 렌터카 회사

어휘 rental 대여, 임대

해설 전체 내용 관련 – 여자의 근무 업체
여자가 첫 대사에서 자신의 미용실(my hair salon)을 언급했으므로 정답은 (A)이다.

60 Why does the woman say, "our current carpeting is a light color"?
(A) To suggest an expense was not justified
(B) To express surprise about a decision
(C) To describe a problem with an order
(D) To indicate the need to make a change

여자는 왜 "현재 카펫이 밝은 색상이에요"라고 말하는가?
(A) 지출이 정당하지 않았음을 시사하기 위해
(B) 결정에 대해 놀라움을 표현하기 위해
(C) 주문 관련 문제를 설명하기 위해
(D) 변화를 줄 필요성을 나타내기 위해

어휘 expense 지출 justify 정당화하다 describe 설명하다 indicate 나타내다, 가리키다

해설 화자의 의도 파악 – 현재 카펫이 밝은 색상이라는 말의 의도
남자가 첫 대사에서 뭔가 다른 것을 찾고 있는지(Are you looking for something different?) 묻자, 여자가 오고 가는 손님들이 많다(we get a lot of customers walking through)며 인용문을 언급하고 있다. 이는 유동 인구가 많은 장소라 밝은 색상의 카펫이 어울리지 않는다고 생각한다는 뜻으로 남자의 말대로 뭔가 다른 것, 즉 변화를 원하고 있음을 알 수 있다. 따라서 정답은 (D)이다.

61 What does the man's business offer?
(A) A bulk discount
(B) Same-day delivery
(C) Free cleaning services
(D) Monthly inspections

남자의 업체는 무엇을 제공하는가?
(A) 대량 주문 할인
(B) 당일 배송
(C) 무료 세척 서비스
(D) 월간 점검

어휘 bulk 대량의 inspection 점검, 검사

해설 세부 사항 관련 – 남자의 업체가 제공하는 것
남자가 마지막 대사에서 모든 구매에 대해 1년간 무료 세척 서비스를 제공한다(I offer free cleaning services for a year for all purchases)고 했으므로 정답은 (C)이다.

62-64 대화 + 메뉴 M-Au / W-Br

M I really need this coffee break. My morning meeting with my client was really challenging.
W What were you discussing?
M The project schedule. **62 They asked us to provide the prototype design to them three weeks earlier than originally planned.**
W Well. Then today's cup is my treat. Which one would you like?
M That's so nice of you! **63 I'll go with the White Cloud Coffee.** I like a little milk in mine.
W Good choice. So, I have some news to share with you. Did you hear about David?
M No, what's going on?
W Apparently, **64 he's planning to retire next month.**

남 커피 한잔할 시간이 정말 필요해요. 오전에 있었던 고객 미팅이 굉장히 힘들었어요.
여 무엇을 논의하셨는데요?
남 프로젝트 일정이요. **그쪽에서 원래 계획했던 것보다 3주나 더 빨리 시제품 디자인을 달라고 요청했어요.**
여 음, 그럼 오늘 커피는 제가 살게요. 뭘로 하시겠어요?
남 정말 고마워요! **전 화이트 클라우드 커피로 할게요.** 저는 우유가 약간 들어간 걸 좋아하거든요.
여 좋은 선택이에요. 자, 저도 공유할 소식이 있어요. 데이비드 얘기 들으셨어요?
남 아니요, 무슨 일이죠?
여 듣자 하니, **다음 달에 은퇴할 계획을 세우고 있더라고요.**

어휘 challenging 힘들게 하는 prototype 시제품, 원형 originally 원래, 애초에 treat 대접, 한턱 share 공유하다 apparently 듣자 하니, 분명히 retire 은퇴하다, 퇴직하다

62 What did the man's client request?
(A) A large shipment
(B) A shortened timeline
(C) A change in design
(D) A more expensive material

남자의 고객은 무엇을 요청했는가?
(A) 대량 배송
(B) 진행 일정 단축
(C) 디자인 변경
(D) 더 비싼 소재

어휘 shipment 배송 shorten 단축하다, 짧게 하다
timeline 진행 일정 material 소재, 재료

해설 세부 사항 관련 – 남자의 고객의 요청 사항
남자가 두 번째 대사에서 그들이 원래 계획했던 것보다 3주나 더 빨리 시제품 디자인을 달라고 요청했다(They asked us to provide the prototype design to them three weeks earlier than originally planned)고 말하는 것으로 보아 고객이 프로젝트 진행 일정을 당겨줄 것을 요청했음을 알 수 있다. 따라서 정답은 (B)이다.

Paraphrasing
대화의 three weeks earlier than originally planned
→ 정답의 A shortened timeline

63 Look at the graphic. How much does the man's coffee cost?
(A) $2.00
(B) $3.25
(C) $3.75
(D) $4.25

시각 정보에 의하면, 남자가 선택한 커피의 가격은 얼마인가?
(A) 2달러
(B) 3.25달러
(C) 3.75달러
(D) 4.25달러

해설 시각 정보 연계 – 남자의 커피 가격
남자가 세 번째 대사에서 화이트 클라우드 커피로 하겠다(I'll go with the White Cloud Coffee)고 했고, 메뉴에서 화이트 클라우드 커피의 가격은 3.75달러이므로 정답은 (C)이다.

64 What does the woman say about David?
(A) He is retiring.
(B) He is organizing a party.
(C) He is on vacation.
(D) He accepted another position.

여자는 데이비드에 대해 무엇이라고 말하는가?
(A) 은퇴할 예정이다.
(B) 파티를 준비하고 있다.
(C) 휴가 중이다.
(D) 다른 일자리를 수락했다.

어휘 organize 준비하다, 조직하다 on vacation 휴가 중인
accept 수락하다, 받아들이다 position 일자리, 직책

해설 세부 사항 관련 – 여자가 데이비드에 대해 하는 말
여자가 마지막 대사에서 데이비드가 다음 달에 은퇴할 계획을 세우고 있다(~ he's planning to retire next month)고 말하고 있으므로 정답은 (A)이다.

65-67 대화 + 일정표 M-Au / W-Am

M This is Bradley from Windows Galore. How can I help you?

W Hello! **65 I'd like to have screens added to my windows at home.** I was wondering if you would be available to stop by and take a look. **66 I live at 42 West Third Street**, by the way.

M OK—that's not far. Let me see. I could come any morning this week.

W How about in the afternoon?

M Hmm. **67 I could reschedule my Tuesday afternoon appointment.** I'll check and get back to you—I have your number now. And your name is?

W Hoffman—Claudia Hoffman. Thank you. Talk to you soon.

남 윈도우즈 갤로어의 브래들리입니다. 무엇을 도와드릴까요?

여 안녕하세요! **저희 집 창문에 방충망을 설치하고 싶습니다.** 잠깐 들르셔서 직접 봐주실 수 있을까 해서요. 아, **저는 웨스트 써드가 42번지에 살고 있습니다.**

남 알겠습니다. 멀지 않은 곳이네요. 잠시만요. 이번 주 중 어느 아침이든 방문 가능합니다.

여 오후에는 어떠신가요?

남 흠. **화요일 오후 약속을 조정할 수도 있겠네요.** 제가 확인해 보고 다시 연락 드리겠습니다. 이제 고객님 전화번호는 가지고 있고요. 그리고 성함이 어떻게 되시죠?

여 호프먼이요, 클라우디아 호프먼. 감사합니다. 곧 다시 통화하시죠.

어휘 stop by 잠깐 들르다   reschedule (일정, 약속을) 조정하다
appointment 약속, 예약   inspector 검사관   loan 대출
dental 치아의, 치과의

Bradley's Schedule	
67 Tuesday	Inspector's visit (2-5 P.M.)
Wednesday	Bank loan meeting (1-4 P.M.)
Thursday	Dental cleaning (2-4 P.M.)
Friday	Café project (1-4 P.M.)

브래들리의 일정	
화요일	검사관 방문 (오후 2-5시)
수요일	은행 대출 회의 (오후 1-4시)
목요일	치아 스케일링 (오후 2-4시)
금요일	카페 프로젝트 (오후 1-4시)

65 What does the man most likely do?
(A) Install windows
(B) Repair roofs
(C) Remove trees
(D) Plant gardens

남자는 무슨 일을 하는 것 같은가?
(A) 창문 설치하기
(B) 지붕 수리하기
(C) 나무 제거하기
(D) 정원 가꾸기

어휘 install 설치하다   repair 수리하다   remove 제거하다, 없애다
plant 가꾸다, 심다

해설 전체 내용 관련 – 남자가 하는 일
여자가 첫 대사에서 남자에게 자신의 집 창문에 방충망을 설치하고 싶다(I'd like to have screens added to my windows at home)고 했으므로 정답은 (A)이다.

Paraphrasing
대화의 have screens added to my windows
→ 정답의 Install windows

66 What does the woman provide?
(A) A floor layout
(B) An address
(C) A form of payment
(D) Proof of insurance

여자는 무엇을 제공하는가?
(A) 층별 배치도
(B) 주소
(C) 결제 수단
(D) 보험 증서

어휘 layout 배치도, 구획   proof 증명(서)   insurance 보험

해설 세부 사항 관련 – 여자가 제공하는 것
여자가 첫 대사에서 웨스트 써드 가 42번지에 살고 있다(I live at 42 West Third Street, ~)고 언급하고 있으므로 정답은 (B)이다.

Paraphrasing
대화의 live at 42 West Third Street → 정답의 An address

67 Look at the graphic. Which appointment will the man try to reschedule?
(A) The inspector's visit
(B) The bank loan meeting
(C) The dental cleaning
(D) The café project

시각 정보에 의하면, 남자는 어떤 약속을 조정하려고 하는가?
(A) 검사관 방문
(B) 은행 대출 회의
(C) 치아 스케일링
(D) 카페 프로젝트

해설 시각 정보 연계 – 남자가 조정하려는 약속
남자가 마지막 대사에서 화요일 오후 약속을 조정할 수 있을 것(I could reschedule my Tuesday afternoon appointment)이라고 했고, 일정표에서 화요일 오후 약속은 검사관 방문이므로 정답은 (A)이다.

68-70 대화 + 유인물   M-Au / W-Br

M   Ms. Kwon, **68 thank you for sending me to the upcoming robotics conference.** I didn't expect an opportunity like this so soon after being hired here.

W   **69 It's important for you to be familiar with current robot designs.** There are always new trends and technologies coming out, and I want you to stay ahead of developments in our industry.

M   I agree. Plus, it'll give me the chance to introduce myself to potential clients.

W   Oh, about that: here's a handout I provide to all new hires. It includes some helpful tips—especially this one. **70 Do you have your business cards yet?**

M   Hmm. I haven't received them, but I'll call the printer today for an update.

남   권 씨, **저를 곧 있을 로봇 공학 콘퍼런스에 보내 주셔서 감사합니다.** 입사하고 나서 이렇게 금방 이런 기회를 얻게 될 줄은 예상하지 못했어요.

여   **최신 로봇 디자인에 익숙해지는 게 중요해요.** 새로운 트렌드와 기술이 계속 나오니, 우리 업계의 발전에 앞서 나가시길 바랍니다.

남 저도 동의해요. 게다가, 저를 잠재 고객들에게 소개할 수 있는 기회도 될 겁니다.

여 아, 그 부분이요. 여기 제가 모든 신입 직원들에게 드리는 유인물이에요. 유용한 팁들을 포함하고 있는데, 특히 이거요. **명함은 이미 받았나요?**

남 흠. 받지 못했는데, 새로운 소식이 있는지 오늘 인쇄소에 전화해 보겠습니다.

어휘 upcoming 곧 있을, 다가오는 robotics 로봇 공학 opportunity 기회 trend 경향, 추세 ahead of ~보다 앞선 development 발전 potential 잠재적인 handout 유인물 especially 특히 upbeat 낙관적인 brief 간결한, 짧은

68 What industry do the speakers most likely work in?
(A) Legal
(B) Construction
(C) Agriculture
(D) Robotics

화자들은 어떤 업계에서 일하는 것 같은가?
(A) 법률
(B) 건설
(C) 농업
(D) 로봇 공학

해설 전체 내용 관련 - 화자들의 근무 업계
남자가 첫 대사에서 자신을 곧 있을 로봇 공학 콘퍼런스에 보내 주어 감사하다(~ thank you for sending me to the upcoming robotics conference)고 인사하고 있으므로 정답은 (D)이다.

69 Why does the woman want the man to attend a conference?
(A) To learn more about the latest industry trends
(B) To accept a reward on behalf of the company
(C) To host a panel discussion
(D) To screen job candidates

여자는 왜 남자가 콘퍼런스에 참석하기를 원하는가?
(A) 최신 업계 경향에 대해 더 배우기 위해
(B) 회사를 대표해서 포상을 받기 위해
(C) 패널 토론을 주최하기 위해
(D) 입사 지원자들을 선별하기 위해

어휘 accept 받아들이다 on behalf of ~을 대표해 screen 선별하다, 가려내다 candidate 지원자, 후보자

해설 세부 사항 관련 - 여자가 남자의 콘퍼런스 참석을 원하는 이유
여자가 첫 대사에서 남자에게 콘퍼런스 참석과 관련해 최신 로봇 디자인에 익숙해지는 게 중요하다(It's important for you to be familiar with current robot designs)고 조언하고 있다. 이는 최신 업계 경향을 익혀야 한다는 의미이므로 정답은 (A)이다.

Paraphrasing
대화의 be familiar with current robot designs
→ 정답의 learn more about the latest industry trends

70 Look at the graphic. Which tip does the woman point out?
(A) Tip 1
(B) Tip 2
(C) Tip 3
(D) Tip 4

시각 정보에 의하면, 여자는 어느 팁을 가리키고 있는가?
(A) 1번 팁
(B) 2번 팁
(C) 3번 팁
(D) 4번 팁

해설 시각 정보 연계 - 여자가 가리키는 팁
여자가 두 번째 대사에서 특정 팁을 가리키면서 명함을 이미 받았는지(Do you have your business cards yet?) 묻고 있고, 유인물에서 명함과 관련된 내용은 4번 팁이므로 정답은 (D)이다.

PART 4

71-73 담화

> M-Cn Crew, **71 please stop working on that truck repair for a second.** Many of you complained about how slow and hard it is to use the car lift, so I purchased a new one and it was delivered this morning! It can lift much heavier vehicles, and it's faster. **72 The only problem is we're missing the bottles of hydraulic fluid that were supposed to be included in the shipment.** So, we're stuck using the old car lift for a few more days. Oh, and one more thing—when talking to customers, **73 please remember to mention that we're now offering a discount on oil changes** if they schedule a vehicle inspection with us.

> 팀원 여러분, **그 트럭 수리 작업을 잠시 멈춰 주시기 바랍니다.** 많은 분들이 자동차 리프트를 이용하는 것이 얼마나 느리고 힘든지 불만을 제기하셔서, 새로운 것을 구매했고, 오늘 아침 배송되었습니다! 이건 훨씬 무거운 차량들을 들어 올릴 수 있고, 더 빠릅니다. **유일한 문제는 배송에 포함되어 있어야 할 유압유 병들이 빠져 있다는 겁니다.** 그래서 며칠 더 기존의 자동차 리프트를 이용할 수 밖에 없어요. 아, 그리고 한 가지 더 있는데, 고객 응대 시 차량 점검을 예약하실 경우 **오일 교환을 할인해 드리고 있다는 점을 꼭 안내해 주세요.**

> 어휘 crew 작업 팀, 조 lift 리프트(들어 올리는 기계); 들어 올리다 vehicle 차량 miss 빠뜨리다 hydraulic fluid 유압유 be supposed to ~하기로 되어 있다 shipment 배송(품) be stuck -ing 어쩔 수 없이 ~하게 되다 mention 언급하다 discount 할인 inspection 점검, 검사

71 Where do the listeners most likely work?
(A) At a taxi service
(B) At a car repair shop
(C) At a shipping company
(D) At a driving school

청자들은 어디에서 일하는 것 같은가?
(A) 택시 서비스 업체
(B) 자동차 정비소
(C) 배송 회사
(D) 자동차 운전 학원

해설 전체 내용 관련 – 청자들의 근무 장소

화자가 초반부에 청자들에게 그 트럭 수리 작업을 잠시 멈춰 달라(~ please stop working on that truck repair for a second)고 요청하고 있는 것으로 보아 청자들은 자동차 정비소에 근무하고 있음을 알 수 있다. 따라서 정답은 (B)이다.

72 What problem does the speaker mention?
(A) A training manual should be updated.
(B) An invoice was incorrect.
(C) Frequent maintenance is required.
(D) Some supplies are missing.

화자는 어떤 문제를 언급하는가?
(A) 교육 매뉴얼이 업데이트되어야 한다.
(B) 거래 내역서가 정확하지 않다.
(C) 잦은 정비가 필요하다.
(D) 일부 물품이 빠져 있다.

어휘 invoice 거래 내역서 incorrect 부정확한, 맞지 않는 frequent 잦은, 빈번한 maintenance 정비, 유지 보수 missing 빠진, 없는

해설 세부 사항 관련 – 화자가 언급하는 문제

화자가 중반부에 유일한 문제가 배송에 포함되어 있어야 할 유압유 병들이 빠져 있다는 것(The only problem is we're missing the bottles of hydraulic fluid that were supposed to be included in the shipment)이라고 말하고 있으므로 정답은 (D)이다.

Paraphrasing
담화의 we're missing the bottles of hydraulic fluid
→ 정답의 Some supplies are missing

73 What should the listeners remind customers about?
(A) Some schedule changes
(B) An online survey
(C) A promotional offer
(D) A safety policy

청자들은 고객들에게 무엇에 대해 상기시켜야 하는가?
(A) 일정 변경
(B) 온라인 설문 조사
(C) 판촉 할인
(D) 안전 정책

해설 세부 사항 관련 – 고객들에게 상기시켜야 하는 것

화자가 후반부에 오일 교환을 할인하고 있다는 점을 꼭 안내해 달라(~ please remember to mention that we're now offering a discount on oil changes ~)고 당부하고 있으므로 정답은 (C)이다.

Paraphrasing
담화의 mention → 질문의 remind
담화의 offering a discount on oil changes
→ 정답의 A promotional offer

74-76 회의 발췌

W-Br As you know, we've had an extremely successful fourth quarter **74 selling desks and chairs to our corporate clients** on the West Coast. In fact, we've done so well that **75 we're planning to give ten percent of this month's profits to a local charity in December.** They have a great reputation for teaching computer skills to children for free. **76 If you'd like to see a video clip of our CEO talking about this initiative, just visit our social media site.**

아시다시피, 우리는 서부 해안 지역 기업 고객들에게 책상과 의자를 판매하며 매우 성공적인 4분기를 보냈습니다. 실제로 실적이 아주 좋아서, 이달 수익의 10퍼센트를 12월에 지역 자선 단체에 기부할 계획이에요. 이곳은 아이들에게 무료로 컴퓨터 교육을 하는 것으로 좋은 평판을 받고 있습니다. CEO가 이 계획에 대해 이야기하는 동영상을 보고 싶으시면, 저희 소셜 미디어 사이트를 방문해 주세요.

어휘 extremely 매우 successful 성공적인 quarter 분기 corporate 기업의 profit 수익, 수입 local 지역의, 현지의 charity 자선 단체, 자선 활동 reputation 평판 initiative 계획

74 What does the company sell?
(A) Office furniture
(B) Kitchen appliances
(C) Garden tools
(D) Tablet computers

회사는 무엇을 판매하는가?
(A) 사무용 가구
(B) 주방 기기
(C) 원예 도구
(D) 태블릿 컴퓨터

해설 세부 사항 관련 – 회사가 판매하는 것
화자가 초반부에 회사의 실적에 대해 이야기하면서 기업 고객들에게 책상과 의자를 판매하는 것(~ selling desks and chairs to our corporate clients)을 언급하고 있으므로 정답은 (A)이다.

Paraphrasing
담화의 desks and chairs to our corporate clients → 정답의 Office furniture

75 What does the speaker say will happen in December?
(A) A promotional sale will begin.
(B) Special equipment will be delivered.
(C) Some temporary staff will be hired.
(D) Some profits will be donated to a charity.

화자는 12월에 무슨 일이 있을 것이라고 말하는가?
(A) 판촉 세일이 시작될 것이다.
(B) 특수 장비가 배송될 것이다.
(C) 임시 직원들이 고용될 것이다.
(D) 일부 수익이 자선 단체에 기부될 것이다.

어휘 promotional 판촉의, 홍보의 temporary 임시의, 일시적인 donate 기부하다

해설 세부 사항 관련 – 12월에 있을 일
화자가 중반부에 이달 수익의 10퍼센트를 12월에 지역 자선 단체에 기부할 계획(~ we're planning to give ten percent of this month's profits to a local charity in December)이라고 했으므로 정답은 (D)이다.

Paraphrasing
담화의 give ten percent of this month's profits to a local charity → 정답의 Some profits will be donated to a charity

76 According to the speaker, what can the listeners find on a social media site?
(A) A manual
(B) A video
(C) Some photographs
(D) A price list

화자에 따르면, 청자들은 소셜 미디어 사이트에서 무엇을 찾을 수 있는가?
(A) 설명서
(B) 동영상
(C) 사진
(D) 가격 목록

해설 세부 사항 관련 – 청자들이 소셜 미디어 사이트에서 찾을 수 있는 것
화자가 후반부에 CEO가 이 계획에 대해 이야기하는 동영상을 보고 싶다면, 소셜 미디어 사이트를 방문하라(If you'd like to see a video clip of our CEO talking about this initiative, just visit our social media site)고 했으므로 정답은 (B)이다.

77-79 팟캐스트

M-Au Welcome to *Impact Unlocked*, the podcast for businesses wanting to streamline their operations with new technology. **77 In today's episode, I'll talk about how to raise money by leveraging social media applications to get donations. 78 I could focus on specific applications, but these things are constantly changing. 78 Instead, I'll speak generally** about how these types of applications can help you connect with potential donors. **79 Some organizations keep using the same familiar fund-raising strategies.** I see this often, **79 but it's important to also incorporate the latest approaches.**

새로운 기술을 통해 운영을 간소화하고자 하는 기업들을 위한 팟캐스트, 〈임팩트 언락트〉에 오신 것을 환영합니다. 오늘 에피소드에서는, 소셜 미디어 애플리케이션을 활용하여 기부금을 모금하는 방법에 대해 이야기해 보겠습니다. 특정 애플리케이션에 초점을 맞출 수도 있겠지만, 이런 것들은 지속적으로 변화하고 있죠. 대신, 이런 종류의 애플리케이션이 어떻게 잠재적인 기부자들과 연결되는 데 도움을 줄 수 있는지에 대해 일반적으로 말씀드리겠습니다. 어떤 단체들은 익숙한 모금 전략을 고수합니다. 이런 경우를 자주 보는데, 최신 접근 방식도 포함하는 것이 중요합니다.

어휘 streamline 간소화하다 operation 운영, 영업 raise money 모금하다 leverage 활용하다 donation 기부 specific 특정한, 구체적인 constantly 지속적으로, 꾸준히 generally 일반적으로, 전체적으로 potential 잠재적인 donor 기부자 organization 단체, 기관 fund-raising 모금 strategy 전략 incorporate 포함하다, 통합하다 latest 최근의, 최신의 approach 접근(법)

77 What is the episode mainly about?
(A) Hiring
(B) Accounting
(C) Fund-raising
(D) Publishing

에피소드는 주로 무엇에 대한 것인가?
(A) 고용
(B) 회계
(C) 모금
(D) 출판

해설 전체 내용 관련 – 방송 주제

화자가 초반부에 오늘 에피소드에서는 소셜 미디어 애플리케이션을 활용하여 기부금을 모금하는 방법에 대해 이야기해 보겠다(In today's episode, I'll talk about how to raise money by leveraging social media applications to get donations)고 했으므로 정답은 (C)이다.

Paraphrasing
담화의 raise money → 정답의 Fund-raising

78 What does the speaker mean when he says, "these things are constantly changing"?
(A) He recommends professional development courses.
(B) He questions the value of an investment.
(C) Some information will be excluded.
(D) Using technology is important.

화자가 "이런 것들은 지속적으로 변화하고 있죠"라고 말할 때 무엇을 의미하는가?
(A) 직무 능력 개발 과정을 추천한다.
(B) 투자의 가치에 대해 의문을 제기한다.
(C) 일부 정보가 제외될 것이다.
(D) 기술을 이용하는 것이 중요하다.

어휘 question 의문을 제기하다 value 가치, 값어치 investment 투자(금) exclude 제외하다

해설 화자의 의도 파악 – 이런 것들은 지속적으로 변화하고 있다는 말의 의도

화자가 중반부에 특정 애플리케이션에 초점을 맞출 수도 있겠지만(I could focus on specific applications, but ~)이라고 말한 뒤 인용문을 언급하고, 대신 일반적으로 말씀드리겠다(Instead, I'll speak generally ~)고 하는 것으로 보아 특정 애플리케이션에 대한 정보는 변동될 수 있으니 제공하지 않겠다는 의도로 한 말임을 알 수 있다. 따라서 정답은 (C)이다.

79 What does the speaker say is important for organizations to do?
(A) Be leaders in their industries
(B) Establish successful advertising methods
(C) Collect community feedback
(D) Use familiar and current strategies

화자는 단체들이 무엇을 하는 것이 중요하다고 말하는가?
(A) 소속 업계에서 리더가 되는 것
(B) 성공적인 광고 기법을 확립하는 것
(C) 지역 사회 의견을 수렴하는 것
(D) 익숙한 전략과 최신의 전략을 이용하는 것

어휘 establish 확립하다 advertising 광고 method 방식, 방법 collect 수집하다, 모으다 community 지역 사회, 지역 공동체

해설 세부 사항 관련 – 단체들에게 중요한 것

화자가 후반부에 어떤 단체들은 익숙한 모금 전략을 고수한다(Some organizations keep using the same familiar fund-raising strategies)며 그렇지만 최신 접근 방식도 포함하는 것이 중요하다(~ but it's important to also incorporate the latest approaches)고 말하고 있다. 이는 그 두 가지 전략을 모두 이용해야 한다는 뜻이므로 정답은 (D)이다.

Paraphrasing
담화의 using the same familiar fund-raising strategies ~ incorporate the latest approaches
→ 정답의 Use familiar and current strategies

80-82 담화

W-Am As the company president, I'm excited to share that **80** we've sold a record number of home appliances for two years in a row, and I'd like to reward your hard work. First, **81** everyone will be eligible for a one-time monetary bonus. Your supervisor will speak with you about how it'll be calculated and when you'll receive it. Also, **82** I'd like to offer more flexibility in your schedule, so all employees will be permitted to work remotely twice a week. You'll just need to note those days on your calendar, so everyone knows where you are.

TEST 2

회사 사장으로서, 우리가 2년 연속으로 기록적인 수의 가전제품을 판매했다는 소식을 공유해 드리게 되어 기쁘게 생각하며, 여러분의 노고에 보상해 드리고자 합니다. 우선, 모든 직원이 일회성 금전적 보너스를 받을 자격을 얻게 될 것입니다. 금액 산정 방식과 지급 시점에 대해서는 여러분의 부서장께서 말씀해 주실 겁니다. 또한, 여러분의 일정에 더 많은 유연성을 드리고자, 전 직원이 주 2회 원격 근무를 할 수 있도록 허용할 예정입니다. 해당 요일을 캘린더에 표시만 해주시면, 동료들이 여러분이 계신 곳을 알게 됩니다.

어휘 a record number of 기록적인 숫자의
home appliance 가전제품 in a row 연속으로
reward 보상하다 be eligible for ~에 대한 자격이 있다
monetary 금전적인 supervisor 부서장, 상사
calculate 계산하다 flexibility 탄력성, 유연성
be permitted to ~하도록 허용되다 remotely 원격으로

80 What does the speaker say the company sells?
(A) Home appliances
(B) Office supplies
(C) Sporting goods
(D) Entertainment systems

화자는 회사가 무엇을 판매한다고 말하는가?
(A) 가전제품
(B) 사무용품
(C) 스포츠용품
(D) 엔터테인먼트 시스템

해설 세부 사항 관련 – 회사가 판매하는 것
화자가 초반부에 우리가 2년 연속으로 기록적인 수의 가전제품을 판매했다(~ we've sold a record number of home appliances for two years in a row ~)고 했으므로 정답은 (A)이다.

81 What will the listeners discuss with their supervisors?
(A) A new sales goal
(B) Training opportunities
(C) A financial bonus
(D) Increasing efficiency

청자들은 자신의 부서장과 무엇을 이야기할 것인가?
(A) 새로운 판매 목표
(B) 교육 기회
(C) 금전적인 보너스
(D) 효율성 증대

어휘 opportunity 기회 efficiency 효율성

해설 세부 사항 관련 – 청자들이 부서장과 이야기할 것
화자가 중반부에 모든 직원이 일회성 금전적 보너스를 받을 자격을 얻게 될 것(~ everyone will be eligible for a one-time monetary bonus)이라며 부서장이 이야기해 줄 것(Your supervisor will speak with you ~)이라고 했으므로 정답은 (C)이다.

Paraphrasing
담화의 a one-time monetary bonus
→ 정답의 A financial bonus

82 How will the company offer more flexibility?
(A) By introducing shared workspaces
(B) By allowing employees to switch assignments
(C) By permitting remote work
(D) By increasing vacation time

회사는 어떻게 더 많은 유연성을 제공할 것인가?
(A) 공용 업무 공간을 도입함으로써
(B) 직원들에게 업무를 맞바꾸도록 허용함으로써
(C) 원격 근무를 허용함으로써
(D) 휴가 시간을 늘림으로써

어휘 introduce 도입하다, 소개하다 shared 공용의, 공동의
switch 맞바꾸다, 전환하다 assignment 업무, 과제
remote 원격의, 멀리 떨어진

해설 세부 사항 관련 – 회사가 유연성을 제공하는 방법
화자가 후반부에 일정에 더 많은 유연성을 제공하고자, 전 직원이 주 2회 원격 근무를 할 수 있도록 허용할 예정(~ I'd like to offer more flexibility in your schedule, so all employees will be permitted to work remotely twice a week)이라고 했으므로 정답은 (C)이다.

Paraphrasing
담화의 be permitted to work remotely
→ 정답의 permitting remote work

83-85 회의 발췌

M-Cn **83** I called this meeting today because I wanted to talk about changes to how our company hires new employees. It came to my attention that some people were confused when reading about these new hiring policies in the latest company newsletter. I posted a link in the meeting invitation to this information, and **84** I asked you to bring your laptops so that you can follow along on your own screen. After we review the policies, **85** you can see Sumit in the back of the room if you'd like a printed copy. He has several of them.

제가 오늘 이 회의를 소집한 이유는 우리 회사의 신입 직원 채용 방식 변화에 대해 이야기하고 싶었기 때문입니다. 최근 회사 뉴스레터에서 새로운 채용 정책에 관한 글을 읽고 일부 직원들이 혼란스러워했다는 걸 알게 됐거든요. 제가 회의 초대장에 관련 정보로 연결되는 링크를 첨부했고, 각자 화면을 보면서 따라하실 수 있도록 **노트북 컴퓨터를 지참해 달라고** 요청했었죠. 정책을 함께 살펴본 뒤에, **인쇄된 자료가 필요하신 분은 회의실 뒤쪽에 있는 수미트에게 말씀해 주세요.** 여러 부 가지고 계십니다.

어휘 it comes to one's attention that ~라는 사실을 알게 되다
confused 혼란스러워하는, 헷갈린 policy 정책, 방침
post 게시하다 invitation 초대(장)

83 What is the purpose of the meeting?
(A) To evaluate vendor contracts
(B) To review hiring policies
(C) To revise budget proposals
(D) To assess editing software

회의의 목적은 무엇인가?
(A) 판매업체 계약을 평가하는 것
(B) 채용 정책을 살펴보는 것
(C) 예산 제안서를 수정하는 것
(D) 편집 소프트웨어를 평가하는 것

어휘 evaluate 평가하다 vendor 판매업체, 판매업자
revise 수정하다 budget 예산 assess 평가하다
editing 편집

해설 전체 내용 관련 – 회의의 목적
화자가 초반부에 오늘 회의를 소집한 이유는 회사의 신입 직원 채용 방식 변화에 대해 이야기하고 싶었기 때문(I called this meeting today because I wanted to talk about changes to how our company hires new employees)이라고 했으므로 정답은 (B)이다.

Paraphrasing
담화의 talk about changes to how our company hires new employees → 정답의 review hiring policies

84 What did the speaker ask the listeners to bring to the meeting?
(A) A list of concerns
(B) A completed survey
(C) A project timeline
(D) A laptop computer

화자는 청자들에게 회의에 무엇을 가져오라고 요청했는가?
(A) 우려 사항 목록
(B) 작성 완료된 설문지
(C) 프로젝트 진행 일정표
(D) 노트북 컴퓨터

어휘 concern 우려, 걱정 timeline 진행 일정표

해설 세부 사항 관련 – 화자가 가져오도록 요청한 것
화자가 중반부에 노트북 컴퓨터를 지참해 달라고 요청했었다(~ I asked you to bring your laptops ~)고 했으므로 정답은 (D)이다.

85 Why might some of the listeners look for Sumit?
(A) To get a document
(B) To ask additional questions
(C) To volunteer for an event
(D) To check the status of a request

일부 청자들은 왜 수미트를 찾을 수도 있는가?
(A) 문서를 받기 위해
(B) 추가 질문을 하기 위해
(C) 행사에 자원봉사를 하기 위해
(D) 요청 사항의 상태를 확인하기 위해

어휘 additional 추가적인 status 상태, 현황

해설 세부 사항 관련 – 청자들이 수미트를 찾는 이유
화자가 후반부에 인쇄된 자료가 필요한 사람은 회의실 뒤쪽에 있는 수미트에게 가면 된다(~ you can see Sumit in the back of the room if you'd like a printed copy)며 그가 여러 부 갖고 있다(He has several of them)고 했으므로 정답은 (A)이다.

Paraphrasing
담화의 would like a printed copy → 정답의 get a document

86-88 회의 발췌

M-Au As head of the product design team, ⁸⁶**I have the sales results from the last quarter**, and they're disappointing. It's clear that consumers are no longer interested in the types of toys and games we've been producing. ⁸⁷**My guess is that people are getting tired of noisy, blinking electronics. We have a lot of work to do.** There's a new trend toward outdoor toys and games, where people can be physically active. I've already come up with some prototypes of new games. I brought a few of them, and ⁸⁸**now I'll show you how they work.**

제품 디자인 팀장으로서, **지난 분기 판매 실적을 갖고 있는데**, 실망스럽네요. 소비자들이 더 이상 우리가 생산해 온 장난감과 게임에 관심이 없는 게 분명합니다. **제 추측으로는 사람들이 시끄럽고 불빛이 깜빡거리는 전자 제품에 싫증이 나고 있는 것 같아요. 우리가 할 일이 많습니다.** 야외용 장난감과 게임 쪽으로 새로운 트렌드가 있어요. 사람들이 신체 활동을 할 수 있는 것들이요. 제가 이미 몇 가지 새로운 게임의 시제품을 만들어 두었습니다. 그중 몇 개를 가져왔는데요, **이제 그것들이 어떻게 작동하는지 보여 드리겠습니다.**

어휘 quarter 분기 disappointing 실망시키는
consumer 소비자 blinking 불빛이 깜빡거리는
electronics 전자 제품 physically 신체적으로
active 활동적인, 적극적인 come up with ~을 고안하다
prototype 시제품, 원형

86 What did the speaker recently receive?
(A) Sales results
(B) Production schedules
(C) An inspection report
(D) An advertising proposal

화자는 최근에 무엇을 받았는가?
(A) 판매 실적
(B) 생산 일정표
(C) 점검 보고서
(D) 광고 제안서

해설 세부 사항 관련 – 화자가 최근에 받은 것
화자가 초반부에 지난 분기 판매 실적을 갖고 있다(~ I have the sales results from the last quarter ~)고 언급하는 것으로 보아 최근에 판매 실적 관련 자료를 받았음을 알 수 있다. 따라서 정답은 (A)이다.

87 What does the speaker mean when he says, "We have a lot of work to do"?
(A) Extra shifts will be scheduled.
(B) A job opening will be posted soon.
(C) Customer orders have increased.
(D) A change is necessary.

화자가 "우리가 할 일이 많습니다"라고 말할 때 무엇을 의미하는가?
(A) 추가 교대 근무 일정이 잡힐 것이다.
(B) 공석이 곧 게시될 것이다.
(C) 고객 주문이 증가했다.
(D) 변화가 필수적이다.

어휘 shift 교대 근무 job opening 공석, 빈자리

해설 화자의 의도 파악 – 우리가 할 일이 많다는 말의 의도
화자가 중반부에 자신의 추측으로는 사람들이 시끄럽고 불빛이 깜빡거리는 전자 제품에 싫증이 나고 있는 것 같다(My guess is that people are getting tired of noisy, blinking electronics)고 말한 뒤 인용문을 언급하고 있다. 이는 이러한 제품들 대신에 다른 것을 만들어야 한다는 뜻이므로, 변화의 필요성을 표현하려는 의도로 한 말임을 알 수 있다. 따라서 정답은 (D)이다.

88 What will the speaker do next?
(A) Distribute some manuals
(B) Give a demonstration
(C) Answer some questions
(D) Show a video

화자는 다음에 무엇을 할 것인가?
(A) 설명서 배부하기
(B) 시연하기
(C) 질문에 답변하기
(D) 동영상 보여 주기

어휘 distribute 배부하다, 나눠 주다 manual 설명서, 안내서
demonstration 시연, 시범

해설 세부 사항 관련 – 화자가 다음에 할 일
화자가 후반부에 앞서 언급한 시제품을 몇 개 가져왔다며 이제 그것들이 어떻게 작동하는지 보여 주겠다(~ now I'll show you how they work)고 했으므로 정답은 (B)이다.

Paraphrasing
담화의 show you how they work
→ 정답의 Give a demonstration

89-91 녹음 메시지

M-Cn Hello. **89**You've reached Ji-Soo Yoon at the visitor center of the Pine Valley Nature Preserve. I am currently out of the office. Please be aware that **90**visitor access to the park will be limited during the month of March while our facilities are undergoing renovations. **91**If you are calling for information about helping to maintain our hiking trails, please refer to the volunteer page on our Web site. We welcome the assistance of motivated individuals. For all other inquiries, please leave a message after the tone.

안녕하세요. 파인 밸리 자연 보호 구역 방문자 센터의 윤지수입니다. 저는 현재 사무실에 있지 않습니다. 시설 보수 작업이 진행되는 3월 한 달간 공원 방문객의 출입이 제한될 예정이라는 점 양해 부탁드립니다. 등산로 관리를 돕는 것에 대한 정보를 위해 전화하신 경우에는 저희 웹사이트의 자원봉사 페이지를 참고해 주세요. 저희는 적극적인 분들의 도움을 환영합니다. 기타 모든 문의 사항은, 신호음이 울린 후에 메시지를 남겨 주세요.

어휘 reach 연락하다 be aware 알다 access 이용, 접근
limited 제한된, 한정된 undergo 거치다, 경험하다
renovation 보수, 개조 maintain 관리하다 trail 등산로, 산길
refer to ~을 참고하다 assistance 지원, 도움, 원조
motivated 적극적인 individual 사람, 개인 inquiry 문의
tone 신호음

89 Where does the speaker work?
(A) At a museum
(B) At a park
(C) At a library
(D) At a theater

화자는 어디에서 일하는가?
(A) 박물관
(B) 공원
(C) 도서관
(D) 극장

해설 | 전체 내용 관련 – 화자의 근무 장소
화자가 초반부에 파인 밸리 자연 보호 구역 방문자 센터의 윤지수(You've reached Ji-Soo Yoon at the visitor center of the Pine Valley Nature Preserve)라고 자신을 소개하고 있으므로 정답은 (B)이다.

90 What will happen in March?
(A) A new facility will open.
(B) An exhibition will be held.
(C) Renovations will take place.
(D) Operating hours will be extended.

3월에 무슨 일이 있을 것인가?
(A) 새로운 시설이 개장할 것이다.
(B) 전시회가 개최될 것이다.
(C) 개조 공사가 진행될 것이다.
(D) 운영 시간이 연장될 것이다.

어휘 | exhibition 전시회 extend 연장하다, 확장하다

해설 | 세부 사항 관련 – 3월에 있을 일
화자가 중반부에 시설 보수 작업이 진행되는 3월 한 달간 공원 방문객의 출입이 제한될 예정(~ visitor access to the park will be limited during the month of March while our facilities are undergoing renovations)이라고 했으므로 정답은 (C)이다.

Paraphrasing
담화의 are undergoing renovations
→ 정답의 Renovations will take place

91 What does the speaker say can be found online?
(A) Volunteer information
(B) A calendar of upcoming events
(C) Ticket prices
(D) An area map

화자는 온라인에서 무엇을 찾을 수 있다고 말하는가?
(A) 자원봉사 정보
(B) 곧 있을 행사의 일정표
(C) 티켓 가격
(D) 지역 안내도

어휘 | upcoming 곧 있을, 다가오는

해설 | 세부 사항 관련 – 온라인에서 찾을 수 있는 것
화자가 후반부에 등산로 관리를 돕는 것에 대한 정보를 위해 전화한 경우에는 웹사이트의 자원봉사 페이지를 참고해 달라(If you are calling for information about helping to maintain our hiking trails, please refer to the volunteer page on our Web site)고 했으므로 정답은 (A)이다.

Paraphrasing
담화의 on our Web site → 질문의 online

92-94 팟캐스트

W-Am **92** Today, I'll be interviewing the owners of Salazar Olive Oil, one of the best in California for the past two decades. **93** Now—if you're hearing about this olive oil for the first time, you're not alone. The Salazar family has kept the operation small. I'm interested in discussing their business philosophy as well as their new project: **94** an olive oil tasting class on their farm. You'll find out how to register during the interview so you can sign up!

오늘은, 지난 20년간 캘리포니아 최고의 올리브 오일 중 하나로 꼽혀 온 살라자르 올리브 오일의 소유주들을 인터뷰해 보겠습니다. 자, 이 올리브 오일에 대해 처음 들어 보신다면, 여러분만 그런 것이 아닙니다. 살라자르 가문은 이 사업을 소규모로 유지해 왔습니다. 저는 그들의 사업 철학뿐만 아니라 새로운 프로젝트인 농장에서의 올리브 오일 맛보기 수업에 대해서도 이야기해 보고 싶어요. 인터뷰 중에 등록하는 방법을 알게 되실 테니, 여러분도 신청하실 수 있습니다!

어휘 | owner 소유주 operation 사업, 운영 philosophy 철학 tasting 시음, 시식 register 등록하다 sign up 신청하다, 등록하다

92 Who are today's guests on the podcast?
(A) Government officials
(B) Business owners
(C) Real estate developers
(D) Cooking-school instructors

오늘 팟캐스트의 초대 손님은 누구인가?
(A) 정부 관계자
(B) 업체 소유주
(C) 부동산 개발업자
(D) 요리 학원 강사

해설 | 세부 사항 관련 – 초대 손님의 직업
화자가 초반부에 오늘은 살라자르 올리브 오일의 소유주들을 인터뷰해 보겠다(Today, I'll be interviewing the owners of Salazar Olive Oil, ~)고 했으므로 정답은 (B)이다.

93 Why does the speaker say, "The Salazar family has kept the operation small"?
(A) To indicate why a product is only sold online
(B) To justify the high price of a product
(C) To suggest that a company is having financial difficulties
(D) To explain why a product is not well-known

화자는 왜 "살라자르 가문은 이 사업을 소규모로 유지해 왔습니다"라고 말하는가?
(A) 제품이 온라인에서만 판매되는 이유를 알려 주려고
(B) 제품의 높은 가격을 정당화하려고
(C) 회사가 재정적으로 어려움을 겪고 있다는 점을 암시하려고
(D) 제품이 잘 알려지지 않은 이유를 설명하려고

어휘 well-known 잘 알려진

해설 화자의 의도 파악 – 살라자르 가문이 사업을 소규모로 유지해 왔다는 말의 의도

화자가 중반부에 이 올리브 오일에 대해 처음 들어 본다면, 여러분만 그런 것이 아니다(Now—if you're hearing about this olive oil for the first time, you're not alone)라고 말한 뒤 인용문을 언급하고 있으므로, 많은 사람들이 처음 들어 볼 정도로 잘 알려져 있지 않은 이유를 설명하려는 의도임을 알 수 있다. 따라서 정답은 (D)이다.

94 What will the listeners be able to do after the podcast?
(A) Request some product samples
(B) Subscribe to a newsletter
(C) Enter a contest
(D) Sign up for a class

청자들은 팟캐스트 후에 무엇을 할 수 있을 것인가?
(A) 제품 샘플 요청하기
(B) 뉴스레터 구독하기
(C) 콘테스트 참가하기
(D) 수업 신청하기

어휘 subscribe to ~을 구독하다

해설 세부 사항 관련 – 청자들이 팟캐스트 후에 할 수 있는 것

화자가 후반부에 농장에서의 올리브 오일 맛보기 수업(~ an olive oil tasting class on their farm)에 대해 언급한 뒤, 인터뷰 중에 등록하는 방법을 알게 될 테니 여러분도 신청할 수 있다(You'll find out how to register during the interview so you can sign up!)고 했으므로 정답은 (D)이다.

95-97 공지 + 지도 ▶동영상 강의

W-Br Welcome to the Abingdon Transit Station. Please be advised that **95the Circle Route bus is not currently stopping at the station entrance because of some street resurfacing work. 96A temporary bus stop has been set up around the corner in front of the post office.** Signs are posted directing you to the new stop. Bus timetables will be affected by the change in the route. **97Use the Abingdon Transit mobile phone app to view live updates for when the next bus is due.**

애빙던 트랜짓 역에 오신 것을 환영합니다. **도로 재포장 공사로 인해 서클 루트 버스가 현재 역 입구에 정차하지 않으니 참고하시기 바랍니다. 우체국 앞 바로 근처에 임시 버스 정류장이 마련되었습니다.** 새로운 정류장으로 안내하는 표지판이 게시되어 있습니다. 버스 운행 시간표는 노선 변경에 영향을 받게 됩니다. **애빙던 트랜짓 휴대전화 앱을 이용해 다음 버스가 언제 도착할지 실시간 업데이트를 확인하세요.**

어휘 currently 현재 resurfacing (도로 등의) 재포장 temporary 임시의 around the corner 바로 근처에, 모퉁이에 direct (길을) 안내하다 affect 영향을 미치다 due ~로 예정된

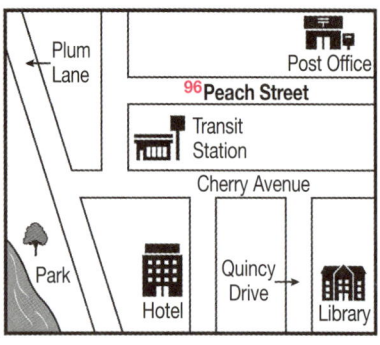
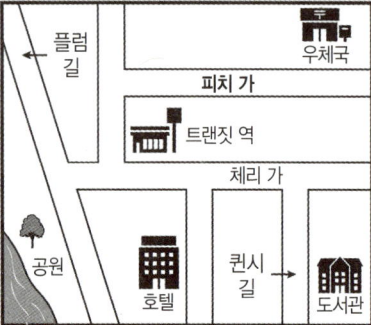

95 According to the speaker, why was a transit route changed?
(A) Some streets are being resurfaced.
(B) Some roads are closed for a bicycle race.
(C) A group of residents is hosting a fund-raising concert.
(D) A local politician will be speaking in a park.

화자에 따르면, 교통 노선은 왜 변경되었는가?
(A) 거리가 재포장되고 있다.
(B) 도로가 자전거 경주로 인해 폐쇄되어 있다.
(C) 한 주민 모임에서 모금 콘서트를 개최하고 있다.
(D) 지역 정치인이 공원에서 연설할 것이다.

어휘 resident 주민 host 개최하다 fund-raising 모금, 기금 마련 politician 정치인

해설 세부 사항 관련 – 교통 노선이 변경된 이유

화자가 초반부에 도로 재포장 공사로 인해 서클 루트 버스가 현재 역 입구에 정차하지 않는다(~ the Circle Route bus is not currently stopping at the station entrance because of some street resurfacing work)고 알리고 있으므로 정답은 (A)이다.

Paraphrasing
담화의 some street resurfacing work
→ 정답의 Some streets are being resurfaced.

96 Look at the graphic. Where will the listeners find a new bus stop?
(A) On Plum Lane
(B) On Peach Street
(C) On Cherry Avenue
(D) On Quincy Drive

시각 정보에 의하면, 청자들은 어디에서 새로운 버스 정류장을 찾을 것인가?
(A) 플럼 길
(B) 피치 가
(C) 체리 가
(D) 퀸시 길

해설 시각 정보 연계 – 새로운 버스 정류장의 위치
화자가 중반부에 우체국 앞 바로 근처에 임시 버스 정류장이 마련되었다(A temporary bus stop has been set up around the corner in front of the post office)고 말하고 있고, 지도에서 우체국 앞 바로 근처에 해당하는 거리는 피치 가이므로 정답은 (B)이다.

Paraphrasing
담화의 A temporary bus stop → 질문의 a new bus stop

97 Why should the listeners check a mobile phone application?
(A) To apply for a job
(B) To scan a promotional code
(C) To view bus schedule updates
(D) To purchase bus tickets

청자들은 왜 휴대전화 애플리케이션을 확인해야 하는가?
(A) 일자리에 지원하기 위해
(B) 프로모션 코드를 스캔하기 위해
(C) 버스 스케줄 업데이트를 확인하기 위해
(D) 버스 승차권을 구입하기 위해

어휘 apply for ~에 지원하다, ~을 신청하다

해설 세부 사항 관련 – 휴대전화 애플리케이션을 확인해야 하는 이유
화자가 후반부에 애빙던 트랜짓 휴대전화 앱을 이용해 다음 버스가 언제 도착할지 실시간 업데이트를 확인하라(Use the Abingdon Transit mobile phone app to view live updates for when the next bus is due)고 했으므로 정답은 (C)이다.

Paraphrasing
담화의 view live updates for when the next bus is due
→ 정답의 view bus schedule updates

98-100 공지 + 워크숍 일정표

M-Cn Hello, everyone! **98 We're happy to announce that the February continuing education workshops here at the community center were very successful.** Thank you for working so hard to make sure they ran smoothly. Every workshop was completely full. **99 In fact, we had to create a waiting list for the Monday night workshop. Beginning in March, we'll offer that same workshop on Fridays.** Now, many participants complained about the lack of vending machines in the building. **100 Bianca will be contacting vending services next week to ask about pricing.**

안녕하세요, 여러분! 이곳 커뮤니티 센터의 2월 평생 교육 워크숍이 매우 성공적이었음을 알려 드리게 되어 기쁩니다. 워크숍이 순조롭게 진행되도록 열심히 일해 주셔서 감사합니다. 모든 워크숍이 완전히 만원이었습니다. 사실, 월요일 야간 워크숍은 대기자 명단을 만들어야 했어요. 3월부터는 같은 워크숍을 금요일에도 제공할 예정입니다. 그리고 많은 참가자들이 건물 내 자판기 부족에 대해 불만을 제기했어요. 비앙카가 다음 주에 자판기 서비스 업체에 연락해 가격에 대해 문의할 예정입니다.

어휘 announce 알리다 continuing education 평생 교육 successful 성공적인 run 진행되다 smoothly 순조롭게 completely 완전히 participant 참가자 lack 부족 vending machine 자판기 contact 연락하다 pricing 가격 entrepreneurship 기업가 정신 introduction 입문, 소개 accounting 회계

Workshop (February)	Days
99 Podcasting	**Mondays**
Entrepreneurship for Beginners	Tuesdays
Introduction to Coding	Wednesdays
Accounting for Small Businesses	Thursdays

워크숍 (2월)	요일
팟캐스트하기	**월요일**
초보자를 위한 기업가 정신	화요일
코딩 입문	수요일
소기업을 위한 회계	목요일

98 Where does the speaker work?
(A) At a restaurant
(B) At a public library
(C) At a community center
(D) At a hospital

화자는 어디에서 일하는가?
(A) 레스토랑
(B) 공공 도서관
(C) 커뮤니티 센터
(D) 병원

해설 전체 내용 관련 – 화자의 근무 장소

화자가 초반부에 이곳 커뮤니티 센터의 2월 평생 교육 워크숍이 매우 성공적이었음을 알리게 되어 기쁘다(We're happy to announce that the February continuing education workshops here at the community center were very successful)고 말하고 있으므로 정답은 (C)이다.

99 Look at the graphic. Which workshop will be offered on Fridays starting in March?
(A) Podcasting
(B) Entrepreneurship for Beginners
(C) Introduction to Coding
(D) Accounting for Small Businesses

시각 정보에 의하면, 3월부터 금요일에 어느 워크숍이 제공될 것인가?
(A) 팟캐스트하기
(B) 초보자를 위한 기업가 정신
(C) 코딩 입문
(D) 소기업을 위한 회계

해설 시각 정보 연계 – 3월부터 금요일에 제공되는 워크숍

화자가 중반부에 사실 월요일 야간 워크숍은 대기자 명단을 만들어야 했다(In fact, we had to create a waiting list for the Monday night workshop)며 3월부터는 같은 워크숍을 금요일에도 제공할 예정(Beginning in March, we'll offer that same workshop on Fridays)이라고 했고, 워크숍 일정표에서 현재 월요일 워크숍은 팟캐스트하기이므로 정답은 (A)이다.

100 What will Bianca do next week?
(A) Request feedback from participants
(B) Order office supplies
(C) Update registration information
(D) Contact some vendors

비앙카는 다음 주에 무엇을 할 것인가?
(A) 참가자들에게 의견 요청하기
(B) 사무용품 주문하기
(C) 등록 정보 업데이트하기
(D) 판매업체에 연락하기

어휘 registration 등록

해설 세부 사항 관련 – 비앙카가 다음 주에 할 일

화자가 후반부에 비앙카가 다음 주에 자판기 서비스 업체에 연락해 가격에 대해 문의할 예정(Bianca will be contacting vending services next week to ask about pricing)이라고 했으므로 정답은 (D)이다.

Paraphrasing
담화의 will be contacting vending services
→ 정답의 Contact some vendors

기출 TEST 3

동영상 강의

1 (D)	2 (A)	3 (D)	4 (B)	5 (C)
6 (A)	7 (A)	8 (B)	9 (B)	10 (B)
11 (A)	12 (A)	13 (C)	14 (C)	15 (C)
16 (B)	17 (C)	18 (B)	19 (C)	20 (C)
21 (C)	22 (B)	23 (C)	24 (A)	25 (B)
26 (B)	27 (A)	28 (A)	29 (C)	30 (C)
31 (C)	32 (B)	33 (C)	34 (B)	35 (C)
36 (A)	37 (D)	38 (B)	39 (D)	40 (C)
41 (B)	42 (B)	43 (D)	44 (C)	45 (A)
46 (D)	47 (D)	48 (B)	49 (B)	50 (C)
51 (D)	52 (C)	53 (B)	54 (C)	55 (D)
56 (D)	57 (A)	58 (C)	59 (B)	60 (C)
61 (D)	62 (A)	63 (C)	64 (D)	65 (C)
66 (A)	67 (C)	68 (A)	69 (A)	70 (C)
71 (B)	72 (C)	73 (D)	74 (A)	75 (C)
76 (B)	77 (C)	78 (D)	79 (A)	80 (B)
81 (D)	82 (A)	83 (B)	84 (D)	85 (D)
86 (B)	87 (A)	88 (B)	89 (B)	90 (C)
91 (A)	92 (C)	93 (C)	94 (A)	95 (C)
96 (B)	97 (C)	98 (A)	99 (B)	100 (C)

PART 1

1

W-Am

(A) He's fixing a file drawer.
(B) He's rolling up his sleeves.
(C) He's closing a laptop computer.
(D) He's drinking from a mug.

(A) 남자가 파일 서랍을 고치고 있다.
(B) 남자가 소매를 걷어 올리고 있다.
(C) 남자가 노트북 컴퓨터를 닫고 있다.
(D) 남자가 머그잔에 든 것을 마시고 있다.

어휘 fix 고치다, 바로잡다 roll up one's sleeves 소매를 걷어 올리다

해설 1인 등장 사진 – 사람의 동작/상태 묘사
(A) 동사 오답. 남자가 파일 서랍을 고치고 있는(is fixing a file drawer) 모습이 아니므로 오답.
(B) 동사 오답. 남자가 소매를 걷어 올리고 있는(is rolling up his sleeves) 모습이 아니므로 오답.
(C) 동사 오답. 남자가 노트북 컴퓨터를 닫고 있는(is closing a laptop computer) 모습이 아니므로 오답.
(D) 정답. 남자가 머그잔에 든 것을 마시고 있는(is drinking from a mug) 모습이므로 정답.

2

M-Cn

(A) Some bushes are covered with snow.
(B) Some flowers are being planted.
(C) A person is walking in the road.
(D) A person is cleaning some windows.

(A) 관목들이 눈으로 덮여 있다.
(B) 꽃들이 심어지고 있다.
(C) 사람이 도로를 걷고 있다.
(D) 사람이 창문을 닦고 있다.

어휘 bush 관목, 덤불 be covered with ~로 덮여 있다 plant 심다, 가꾸다

해설 1인 등장 사진 – 사람/사물/풍경 혼합 묘사
(A) 정답. 관목들(Some bushes)이 눈으로 덮여 있는(are covered with snow) 모습이므로 정답.
(B) 사진에 없는 명사를 이용한 오답. 사진에 꽃들(Some flowers)의 모습이 보이지 않으므로 오답.
(C) 동사 오답. 사람이 도로를 걷고 있는(is walking in the road) 모습이 아니므로 오답.
(D) 동사 오답. 사람이 창문을 닦고 있는(is cleaning some windows) 모습이 아니므로 오답.

3

M-Au

(A) A man is changing a tire on his car.
(B) A man is opening a car door.
(C) A man is putting fuel into his car.
(D) A man is spreading out a map on top of his car.

(A) 남자가 자동차의 타이어를 교체하고 있다.
(B) 남자가 자동차 문을 열고 있다.
(C) 남자가 자동차에 연료를 넣고 있다.
(D) 남자가 자동차 위에 지도를 펼치고 있다.

어휘 put ~ into ... ~을 …에 넣다 fuel 연료 spread out 펼치다

해설 1인 등장 사진 – 사람의 동작/상태 묘사
(A) 동사 오답. 남자가 자동차의 타이어를 교체하고 있는(is changing a tire on his car) 모습이 아니므로 오답.
(B) 동사 오답. 남자가 자동차 문을 열고 있는(is opening a car door) 모습이 아니므로 오답.

TEST 3 61

(C) 동사 오답. 남자가 자동차에 연료를 넣고 있는(is putting fuel into his car) 모습이 아니므로 오답.
(D) 정답. 남자가 자동차 위에 지도를 펼치고 있는(is spreading out a map on top of his car) 모습이므로 정답.

(B) 사진에 없는 명사를 이용한 오답. 사진에 서류(some papers)와 책상(a desk)의 모습이 보이지 않으므로 오답.
(C) 정답. 상자들(Some boxes)이 전등들 밑에 정돈되어 있는 (are arranged under some lamps) 모습이므로 정답.
(D) 사진에 없는 명사를 이용한 오답. 사진에 전선(Some wire)의 모습이 보이지 않으므로 오답.

4

W-Br

(A) They're leaving a restaurant.
(B) They're seated next to each other.
(C) One of the women is looking in her handbag.
(D) One of the women is folding a scarf.

(A) 사람들이 레스토랑에서 나가고 있다.
(B) 사람들이 나란히 앉아 있다.
(C) 여자들 중 한 명이 핸드백 속을 들여다보고 있다.
(D) 여자들 중 한 명이 스카프를 접고 있다.

어휘 fold 접다, 개다

해설 2인 이상 등장 사진 – 사람의 동작/상태 묘사
(A) 동사 오답. 사람들이 레스토랑에서 나가고 있는(are leaving a restaurant) 모습이 아니므로 오답.
(B) 정답. 사람들이 나란히 앉아 있는(are seated next to each other) 모습이므로 정답.
(C) 동사 오답. 여자들 중 한 명이 핸드백 속을 들여다보고 있는(is looking in her handbag) 모습이 아니므로 오답.
(D) 동사 오답. 여자들 중 한 명이 스카프를 접고 있는(is folding a scarf) 모습이 아니므로 오답.

5

▶동영상 강의
W-Am

(A) A selection of luggage is on display.
(B) A lamp and some papers are on a desk.
(C) Some boxes are arranged under some lamps.
(D) Some wire has been rolled up on the floor.

(A) 다양한 여행 가방이 진열되어 있다.
(B) 전등과 서류들이 책상 위에 있다.
(C) 상자들이 전등들 밑에 정돈되어 있다.
(D) 전선이 바닥에 둥글게 말려 있다.

어휘 a selection of 다양한, 선별된   luggage 여행 가방, 수하물
on display 진열된, 전시된   papers 서류   arrange 정돈하다
roll up 둥글게 말다

해설 사물/풍경 사진 – 사물 묘사
(A) 사진에 없는 명사를 이용한 오답. 사진에 여행 가방(luggage)의 모습이 보이지 않으므로 오답.

6

M-Au

(A) A cyclist is riding past a pedestrian.
(B) A tent is set up next to a lake.
(C) Some people are resting on a stone wall.
(D) Some people are swimming in a lake.

(A) 자전거를 탄 사람이 보행자를 지나쳐 달리고 있다.
(B) 텐트가 호수 옆에 설치되어 있다.
(C) 사람들이 돌담 위에서 쉬고 있다.
(D) 사람들이 호수에서 수영하고 있다.

어휘 ride 타다   past ~을 지나쳐   pedestrian 보행자
set up 설치하다, 마련하다   rest 쉬다, 휴식하다

해설 2인 이상 등장 사진 – 사람/사물/풍경 혼합 묘사
(A) 정답. 자전거를 탄 사람(A cyclist)이 보행자를 지나쳐 달리고 있는(is riding past a pedestrian) 모습이므로 정답.
(B) 사진에 없는 명사를 이용한 오답. 사진에 텐트(A tent)의 모습이 보이지 않으므로 오답.
(C) 동사 오답. 돌담 위에서 쉬고 있는(are resting on a stone wall) 사람들의 모습이 보이지 않으므로 오답.
(D) 동사 오답. 호수에서 수영하고 있는(are swimming in a lake) 사람들의 모습이 보이지 않으므로 오답.

PART 2

7
W-Br / M-Cn

Where's the coffeemaker?

(A) On the bottom shelf.
(B) A large serving spoon.
(C) It was discounted.

커피메이커는 어디 있나요?

(A) 맨 아래 선반이에요.
(B) 큰 서빙 스푼이요.
(C) 그건 할인되었어요.

어휘 bottom 맨 아래의, 하단의

해설 커피메이커가 있는 곳을 묻는 Where 의문문
(A) 정답. 커피메이커가 있는 곳을 묻는 질문에 맨 아래 선반이라고 구체적인 위치로 응답하고 있으므로 정답.
(B) 질문과 상관없는 오답.
(C) 질문과 상관없는 오답.

8   M-Cn / M-Au

Why are you calling the clients?

(A) A spreadsheet with their contact information.
(B) Because they canceled their order.
(C) I can walk you there.

고객들에게 왜 전화하시나요?
(A) 그분들의 연락처가 담긴 스프레드시트요.
(B) 그분들이 주문을 취소했기 때문입니다.
(C) 제가 안내해 드릴게요.

어휘   spreadsheet 스프레드시트   contact information 연락처

해설   고객들에게 전화하는 이유를 묻는 Why 의문문
(A) 연상 단어 오답. 질문의 calling에서 연상 가능한 contact를 이용한 오답.
(B) 정답. 고객들에게 전화하는 이유를 묻는 질문에 그 사람들이 주문을 취소해서라고 구체적인 이유를 제시하고 있으므로 정답.
(C) 질문과 상관없는 오답.

9   W-Br / M-Au

Would you like to attend our next company retreat?

(A) I'm parked next to that tree.
(B) Yes, I'd like that.
(C) Just some grilled vegetables.

다음 회사 야유회에 참석하시겠어요?
(A) 저 나무 옆에 주차했어요.
(B) 네, 그러고 싶어요.
(C) 그릴에 구운 채소만요.

어휘   attend 참석하다   retreat 야유회, 짧은 여행

해설   제안/권유의 의문문
(A) 유사 발음 오답. 질문의 retreat와 부분적으로 발음이 유사한 tree를 이용한 오답.
(B) 정답. 다음 회사 야유회에 참석할지 묻는 질문에 네(Yes)라고 대답한 뒤, 그러고 싶다고 긍정 답변과 일관된 내용을 덧붙였으므로 정답.
(C) 연상 단어 오답. 질문의 Would you like를 음식 주문과 관련된 것으로 잘못 이해했을 경우 연상 가능한 grilled vegetables를 이용한 오답.

10   W-Am / W-Br

Who can update the Web site?

(A) I like the new Web site, too.
(B) Kento said he could do it.
(C) That's the right password.

누가 웹사이트를 업데이트할 수 있죠?
(A) 저도 새 웹사이트가 마음에 듭니다.
(B) 켄토가 할 수 있다고 말했어요.
(C) 그게 맞는 비밀번호입니다.

해설   웹사이트를 업데이트할 수 있는 사람을 묻는 Who 의문문
(A) 단어 반복 오답. 질문의 Web site를 반복 이용한 오답.
(B) 정답. 웹사이트를 업데이트할 수 있는 사람을 묻는 질문에 켄토가 할 수 있다고 말했다고 구체적인 사람을 알려 주고 있으므로 정답.
(C) 연상 단어 오답. 질문의 Web site에서 연상 가능한 password를 이용한 오답.

11   M-Au / W-Am

Does your desk face the door or the window?

(A) It faces the door.
(B) About forty minutes.
(C) Because the room is too small.

당신 책상은 문을 향해 있나요, 아니면 창을 향해 있나요?
(A) 문을 향해 있습니다.
(B) 약 40분이요.
(C) 방이 너무 작아서요.

어휘   face 향하다, 마주보다

해설   책상이 향해 있는 방향을 묻는 선택 의문문
(A) 정답. 책상이 문과 창 중 어디를 향해 있는지 묻는 질문에 문을 향해 있다고 둘 중 하나를 선택해 응답하고 있으므로 정답.
(B) 질문과 상관없는 오답. How long 의문문에 대한 응답이므로 오답.
(C) 질문과 상관없는 오답. Why 의문문에 대한 응답이므로 오답.

12   W-Am / M-Au

When will your performance take place?

(A) Next Tuesday.
(B) No, I just checked.
(C) We shopped there yesterday.

당신 공연은 언제 하나요?
(A) 다음 주 화요일이요.
(B) 아니요, 제가 방금 확인했어요.
(C) 저희는 어제 그곳에서 쇼핑했어요.

어휘   take place 열리다, 개최되다

해설   공연 시점을 묻는 When 의문문
(A) 정답. 공연 시점을 묻는 질문에 다음 주 화요일이라고 구체적인 시점으로 응답하고 있으므로 정답.
(B) Yes/No 불가 오답. When 의문문에는 Yes/No 응답이 불가능하므로 오답.
(C) 질문과 상관없는 오답.

13   M-Au / M-Cn

What will you get for completing the program?

(A) How many hours a week?
(B) OK, thanks for asking.
(C) A certificate in accounting.

프로그램을 수료하면 무엇을 받으시나요?
(A) 일주일에 몇 시간이요?
(B) 괜찮아요. 물어봐 주셔서 감사합니다.
(C) 회계 분야의 자격증이요.

어휘 complete 수료하다, 완료하다   certificate 자격증, 증명(서)
accounting 회계

해설 프로그램을 수료하면 받는 것을 묻는 What 의문문
(A) 질문과 상관없는 오답.
(B) Yes/No 불가 오답. What 의문문에는 Yes/No 응답이 불가능한데, OK도 일종의 Yes 응답이라고 볼 수 있으므로 오답.
(C) 정답. 프로그램을 수료하면 받는 것을 묻는 질문에 회계 분야의 자격증이라고 구체적으로 응답하고 있으므로 정답.

14 M-Cn / W-Am

How did the company get its name?
(A) There's a new guest list.
(B) Oh, about three years ago.
(C) It's named after the owner.

회사는 어떻게 그 이름을 갖게 되었나요?
(A) 신규 초대 손님 명단이 있어요.
(B) 아, 약 3년 전에요.
(C) 소유주의 이름을 따서 지었어요.

어휘 be named after ~의 이름을 따서 지어지다

해설 회사 이름을 갖게 된 배경을 묻는 How 의문문
(A) 연상 단어 오답. 질문의 name에서 연상 가능한 guest list를 이용한 오답.
(B) 질문과 상관없는 오답. When 의문문에 대한 응답이므로 오답.
(C) 정답. 회사 이름을 갖게 된 배경을 묻는 질문에 소유주의 이름을 따서 지었다고 구체적으로 설명하고 있으므로 정답.

15 W-Br / M-Au

Your kitchen looks nice painted in this shade of yellow.
(A) Twenty color copies, please.
(B) Dinner will be ready in ten minutes.
(C) Yes, it really brightens up the room.

이 노란 색조로 칠해진 주방이 멋져 보이네요.
(A) 컬러 복사로 20장 부탁합니다.
(B) 저녁 식사가 10분 후에 준비될 겁니다.
(C) 네, 공간을 정말로 화사하게 만들어 줘요.

어휘 look ~하게 보이다, ~한 것 같다   shade 색조
brighten up 화사하게 만들다, 밝혀 주다

해설 의견 전달의 평서문
(A) 연상 단어 오답. 평서문의 yellow에서 연상 가능한 color를 이용한 오답.
(B) 연상 단어 오답. 평서문의 kitchen에서 연상 가능한 Dinner를 이용한 오답.
(C) 정답. 노란 색조로 칠해진 주방이 멋져 보인다는 평서문에 네(Yes)라고 대답한 뒤, 공간을 화사하게 만들어 준다는 장점을 덧붙이고 있으므로 정답.

16 W-Am / W-Br

Are you considering hiring a public relations firm?
(A) I wasn't at that press conference.
(B) No, we decided not to.
(C) It's in the closet.

홍보 전문 업체를 고용하는 것을 고려하고 계신가요?
(A) 저는 그 기자 회견에 없었어요.
(B) 아니요, 그러지 않기로 결정했어요.
(C) 그건 수납장에 있어요.

어휘 consider 고려하다   public relations 홍보 (활동)
firm 업체, 회사   press conference 기자 회견

해설 홍보 전문 업체 고용을 고려하고 있는지 묻는 Be동사 의문문
(A) 연상 단어 오답. 질문의 public relations에서 연상 가능한 press conference를 이용한 오답.
(B) 정답. 홍보 전문 업체 고용을 고려하고 있는지 묻는 질문에 아니요(No)라고 대답한 뒤, 그러지 않기로 결정했다며 부정 답변과 일관된 내용을 덧붙이고 있으므로 정답.
(C) 질문과 상관없는 오답. Where 의문문에 대한 응답이므로 오답.

17 M-Au / M-Cn

Does this hallway lead to the lobby or to the courtyard?
(A) My brother mentioned that.
(B) How much does the box weigh?
(C) To the lobby, I think.

이 복도가 로비로 이어지나요, 아니면 안뜰로 이어지나요?
(A) 제 남동생이 그 얘기 했어요.
(B) 상자 무게가 얼마나 되나요?
(C) 로비인 것 같아요.

어휘 hallway 복도   lead to ~로 이어지다   courtyard 안뜰
mention 언급하다   weigh 무게가 ~이다

해설 복도가 이어지는 곳을 묻는 선택 의문문
(A) 질문과 상관없는 오답.
(B) 유사 발음 오답. 질문의 hallway와 부분적으로 발음이 유사한 weigh를 이용한 오답.
(C) 정답. 복도가 로비와 안뜰 중 어디로 이어지는지 묻는 질문에 로비인 것 같다고 둘 중 하나를 선택해 응답하고 있으므로 정답.

18 M-Cn / W-Br

The company's headquarters is in Houston, right?
(A) This quarter's budget.
(B) Let me look at the directory.
(C) From nine to three.

회사 본사가 휴스턴에 있죠, 그렇죠?
(A) 이번 분기 예산이요.
(B) 안내 책자를 확인해 볼게요.
(C) 9시부터 3시까지요.

어휘 **headquarters** 본사, 본부 **quarter** 분기 **budget** 예산
directory 안내 책자, 주소록

해설 회사 본사가 휴스턴에 있는지 확인하는 부가 의문문
(A) 유사 발음 오답. 질문의 headquarters와 부분적으로 발음이 유사한 quarter를 이용한 오답.
(B) 정답. 회사 본사가 휴스턴에 있는지 확인하는 질문에 안내 책자를 확인해 보겠다고 응답했으므로 정답.
(C) 질문과 상관없는 오답. When 의문문에 대한 응답이므로 오답.

19 W-Br / W-Am

Aren't the windows in the warehouse supposed to be replaced?
(A) Sure, I'll frame the picture.
(B) No, I don't have any.
(C) Mr. Bora ordered them.

창고 창문들을 교체하기로 되어 있지 않나요?
(A) 네, 제가 그 사진을 액자에 넣을게요.
(B) 아니요, 저는 없어요.
(C) 보라 씨가 그것들을 주문했습니다.

어휘 **be supposed to** ~하기로 되어 있다, ~해야 하다
warehouse 창고 **replace** 교체하다 **frame** 액자에 넣다

해설 창고 창문을 교체할 예정인지 확인하는 부정 의문문
(A) 연상 단어 오답. 질문의 windows에서 연상 가능한 frame을 이용한 오답.
(B) 질문과 상관없는 오답.
(C) 정답. 창고 창문을 교체할 예정인지 확인하는 질문에 보라 씨가 그것들을 주문했다며 네(Yes)를 생략한 긍정 답변을 하고 있으므로 정답.

20 W-Br / M-Cn   ▶ 동영상 강의

Who's leading the workshop on Friday?
(A) Nice seeing you, too!
(B) The other team has a ten-point lead.
(C) It'll be Olga.

누가 금요일에 워크숍을 진행하나요?
(A) 저도 만나서 반가웠습니다!
(B) 상대팀이 10점 앞서고 있습니다.
(C) 올가일 거예요.

어휘 **lead** 진행하다, 이끌다; 리드, 우세

해설 금요일 워크숍 진행자를 묻는 Who 의문문
(A) 질문과 상관없는 오답.
(B) 파생어 오답. 질문의 leading과 파생어 관계인 lead를 이용한 오답.
(C) 정답. 금요일 워크숍 진행자를 묻는 질문에 올가일 거라고 구체적인 사람 이름으로 응답하고 있으므로 정답.

21 M-Cn / W-Br

Should we join our department's book club?
(A) An award-winning author.
(B) The office supplies are in the storage room.
(C) They could use a few more people.

우리 부서의 독서 동호회에 가입해야 할까요?
(A) 수상 경력이 있는 작가요.
(B) 사무용품은 창고에 있어요.
(C) 그곳에 사람이 좀 더 필요할 거예요.

어휘 **join** 가입하다, 합류하다 **award-winning** 수상 경력이 있는
supplies 용품, 물품 **storage** 보관, 저장
could use ~가 필요하다, ~가 있으면 좋겠다

해설 독서 동호회에 가입해야 할지 묻는 조동사(Should) 의문문
(A) 연상 단어 오답. 질문의 book에서 연상 가능한 author를 이용한 오답.
(B) 연상 단어 오답. 질문의 department에서 연상 가능한 office를 이용한 오답.
(C) 정답. 독서 동호회에 가입해야 할지 묻는 질문에 사람이 좀 더 필요할 거라는 말로 가입을 권유하고 있으므로 정답.

22 W-Am / M-Au

Shouldn't this package be returned?
(A) Several packets of stamps from the post office.
(B) Yes, it has to go back to the manufacturer.
(C) Didn't she return from her trip last week?

이 소포는 반송되어야 하지 않나요?
(A) 우체국에서 우표 여러 묶음이요.
(B) 네, 제조사로 다시 보내야 해요.
(C) 그녀는 여행에서 지난주에 돌아오지 않았나요?

어휘 **package** 소포, 상자 **return** 반송하다, 돌아오다
packet 묶음, 다발 **manufacturer** 제조사

해설 소포가 반송되어야 하는지 확인하는 부정 의문문
(A) 유사 발음 오답. 질문의 package와 부분적으로 발음이 유사한 packets를 이용한 오답.
(B) 정답. 소포가 반송되어야 하는지 확인하는 질문에 네(Yes)라고 대답한 뒤, 제조사로 다시 보내야 한다고 긍정 답변과 일관된 내용을 덧붙이고 있으므로 정답.
(C) 파생어 오답. 질문의 returned와 파생어 관계인 return을 이용한 오답.

23 W-Br / M-Au

When will the training sessions for the new security measures take place?
(A) Yes, it was a complete success.
(B) The upstairs conference room is large enough.
(C) Not until the start of next month.

새 보안 조치를 위한 교육이 언제 열리나요?
(A) 네, 그건 완벽한 성공이었어요.
(B) 위층에 있는 대회의실은 충분히 넓어요.
(C) 다음 달 초나 되어야 합니다.

어휘 session (특정 활동을 위한) 시간   measures 조치, 수단
complete 완전한   success 성공(작)   upstairs 위층의

해설 새 보안 조치를 위한 교육이 열리는 시기를 묻는 When 의문문
(A) Yes/No 불가 오답. When 의문문에는 Yes/No 응답이 불가능하므로 오답.
(B) 연상 단어 오답. 질문의 training sessions에서 연상 가능한 conference room을 이용한 오답.
(C) 정답. 새 보안 조치를 위한 교육이 열리는 시기를 묻는 질문에 다음 달 초나 되어야 한다고 응답하고 있으므로 정답.

24 M-Cn / W-Am   ▶동영상 강의

Do you want the draft of the proposal e-mailed to you or printed out?
(A) Erina will be the one reviewing it.
(B) They're too expensive.
(C) I can arrange a client dinner.

제안서 초안을 이메일로 받길 원하세요, 아니면 출력된 것을 원하세요?
(A) 에리나가 검토할 사람이에요.
(B) 그것들은 너무 비싸요.
(C) 제가 고객 저녁 식사 자리를 마련할 수 있어요.

어휘 draft 초안   proposal 제안(서)   review 검토하다, 살펴보다
arrange 마련하다, 조치하다

해설 제안서 초안을 받을 방법을 묻는 선택 의문문
(A) 정답. 제안서 초안을 이메일로 받고 싶은지, 아니면 출력된 것을 원하는지 묻는 질문에 에리나가 검토할 사람이라며 질문에 답해 줄 수 있는 다른 사람을 알려 주고 있으므로 정답.
(B) 질문과 상관없는 오답. 질문에 3인칭 복수 대명사 They로 지칭할 사물이 언급된 적이 없으므로 오답.
(C) 질문과 상관없는 오답.

25 W-Am / W-Br

Which day is most convenient for you?
(A) Yes, I'd appreciate it.
(B) Well, the conference begins on Thursday.
(C) Yes, it's under the passenger seat.

어느 요일이 가장 편하신가요?
(A) 네, 감사합니다.
(B) 음, 콘퍼런스가 목요일에 시작해요.
(C) 네, 조수석 밑에 있어요.

어휘 convenient 편리한   appreciate 감사하다
passenger seat (자동차의) 조수석

해설 가장 편한 요일을 묻는 Which 의문문
(A) Yes/No 불가 오답. Which 의문문에는 Yes/No 응답이 불가능하므로 오답.
(B) 정답. 가장 편한 요일을 묻는 질문에 콘퍼런스가 목요일에 시작한다고 기준으로 삼을 수 있는 시점을 알려 주고 있으므로 정답.
(C) Yes/No 불가 오답. Which 의문문에는 Yes/No 응답이 불가능하므로 오답.

26 M-Au / M-Cn

Our department's looking for more interns.
(A) My phone has an extended warranty.
(B) What are the qualifications?
(C) Yes, you completed your project.

우리 부서는 인턴을 더 모집하고 있어요.
(A) 제 전화기는 보증 기간이 연장되었습니다.
(B) 자격 요건이 어떻게 되나요?
(C) 네, 당신은 프로젝트를 완료했습니다.

어휘 look for ~을 구하다, 찾다   extend 연장하다, 확장하다
warranty 품질 보증(서)   qualification 자격 (요건), 자격증

해설 정보 전달의 평서문
(A) 평서문과 상관없는 오답.
(B) 정답. 부서에서 인턴을 더 모집하고 있다는 평서문에 자격 요건이 어떻게 되는지 되물으며, 관련된 정보를 확인하고 있으므로 정답.
(C) 평서문과 상관없는 오답.

27 M-Cn / W-Am

How was your lunch at the park?
(A) I had an unexpected client meeting.
(B) Three sugars, please.
(C) It's on the top shelf.

공원에서의 점심 식사는 어떠셨나요?
(A) 예기치 못한 고객 회의가 있었어요.
(B) 설탕 세 스푼 넣어 주세요.
(C) 그건 맨 위쪽 선반에 있어요.

어휘 unexpected 예기치 못한, 뜻밖의

해설 공원에서의 점심 식사가 어땠는지 묻는 How 의문문
(A) 정답. 공원에서의 점심 식사가 어땠는지 묻는 질문에 예기치 못한 고객 회의가 있었다며 공원에서 식사하지 못했음을 우회적으로 나타내고 있으므로 정답.
(B) 연상 단어 오답. 질문의 lunch에서 연상 가능한 sugars를 이용한 오답.
(C) 질문과 상관없는 오답. Where 의문문에 대한 응답이므로 오답.

28 W-Am / M-Au

Does your company send out the same promotional material every month?
(A) We're going to try something new.
(B) The bank across the street.
(C) Niko just got promoted.

귀사에서는 매달 같은 홍보물을 발송하나요?
(A) 새로운 것을 시도해 보려고 해요.
(B) 길 건너편에 있는 은행이요.
(C) 니코가 막 승진했어요.

어휘 send out 발송하다　promotional 홍보의, 판촉의
material 자료, 재료　promote 승진시키다

해설 매달 같은 홍보물을 발송하는지 묻는 조동사(Does) 의문문
(A) 정답. 매달 같은 홍보물을 발송하는지 묻는 질문에 새로운 것을 시도해 보려고 한다며 지금까지는 같은 홍보물을 보냈으나 변화를 줄 계획이 있음을 우회적으로 나타내고 있으므로 정답.
(B) 질문과 상관없는 오답. Where 의문문에 대한 응답이므로 오답.
(C) 유사 발음 오답. 질문의 promotional과 부분적으로 발음이 유사한 promoted를 이용한 오답.

29 W-Br / M-Cn

Where can I look at floor plans for our new office building?
(A) Yes, I'd like some coffee.
(B) A few more résumés.
(C) I can ask the architect.

어디서 저희 새 사무실 건물의 평면도를 볼 수 있나요?
(A) 네, 커피로 할게요.
(B) 이력서 몇 장 더요.
(C) 건축가에게 물어볼게요.

어휘 floor plan 평면도, 도면　résumé 이력서　architect 건축가

해설 새 사무실 건물의 평면도를 볼 수 있는 곳을 묻는 Where 의문문
(A) Yes/No 불가 오답. Where 의문문에는 Yes/No 응답이 불가능하므로 오답.
(B) 질문과 상관없는 오답.
(C) 정답. 새 사무실 건물의 평면도를 볼 수 있는 곳을 묻는 질문에 건축가에게 물어보겠다며 자신도 알지 못함을 우회적으로 나타내고 있으므로 정답.

30 M-Cn / W-Br　▶동영상 강의

Can I use the company car to pick up the clients from the airport?
(A) Shenchao is the best project manager I know.
(B) No, thanks—I've already been there.
(C) The keys are on the desk over there.

공항에서 고객들을 모시고 오기 위해 회사 차를 써도 될까요?
(A) 센차오가 제가 아는 최고의 프로젝트 관리자입니다.
(B) 아니요, 괜찮습니다. 저는 이미 그곳에 가 봤어요.
(C) 열쇠는 저기 책상 위에 있어요.

어휘 pick up 데려오다, 가져오다

해설 부탁/요청의 의문문
(A) 질문과 상관없는 오답.
(B) 질문과 상관없는 오답. 제안 의문문에 대한 응답이므로 오답.
(C) 정답. 공항에서 고객들을 데려오기 위해 회사 차를 써도 되는지 묻는 질문에 열쇠는 책상 위에 있다며 우회적으로 수락의 의미를 나타내고 있으므로 정답.

31 M-Au / W-Am

How often should our heating system be inspected?
(A) Approximately $400.
(B) Because I have a meeting at that time.
(C) The recommendation is in the manual.

우리 난방 시스템은 얼마나 자주 점검되어야 하나요?
(A) 약 400달러요.
(B) 제가 그 시간에 회의가 있어서요.
(C) 권장 사항이 설명서에 나와 있어요.

어휘 inspect 점검하다, 검사하다　approximately 약, 대략
recommendation 권장, 추천　manual (사용) 설명서, 안내서

해설 난방 시스템 점검 빈도를 묻는 How often 의문문
(A) 질문과 상관없는 오답. How much 의문문에 대한 응답이므로 오답.
(B) 질문과 상관없는 오답. Why 의문문에 대한 응답이므로 오답.
(C) 정답. 난방 시스템 점검 빈도를 묻는 질문에 권장 사항이 설명서에 나와 있다며 알 수 있는 방법을 제시하고 있으므로 정답.

PART 3

32-34 M-Cn / W-Am

M Hi, **32 Chef Ayaka.** I was looking over this week's sales, and I noticed that a lot of people ordered the beef stew special.

W Yeah. It's been very popular with patrons. In fact, I want to add it to the regular menu.

M Good idea. **33 Beef prices change frequently,** though, so we might need to consider that when we set the price for the dish if we're going to offer it daily.

W OK. **34 I'll call our supplier too.** We need to make sure they can get us enough beef each week.

남 안녕하세요, **아야카 셰프님.** 이번 주 판매량을 살펴보다가, 많은 분들이 비프 스튜 특선 요리를 주문하신 것을 알게 됐어요.

여 네. 손님들에게 아주 인기가 많아요. 사실, 그걸 일반 메뉴에 추가하고 싶어요.

남 좋은 생각이에요. 하지만 **소고기 가격이 자주 바뀌기 때문에,** 그 요리를 매일 제공하려 한다면 가격을 정할 때 그 부분을 고려해야 할 거예요.

여 알겠습니다. **제가 공급업체에도 전화할게요.** 그들이 매주 충분한 양의 소고기를 공급해 줄 수 있어야 합니다.

> 어휘 look over ~을 살펴보다, ~을 검토하다 notice 알게 되다 popular 인기 있는 patron 손님 add 추가하다, 더하다 regular 보통의 frequently 자주, 빈번히 consider 고려하다 set 정하다 supplier 공급업체, 공급자

32 Where do the speakers most likely work?
(A) At a shipping company
(B) At a restaurant
(C) At a gift shop
(D) At a farm

화자들은 어디에서 일하는 것 같은가?
(A) 배송 회사
(B) 레스토랑
(C) 선물 매장
(D) 농장

해설 전체 내용 관련 – 화자들의 근무 장소
남자가 첫 대사에서 여자를 셰프라고 부르고 있고, 많은 사람들이 비프 스튜 특선 요리를 주문한 것(Chef Ayaka. ~ I noticed that a lot of people ordered the beef stew special)과 관련해 이야기하고 있으므로 정답은 (B)이다.

33 What does the man suggest considering?
(A) An advertising strategy
(B) An online menu
(C) The price of an item
(D) The results of a survey

남자는 무엇을 고려하라고 제안하는가?
(A) 광고 전략
(B) 온라인 메뉴
(C) 제품 가격
(D) 설문 조사 결과

어휘 advertising 광고 (활동) strategy 전략 result 결과(물) survey 설문 조사(지)

해설 세부 사항 관련 – 남자가 제안하는 고려 사항
남자가 두 번째 대사에서 소고기 가격이 자주 바뀌기 때문에, 가격을 정할 때 그 부분을 고려해야 할 것(Beef prices change frequently, though, so we might need to consider that when we set the price for the dish ~)이라고 했으므로 정답은 (C)이다.

Paraphrasing
대화의 Beef prices → 정답의 The price of an item

34 What does the woman say she will do?
(A) Pay a deposit
(B) Contact a supplier
(C) Reschedule a delivery
(D) Arrange some merchandise

여자는 무엇을 할 것이라고 말하는가?
(A) 선금 지불하기
(B) 공급업체에 연락하기
(C) 배송 일정 재조정하기
(D) 상품 정리하기

어휘 deposit 선금, 보증금 contact 연락하다 reschedule 일정을 재조정하다 arrange 정리하다, 마련하다 merchandise 상품

해설 세부 사항 관련 – 여자가 할 일
여자가 마지막 대사에서 자신이 공급업체에 전화할 것(I'll call our supplier too)이라고 했으므로 정답은 (B)이다.

Paraphrasing
대화의 call → 정답의 Contact

35-37 3인 대화 M-Au / W-Br / M-Cn

M1 Excuse me, **35 does train 1401 stop at the Lexington Street station?**
W Yes. It's a twenty-minute ride.
M2 Oh good, that gives us plenty of time to get to the party.
W **35 The train leaves from platform twelve in three minutes.**
M2 Let's head over there now, Sergey. **36 I'm really looking forward to our company gala event tonight.**
M1 Me too. **37 Hey did you happen to bring an umbrella? I forgot mine.** It might rain on our walk from the station.
M2 I did! We can share it.

남1 실례합니다. 1401번 열차가 렉싱턴 가 역에 정차하나요?
여 네. 20분 정도 걸립니다.
남2 아, 잘됐네요. 그럼 파티에 가는 시간이 넉넉하네요.
여 그 열차는 3분 후에 12번 승강장에서 출발합니다.
남2 지금 그쪽으로 갑시다, 세르게이. 오늘 밤 우리 회사 축하 행사가 정말 기대돼요.
남1 저도요. 저기, 혹시 우산 가져왔어요? 저는 깜빡했네요. 역에서 걸어가는 동안 비가 올지도 몰라요.
남2 가져왔어요! 같이 써요.

어휘 ride 타고 가기 plenty of 많은 head over 향하다 look forward to ~을 고대하다 gala 축하 행사, 기념 행사 forget 잊다 share 함께 사용하다, 공유하다

35 Where is the conversation most likely taking place?
(A) At a fitness center
(B) At a hotel
(C) At a train station
(D) At a corporate office

대화는 어디에서 이루어지는 것 같은가?
(A) 피트니스 센터
(B) 호텔
(C) 기차역
(D) 기업 사무실

해설 전체 내용 관련 – 대화 장소
첫 번째 남자가 첫 대사에서 1401번 열차가 렉싱턴 가 역에 정차하는지(~ does train 1401 stop at the Lexington Street station?) 물은 것과 여자가 두 번째 대사에서 열차가 3분 후에 12번 승강장에서 출발한다(The train leaves from platform twelve in three minutes)고 말한 것을 통해 기차역에서 대화 중임을 짐작할 수 있다. 따라서 정답은 (C)이다.

36 What type of event will the men attend this evening?
(A) A company gala
(B) An opera
(C) A sports match
(D) A lecture

남자들은 오늘 저녁에 어떤 종류의 행사에 참석할 것인가?
(A) 회사 축하 행사
(B) 오페라
(C) 스포츠 경기
(D) 강연

어휘 attend 참석하다

해설 세부 사항 관련 – 남자들이 오늘 저녁에 참석하는 행사
두 번째 남자가 두 번째 대사에서 오늘 밤 회사 축하 행사가 정말 기대된다(I'm really looking forward to our company gala event tonight)고 했으므로 정답은 (A)이다.

Paraphrasing
대화의 tonight → 질문의 this evening

37 What did Sergey forget to bring?
(A) Gloves
(B) Sunglasses
(C) A hat
(D) An umbrella

세르게이는 무엇을 가져오는 것을 잊었는가?
(A) 장갑
(B) 선글라스
(C) 모자
(D) 우산

해설 세부 사항 관련 – 세르게이가 잊은 것
두 번째 남자가 첫 번째 남자를 세르게이라고 불렀고, 첫 번째 남자가 두 번째 대사에서 우산을 가져왔는지 물으며, 자신은 깜빡했다(Hey did you happen to bring an umbrella? I forgot mine)고 했으므로 정답은 (D)이다.

38-40 W-Am / M-Cn

W **38** I talked to Mr. Hoffman this morning, and he said he's decided to start a delivery service for our customers who have a difficult time picking up their prescriptions.

M That's a good idea. **39** I know a lot of people find it inconvenient to come in person to get their medications. But many of our customers buy other things while they're here.

W Oh, they'll be able to make other purchases too, to be delivered with their medicine. In fact, **40** I'm supposed to draft a job posting for delivery drivers. Could you help me do that?

여 오늘 오전에 호프먼 씨와 이야기했는데, 처방 약을 가져가기 힘든 고객들을 위해 배송 서비스를 시작하기로 하셨대요.

남 좋은 생각입니다. 많은 사람들이 약을 받기 위해 직접 오는 걸 불편하게 생각한다는 것을 알고 있어요. 하지만 우리 고객 중 많은 분들께서 이곳에 오시면 다른 것들도 구매하시잖아요.

여 아, 다른 것들도 구매해서 약과 함께 배송받을 수 있을 겁니다. 사실, 제가 배송 기사를 찾는 구인 공고 초안을 작성해야 해요. 그 일을 도와주실 수 있으신가요?

어휘 have a difficult time -ing ~하는 데 어려움을 겪다
pick up 가져가다, 가져오다 prescription 처방(약), 처방전
inconvenient 불편한 in person 직접 medication 약(품)
in fact 사실 be supposed to ~해야 하다, ~하기로 되어 있다
draft 초안을 작성하다 job posting 구인 공고

38 What has Mr. Hoffman decided to do?
(A) Extend store hours
(B) Start a delivery service
(C) Offer a rewards program
(D) Stop selling certain products

호프먼 씨는 무엇을 하기로 결정했는가?
(A) 매장 운영 시간 연장하기
(B) 배송 서비스 시작하기
(C) 고객 보상 프로그램 제공하기
(D) 특정 제품 판매 중단하기

어휘 reward 보상 certain 특정한, 일정한

해설 세부 사항 관련 – 호프먼 씨가 결정한 일
여자가 첫 대사에서 호프먼 씨가 배송 서비스를 시작하기로 했다(~ he said he's decided to start a delivery service for our customers ~)고 했으므로 정답은 (B)이다.

39 What business do the speakers most likely work for?
(A) A bakery
(B) A flower shop
(C) A grocery store
(D) A pharmacy

화자들은 어떤 업체에서 일하는 것 같은가?
(A) 제과점
(B) 꽃집
(C) 식료품점
(D) 약국

해설 전체 내용 관련 – 화자들의 근무 장소
남자가 첫 대사에서 많은 사람들이 약을 받기 위해 직접 오는 걸 불편하게 생각한다는 것을 알고 있다(I know a lot of people find it inconvenient to come in person to get their medications)고 했으므로 정답은 (D)이다.

40 What does the woman ask the man to help her do?
(A) Mail some packages
(B) Take inventory
(C) Create a job posting
(D) Help some customers

여자는 남자에게 무엇을 하는 것을 도와달라고 요청하는가?
(A) 우편으로 소포 보내기
(B) 재고 조사하기
(C) 구인 공고 만들기
(D) 고객 돕기

어휘 inventory 재고 조사, 재고 (목록)

해설 세부 사항 관련 – 여자가 도움을 요청하는 일
여자가 마지막 대사에서 배송 기사를 찾는 구인 공고 초안을 작성해야 한다며 그 일을 도와줄 수 있는지(~ I'm supposed to draft a job posting for delivery drivers. Could you help me do that?) 묻고 있으므로 정답은 (C)이다.

Paraphrasing
대화의 draft → 정답의 Create

41-43 W-Am / M-Au

W Marcel, I don't know if you reviewed the latest report. **41 Unfortunately, our sales are continuing to drop.**
M Yes, competition is at an all-time high. More and more companies are selling clothing and gear for outdoor recreation.
W We need better ways to make our brand stand out.
M Well, **42 we could probably benefit from having more direct input from athletes who use our gear.** I was thinking maybe we could hire a professional rock climber to consult with our designers.
W That's an interesting idea. Is there anyone you have in mind?
M **43 I'll e-mail you a list this afternoon.**

여 마르셀, 최신 보고서를 살펴보셨는지 모르겠네요. **안타깝게도, 우리 매출이 계속 하락하고 있어요.**
남 네, 경쟁이 사상 최고 수준이에요. 점점 더 많은 회사들이 야외 여가 활동을 위한 의류와 장비를 판매하고 있어요.
여 우리 브랜드를 돋보이게 만들 더 좋은 방안들이 필요해요.
남 음, **어쩌면 우리 장비를 이용하는 운동선수들에게 좀 더 직접적인 의견을 받으면 도움이 될 수 있을 거예요.** 전문 암벽 등반 선수를 고용해 우리 디자이너들과 상의하면 어떨까 하는 생각을 했었어요.
여 흥미로운 아이디어군요. 생각해 두신 분이 있나요?
남 **오늘 오후에 명단을 이메일로 보내 드릴게요.**

어휘 unfortunately 안타깝게도 drop 하락하다, 감소하다 competition 경쟁, 경연 at an all-time high 사상 최고 수준인 gear 장비, 복장 outdoor recreation 야외 여가 활동 stand out 돋보이다 benefit from ~로부터 혜택을 보다 input 의견 athlete 운동선수 consult 상의하다

41 What problem does the woman mention?
(A) A product is faulty.
(B) A company's sales are decreasing.
(C) Some materials are damaged.
(D) A sales department is understaffed.

여자는 어떤 문제를 언급하는가?
(A) 제품에 결함이 있다.
(B) 회사 매출이 감소하고 있다.
(C) 일부 재료가 손상되었다.
(D) 영업부에 직원이 부족하다.

어휘 faulty 결함이 있는 decrease 감소하다 damaged 손상된 understaffed 직원이 부족한

해설 전체 내용 관련 – 여자가 언급하는 문제
여자가 첫 대사에서 안타깝게도 회사 매출이 계속 하락하고 있다(Unfortunately, our sales are continuing to drop)고 했으므로 정답은 (B)이다.

Paraphrasing
대화의 are continuing to drop → 정답의 are decreasing

42 Where do the speakers most likely work?
(A) At a publishing firm
(B) At a sporting goods company
(C) At a travel agency
(D) At a state park

화자들은 어디에서 일하는 것 같은가?
(A) 출판사
(B) 스포츠 용품 회사
(C) 여행사
(D) 주립 공원

해설 전체 내용 관련 – 화자들의 근무 장소
남자가 두 번째 대사에서 회사의 장비를 이용하는 운동선수들에게 좀 더 직접적인 의견을 받으면 도움이 될 수 있을 것(we could probably benefit from having more direct input from athletes who use our gear)이라고 한 것에서 스포츠 용품 회사의 직원들임을 알 수 있으므로 정답은 (B)이다.

43 What does the man say he will do this afternoon?
(A) Sign a document
(B) Ship an order
(C) Review customer feedback
(D) Send a list

남자는 오늘 오후에 무엇을 할 것이라고 말하는가?
(A) 서류에 서명하기
(B) 주문품 배송하기
(C) 고객 의견 검토하기
(D) 명단 보내기

해설 세부 사항 관련 – 남자가 오늘 오후에 할 일
남자가 마지막 대사에서 오늘 오후에 명단을 이메일로 보내겠다(I'll e-mail you a list this afternoon)고 했으므로 정답은 (D)이다.

Paraphrasing
대화의 e-mail → 정답의 Send

44-46 W-Br / M-Cn

W Hello. **44 I was featured in an article in your newspaper about five years ago. And now when I click on the link, nothing happens.**

M Oh, the public links expire after three years, but **45 I can search for your article in our database.** I just need keywords from the article to use in the search.

W It was about my internship at a dental office.

M OK. Let me check our archives.

W Thanks. I was still in college when the article came out, but **46 now I'm starting my own practice. And I'd like to hang the article on the wall.**

M Oh! Congratulations.

여 안녕하세요. 제가 약 5년 전에 귀사의 신문 기사에 특집으로 실렸습니다. 그리고 지금 그 링크를 클릭하면, 아무것도 나오지 않습니다.
남 아, 공개 링크는 3년이 지나면 만료되지만, **저희 데이터베이스에서 그 기사를 검색해 드릴 수 있습니다.** 검색에 사용할 기사의 키워드만 있으면 됩니다.
여 치과에서의 인턴십에 관한 것이었어요.
남 알겠습니다. 저희 기록을 확인해 보겠습니다.
여 감사합니다. 제가 아직 대학교에 다니고 있을 때 그 기사가 나왔는데, **이제 제 개인 병원을 열어요. 그래서 그 기사를 벽에 걸어 놓고 싶어요.**
남 아! 축하드립니다.

어휘 feature 특집으로 싣다, 특징으로 하다 public 공개적인 expire 만료되다, 끝나다 search for ~을 검색하다, ~을 찾다 dental 치과의, 치아의 archive 기록 보관소 practice 병원 hang 걸다, 매달다

44 Why is the woman calling?
(A) To verify some facts
(B) To confirm a deadline
(C) To inquire about an article
(D) To apply for a position

여자는 왜 전화하는가?
(A) 사실을 확인하기 위해
(B) 마감 기한을 확인하기 위해
(C) 기사에 관해 문의하기 위해
(D) 일자리에 지원하기 위해

어휘 verify 확인하다 fact 사실 confirm 확인하다, 확정하다 deadline 마감 기한 inquire about ~에 관해 문의하다 apply for ~에 지원하다, ~을 신청하다 position 일자리, 직책

해설 전체 내용 관련 – 여자가 전화하는 목적
여자가 첫 대사에서 약 5년 전에 자신이 신문 기사에 특집으로 실렸는데, 지금은 그 링크를 클릭하면 아무것도 나오지 않는다(I was featured in an article in your newspaper about five years ago. And now when I click on the link, nothing happens)고 했으므로 정답은 (C)이다.

45 What does the man offer to do?
(A) Search a database
(B) Renew a subscription
(C) Consult with colleagues
(D) Send an updated schedule

남자는 무엇을 하겠다고 제안하는가?
(A) 데이터베이스 검색하기
(B) 구독 갱신하기
(C) 동료들과 상의하기
(D) 업데이트된 일정표 보내기

어휘 renew 갱신하다 subscription 구독, 가입 colleague 동료

해설 세부 사항 관련 – 남자의 제안 사항
남자가 첫 대사에서 자사의 데이터베이스에서 여자가 말한 기사를 검색해 줄 수 있다(~ I can search for your article in our database)고 했으므로 정답은 (A)이다.

---

46 Why does the man congratulate the woman?
(A) She appeared on television.
(B) She was nominated for an award.
(C) She is publishing a book.
(D) She is starting her own business.

남자는 왜 여자를 축하하는가?
(A) 텔레비전에 출연했다.
(B) 상의 후보로 지명되었다.
(C) 책을 출간한다.
(D) 개인 업체를 시작한다.

어휘 appear 출연하다, 나타나다 nominate 후보로 지명하다

해설 세부 사항 관련 – 남자가 여자를 축하하는 이유
여자가 세 번째 대사에서 개인 병원을 열기 때문에 기사를 벽에 걸어 놓고 싶다(~ now I'm starting my own practice. And I'd like to hang the article on the wall)고 설명하자, 남자가 축하 인사를 건네고 있으므로 정답은 (D)이다.

Paraphrasing
대화의 my own practice → 정답의 her own business

47-49 W-Am / M-Cn   ▶ 동영상 강의

W Welcome to Scott's Supplies! Just so you know, **⁴⁷all our power tools and ladders are twenty percent off today.** Is there something I can help you with?

M Yes. I came in last week to get some lumber for a home project I was working on, but **⁴⁸the boards I purchased are the wrong width.** I was wondering if I could get a refund.

W Sure. **⁴⁹Do you have the receipt?**

M **⁴⁹No, unfortunately. I must've lost it.**

W Hmm, OK. Let me find the manager.

여 스캇츠 서플라이즈에 오신 것을 환영합니다! 참고로 말씀드리자면, **모든 전동 공구와 사다리가 오늘 20퍼센트 할인됩니다.** 제가 도와드릴 게 있나요?

남 네. 지난주에 와서 제가 작업하고 있던 주택 프로젝트에 필요한 목재를 샀는데, **구입한 판자가 너비가 맞지 않아요.** 환불을 받을 수 있는지 궁금했습니다.

여 물론입니다. **영수증을 갖고 계신가요?**

남 **안타깝게도 없어요. 잃어버린 것 같아요.**

여 흠, 알겠습니다. 제가 점장님을 찾아보겠습니다.

어휘 power tool 전동 공구 ladder 사다리 lumber 목재 width 너비, 폭 refund 환불(액) receipt 영수(증)

---

47 Where does the conversation most likely take place?
(A) At a furniture store
(B) At an electronics store
(C) At a sporting goods store
(D) At a building supply store

대화는 어디에서 진행되고 있을 것 같은가?
(A) 가구 매장
(B) 전자 제품 매장
(C) 스포츠용품 매장
(D) 건축용품 매장

어휘 goods 상품 supply 용품, 공급(품)

해설 전체 내용 관련 – 대화 장소
여자가 첫 대사에서 모든 전동 공구와 사다리가 오늘 20퍼센트 할인된다(~ all our power tools and ladders are twenty percent off today)고 했으므로 정답은 (D)이다.

Paraphrasing
대화의 power tools and ladders → 정답의 building supply

---

48 Why does the man want a refund?
(A) He found a less expensive option.
(B) He bought the wrong size.
(C) He does not like the color of an item.
(D) He noticed an item is damaged.

남자는 왜 환불을 원하는가?
(A) 더 저렴한 옵션을 발견했다.
(B) 맞지 않는 사이즈를 구입했다.
(C) 제품 색상이 마음에 들지 않는다.
(D) 제품이 손상된 것을 발견했다.

해설 세부 사항 관련 – 남자가 환불을 원하는 이유
남자가 첫 대사에서 구입한 판자가 너비가 맞지 않는다(~ the boards I purchased are the wrong width)고 했으므로 정답은 (B)이다.

Paraphrasing
대화의 the boards I purchased are the wrong width → 정답의 bought the wrong size

49 What does the woman imply when she says, "Let me find the manager"?
(A) She needs to attend to other customers.
(B) She does not have the authority to complete a request.
(C) A transaction was not processed correctly.
(D) A quality complaint needs to be documented.

여자가 "제가 점장님을 찾아보겠습니다"라고 말할 때 무엇을 의미하는가?
(A) 다른 고객들을 챙겨야 한다.
(B) 요청을 완료할 권한이 없다.
(C) 거래가 제대로 처리되지 않았다.
(D) 품질 관련 불만 사항이 문서화되어야 한다.

어휘 attend to ~을 챙기다, ~을 처리하다 authority 권한, 권위(자) transaction 거래 process 처리하다 correctly 제대로 complaint 불만 document 문서화하다

해설 화자의 의도 파악 – 점장님을 찾아보겠다는 말의 의도
여자가 두 번째 대사에서 영수증을 갖고 있는지(Do you have the receipt?) 묻는 것에 대해 남자가 그렇지 않다는 말과 함께 잃어버렸다(No, unfortunately. I must've lost it)고 대답하자, 여자가 인용문을 언급하고 있다. 이는 여자는 권한이 없으므로 권한이 있는 점장을 찾아보겠다는 뜻이므로 정답은 (B)이다.

50-52 W-Br / M-Au

W Welcome back! **⁵⁰How were your lunch deliveries?**

M All right, except one bag broke and the food container fell out right as I was walking up to a customer's door. The container was still sealed, and the customer accepted it, so it turned out OK in the end.

W Well, I'm glad everything worked out. By the way, take a look at my screen! **⁵¹I got the new delivery software installed and running while you were gone.**

M This looks great! I like how different areas can be grouped together so drivers can deliver more efficiently.

W Me too. **⁵²And since we've recently had such a significant increase in customers**, this will be really useful.

여 돌아온 것을 환영합니다! **점심 식사 배달은 어떠셨나요?**
남 괜찮았습니다. 봉투 하나가 찢어져서, 제가 고객의 집 앞으로 걸어 올라가고 있던 딱 그때 음식 용기가 떨어진 것만 빼면요. 용기가 그대로 밀봉되어 있었고, 고객께서 그것을 받아 주셔서 결과적으로는 괜찮았어요.
여 음, 모든 게 잘돼서 다행이네요. 그건 그렇고, 제 화면을 한번 보세요! **자리를 비우신 동안 새로운 배달 소프트웨어를 설치해 작동시키고 있어요.**
남 이거 굉장해 보이네요! 기사들이 더 효율적으로 배달할 수 있도록 여러 구역들을 함께 묶을 수 있다는 점이 마음에 듭니다.
여 저도요. **그리고 최근에 고객이 많이 증가해서**, 이게 정말 유용할 거예요.

어휘 break 망가지다, 고장 나다 container 용기, 그릇 seal 밀봉하다, 봉하다 accept 받아들이다, 수용하다 turn out ~한 것으로 드러나다, ~한 것으로 판명되다 work out 잘되다, 잘 해결되다 install 설치하다 run 작동하다 group (그룹으로) 묶다, 분류하다 efficiently 효율적으로 significant 많은, 상당한 increase 증가; 증가하다, 증가시키다 useful 유용한

50 What most likely is the man's job?
(A) Plumber
(B) Auto mechanic
(C) Food delivery person
(D) Computer technician

남자의 직업은 무엇인 것 같은가?
(A) 배관공
(B) 자동차 정비사
(C) 음식 배달원
(D) 컴퓨터 기술자

해설 전체 내용 관련 – 남자의 직업
여자가 첫 대사에서 남자에게 점심 식사 배달이 어땠는지(How were your lunch deliveries?) 묻고 있으므로 정답은 (C)이다.

51 What did the woman do while the man was gone?
(A) She created an advertisement.
(B) She finalized a contract.
(C) She addressed a customer complaint.
(D) She had new software installed.

남자가 자리를 비운 동안 여자는 무엇을 했는가?
(A) 광고를 만들었다.
(B) 계약을 마무리했다.
(C) 고객 불만을 처리했다.
(D) 새로운 소프트웨어를 설치했다.

어휘 create 만들다 advertisement 광고 finalize 마무리하다 contract 계약(서) address 처리하다, 다루다

해설 세부 사항 관련 – 남자가 자리를 비운 동안 여자가 한 일
여자가 두 번째 대사에서 남자가 자리를 비운 동안 새로운 배달 소프트웨어를 설치해 작동시키고 있다(I got the new delivery software installed and running while you were gone)고 했으므로 정답은 (D)이다.

Paraphrasing
대화의 got the new delivery software installed
→ 정답의 had new software installed

52 What does the woman say has recently changed?
(A) Costs have been reduced.
(B) A competitor has opened a location nearby.
(C) The number of customers has increased.
(D) Safety regulations have been introduced.

여자는 최근에 무엇이 바뀌었다고 말하는가?
(A) 비용이 감소되었다.
(B) 경쟁사가 근처에 지점을 열었다.
(C) 고객 수가 증가했다.
(D) 안전 규정이 도입되었다.

어휘 reduce 감소시키다   competitor 경쟁사, 경쟁자   location 지점, 위치   nearby 근처에   regulation 규제, 규정   introduce 도입하다, 소개하다

해설 세부 사항 관련 – 여자가 최근에 바뀌었다고 말하는 것
여자가 마지막 대사에서 최근에 고객이 많이 증가했다(And since we've recently had such a significant increase in customers ~)고 했으므로 정답은 (C)이다.

Paraphrasing
대화의 had such a significant increase in customers
→ 정답의 The number of customers has increased

53-55 M-Cn / W-Br

M Hi, Jin-Ah. I've got good news. ⁵³**We signed a contract to create an ad campaign for a new client.**

W That's great! Who is it?

M ⁵⁴**It's HMD Incorporated, an organic snack company. They just developed a new line of snacks made entirely from vegetables.** They want to market the snacks to sports teams as well as individuals.

W Well, that sounds exciting but hard to understand. I guess we'll need to learn more about the products first.

M Exactly. We'll have the client come in to give us nutritional information, and provide us with some samples. ⁵⁵**I'll schedule a meeting with them soon.**

남 안녕하세요, 진아. 좋은 소식이 있어요. **새로운 고객과 광고 제작 계약을 체결했어요.**

여 잘됐네요! 그게 누구죠?

남 **HMD 주식회사인데, 유기농 스낵 회사입니다. 그곳에서 완전히 채소로만 만들어진 스낵 신제품을 막 개발했어요.** 개인뿐 아니라 스포츠 팀들에게도 이 스낵을 마케팅하고 싶어 해요.

여 음, 흥미롭게 들리지만 이해하기 어렵네요. 먼저 그 제품에 관해 더 많이 알아야 할 것 같아요.

남 맞아요. 고객이 방문하여 영양 정보를 전달하고 샘플을 제공하도록 할 것입니다. **제가 곧 회의 일정을 잡을 것입니다.**

어휘 sign a contract 계약을 맺다   ad campaign 광고 캠페인   organic 유기농의   develop 개발하다   entirely 완전히   market 마케팅하다, 시장에 내놓다   individual 사람, 개인   nutritional 영양의

53 What type of company do the speakers work for?
(A) An investment firm
(B) An advertising agency
(C) A staffing service
(D) A construction company

화자들은 어떤 종류의 회사에서 일하는가?
(A) 투자 회사
(B) 광고 대행사
(C) 인력 모집 서비스 업체
(D) 건설 회사

어휘 investment 투자   firm 회사, 업체   staffing 인력 모집

해설 전체 내용 관련 – 화자들의 근무 회사
남자가 첫 대사에서 새로운 고객과 광고 제작 계약을 체결했다(We signed a contract to create an ad campaign for a new client)고 했으므로 정답은 (B)이다.

54 What has HMD Incorporated recently done?
(A) It has built a new headquarters.
(B) It has donated to a charity.
(C) It has developed a new line of products.
(D) It has won an industry award.

HMD 주식회사는 최근에 무엇을 했는가?
(A) 새로운 본사를 지었다.
(B) 자선 단체에 기부했다.
(C) 신제품 라인을 개발했다.
(D) 업계 상을 받았다.

어휘 donate 기부하다   charity 자선 (단체)   win an award 상을 받다

해설 세부 사항 관련 – HMD 주식회사가 최근에 한 일
남자가 두 번째 대사에서 HMD 주식회사가 유기농 스낵 회사라는 말과 함께 완전히 채소로만 만들어진 스낵 신제품을 막 개발했다(It's HMD Incorporated, an organic snack company. They just developed a new line of snacks made entirely from vegetables)고 했으므로 정답은 (C)이다.

Paraphrasing
대화의 just → 질문의 recently
대화의 snacks → 정답의 products

55 What does the man say he will do?
(A) Update his team's goals
(B) Conduct some research
(C) Apply for a permit
(D) Arrange for a meeting

남자는 무엇을 할 것이라고 말하는가?
(A) 팀의 목표 업데이트하기
(B) 조사 실시하기
(C) 허가증 신청하기
(D) 회의 잡기

어휘 conduct 실시하다   arrange for ~을 주선하다, ~을 준비하다

해설 세부 사항 관련 – 남자가 할 일
남자가 마지막 대사에서 곧 회의 일정을 잡을 것(I'll schedule a meeting with them soon)이라고 했으므로 정답은 (D)이다.

Paraphrasing
대화의 schedule a meeting → 정답의 Arrange for a meeting

56-58 3인 대화 W-Am / M-Au / W-Br

> **W1** ⁵⁶**Oliver, have you finished the maintenance check on the small airplane that came in this morning?** The owner's hoping to fly it this weekend.
>
> **M** ⁵⁶**I finished checking it earlier this morning.** It needs a new fuel injection pump, so I've asked Camille to order one. Oh, here she comes. ⁵⁷**Camille, will the new pump arrive today?**
>
> **W2** ⁵⁷**Unfortunately, no. The manufacturer said there'll be a delay**, and it won't arrive until Monday.
>
> **W1** I better let the customer know. ⁵⁸**She was planning to fly the plane to Toronto this weekend for a friend's wedding.** She'll need to find another way to get there.

여1 올리버, 오늘 오전에 들어온 소형 비행기의 관리 점검을 마치셨나요? 주인이 이번 주말에 비행기를 원해요.
남 오늘 아침 일찍 점검을 마쳤어요. 새 연료 주입 펌프가 필요해서, 카밀에게 하나 주문해 달라고 요청했어요. 아, 여기 오네요. 카밀, 새 펌프가 오늘 도착할까요?
여2 유감스럽지만, 아니요. 제조사에서 지연될 거라고 했어요. 월요일에나 도착할 거예요.
여1 고객님께 알려 드리는 게 좋겠군요. 이번 주말에 친구 결혼식에 참석하기 위해 그 비행기를 타고 토론토에 가실 계획이셨거든요. 그곳에 갈 다른 방법을 찾으셔야 하겠네요.

어휘 maintenance 유지 관리, 시설 관리   owner 소유주, 주인   injection 주입   delay 지연, 지체; 지연시키다

---

56 What did the man perform a maintenance check on?
(A) A motorcycle
(B) A car
(C) A bus
(D) An airplane

남자는 무엇의 관리 점검을 했는가?
(A) 오토바이
(B) 자동차
(C) 버스
(D) 비행기

해설 전체 내용 관련 – 남자가 점검한 것
첫 번째 여자가 첫 대사에서 남자의 이름을 부르면서 소형 비행기의 관리 점검을 마쳤는지(Oliver, have you finished the maintenance check on the small airplane ~?) 물었고, 남자가 점검을 마쳤다(I finished checking it ~)고 했으므로 정답은 (D)이다.

---

57 What news does Camille share?
(A) A delivery will be delayed.
(B) An expense will increase.
(C) A staff member is unavailable.
(D) A rainstorm is predicted.

카밀은 어떤 소식을 공유하는가?
(A) 배송이 지연될 것이다.
(B) 비용이 증가할 것이다.
(C) 직원이 부재중이다.
(D) 폭풍우가 예상된다.

어휘 expense 비용, 경비   unavailable 부재중인, 이용할 수 없는   predict 예상하다

해설 세부 사항 관련 – 카밀이 공유하는 소식
남자가 첫 대사에서 카밀에게 새 펌프가 오늘 도착할지(Camille, will the new pump arrive today?) 묻자, 두 번째 여자가 유감스럽게도 아니라며, 제조사에서 지연될 거라고 했다(Unfortunately, no. The manufacturer said there'll be a delay, ~)고 답하므로 정답은 (A)이다.

Paraphrasing
대화의 there'll be a delay
→ 정답의 A delivery will be delayed.

---

58 Why is the customer traveling to Toronto?
(A) To participate in a competition
(B) To present at a conference
(C) To attend a wedding
(D) To sign a contract

고객은 왜 토론토로 가는가?
(A) 경연 대회에 참가하기 위해
(B) 콘퍼런스에서 발표하기 위해
(C) 결혼식에 참석하기 위해
(D) 계약을 맺기 위해

어휘 participate in ~에 참가하다   present 발표하다

해설 세부 사항 관련 – 고객이 토론토에 가는 목적
첫 번째 여자가 마지막 대사에서 고객이 이번 주말에 친구 결혼식에 참석하기 위해 그 비행기를 타고 토론토에 갈 계획이었다(She was planning to fly the plane to Toronto this weekend for a friend's wedding)고 했으므로 정답은 (C)이다.

Paraphrasing
대화의 to fly the plane to → 질문의 traveling to
대화의 for a friend's wedding → 정답의 To attend a wedding

59-61 M-Au / W-Br

M Hello, ⁵⁹**you've reached the customer service line for Quality Internet Service.** How can I help you?

W I'm Mona Shannak, and my account number's PK62H5. I'd like to close my account on June thirtieth.

M Oh, ⁶⁰**have you been experiencing issues with the service?**

W Actually, my company has asked me to relocate to Spain.

M That's exciting! I'll take care of your request for you then.

W Thank you—I appreciate that.

M When I'm done updating your records, ⁶¹**would you be willing to stay on the phone line to take a survey about your experience as a customer?**

W ⁶¹**Certainly.**

남 안녕하세요, **퀄리티 인터넷 서비스의 고객 서비스입니다.** 무엇을 도와드릴까요?
여 저는 모나 샤낙이고, 계정 번호는 PK62H5입니다. 6월 30일에 계정을 해지하고 싶어요.
남 아, **서비스에 문제가 있었나요?**
여 실은, 회사에서 스페인으로 전근을 요청했어요.
남 멋지네요! 그럼 요청 사항을 처리해 드리겠습니다.
여 감사합니다.
남 제가 기록 업데이트를 마치면, **전화를 끊지 마시고 고객 경험에 관한 설문 조사에 응해 주시겠어요?**
여 **물론입니다.**

어휘 account 계정, 계좌   experience 겪다, 경험하다
issue 문제, 사안   relocate 옮기다   take care of ~을 처리하다
stay on the phone line 전화를 끊지 않고 기다리다

---

59 What type of business does the man work for?
(A) An electric company
(B) An Internet provider
(C) A landscaping service
(D) A water supplier

남자는 어떤 종류의 업체에서 일하는가?
(A) 전기 회사
(B) 인터넷 공급업체
(C) 조경 서비스 업체
(D) 상수도 공급업체

해설 전체 내용 관련 – 남자의 근무 업체
남자가 첫 대사에서 여자에게 퀄리티 인터넷 서비스의 고객 서비스(~ you've reached the customer service line for Quality Internet Service)라고 했으므로 정답은 (B)이다.

60 What does the woman imply when she says, "my company has asked me to relocate to Spain"?
(A) She enjoys traveling for business.
(B) She was surprised by a job transfer.
(C) She has no complaints about a service.
(D) She would like paperwork sent to a different address.

여자가 "회사에서 스페인으로 전근을 요청했어요"라고 말할 때 무엇을 의미하는가?
(A) 출장을 떠나는 것을 즐긴다.
(B) 직무 전환에 놀랐다.
(C) 서비스에 대한 불만이 없다.
(D) 문서가 다른 주소로 보내지기를 원한다.

어휘 be surprised by ~에 놀라다   job transfer 직무 전환
paperwork 문서 (작업)

해설 화자의 의도 파악 – 회사에서 스페인으로 전근을 요청했다는 말의 의도
남자가 두 번째 대사에서 서비스에 문제가 있었는지(~ have you been experiencing issues with the service?) 묻자 여자가 인용문을 언급하고 있다. 이는 계정 해지의 이유가 서비스 문제가 아닌 다른 것임을 밝히는 말이므로 정답은 (C)이다.

61 What does the woman agree to do?
(A) Pay a bill
(B) Read a policy
(C) Return a call
(D) Complete a survey

여자는 무엇을 하는 것에 동의하는가?
(A) 청구서 납부하기
(B) 정책 읽기
(C) 답신 전화하기
(D) 설문 조사 완료하기

어휘 bill 청구서, 계산서   policy 정책, 방침

해설 세부 사항 관련 – 여자가 동의하는 것
남자가 네 번째 대사에서 전화를 끊지 말고 고객 경험에 관한 설문 조사에 응해 줄 것인지(~ would you be willing to stay on the phone line to take a survey about your experience as a customer?) 묻자, 여자가 물론(Certainly)이라고 했으므로 정답은 (D)이다.

Paraphrasing
대화의 take a survey → 정답의 Complete a survey

62-64 대화 + 매장 선반 W-Am / M-Cn   ▶동영상 강의

W Marco, you'll be restocking the cleaning products this morning, right? While you're doing that, ⁶²could you also put the updated sale-price labels on the hand soap dispensers? They're on the shelf right above the laundry detergent.

M No problem—that shouldn't take long. What else can I help with?

W ⁶³Can you make room for our new international foods section at the front of the store?

M ⁶⁴Oh, did the shipment finally arrive? That snowstorm up north really affected delivery schedules.

여 마르코, 오늘 오전에 청소용 제품들을 다시 채워 넣으실 거죠, 그렇죠? 그 일을 하시면서, 손 세정제 디스펜서에 업데이트된 할인가 라벨도 부착해 주실 수 있으세요? 세탁 세제 바로 위쪽 선반에 있어요.
남 알겠습니다. 그 일은 오래 걸리지 않을 거예요. 또 무엇을 도와드릴까요?
여 매장 앞쪽에 새 해외 식품 코너를 위한 공간을 만들어 주시겠어요?
남 아, 배송품이 드디어 도착했나요? 북부 지역의 폭설이 배송 일정에 큰 영향을 미쳤잖아요.

어휘 restock 다시 채우다, 보충하다 dispenser 디스펜서, 용기 detergent 세제 room 공간, 자리 shipment 배송(품) affect 영향을 미치다 disinfectant 살균성의

62 Look at the graphic. Which dollar amount will the man change?
(A) $2.37
(B) $4.55
(C) $7.86
(D) $2.91

시각 정보에 의하면, 남자는 몇 달러의 금액을 변경할 것인가?
(A) 2.37달러
(B) 4.55달러
(C) 7.86달러
(D) 2.91달러

해설 시각 정보 연계 – 남자가 변경할 금액
여자가 첫 대사에서 남자에게 손 세정제 디스펜서에 업데이트된 할인가 라벨을 부착해 줄 것(~ could you also put the updated sale-price labels on the hand soap dispensers?)을 요청하고 있다. 매장 선반에서 손 세정제 가격이 2.37달러로 표기되어 있으므로 정답은 (A)이다.

63 What will be added at the front of the store?
(A) An additional checkout stand
(B) A holiday display
(C) A special food section
(D) A seating area

매장 앞쪽에 무엇이 추가될 것인가?
(A) 추가 계산대
(B) 휴일 장식
(C) 특별 식품 코너
(D) 좌석 공간

어휘 additional 추가적인 checkout stand 계산대 display 진열(품), 전시(품)

해설 세부 사항 관련 – 매장 앞쪽에 추가될 것
여자가 두 번째 대사에서 매장 앞쪽에 새 해외 식품 코너를 위한 공간을 만들어 줄 것(Can you make room for our new international foods section at the front of the store?)을 요청하고 있으므로 정답은 (C)이다.

Paraphrasing
대화의 our new international foods section
→ 정답의 A special food section

TEST 3 77

64 According to the man, why did a shipment arrive late?
(A) He forgot to place an order.
(B) It was delivered to the wrong address.
(C) Some supplies were unavailable.
(D) Weather conditions were poor.

남자에 따르면, 배송품은 왜 늦게 도착했는가?
(A) 주문하는 것을 잊었다.
(B) 엉뚱한 주소로 배송되었다.
(C) 일부 물품을 구할 수 없었다.
(D) 날씨 상태가 좋지 못했다.

어휘 place an order 주문하다 condition 상태, 조건

해설 세부 사항 관련 – 배송품이 늦게 도착한 이유
남자가 마지막 대사에서 배송품이 드디어 도착했는지 물으며, 북부 지역의 폭설이 배송 일정에 큰 영향을 미쳤다(Oh, did the shipment finally arrive? That snowstorm up north really affected delivery schedules)고 했으므로 정답은 (D)이다.

Paraphrasing
대화의 snowstorm → 정답의 Weather conditions were poor

65-67 대화 + 일정표 W-Br / M-Au

W Thanks for calling Kwon Photography Studio.
M Hello. ⁶⁵**I need to have a photo taken for a Canadian passport.**
W OK. You can make an appointment Monday through Friday. ⁶⁶**Just bring in a copy of the application so we can see the size requirements.**
M I work nine to five every day at my current job. Do you have any openings after five P.M.?
W No problem. ⁶⁷**We're open until six P.M. one day a week.**

여 권 포토 스튜디오에 전화해 주셔서 감사합니다.
남 안녕하세요. **캐나다 여권용 사진을 찍어야 해요.**
여 알겠습니다. 월요일부터 금요일까지 예약하실 수 있어요. **사이즈 요구 사항을 확인할 수 있도록 신청서만 한 부 가져오시면 됩니다.**
남 제가 현재 직장에서 매일 9시부터 5시까지 근무를 해요. 오후 5시 후에 빈 시간대가 있을까요?
여 문제없습니다. **저희는 일주일에 하루 오후 6시까지 문을 열어요.**

어휘 passport 여권 make an appointment 예약하다 application 신청(서), 지원(서) requirements 요건, 필수 조건 current 현재의 opening 빈 시간대, 빈자리 operation 운영, 영업

Hours of Operation	
Monday	9 A.M.–5 P.M.
Tuesday	8 A.M.–4 P.M.
⁶⁷**Wednesday**	**10 A.M.–6 P.M.**
Thursday	8 A.M.–5 P.M.
Friday	9 A.M.–Noon

운영 시간	
월요일	오전 9시–오후 5시
화요일	오전 8시–오후 4시
수요일	**오전 10시–오후 6시**
목요일	오전 8시–오후 5시
금요일	오전 9시–정오

65 What does the man say he needs to have done?
(A) He needs to schedule a job interview.
(B) He needs to cancel a doctor's appointment.
(C) He needs to have his photograph taken.
(D) He needs to renew his driver's license.

남자는 무엇을 해야 한다고 말하는가?
(A) 구직 면접 일정을 잡아야 한다.
(B) 의사 진료 예약을 취소해야 한다.
(C) 사진을 찍어야 한다.
(D) 운전 면허증을 갱신해야 한다.

해설 세부 사항 관련 – 남자가 해야 하는 것
남자가 첫 대사에서 캐나다 여권용 사진을 찍어야 한다(I need to have a photo taken for a Canadian passport)고 했으므로 정답은 (C)이다.

66 What does the woman ask the man to bring to an appointment?
(A) An application form
(B) Some references
(C) A study guide
(D) A payment receipt

여자는 남자에게 예약 시간에 무엇을 가져오라고 요청하는가?
(A) 신청서
(B) 추천서
(C) 학습 가이드
(D) 지불 영수증

어휘 form 양식, 서식 reference 추천(서), 추천인

해설 세부 사항 관련 – 여자의 요청 사항
여자가 두 번째 대사에서 사이즈 요구 사항을 확인할 수 있도록 신청서만 한 부 가져오면 된다(Just bring in a copy of the application so we can see the size requirements)고 했으므로 정답은 (A)이다.

Paraphrasing
대화의 a copy of the application
→ 정답의 An application form

78

67 Look at the graphic. Which day will the man request an appointment for?
(A) Monday
(B) Tuesday
(C) Wednesday
(D) Thursday

시각 정보에 의하면, 남자는 어느 요일로 예약을 요청할 것인가?
(A) 월요일
(B) 화요일
(C) 수요일
(D) 목요일

해설 시각 정보 연계 – 남자가 예약을 요청할 요일
여자가 마지막 대사에서 남자가 원하는 예약 시간과 관련해 일주일에 하루 오후 6시까지 문을 연다(We're open until six P.M. one day a week)고 했다. 일정표에서 영업 종료 시간이 오후 6시로 표기된 요일은 수요일이므로 정답은 (C)이다.

Transportation Reimbursement Form

Section 1: Full name
Section 2: Transportation type
Section 3: Payment method
70 Section 4: Department code
Section 5: Amount to be reimbursed

교통 비용 환급 양식

섹션 1: 전체 성명
섹션 2: 교통편 종류
섹션 3: 결제 수단
섹션 4: 부서 코드
섹션 5: 환급될 금액

68-70 대화 + 양식 M-Au / W-Am

M   Hi, Marina. **68** Do you have receipts for your expenses from the dental hygienists' conference you attended last week?

W   Yes, I have them. I was just going to scan them and send them to you by e-mail.

M   Thanks very much. **69** Once I receive them, I'll process your request for reimbursement. Don't forget to fill out the travel expenses form and include it in your e-mail, too.

W   OK. **70** Remind me, what should I use for the department code?

M   Oh, sorry. I forgot to tell you. Use number 1009.

남   안녕하세요, 마리나. **지난주에 참석하셨던 치과 위생사 콘퍼런스에서 지출한 비용에 대한 영수증을 갖고 계신가요?**
여   네, 갖고 있어요. 그것들을 스캔해서 이메일로 보내려고 했어요.
남   대단히 감사합니다. **제가 받는 대로, 환급 요청을 처리해 드리겠습니다.** 출장 경비 양식을 작성해서 이메일에 첨부하는 것도 잊지 마세요.
여   네. **부서 코드에 무엇을 사용해야 하는지 알려 주시겠어요?**
남   아, 죄송합니다. 말씀드리는 걸 잊었네요. 1009번을 이용하시면 됩니다.

어휘 receipt 영수(증) expense 비용 dental 치과의, 치아의 hygienist 위생사 process 처리하다 request 요청, 요구 reimbursement (비용) 환급 fill out 작성하다, 기입하다 include 포함하다 remind 다시 알려 주다, 상기시키다 transportation 교통(편) type 종류 method 수단, 방식 amount 금액, 양

---

68 What event did the woman attend last week?
(A) A professional conference
(B) A training workshop
(C) A car auction
(D) A product demonstration

여자는 지난주에 어떤 행사에 참석했는가?
(A) 전문 콘퍼런스
(B) 교육 워크숍
(C) 자동차 경매
(D) 제품 시연회

어휘 auction 경매 demonstration 시연(회), 시범

해설 세부 사항 관련 – 여자가 지난주에 참석한 행사
남자가 첫 대사에서 여자에게 지난주에 참석한 치과 위생사 콘퍼런스에서 지출한 비용에 대한 영수증을 갖고 있는지(Do you have receipts for your expenses from the dental hygienists' conference you attended last week?) 묻고 있으므로 정답은 (A)이다.

Paraphrasing
대화의 the dental hygienists' conference
→ 정답의 A professional conference

---

69 What will the man do with the documents the woman provides?
(A) Process a request
(B) Postpone a reservation
(C) Make a schedule
(D) Finalize a report

남자는 여자가 제공하는 서류로 무엇을 할 것인가?
(A) 요청 처리하기
(B) 예약 연기하기
(C) 일정표 만들기
(D) 보고서 마무리하기

어휘 postpone 연기하다, 미루다 reservation 예약

해설 세부 사항 관련 – 여자가 제공하는 서류로 남자가 할 일

남자가 두 번째 대사에서 여자가 보내는 영수증들을 받는 대로 환급 요청을 처리해 주겠다(Once I receive them, I'll process your request for reimbursement)고 했으므로 정답은 (A)이다.

70 Look at the graphic. Which section does the woman ask about?
(A) Section 2
(B) Section 3
(C) Section 4
(D) Section 5

시각 정보에 의하면, 여자는 어느 섹션에 대해 묻는가?
(A) 섹션 2
(B) 섹션 3
(C) 섹션 4
(D) 섹션 5

해설 시각 정보 연계 – 여자가 묻는 섹션

여자가 두 번째 대사에서 부서 코드에 무엇을 사용해야 하는지(Remind me, what should I use for the department code?) 물었다. 양식에서 부서 코드가 쓰여 있는 섹션은 섹션 4이므로 정답은 (C)이다.

PART 4

71-73 회의 발췌

> W-Am **71 The town's annual music festival is only a few months away**, and our committee still has a lot of planning to do. We already have a list of performers who have agreed to appear. Fortunately, we can use the same stage and equipment we've used in the past. **72 However, we don't have enough fencing to create a larger seating area.** **73 Eniola, since you're in charge of accounts, would you check sometime today to see whether we have money for extra fencing?**

시의 연례 음악 축제가 불과 몇 달밖에 남지 않았는데, 우리 위원회는 여전히 계획해야 할 일이 많습니다. 우리는 이미 출연에 동의한 공연자들의 명단을 갖고 있습니다. 다행히, 우리가 과거에 이용했던 것과 동일한 무대와 장비를 이용할 수 있습니다. 하지만 좌석 공간을 더 크게 만들 울타리가 충분하지 않습니다. 에니올라, 회계를 책임지고 계시니, 울타리를 추가하기 위해 쓸 수 있는 자금이 있는지 오늘 중으로 확인해 주시겠어요?

어휘 annual 연례적인, 해마다의 committee 위원회
planning 계획 agree 동의하다 appear 출연하다, 나타나다
fortunately 다행히 equipment 장비 fencing 울타리
in charge of ~을 책임지고 있는 accounts 회계 extra 추가의

71 Which event is being planned?
(A) A holiday parade
(B) A music festival
(C) A sports competition
(D) A company picnic

어느 행사가 계획되고 있는가?
(A) 휴일 퍼레이드
(B) 음악 축제
(C) 스포츠 대회
(D) 회사 야유회

해설 전체 내용 관련 – 계획되고 있는 행사

화자가 초반부에 연례 음악 축제가 불과 몇 달밖에 남지 않았다(The town's annual music festival is only a few months away ~)고 언급하면서 그 행사의 계획과 관련해 이야기하고 있으므로 정답은 (B)이다.

72 What problem does the speaker mention?
(A) A stage needs to be repainted.
(B) Some participants have canceled.
(C) There is not enough fencing.
(D) A parking area cannot be used.

화자는 어떤 문제를 언급하는가?
(A) 무대에 페인트칠이 다시 되어야 한다.
(B) 일부 참가자들이 취소했다.
(C) 울타리가 충분하지 않다.
(D) 주차 공간을 이용할 수 없다.

어휘 participant 참가자

해설 세부 사항 관련 – 화자가 언급하는 문제

화자가 중반부에 좌석 공간을 더 크게 만들 울타리가 충분하지 않다(However, we don't have enough fencing to create a larger seating area)는 했으므로 정답은 (C)이다.

Paraphrasing
담화의 don't have enough fencing
→ 정답의 There is not enough fencing.

73 What will Eniola most likely do today?
(A) Select a caterer
(B) Hire a maintenance worker
(C) Confirm a start time
(D) Check a budget

에니올라는 오늘 무엇을 할 것 같은가?
(A) 출장 요리 업체 선정하기
(B) 유지 관리 직원 고용하기
(C) 시작 시간 확인하기
(D) 예산 확인하기

어휘 select 선정하다, 선택하다   caterer 출장 요리 업체

해설 세부 사항 관련 – 에니올라가 오늘 할 일

화자가 후반부에 에니올라의 이름을 부르면서 울타리를 추가하기 위해 쓸 수 있는 자금이 있는지 오늘 중으로 확인해 줄 것(Eniola, ~ would you check sometime today to see whether we have money for extra fencing?)을 요청하고 있다. 이는 예산이 충분한지 확인해 달라는 의미이므로 정답은 (D)이다.

Paraphrasing
담화의 to see whether we have money for extra fencing
→ 정답의 Check a budget

74-76 담화

W-Br Hello, everyone! **74 Thanks for stopping by my booth. I hope you've been enjoying all the manufacturing exhibits and demonstrations.** I'm Carmen Fuentes, and I'm a sales representative at LT Plastic Injectors. Today I'm delighted to show you one of our new injection molding machines. It's currently fitted with a mold to make plastic bottle caps. **75 This machine is able to create 96 bottle caps every two seconds. That's incredibly fast!** And for today only, **76 we're offering a ten percent discount on orders for this machine** just for attending our demonstration.

안녕하세요, 여러분! 저희 부스에 들러 주셔서 감사합니다. 모든 제조 관련 전시와 시연을 즐기셨기를 바랍니다. 저는 카르멘 푸엔테스이고, LT 플라스틱 인젝터스의 영업 사원입니다. 오늘 여러분께 새로운 사출 성형 기계 중 하나를 보여 드리게 되어 기쁩니다. 이 제품은 현재 플라스틱 병뚜껑을 만들기 위한 틀이 장착되어 있습니다. 이 기계는 2초마다 96개의 병뚜껑을 만들어 낼 수 있습니다. 믿을 수 없을 정도로 빠릅니다! 그리고 오늘 단 하루, 시연회에 참석하신 분들에게만 이 기계를 주문하시면 10퍼센트 할인해 드립니다.

어휘 stop by ~에 들르다   booth 부스, 임시 칸막이 공간   manufacturing 제조(업)   exhibit 전시(품); 전시하다   representative 직원, 대표자   be delighted to ~해서 기쁘다   injection molding 사출 성형   currently 현재   fitted with ~가 갖춰진, ~가 설치된   mold 틀, 거푸집   cap 뚜껑, 마개   incredibly 믿을 수 없을 정도로

74 What type of event are the listeners most likely attending?
(A) A trade show
(B) A press conference
(C) A charity auction
(D) A grand opening ceremony

청자들은 어떤 종류의 행사에 참석하고 있는 것 같은가?
(A) 무역 박람회
(B) 기자 회견
(C) 자선 경매
(D) 개장 기념 행사

어휘 ceremony 기념 행사, 축하 행사

해설 전체 내용 관련 – 청자들이 참석하는 행사

화자가 초반부에 청자들에게 부스에 들러 줘서 감사하다며, 모든 제조 관련 전시와 시연을 즐겼기를 바란다(~ I hope you've been enjoying all the manufacturing exhibits and demonstrations)고 했으므로 정답은 (A)이다.

75 What does the speaker emphasize about a machine?
(A) Its durability
(B) Its ease of use
(C) Its speed
(D) Its energy efficiency

화자는 기계에 대해 무엇을 강조하는가?
(A) 내구성
(B) 이용 편의성
(C) 속도
(D) 에너지 효율성

어휘 emphasize 강조하다   durability 내구성   efficiency 효율성

해설 세부 사항 관련 – 화자가 기계에 대해 강조하는 것

화자가 중반부에 자사의 기계가 2초마다 96개의 병뚜껑을 만들어 낼 수 있다며 믿을 수 없을 정도로 빠르다(This machine is able to create 96 bottle caps every two seconds. That's incredibly fast!)는 말을 덧붙이고 있으므로 정답은 (C)이다.

Paraphrasing
담화의 incredibly fast → 정답의 speed

76 What does the speaker offer the listeners?
(A) A free sample
(B) A product discount
(C) A meal voucher
(D) A training brochure

화자는 청자들에게 무엇을 제공하는가?
(A) 무료 샘플
(B) 제품 할인
(C) 식권
(D) 교육 안내 책자

어휘 free 무료의 voucher 상품권, 쿠폰 brochure 안내 책자

해설 세부 사항 관련 – 화자가 제공하는 것
화자가 후반부에 이 기계를 주문하면 10퍼센트 할인해 준다(~ we're offering a ten percent discount on orders for this machine ~)고 했으므로 정답은 (B)이다.

> **Paraphrasing**
> 담화의 a ten percent discount on orders for this machine
> → 정답의 A product discount

77-79 공지

> W-Am The company leadership here at PCF Technologies has decided to make a major change. Historically, **77 we've been one of the largest manufacturers of computer chips.** However, starting next month, our company will launch a research and development division and start designing chips, too. **78 We've decided to make this change to allow us to have more control over the quality of the technology we produce.** As a result, **79 some employees will have new work assignments going forward. Those assignments will be communicated later in the morning.**
>
> PCF 테크놀로지스의 회사 경영진은 큰 변화를 주기로 결정했습니다. 역사적으로, 우리는 가장 큰 컴퓨터 칩 제조사 중 하나였습니다. 하지만 다음 달부터 우리 회사는 연구 개발부를 출범해 칩을 설계하는 일도 시작할 것입니다. 우리가 생산하는 기술의 품질을 더 잘 통제하기 위해 이러한 변경을 결정했습니다. 그 결과, 일부 직원들은 앞으로 새로운 업무를 배정받게 됩니다. 그렇게 배정된 업무는 오전 중으로 전달될 예정입니다.
>
> 어휘 leadership 경영진, 지도부 major 큰, 주요한 manufacturer 제조사 launch 출범하다, 출시하다 research 연구, 조사 development 개발 division 부서 allow 허용하다, ~할 수 있게 해 주다 control 통제, 관리 assignment 배정(되는 것), 할당(되는 것)

77 What industry does the speaker work in?
(A) Food manufacturing
(B) Building construction
(C) Computer technology
(D) Entertainment

화자는 어떤 업계에서 일하고 있는가?
(A) 식품 제조
(B) 건물 건축
(C) 컴퓨터 기술
(D) 연예

해설 전체 내용 관련 – 화자의 근무 업계
화자가 초반부에 소속 회사가 가장 큰 컴퓨터 칩 제조사 중 하나였다(we've been one of the largest manufacturers of computer chips)고 했으므로 정답은 (C)이다.

78 Why is the company making a change?
(A) To create employment opportunities
(B) To reduce manufacturing costs
(C) To comply with a government policy
(D) To increase control over quality

회사는 왜 변화를 주는가?
(A) 고용 기회를 만들기 위해
(B) 제조 비용을 줄이기 위해
(C) 정부 정책을 준수하기 위해
(D) 품질에 대한 통제를 높이기 위해

어휘 employment 고용, 취업 opportunity 기회 comply with ~을 준수하다

해설 세부 사항 관련 – 회사가 변화를 주는 이유
화자가 중반부에 생산하는 기술의 품질을 더 잘 통제하기 위해 이러한 변경을 결정했다(We've decided to make this change to allow us to have more control over the quality of the technology we produce)고 했으므로 정답은 (D)이다.

> **Paraphrasing**
> 담화의 have more control over the quality
> → 정답의 increase control over quality

79 What will be sent out later in the morning?
(A) Work assignments
(B) Calendar invitations
(C) A press release
(D) Product specifications

무엇이 오전 중으로 보내질 것인가?
(A) 배정된 업무
(B) 일정 초대장
(C) 보도 자료
(D) 제품 사양

어휘 invitation 초대(장) press release 보도 자료 specifications 사양, (설계 등의) 설명서

해설 세부 사항 관련 – 오전 중으로 보내질 것
화자가 후반부에 일부 직원들은 앞으로 새로운 업무를 배정받을 것이며, 그렇게 배정된 업무는 오전 중으로 전달될 것(~ some employees will have new work assignments going forward. Those assignments will be communicated later in the morning)이라고 했으므로 정답은 (A)이다.

> **Paraphrasing**
> 담화의 will be communicated → 질문의 will be sent out

80-82 팟캐스트

M-Au Hello! Welcome to *Ag-Cast*—80 **a podcast all about the latest news in agriculture.** Before we get started with today's episode, 81 **I'd like to note that I provided the wrong dates for the Farming Exposition during last week's episode.** The start date of the event is March thirty-first, not the twenty-first. I'm sorry about that. OK, let's move on to today's guest. 82 **Ms. Junko Adachi is the director at Fertilizer-ONE—a nonprofit organization that provides small farms with low-cost fertilizer.** During her time as director, the organization has helped over 1,000 small farms increase their yields!

안녕하세요! **농업 분야의 모든 최신 뉴스를 다루는 팟캐스트**, 〈애그 캐스트〉에 오신 것을 환영합니다. 오늘 방송을 시작하기에 앞서, **지난주 방송에서 농업 박람회의 날짜를 잘못 알려 드렸다는 점 말씀드립니다.** 이 행사의 시작 날짜는 3월 21일이 아니라 31일입니다. 이에 대해 사과드립니다. 자, 오늘 초대 손님 순서로 넘어가겠습니다. **준코 아다치 씨는 소규모 농장에 저가 비료를 제공하는 비영리 단체인 퍼틸라이저 원의 이사입니다.** 이분이 이사로 재직하는 동안, 이 단체는 1,000개가 넘는 소규모 농장의 수확량 증대를 도왔습니다!

어휘 agriculture 농업 episode 1회 방송분 note 언급하다 exposition 박람회 move on to ~로 넘어가다, ~로 이동하다 nonprofit 비영리의 organization 단체 low-cost 저가의 fertilizer 비료 yield 수확량, 산출량

80 What is the focus of the podcast?
(A) Technology
(B) Agriculture
(C) Finance
(D) Cooking

팟캐스트의 초점은 무엇인가?
(A) 기술
(B) 농업
(C) 금융
(D) 요리

해설 전체 내용 관련 – 팟캐스트의 초점
화자가 초반부에 농업 분야의 모든 최신 뉴스를 다루는 팟캐스트(~ a podcast all about the latest news in agriculture)라고 했으므로 정답은 (B)이다.

81 Why does the speaker apologize?
(A) For having some audio problems
(B) For delaying some Web site updates
(C) For forgetting to thank a sponsor
(D) For providing an incorrect date

화자는 왜 사과하는가?
(A) 음향 문제가 있었기 때문에
(B) 웹사이트 업데이트가 지연됐기 때문에
(C) 후원사에 감사하는 것을 잊었기 때문에
(D) 잘못된 날짜를 알려 주었기 때문에

어휘 sponsor 후원사, 후원자 incorrect 잘못된, 맞지 않는

해설 세부 사항 관련 – 화자가 사과하는 이유
화자가 중반부에 지난주 방송에서 농업 박람회의 날짜를 잘못 알려 준 것(I'd like to note that I provided the wrong dates for the Farming Exposition during last week's episode)을 언급하면서, 날짜를 정정하고 사과했으므로 정답은 (D)이다.

Paraphrasing
담화의 provided the wrong dates
→ 정답의 providing an incorrect date

82 Who is Junko Adachi?
(A) The director of a nonprofit organization
(B) The president of a national bank
(C) A successful inventor
(D) A well-known author

준코 아다치는 누구인가?
(A) 비영리 단체의 이사
(B) 국립 은행장
(C) 성공한 발명가
(D) 유명한 작가

어휘 inventor 발명가 well-known 유명한, 잘 알려진

해설 세부 사항 관련 – 준코 아다치의 직업
화자가 후반부에 준코 아다치 씨는 소규모 농장에 저가 비료를 제공하는 비영리 단체인 퍼틸라이저 원의 이사(Ms. Junko Adachi is the director at Fertilizer-ONE—a nonprofit organization that provides small farms with low-cost fertilizer)라고 했으므로 정답은 (A)이다.

83-85 전화 메시지

W-Br Hi, Mr. Flores. 83 **This is Susana, the supervisor of the construction crew working on your renovation project.** I'm calling because we've run into an issue with the front window replacements. 84 **Your house was built a long time ago and has settled over the years. Unfortunately, this has caused some frame alignment issues.** We will not be able to install the new bay window you requested for the front room without more extensive work than the budget will cover. Our work is done for today, but 85 **we'll need to know how to proceed by tomorrow.** I'll be available for the next couple of hours.

> 안녕하세요, 플로레스 씨. 귀하의 개조 공사 프로젝트 작업을 하고 있는 공사팀 감독, 수잔나입니다. 전면 창 교체와 관련된 문제가 발생하여 전화를 드립니다. **귀하의 주택은 오래 전에 지어져 수년에 걸쳐 내려앉았습니다.** 유감스럽게도, 이로 인해 일부 창틀에 정렬 문제가 발생했습니다. 예산으로 충당할 수 있는 범위보다 더 광범위한 작업을 하지 않고는 앞쪽 방에 요청하신 새 돌출형 창을 설치할 수 없을 겁니다. 오늘 작업은 끝났지만, **내일까지는 어떻게 진행할지 알아야 합니다.** **저는 앞으로 두어 시간 동안 연락 가능합니다.**

> 어휘 supervisor 감독(관), 책임자 crew 작업팀, 조 renovation 개조, 보수 run into ~와 맞닥뜨리다 replacement 교체(품), 대체(품) settle 내려앉다, 자리잡다 cause 초래하다 frame 틀, 테두리 alignment 조정, 정렬 bay window 돌출형 창문 extensive 광범위한, 폭넓은 cover 충당하다, 포함하다 proceed 진행하다, 나아가다 available 시간이 있는, 이용할 수 있는

83 What industry does the speaker work in?
(A) Real estate
(B) Construction
(C) Technology
(D) Manufacturing

화자는 어떤 업계에서 일하고 있는가?
(A) 부동산
(B) 건설
(C) 기술
(D) 제조

해설 전체 내용 관련 – 화자의 근무 업계
화자가 초반부에 자신의 이름을 언급하면서 개조 공사 프로젝트 작업을 하고 있는 공사팀 감독(This is Susana, the supervisor of the construction crew working on your renovation project)이라고 했으므로 정답은 (B)이다.

84 According to the speaker, what has caused a problem?
(A) Bad weather
(B) An employee absence
(C) A supply shortage
(D) The age of a building

화자에 따르면, 무엇이 문제를 초래했는가?
(A) 좋지 못한 날씨
(B) 직원 결근
(C) 공급 부족
(D) 건물의 나이

어휘 absence 결근, 부재 shortage 부족

해설 세부 사항 관련 – 문제의 원인
화자가 중반부에 청자의 주택은 오래 전에 지어져 수년에 걸쳐 내려앉았고, 이로 인해 일부 창틀에 정렬 문제가 발생했다(Your house was built a long time ago and has settled over the years. Unfortunately, this has caused some frame alignment issues)고 했으므로 정답은 (D)이다.

Paraphrasing
담화의 Your house was built a long time ago
→ 정답의 The age of a building

85 Why does the speaker say, "I'll be available for the next couple of hours"?
(A) To inform the listener of new business hours
(B) To confirm the listener's appointment
(C) To remind the listener to submit a payment
(D) To encourage the listener to call back soon

화자는 왜 "저는 앞으로 두어 시간 동안 연락 가능합니다"라고 말하는가?
(A) 청자에게 새로운 영업시간을 알려 주기 위해
(B) 청자의 예약을 확인해 주기 위해
(C) 청자에게 대금을 결제하도록 상기시키기 위해
(D) 청자에게 곧 다시 전화하도록 권하기 위해

어휘 appointment 예약, 약속

해설 화자의 의도 파악 – 앞으로 두어 시간 동안 연락 가능하다는 말의 의도
화자가 후반부에 내일까지는 어떻게 진행할지 알아야 한다(~ we'll need to know how to proceed by tomorrow)면서 인용문을 언급하고 있다. 이는 자신과 통화 가능한 시간대를 알려줌으로써 결정 사항과 관련해 회신해 달라는 뜻이므로 정답은 (D)이다.

86-88 회의 발췌

> M-Cn **86 You may remember that our bank branch was evaluated by auditors from our headquarters last week.** Well, I received their report today. They looked at everything from how we handle recordkeeping for accounts and transactions to how our bank tellers interact with individual customers. Above all, **87 they were impressed with the quality of our customer service, specifically how we greet customers and direct them to the right associate.** However, we received low ratings on marketing our other products. **88 I'd like all supervisors to talk to their staff about strategies to pitch our products and services to customers.**

> 지난주에 우리 은행 지점이 본사 회계 감사관으로부터 평가를 받은 것을 기억하실 것입니다. 음, 오늘 그들의 보고서를 받았습니다. 그들은 계좌와 거래의 기록을 보관하는 방식부터 은행원들이 개별 고객과 소통하는 방식까지 모든 부분을 살펴봤습니다. 무엇보다, **그들은 고객 서비스 품질, 특히 우리가 고객들을 맞이하고 적절한 직원에게 안내해 드리는 방식에 깊은 인상을 받았습니다.** 하지만 우리의 다른 상품을 마케팅하는 일에 대해서는 낮은 등급을 받았습니다. **모든 책임자들은 우리 상품과 서비스를 고객들께 홍보할 전략에 대해 소속 직원들과 이야기해 주셨으면 합니다.**

어휘 branch 지점 evaluate 평가하다 auditor 회계 감사관 handle 처리하다, 다루다 recordkeeping 기록 보관 interact with ~와 소통하다, ~와 교류하다 quality 품질 specifically 특히, 구체적으로 greet 맞이하다 direct 안내하다 associate 직원, 동료 rating 등급, 평점 pitch 홍보하다

86 Who most likely is the speaker?
(A) A marketing consultant
(B) A bank manager
(C) A hospital director
(D) A factory owner

화자는 누구인 것 같은가?
(A) 마케팅 컨설턴트
(B) 은행장
(C) 병원장
(D) 공장 소유주

해설 전체 내용 관련 – 화자의 직업
화자가 초반부에 소속 은행 지점이 본사 감사관으로부터 평가를 받았던 것(~ our bank branch was evaluated by auditors from our headquarters last week)을 언급했고, 이어 그 결과에 대해서 말하고 있다. 따라서 정답은 (B)이다.

87 According to the speaker, what were some auditors impressed with?
(A) Customer service
(B) Employee satisfaction
(C) Community outreach
(D) Worker safety

화자에 따르면, 회계 감사관들은 무엇에 깊은 인상을 받았는가?
(A) 고객 서비스
(B) 직원 만족도
(C) 지역 봉사 활동
(D) 직원 안전

어휘 satisfaction 만족(도) community 지역 사회, 지역 공동체 outreach 봉사 활동

해설 세부 사항 관련 – 회계 감사관들이 깊은 인상을 받은 부분
화자가 중반부에 회계 감사관들이 고객 서비스 품질에 깊은 인상을 받았다(~ they were impressed with the quality of our customer service, ~)고 했으므로 정답은 (A)이다.

88 What does the speaker ask supervisors to do?
(A) Reward staff for their efficiency
(B) Review marketing strategies with their teams
(C) Schedule team-building exercises
(D) Recommend staff for promotions

화자는 책임자들에게 무엇을 하도록 요청하는가?
(A) 직원들의 효율성에 대해 보상하기
(B) 팀원들과 마케팅 전략 살펴보기
(C) 팀 단합 활동 일정 잡기
(D) 승진 대상 직원 추천하기

어휘 reward 보상하다 efficiency 효율성 exercise 활동, 운동 promotion 승진, 홍보

해설 세부 사항 관련 – 화자의 요청 사항
화자가 후반부에 모든 책임자들은 상품과 서비스를 고객에게 홍보할 전략에 대해 소속 직원들과 이야기해 주길 원한다(I'd like all supervisors to talk to their staff about strategies to pitch our products and services to customers)고 했으므로 정답은 (B)이다.

Paraphrasing
담화의 talk to their staff about strategies to pitch our products and services
→ 정답의 Review marketing strategies with their teams

89-91 담화

M-Au Oh good. I'm glad to see everyone is here early, as requested. **89** We have an unusually busy night ahead of us—due to the addition of six large group reservations. We'll set up for those first in the overflow room. **90** Tables will need to come out of storage. I'll unlock the door after this meeting. But before you start your shift, make sure to try tonight's specials. They're in their usual spot under the heat lamps. Be sure you promote the truffles dish in particular. **91** We'd like to see if this could be a permanent menu item. Management will be watching closely. Its price point is high, but it really is delicious.

아, 좋습니다. 요청대로, 모두 이곳에 일찍 와 계신 것을 보니 기쁩니다. **여섯 개의 대규모 단체 예약이 추가되어 이례적으로 바쁜 밤을 앞두고 있습니다.** 우리는 먼저 초과 인원을 위한 공간에 자리를 마련할 것입니다. **테이블은 창고에서 꺼내 와야 합니다.** 회의가 끝나고 그 문을 열어 드릴게요. 그런데 근무를 시작하시기 전에, 오늘 밤의 특별 메뉴를 꼭 시식해 보세요. 평소와 같은 자리인 보온용 전등 아래에 있습니다. 특히 송로 버섯 요리를 적극 홍보해 주세요. **정식 메뉴로 도입할 수 있을지 알아보려고 합니다. 경영진이 면밀히 지켜볼 예정입니다.** 가격대가 높긴 하지만, 정말 맛있습니다.

어휘 unusually 이례적으로, 평소와 달리 ahead of ~ 앞에 addition 추가(되는 것) overflow 초과, 과잉 shift 교대 근무(조) usual 평소의, 일반적인 spot 자리, 장소 promote 홍보하다 in particular 특히 permanent 영구적인, 종신의 management 경영(진), 관리(진) closely 면밀히, 밀접하게 price point 가격대

89 Why does the speaker call employees in early?
(A) He wants to pass out some gifts.
(B) He expects a busy night.
(C) The owner will give a speech.
(D) New uniforms have arrived.

화자는 왜 일찍 직원들을 소집했는가?
(A) 선물을 나눠 주고 싶어 한다.
(B) 바쁜 밤이 될 것으로 예상한다.
(C) 소유주가 연설할 것이다.
(D) 새로운 유니폼이 도착했다.

어휘 pass out 나눠 주다 expect 예상하다, 기대하다

해설 전체 내용 관련 – 화자가 일찍 직원들을 소집한 이유
화자가 초반부에 청자들이 일찍 와서 기쁘다는 말과 함께 여섯 개의 대규모 단체 예약이 추가되어 이례적으로 바쁜 밤을 앞두고 있다(We have an unusually busy night ahead of us—due to the addition of six large group reservations)고 했으므로 정답은 (B)이다.

90 What should be retrieved from storage?
(A) Promotional signs
(B) Heat lamps
(C) Extra tables
(D) Storage containers

창고에서 무엇을 꺼내야 하는가?
(A) 홍보용 표지판
(B) 보온용 전등
(C) 추가 테이블
(D) 보관 용기

어휘 retrieve 되찾다, 회수하다

해설 세부 사항 관련 – 창고에서 꺼내야 하는 것
화자가 중반부에 테이블들을 창고에서 꺼내 와야 할 것(Tables will need to come out of storage, ~)이라고 했으므로 정답은 (C)이다.

Paraphrasing
담화의 come out of storage
→ 질문의 be retrieved from storage

91 What does the speaker mean when he says, "Management will be watching closely"?
(A) A decision about an item will be made soon.
(B) A client may not renew a contract.
(C) A large profit is expected.
(D) More people might be hired.

화자가 "경영진이 면밀히 지켜볼 예정입니다"라고 말할 때 무엇을 의미하는가?
(A) 품목에 대한 결정이 곧 내려질 것이다.
(B) 고객이 계약을 갱신하지 않을 수도 있다.
(C) 많은 수익이 예상된다.
(D) 더 많은 사람들이 고용될 수도 있다.

해설 화자의 의도 파악 – 경영진이 면밀히 지켜볼 예정이라는 말의 의도
화자가 후반부에 송로 버섯 요리 홍보를 강조하며, 정식 메뉴로 도입할 수 있을지 알아보려고 한다(We'd like to see if this could be a permanent menu item)는 말과 함께 인용문을 언급했다. 따라서 경영진이 해당 메뉴에 대한 결정을 내리려고 한다는 것을 알 수 있으므로 (A)가 정답이다.

92-94 방송

W-Am Hello, and **92welcome to WBCO financial news.** Tonight, we're talking about the prices we pay online for goods and services. In particular, we'll look at why you may pay more if you shop during times of peak demand. **93Called surge pricing, this trend first started with computer software that allowed large airlines to track demand and quickly change their ticket prices.** That technology is now widely available. You may find that even small businesses charge more when demand is higher. Our guest today is Professor Yun Hang, a leading expert on the topic. **94Last month he was the featured speaker at the International Economics Summit.**

안녕하세요. WBCO 경제 뉴스에 오신 것을 환영합니다. 오늘 밤, 온라인에서 상품과 서비스를 구매할 때 지불하는 가격에 대해 이야기해보겠습니다. 특히, 수요가 많은 시기에 쇼핑을 하면 더 많은 비용을 지불하게 되는 이유를 살펴볼 것입니다. 가격 급등 현상이라고 부르는 이런 경향은 대형 항공사가 수요를 추적하여 항공권 가격을 신속하게 변경할 수 있게 하는 컴퓨터 소프트웨어에서 처음 시작되었습니다. 이 기술은 이제 널리 이용되고 있습니다. 심지어 작은 업체들도 수요가 많을 때 더 많은 비용을 청구하는 경우를 볼 수 있습니다. 오늘 초대 손님은 윤 항 교수님이며, 이 분야의 손꼽히는 전문가입니다. 지난 달에는 국제 경제 정상 회의에서 특별 연사로 참여했습니다.

어휘 financial 경제의, 금융의 peak 절정의, 최고조의 demand 수요, 요구 surge 급등, 급증 pricing 가격 (책정) trend 경향, 추세 track 파악하다, 추적하다 widely 널리 charge 청구하다, 부과하다 leading 손꼽히는, 선도적인 featured speaker 특별 연사

92 What type of news is the broadcast about?
(A) Travel
(B) Art
(C) Financial
(D) Sports

방송은 어떤 종류의 뉴스에 관한 것인가?
(A) 여행
(B) 예술
(C) 경제
(D) 스포츠

해설 전체 내용 관련 – 방송 주제
화자가 초반부에 WBCO 경제 뉴스에 온 것을 환영한다(~ welcome to WBCO financial news)고 했으므로 정답은 (C)이다.

93 Why does the speaker say, "That technology is now widely available"?
(A) To praise a marketing plan
(B) To recommend a computer application
(C) To explain the growth of a trend
(D) To correct some wrong information

화자는 왜 "이 기술은 이제 널리 이용되고 있습니다"라고 말하는가?
(A) 마케팅 계획을 칭찬하기 위해
(B) 컴퓨터 애플리케이션을 추천하기 위해
(C) 경향의 증가를 설명하기 위해
(D) 잘못된 정보를 바로잡기 위해

어휘 praise 칭찬하다 explain 설명하다 growth 증가, 성장 correct 바로잡다, 정정하다

해설 화자의 의도 파악 – 이 기술이 이제 널리 이용되고 있다는 말의 의도
화자가 중반부에 이런 경향은 대형 항공사가 수요를 추적하여 항공권 가격을 신속하게 변경할 수 있게 하는 컴퓨터 소프트웨어에서 처음 시작되었다(~ this trend first started with computer software that allowed large airlines ~)면서 인용문을 언급하고 있다. 따라서 그러한 경향이 현재 널리 이용되고 있을 정도로 증가했음을 알리기 위해 한 말이라는 것을 알 수 있으므로 정답은 (C)이다.

94 What did Professor Yun Hang do last month?
(A) He spoke at a conference.
(B) He published a book.
(C) He started a business.
(D) He won an award.

윤 항 교수는 지난달에 무엇을 했는가?
(A) 콘퍼런스에서 연설했다.
(B) 책을 출간했다.
(C) 사업을 시작했다.
(D) 상을 받았다.

어휘 publish 출간하다, 펴내다, 싣다

해설 세부 사항 관련 – 윤 항 교수가 지난달에 한 일
화자가 후반부에 윤 항 교수를 소개하면서 지난달에는 국제 경제 정상 회의에서 특별 연사로 참여했다(Last month he was the featured speaker at the International Economics Summit)고 했으므로 정답은 (A)이다.

Paraphrasing
담화의 the featured speaker at the International Economics Summit → 정답의 spoke at a conference

95-97 전화 메시지 + 쿠폰

M-Au Hi. This is Liam from Oceania Flowers. I'm calling about our print order for coupons. **⁹⁵We originally said we needed the coupons by Friday, but we now need them to be ready by Wednesday instead.** ⁹⁶We just found out yesterday that our application to the National Florists Association was approved. We'll be attending their annual Floral Show in Richmond this weekend. Oh, one other thing—⁹⁷**we'd also like to change the limit to five items on the coupon.** Can you take care of that before you start printing? Thank you!

안녕하세요. 저는 오셔니아 플라워즈의 리암입니다. 저희 쿠폰 출력 주문과 관련해 전화를 드립니다. **원래는 금요일까지 쿠폰이 필요하다고 말씀을 드렸었는데, 이제는 수요일까지 준비되어야 합니다.** 전국 플로리스트 협회에 낸 신청서가 승인되었다는 사실을 어제 막 알게 되었어요. 이번 주말 리치몬드에서 열리는 이 협회의 연례 꽃 박람회에 참석할 예정입니다. 아, 다른 한 가지가 더 있는데, **쿠폰의 적용 한도를 5개 제품으로 변경하고 싶어요.** 출력을 시작하기 전에 이 부분을 처리해 주시겠어요? 감사합니다!

어휘 originally 원래, 애초에 instead 대신 approve 승인하다 limit 한정, 제한

Oceania Flowers Since 2005
25% off Daisies!
⁹⁷**Limit of 2 items**
Open 8 A.M.–6 P.M.

오셔니아 플라워즈 2005년 개업
데이지 25% 할인!
2개 제품 한정
영업시간 오전 8시–오후 6시

95 Why is the speaker calling?
(A) To file a complaint
(B) To purchase some tickets
(C) To revise an order
(D) To promote a product

화자는 왜 전화하는가?
(A) 불만을 제기하기 위해
(B) 티켓을 구입하기 위해
(C) 주문을 변경하기 위해
(D) 제품을 홍보하기 위해

어휘 file a complaint 불만을 제기하다 revise 변경하다, 수정하다

해설 **전체 내용 관련 – 화자의 전화 목적**
화자가 초반부에 원래 금요일까지 필요하다고 말한 쿠폰이 이제는 수요일까지 준비되어야 한다(We originally said we needed the coupons by Friday, but we now need them to be ready by Wednesday instead)고 말하고 있다. 이는 쿠폰 출력 주문에 대한 기한을 변경하겠다는 뜻이므로 정답은 (C)이다.

96 What did the speaker find out yesterday?
(A) A printer was replaced.
(B) An application was approved.
(C) A sales event was announced.
(D) A lease was extended.

화자는 어제 무엇을 알게 되었는가?
(A) 프린터가 교체되었다.
(B) 신청서가 승인되었다.
(C) 할인 행사가 공지되었다.
(D) 임대 계약이 연장되었다.

어휘 lease 임대 계약(서)

해설 **세부 사항 관련 – 화자가 어제 알게 된 것**
화자가 중반부에 전국 플로리스트 협회에 낸 신청서가 승인되었다는 사실을 어제 막 알게 되었다(We just found out yesterday that our application to the National Florists Association was approved)고 했으므로 정답은 (B)이다.

97 Look at the graphic. Which number does the speaker want to change?
(A) 2005
(B) 25
(C) 2
(D) 6

시각 정보에 의하면, 화자는 어느 숫자를 변경하고 싶어 하는가?
(A) 2005
(B) 25
(C) 2
(D) 6

해설 **시각 정보 연계 – 화자가 변경하려는 숫자**
화자가 후반부에 쿠폰의 적용 한도를 5개 제품으로 변경하고 싶다(~ we'd also like to change the limit to five items on the coupon)고 했는데, 쿠폰에 한정 제품 수량이 2로 나와 있으므로 정답은 (C)이다.

98-100 메시지 + 버스 노선도

M-Cn Hi, Takuma. **98 Good news—you got your first television audition! It's for a role in a TV drama.** I've sent an e-mail with the script and details. Since you're auditioning to join the cast of an ongoing show, **99 you should watch some videos of previous episodes so you understand the role.** One last note—since you're new to the city, you might be wondering about the best bus route to take. You could take the green line to Orchard, but **100 I'd recommend taking the yellow line to the last stop.** It's a longer route, but the last stop is closer to the studio.

안녕하세요, 타쿠마. **좋은 소식이 있어요. 첫 번째 텔레비전 오디션 기회를 얻으셨어요! TV 드라마 배역이에요.** 대본과 상세 정보를 이메일로 보냈어요. 진행 중인 프로그램의 출연진에 합류하기 위해 오디션을 보는 것이라서, **이전 방송분을 시청해서 배역을 이해해야 해요.** 마지막 한 가지 전달 사항이에요. 이 도시에 처음이시니, 어떤 버스를 타야 가장 좋을지 궁금하실 거예요. 녹색 노선을 타고 오차드로 가실 수도 있겠지만, **황색 노선을 이용해 마지막 정거장까지 가시는 것을 권해 드려요.** 경로가 더 길지만, 마지막 정거장이 스튜디오와 더 가깝습니다.

어휘 audition 오디션; 오디션을 보다 script 대본, 원고 details 상세 정보, 세부 사항 join 합류하다, 함께하다 cast 출연진 ongoing 진행 중인 previous 이전의 note 전달 사항, 메모 wonder 궁금해하다 route 경로, 노선 close 가까운

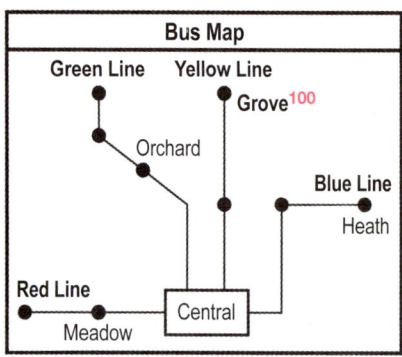

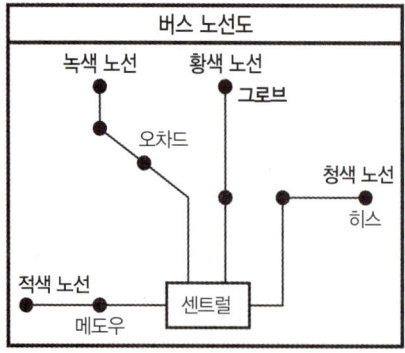

98 Who most likely is the listener?
(A) An actor
(B) A photographer
(C) A writer
(D) An athlete

청자는 누구인 것 같은가?
(A) 배우
(B) 사진가
(C) 작가
(D) 운동선수

해설 전체 내용 관련 – 청자의 직업

화자가 초반부에 좋은 소식이라는 말과 함께 청자가 첫 번째 텔레비전 오디션 기회를 얻었고, 그것이 TV 드라마 배역(Good news—you got your first television audition! It's for a role in a TV drama)이라고 했으므로 정답은 (A)이다.

99 According to the speaker, what should the listener do to prepare?
(A) Update a résumé
(B) Review some videos
(C) Contact a colleague
(D) Make a recording

화자에 따르면, 청자는 준비하기 위해 무엇을 해야 하는가?
(A) 이력서 업데이트하기
(B) 영상 살펴보기
(C) 동료에게 연락하기
(D) 녹화본 만들기

해설 세부 사항 관련 – 청자가 준비를 위해 할 일

화자가 중반부에 이전 방송분을 시청해서 배역을 이해해야 한다(~ you should watch some videos of previous episodes so you understand the role)고 했으므로 정답은 (B)이다.

Paraphrasing
담화의 watch some videos of previous episodes
→ 정답의 Review some videos

100 Look at the graphic. Which bus stop does the speaker recommend getting off at?
(A) Orchard
(B) Heath
(C) Grove
(D) Meadow

시각 정보에 의하면, 화자는 어느 버스 정거장에서 하차하도록 권하는가?
(A) 오차드
(B) 히스
(C) 그로브
(D) 메도우

해설 시각 정보 연계 – 화자가 하차를 권하는 정거장

화자가 후반부에 황색 노선을 이용해 마지막 정거장까지 가는 것을 권한다(~ I'd recommend taking the yellow line to the last stop)고 했는데, 버스 노선도에서 황색 노선의 마지막 정거장은 그로브이므로 정답은 (C)이다.

기출 TEST 4

1 (C)	2 (D)	3 (A)	4 (B)	5 (A)
6 (B)	7 (C)	8 (C)	9 (C)	10 (B)
11 (C)	12 (A)	13 (A)	14 (B)	15 (C)
16 (A)	17 (A)	18 (B)	19 (A)	20 (C)
21 (B)	22 (A)	23 (B)	24 (C)	25 (B)
26 (A)	27 (A)	28 (A)	29 (B)	30 (C)
31 (B)	32 (C)	33 (A)	34 (C)	35 (D)
36 (C)	37 (A)	38 (B)	39 (D)	40 (A)
41 (C)	42 (A)	43 (C)	44 (B)	45 (A)
46 (A)	47 (B)	48 (C)	49 (A)	50 (B)
51 (D)	52 (C)	53 (D)	54 (C)	55 (A)
56 (C)	57 (D)	58 (D)	59 (B)	60 (D)
61 (C)	62 (B)	63 (A)	64 (B)	65 (C)
66 (B)	67 (D)	68 (C)	69 (A)	70 (B)
71 (B)	72 (D)	73 (A)	74 (A)	75 (D)
76 (B)	77 (D)	78 (A)	79 (B)	80 (C)
81 (C)	82 (B)	83 (D)	84 (A)	85 (A)
86 (C)	87 (B)	88 (B)	89 (D)	90 (C)
91 (C)	92 (A)	93 (C)	94 (D)	95 (D)
96 (A)	97 (D)	98 (C)	99 (B)	100 (D)

PART 1

1

M-Cn

(A) She's crossing a busy street.
(B) She's removing her eyeglasses.
(C) She's standing next to a bin.
(D) She's getting into a taxicab.

(A) 여자가 분주한 거리를 건너고 있다.
(B) 여자가 안경을 벗고 있다.
(C) 여자가 쓰레기통 옆에 서 있다.
(D) 여자가 택시에 타고 있다.

어휘 cross 건너다, 가로지르다 remove 벗다, 제거하다
bin 쓰레기통 get into ~에 타다

해설 1인 등장 사진 – 사람의 동작/상태 묘사
(A) 오답. 여자가 분주한 거리를 건너고 있는(is crossing a busy street) 모습이 아니므로 오답.
(B) 오답. 여자가 안경을 벗는(is removing her eyeglasses) 모습이 아니므로 오답.
(C) 정답. 여자가 쓰레기통 옆에 서 있는(is standing next to a bin) 모습이므로 정답.
(D) 오답. 여자가 택시에 타는(is getting into a taxicab) 모습이 아니므로 오답.

2

W-Br

(A) Some trucks have stopped at a traffic signal.
(B) Some lights are being installed above a garage door.
(C) A garden is being planted along a fence.
(D) Several vehicles are parked outside a building.

(A) 트럭들이 교통 신호등 앞에 정차해 있다.
(B) 전등들이 차고 문 위에 설치되고 있다.
(C) 정원에 울타리를 따라 식물이 심어지고 있다.
(D) 여러 대의 차량들이 건물 밖에 주차되어 있다.

어휘 traffic 교통(량), 차량들 install 설치하다 garage 차고
plant (식물을) 심다 vehicle 차량

해설 사물/풍경 사진 – 풍경 묘사
(A) 사진에 없는 명사를 이용한 오답. 사진에 교통 신호등(a traffic signal)의 모습이 보이지 않으므로 오답.
(B) 동사 오답. 전등들(Some lights)이 설치되고 있는(are being installed) 모습이 아니므로 오답.
(C) 동사 오답. 식물이 심어지고 있는(is being planted) 모습이 아니므로 오답.
(D) 정답. 여러 대의 차량들(Several vehicles)이 건물 밖에 주차되어 있는(are parked outside a building) 모습이므로 정답.

3

M-Cn

(A) A woman is following a man down a corridor.
(B) A woman is putting together some cardboard boxes.
(C) A man is emptying a large container.
(D) A man is climbing up a ladder.

(A) 여자가 복도에서 남자를 따라가고 있다.
(B) 여자가 판지 상자들을 조립하고 있다.
(C) 남자가 대형 용기를 비우고 있다.
(D) 남자가 사다리 위로 올라가고 있다.

어휘 follow 따라가다 corridor 복도 put together 조립하다
empty 비우다 container 용기 climb up 위로 올라가다
ladder 사다리

해설 2인 이상 등장 사진 - 사람의 동작/상태 묘사
(A) 정답. 여자가 복도에서 남자를 따라가고 있는(is following a man down a corridor) 모습이므로 정답.
(B) 동사 오답. 여자가 판지 상자들을 조립하고 있는(is putting together some cardboard boxes) 모습이 아니므로 오답.
(C) 동사 오답. 남자가 대형 용기를 비우고 있는(is emptying a large container) 모습이 아니므로 오답.
(D) 동사 오답. 남자가 사다리 위로 올라가고 있는(is climbing up a ladder) 모습이 아니므로 오답.

4

M-Au

(A) He's clearing some snow off a path.
(B) He's pulling a cart on a walkway.
(C) He's leaning over to tie his shoe.
(D) He's taking some items out of a basket.

(A) 남자가 길에서 눈을 치우고 있다.
(B) 남자가 보도에서 카트를 끌고 있다.
(C) 남자가 신발끈을 묶기 위해 몸을 숙이고 있다.
(D) 남자가 바구니에서 물품을 꺼내고 있다.

어휘 path 길, 보도 walkway 보도, 통로 lean over 몸을 숙이다
take ~ out of ... …에서 ~을 꺼내다

해설 1인 등장 사진 - 사람의 동작/상태 묘사
(A) 동사 오답. 남자가 눈을 치우고 있는(is clearing some snow off a path) 모습이 아니므로 오답.
(B) 정답. 남자가 보도에서 카트를 끌고 있는(is pulling a cart on a walkway) 모습이므로 정답.
(C) 동사 오답. 남자가 몸을 숙이고 있는(is leaning over) 모습이 아니므로 오답.
(D) 동사 오답. 남자가 바구니에서 물품을 꺼내고 있는(is taking some items out of a basket) 모습이 아니므로 오답.

5

W-Br

(A) One of the women is carrying a bag on her shoulder.
(B) One of the women is placing her luggage on a scale.
(C) Some suitcases have been lined up against the wall.
(D) Some clothes are being packed in a bag.

(A) 여자들 중 한 명이 어깨에 가방을 메고 있다.
(B) 여자들 중 한 명이 짐을 저울에 올려 놓고 있다.
(C) 여행 가방들이 벽 쪽에 줄지어 있다.
(D) 옷들이 가방에 담기고 있다.

어휘 place 놓다, 두다 scale 저울 suitcase 여행 가방
line up ~을 한 줄로 세우다 pack (짐 등을) 꾸리다, 싸다

해설 2인 이상 등장 사진 - 사람/사물/풍경 혼합 묘사
(A) 정답. 여자들 중 한 명이 어깨에 가방을 메고 있는(is carrying a bag on her shoulder) 모습이므로 정답.
(B) 사진에 없는 명사를 이용한 오답. 사진에 저울(a scale)의 모습이 보이지 않으므로 오답.
(C) 동사 오답. 여행 가방들(Some suitcases)이 벽 쪽에 줄지어 있는(have been lined up against the wall) 모습이 아니므로 오답.
(D) 동사 오답. 옷들(Some clothes)이 가방에 담기고 있는(are being packed in a bag) 모습이 아니므로 오답.

6

W-Am

(A) Some customers are drinking from coffee cups.
(B) Some coffee cups have been placed on a counter.
(C) Some aprons are hanging from hooks.
(D) One of the workers is wiping down a counter.

(A) 고객들이 커피잔에 든 것을 마시고 있다.
(B) 커피잔들이 카운터에 놓여 있다.
(C) 앞치마들이 고리에 걸려 있다.
(D) 직원들 중 한 명이 카운터를 닦고 있다.

어휘 apron 앞치마 hang from ~에 걸려 있다 wipe down 닦다

해설 2인 이상 등장 사진 - 사람/사물/풍경 혼합 묘사
(A) 동사 오답. 고객들이 커피잔에 든 것을 마시고 있는(are drinking from coffee cups) 모습이 아니므로 오답.
(B) 정답. 커피잔들(Some coffee cups)이 카운터에 놓여 있는(have been placed on a counter) 모습이므로 정답.
(C) 동사 오답. 앞치마들(Some aprons)이 고리에 걸려 있는(are hanging from hooks) 모습이 아니므로 오답.
(D) 동사 오답. 직원들 중 한 명이 카운터를 닦고 있는(is wiping down a counter) 모습이 아니므로 오답.

PART 2

7 M-Au / W-Br

Will you let me know when the catering order arrives?
(A) A reservation for two.
(B) The front office.
(C) Sure, I'll text you.

출장 요리 주문이 도착하면 알려 주실래요?
(A) 두 명 예약이요.
(B) 접수처요.
(C) 물론이죠, 문자 메시지를 보내 드리겠습니다.

어휘 let ~ know ~에게 알리다 catering 출장 요리 제공(업) reservation 예약 front office 접수처, 고객 대면 부서 text 문자 메시지를 보내다

해설 부탁/요청의 의문문
(A) 연상 단어 오답. 질문의 order에서 연상 가능한 reservation을 이용한 오답.
(B) 질문과 상관없는 오답.
(C) 정답. 출장 요리 주문이 도착하면 알려 달라는 요청에 물론이죠(Sure)라고 수락한 뒤, 문자 메시지를 보내겠다며 긍정 답변과 일관된 내용을 덧붙이고 있으므로 정답.

8 W-Am / W-Br

Why is the manager being replaced?
(A) Let's do that.
(B) I prefer working with a team.
(C) Because she's leaving the company.

관리자가 왜 교체되는 건가요?
(A) 그렇게 합시다.
(B) 팀과 함께 일하는 것을 선호합니다.
(C) 그분께서 회사를 그만두시기 때문입니다.

어휘 replace 교체하다, 대체하다 prefer 선호하다

해설 관리자가 교체되는 이유를 묻는 Why 의문문
(A) 질문과 상관없는 오답. 제안 의문문에 대한 응답이므로 오답.
(B) 연상 단어 오답. 질문의 manager에서 연상 가능한 working과 team을 이용한 오답.
(C) 정답. 관리자가 교체되는 이유를 묻는 질문에 그 사람이 회사를 그만두기 때문이라고 이유를 제시하고 있으므로 정답.

9 W-Br / M-Cn ▶동영상 강의

Ms. Cho should close the store early on Friday.
(A) I prefer a salad.
(B) Cash register four.
(C) Yes, I agree.

조 씨는 금요일에 매장을 일찍 닫아야 해요.
(A) 저는 샐러드를 선호합니다.
(B) 4번 계산대요.
(C) 네, 동의합니다.

어휘 cash register 계산대 agree 동의하다, 합의하다

해설 정보 전달의 평서문
(A) 연상 단어 오답. 평서문의 store에서 연상 가능한 salad를 이용한 오답.
(B) 연상 단어 오답. 평서문의 store에서 연상 가능한 Cash register를 이용한 오답.
(C) 정답. 조 씨가 금요일에 매장을 일찍 닫아야 한다는 평서문에 동의한다는 뜻을 나타내고 있으므로 정답.

10 W-Am / M-Au

Why did you decide to become a pilot?
(A) Is there free Internet access?
(B) I enjoy traveling.
(C) He's on vacation in Argentina.

왜 조종사가 되기로 결정하셨나요?
(A) 무료 인터넷 접속이 가능한가요?
(B) 여행을 즐깁니다.
(C) 그는 아르헨티나에서 휴가 중이에요.

어휘 decide 결정하다 access 접속, 접근 on vacation 휴가 중인

해설 조종사가 되기로 결정한 이유를 묻는 Why 의문문
(A) 질문과 상관없는 오답.
(B) 정답. 조종사가 되기로 결정한 이유를 묻는 질문에 여행을 즐긴다고 이유를 밝히고 있으므로 정답.
(C) 질문과 상관없는 오답. 질문에 3인칭 대명사 He로 지칭할 인물이 언급된 적이 없으므로 오답.

11 M-Cn / W-Br

Have you always commuted by train?
(A) The training starts at two o'clock.
(B) I think the station is on Mulberry Avenue.
(C) Yes, because I don't have a car.

항상 기차로 통근하셨나요?
(A) 그 교육은 2시에 시작해요.
(B) 그 역은 멀베리 가에 있는 것 같아요.
(C) 네, 차가 없어서요.

어휘 commute 통근하다, 통학하다

해설 항상 기차로 통근했는지 묻는 조동사(Have) 의문문
(A) 유사 발음 오답. 질문의 train과 부분적으로 발음이 유사한 training을 이용한 오답.
(B) 연상 단어 오답. 질문의 train에서 연상 가능한 station을 이용한 오답.
(C) 정답. 항상 기차로 통근했는지 묻는 질문에 네(Yes)라고 대답한 뒤, 차가 없기 때문이라고 긍정 답변과 일관된 내용을 덧붙이고 있으므로 정답.

12 W-Am / W-Br

When does your manager usually come in?
(A) Early in the morning.
(B) No, I just left it there.
(C) I haven't—thanks.

매니저는 보통 언제 오시나요?
(A) 아침 일찍이요.
(B) 아니요, 방금 거기에 두었어요.
(C) 그런 적 없어요. 감사합니다.

어휘 usually 평소에, 보통

해설 매니저가 평소 오는 시간을 묻는 When 의문문
(A) 정답. 매니저가 평소 오는 시간을 묻는 질문에 아침 일찍이라고 시간을 알려 주고 있으므로 정답.
(B) Yes/No 불가 오답. When 의문문에는 Yes/No 응답이 불가능하므로 오답.
(C) 질문과 상관없는 오답. Have로 시작하는 의문문에 대한 응답이므로 오답.

13 W-Br / M-Au

Isn't there a discount on this computer monitor?
(A) Yes, a ten percent discount.
(B) An inventory check.
(C) Mine is broken.

이 컴퓨터 모니터는 할인하지 않나요?
(A) 네, 10퍼센트 할인됩니다.
(B) 재고 확인이요.
(C) 제 것은 고장 났어요.

어휘 inventory 재고(품), 재고 목록   broken 고장 난, 망가진

해설 모니터 할인 여부를 확인하는 부정 의문문
(A) 정답. 모니터 할인 여부를 확인하는 질문에 네(Yes)라고 대답한 뒤, 10퍼센트 할인된다고 긍정 답변과 일관된 내용을 덧붙이고 있으므로 정답.
(B) 질문과 상관없는 오답.
(C) 질문과 상관없는 오답.

14 W-Am / M-Cn

How is the new group of interns doing?
(A) No, we have five people in total.
(B) I haven't heard any negative feedback at all.
(C) Let's pose for a group photo over there.

신입 인턴은 어떻게 지내고 있나요?
(A) 아니요, 저희는 총 다섯 명입니다.
(B) 부정적인 의견은 전혀 듣지 못했어요.
(C) 저쪽에서 단체 사진을 찍을 수 있게 포즈를 취합시다.

어휘 in total 총   negative 부정적인   feedback 의견
pose 포즈를 취하다

해설 신입 인턴들이 어떻게 지내는지 묻는 How 의문문
(A) Yes/No 불가 오답. How 의문문에는 Yes/No 응답이 불가능하므로 오답.
(B) 정답. 신입 인턴들이 어떻게 지내는지 묻는 질문에 부정적인 의견은 전혀 듣지 못했다며 잘 지내고 있음을 우회적으로 알려 주고 있으므로 정답.
(C) 단어 반복 오답. 질문의 group을 반복 이용한 오답.

15 W-Br / M-Cn

They're carrying those boxes to the storage room.
(A) That's a good price.
(B) No, the store opens at noon today.
(C) I'll go with them.

그들이 그 상자들을 창고로 옮기고 있어요.
(A) 좋은 가격이네요.
(B) 아니요, 그 매장은 오늘 정오에 열어요.
(C) 제가 그들과 함께 갈게요.

어휘 carry 나르다, 옮기다   storage 보관, 저장

해설 정보 전달의 평서문
(A) 평서문과 상관없는 오답.
(B) 유사 발음 오답. 평서문의 storage와 부분적으로 발음이 유사한 store를 이용한 오답.
(C) 정답. 사람들이 상자들을 창고로 옮기고 있다고 알리는 평서문에 그들과 함께 가겠다는 말로 도움을 제공하겠다는 의사를 나타내고 있으므로 정답.

16 M-Au / W-Am

Where can I send the money?
(A) To my bank account.
(B) I think that's expensive, too.
(C) By next Tuesday.

돈을 어디로 보내면 될까요?
(A) 제 은행 계좌로요.
(B) 그것도 비싼 것 같아요.
(C) 다음 주 화요일까지요.

어휘 account 계좌, 계정

해설 돈을 보낼 곳을 묻는 Where 의문문
(A) 정답. 돈을 보낼 곳을 묻는 질문에 자신의 계좌로 보내라고 알려 주고 있으므로 정답.
(B) 연상 단어 오답. 질문의 money에서 연상 가능한 expensive를 이용한 오답.
(C) 질문과 상관없는 오답. When 의문문에 대한 응답이므로 오답.

17 M-Au / M-Cn

Who's coming in tomorrow to help us prepare for the grand opening?
(A) Rebecca and Malik.
(B) An online job posting.
(C) Some sales data.

개장식 준비를 돕기 위해 내일 누가 오나요?
(A) 레베카와 말릭이요.
(B) 온라인 구인 광고요.
(C) 매출 자료요.

어휘 prepare 준비하다   job posting 구인 광고
sales 매출, 판매(량)

해설 개장식 준비를 돕기 위해 오는 사람을 묻는 Who 의문문
(A) 정답. 개장식 준비를 돕기 위해 오는 사람을 묻는 질문에 레베카와 말릭이라고 구체적인 사람 이름을 알려 주고 있으므로 정답.
(B) 연상 단어 오답. 질문의 opening을 공석으로 이해하는 경우에 연상 가능한 job posting을 이용한 오답.
(C) 질문과 상관없는 오답.

18 W-Am / M-Cn

How often does the bus stop at this location?
(A) I'll be visiting the office.
(B) About every twenty minutes.
(C) A city council meeting.

버스가 이곳에 얼마나 자주 정차하나요?
(A) 저는 그 사무실을 방문할 예정입니다.
(B) 약 20분마다요.
(C) 시 의회 회의요.

어휘 location 곳, 위치   council 의회

해설 버스의 정차 빈도를 묻는 How often 의문문
(A) 질문과 상관없는 오답.
(B) 정답. 버스의 정차 빈도를 묻는 질문에 약 20분마다라고 빈도로 응답하고 있으므로 정답.
(C) 질문과 상관없는 오답.

19 W-Am / M-Au

What's the candidate review process?
(A) We review the résumés first.
(B) A few good reviews.
(C) OK—I'll just follow them.

지원자 평가 과정이 어떻게 되나요?
(A) 우선 이력서를 검토합니다.
(B) 몇몇 좋은 평가들이요.
(C) 알겠어요, 그냥 따라갈게요.

어휘 candidate 지원자, 후보자   review 평가; 검토하다, 평가하다
process (처리) 과정   follow 따르다, 따라가다

해설 지원자 평가 과정을 묻는 What 의문문
(A) 정답. 지원자 평가 과정을 묻는 질문에 우선 이력서를 검토한다며 첫 번째 단계를 알려 주고 있으므로 정답.
(B) 단어 반복 오답. 질문의 review를 반복 이용한 오답.
(C) Yes/No 불가 오답. What 의문문에는 Yes/No 응답이 불가능한데, OK도 일종의 Yes 응답이라고 볼 수 있으므로 오답.

20 W-Am / M-Cn

There's coffee in the break room, right?
(A) That shift starts at noon.
(B) We decided to paint this room gray.
(C) Yes—I just made a fresh pot.

휴게실에 커피 있죠, 그렇죠?
(A) 그 근무는 정오에 시작합니다.
(B) 이 방을 회색으로 칠하기로 했어요.
(C) 네, 제가 방금 새로 끓여 놨습니다.

어휘 break room 휴게실   shift 교대 근무(조)
make a fresh pot (차 등을) 새로 끓이다

해설 휴게실에 커피가 있는지 확인하는 부가 의문문
(A) 질문과 상관없는 오답. When 의문문에 대한 응답이므로 오답.
(B) 단어 반복 오답. 질문의 room을 반복 이용한 오답.
(C) 정답. 휴게실에 커피가 있는지 확인하는 질문에 네(Yes)라고 대답한 뒤, 자신이 막 새로 끓였다고 긍정 답변과 일관된 내용을 덧붙이고 있으므로 정답.

21 M-Au / W-Am

Who's going to the company picnic today?
(A) About two hours long.
(B) I'm leaving in a few minutes.
(C) A two-year maintenance contract.

오늘 회사 야유회에 누가 가나요?
(A) 약 두 시간이요.
(B) 제가 몇 분 후에 출발할 거예요.
(C) 2년 유지 관리 계약이요.

어휘 maintenance 유지 관리, 정비   contract 계약(서)

해설 회사 야유회에 가는 사람을 묻는 Who 의문문
(A) 질문과 상관없는 오답. How long 의문문에 대한 응답이므로 오답.
(B) 정답. 회사 야유회에 가는 사람을 묻는 질문에 자신이 곧 출발한다고 알려 주고 있으므로 정답.
(C) 질문과 상관없는 오답. How long 의문문에 대한 응답이므로 오답.

22 W-Br / M-Cn

Will the bakery be open tomorrow?
(A) No, it's closed until mid-August.
(B) Have you checked the oven?
(C) The pound cake is delicious.

그 제과점이 내일 문을 열까요?
(A) 아니요, 8월 중순까지 문을 닫아요.
(B) 오븐은 확인하셨어요?
(C) 파운드 케이크가 맛있어요.

해설 제과점이 내일 문을 여는지 묻는 조동사(Will) 의문문
(A) 정답. 제과점이 내일 문을 여는지 묻는 질문에 아니요(No)라고 대답한 뒤, 8월 중순까지 문을 닫는다며 부정 답변과 일관된 내용을 덧붙이고 있으므로 정답.

(B) 연상 단어 오답. 질문의 bakery에서 연상 가능한 oven을 이용한 오답.
(C) 연상 단어 오답. 질문의 bakery에서 연상 가능한 pound cake를 이용한 오답.

23 M-Cn / M-Au ▶동영상 강의

Are you installing the new software on Monday or Tuesday?

(A) Thanks, but they already have one.
(B) I'll be out of the office all week.
(C) It was an older model laptop.

새 소프트웨어를 월요일에 설치하실 건가요, 아니면 화요일에 하실 건가요?
(A) 감사하지만, 그분들은 이미 갖고 있어요.
(B) 저는 이번 주 내내 사무실을 비울 거예요.
(C) 구형 노트북이었어요.

해설 소프트웨어를 설치할 요일을 묻는 선택 의문문
(A) 질문과 상관없는 오답. 질문에 3인칭 복수 대명사 they로 지칭할 인물이 언급된 적이 없으므로 오답.
(B) 정답. 월요일과 화요일 중 언제 새 소프트웨어를 설치할지 묻는 질문에 이번 주 내내 사무실을 비울 것이라며 월요일과 화요일 모두 불가능하다는 제3의 답변을 한 정답.
(C) 연상 단어 오답. 질문의 software에서 연상 가능한 laptop을 이용한 오답.

24 M-Cn / W-Br

Let me find a sales associate to help you.

(A) At the top of the list.
(B) My article is ready to be uploaded.
(C) I just found what I'm looking for.

도와드릴 영업 사원을 찾아 드리겠습니다.
(A) 목록 상단에요.
(B) 제 기사를 업로드할 준비가 되었습니다.
(C) 제가 찾는 것을 방금 발견했어요.

어휘 associate 사원, 동료 look for ~을 찾다

해설 제안/권유의 평서문
(A) 평서문과 상관없는 오답. Where 의문문에 대한 응답이므로 오답.
(B) 평서문과 상관없는 오답.
(C) 정답. 도와줄 영업 사원을 찾아 주겠다고 제안하는 평서문에 찾는 것을 막 발견했다며 영업 사원이 필요하지 않음을 우회적으로 알려 주고 있으므로 정답.

25 M-Au / W-Am

You're offering discounts to students, right?

(A) No, that's not my wallet.
(B) You'll need valid identification.
(C) I'm doing inventory this weekend.

학생에게 할인을 제공하죠, 그렇죠?
(A) 아니요, 제 지갑이 아닙니다.
(B) 유효한 신분증이 필요할 거예요.
(C) 이번 주말에 재고 조사를 할 거예요.

어휘 valid 유효한 identification 신분 증명(서)

해설 학생 할인 제공 여부를 확인하는 부가 의문문
(A) 질문과 상관없는 오답.
(B) 정답. 학생 할인 제공 여부를 확인하는 질문에 유효한 신분증이 필요하다며 학생 할인을 제공함을 우회적으로 알려 주고 있으므로 정답.
(C) 질문과 상관없는 오답.

26 W-Br / W-Am

The sales department posted an advertisement for an assistant.

(A) I didn't know they were hiring.
(B) An additional charge for shipping.
(C) No, I haven't been there.

영업부에서 업무 보조를 구하는 광고를 게시했어요.
(A) 그곳에서 사람을 고용하는 줄 몰랐어요.
(B) 추가 배송 요금이요.
(C) 아니요, 그곳에 가 본 적 없어요.

어휘 post 게시하다 advertisement 광고 assistant 보조, 조수 additional 추가적인 charge (청구) 요금 shipping 배송

해설 정보 전달의 평서문
(A) 정답. 영업부에서 업무 보조를 구하는 광고를 게시했다고 알리는 평서문에 그 부서에서 사람을 고용하는 줄 몰랐다고 호응하고 있으므로 정답.
(B) 평서문과 상관없는 오답.
(C) 평서문과 상관없는 오답.

27 W-Br / M-Cn ▶동영상 강의

Does the new accounting software work well?

(A) I haven't downloaded it yet.
(B) We're not offering a discount.
(C) That was my reaction too.

새 회계 소프트웨어가 잘 작동하나요?
(A) 아직 다운로드하지 않았어요.
(B) 저희는 할인을 제공하고 있지 않아요.
(C) 저도 그런 반응이었어요.

어휘 accounting 회계(부) work 작동하다 reaction 반응

해설 회계 소프트웨어가 잘 작동하는지 묻는 조동사(Does) 의문문
(A) 정답. 회계 소프트웨어가 잘 작동하는지 묻는 질문에 아직 다운로드하지 않았다며 모른다는 사실을 우회적으로 알려 주고 있으므로 정답.
(B) 유사 발음 오답. 질문의 accounting과 부분적으로 발음이 유사한 discount를 이용한 오답.
(C) 질문과 상관없는 오답.

28 W-Am / M-Cn

When's the finance department going to confirm our first-quarter budget?
(A) Their deadline is next week.
(B) Yes, I'll be there.
(C) In the mail room.

재무 부서에서 언제 1분기 예산을 확정할 건가요?
(A) 마감 기한이 다음 주예요.
(B) 네, 그곳에 갈 거예요.
(C) 우편실에요.

어휘 finance 재무, 재정 confirm 확정하다, 확인해 주다 quarter 분기 budget 예산 deadline 마감 기한

해설 재무 부서에서 1분기 예산을 확정하는 시기를 묻는 When 의문문
(A) 정답. 재무 부서에서 1분기 예산을 확정하는 시기를 묻는 질문에 그 부서의 마감 기한이 다음 주라며 그때까지는 확정될 것이라는 뜻을 우회적으로 나타내고 있으므로 정답.
(B) Yes/No 불가 오답. When 의문문에는 Yes/No 응답이 불가능하므로 오답.
(C) 질문과 상관없는 오답. Where 의문문에 대한 응답이므로 오답.

29 M-Cn / M-Au

Who canceled the conference call?
(A) The upstairs conference room.
(B) It's been rescheduled.
(C) Yes, you can.

누가 전화 회의를 취소했나요?
(A) 위층에 있는 대회의실이요.
(B) 일정이 재조정되었습니다.
(C) 네, 그러셔도 됩니다.

어휘 conference call 전화 회의 upstairs 위층의 reschedule 일정을 재조정하다

해설 전화 회의를 취소한 사람을 묻는 Who 의문문
(A) 단어 반복 오답. 질문의 conference를 반복 이용한 오답.
(B) 정답. 전화 회의를 취소한 사람을 묻는 질문에 일정이 재조정되었다며 취소된 것이 아님을 우회적으로 알려 주고 있으므로 정답.
(C) Yes/No 불가 오답. Who 의문문에는 Yes/No 응답이 불가능하므로 오답.

30 M-Au / W-Am

Can you please transfer the service to my new phone?
(A) Let's put it in the backseat.
(B) At the Maple Street station.
(C) There is a processing fee.

새 휴대폰으로 서비스를 이전해 주실 수 있나요?
(A) 뒷자리에 둡시다.
(B) 메이플 가 역에요.
(C) 처리 수수료가 있습니다.

어휘 transfer 이전하다, 전근시키다 backseat 뒷자리 processing fee 처리 수수료

해설 부탁/요청의 의문문
(A) 질문과 상관없는 오답.
(B) 질문과 상관없는 오답. Where 의문문에 대한 응답이므로 오답.
(C) 정답. 새 휴대폰으로 서비스 이전을 요청하는 질문에 처리 수수료가 있다며 수수료를 내면 이전이 가능함을 우회적으로 알려 주고 있으므로 정답.

31 W-Br / M-Cn

How was today's manufacturing seminar?
(A) A new pair of shoes.
(B) We didn't get there in time.
(C) There's a user's manual in the drawer.

오늘 있었던 제조 세미나는 어땠나요?
(A) 새 신발 한 켤레요.
(B) 저희는 제때 도착하지 못했어요.
(C) 서랍에 사용자 설명서가 있어요.

어휘 manufacturing 제조(업) in time 제때, 시간에 맞춰 manual 설명서, 안내서 drawer 서랍

해설 오늘 있었던 제조 세미나에 대한 의견을 묻는 How 의문문
(A) 질문과 상관없는 오답.
(B) 정답. 오늘 있었던 제조 세미나에 대한 의견을 묻는 질문에 제때 도착하지 못했다며 참석하지 못해서 알지 못함을 우회적으로 나타내고 있으므로 정답.
(C) 유사 발음 오답. 질문의 manufacturing과 부분적으로 발음이 유사한 manual을 이용한 오답.

PART 3

32-34 W-Am / M-Au ▶동영상 강의

W Good morning. **32 Thanks for coming to tour this apartment building.**

M I'm glad I could visit in person. **33 I've always wanted to live in this neighborhood**—it's so beautiful. This building is brand-new, isn't it?

W Yes. In fact, you'd be among the very first tenants if you decide to move here. Before you look at some apartments, **34 would you please sign your name here in our guest book?**

M Oh, of course.

여 안녕하세요. **이 아파트를 둘러보러 와 주셔서 감사합니다.**
남 직접 방문할 수 있어서 기뻐요. **항상 이 동네에 살고 싶었거든요.** 너무 아름답네요. 이 건물은 신축이죠, 아닌가요?

여 네. 실제로, 이곳으로 이사하기로 결정하시면 첫 입주자들 중 한 명이 될 것입니다. 아파트를 보시기 전에, **여기 방명록에 서명해 주시겠어요?**
남 아, 물론입니다.

어휘 tour 둘러보다, 견학하다 in person 직접 (가서)
neighborhood 지역, 인근 brand-new 새로운
tenant 세입자 sign 서명하다

32 Who most likely is the woman?
(A) A landscape architect
(B) An interior designer
(C) A real estate agent
(D) A building inspector

여자는 누구인 것 같은가?
(A) 조경 건축가
(B) 인테리어 디자이너
(C) 부동산 중개업자
(D) 건물 조사관

해설 전체 내용 관련 – 여자의 직업
여자가 첫 대사에서 남자에게 아파트를 둘러보러 와 줘서 감사하다 (Thanks for coming to tour this apartment building)고 했다. 이는 부동산 중개업자가 아파트를 보러 온 사람에게 할 수 있는 말이므로 정답은 (C)이다.

33 What is the man looking forward to?
(A) Living in a particular area
(B) Walking to work
(C) Going on vacation
(D) Saving money for a house

남자는 무엇을 고대하고 있는가?
(A) 특정 지역에 살기
(B) 걸어서 출근하기
(C) 휴가 떠나기
(D) 집을 위해 돈 모으기

어휘 look forward to ~을 고대하다 particular 특정한, 특별한

해설 세부 사항 관련 – 남자가 고대하는 것
남자가 첫 대사에서 항상 이 동네에 살고 싶었다(I've always wanted to live in this neighborhood)고 했으므로 정답은 (A)이다.

Paraphrasing
대화의 this neighborhood → 정답의 a particular area

34 What does the woman ask for?
(A) Some references
(B) Some identification
(C) A signature
(D) A payment

여자는 무엇을 요청하는가?
(A) 추천서
(B) 신분증
(C) 서명
(D) 결제

어휘 ask for ~을 요청하다 reference 추천(서), 추천인
identification 신분 증명(서)

해설 세부 사항 관련 – 여자의 요청 사항
여자가 두 번째 대사에서 방명록에 서명할 것(~ would you please sign your name here in our guest book?)을 요청하고 있으므로 정답은 (C)이다.

Paraphrasing
대화의 sign your name → 정답의 A signature

35-37 W-Am / M-Cn

W Chen, I hope all is going well on your first day. **35 I saw you have some scheduled seafood deliveries across the bay in the Morgan District. Why haven't you left yet?**
M I wasn't going to head over to that particular area for another hour. Do the restaurants in the Morgan District want their deliveries earlier than scheduled?
W No, but **36 I'm concerned about Bay Bridge traffic. It's routinely congested with vehicles. So you should always add at least an extra hour to your trip out there.**
M Thanks for the tip. **37 I'll also check traffic Webcams** on the highway agency's Web site.

여 첸, 근무 첫날인데 모든 일이 순조롭게 진행되고 있기를 바랍니다. **만 건너편의 모건 지역에 해산물 배송 업무가 예정되어 있는 걸 봤어요. 왜 아직 출발하지 않았나요?**
남 한 시간 더 있다가 그 지역으로 갈 생각이었어요. 모건 지역에 있는 레스토랑들이 예정보다 빨리 배송받길 원하나요?
여 아니요, 하지만 **베이 브리지의 교통량이 걱정됩니다. 차량들로 혼잡한 게 일상적이거든요. 그래서 거기에 갈 때는 항상 최소 한 시간은 더 잡아야 해요.**
남 팁 감사합니다. 고속도로 관리국의 웹사이트에서 **교통 웹캠들도 확인해 볼게요.**

어휘 go well 잘되다, 잘 진행되다 bay 만 district 지역, 구역
head over to ~로 향하다 traffic 교통(량), 차량들
routinely 일상적으로 congested 혼잡한 add 추가하다
at least 최소한 extra 추가의 agency (정부) 기관, 대행사

35 What most likely is the man's job?
(A) Boat crew member
(B) Restaurant owner
(C) Seafood inspector
(D) Delivery truck driver

남자의 직업은 무엇인 것 같은가?
(A) 보트 승무원
(B) 레스토랑 소유주
(C) 해산물 검사관
(D) 배송 트럭 기사

해설 전체 내용 관련 – 남자의 직업
여자가 첫 대사에서 남자에게 모건 지역에 해산물 배송 업무가 예정되어 있는 걸 봤다며, 왜 아직 출발하지 않았는지(I saw you have some scheduled seafood deliveries ~. Why haven't you left yet?) 묻고 있으므로 정답은 (D)이다.

36 Why is the woman concerned?
(A) A road has been temporarily closed.
(B) A permit has expired.
(C) Traffic may cause a delay.
(D) Some supplies are no longer available.

여자는 왜 걱정하는가?
(A) 도로가 일시적으로 폐쇄되었다.
(B) 허가증이 만료되었다.
(C) 교통량으로 인해 지연될 수 있다.
(D) 일부 물품을 더 이상 이용할 수 없다.

어휘 temporarily 일시적으로, 임시로   permit 허가증
expire 만료되다   cause 초래하다   delay 지연, 지체
supplies 물품, 용품   available 이용할 수 있는, 시간이 있는

해설 세부 사항 관련 – 여자가 걱정하는 이유
여자가 두 번째 대사에서 베이 브리지의 교통량이 걱정된다며, 차량들로 혼잡한 게 일상적이라서 거기에 갈 때는 항상 최소 한 시간은 더 잡아야 한다(I'm concerned about Bay Bridge traffic. It's routinely congested with vehicles. So you should always add at least an extra hour ~)고 덧붙이고 있으므로 정답은 (C)이다.

Paraphrasing
대화의 congested with vehicles → 정답의 Traffic

37 What does the man say he will check?
(A) Some webcams
(B) A list of ingredients
(C) An address
(D) Some maps

남자는 무엇을 확인할 것이라고 말하는가?
(A) 웹캠
(B) 재료 목록
(C) 주소
(D) 지도

어휘 ingredient (음식) 재료, 성분

해설 세부 사항 관련 – 남자가 확인할 것
남자가 마지막 대사에서 교통 웹캠들도 확인해 보겠다(I'll also check traffic Webcams ~)고 했으므로 정답은 (A)이다.

38-40 M-Au / W-Br

M This morning I got an e-mail from ³⁸**Pelicon, a local producer of beauty products.** They're interested in purchasing lanolin from us to use in their new line of all-natural makeup.

W I'm not sure about that. We're a fairly small farm, and we already sell lanolin to another local business. ³⁹**I'm worried that we don't produce enough lanolin to meet the demand of another client.** I don't want to expand and take on more wool production.

M But ⁴⁰**our contract with the business we currently supply lanolin to has almost expired**—there's no guarantee it will be renewed. I think you should at least read Pelicon's proposal.

W Sure. Can you forward me the e-mail?

남 오늘 아침에 **지역 화장품 생산업체인 펠리컨으로부터 이메일을** 하나 받았어요. 새로운 천연 화장품 라인에 사용할 라놀린을 구매하는 데 관심이 있네요.

여 잘 모르겠네요. 우리는 꽤 작은 농장이고, 이미 라놀린을 다른 지역 업체에 판매하고 있잖아요. **다른 고객의 수요를 충족할 수 있을 만큼 라놀린을 충분히 생산하지 못할까 봐 걱정입니다.** 확장해서 더 많은 양모 생산을 맡고 싶지 않아요.

남 하지만 **현재 라놀린을 공급하는 업체와의 계약이 거의 만료되었고**, 갱신될 거라는 보장도 없어요. 최소한 펠리컨의 제안서를 읽어는 봐야 한다고 생각합니다.

여 좋아요. 제게 그 이메일을 전달해 주시겠어요?

어휘 local 지역의, 현지의   all-natural 천연 원료만으로 만드는
fairly 꽤, 상당히   meet 충족하다   demand 수요, 요구
expand 확장하다   take on ~을 떠맡다   currently 현재
supply 공급하다   guarantee 보장, 보증   renew 갱신하다
proposal 제안(서)   forward 전송하다, 다시 보내다

38 According to the man, what does Pelicon produce?
(A) Household cleaners
(B) Cosmetics
(C) Industrial textiles
(D) Pharmaceuticals

남자에 따르면, 펠리컨은 무엇을 생산하는가?
(A) 가정용 세척제
(B) 화장품
(C) 산업용 섬유
(D) 의약품

어휘 household 가정; 가정의   industrial 산업의, 공업의
textile 섬유, 직물   pharmaceutical 의약(품), 제약

해설 세부 사항 관련 – 펠리컨이 생산하는 것
남자가 첫 대사에서 지역 화장품 생산업체인 펠리컨(Pelicon, a local producer of beauty products)이라고 했으므로 정답은 (B)이다.

Paraphrasing
대화의 beauty products → 정답의 Cosmetics

39 What does the woman say she is concerned about?
(A) Hiring skilled workers
(B) Securing a bank loan
(C) Finding transportation
(D) Making enough product

여자는 무엇이 걱정된다고 말하는가?
(A) 숙련된 직원 고용하기
(B) 은행 대출 받기
(C) 교통편 찾기
(D) 충분한 제품 만들기

어휘 skilled 숙련된, 능숙한   secure 받다, 확보하다   loan 대출
transportation 교통(편)

해설 세부 사항 관련 – 여자가 걱정하는 것
여자가 첫 대사에서 다른 고객의 수요를 충족할 수 있을 만큼 라놀린을 충분히 생산하지 못할까 봐 걱정(I'm worried that we don't produce enough lanolin to meet the demand of another client)이라고 했으므로 정답은 (D)이다.

Paraphrasing
대화의 produce enough lanolin
→ 정답의 Making enough product

40 Why does the man recommend reading an e-mail?
(A) To consider a business proposal
(B) To prepare for a client meeting
(C) To view some construction plans
(D) To learn the details of a complaint

남자는 왜 이메일을 읽어 보라고 권하는가?
(A) 사업 제안을 고려해 보기 위해
(B) 고객 회의를 준비하기 위해
(C) 건설 설계도를 확인해 보기 위해
(D) 불만에 대한 상세한 정보를 알기 위해

어휘 consider 고려하다   plan 설계도   details 상세 정보, 세부 사항
complaint 불만, 불평

해설 세부 사항 관련 – 남자가 이메일을 읽도록 권하는 이유
남자가 두 번째 대사에서 현재 업체와의 계약이 거의 만료되었고, 갱신될 거라는 보장도 없다(our contract ~ has almost expired—there's no guarantee it will be renewed)며, 펠리컨의 제안서를 읽어는 봐야 한다(I think you should at least read Pelicon's proposal)고 했다. 이는 현재 사업이 어떻게 될지 모르니 펠리컨의 사업 제안을 고려해 보라는 것이므로 (A)가 정답이다.

41-43 M-Cn / W-Am

M Nisreen? This is Lewis. **⁴¹I heard you're going to be working for our company overseas, in the New Zealand office.** What a great opportunity!

W Yes, thank you. I start next month, and I'm really excited.

M I'm calling to touch base with you about some of our vendor contracts. **⁴²It's time to renew the contracts, and I wanted to ask you to take care of that before you left.**

W No problem. I know where those files are located on our shared computer drive. **⁴³I'll just need the password to access them.**

남 니즈린? 루이스입니다. **뉴질랜드 지사에서 해외 근무를 하게 된다고 들었어요.** 정말 좋은 기회입니다!
여 네, 감사합니다. 다음 달에 시작하는데, 정말 기대됩니다.
남 판매업체 계약과 관련해 몇 가지 협의하기 위해 전화했어요. **계약을 갱신할 때가 되어서, 떠나시기 전에 그 건의 처리를 요청하고 싶었어요.**
여 문제없습니다. 우리 공용 컴퓨터 드라이브에서 그 파일들이 어디에 있는지 알아요. **이용하려면 비밀번호만 있으면 될 거예요.**

어휘 overseas 해외에서, 해외로   opportunity 기회
touch base with ~와 협의하다   vendor 판매업체, 판매업자
take care of ~을 처리하다, ~을 돌보다   be located 위치해 있다
access 이용하다, 접근하다

41 What will the woman do next month?
(A) Reorganize a department
(B) Attend a conference
(C) Relocate to an overseas office
(D) Take a vacation

여자는 다음 달에 무엇을 할 것인가?
(A) 부서 개편하기
(B) 콘퍼런스 참석하기
(C) 해외 지사로 옮기기
(D) 휴가 떠나기

어휘 reorganize 개편하다, 구조 조정하다   relocate 옮기다

TEST 4   99

해설 세부 사항 관련 – 여자가 다음 달에 할 것
남자가 첫 대사에서 여자가 뉴질랜드 지사에서 해외 근무를 하게 된다고 들었다(I heard you're going to be working for our company overseas, in the New Zealand office)고 했으므로 정답은 (C)이다.

Paraphrasing
대화의 working for our company overseas, in the New Zealand office → 정답의 Relocate to an overseas office

42 What does the man want the woman to do?
(A) Help with some contracts
(B) Prepare a project timeline
(C) Update some software
(D) Call a sales representative

남자는 여자가 무엇을 하기를 원하는가?
(A) 계약 관련 도움 주기
(B) 프로젝트 진행 일정표 준비하기
(C) 소프트웨어 업데이트하기
(D) 영업 직원에게 전화하기

어휘 timeline 진행 일정(표) representative 직원, 대표자

해설 세부 사항 관련 – 남자가 여자에게 원하는 것
남자가 두 번째 대사에서 여자에게 계약을 갱신할 때가 되어서, 떠나기 전에 그 건의 처리를 요청하고 싶었다(It's time to renew the contracts, and I wanted to ask you to take care of that before you left)고 했으므로 정답은 (A)이다.

43 What does the woman ask the man for?
(A) Some employee names
(B) Some credit card information
(C) A file password
(D) A telephone number

여자는 남자에게 무엇을 요청하는가?
(A) 직원 이름
(B) 신용카드 정보
(C) 파일 비밀번호
(D) 전화번호

해설 세부 사항 관련 – 여자의 요청 사항
여자가 마지막 대사에서 파일들을 언급하며, 이용하려면 비밀번호만 있으면 될 것(~ I'll just need the password to access them)이라고 했으므로 정답은 (C)이다.

44-46 W-Br / M-Cn

W Hi. **44 This is Giovanni Marino's agent. I'm calling to reschedule his planned appearance on the *Sunday Morning Show*.**

M Right. We have him booked to appear on the show in July to promote **45 his new movie.**

W Unfortunately, **45 the movie he's acting in** is behind schedule, and he'll now be on location through the end of August.

M Hmm, I see. Let me look at our guest calendar. I have a slot I'm looking to fill on September fourteenth—would that work?

W Yes, that would be great, thanks.

M All right. **46 I'll update the contract with the new date and e-mail it to you.**

여 안녕하세요. 지오바니 마리노의 대리인입니다. 계획되어 있는 〈선데이 모닝 쇼〉 출연 일정을 재조정하기 위해 전화했습니다.

남 맞아요. 신작 영화를 홍보하실 수 있게 7월에 프로그램 출연을 예약해 드렸습니다.

여 안타깝게도, 출연 중인 영화의 촬영이 예정보다 늦어져, 이제는 8월 말까지 현지 촬영이 진행될 예정이에요.

남 흠, 알겠습니다. 저희 초대 손님 일정표를 확인해 보겠습니다. 9월 14일에 채우려고 하는 자리가 하나 있는데, 그 날짜 괜찮을까요?

여 네, 그럼 아주 좋겠네요. 감사합니다.

남 좋습니다. 새로운 날짜로 계약서를 업데이트해서 이메일로 보내드리겠습니다.

어휘 agent 대리인, 중개인 appearance 출연, 등장 promote 홍보하다, 촉진하다 unfortunately 안타깝게도 act 연기하다, 행동하다 behind schedule 일정보다 늦은 on location 현지촬영 중인, 촬영지에 가 있는 slot 시간대, 자리 look to ~하려고 하다 fill 채우다, 메우다 work 괜찮다, 잘되다

44 Why is the woman calling?
(A) To negotiate a payment
(B) To reschedule an appearance
(C) To book a venue
(D) To ask about security

여자는 왜 전화하는가?
(A) 지불액을 협의하기 위해
(B) 출연 일정을 재조정하기 위해
(C) 행사장을 예약하기 위해
(D) 보안에 관해 묻기 위해

어휘 negotiate 협의하다, 협상하다 payment 지불(액) venue 행사장, 개최 장소

해설 전체 내용 관련 – 여자가 전화하는 이유
여자가 첫 대사에서 자신이 지오바니 마리노의 대리인이라며, 〈선데이 모닝 쇼〉 출연 일정을 재조정하기 위해 전화했다(This is Giovanni Marino's agent. I'm calling to reschedule his planned appearance on the *Sunday Morning Show*)고 했으므로 정답은 (B)이다.

45 Who most likely is Giovanni Marino?
(A) An actor
(B) A politician
(C) A writer
(D) A photographer

지오바니 마리노는 누구인 것 같은가?
(A) 배우
(B) 정치인
(C) 작가
(D) 사진가

해설 세부 사항 관련 – 지오바니 마리노의 직업
남자가 첫 대사에서 지오바니 마리노의 신작 영화(his new movie)를 언급했고, 여자도 그가 출연 중인 영화(the movie he's acting in)라고 했으므로 정답은 (A)이다.

46 What will the man send in an e-mail?
(A) A revised contract
(B) A reimbursement form
(C) An invitation to a video conference
(D) Directions to a location

남자는 이메일로 무엇을 보낼 것인가?
(A) 수정된 계약서
(B) 비용 환급 양식
(C) 화상 회의 초대장
(D) 어느 장소로 가는 길 안내

어휘 revised 수정된, 변경된 reimbursement (비용) 환급 form 양식, 서식 video conference 화상 회의 directions 길 안내 (정보)

해설 세부 사항 관련 – 남자가 이메일로 보낼 것
남자가 마지막 대사에서 새로운 날짜로 계약서를 업데이트해서 이메일로 보낼 것(I'll update the contract with the new date and e-mail it to you)이라고 했으므로 정답은 (A)이다.

Paraphrasing
대화의 update the contract with the new date
→ 정답의 A revised contract

47-49 3인 대화 M-Cn / W-Br / M-Au

M1 Hello, Usha. Hi, Pablo.

W Hey, Konstantin. **47 We're talking about our thoughts on the new company policy for remote workers.** On the days I have to come into the office, I always worry about finding an appropriate workstation.

M2 Yeah, I don't like the unpredictability either. Why can't we just sign up for our workstation sometime in advance? What do you think about it?

M1 These are good points. **48 Let's all go to the director to discuss this with her.**

M2 **48 I believe she's in her office, so now's a good time.**

W Oh, I can't go now. **49 I have a report to finalize by noon.**

남1 안녕하세요, 우샤. 안녕하세요, 파블로.
여 안녕하세요, 콘스탄틴. 저희는 원격 근무자들을 대상으로 하는 새로운 회사 정책에 대한 생각을 이야기하고 있어요. 회사에 출근해야 하는 날에는, 항상 적당한 업무 자리를 찾는 게 걱정이에요.
남2 네, 저도 예측 불가능성이 마음에 들지 않아요. 왜 저희가 미리 저희 업무 자리를 신청할 수 없는 건가요? 이 부분에 대해 어떻게 생각하세요?
남1 좋은 지적입니다. 다같이 이사님께 가서 함께 이 문제를 논의해 봅시다.
남2 사무실에 계신 것 같으니, 지금이 좋은 때입니다.
여 아, 저는 지금 갈 수 없어요. 정오까지 마무리해야 하는 보고서가 있어요.

어휘 thought 생각 policy 정책, 방침 remote 원격의, 먼 appropriate 적당한, 적절한 workstation 업무 자리, 작업대 unpredictability 예측 불가능성 sign up for ~을 신청하다 in advance 미리, 사전에 good point 좋은 지적 finalize 마무리하다, 최종 확정하다

47 What are the speakers discussing?
(A) A conference schedule
(B) A company policy
(C) A catering menu
(D) A supply order

화자들은 무엇을 이야기하고 있는가?
(A) 콘퍼런스 일정
(B) 회사 정책
(C) 출장 요리 메뉴
(D) 물품 주문

어휘 supply 물품, 공급(품)

해설 전체 내용 관련 – 대화 주제
여자가 첫 대사에서 원격 근무자들을 대상으로 하는 새로운 회사 정책에 대한 생각을 이야기하고 있다(We're talking about our thoughts on the new company policy for remote workers)고 했으므로 정답은 (B)이다.

48 What do the men want to do?
(A) Rent a car
(B) Go to a restaurant
(C) Speak with a manager
(D) Change some flight reservations

남자들은 무엇을 하고 싶어 하는가?
(A) 자동차 대여하기
(B) 레스토랑에 가기
(C) 책임자와 이야기하기
(D) 항공편 예약 변경하기

어휘 rent 대여하다

해설 세부 사항 관련 – 남자들이 하고 싶어 하는 일
첫 번째 남자가 두 번째 대사에서 다같이 이사에게 가서 함께 문제를 논의하자(Let's all go to the director to discuss this with her)고 제안하자, 두 번째 남자가 그 이사가 사무실에 있는 것 같으니 지금이 좋은 때(I believe she's in her office, so now's a good time)라며 동의하고 있으므로 정답은 (C)이다.

Paraphrasing
대화의 go to the director to discuss this with her
→ 정답의 Speak with a manager

49 What does the woman say she needs to do now?
(A) Work on a report
(B) Meet with a client
(C) Print some materials
(D) Check her e-mails

여자는 지금 무엇을 해야 한다고 말하는가?
(A) 보고서 작업하기
(B) 고객 만나기
(C) 자료 출력하기
(D) 이메일 확인하기

어휘 material 자료, 재료

해설 세부 사항 관련 – 여자가 지금 해야 할 일
여자가 마지막 대사에서 정오까지 마무리해야 하는 보고서가 있다(I have a report to finalize by noon)고 했으므로 정답은 (A)이다.

Paraphrasing
대화의 a report to finalize → 정답의 Work on a report

50-52 W-Br / M-Cn

W OK, Mr. Jebreen. ⁵⁰**Here's your new library card.** Remember that you can borrow books, CDs, and DVDs from our collection with it.

M Thank you. I read somewhere that people can also borrow digital items.

W Yes! ⁵¹**We offer the Cloud-Camel application. All you have to do is download the app and use the information on your card to set up an account.**

M That's great. ⁵²**I go on a business trip every month**, so having easy access to online content will be convenient.

여 자, 제브린 씨. **여기 새 도서관 카드입니다.** 이 카드로 저희 소장 자료 중 도서와 CD, DVD를 빌리실 수 있다는 점을 기억해 주세요.

남 감사합니다. 어디선가 디지털 자료도 빌릴 수 있다고 읽었어요.

여 네! **클라우드-캐멀 애플리케이션을 제공합니다. 이 앱을 다운로드해서 갖고 계신 카드에 있는 정보를 이용해 계정을 설정하기만 하면 됩니다.**

남 아주 좋네요. **저는 매달 출장을 떠나기 때문에**, 온라인 콘텐츠를 쉽게 이용할 수 있다면 편리할 거예요.

어휘 borrow 빌리다 collection (도서관 등의) 소장 자료, 수집(품) set up 설정하다, 설치하다 have access to ~을 이용할 수 있다 convenient 편리한

50 Who most likely is the woman?
(A) A journalist
(B) A librarian
(C) A musician
(D) A software developer

여자는 누구인 것 같은가?
(A) 기자
(B) 사서
(C) 음악가
(D) 소프트웨어 개발자

해설 전체 내용 관련 – 여자의 직업
여자가 첫 대사에서 남자에게 새 도서관 카드(Here's your new library card)를 건네며, 도서관에서 빌릴 수 있는 자료들에 대해 설명하고 있으므로 정답은 (B)이다.

51 What does the woman recommend that the man do?
(A) Consult a manual
(B) Sign up for a class
(C) Listen to some music
(D) Use a particular mobile app

여자는 남자에게 무엇을 하도록 권하는가?
(A) 설명서 참고하기
(B) 강좌에 등록하기
(C) 음악 듣기
(D) 특정 모바일 앱 이용하기

어휘 consult 참고하다, 상담하다 manual 설명서, 안내서

해설 세부 사항 관련 – 여자가 권하는 것
여자가 두 번째 대사에서 클라우드-캐멀 애플리케이션을 다운로드해서 카드에 있는 정보를 이용해 계정을 설정하기만 하면 된다(We offer the Cloud-Camel application. All you have to do is download the app ~)고 설명하고 있으므로 정답은 (D)이다.

52 What does the man say happens each month?
(A) He publishes a blog post.
(B) He meets with a social group.
(C) He travels for work.
(D) He volunteers for a community event.

남자는 매달 무슨 일이 있다고 말하는가?
(A) 블로그 게시글을 올린다.
(B) 사회 단체와 만난다.
(C) 출장을 간다.
(D) 지역 사회 행사에서 자원봉사를 한다.

어휘 post 게시글 volunteer 자원봉사를 하다, 자원하다
community 지역 사회, 지역 공동체

해설 세부 사항 관련 – 남자가 매달 있다고 말하는 일
남자가 마지막 대사에서 매달 출장을 떠난다(I go on a business trip every month ~)고 했으므로 정답은 (C)이다.

Paraphrasing
대화의 go on a business trip → 정답의 travels for work

53-55 W-Am / M-Cn

W **53 Have you reviewed the data from the workplace survey? You really should.** It looks like most staff feel positive about the direction that the company is going in. **54 But almost 40 percent feel like their individual contributions aren't being recognized.**

M Well, the company's certainly had other priorities. I wonder how the management team's going to respond.

W **55 I've suggested many times that they give out awards every quarter for exceptional performance.** Maybe now they'll finally start doing it.

여 사내 설문 조사 데이터를 검토하셨나요? 꼭 검토해야 해요. 대부분의 직원들이 회사가 나아가고 있는 방향에 대해 긍정적으로 생각하는 것 같아요. 하지만 거의 40퍼센트는 개인의 기여를 인정받지 못하고 있다고 느끼고 있어요.
남 음, 회사에 분명 다른 우선 순위들이 있었죠. 경영진이 어떻게 반응할지 궁금하네요.
여 제가 매 분기마다 뛰어난 성과에 대해 상을 수여해야 한다고 여러 번 제안했어요. 이제야 드디어 그걸 시작할지도 모르겠네요.

어휘 positive 긍정적인 individual 개별적인, 개인의
contribution 기여, 공헌 recognize 인정하다, 표창하다
certainly 분명히 priority 우선 순위 respond 반응하다
give out ~을 나눠 주다 exceptional 뛰어난, 이례적인
performance 성과, 실적

---

53 What does the woman want the man to look at?
(A) A marketing plan
(B) A conference calendar
(C) Schedule changes
(D) Survey results

여자는 남자가 무엇을 보기를 원하는가?
(A) 마케팅 계획
(B) 콘퍼런스 일정표
(C) 일정 변동
(D) 설문 조사 결과

해설 세부 내용 관련 – 여자가 남자에게 보라고 하는 것
여자가 첫 대사에서 남자에게 사내 설문 조사 데이터를 검토했는 지 물으며, 꼭 검토해야 한다(Have you reviewed the data from the workplace survey? You really should)고 했으므로 정답은 (D)이다.

Paraphrasing
대화의 the data from the workplace survey
→ 정답의 Survey results

---

54 What does the man imply when he says, "the company's certainly had other priorities"?
(A) His workload has decreased.
(B) He is not responsible for some results.
(C) Some criticism is accurate.
(D) Some decisions led to a successful outcome.

남자가 "회사에 분명 다른 우선 순위들이 있었죠"라고 말할 때 무엇 을 암시하는가?
(A) 자신의 업무량이 감소했다.
(B) 일부 결과에 대한 책임이 없다.
(C) 비판이 정확하다.
(D) 결정이 성공적인 결과로 이어졌다.

어휘 decrease 감소하다 be responsible for ~에 대한 책임이 있다
criticism 비판, 비평 accurate 정확한 lead to ~로 이어지다
outcome 결과

해설 화자의 의도 파악 – 회사에 다른 우선 순위들이 있었다는 말의 의도
여자가 첫 대사에서 거의 40퍼센트는 개인의 기여를 인정받지 못 하고 있다고 느낀다(But almost 40 percent feel like their individual contributions aren't being recognized)고 말하자, 남자가 인용문을 언급하고 있다. 이는 40퍼센트의 직원들 이 갖고 있는 부정적인 의견에 대해 공감한다는 뜻을 나타내는 것이 므로 정답은 (C)이다.

---

55 What has the woman suggested in the past?
(A) Rewarding staff performance
(B) Extending business hours
(C) Encouraging professional development
(D) Organizing team-building events

여자는 과거에 무엇을 제안한 적이 있는가?
(A) 직원 성과에 대해 보상하기
(B) 영업시간 연장하기
(C) 직업 능력 개발 장려하기
(D) 팀 단합 행사 마련하기

어휘 reward 보상하다 extend 연장하다 encourage 장려하다 organize 마련하다, 조직하다

해설 세부 사항 관련 – 여자가 과거에 제안한 것
여자가 마지막 대사에서 매 분기마다 뛰어난 성과에 대해 상을 수여해야 한다고 여러 번 제안했다(I've suggested many times that they give out awards every quarter for exceptional performance)고 했으므로 정답은 (A)이다.

> **Paraphrasing**
> 대화의 give out awards every quarter for exceptional performance
> → 정답의 Rewarding staff performance

56-58 3인 대화 W-Am / M-Au / W-Br

W1 Hi, Ajiola. As I mentioned on the phone, ⁵⁶**my colleague and I recently started a clothing company** and are hoping your branding firm can help us promote our line of athletic apparel. You think we should focus on advertising on social media, right?

M Right. Contrary to popular belief, ⁵⁷**television is definitely not the entire advertising landscape.** Advertising on the Internet is also a great way for a company to increase its visibility.

W2 I heard you recommended working with an online influencer.

M Yes—Saskia Hoffman. Saskia's very knowledgeable about exercise, and ⁵⁸**lots of people use her online exercise routines. Her viewers will pay attention to what she recommends and wears.**

여1 안녕하세요, 아지올라. 전화상으로 말씀드렸듯이, **제 동료와 제가 최근에 의류 회사를 시작해서**, 귀하의 브랜딩 회사에서 저희 운동복 라인을 홍보하는 데 도움을 줄 수 있기를 바랍니다. 저희가 소셜 미디어 광고에 초점을 맞춰야 한다고 생각하시는 거죠, 그렇죠?

남 그렇습니다. 일반적인 생각과 달리, **텔레비전이 광고 분야의 전부는 아닙니다.** 인터넷 광고 또한 회사의 인지도를 높일 수 있는 훌륭한 방법입니다.

여2 온라인 인플루언서와 협업하는 것을 추천한다고 들었어요.

남 네, 사스키아 호프먼이요. 사스키아는 운동에 대해 아는 것이 많고, **많은 사람들이 그녀의 온라인 운동 루틴을 활용하고 있어요. 시청자들은 그녀가 추천하고 착용하는 것에 관심을 기울일 것입니다.**

어휘 colleague 동료 (직원) branding 브랜드 구축 firm 회사 athletic 운동의 focus on ~에 초점을 맞추다 advertising 광고 (활동) contrary to ~와 달리 popular belief 일반적인 생각 definitely 분명히, 확실히 entire 전체의 landscape 분야, 풍경 increase 높이다 visibility 눈에 보이는 정도, 가시성 influencer 인플루언서 knowledgeable 아는 것이 많은 routine 루틴, 일상(적인 것) pay attention to ~에 관심을 기울이다, ~에 주목하다

56 What type of business do the women own?
(A) A hair salon
(B) A recording studio
(C) A clothing company
(D) A fitness center

여자들은 어떤 종류의 업체를 소유하고 있는가?
(A) 미용실
(B) 녹음 스튜디오
(C) 의류 회사
(D) 피트니스 센터

어휘 own 소유하다

해설 세부 사항 관련 – 여자들이 소유한 업체
첫 번째 여자가 첫 대사에서 최근에 의류 회사를 시작했다(~ my colleague and I recently started a clothing company ~)고 했으므로 정답은 (C)이다.

57 What does the man say regarding television?
(A) It is an industry he once worked in.
(B) It reaches more people than magazines.
(C) It needs more programs about sports.
(D) It is not the only advertising platform available.

남자는 텔레비전과 관련해 무슨 말을 하는가?
(A) 자신이 한때 일했던 업계이다.
(B) 잡지보다 더 많은 사람들에게 도달한다.
(C) 더 많은 스포츠 프로그램을 필요로 한다.
(D) 이용 가능한 유일한 광고 플랫폼이 아니다.

어휘 industry 업계, 산업 reach 도달하다

해설 세부 사항 관련 – 남자가 텔레비전과 관련해 하는 말
남자가 첫 대사에서 텔레비전이 광고 분야의 전부는 아니다(~ television is definitely not the entire advertising landscape)라고 했으므로 정답은 (D)이다.

> **Paraphrasing**
> 대화의 not the entire advertising landscape
> → 정답의 not the only advertising platform available

58 According to the man, why would Saskia Hoffman be a good choice?
(A) She recently won an award.
(B) She lives nearby.
(C) She charges affordable rates.
(D) She is well known in her field.

남자에 따르면, 사스키아 호프먼이 왜 좋은 선택이 될 것인가?
(A) 최근에 상을 받았다.
(B) 근처에 산다.
(C) 알맞은 요금을 청구한다.
(D) 자신의 분야에서 잘 알려져 있다.

어휘 nearby 근처에 charge 청구하다 affordable 알맞은 rate 요금 field 분야

해설 세부 사항 관련 – 사스키아 호프먼이 좋은 선택인 이유
남자가 마지막 대사에서 많은 사람들이 그녀의 온라인 운동 루틴을 활용하고 있고, 시청자들은 그녀가 추천하고 착용하는 것에 관심을 기울일 것(~ lots of people use her online exercise routines. Her viewers will pay attention to what she recommends and wears)이라고 했다. 이는 호프먼이 많은 사람들에게 영향을 미치고 있다는 뜻으로, 자신의 분야에서 잘 알려져 있음을 나타내는 말이므로 정답은 (D)이다.

어휘 stock 재고로 갖추다; 재고(품) timeline 진행 일정(표) illustrator 삽화가 illustration 삽화 special edition 특별판

59 What does the speakers' company manufacture?
(A) Art supplies
(B) Puzzles
(C) Shipping materials
(D) Power tools

화자들의 회사는 무엇을 제조하는가?
(A) 미술용품
(B) 퍼즐
(C) 배송용 물품
(D) 전동 공구

어휘 manufacture 제조하다

해설 전체 내용 관련 – 화자들의 회사가 제조하는 것
여자가 첫 대사에서 백화점 체인에서 받은 주문(~ the order we got from the department store chain)을 언급하며, 조각 퍼즐 5,000개를 주문한 곳(~ the one that placed an order for 5,000 jigsaw puzzles)이라고 했으므로 정답은 (B)이다.

59-61 W-Br / M-Au

W Hi, Shinji. I wanted to ask you about **⁵⁹the order we got from the department store chain.** You know, **⁵⁹the one that placed an order for 5,000 jigsaw puzzles?**

M Yes. **⁶⁰They want the order in a week so they can stock them before the holiday.**

W **A week is not a long time.**

M We've had short timelines before. Anyway, **⁶¹our illustrators sent some new puzzle illustrations, right?** I heard they're making a special edition.

W Yes, and I'm so excited! **⁶¹I've got the sketches right here. Let me show you.**

여 안녕하세요, 신지. 우리가 **백화점 체인에서 받은 주문**에 대해 물어보고 싶었어요. 그러니까, **조각 퍼즐 5,000개를 주문한 곳** 있잖아요?
남 네. **그곳에서 연휴 전에 재고를 갖출 수 있도록 일주일 후에 주문한 것을 받기를 원해요.**
여 **일주일은 긴 시간이 아닙니다.**
남 전에도 일정이 짧았던 적이 있었어요. 그건 그렇고, **우리 삽화가들이 새 퍼즐용 삽화를 보냈죠, 그렇죠?** 특별판을 만들고 있다고 들었어요.
여 네, 너무 기대돼요! **바로 여기 그 스케치가 있어요. 제가 보여드릴게요.**

60 What does the woman imply when she says, "A week is not a long time"?
(A) Some prices will likely increase.
(B) Some temporary employees have been hired.
(C) A colleague's work is excellent.
(D) An order may not be filled.

여자가 "일주일은 긴 시간이 아닙니다"라고 말할 때 무엇을 의미하는가?
(A) 일부 가격이 인상될 가능성이 있다.
(B) 임시직 직원들이 고용되었다.
(C) 동료의 작업물이 훌륭하다.
(D) 주문이 이행되지 않을 수도 있다.

어휘 temporary 임시의, 일시적인 fill 이행하다, 채우다

해설 화자의 의도 파악 – 일주일은 긴 시간이 아니라는 말의 의도
남자가 첫 대사에서 주문한 업체가 연휴 전에 재고를 갖출 수 있도록 일주일 후에 주문한 것을 받기를 원한다(They want the order in a week so they can stock them before the holiday)고 말하자, 여자가 인용문을 언급하고 있다. 이는 일주일이 긴 시간이 아니기 때문에 주문을 이행하지 못할 수도 있다고 말하는 것이므로 정답은 (D)이다.

61 What will the woman do next?
(A) Review a contract
(B) Print out an invoice
(C) Share some illustrations
(D) Confirm a client meeting

여자는 다음에 무엇을 할 것인가?
(A) 계약서 검토하기
(B) 거래 내역서 인쇄하기
(C) 삽화 공유하기
(D) 고객 회의 확정하기

어휘 **invoice** 거래 내역서 **confirm** 확정하다, 확인해 주다

해설 **세부 사항 관련 – 여자가 다음에 할 일**
남자가 두 번째 대사에서 삽화가들이 새 퍼즐용 삽화를 보냈는지(~ our illustrators sent some new puzzle illustrations, right?) 묻자, 여자가 그 스케치를 갖고 있다며 보여 주겠다(I've got the sketches right here. Let me show you)고 했으므로 정답은 (C)이다.

Paraphrasing
대화의 Let me show you → 정답의 Share

62-64 대화 + 청구 내역서 M-Au / W-Am

M Hi, Ms. Rossi. **62 I understand you're concerned about a charge that appears on the statement for your business account.**

W Yes, **63 I have a question about the charge on May 3.** I don't remember purchasing anything for that amount.

M Let me review your statement now. Hmm. It looks like that purchase was made abroad. So an international transaction fee was added to the purchase amount.

W Oh, yes—I was out of the country at that time. Thanks for clarifying. **64 Can you provide me with a list of all the bank fees for transactions made abroad?**

M **64 Yes, of course.** Here's a document that lists all the information.

남 안녕하세요, 로시 씨. **사업자용 계좌 명세서에 표시되어 있는 청구 금액에 대해 우려하시는 것으로 알고 있습니다.**

여 네, **5월 3일 청구 금액에 대해 질문이 있습니다.** 해당 금액으로 아무것도 구매한 기억이 없습니다.

남 지금 그 내역서를 살펴보겠습니다. 흠. 그 구매가 해외에서 이뤄진 것으로 보입니다. 그래서 해외 거래 수수료가 그 구매 금액에 추가되었습니다.

여 아, 네. 제가 그때 해외에 있었습니다. 명확히 해 주셔서 감사합니다. **해외 거래에 대한 모든 은행 수수료 목록을 제공해 주실 수 있나요?**

남 **네, 물론입니다.** 여기 모든 정보가 나열된 문서입니다.

어휘 **concerned** 우려하는, 걱정하는 **appear** 나타나다, 보이다 **statement** 내역서, 명세서 **amount** 총액, 액수, 양 **abroad** 해외에(서) **transaction** 거래 **fee** 수수료, 요금 **clarify** 명확히 하다, 분명히 말하다

Axiom Bank
Billing Statement
Name: Lola Rossi

Transaction Date	Amount
63 May 3	$203.00
May 15	$350.00
May 18	$75.50
May 29	$83.15

액시엄 은행
청구 내역서
성명: 롤라 로시

거래 날짜	총액
5월 3일	203.00달러
5월 15일	350.00달러
5월 18일	75.50달러
5월 29일	83.15달러

62 Where does the man most likely work?
(A) At an airport
(B) At a bank
(C) At a real estate agency
(D) At a department store

남자는 어디에서 일하는 것 같은가?
(A) 공항
(B) 은행
(C) 부동산 중개업체
(D) 백화점

해설 **전체 내용 관련 – 남자의 근무 장소**
남자가 첫 대사에서 여자가 사업자용 계좌 명세서에 표시되어 있는 청구 금액에 대해 우려하는 것으로 안다(I understand you're concerned about a charge that appears on the statement for your business account)고 했고, 관련 질문에 응답하고 있으므로 정답은 (B)이다.

63 Look at the graphic. Which amount does the woman ask about?
(A) $203.00
(B) $350.00
(C) $75.50
(D) $83.15

시각 정보에 의하면, 여자는 어느 금액에 대해 묻는가?
(A) 203.00달러
(B) 350.00달러
(C) 75.50달러
(D) 83.15달러

해설 **시각 정보 연계 – 여자가 묻는 금액**
여자가 첫 대사에서 5월 3일 청구 금액에 대해 질문이 있다(I have a question about the charge on May 3)고 했고, 청구 내역서에서 5월 3일 총액은 203.00달러이므로 정답은 (A)이다.

64 What does the man give the woman?
(A) An updated statement
(B) A list of fees
(C) A discount card
(D) A brochure

남자는 여자에게 무엇을 주는가?
(A) 업데이트된 내역서
(B) 수수료 목록
(C) 할인 카드
(D) 안내 책자

해설 세부 사항 관련 – 남자가 여자에게 주는 것

여자가 두 번째 대사에서 해외 거래에 대한 모든 은행 수수료 목록을 제공해 줄 것(Can you provide me with a list of all the bank fees for transactions made abroad?)을 요청했고, 남자가 알겠다(Yes, of course)고 했으므로 정답은 (B)이다.

어휘 reserve 예약하다 hopefully 바라건대, 잘하면 celebrity 유명 인사 sign autographs 사인해 주다

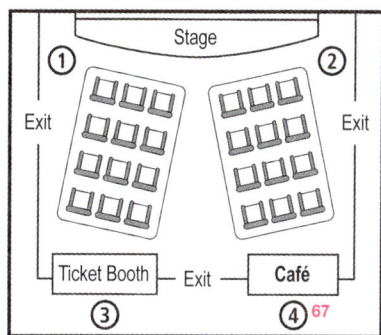

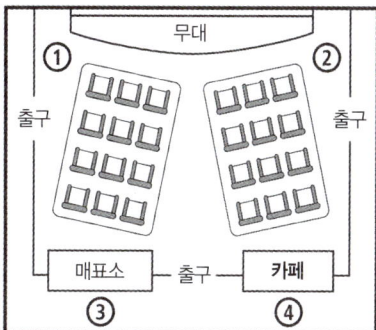

65-67 대화 + 안내도 M-Cn / W-Am ▶ 동영상 강의

M Magali, were you able to reserve the performing arts center for the piano concert?

W Yes. **65 I booked their main auditorium for that day.** They're sending me the contract.

M **65 Thanks for doing that.**

W No problem. Hopefully, it'll be as successful as last year.

M We sold 2,000 tickets last year, but we had three celebrity performers. **66 I'm worried we won't sell as many tickets this year.**

W Well, Xinyu Gu is a very popular pianist. And she's staying after the concert to sign autographs. Which reminds me, where should we set up the table for that?

M Good question. Hmm. The café should be closed by then. **67 Let's set it up next to the café.**

남 마갈리, 피아노 콘서트를 위해 공연 예술 센터를 예약하실 수 있었나요?
여 네. **그날 대강당을 예약했어요.** 제게 계약서를 보내 줄 거예요.
남 **그렇게 해 주셔서 감사합니다.**
여 별말씀을요. 작년처럼 성공적인 행사가 되길 바랍니다.
남 작년에는 티켓을 2,000장 판매했는데, 유명 연주자가 세 명 있었잖아요. **올해는 티켓을 그만큼 많이 판매하지 못할까 봐 걱정이에요.**
여 음, 신유 구는 매우 유명한 피아니스트입니다. 그리고 공연이 끝난 후에 남아서 사인을 해 줄 거예요. 그러고 보니 그것을 위한 테이블을 어디에 설치해야 할까요?
남 좋은 질문입니다. 흠. 카페가 그때쯤 문을 닫을 거예요. **카페 옆에 설치합시다.**

---

65 What does the man thank the woman for doing?
(A) Printing programs
(B) Setting up lighting
(C) Reserving a venue
(D) Paying a performer

남자는 여자가 무엇을 한 것에 대해 고마워하는가?
(A) 프로그램 인쇄하기
(B) 조명 설치하기
(C) 행사장 예약하기
(D) 연주자에게 비용 지급하기

해설 전체 내용 관련 – 남자가 고마워하는 것

여자가 첫 대사에서 대강당을 예약했다(I booked their main auditorium for that day)고 말하자, 남자가 그렇게 해 주어 고맙다(Thanks for doing that)고 했으므로 정답은 (C)이다.

Paraphrasing
대화의 booked their main auditorium
→ 정답의 Reserving a venue

---

66 What does the man say he is worried about?
(A) Reviews from critics
(B) Ticket sales
(C) A performance schedule
(D) The cost of merchandise

남자는 무엇이 걱정된다고 말하는가?
(A) 평론가들의 평가
(B) 티켓 판매량
(C) 공연 일정
(D) 상품 비용

어휘 critic 평론가, 비평가 merchandise 상품

해설 세부 사항 관련 – 남자가 걱정하는 것
남자가 세 번째 대사에서 작년 티켓 판매량을 언급하면서 올해는 티켓을 그만큼 많이 판매하지 못할까 봐 걱정된다(I'm worried we won't sell as many tickets this year)고 했으므로 정답은 (B)이다.

> **Paraphrasing**
> 대화의 sell as many tickets → 정답의 Ticket sales

67 Look at the graphic. Where will a table be set up?
(A) At location 1
(B) At location 2
(C) At location 3
(D) At location 4

시각 정보에 의하면, 테이블은 어디에 설치될 것인가?
(A) 1번 위치
(B) 2번 위치
(C) 3번 위치
(D) 4번 위치

해설 시각 정보 연계 – 테이블이 설치될 곳
남자가 마지막 대사에서 카페 옆에 설치하자(Let's set it up next to the café)고 했고, 안내도에서 카페 옆은 4번이므로 정답은 (D)이다.

68-70 대화 + 블로그 게시글 목록 M-Au / W-Br

M Welcome to the garden center. Can I help you?

W Hi. ⁶⁸**I've started growing rose bushes**, and I've heard they require special care. ⁶⁸**Are there any products you can recommend?**

M Yes! But first, I'd like to show you a great resource on our Web site. Have you seen our blog?

W No, I haven't.

M We have monthly posts on many gardening topics, and ⁶⁹**there's a recent one about growing roses.**

W ⁶⁹**I'll check it out!** Thanks so much.

M You're welcome. Now—⁷⁰**let me show you our fertilizers.** They're in aisle six.

남 원예 용품점에 오신 것을 환영합니다. 무엇을 도와드릴까요?
여 안녕하세요. **장미 덤불을 기르기 시작했는데**, 특별 관리가 필요하다고 들었어요. **추천해 주실 제품이 있나요?**
남 네! 하지만 우선, 저희 웹사이트에 있는 아주 좋은 자료를 보여 드리고 싶습니다. 저희 블로그를 보신 적 있으세요?
여 아니요, 없어요.
남 다양한 원예 주제에 관해서 매달 게시글을 올리는데, **장미 재배에 관한 최신 글이 있어요.**
여 **확인해 볼게요!** 정말 감사합니다.
남 별말씀을요. 이제 **저희 비료들을 보여 드리겠습니다.** 6번 통로에 있어요.

어휘 grow 기르다 bush 덤불, 관목 require 필요로 하다 care 관리, 돌봄 resource 자료, 자원, 자산 recent 최근의 fertilizer 비료 aisle 통로 natural 자연의 pest 해충 remedy 처리 방안, 해결책, 치료(약) composting 퇴비 제조 drought 가뭄 tolerant 잘 견디는, 내성이 있는

⁶⁹May	Growing roses
June	Natural pest remedies
July	Composting
August	Drought-tolerant plants

5월	장미 재배
6월	천연 해충 처리법
7월	퇴비 제조
8월	가뭄을 잘 견디는 식물

68 Why is the woman at the garden center?
(A) To enroll in a course
(B) To join a gardening club
(C) To buy some supplies
(D) To return a purchase

여자는 왜 원예 용품점에 있는가?
(A) 강좌에 등록하기 위해
(B) 원예 동호회에 가입하기 위해
(C) 용품을 구입하기 위해
(D) 구매품을 반품하기 위해

어휘 enroll in ~에 등록하다 join 가입하다, 합류하다 return 반품하다, 반환하다

해설 전체 내용 관련 – 여자가 원예 용품점에 있는 이유
여자가 첫 대사에서 장미 덤불을 기르기 시작했는데, 추천 제품이 있는지(I've started growing rose bushes, ~ Are there any products you can recommend?) 묻고 있으므로 정답은 (C)이다.

69 Look at the graphic. Which month's post will the woman most likely read?
 (A) May's post
 (B) June's post
 (C) July's post
 (D) August's post

시각 정보에 의하면, 여자는 어느 달의 게시글을 읽을 것 같은가?
 (A) 5월 게시글
 (B) 6월 게시글
 (C) 7월 게시글
 (D) 8월 게시글

해설 시각 정보 연계 – 여자가 읽을 게시글
남자가 세 번째 대사에서 장미 재배에 관한 최신 글이 있다(~ there's a recent one about growing roses)고 하자, 여자가 확인해 보겠다(I'll check it out)고 했으며, 블로그 게시글 목록에서 5월(May) 게시글이 장미 재배(Growing roses)에 관한 것임을 알 수 있으므로 정답은 (A)이다.

70 What kind of products will the man show to the woman?
 (A) Indoor plants
 (B) Plant fertilizers
 (C) Gardening tools
 (D) Irrigation systems

남자는 어떤 종류의 제품을 여자에게 보여 줄 것인가?
 (A) 실내용 식물
 (B) 식물용 비료
 (C) 원예 도구
 (D) 관개 시스템

어휘 irrigation 관개

해설 세부 사항 관련 – 남자가 보여 줄 제품
남자가 마지막 대사에서 비료를 보여 주겠다(~ let me show you our fertilizers)고 했으므로 정답은 (B)이다.

PART 4

71-73 공지

W-Br **71 Attention, Casella Transit customers. Maintenance work on the red and yellow lines will begin next week.** You can expect some disruptions to regular service, so please plan ahead. Use the latest version of our mobile phone application for real-time updates. **72 You can receive notifications regarding delays if your train is impacted.** **73** Want to save on commuter rides? Purchase your e-ticket through the mobile app as well. Printing a ticket at a kiosk is now subject to additional fees.

카셀라 교통 고객 여러분께 알립니다. 적색 및 황색 노선의 유지 관리 작업이 다음 주에 시작될 것입니다. 정규 서비스에 차질이 예상되오니, 미리 계획을 세우시기 바랍니다. 최신 버전의 저희 휴대폰 애플리케이션을 사용하여 실시간 업데이트를 확인하세요. 여러분의 열차가 영향을 받는 경우에 지연과 관련된 알림을 받을 수 있습니다. 통근 교통비를 절약하고 싶으신가요? 모바일 앱을 통해 전자 승차권을 구입하세요. 이제 단말기에서 승차권을 출력하면 추가 요금이 부과됩니다.

어휘 maintenance 유지 관리, 정비 disruption 지장, 방해 regular 정규의, 일반적인 ahead 미리 real-time 실시간의 notification 알림(메시지), 통지(서) impact 영향을 미치다 commuter 통근자 ride 타기, 타고 가기 kiosk 단말기 be subject to ~의 대상이 되다 additional 추가적인

71 What field does the speaker most likely work in?
 (A) Finance
 (B) Transportation
 (C) Construction
 (D) Robotics

화자는 어떤 분야에서 일하는 것 같은가?
 (A) 금융
 (B) 교통
 (C) 건설
 (D) 로봇 공학

해설 전체 내용 관련 – 화자의 근무 분야
화자가 초반부에 카셀라 교통 고객에게 알린다며, 적색 및 황색 노선의 유지 관리 작업이 다음 주에 시작될 것(Attention, Casella Transit customers. Maintenance work on the red and yellow lines will begin next week)이라고 했으므로 정답은 (B)이다.

Paraphrasing
담화의 Transit → 정답의 Transportation

72 What does the speaker say the listeners can receive notifications about?
 (A) Route changes
 (B) Mobile app updates
 (C) New products
 (D) Schedule delays

화자는 청자들이 무엇에 대한 알림을 받을 수 있다고 말하는가?
 (A) 노선 변경
 (B) 모바일 앱 업데이트
 (C) 신제품
 (D) 일정 지연

어휘 route 노선, 경로

해설 세부 사항 관련 – 알림을 받을 수 있는 것
화자가 중반부에 열차가 영향을 받는 경우에 지연과 관련된 알림을 받을 수 있다(You can receive notifications regarding delays if your train is impacted)고 했으므로 정답은 (D)이다.

TEST 4 109

73 According to the speaker, how can the listeners reduce a cost?
(A) By purchasing a digital ticket
(B) By reserving multiple permits
(C) By traveling at less busy hours
(D) By joining a loyalty program

화자에 따르면, 청자들은 어떻게 비용을 줄일 수 있는가?
(A) 디지털 티켓을 구입함으로써
(B) 다양한 허가증을 예약함으로써
(C) 덜 바쁜 시간대에 이동함으로써
(D) 고객 보상 프로그램에 가입함으로써

어휘 reduce 줄이다, 감소시키다   multiple 다양한, 다수의
loyalty program 고객 보상 프로그램

해설 세부 사항 관련 – 비용을 줄이는 방법
화자가 후반부에 통근 교통비를 절약하고 싶은지 물으며, 모바일 앱을 통해 전자 승차권을 구입하라(Want to save on commuter rides? Purchase your e-ticket through the mobile app as well)고 했으므로 정답은 (A)이다.

Paraphrasing
담화의 save → 질문의 reduce a cost
담화의 e-ticket → 정답의 a digital ticket

74-76 회의 발췌

> **W-Am** Good morning, Glenman House Living Museum staff. Recently, researchers discovered the original plans for the house's gardens from the eighteenth century. **⁷⁴So, we're going to restore the gardens based on those plans!** Even though we have the original designs, **⁷⁵making an authentic re-creation won't be an easy task. We don't know what specific varieties of plants were grown back then.** That's why we're so lucky to have **⁷⁶Vivek Hazarika** consulting on this project. **⁷⁶As a gardener who has managed the grounds of many historic estates**, he has extensive expertise in what would have been planted at the time.

안녕하세요, 글렌맨 하우스 리빙 박물관 직원 여러분. 최근에 연구원들이 18세기 이 저택 정원의 원본 설계도를 발견했습니다. **그래서 이 설계도를 바탕으로 정원을 복원할 것입니다!** 우리가 원본 디자인을 갖고 있기는 하지만 **진짜 같이 재현하는 것은 쉬운 작업이 아닙니다. 우리는 당시 어떤 종류의 식물이 재배되었는지 모릅니다.** 그렇기 때문에 **비벡 하자리카**가 이 프로젝트를 컨설팅해 주는 것은 정말 행운입니다. **많은 역사적 저택들의 부지를 관리해 온 정원사로서**, 당시 심었을 식물에 대한 폭넓은 전문 지식을 보유하고 있습니다.

어휘 discover 발견하다, 깨닫다   original 원본의, 원래의
restore 복원하다, 복구하다   based on ~을 바탕으로
authentic 진짜 같은, 진짜의   re-creation 재현, 개조
task 작업, 일   specific 특정한, 구체적인   variety 종류, 품종
gardener 정원사   manage 관리하다   grounds 부지, 구내
estate 저택, 토지, 사유지   extensive 광범위한, 폭넓은
expertise 전문 지식, 전문 기술

74 What is the purpose of the meeting?
(A) To explain a restoration project
(B) To prepare for a public event
(C) To train some new tour guides
(D) To recruit some volunteers

회의의 목적은 무엇인가?
(A) 복원 프로젝트를 설명하는 것
(B) 공개 행사를 준비하는 것
(C) 신입 여행 가이드를 교육하는 것
(D) 자원봉사자를 모집하는 것

어휘 explain 설명하다   restoration 복원, 복구   train 교육하다
recruit 모집하다   volunteer 자원봉사자

해설 전체 내용 관련 – 회의의 목적
화자가 초반부에 원본 설계도를 발견했다며, 이 설계도를 바탕으로 정원을 복원할 것(So, we're going to restore the gardens based on those plans!)이라고 알리면서, 그와 관련해 이야기하고 있으므로 정답은 (A)이다.

75 According to the speaker, why will a task be challenging?
(A) Funding has not been secured.
(B) Unfavorable weather is predicted.
(C) Some permits have been delayed.
(D) Some important information is missing.

화자에 따르면, 작업은 왜 어려울 것인가?
(A) 자금이 확보되지 않았다.
(B) 좋지 못한 날씨가 예상된다.
(C) 허가증이 지연되었다.
(D) 중요한 정보가 빠져 있다.

어휘 challenging 힘든, 까다로운   funding 자금 (제공)
unfavorable 좋지 못한, 호의적이지 않은   predict 예상하다
delay 지연시키다   missing 빠진, 분실된

해설 세부 사항 관련 – 작업이 어려운 이유
화자가 중반부에 진짜 같이 재현하는 것은 쉬운 작업이 아니며, 당시 어떤 종류의 식물이 재배되었는지 모른다(~ making an authentic re-creation won't be an easy task. We don't know what specific varieties of plants were grown back then)고 했으므로 정답은 (D)이다.

Paraphrasing
담화의 won't be an easy task → 질문의 challenging
담화의 don't know what specific varieties of plants were grown → 정답의 Some important information is missing.

76 Who is Vivek Hazarika?
(A) An architect
(B) A gardener
(C) A salesperson
(D) An archaeologist

비벡 하자리카는 누구인가?
(A) 건축가
(B) 정원사
(C) 영업 사원
(D) 고고학자

해설 세부 사항 관련 – 비벡 하자리카의 직업
화자가 후반부에 비벡 하자리카가 많은 역사적 저택들의 부지를 관리해 온 정원사(As a gardener who has managed the grounds of many historic estates ~)라고 했으므로 정답은 (B)이다.

77-79 안내 ▶동영상 강의

M-Cn **77Welcome, new sales representatives, to today's session on cold calling,** a sales technique where we call potential clients who haven't heard of us yet. Toward the end of the session **78you'll each be given a list of prospective parties to call.** Now, the people you're contacting are busy and may not be receptive. Your job's to persuade them that what you have to say is worth their while. Be friendly and avoid using scripts. **79Now we'll listen to some cold call recordings to learn what works and what doesn't.**

신입 영업 사원 여러분, 오늘의 전화 영업 교육에 오신 것을 환영합니다. 전화 영업은 아직 우리에 대해 들어보지 못한 잠재 고객들에게 전화를 거는 영업 기법입니다. 교육이 끝날 무렵에, **여러분은 각자 전화할 잠재 고객 명단을 받을 것입니다.** 자, 여러분이 연락할 사람들이 바쁘고 수용적이지 않을 수도 있습니다. 여러분이 할 일은 여러분이 하는 말이 가치가 있다는 것을 설득하는 것입니다. 친절하게 대하고 원고를 이용하는 것을 피하세요. **이제 전화 영업 녹음을 들어보고 어떤 것이 효과적이고 어떤 것이 효과가 없는지 알아보겠습니다.**

어휘 session (특정 활동을 위한) 시간 cold calling 전화 영업 potential 잠재적인, 가능성 있는 prospective 잠재적인, 유망한 party 사람, 당사자 receptive 수용적인 persuade 설득하다 worth one's while ~에게 가치 있는 avoid 피하다 script 원고

77 What is the purpose of the session?
(A) To discuss customer feedback
(B) To explain an attendance policy
(C) To discourage mobile phone use
(D) To train new sales staff

교육의 목적은 무엇인가?
(A) 고객 의견을 논의하는 것
(B) 출석 정책을 설명하는 것
(C) 휴대전화 사용을 막는 것
(D) 신입 영업 직원들을 교육하는 것

어휘 attendance 출석, 참석 discourage 막다, 단념시키다

해설 전체 내용 관련 – 교육의 목적
화자가 초반부에 오늘의 전화 영업 교육에 온 신입 영업 사원 여러분을 환영한다(Welcome, new sale representatives, to today's session on cold calling, ~)고 했으므로 정답은 (D)이다.

78 What will be on a list that the listeners will receive?
(A) Potential clients to contact
(B) Employees who have exceeded sales goals
(C) Products offered by the company
(D) Departments within the company

청자들이 받을 명단에 무엇이 있을 것인가?
(A) 연락할 잠재 고객들
(B) 영업 목표를 초과한 직원들
(C) 회사에서 제공하는 제품들
(D) 회사 내의 부서들

어휘 exceed 초과하다, 넘어서다

해설 세부 사항 관련 – 명단에 있는 것
화자가 중반부에 청자들이 전화할 잠재 고객 명단을 받을 것(~ you'll each be given a list of prospective parties to call)이라고 했으므로 정답은 (A)이다.

Paraphrasing
담화의 prospective parties to call
→ 정답의 Potential clients to contact

79 What will the listeners do next?
(A) Memorize prepared scripts
(B) Listen to recorded calls
(C) Take a brief survey
(D) Brainstorm conversational topics

청자들은 다음에 무엇을 할 것인가?
(A) 준비된 원고 암기하기
(B) 녹음된 전화 통화 듣기
(C) 간단한 설문 조사 참여하기
(D) 대화 주제에 대한 아이디어 떠올리기

어휘 memorize 암기하다, 외우다 brief 간단한, 짧은 brainstorm 아이디어를 구상하다 conversational 대화의

해설 세부 사항 관련 – 청자들이 다음에 할 일
화자가 후반부에 이제 전화 영업 녹음을 들어보고 어떤 것이 효과적이고 어떤 것이 효과가 없는지 알아보겠다(Now we'll listen to some cold call recordings to learn what works and what doesn't)고 했으므로 정답은 (B)이다.

Paraphrasing
담화의 some cold call recordings → 정답의 recorded calls

80-82 전화 메시지

M-Au Ms. Stewart, this is Rodrigo Gomez, president of Gomez and Sons. **⁸⁰I want to apologize personally for the problems your restaurant experienced using our patio umbrellas.** At our company, we pride ourselves on doing everything in-house, from graphic design to production. This gives us greater control over the quality of our products. But we do use outside suppliers for parts. **⁸¹Apparently, we received some inferior metal components. ⁸²We will send you a replacement set of umbrellas at no cost today, constructed with new metal parts.**

스튜어트 씨, 저는 고메즈 앤 썬즈의 대표, 로드리고 고메즈입니다. 귀하의 레스토랑에서 저희 테라스용 파라솔을 이용하면서 겪은 문제들에 대해 직접 사과드리고자 합니다. 저희 회사에서는 그래픽 디자인부터 생산까지 모든 것을 회사 내에서 하고 있다는 데 자부심을 가지고 있습니다. 이것은 제품의 품질을 더 잘 통제할 수 있게 해 줍니다. 하지만 부품은 외부 공급업체를 이용합니다. 보아하니, 좋지 못한 금속 부품을 받은 것 같습니다. 저희가 오늘 새 금속 부품으로 제작된 파라솔 세트 교체품을 무료로 보내 드리겠습니다.

어휘 personally 직접 patio umbrella 테라스용 파라솔 pride oneself on ~에 대해 자부심을 갖다, ~을 자랑으로 여기다 in-house 회사 내부에서 control 통제(력), 제어 supplier 공급업체, 공급업자 apparently 보아하니, 분명히 inferior 좋지 않은, 열등한 component 부품, 요소 replacement 교체(품), 후임자 at no cost 무료로 construct 제작하다, 만들다

80 What does the speaker's company sell?
(A) Sound systems
(B) Light fixtures
(C) Umbrellas
(D) Refrigerators

화자의 회사는 무엇을 판매하는가?
(A) 음향 시스템
(B) 조명
(C) 파라솔
(D) 냉장고

해설 전체 내용 관련 - 화자의 회사가 판매하는 것
화자가 초반부에 화자의 회사의 테라스용 파라솔을 이용하면서 겪은 문제들에 대해 직접 사과하고자 한다(I want to apologize personally for the problems your restaurant experienced using our patio umbrellas)고 했으므로 정답은 (C)이다.

81 Why does the speaker say, "we do use outside suppliers for parts"?
(A) To recommend a different company
(B) To justify an increased price
(C) To explain the source of a problem
(D) To decline a proposal

화자는 왜 "부품은 외부 공급업체를 이용합니다"라고 말하는가?
(A) 다른 회사를 추천하기 위해
(B) 가격 인상을 정당화하기 위해
(C) 문제의 근원을 설명하기 위해
(D) 제안을 거절하기 위해

어휘 justify 정당화하다, 타당함을 보여 주다 increased 인상된 source 근원, 원천 decline 거절하다

해설 화자의 의도 파악 - 부품은 외부 공급업체를 이용한다는 말의 의도
화자가 중반부에 인용문을 언급하면서 자신의 회사가 좋지 못한 금속 부품을 받은 것 같다(Apparently, we received some inferior metal components)고 했다. 이는 문제가 발생한 원인을 설명하는 말이므로 정답은 (C)이다.

82 What does the speaker say he will do today?
(A) Interview some applicants
(B) Send a shipment
(C) Train some staff
(D) Update a spreadsheet

화자는 오늘 무엇을 할 것이라고 말하는가?
(A) 지원자 면접 보기
(B) 배송품 발송하기
(C) 직원 교육하기
(D) 스프레드시트 업데이트하기

어휘 applicant 지원자, 신청자 shipment 배송(품) spreadsheet 스프레드시트(표 기반의 문서 프로그램)

해설 세부 사항 관련 - 화자가 오늘 할 일
화자가 후반부에 오늘 새 금속 부품으로 제작된 파라솔 세트 교체품을 무료로 보내 주겠다(We will send you a replacement set of umbrellas at no cost today, constructed with new metal parts)고 했으므로 정답은 (B)이다.

Paraphrasing
담화의 send you a replacement set of umbrellas → 정답의 Send a shipment

83-85 광고

W-Br **⁸³Temp-Time Work Solutions has hundreds of qualified, temporary workers available to meet any of your staffing needs.** Please call us to help your business fill open positions. **⁸⁴We are the largest temp agency in the region**, with branch offices in six locations. Let Temp-Time help you find the right person to complete just about any job! Call us at 555-0145 and **⁸⁵mention this ad to get a twenty percent discount off our fee.**

템프-타임 워크 솔루션즈는 모든 직원 채용 필요를 충족할 수 있는 수백 명의 자격을 갖춘 임시직 근로자를 보유하고 있습니다. 전화 주시면 귀사의 공석을 충원하도록 도와드리겠습니다. 저희는 이 지역에서 가장 큰 임시 인력 파견 업체이며, 여섯 곳에 지사가 있습니다. 템프-타임이 어떤 일이든 완수할 수 있는 적합한 인재를 찾을 수 있도록 도와드립니다! 555-0145번으로 저희에게 전화하셔서 이 광고를 언급하시고 20퍼센트 요금 할인을 받으세요.

어휘 qualified 자격을 갖춘, 적격의 staffing 직원 채용, 직원 구성 position 직책, 일자리 temp agency 임시 인력 파견 업체 region 지역 branch office 지사 ad 광고

83 What type of business is being advertised?
(A) An event planning company
(B) A financial advising service
(C) An attorney's office
(D) A staffing agency

어떤 종류의 업체가 광고되고 있는가?
(A) 행사 기획 회사
(B) 재정 자문 서비스
(C) 변호사 사무실
(D) 인력 채용 대행사

해설 전체 내용 관련 - 광고되는 업체의 종류
화자가 초반부에 템프-타임 워크 솔루션즈는 모든 직원 채용 필요를 충족할 수 있는 수백 명의 자격을 갖춘 임시직 근로자를 보유하고 있다(Temp-Time Work Solutions has hundreds of qualified, temporary workers available to meet any of your staffing needs)고 했으므로 정답은 (D)이다.

84 What aspect of a business does the speaker emphasize?
(A) Its large size
(B) Its reasonable prices
(C) Its business hours
(D) Its long history

화자는 업체의 어떤 측면을 강조하는가?
(A) 큰 규모
(B) 합리적인 가격
(C) 영업시간
(D) 긴 역사

어휘 emphasize 강조하다 reasonable 합리적인, 가격이 알맞은

해설 세부 사항 관련 - 화자가 강조하는 측면
화자가 중반부에 이 지역에서 가장 큰 임시 인력 파견 업체(We are the largest temp agency in the region ~)라고 했으므로 정답은 (A)이다.

Paraphrasing
담화의 the largest temp agency in the region
→ 정답의 Its large size

85 How can the listeners receive a discount?
(A) By mentioning an advertisement
(B) By referring friends
(C) By paying with a credit card
(D) By using a coupon

청자들은 어떻게 할인을 받을 수 있는가?
(A) 광고를 언급함으로써
(B) 친구를 소개함으로써
(C) 신용카드로 지불함으로써
(D) 쿠폰을 이용함으로써

어휘 refer 소개하다, 추천하다

해설 세부 사항 관련 - 할인 받는 방법
화자가 후반부에 전화를 걸어 광고를 언급하고 20퍼센트 요금 할인을 받으라(~ mention this ad to get a twenty percent discount off our fee)고 했으므로 정답은 (A)이다.

Paraphrasing
담화의 this ad → 정답의 an advertisement

86-88 회의 발췌

M-Au I've just received details about this year's hospitality conference. It looks like it'll be particularly informative this year. It'll be held at the end of the month. Now, **⁸⁶I know I've set your project due dates for the end of the month as well, but this is an important opportunity.** The conference will feature an expo of vendors who serve hotel chains, which could be useful given that **⁸⁷we'll be opening hotels in two new cities next year!** Speaking of which, **⁸⁸Thilo visited both of those construction sites last week and is now going to give us a progress report.**

올해의 접객업 콘퍼런스에 관한 상세 정보를 방금 받았습니다. 올해는 특히 유익할 것으로 보입니다. 이 행사는 이달 말에 개최될 것입니다. 자, **제가 여러분의 프로젝트 마감 날짜도 이달 말로 정해 놓았다는 사실을 알고 있지만, 이는 중요한 기회입니다.** 이번 콘퍼런스에는 호텔 체인에 서비스를 제공하는 판매업체들의 박람회가 포함될 텐데, **우리가 내년에 두 곳의 새로운 도시에 호텔을 개장할 예정인 것**을 고려하면 유용할 것입니다! 말이 나온 김에, **틸로가 지난주에 그 공사 현장 두 곳을 방문했고, 이제 진행 상황을 보고할 예정입니다.**

어휘 hospitality 접객(업) particularly 특히, 특별히 informative 유익한, 유용한 정보를 주는 hold 개최하다 due date 마감 날짜 feature 특징으로 하다, 특별히 포함하다

expo 박람회 vendor 판매 회사 serve 서비스를 제공하다
given that ~임을 고려해 (볼 때) progress 진행 (상황), 진척

86 What does the speaker mean when he says, "this is an important opportunity"?
(A) A new client has an urgent problem.
(B) Some information is needed from the listeners.
(C) Some deadlines are flexible.
(D) The listeners have done a good job.

화자가 "이는 중요한 기회입니다"라고 말할 때 무엇을 의미하는가?
(A) 신규 고객에게 긴급한 문제가 있다.
(B) 일부 정보가 청자들로부터 필요하다.
(C) 마감 기한이 바뀔 수 있다.
(D) 청자들이 일을 잘 처리해 주었다.

어휘 urgent 긴급한 flexible 융통성 있는, 탄력적인

해설 화자의 의도 파악 – 중요한 기회라는 말의 의도
화자가 중반부에 자신이 청자들의 프로젝트 마감 날짜를 이달 말로 정해 놓았다는 사실을 알고 있지만(I know I've set your project due dates for the end of the month as well, but)이라고 말하면서 인용문을 언급하고 있다. 이는 콘퍼런스가 중요한 기회이니 마감일을 변경해서라도 참석해야 한다는 뜻이므로 정답은 (C)이다.

87 What will the speaker's business do next year?
(A) Redesign advertising materials
(B) Open new locations
(C) Hire a new vendor
(D) Implement a security policy

화자의 업체는 내년에 무엇을 할 것인가?
(A) 광고물 다시 디자인하기
(B) 신규 지점 개점하기
(C) 새 판매업체 고용하기
(D) 보안 정책 시행하기

어휘 advertising 광고 (활동) implement 시행하다

해설 세부 사항 관련 – 화자의 업체가 내년에 할 것
화자가 중반부에 내년에 두 곳의 새로운 도시에 호텔을 개장할 것(~ we'll be opening hotels in two new cities next year)이라고 했으므로 정답은 (B)이다.

Paraphrasing
담화의 opening hotels in two new cities
→ 정답의 Open new locations

88 What will Thilo do next?
(A) Practice his conference presentation
(B) Provide a construction update
(C) Summarize some financial data
(D) Contact a supply vendor

틸로는 다음에 무엇을 할 것인가?
(A) 콘퍼런스 발표 연습하기
(B) 공사 관련 최신 소식 제공하기
(C) 재무 데이터 요약하기
(D) 물품 판매업체에 연락하기

어휘 practice 연습하다 summarize 요약하다

해설 세부 사항 관련 – 틸로가 다음에 할 일
화자가 후반부에 틸로가 지난주에 그 공사 현장 두 곳을 방문했고, 이제 진행 상황을 보고할 예정(Thilo visited both of those construction sites last week and is now going to give us a progress report)이라고 했으므로 정답은 (B)이다.

Paraphrasing
담화의 give us a progress report
→ 정답의 Provide a construction update

89-91 소개

W-Am Welcome to the annual Soundtrack Music Awards show. **89** This year, we're streaming this event live over the Internet for the very first time! Tonight's honoree, **90** Olga Alabi, founded the I-Beat music label in 1996. She has worked tirelessly to bring original soundtrack music to film audiences around the world. Over the years, she has been responsible for discovering and developing some of today's leading composers. In fact, **91** after Ms. Alabi receives her award, some of her most famous clients will perform for us.

연례 사운드트랙 음악 시상식에 오신 것을 환영합니다. 올해는 처음으로 이 행사를 인터넷에서 라이브로 중계합니다! 오늘 밤의 수상자인 올가 앨러비는 1996년에 I-비트 음반사를 설립했습니다. 그녀는 오리지널 사운드트랙 음악을 전 세계의 영화 관람객들에게 전하고자 부단히 노력해 왔습니다. 수년간, 그녀는 오늘날 최고의 작곡가들을 발굴하고 개발하는 일을 담당해 왔습니다. 사실, 앨러비 씨가 상을 받은 후, 그녀의 가장 유명한 고객 중 일부가 공연할 예정입니다.

어휘 annual 연례적인 stream (인터넷에서) 방송하다, 중계하다
honoree 수상자 found 설립하다 music label 음반사
tirelessly 부단히, 지칠 줄 모르고 audience 관객, 청중
develop 성장시키다 leading 선도적인, 손꼽히는
composer 작곡가 perform 공연하다, 연주하다

89 What does the speaker say is new about this year's event?
(A) It takes place outdoors.
(B) It is sponsored by a major publication.
(C) It has been sold out for months.
(D) It is being streamed live.

화자는 올해의 행사와 관련해 무엇이 새롭다고 말하는가?
(A) 야외에서 개최된다.
(B) 대형 출판사의 후원을 받는다.
(C) 수 개월 동안 매진되었다.
(D) 라이브로 중계된다.

어휘 take place 개최되다, 진행되다 sponsor 후원하다, 협찬하다
publication 출판(물) sold out 매진인, 품절인

해설 세부 사항 관련 – 행사와 관련해 새로운 것
화자가 초반부에 올해는 처음으로 이 행사를 인터넷에서 라이브로 중계한다(This year, we're streaming this event live over the Internet for the very first time!)고 했으므로 정답은 (D)이다.

Paraphrasing
담화의 for the very first time → 질문의 new

90
Why is Ms. Alabi being recognized?
(A) She is a talented songwriter.
(B) She invented a musical instrument.
(C) She started a major record label.
(D) She supports several charities.

앨러비 씨는 왜 인정받는가?
(A) 능력 있는 작곡가이다.
(B) 악기를 발명했다.
(C) 주요 음반사를 시작했다.
(D) 여러 자선 단체를 지원한다.

어휘 talented 능력 있는, 재능 있는 invent 발명하다
musical instrument 악기 support 지원하다, 지지하다

해설 세부 사항 관련 – 앨러비 씨가 인정받는 이유
화자가 중반부에 올가 앨러비는 1996년에 I-비트 음반사를 설립했고, 오리지널 사운드트랙 음악을 전 세계의 영화 관람객들에게 전하고자 부단히 노력해 왔다(~ Olga Alabi, founded the I-Beat music label in 1996. She has worked tirelessly to bring original soundtrack music to film audiences around the world)고 했으므로 정답은 (C)이다.

Paraphrasing
담화의 founded the I-Beat music label
→ 정답의 started a major record label

91
According to the speaker, what will happen after Ms. Alabi receives her award?
(A) Photographs will be taken.
(B) Dinner will be served.
(C) Some musicians will perform.
(D) Some interviews will be held.

화자에 따르면, 앨러비 씨가 상을 받은 후에 무슨 일이 있을 것인가?
(A) 사진이 촬영될 것이다.
(B) 저녁 만찬이 제공될 것이다.
(C) 음악가들이 공연할 것이다.
(D) 인터뷰가 있을 것이다.

어휘 serve (음식 등을) 제공하다, 내오다

해설 세부 사항 관련 – 앨러비 씨가 상을 받은 후에 있을 일
화자가 후반부에 앨러비 씨가 상을 받은 후, 그녀의 가장 유명한 고객 중 일부가 공연할 예정(~ after Ms. Alabi receives her award, some of her most famous clients will perform for us)이라고 했으므로 정답은 (C)이다.

92-94 회의 발췌

M-Cn ⁹²OK, team, let's discuss our first-quarter sales figures. Unfortunately, retail sales of our smartwatches and other products have continued to fall. ⁹³Our president has proposed expanding the product line to include a virtual reality headset. And those have been popular lately. You can expect a lot more information at a future meeting. ⁹⁴Next on the agenda, Raya will be demonstrating the new software we'll be using to track consumer purchasing trends.

좋아요, 팀원 여러분, 1분기 매출 수치에 대해 논의해 봅시다. 안타깝게도, 스마트워치와 기타 제품들의 소매 판매가 계속 감소하고 있습니다. 대표님은 가상 현실 헤드셋을 포함하여 제품 라인을 확장할 것을 제안했습니다. 그리고 그것들이 요즘 인기 있습니다. 여러분은 향후 회의에서 더 많은 정보를 기대할 수 있습니다. 다음 안건으로는, 소비자 구매 경향을 파악하기 위해 사용할 새 소프트웨어를 라야가 시연해 줄 것입니다.

어휘 figure 수치, 숫자 retail 소매의 fall 감소하다, 떨어지다
propose 제안하다, 제의하다 include 포함하다
virtual reality 가상 현실 expect 예상하다, 기대하다
agenda 안건, 의제 demonstrate 시연하다, 시범을 보이다
track 파악하다, 추적하다 consumer 소비자 trend 경향, 추세

92
Which department does the speaker most likely work in?
(A) Sales
(B) Accounting
(C) Human resources
(D) Information technology

화자는 어느 부서에서 일하는 것 같은가?
(A) 영업
(B) 회계
(C) 인사
(D) 정보 기술

해설 전체 내용 관련 – 화자의 부서
화자가 초반부에 팀원들에게 1분기 매출 수치에 대해 논의해 보자(OK, team, let's discuss our first-quarter sales figures)고 했으므로 정답은 (A)이다.

TEST 4 115

93 Why does the speaker say, "those have been popular lately"?
(A) To express disbelief
(B) To explain a shortage
(C) To agree with a proposal
(D) To make a correction

화자는 왜 "그것들이 요즘 인기 있습니다"라고 말하는가?
(A) 불신을 나타내기 위해
(B) 부족의 원인을 설명하기 위해
(C) 제안에 동의하기 위해
(D) 잘못을 바로잡기 위해

어휘 express 나타내다, 표현하다 disbelief 불신(감)
shortage 부족 make a correction 잘못을 바로잡다

해설 화자의 의도 파악 – 그것들이 요즘 인기 있다는 말의 의도
화자가 중반부에 대표가 가상 현실 헤드셋을 포함하여 제품 라인을 확장할 것을 제안했다(Our president has proposed expanding the product line to include a virtual reality headset)고 알리면서 인용문을 언급하고 있다. 이는 인기 있는 제품이기 때문에 대표가 제안한 대로 하는 것이 좋겠다는 의미를 나타내는 말이므로 정답은 (C)이다.

94 What will the listeners do next?
(A) Take a lunch break
(B) Ask questions about a policy
(C) Read a report
(D) View a demonstration

청자들은 다음에 무엇을 할 것인가?
(A) 점심 식사 시간 갖기
(B) 정책에 관해 질문하기
(C) 보고서 읽기
(D) 시연 보기

어휘 demonstration 시연(회), 시범

해설 세부 사항 관련 – 청자들이 다음에 할 일
화자가 후반부에 다음 안건으로는, 소비자 구매 경향을 파악하기 위해 사용할 새 소프트웨어를 라야가 시연해 줄 것(Next on the agenda, Raya will be demonstrating the new software we'll be using to track consumer purchasing trends)이라고 했으므로 정답은 (D)이다.

95-97 투어 정보 + 일기 예보

M-Au Please follow me, and ⁹⁵**we'll begin today's tour.** Now, I know not everyone who takes this all-access tour is ⁹⁵**a football fan.** Many of our visitors are just curious about how ⁹⁵**a modern sports facility of this size** operates. Well, you'll get to see that and much more. And fortunately for us, ⁹⁶**today's forecast shows a mix of sun and clouds, with no rain.** That's just the right combination for spending some time outside on the field comfortably. Also, as a heads-up, ⁹⁷**a shuttle bus will meet us at the end of the tour to bring us all back to the parking lot.**

저를 따라오시면, **오늘의 견학을 시작하겠습니다.** 자, 모든 구역에 출입할 수 있는 이번 견학에 참여하는 모든 분들이 **축구 팬**은 아니라는 것을 알고 있습니다. 방문객 중 많은 사람들이 단지 **이 정도 규모의 현대적인 스포츠 시설**이 어떻게 운영되는지 궁금해합니다. 음, 여러분은 그 이상의 것을 보실 것입니다. 그리고 다행스럽게도, **오늘의 예보는 비 없이 햇빛과 구름이 섞인 날씨를 보여줍니다.** 야외 경기장에서 편하게 시간을 보내기에 딱 좋은 조합입니다. 또한, 미리 알려 드리자면, **견학이 끝나면 셔틀버스가 와서 주차장으로 다시 모셔다 드릴 것입니다.**

어휘 all-access 모든 구역에 출입할 수 있는 facility 시설(물)
operate 운영되다, 가동되다 fortunately 다행스럽게도
forecast 예보 a mix of 혼합된 combination 조합
comfortably 편하게 heads-up 공지, 알림

⁹⁶Monday	18°C	☁️
Tuesday	24°C	☀️
Wednesday	21°C	🌧️
Thursday	22°C	☀️

월요일	18°C	☁️
화요일	24°C	☀️
수요일	21°C	🌧️
목요일	22°C	☀️

95 Where are the listeners?
(A) At a farm
(B) At a factory
(C) At a museum
(D) At a stadium

청자들은 어디에 있는가?
(A) 농장
(B) 공장
(C) 박물관
(D) 경기장

해설 　전체 내용 관련 – 청자들이 있는 곳
화자가 초반부에 오늘의 견학을 시작한다(we'll begin today's tour)고 했고, 이어서 축구 팬(a football fan)과 이 정도 규모의 현대적인 스포츠 시설(a modern sports facility of this size)을 언급한 것에서 경기장에 있음을 알 수 있다. 따라서 정답은 (D)이다.

Paraphrasing
담화의 a modern sports facility → 정답의 a stadium

96 Look at the graphic. When is the tour taking place?
(A) On Monday
(B) On Tuesday
(C) On Wednesday
(D) On Thursday

시각 정보에 의하면, 견학은 언제 진행되고 있는가?
(A) 월요일
(B) 화요일
(C) 수요일
(D) 목요일

해설 　시각 정보 연계 – 견학이 진행되는 날
화자가 중반부에 오늘의 예보는 햇빛과 구름이 섞인 날씨를 보여 준다(~ today's forecast shows a mix of sun and clouds, ~)고 했고, 일기 예보에서 해와 구름이 함께 있는 날은 월요일이므로 정답은 (A)이다.

97 What will happen at the end of the tour?
(A) Pictures will be taken.
(B) Food will be served.
(C) Gifts will be given out.
(D) A shuttle bus will arrive.

견학 종료 시에 무슨 일이 있을 것인가?
(A) 사진이 촬영될 것이다.
(B) 음식이 제공될 것이다.
(C) 선물이 증정될 것이다.
(D) 셔틀버스가 도착할 것이다.

해설 　세부 사항 관련 – 견학 종료 시에 있을 일
화자가 후반부에 견학이 끝나면 셔틀버스가 와서 주차장으로 다시 데려다 줄 것(~ a shuttle bus will meet us at the end of the tour to bring us all back to the parking lot)이라고 했으므로 정답은 (D)이다.

Paraphrasing
담화의 meet us → 정답의 arrive

98-100 회의 발췌 + 업무 배정표

W-Br   As you all know, we're hosting a large event tonight. **98 It's a dinner party to celebrate the retirement of a longtime employee of Jalton Incorporated.** The chefs are already prepping dinner, and I need you all to set up the ballroom. Here's the assignment list. There's just one change. **99 Amanda couldn't make it, so Kota's covering for her and will take Amanda's assignment.** Now, **100 I have a meeting with a potential client at noon**, but otherwise, I'll be available all day if anything comes up.

모두 아시다시피, 오늘 밤 큰 행사를 개최합니다. **잴튼 주식회사에서 오랫동안 근무한 직원의 은퇴를 기념하는 저녁 만찬입니다.** 요리사들이 이미 저녁 식사를 준비하고 있으니, 여러분은 모두 연회장을 준비해 주시기 바랍니다. 여기 업무 배정표가 있습니다. 단 한 가지 변동 사항이 있습니다. **아만다가 올 수 없어서, 코타가 대신해 아만다에게 배정된 업무를 맡을 것입니다.** 자, **저는 정오에 잠재 고객과 회의가 있지만**, 그 외에는 무슨 일이 생기면 하루 종일 시간이 있습니다.

어휘 host 주최하다   celebrate 기념하다, 축하하다   retirement 은퇴, 퇴직   prep 준비하다   ballroom 연회실   assignment 배정(되는 것)   make it 오다   cover 대신하다   otherwise 그 외에는, 그렇지 않으면   come up 생기다, 발생하다   organize 준비하다, 조직하다   hang 걸다, 매달다   decoration 장식(물)   flower arrangement 꽃 장식, 꽃꽂이

Name	Assignment
Ji-soo	Organizing the food-serving station
99 Amanda	**Hanging decorations**
Sandrine	Creating flower arrangements
Murat	Setting up tables and chairs

이름	배정 업무
지수	배식대 준비
아만다	**장식물 걸기**
샌드린	꽃 장식 만들기
무랏	탁자 및 의자 설치

98 What type of event is being held tonight?
(A) A grand opening
(B) A company anniversary
(C) A retirement party
(D) A wedding celebration

어떤 종류의 행사가 오늘 밤에 개최되는가?
(A) 개장식
(B) 회사 기념일
(C) 은퇴 기념 파티
(D) 결혼 축하연

어휘 anniversary 기념일   celebration 축하 행사, 기념 행사

해설 **전체 내용 관련 – 오늘 밤에 열리는 행사**
화자가 초반부에 오늘 밤 큰 행사를 개최한다며 잴튼 주식회사에서 오랫동안 근무한 직원의 은퇴를 기념하는 저녁 만찬(It's a dinner party to celebrate the retirement of a longtime employee of Jalton Incorporated)이라고 했으므로 정답은 (C)이다.

---

99 Look at the graphic. Which assignment will Kota be responsible for?
(A) Organizing the food-serving station
(B) Hanging decorations
(C) Creating flower arrangements
(D) Setting up tables and chairs

시각 정보에 의하면, 코타는 어느 업무를 책임질 것인가?
(A) 배식대 준비
(B) 장식물 걸기
(C) 꽃 장식 만들기
(D) 탁자 및 의자 설치

해설 **시각 정보 연계 – 코타가 책임질 일**
화자가 중반부에 아만다가 올 수 없어서, 코타가 대신해 아만다에게 배정된 업무를 맡을 것(Amanda couldn't make it, so Kota's covering for her and will take Amanda's assignment)이라고 했고, 업무 배정표에서 아만다의 업무가 장식물 걸기라는 것을 알 수 있으므로 정답은 (B)이다.

---

100 What does the speaker say she has to do at noon?
(A) Go to the airport
(B) Pick up some tablecloths
(C) Cook a meal
(D) Attend a meeting

화자는 정오에 무엇을 해야 한다고 말하는가?
(A) 공항에 가기
(B) 식탁보 가져오기
(C) 식사 요리하기
(D) 회의 참석하기

어휘 pick up 가져가다, 가져오다

해설 **세부 사항 관련 – 화자가 정오에 할 일**
화자가 후반부에 정오에 잠재 고객과 회의가 있다(I have a meeting with a potential client at noon ~)고 했으므로 정답은 (D)이다.

Paraphrasing
담화의 have a meeting → 정답의 Attend a meeting

기출 TEST 5

동영상 강의

1 (C)	2 (B)	3 (A)	4 (D)	5 (B)
6 (B)	7 (B)	8 (B)	9 (B)	10 (C)
11 (B)	12 (C)	13 (C)	14 (B)	15 (B)
16 (C)	17 (C)	18 (A)	19 (B)	20 (B)
21 (C)	22 (C)	23 (C)	24 (C)	25 (B)
26 (B)	27 (A)	28 (C)	29 (C)	30 (B)
31 (A)	32 (D)	33 (B)	34 (B)	35 (B)
36 (A)	37 (C)	38 (C)	39 (A)	40 (D)
41 (B)	42 (D)	43 (C)	44 (C)	45 (A)
46 (B)	47 (D)	48 (C)	49 (B)	50 (D)
51 (A)	52 (C)	53 (C)	54 (D)	55 (B)
56 (D)	57 (C)	58 (C)	59 (A)	60 (B)
61 (C)	62 (B)	63 (A)	64 (D)	65 (A)
66 (D)	67 (B)	68 (B)	69 (A)	70 (D)
71 (A)	72 (B)	73 (A)	74 (D)	75 (A)
76 (B)	77 (A)	78 (D)	79 (B)	80 (A)
81 (B)	82 (A)	83 (C)	84 (A)	85 (B)
86 (D)	87 (C)	88 (C)	89 (C)	90 (D)
91 (A)	92 (D)	93 (C)	94 (A)	95 (A)
96 (C)	97 (B)	98 (D)	99 (A)	100 (A)

PART 1

1

M-Au

(A) She's pushing a large container down a hallway.
(B) She's looking at information on a laptop screen.
(C) She's sorting through paper files.
(D) She's placing a hat on top of a file cabinet.

(A) 여자가 복도를 따라 대형 용기를 밀고 있다.
(B) 여자가 노트북 화면에 있는 정보를 보고 있다.
(C) 여자가 종이 파일들을 살펴보고 있다.
(D) 여자가 파일 캐비닛 위에 모자를 놓고 있다.

어휘 container 용기 hallway 복도 information 정보
sort through ~을 (자세히) 살펴보다 place 놓다, 두다

해설 1인 등장 사진 – 사람의 동작/상태 묘사
(A) 동사 오답. 여자가 대형 용기를 밀고 있는(is pushing a large container) 모습이 아니므로 오답.
(B) 동사 오답. 여자가 노트북 화면에 있는 정보를 보고 있는(is looking at information on a laptop screen) 모습이 아니므로 오답.
(C) 정답. 여자가 종이 파일들을 살펴보고 있는(is sorting through paper files) 모습이므로 정답.
(D) 동사 오답. 여자가 파일 캐비닛 위에 모자를 놓고 있는(is placing a hat on top of a file cabinet) 모습이 아니므로 오답.

2

W-Br

(A) A worker is painting lines on the floor.
(B) A worker is using a machine to move some boxes.
(C) A worker is sealing some packages.
(D) A worker is repairing a motor.

(A) 작업자가 바닥에 선을 그리고 있다.
(B) 작업자가 기계를 이용해 상자들을 옮기고 있다.
(C) 작업자가 포장물을 밀봉하고 있다.
(D) 작업자가 모터를 수리하고 있다.

어휘 seal 밀봉하다, 봉인하다 package 포장물, 소포

해설 1인 등장 사진 – 사람의 동작/상태 묘사
(A) 동사 오답. 작업자가 선을 그리는(is painting lines) 모습이 아니므로 오답.
(B) 정답. 작업자가 기계를 이용해 상자들을 옮기는(is using a machine to move some boxes) 모습이므로 정답.
(C) 동사 오답. 작업자가 포장물을 밀봉하고 있는(is sealing some packages) 모습이 아니므로 오답.
(D) 동사 오답. 작업자가 모터를 수리하고 있는(is repairing a motor) 모습이 아니므로 오답.

3

W-Am

(A) There are beverages available inside a tent.
(B) There are some people riding in an automobile.
(C) The man is reaching for a water bottle.
(D) The woman is moving some furniture.

(A) 텐트 안에 이용 가능한 음료들이 있다.
(B) 자동차에 타 있는 사람들이 있다.
(C) 남자가 물병을 향해 손을 뻗고 있다.
(D) 여자가 가구를 옮기고 있다.

어휘 beverage 음료 available 이용 가능한 ride 타다
automobile 자동차 reach for ~을 향해 손을 뻗다

TEST 5 119

해설 2인 이상 등장 사진 – 사람/사물/풍경 혼합 묘사
(A) 정답. 텐트 안에 이용 가능한 음료들이 있는(beverages available inside a tent) 모습이므로 정답.
(B) 사진에 없는 명사를 이용한 오답. 사진에 자동차(an automobile)의 모습이 보이지 않으므로 오답.
(C) 동사 오답. 남자가 물병을 향해 손을 뻗는(is reaching for a water bottle) 모습이 아니므로 오답.
(D) 동사 오답. 여자가 가구를 옮기는(is moving some furniture) 모습이 아니므로 오답.

4

M-Cn

(A) The door of a clothing store has been propped open.
(B) Customers are waiting to enter a clothing store.
(C) One of the customers is trying on a jacket.
(D) Clothing is displayed outside on racks.

(A) 옷 가게의 문이 밑부분을 받쳐 열려 있다.
(B) 고객들이 옷 가게에 들어가기 위해 기다리고 있다.
(C) 고객들 중 한 명이 재킷을 입어 보고 있다.
(D) 옷이 외부에 있는 거치대에 진열되어 있다.

어휘 be propped open 밑부분을 받쳐 열어 놓다
try on ~을 입어 보다   display 진열하다, 전시하다
rack 거치대, ~걸이

해설 2인 이상 등장 사진 – 사람/사물/풍경 혼합 묘사
(A) 사진에 없는 명사를 이용한 오답. 사진에 옷 가게 문(The door of a clothing store)의 모습이 보이지 않으므로 오답.
(B) 동사 오답. 고객들이 옷 가게에 들어가기 위해 기다리는(are waiting to enter a clothing store) 모습이 아니므로 오답.
(C) 동사 오답. 고객들 중 한 명이 재킷을 입어 보는(is trying on a jacket) 모습이 아니므로 오답.
(D) 정답. 옷(Clothing)이 외부에 있는 거치대에 진열되어 있는(is displayed outside on racks) 모습이므로 정답.

5

M-Cn

(A) One of the men is lowering some window shades.
(B) One of the men is writing on a poster board.
(C) One of the women is putting on a sweater.
(D) One of the women is reading from a notebook.

(A) 남자들 중 한 명이 창문 블라인드를 내리고 있다.
(B) 남자들 중 한 명이 포스터 보드에 뭔가 쓰고 있다.
(C) 여자들 중 한 명이 스웨터를 입고 있는 중이다.
(D) 여자들 중 한 명이 노트에 쓰여 있는 것을 읽고 있다.

어휘 lower 내리다, 낮추다   shade 블라인드, 차양
put on (동작) ~을 입다

해설 2인 이상 등장 사진 – 사람의 동작/상태 묘사
(A) 동사 오답. 남자들 중 한 명이 창문 블라인드를 내리는(is lowering some window shades) 모습이 아니므로 오답.
(B) 정답. 남자들 중 한 명이 포스터 보드에 뭔가 쓰고 있는(is writing on a poster board) 모습이므로 정답.
(C) 동사 오답. 여자들 중 한 명이 스웨터를 입는(is putting on a sweater) 모습이 아니므로 오답.
(D) 동사 오답. 여자들 중 한 명이 노트에 쓰여 있는 것을 읽는(is reading from a notebook) 모습이 아니므로 오답.

6

W-Br

(A) One of the cars is stopped at a stop sign.
(B) Some tires are stacked against a building.
(C) Some vehicles are being washed.
(D) A motorcycle is going through a gate.

(A) 자동차들 중 한 대가 정지 표지판 앞에 서 있다.
(B) 타이어들이 건물 옆에 쌓여 있다.
(C) 차량들이 세차되고 있다.
(D) 오토바이가 문을 통과해 지나가고 있다.

어휘 sign 표지판, 간판   stack 쌓다   vehicle 차량   gate 문

해설 사물/풍경 사진 – 풍경 묘사
(A) 사진에 없는 명사를 이용한 오답. 사진에 정지 표지판(a stop sign)의 모습이 보이지 않으므로 오답.
(B) 정답. 타이어들(Some tires)이 건물 옆에 쌓여 있는(are stacked against a building) 모습이므로 정답.
(C) 동사 오답. 차량들(Some vehicles)이 세차되고 있는(are being washed) 모습이 아니므로 오답.
(D) 동사 오답. 오토바이(A motorcycle)가 문을 통과해 지나가고 있는(is going through a gate) 모습이 아니므로 오답.

PART 2

7 W-Am / W-Br

Where did you put the invoice from Stanson Incorporated?

(A) No, not yet.
(B) On your desk.
(C) The post office is crowded today.

스탠슨 주식회사에서 보낸 청구서를 어디에 두셨나요?
(A) 아니요, 아직이요.
(B) 당신 책상에요.
(C) 오늘 우체국이 붐벼요.

어휘 invoice 청구서, 송장   crowded 붐비는

해설 청구서를 둔 곳을 묻는 Where 의문문
(A) Yes/No 불가 오답. Where 의문문에는 Yes/No 응답이 불가능하므로 오답.
(B) 정답. 청구서를 둔 곳을 묻는 질문에 상대방의 책상이라고 둔 장소를 알려 주고 있으므로 정답.
(C) 질문과 상관없는 오답.

8 M-Au / W-Am

Is the inspector coming this afternoon or tomorrow morning?
(A) The exterior light isn't working.
(B) He'll be here tomorrow.
(C) I'll take the next right turn.

조사관은 오늘 오후에 오나요, 아니면 내일 오전에 오나요?
(A) 외부 조명이 작동하지 않아요.
(B) 내일 오실 거예요.
(C) 다음번에 우회전할 거예요.

어휘 inspector 조사관, 검사관   exterior 외부의

해설 조사관이 오는 시점을 묻는 선택 의문문
(A) 질문과 상관없는 오답.
(B) 정답. 조사관이 오늘 오후에 오는지, 아니면 내일 오전에 오는지 묻는 질문에 내일 온다며 둘 중 하나를 선택해 응답하고 있으므로 정답.
(C) 질문과 상관없는 오답.

9 M-Au / M-Cn

What's the total cost to remodel the office lobby?
(A) The view from this window is great.
(B) Over 50,000 dollars.
(C) No, a sofa and table.

사무실 로비를 리모델링하는 데 드는 총 비용은 얼마인가요?
(A) 이 창문에서 보이는 경관이 아주 멋져요.
(B) 5만 달러가 넘어요.
(C) 아니요, 소파와 테이블이요.

어휘 cost 비용   remodel 리모델링하다, 개조하다

해설 사무실 로비 리모델링 총 비용을 묻는 What 의문문
(A) 연상 단어 오답. 질문의 office lobby에서 연상 가능한 view와 window를 이용한 오답.
(B) 정답. 사무실 로비 리모델링 총 비용을 묻는 질문에 5만 달러가 넘는다며 대략적인 금액을 알려 주고 있으므로 정답.
(C) Yes/No 불가 오답. What 의문문에는 Yes/No 응답이 불가능하므로 오답.

10 W-Am / M-Cn

Are you getting the same type of desk or a different one?
(A) It's conveniently located.
(B) I can pick it up for you.
(C) The same type.

같은 종류의 책상을 구입하시나요, 아니면 다른 것으로 하시나요?
(A) 편리한 곳에 위치해 있어요.
(B) 제가 갖다드릴 수 있어요.
(C) 같은 종류요.

어휘 conveniently located 편리한 곳에 위치한
pick up 가져오다, 찾아오다

해설 구입하는 책상의 종류를 묻는 선택 의문문
(A) 질문과 상관없는 오답.
(B) 질문과 상관없는 오답.
(C) 정답. 같은 종류의 책상을 구입하는지, 아니면 다른 것으로 하는지 묻는 질문에 같은 종류라며 둘 중 하나를 선택해 응답하고 있으므로 정답.

11 M-Cn / M-Au

We're taking the clients to the theater this evening.
(A) He already ate.
(B) I'll reserve a taxi.
(C) From Australia.

우리가 오늘 저녁에 고객들을 극장에 데려갈 거예요.
(A) 그는 이미 식사했어요.
(B) 제가 택시를 예약할게요.
(C) 호주에서요.

어휘 reserve 예약하다

해설 정보 전달의 평서문
(A) 평서문과 상관없는 오답. 평서문에 3인칭 대명사 He로 지칭할 인물이 언급된 적이 없으므로 오답.
(B) 정답. 오늘 저녁에 고객들을 극장에 데려간다고 알리는 평서문에 택시를 예약하겠다는 말로 극장으로 가는 데 필요한 조치를 언급하고 있으므로 정답.
(C) 평서문과 상관없는 오답. Where 의문문에 대한 응답이므로 오답.

12 M-Cn / W-Br

When is your budget report due?
(A) It was too expensive.
(B) I don't need one.
(C) By Tuesday at the latest.

예산 보고서 제출 기한이 언제인가요?
(A) 그건 너무 비쌌어요.
(B) 저는 필요 없어요.
(C) 늦어도 화요일까지요.

어휘 budget 예산   due ~가 기한인   at the latest 늦어도

해설 예산 보고서 제출 기한을 묻는 When 의문문
(A) 연상 단어 오답. 질문의 budget에서 연상 가능한 expensive를 이용한 오답.
(B) 질문과 상관없는 오답.
(C) 정답. 예산 보고서 제출 기한을 묻는 질문에 화요일까지라고 구체적인 시점을 알려 주고 있으므로 정답.

13 M-Au / W-Am

Who can I talk to about getting a membership at this fitness center?

(A) A monthly bill.
(B) Some new workout equipment.
(C) I can help you with that.

여기 피트니스 센터의 회원 가입에 대해 누구와 상담할 수 있나요?
(A) 월간 고지서요.
(B) 새 운동 장비요.
(C) 제가 도와드릴 수 있어요.

어휘 bill 고지서, 계산서 workout 운동 equipment 장비

해설 회원 가입에 대해 상담할 사람을 묻는 Who 의문문
(A) 연상 단어 오답. 질문의 membership에서 연상 가능한 monthly bill을 이용한 오답.
(B) 연상 단어 오답. 질문의 fitness center에서 연상 가능한 workout equipment를 이용한 오답.
(C) 정답. 회원 가입에 대해 상담할 사람을 묻는 질문에 자신이 도와줄 수 있다고 응답하고 있으므로 정답.

14 M-Au / M-Cn

Are you planning to buy a house in the city?

(A) A housecleaning company.
(B) I don't want to move.
(C) I'll be waiting at the post office.

도시에 있는 집을 구입할 계획이신가요?
(A) 주택 청소 회사요.
(B) 저는 이사하고 싶지 않아요.
(C) 우체국에서 기다리고 있을게요.

해설 도시에 있는 집을 구입할 계획인지 묻는 Be동사 의문문
(A) 유사 발음 오답. 질문의 house와 부분적으로 발음이 유사한 housecleaning을 이용한 오답.
(B) 정답. 도시에 있는 집을 구입할 계획인지 묻는 질문에 이사하고 싶지 않다며 집을 구입할 계획이 없음을 우회적으로 알려 주고 있으므로 정답.
(C) 질문과 상관없는 오답.

15 M-Au / W-Br

How did you decide on a venue for the fund-raising event?

(A) A small contribution.
(B) I got a recommendation from a friend.
(C) To buy books for the library.

기금 마련 행사 장소는 어떻게 결정하셨나요?
(A) 소액 기부금이요.
(B) 친구에게 추천을 받았어요.
(C) 도서관에 필요한 책들을 구입하기 위해서요.

어휘 venue (행사) 장소 fund-raising 기금 마련, 모금 contribution 기부(금), 기여

해설 행사 장소를 어떻게 결정했는지 묻는 How 의문문
(A) 연상 단어 오답. 질문의 fund-raising에서 연상 가능한 contribution을 이용한 오답.
(B) 정답. 행사 장소를 어떻게 결정했는지 묻는 질문에 친구에게 추천을 받았다고 알려 주고 있으므로 정답.
(C) 질문과 상관없는 오답. Why 의문문에 대한 응답이므로 오답.

16 M-Cn / M-Au

Could you help Ms. Ishida update the expense reports?

(A) It's an electric vehicle.
(B) This restaurant is expensive.
(C) I'll have time after my meeting.

이시다 씨가 지출 보고서를 업데이트하는 것을 도와주시겠어요?
(A) 그건 전기 자동차예요.
(B) 이 레스토랑은 비싸요.
(C) 회의 후에 시간이 있을 거예요.

어휘 expense 지출 (비용), 경비

해설 부탁/요청의 의문문
(A) 질문과 상관없는 오답.
(B) 유사 발음 오답. 질문의 expense와 부분적으로 발음이 유사한 expensive를 이용한 오답.
(C) 정답. 이시다 씨가 지출 보고서를 업데이트하는 것을 도와줄 수 있는지 묻는 질문에 회의 후에 시간이 있다는 말로 도와줄 수 있는 시점을 알려 주고 있으므로 정답.

17 W-Br / W-Am

The sales representatives really appreciated the training we led.

(A) The new transportation center nearby.
(B) No, but there is a manual online.
(C) Yes, they seemed to find it helpful.

영업 직원들이 우리가 진행한 교육에 대해 정말로 감사해했어요.
(A) 근처에 있는 새 교통 센터요.
(B) 아니요, 하지만 온라인에 설명서가 있습니다.
(C) 네, 그분들이 도움이 된다고 생각한 것 같았어요.

어휘 sales 영업, 판매(량) representative 직원, 대표자 lead 진행하다, 이끌다 nearby 근처에 manual (사용) 설명서 seem to ~하는 것 같다, ~하는 것처럼 보이다

해설 정보 전달의 평서문
(A) 평서문과 상관없는 오답.
(B) 연상 단어 오답. 평서문의 training에서 연상 가능한 manual을 이용한 오답.

(C) 정답. 영업 직원들이 교육에 대해 정말로 감사해했다는 평서문에 네(Yes)라고 대답한 뒤, 도움이 된다고 생각한 것 같았다며 긍정 답변과 일관된 내용을 덧붙이고 있으므로 정답.

18 M-Au / W-Am

Do you know who was promoted to senior director?
(A) It hasn't been announced yet.
(B) I received my promotional gift yesterday.
(C) I've seen that film.

누가 선임 이사로 승진되었는지 아세요?
(A) 아직 발표되지 않았어요.
(B) 어제 홍보용 선물을 받았어요.
(C) 그 영화 봤어요.

어휘 promote 승진시키다, 홍보하다   promotional 홍보의, 판촉의

해설 선임 이사로 승진된 사람을 아는지 묻는 간접 의문문
(A) 정답. 선임 이사로 승진된 사람을 아는지 묻는 질문에 아직 발표되지 않았다며 자신도 모름을 우회적으로 나타내고 있으므로 정답.
(B) 유사 발음 오답. 질문의 promoted와 부분적으로 발음이 유사한 promotional을 이용한 오답.
(C) 연상 단어 오답. 질문의 director를 감독으로 이해했을 경우 연상 가능한 film을 이용한 오답.

19 W-Br / M-Au

Isn't the registration deadline tomorrow?
(A) Here's a map that you can use.
(B) No, it's next week.
(C) My office is on the ninth floor.

등록 마감일은 내일 아닌가요?
(A) 여기 이용하실 수 있는 안내도입니다.
(B) 아니요, 다음 주예요.
(C) 제 사무실은 9층에 있어요.

어휘 registration 등록   deadline 마감 기한

해설 등록 마감일이 내일인지 확인하는 부정 의문문
(A) 질문과 상관없는 오답.
(B) 정답. 등록 마감일이 내일인지 확인하는 질문에 아니요(No)라고 대답한 뒤, 다음 주라며 부정 답변과 일관된 내용을 덧붙이고 있으므로 정답.
(C) 질문과 상관없는 오답. Where 의문문에 대한 응답이므로 오답.

20 M-Cn / W-Br

Would you like some help installing that new software?
(A) No, I'm sure we sent it out yesterday.
(B) Thanks, but I know how to do it.
(C) He can type very fast.

새 소프트웨어를 설치하는 데 도움이 필요하신가요?
(A) 아니요, 우리가 어제 발송한 게 확실해요.
(B) 감사하지만, 어떻게 하는지 알아요.
(C) 그는 아주 빨리 타자를 칠 수 있어요.

어휘 install 설치하다   type 타자를 치다

해설 제안/권유의 의문문
(A) 질문과 상관없는 오답.
(B) 정답. 새 소프트웨어를 설치하는 데 도움이 필요한지 묻는 질문에 어떻게 하는지 안다며 거절 의사를 우회적으로 표현하고 있으므로 정답.
(C) 질문과 상관없는 오답. 질문에 3인칭 대명사 He로 지칭할 인물이 언급된 적이 없으므로 오답.

21 W-Am / M-Cn   ▶동영상 강의

Our factory makes the best cookies in the city.
(A) A cup of sugar.
(B) He worked an afternoon shift.
(C) Aren't they delicious?

우리 공장이 이 도시에서 가장 맛있는 쿠키를 만듭니다.
(A) 설탕 한 컵이요.
(B) 그는 오후 교대 근무를 했어요.
(C) 정말 맛있지 않아요?

어휘 shift 교대 근무(조)

해설 정보 전달의 평서문
(A) 연상 단어 오답. 평서문의 cookies에서 연상 가능한 sugar를 이용한 오답.
(B) 평서문과 상관없는 오답. 평서문에 3인칭 대명사 He로 지칭할 인물이 언급된 적이 없으므로 오답.
(C) 정답. 공장이 이 도시에서 가장 맛있는 쿠키를 만든다는 평서문에 정말 맛있지 않냐고 되물으며 우회적으로 동의하고 있으므로 정답.

22 M-Cn / M-Au

The fruit market is still selling mangoes, isn't it?
(A) No thanks—I don't need anything.
(B) There's a waiting area in the lobby.
(C) Yes, I bought some there yesterday.

과일 시장에서 아직 망고를 팔고 있죠, 그렇지 않나요?
(A) 괜찮습니다. 아무것도 필요하지 않아요.
(B) 로비에 대기 구역이 있어요.
(C) 네, 어제 거기서 몇 개 샀어요.

해설 과일 시장에서 아직 망고를 파는지 여부를 확인하는 부가 의문문
(A) 질문과 상관없는 오답. 제안 의문문에 대한 응답이므로 오답.
(B) 질문과 상관없는 오답.
(C) 정답. 과일 시장에서 아직 망고를 파는지 여부를 확인하는 질문에 네(Yes)라고 대답한 뒤, 어제 거기서 샀다며 긍정 답변과 일관된 내용을 덧붙이고 있으므로 정답.

23 W-Br / M-Cn

Why are you staying in the office for lunch?
(A) No, they weren't.
(B) Just a salad and soup, please.
(C) Because it is raining.

점심시간에 왜 사무실에 남아 있나요?
(A) 아니요, 그렇지 않았어요.
(B) 샐러드와 수프만 주세요.
(C) 비가 내리고 있어서요.

해설 점심시간에 사무실에 남아 있는 이유를 묻는 Why 의문문
(A) Yes/No 불가 오답. Why 의문문에는 Yes/No 응답이 불가능하므로 오답.
(B) 연상 단어 오답. 질문의 lunch에서 연상 가능한 salad and soup를 이용한 오답.
(C) 정답. 점심시간에 사무실에 남아 있는 이유를 묻는 질문에 비가 내리고 있어서라고 구체적인 이유를 제시하고 있으므로 정답.

24 W-Am / W-Br

How did the company basketball team play last night?
(A) Sure, I'll have a few.
(B) How can I sign up?
(C) The game was canceled.

어젯밤 회사 농구팀의 경기는 어땠나요?
(A) 물론이죠, 몇 개 먹을게요.
(B) 어떻게 신청할 수 있죠?
(C) 그 경기는 취소되었어요.

어휘 sign up 신청하다, 등록하다 cancel 취소하다

해설 회사 농구팀의 경기가 어땠는지 묻는 How 의문문
(A) Yes/No 불가 오답. How 의문문에는 Yes/No 응답이 불가능한데, Sure도 일종의 Yes 응답이라고 볼 수 있으므로 오답.
(B) 단어 반복 오답. 질문의 How를 반복 이용한 오답.
(C) 정답. 회사 농구팀의 경기가 어땠는지 묻는 질문에 취소되었다며 경기가 진행되지 않았음을 알려 주고 있으므로 정답.

25 M-Au / M-Cn

Isn't our department's quarterly report supposed to be sent out today?
(A) No, he drinks coffee.
(B) There's a lot of information to include.
(C) Some office supplies.

우리 부서의 분기 보고서가 오늘 발송되어야 하지 않나요?
(A) 아니요, 그는 커피를 마셔요.
(B) 포함해야 할 정보가 많아요.
(C) 사무용품이요.

어휘 be supposed to ~하기로 되어 있다 quarterly 분기의 include 포함하다 supplies 용품, 물품

해설 분기 보고서가 오늘 발송되어야 하는지 확인하는 부정 의문문
(A) 질문과 상관없는 오답. 질문에 3인칭 대명사 he로 지칭할 인물이 언급된 적이 없으므로 오답.
(B) 정답. 분기 보고서가 오늘 발송되어야 하는지 확인하는 질문에 포함해야 할 정보가 많다며 아직 보낼 수 없음을 우회적으로 나타내고 있으므로 정답.
(C) 연상 단어 오답. 질문의 department에서 연상 가능한 office를 이용한 오답.

26 M-Cn / W-Am

Would you like a copy of the article I mentioned?
(A) No, I'm not.
(B) Yes, I'd appreciate that.
(C) A Thursday morning appointment.

제가 언급했던 기사의 사본을 드릴까요?
(A) 아니요, 저는 그렇지 않아요.
(B) 네, 그렇게 해 주시면 감사하겠습니다.
(C) 목요일 오전 예약이요.

어휘 mention 언급하다 appointment 예약, 약속

해설 제안/권유의 의문문
(A) 질문과 상관없는 오답.
(B) 정답. 기사의 사본을 원하는지 묻는 질문에 네(Yes)라고 대답한 뒤, 그렇게 해 주면 감사하겠다며 긍정 답변과 일관된 내용을 덧붙이고 있으므로 정답.
(C) 질문과 상관없는 오답.

27 M-Au / W-Am   ▶ 동영상 강의

Did you decide on the design for the new logo?
(A) There are so many good options.
(B) Please adjust that sign by the door.
(C) Maybe he'll arrive today.

새 로고 디자인은 결정했나요?
(A) 좋은 선택지가 너무 많아요.
(B) 문 옆에 있는 간판을 조정해 주세요.
(C) 그는 아마 오늘 도착할 거예요.

어휘 adjust 조정하다, 조절하다

해설 새 로고 디자인을 결정했는지 묻는 조동사(Did) 의문문
(A) 정답. 새 로고 디자인을 결정했는지 묻는 질문에 좋은 선택지가 너무 많다며 아직 결정하지 못했음을 우회적으로 나타내고 있으므로 정답.
(B) 유사 발음 오답. 질문의 design과 부분적으로 발음이 유사한 sign을 이용한 오답.
(C) 질문과 상관없는 오답. 질문에 3인칭 대명사 he로 지칭할 인물이 언급된 적이 없으므로 오답.

28 M-Cn / M-Au

Our bookstore is having a sale today, isn't it?

(A) Sure, you can use my printer.
(B) I really enjoyed that book.
(C) It's only a small discount.

우리 서점이 오늘 세일을 하죠, 그렇지 않나요?
(A) 물론이죠, 제 프린터를 이용하셔도 돼요.
(B) 그 책을 정말 재미있게 읽었어요.
(C) 약간 할인할 뿐이에요.

해설 서점이 세일하는지 여부를 묻는 부가 의문문
(A) 질문과 상관없는 오답.
(B) 연상 단어 오답. 질문의 bookstore에서 연상 가능한 book을 이용한 오답.
(C) 정답. 서점이 세일하는지 여부를 묻는 질문에 약간 할인할 뿐이라며 세일을 한다는 것을 우회적으로 알려 주고 있으므로 정답.

29 W-Br / M-Cn

Why haven't the painters arrived yet?

(A) The keys are in the desk drawer.
(B) No, that's all right.
(C) I heard that traffic is heavy this morning.

페인트 작업자들이 왜 아직 도착하지 않았나요?
(A) 열쇠는 책상 서랍 안에 있어요.
(B) 아니요, 괜찮습니다.
(C) 오늘 아침에 교통 체증이 극심하다고 들었어요.

어휘 drawer 서랍   traffic 교통(량), 차량들
해설 페인트 작업자들이 도착하지 않은 이유를 묻는 Why 의문문
(A) 질문과 상관없는 오답.
(B) Yes/No 불가 오답. Why 의문문에는 Yes/No 응답이 불가능하므로 오답.
(C) 정답. 페인트 작업자들이 도착하지 않은 이유를 묻는 질문에 교통 체증이 극심하다고 들었다고 이유를 제시하고 있으므로 정답.

30 M-Cn / M-Au   ▶ 동영상 강의

Should I bring some flowers or some food to the party?

(A) He's right down the hall.
(B) Don't you live next to a florist's shop?
(C) A few more hours.

파티에 꽃을 좀 가져가야 할까요, 아니면 음식을 좀 가져가야 할까요?
(A) 그는 복도 바로 저쪽에 있습니다.
(B) 꽃집 옆에 살지 않나요?
(C) 몇 시간 더요.

해설 파티에 가져갈 물품과 관련해 묻는 선택 의문문
(A) 질문과 상관없는 오답. 질문에 3인칭 대명사 He로 지칭할 인물이 언급된 적이 없으므로 오답.
(B) 정답. 파티에 꽃을 가져가야 할지, 아니면 음식을 가져가야 할지 묻는 질문에 꽃집 옆에 살지 않냐며 꽃을 가져가라는 뜻을 우회적으로 나타내고 있으므로 정답.
(C) 질문과 상관없는 오답. How long 또는 When 의문문에 대한 응답이므로 오답.

31 W-Am / W-Br

The meeting can wait until tomorrow.

(A) I'll make sure the room is set up.
(B) Did you bring an umbrella?
(C) No, he wasn't.

회의는 내일로 미뤄도 돼요.
(A) 제가 회의실을 준비해 둘게요.
(B) 우산 가져오셨나요?
(C) 아니요, 그는 그렇지 않았어요.

어휘 make sure 반드시 ~하도록 하다   set up 준비하다, 설정하다
해설 제안/권유의 평서문
(A) 정답. 회의를 내일로 미뤄도 된다는 평서문에 회의실을 준비해 두겠다며 제안을 우회적으로 수용하고 있으므로 정답.
(B) 평서문과 상관없는 오답.
(C) 평서문과 상관없는 오답. 평서문에 3인칭 대명사 he로 지칭할 인물이 언급된 적이 없으므로 오답.

PART 3

32-34 W-Am / M-Cn

W Hello, Tariq. **32 Could you do me a favor?**

M Sure—what is it?

W I'm meeting with the Gerhard Group at ten A.M. for the product pitch, and **32 I need copies of your market analysis report made for each representative.**

M Aren't you at the office right now?

W Actually, I came in early today, but **33 I couldn't get the copy machine to work.**

M Seriously? **33 We bought it last month!**

W I'm afraid so.

M **34 I just got off the train**. I'll stop at Business Express on McAllister Street and take care of it on my way to the office.

여 안녕하세요, 타리크. **제 부탁 하나만 들어주시겠어요?**
남 물론이죠, 뭔가요?
여 제가 오전 10시에 제품 홍보용 발표 때문에 게르하르드 그룹을 만나는데, **각 직원을 위해 당신의 시장 분석 보고서 복사본이 필요해요.**
남 지금 사무실에 계시지 않나요?
여 실은, 오늘 일찍 출근했는데, **복사기를 작동시킬 수 없었어요.**
남 정말요? **지난달에 구입했잖아요!**
여 안타깝게도 그래요.
남 **제가 방금 기차에서 내렸어요.** 사무실로 가는 길에 맥앨리스터 가에 있는 비즈니스 익스프레스에 들러서 처리할게요.

> 어휘 pitch (영업을 위한) 홍보용 발표, 구매 권유 analysis 분석
> work (기계 등이) 작동하다 take care of ~을 처리하다

32 What does the woman ask the man to do for her?
(A) Greet a client in the lobby
(B) Present a product pitch
(C) Organize some binders
(D) Make some photocopies

여자는 남자에게 무엇을 해 달라고 요청하는가?
(A) 로비에서 고객을 맞이하기
(B) 제품 홍보용 발표하기
(C) 바인더 정리하기
(D) 복사하기

어휘 greet 맞이하다 organize 정리하다, 조직하다

해설 세부 사항 관련 – 여자의 요청 사항
여자가 첫 대사에서 부탁을 들어줄 수 있는지(Could you do me a favor) 물은 후, 두 번째 대사에서 각 직원을 위해 당신의 시장 분석 보고서 복사본이 필요하다(~ I need copies of your market analysis report made for each representative)고 했으므로 정답은 (D)이다.

Paraphrasing
대화의 need copies of your market analysis report
→ 정답의 Make some photocopies

33 What does the man say about some equipment?
(A) It is operating smoothly.
(B) It was purchased recently.
(C) It needs to be plugged in.
(D) It has not yet been updated.

남자는 장비에 대해 무엇이라고 말하는가?
(A) 순조롭게 작동되고 있다.
(B) 최근에 구입했다.
(C) 플러그가 꽂혀야 한다.
(D) 아직 업데이트되지 않았다.

어휘 operate 작동되다, 가동되다 smoothly 순조롭게 recently 최근에 plug in 플러그를 꽂다

해설 세부 사항 관련 – 남자가 장비에 대해 하는 말
여자가 세 번째 대사에서 복사기를 작동시킬 수 없었다(I couldn't get the copy machine to work)고 하자, 남자가 지난달에 구입했다(We bought it last month!)며 놀라움을 나타내고 있으므로 정답은 (B)이다.

Paraphrasing
대화의 bought it last month
→ 정답의 It was purchased recently

34 Where is the man?
(A) At the office
(B) At a train station
(C) At a store
(D) At a client's headquarters

남자는 어디에 있는가?
(A) 사무실
(B) 기차역
(C) 상점
(D) 고객사의 본사

어휘 headquarters 본사

해설 세부 사항 관련 – 남자가 있는 곳
남자가 마지막 대사에서 방금 기차에서 내렸다(I just got off the train)고 했으므로 정답은 (B)이다.

35-37 W-Br / M-Cn

W Delton Van Lines. How can I help you?

M Hello. I'm the office manager at Woodsom Insurance Company. ³⁵**We are relocating to a new office in June and would like to book your services.**

W Certainly! But before we reserve a date for the move, ³⁶**we'll need to come to your current location and estimate the cost of moving your furniture and equipment.**

M We have a staff meeting tomorrow morning, so no one's available to show you around then. But tomorrow afternoon works.

W Perfect! ³⁶**Our representative can be there at two.** ³⁷**I'll just need to know where you're located.**

여 델튼 밴 라인즈입니다. 무엇을 도와드릴까요?

남 안녕하세요. 우드섬 보험회사의 사무실 관리자입니다. **6월에 새 사무실로 이전하는데, 귀사의 서비스를 예약하고 싶습니다.**

여 알겠습니다! 하지만 이사 날짜를 예약하기 전에, **현재 위치로 가서 가구와 장비를 옮기는 데 드는 비용을 견적해야 할 겁니다.**

남 내일 오전에 직원회의가 있어서, 그때는 안내해 드릴 수 있는 사람이 없습니다. 하지만 내일 오후는 괜찮습니다.

여 아주 좋습니다! **저희 직원이 2시에 갈 수 있습니다. 위치만 알면 됩니다.**

어휘 relocate 이전하다, 이사하다 book 예약하다 certainly (대답으로) 물론입니다, 알았습니다 current 현재의 estimate 견적하다, 추산하다 available 시간이 나는, 이용 가능한 work (일정 등이) 괜찮다, 좋다 be located 위치해 있다

35 Where does the woman most likely work?
(A) At a furniture store
(B) At a moving company
(C) At a post office
(D) At an office supply store

해설 여자는 어디에서 일하는 것 같은가?
(A) 가구 매장
(B) 이사 회사
(C) 우체국
(D) 사무용품 매장

해설 전체 내용 관련 – 여자의 근무 장소
남자가 첫 대사에서 여자에게 6월에 새 사무실로 이전하는데 귀사의 서비스를 예약하고 싶다(We are relocating to a new office in June and would like to book your services)고 했으므로 정답은 (B)이다.

36 Why will a representative visit the man's company tomorrow?
(A) To provide an estimate
(B) To sign a contract
(C) To give a presentation
(D) To place an order

왜 직원이 내일 남자의 회사를 방문할 것인가?
(A) 견적을 제공하기 위해
(B) 계약서에 서명하기 위해
(C) 발표하기 위해
(D) 주문하기 위해

어휘 estimate 견적(서) contract 계약(서)
place an order 주문하다

해설 세부 사항 관련 – 직원이 남자의 회사를 방문하는 목적
여자가 두 번째 대사에서 현재 위치로 가서 가구와 장비를 옮기는 데 드는 비용을 견적해야 할 것(we'll need to come to your current location and estimate the cost of moving your furniture and equipment)이라고 했고, 마지막 대사에서 직원이 2시에 갈 수 있다(Our representative can be there at two)고 했다. 따라서 비용 견적을 위해 방문할 것임을 알 수 있으므로 정답은 (A)이다.

Paraphrasing
대화의 estimate the cost → 정답의 provide an estimate

37 What information will the man most likely provide next?
(A) A company's operating hours
(B) An account number
(C) A street address
(D) A telephone number

남자는 다음에 어떤 정보를 제공할 것 같은가?
(A) 회사의 운영 시간
(B) 계좌 번호
(C) 거리 주소
(D) 전화번호

해설 세부 사항 관련 – 남자가 제공할 정보
여자가 마지막 대사에서 위치만 알면 된다(I'll just need to know where you're located)고 했으므로 정답은 (C)이다.

Paraphrasing
대화의 where you're located → 정답의 A street address

38-40 M-Au / W-Br

M Doctor MacMillan, ³⁸**I'm calling from the human resources department.** I'm in charge of your onboarding, and I wanted to confirm your start date. It's the first of April, right?

W Right. That's when ³⁹**I'll be joining the scientific research team.** And as you probably know, I'm still finishing up a research paper with my current institution.

M Yes, the director did tell me that. ⁴⁰**Your contract includes time for you to finish up your previous commitments. I can send it to you this afternoon.**

남 맥밀란 박사님, **인사부에서 전화를 드립니다.** 제가 박사님의 신규 입사자 교육을 담당하고 있는데, 시작 날짜를 확인하고 싶어요. 4월 1일이 맞죠?

여 그렇습니다. 그때 **제가 과학 연구팀에 합류할 예정입니다.** 그리고 아마 아시겠지만, 제가 아직 현재 기관의 연구 논문을 마무리하고 있습니다.

남 네, 소장님께서 말씀하셨습니다. **계약서에 이전 업무들을 마무리하기 위한 시간이 포함되어 있습니다. 그것을 오늘 오후에 보내 드릴게요.**

어휘 in charge of ~을 담당하고 있는, ~을 책임지고 있는
onboarding (적응을 위한) 신규 입사자 교육, 정착 교육
confirm 확인하다 join 합류하다 finish up 마무리하다
research paper 연구 논문 institution 기관, 협회
previous 이전의, 과거의 commitment 책무, 헌신

38 What department does the man work in?
(A) Legal
(B) Accounting
(C) Human resources
(D) Public relations

남자는 어느 부서에서 일하고 있는가?
(A) 법무
(B) 회계
(C) 인사
(D) 홍보

해설 전체 내용 관련 – 남자의 근무 부서
남자가 첫 대사에서 인사부에서 전화한다(I'm calling from the human resources department)고 했으므로 정답은 (C)이다.

39 What kind of work has the woman been hired to do?
(A) Scientific research
(B) Book editing
(C) Office management
(D) Legal advising

여자는 무슨 일을 하도록 고용되었는가?
(A) 과학 연구
(B) 도서 편집
(C) 사무실 관리
(D) 법무 조언

어휘 hire 고용하다

해설 세부 사항 관련 – 여자의 업무
여자가 첫 대사에서 과학 연구팀에 합류할 예정(~ I'll be joining the scientific research team)이라고 했으므로 정답은 (A)이다.

40 What will the man send the woman this afternoon?
(A) A password
(B) A travel reimbursement
(C) A security badge
(D) A contract

남자는 오늘 오후에 여자에게 무엇을 보낼 것인가?
(A) 비밀번호
(B) 출장 비용 환급액
(C) 보안 출입증
(D) 계약서

어휘 reimbursement 환급(액)

해설 세부 사항 관련 – 남자가 오늘 오후에 보낼 것
남자가 마지막 대사에서 여자의 계약서에 대해 이야기하면서 오늘 오후에 보내겠다(Your contract ~ I can send it to you this afternoon)고 했으므로 정답은 (D)이다.

41-43 3인 대화 W-Br / M-Cn / W-Am

W1 **41 We've been getting a lot of online orders for our chocolate candies lately.** I'm glad to see the increase in orders, but I'm worried about meeting the demands. Are we going to be able to fill and ship all these orders?

M **42 I think we should hire a few more people to work in the mornings. They could help with packaging and shipping.** What do you think, Rebecca?

W2 I agree. **43 I also think that we should ask if our delivery service can pick up our packages twice a day instead of just once a day**—maybe every morning and afternoon. I'll call them today.

여1 최근 초콜릿 캔디의 온라인 주문을 많이 받고 있습니다. 주문이 증가해서 기쁘지만 수요를 충족할 수 있을지 걱정입니다. 이 주문을 모두 처리하고 배송할 수 있을까요?

남 오전에 근무할 사람을 몇 명 더 고용해야 할 것 같아요. 포장과 배송을 도와줄 수 있을 거예요. 어떻게 생각하세요, 레베카?

여2 동의합니다. 그리고 배송 서비스 업체가 하루에 단 한 번이 아니라 하루에 두 번씩, 아마 매일 아침과 오후에 배송품을 가져갈 수 있을지도 물어보는 게 좋겠어요. 제가 오늘 전화할게요.

어휘 increase 증가, 인상 meet (요구, 조건 등을) 충족하다 demand 수요, 요구 fill 충족하다, 채우다 ship 발송하다 package 포장하다, 꾸리다; 소포, 포장물 agree 동의하다 instead of ~ 대신

41 What recently happened at the business?
(A) Its monthly rent increased.
(B) It received many orders.
(C) It was featured in a magazine.
(D) It passed an inspection.

최근 업체에 무슨 일이 있었는가?
(A) 월 임대료가 인상되었다.
(B) 주문을 많이 받았다.
(C) 잡지에 특집으로 실렸다.
(D) 점검을 통과했다.

어휘 rent 임대료 feature 특집으로 싣다, 특징으로 하다 pass 통과하다, 합격하다 inspection 점검, 검사

해설 세부 사항 관련 – 최근 업체에 있었던 일
첫 번째 여자가 첫 대사에서 소속 회사가 최근 초콜릿 캔디의 온라인 주문을 많이 받고 있다(We've been getting a lot of online orders for our chocolate candies lately)고 했으므로 정답은 (B)이다.

Paraphrasing
대화의 lately → 질문의 recently
대화의 getting a lot of online orders
→ 정답의 received many orders

42 According to the man, what will help the business?
(A) Purchasing updated equipment
(B) Offering different products
(C) Extending store hours
(D) Hiring more employees

남자에 따르면, 무엇이 업체에 도움이 될 것인가?
(A) 업데이트된 장비 구입하기
(B) 다른 제품 제공하기
(C) 매장 영업시간 연장하기
(D) 추가 직원 고용하기

어휘 extend 연장하다, 확장하다

해설 세부 사항 관련 - 업체에 도움이 될 것

남자가 첫 대사에서 오전에 근무할 사람을 몇 명 더 고용해야 할 것 같다며, 포장과 배송을 도와줄 수 있을 것(I think we should hire a few more people to work in the mornings. They could help with packaging and shipping)이라고 했으므로 정답은 (D)이다.

Paraphrasing
대화의 hire a few more people
→ 정답의 Hiring more employees

43 Who does Rebecca say she will call today?
(A) A packaging designer
(B) An Internet service provider
(C) A delivery service
(D) A bank

레베카는 오늘 누구에게 전화할 것이라고 말하는가?
(A) 포장 디자이너
(B) 인터넷 서비스 제공업체
(C) 배송 서비스 업체
(D) 은행

해설 세부 사항 관련 - 레베카가 오늘 전화할 곳

두 번째 여자(레베카)가 첫 대사에서 배송 서비스 업체가 하루에 두 번씩 배송품을 가져갈 수 있을지 물어보는 게 좋겠다며, 오늘 전화하겠다(I also think that we should ask if our delivery service can pick up our packages twice a day ~ I'll call them today)고 했으므로 정답은 (C)이다.

44-46 W-Am / M-Cn

W I spoke to the Mancini brothers. They just shipped our leather order—the hazelnut color. But it'll take a while to arrive. We don't have enough in stock to complete **44the ten sofa orders that we've received the past few days.**

M **45What about the local leather supplier that brought us some samples last week? We could ask them whether they have enough for ten sofas.**

W To be honest, **46I wasn't very impressed with the quality of their leather. I'd rather wait.** I'll reach out to the customers about the delay.

여 맨시니 브라더스와 이야기했습니다. 헤이즐넛 색상 가죽 주문을 막 발송했대요. 그런데 도착하려면 시간이 좀 걸릴 거예요. **지난 며칠 동안 받은 10개의 소파 주문을 완료할 수 있을 만큼 재고가 충분하지 않아요.**

남 **지난주에 샘플을 가져온 지역 가죽 공급업체는 어떤가요? 소파 10개를 만들 만큼 충분한 양이 있는지 물어볼 수 있을 거예요.**

여 솔직히, **그곳 가죽의 품질이 그렇게 인상적이지 않았어요. 차라리 기다리는 게 좋겠어요.** 지연에 대해 고객들께 연락을 드릴게요.

어휘 leather 가죽 take a while 시간이 좀 걸리다
have ~ in stock ~을 재고로 보유하다 complete 완료하다
local 지역의, 현지의 supplier 공급업체 to be honest 솔직히
be impressed with ~에 깊은 인상을 받다
reach out to ~에게 연락하다 delay 지연, 지체

44 What do the speakers manufacture?
(A) Shoes
(B) Luggage
(C) Furniture
(D) Sports equipment

화자들은 무엇을 제조하는가?
(A) 신발
(B) 여행 가방
(C) 가구
(D) 스포츠 장비

해설 전체 내용 관련 - 화자들이 제조하는 것

여자가 첫 대사에서 지난 며칠 동안 10개의 소파 주문을 받은(~ the ten sofa orders that we've received the past few days) 것을 언급했으므로 정답은 (C)이다.

Paraphrasing
대화의 sofa → 정답의 Furniture

45 Who does the man suggest contacting?
(A) A leather supplier
(B) A delivery driver
(C) An interior designer
(D) A machine technician

남자는 누구에게 연락하기를 권하는가?
(A) 가죽 공급업체
(B) 배송 기사
(C) 인테리어 디자이너
(D) 기계 기술자

해설 세부 사항 관련 – 남자가 연락을 권하는 곳
남자가 첫 대사에서 지역 가죽 공급업체를 언급하며, 소파 10개를 만들 만큼 충분한 양이 있는지 물어볼 수 있을 것(What about the local leather supplier ~ We could ask them whether they have enough for ten sofas)이라고 했으므로 정답은 (A)이다.

---

46 Why is the woman opposed to making a change?
(A) She has contracts with clients.
(B) She is concerned about quality.
(C) Overhead expenses will increase.
(D) A license will expire soon.

여자는 왜 변화를 주는 것에 반대하는가?
(A) 고객들과 계약이 되어 있다.
(B) 품질을 우려하고 있다.
(C) 일반 경비가 늘어날 것이다.
(D) 허가증이 곧 만료될 것이다.

어휘 be opposed to ~하는 것에 반대하다
be concerned about ~을 우려하다
overhead expenses 일반 경비   expire 만료되다

해설 세부 사항 관련 – 여자가 변화에 반대하는 이유
여자가 마지막 대사에서 남자가 언급한 공급업체의 가죽 품질이 그렇게 인상적이지 않았다며, 차라리 기다리는 게 좋겠다(I wasn't very impressed with the quality of their leather. I'd rather wait)고 했으므로 정답은 (B)이다.

Paraphrasing
대화의 wasn't very impressed with the quality
→ 정답의 is concerned about quality

47-49 W-Am / M-Au ▶ 동영상 강의

W Thanks for coming in, Marcos. **47 I just got the results from the consulting firm we hired. They have some ideas about how we can increase sales of our denim blue jeans.**

M I hope so. What does our target audience want?

W Well, **48 they think it's time we updated our brand with new styles or colors.**

M You know, **it takes a lot of effort to develop and launch new styles.**

W Yes. But, if we don't do it, another company will.

M You're right. **49 I'll ask Junko to come up with some new designs for us to consider.**

여 와 주셔서 감사합니다, 마르코스. 우리가 고용한 컨설팅 업체로부터 막 결과를 받았어요. 데님 청바지의 판매를 늘릴 수 있는 방법에 대한 몇 가지 아이디어가 있더군요.
남 그렇기를 바랍니다. 우리 목표 고객들은 무엇을 원하나요?
여 음, 그들은 우리가 새로운 스타일이나 색상으로 브랜드를 업데이트할 시기라고 생각해요.
남 알잖아요. 새로운 스타일을 개발하고 출시하려면 많은 노력이 필요해요.
여 네. 하지만 우리가 그렇게 하지 않으면, 다른 회사가 할 겁니다.
남 맞는 말씀입니다. 준코에게 우리가 고려할 수 있게 새로운 디자인 몇 개를 제안해 달라고 요청할게요.

어휘 result 결과(물)   target audience 목표 고객, 주 대상
effort 노력   develop 개발하다   launch 출시하다, 시작하다
come up with ~을 제시하다   consider 고려하다

---

47 What are the speakers meeting to discuss?
(A) Safety regulations
(B) Equipment upgrades
(C) Budget cuts
(D) Consultant recommendations

화자들은 무엇을 논의하기 위해 만나고 있는가?
(A) 안전 규정
(B) 장비 업그레이드
(C) 예산 절감
(D) 컨설턴트 권고 사항

어휘 regulation 규정, 규제   cut 절감, 감소

해설 전체 내용 관련 – 논의 주제
여자가 첫 대사에서 컨설팅 업체로부터 결과를 받았다며, 데님 청바지의 판매를 늘릴 수 있는 방법에 대한 몇 가지 아이디어가 있다(I just got the results from the consulting firm we hired. They have some ideas ~)고 했고, 관련된 이야기를 이어 가고 있으므로 정답은 (D)이다.

---

48 What does the man mean when he says, "it takes a lot of effort to develop and launch new styles"?
(A) He is excited about a challenge.
(B) He is surprised at a competitor's choices.
(C) He is doubtful about a suggestion.
(D) He thinks more employees should be hired.

남자가 "새로운 스타일을 개발하고 출시하려면 많은 노력이 필요해요"라고 말할 때 무엇을 의미하는가?
(A) 도전에 대해 들떠 있다.
(B) 경쟁사의 선택에 대해 놀라고 있다.
(C) 제안에 대해 의구심을 갖고 있다.
(D) 더 많은 직원이 고용되어야 한다고 생각한다.

어휘 challenge 도전 (과제), 어려운 일 competitor 경쟁사, 경쟁자 doubtful 의구심을 갖고 있는, 확신이 없는 suggestion 제안, 의견

해설 화자의 의도 파악 – 새로운 스타일의 개발 및 출시에 많은 노력이 필요하다는 말의 의도
여자가 두 번째 대사에서 그들은 우리가 새로운 스타일이나 색상으로 브랜드를 업데이트할 시기라고 생각한다(they think it's time we updated our brand with new styles or colors)고 말한 것에 대해 남자가 인용문을 언급하고 있다. 이는 브랜드 업데이트가 어려운 일이라는 뜻으로, 브랜드 업데이트 제안을 부정적인 시각으로 바라보는 것이므로 정답은 (C)이다.

49 Who most likely is Junko?
(A) A focus group leader
(B) A clothing designer
(C) A sales associate
(D) An accountant

준코는 누구인 것 같은가?
(A) 포커스 그룹 대표자
(B) 의류 디자이너
(C) 영업 사원
(D) 회계사

어휘 focus group 포커스 그룹 associate 직원, 동료

해설 세부 사항 관련 – 준코의 직업
남자가 마지막 대사에서 준코에게 새로운 디자인 몇 개를 제안해 달라고 요청하겠다(I'll ask Junko to come up with some new designs for us to consider)고 했으므로 정답은 (B)이다.

50-52 M-Cn / W-Am

M Hi, Gabriela. Thanks for agreeing to give me the highlights of the budget discussion from the monthly meeting. ⁵⁰**I'm back from vacation and still catching up.**

W Sure. Here's a copy of the report. Everyone on our organization's board at Tennis United agreed to the fee increase for ⁵¹**the tennis camp for young players.**

M Good. And why do we have T-shirts listed as an expense item?

W Although the next tournament's in the fall, ⁵²**the T-shirts were ordered very early. That way we received half off the price**, since the supplier wanted to get rid of his summer inventory.

남 안녕하세요, 가브리엘라. 월간 회의의 예산 논의 관련 중점 사항들을 알려 주시는 데 동의해 주셔서 감사합니다. **휴가에서 복귀해서 아직 업무를 따라잡고 있어요.**

여 별말씀을요. 여기 보고서 사본입니다. 테니스 유나이티드의 이사회 구성원 모두가 **젊은 선수들을 위한 테니스 캠프**의 요금 인상에 동의했습니다.

남 좋습니다. 그리고 왜 지출 항목에 티셔츠가 있나요?

여 다음 토너먼트가 가을에 있긴 하지만, **티셔츠를 아주 일찍 주문했습니다. 그렇게 해서 가격의 절반을 할인받았어요.** 공급업자가 여름 재고를 소진하고 싶어 했거든요.

어휘 agree 동의하다 highlight 중점 사항, 강조 사항; 강조하다 catch up (진행, 속도 등) 따라잡다 organization 단체, 조직 board 이사회 list 기재하다, 목록에 올리다 that way 그렇게 해서 get rid of ~을 없애다 inventory 재고(품), 재고 목록

50 Why did the man miss a meeting?
(A) He was stuck in traffic.
(B) He had a medical appointment.
(C) He was speaking with a client.
(D) He was away on vacation.

남자는 왜 회의를 놓쳤는가?
(A) 교통 체증에 갇혀 있었다.
(B) 진료 예약이 있었다.
(C) 고객과 이야기하고 있었다.
(D) 휴가로 자리를 비웠다.

어휘 miss (회의, 수업 등) 놓치다, 결석하다 be stuck in ~에 갇혀 있다

해설 세부 사항 관련 – 남자가 회의에 놓친 이유
남자가 첫 대사에서 월간 회의와 관련해 이야기하면서 휴가에서 복귀해서 아직 업무를 따라잡고 있다(I'm back from vacation and still catching up)고 했으므로 정답은 (D)이다.

51 Which sport does the speakers' organization promote?
(A) Tennis
(B) Volleyball
(C) Swimming
(D) Gymnastics

화자들의 단체는 어느 스포츠를 장려하는가?
(A) 테니스
(B) 배구
(C) 수영
(D) 체조

어휘 promote 장려하다, 홍보하다

해설 세부 사항 관련 – 화자들의 단체가 장려하는 스포츠
여자가 첫 대사에서 젊은 선수들을 위한 테니스 캠프(the tennis camp for young players)와 관련해 이야기하고 있으므로 정답은 (A)이다.

52 Why were T-shirts ordered early?
(A) To avoid potential delays
(B) To get free delivery
(C) To receive a discount
(D) To meet heavy demand

티셔츠를 왜 일찍 주문했는가?
(A) 잠재적인 지연을 피하기 위해
(B) 무료 배송 서비스를 받기 위해
(C) 할인을 받기 위해
(D) 많은 수요를 충족하기 위해

어휘 avoid 피하다　potential 잠재적인　free 무료의

해설 세부 사항 관련 – 티셔츠를 일찍 주문한 이유
여자가 마지막 대사에서 티셔츠를 아주 일찍 주문했다며, 그렇게 해서 가격의 절반을 할인받았다(~ the T-shirts were ordered very early. That way we received half off the price ~)고 했으므로 정답은 (C)이다.

Paraphrasing
대화의 half off the price → 정답의 a discount

53-55 3인 대화　W-Am / M-Au / M-Cn

W　The first item on today's meeting agenda is ⁵³**our bid to renovate the Morrisville Bridge.** Do we have an update on that yet?

M1　Yes—unfortunately we didn't get the contract.

M2　Yes, the only explanation given was that ⁵⁴**another construction company submitted a proposal with a shorter timeline.**

W　So, what do we know about this competitor? Have they worked on other local projects?

M1　The only thing I heard was their name—CDQ Construction Company.

W　Well, I'd like to know more about them. ⁵⁵**Can you two do some research before our next meeting?**

여　오늘 회의의 첫 번째 안건은 **모리스빌 다리의 보수를 위한 우리의 입찰** 건입니다. 혹시 이에 관한 새로운 소식이 있나요?

남1　네, 유감스럽게도 계약을 따내지 못했습니다.

남2　네, 전달받은 유일한 설명은 **다른 건설 회사가 더 짧은 일정으로 제안서를 제출했다는 것**이었습니다.

여　그럼, 그 경쟁사에 대해 우리가 알고 있는 건 무엇인가요? 지역 내 다른 프로젝트들도 작업했나요?

남1　유일하게 들은 것은 그곳 이름인데, CDQ 건설 회사입니다.

여　음, 그 회사에 대해 더 많이 알았으면 합니다. **두 분이 다음 회의 전까지 조사를 해 주시겠어요?**

어휘 agenda 안건　bid 입찰(액)　renovate 개조하다, 보수하다
unfortunately 유감스럽게도, 안타깝게도　explanation 설명
submit 제출하다　proposal 제안(서)　timeline 진행 일정

---

53 What industry do the speakers most likely work in?
(A) Energy
(B) Finance
(C) Construction
(D) Manufacturing

화자들은 어떤 업계에서 일하는 것 같은가?
(A) 에너지
(B) 금융
(C) 건설
(D) 제조

해설 전체 내용 관련 – 화자들의 근무 업계
여자가 첫 대사에서 모리스빌 다리의 보수를 위한 회사의 입찰(our bid to renovate the Morrisville Bridge)을 언급했으므로 정답은 (C)이다.

---

54 What is the reason a company did not get a contract?
(A) Some costs were too high.
(B) A facility failed an inspection.
(C) Some paperwork was submitted late.
(D) A competitor can complete a project faster.

회사에서 계약을 따내지 못한 이유는 무엇인가?
(A) 비용이 너무 높았다.
(B) 시설이 점검에서 불합격했다.
(C) 서류가 늦게 제출되었다.
(D) 경쟁사가 프로젝트를 더 빨리 완료할 수 있다.

어휘 facility 시설(물)　fail 불합격하다, 실패하다

해설 세부 사항 관련 – 계약을 따내지 못한 이유
두 번째 남자가 첫 대사에서 계약을 따내지 못한 이유에 대해 다른 건설 회사가 더 짧은 일정으로 제안서를 제출했다(~ another construction company submitted a proposal with a shorter timeline)고 했으므로 정답은 (D)이다.

Paraphrasing
대화의 another construction company submitted a proposal with a shorter timeline
→ 정답의 A competitor can complete a project faster.

---

55 What does the woman ask the men to do?
(A) Visit a facility
(B) Conduct some research
(C) Rewrite a proposal
(D) Contact some vendors

여자는 남자들에게 무엇을 하도록 요청하는가?
(A) 시설 방문하기
(B) 조사 실시하기
(C) 제안서 다시 쓰기
(D) 판매업체에 연락하기

어휘 conduct 실시하다, 수행하다 contact 연락하다
vendor 판매업체, 판매업자

해설 세부 사항 관련 – 여자의 요청 사항
여자가 마지막 대사에서 남자들에게 다음 회의 전까지 조사를 해 줄 것(Can you two do some research before our next meeting?)을 요청했으므로 정답은 (B)이다.

Paraphrasing
대화의 do → 정답의 Conduct

56-58 W-Br / M-Au

W ⁵⁶**Did you see that the results of last month's employee survey have been compiled?** All the staff feedback is available.

M Yes, and I just finished reviewing the comments.

W You know, I noticed one recurring complaint. The size of the break room is too small. ⁵⁷**Perhaps we could enlarge the break room by having the wall taken down between it and the meeting room next door.**

M Well, we do have money available in the budget.

W Then could you reach out to your contact at the construction company?

M ⁵⁸**I can't do it this afternoon, since I need to see a dentist**, but I will definitely make the call.

여 지난달 직원 설문 조사 결과가 정리된 걸 보셨나요? 모든 직원 의견을 확인할 수 있어요.
남 네, 방금 의견 검토를 마쳤습니다.
여 있잖아요, 한 가지 반복되는 불만을 알게 되었어요. 휴게실의 크기가 너무 작아요. **아마 휴게실과 옆에 있는 회의실 사이의 벽을 철거해서 확장할 수 있을 거예요.**
남 음, 예산에 쓸 수 있는 돈이 있어요.
여 그렇다면 건설 회사의 담당자에게 연락해 주시겠어요?
남 **치과 진료를 받아야 해서 오늘 오후에는 할 수 없지만** 꼭 전화할게요.

어휘 survey 설문 조사(지) compile (자료 등을 모아) 정리하다
feedback 의견 review 살펴보다, 검토하다 comment 의견
notice 알게 되다, 주목하다 recurring 반복되는, 되풀이되는
complaint 불만 enlarge 확장하다 take down 철거하다
contact 연락; 관계에 있는 사람 definitely 꼭, 분명히

56 What did the company do last month?
(A) It opened a second location.
(B) It merged with another business.
(C) It launched a new product.
(D) It conducted an employee survey.

회사는 지난달에 무엇을 했는가?
(A) 두 번째 지점을 열었다.
(B) 다른 업체와 합병했다.
(C) 신제품을 출시했다.
(D) 직원 설문 조사를 실시했다.

어휘 merge with ~와 합병하다

해설 세부 사항 관련 – 회사가 지난달에 한 일
여자가 첫 대사에서 지난달 직원 설문 조사 결과가 정리된 걸 봤는지(Did you see that the results of last month's employee survey have been compiled?) 물었으므로 정답은 (D)이다.

57 Why does the man say, "we do have money available in the budget"?
(A) To request another budget analysis
(B) To suggest hiring additional employees
(C) To agree with a proposed renovation
(D) To recommend an increase in advertising

남자는 왜 "예산에 쓸 수 있는 돈이 있어요"라고 말하는가?
(A) 예산 분석을 한 번 더 요청하기 위해
(B) 추가 직원 고용을 제안하기 위해
(C) 제안된 개조 공사에 동의하기 위해
(D) 광고 증가를 권하기 위해

어휘 propose 제안하다

해설 화자의 의도 파악 – 예산에 쓸 수 있는 돈이 있다는 말의 의도
여자가 두 번째 대사에서 벽을 철거해서 휴게실을 확장할 수 있을 것(~ we could enlarge the break room by having the wall taken down ~)이라고 제안하는 것에 대해 남자가 인용문을 언급하고 있다. 이는 예산에 남은 돈이 있기 때문에 여자가 제안하는 확장 공사를 할 수 있다는 뜻이므로 정답은 (C)이다.

58 What does the man say he has to do this afternoon?
(A) Have his car repaired
(B) Give a presentation
(C) Go to a dentist appointment
(D) Attend a reception

남자는 오늘 오후에 무엇을 해야 한다고 말하는가?
(A) 자동차 수리받기
(B) 발표하기
(C) 치과 예약에 가기
(D) 환영회 참석하기

어휘 reception 환영회

TEST 5 **133**

해설 **세부 사항 관련 – 남자가 오늘 오후에 할 일**
남자가 마지막 대사에서 치과 진료를 받아야 해서 오늘 오후에는 할 수 없다(I can't do it this afternoon, since I need to see a dentist ~)고 했으므로 정답은 (C)이다.

> **Paraphrasing**
> 대화의 see a dentist → 정답의 Go to a dentist appointment

59-61 W-Am / M-Au

> W **59 Thanks for calling Hang's Metal Recycling Company.** How can I help you?
>
> M Hi. I'm with Shannak Construction Company. We've got a lot of brass metal scrap from a recent remodeling job. Are you currently buying metal scrap?
>
> W Yes, we are. We currently pay two dollars a pound.
>
> M Oh, **60 there's another recycling center that pays two dollars and twenty-five cents a pound. Would you be willing to match their price?**
>
> W Yes, we have a price-match guarantee.
>
> M Great. **61 I'll bring the metal to you this afternoon, then.**

여 항스 금속 재활용 회사에 전화해 주셔서 감사합니다. 무엇을 도와드릴까요?
남 안녕하세요. 저는 샤낙 건설 회사에 근무하는 사람입니다. 최근 리모델링 공사에서 황동 고철이 많이 생겼어요. 현재 고철을 매입하고 계신가요?
여 네, 그렇습니다. 현재 1파운드당 2달러를 지급하고 있습니다.
남 아, 1파운드당 2달러 25센트를 지급하는 다른 재활용 센터가 있어요. 그곳 가격에 맞춰 주실 의향이 있으신가요?
여 네, 저희는 가격 일치 보장제를 시행합니다.
남 잘됐네요. 그럼 오늘 오후에 고철을 가져갈게요.

어휘 recycling 재활용 brass 황동 metal scrap 고철 recent 최근의 remodeling 리모델링, 개조 currently 현재 be willing to ~할 의향이 있다, 기꺼이 ~하다 match 맞추다, 일치시키다 guarantee 보장(하는 것), 보증(서)

59 Where does the woman work?
(A) At a recycling company
(B) At an appliance store
(C) At a manufacturing company
(D) At an architectural firm

여자는 어디에서 일하는가?
(A) 재활용 회사
(B) 가전기기 매장
(C) 제조 회사
(D) 건축 회사

해설 **전체 내용 관련 – 여자의 근무 장소**
여자가 첫 대사에서 항스 금속 재활용 회사에 전화해 줘서 감사하다(Thanks for calling Hang's Metal Recycling Company)고 했으므로 정답은 (A)이다.

60 What does the man ask the woman to do?
(A) Revise a contract
(B) Match a competitor's offer
(C) Refund a delivery fee
(D) Sign in at a security desk

남자는 여자에게 무엇을 해 달라고 요청하는가?
(A) 계약서 수정하기
(B) 경쟁사 제공 가격에 맞추기
(C) 배송료 환불해 주기
(D) 보안 데스크에서 서명하고 들어가기

어휘 revise 수정하다, 정정하다 refund 환불해 주다 sign in 서명하고 들어가다

해설 **세부 사항 관련 – 남자의 요청 사항**
남자가 두 번째 대사에서 다른 재활용 센터를 언급하면서 그곳 가격에 맞춰 줄 의향이 있는지(there's another recycling center ~ Would you be willing to match their price?) 묻고 있으므로 정답은 (B)이다.

> **Paraphrasing**
> 대화의 match their price
> → 정답의 Match a competitor's offer

61 What does the man say he will do this afternoon?
(A) Conduct an inspection
(B) Sign a document
(C) Deliver some materials
(D) Update a Web site

남자는 오늘 오후에 무엇을 할 것이라고 말하는가?
(A) 점검 실시하기
(B) 문서에 서명하기
(C) 물품 전달하기
(D) 웹사이트 업데이트하기

어휘 material 물품, 재료, 자료

해설 **세부 사항 관련 – 남자가 오늘 오후에 할 일**
남자가 마지막 대사에서 오늘 오후에 고철을 가져가겠다(I'll bring the metal to you this afternoon, then)고 했으므로 정답은 (C)이다.

> **Paraphrasing**
> 대화의 bring the metal → 정답의 Deliver some materials

62-64 대화 + 프로젝트 계획표 W-Br / M-Cn

W Hi. I just got off the phone with management. They're not happy. The construction of the train tunnel isn't progressing fast enough.

M Yeah, I'm not surprised. ⁶²**The drilling is done now.** The thing is, we can't start installing the support columns until we have all the materials for the concrete.

W When are the materials going to get here?

M A week, maybe two.

W ⁶³**Let's see if the shipment can be expedited. Can you do that?**

M Sure. I'll call the supplier to ask about getting it here sooner.

W In the meantime, ⁶⁴**I'm going to write an e-mail to management** to explain how we're attempting to resolve the situation.

여 안녕하세요. 방금 경영진과 통화를 마쳤어요. 기분이 좋지 않으시네요. 기차 터널 공사가 충분히 빠르게 진행되고 있지 않아요.

남 네, 놀랍지 않아요. **이제 굴착 작업이 끝났어요.** 문제는 콘크리트를 위한 재료가 모두 준비되기 전에는 지지 기둥 설치를 시작할 수 없다는 것입니다.

여 재료는 언제 오나요?

남 일주일, 어쩌면 2주요.

여 배송이 더 신속히 될 수 있는지 확인해 봅시다. 그렇게 해 주실 수 있으세요?

남 물론이죠. 공급 업체에 전화해서 더 빨리 도착할 수 있는지 물어볼게요.

여 그동안, **저는 경영진에 이메일을 써서** 상황을 어떻게 해결하려고 하는지 설명하겠습니다.

어휘 management 경영(진), 관리(진) progress 진행되다 drilling 굴착, 구멍 뚫기 column 기둥 concrete 콘크리트 expedite 더 신속히 처리하다 in the meantime 그동안 explain 설명하다 attempt 시도하다 resolve 해결하다 assemble 조립하다 lay down 부설하다, 설치하다

Train Tunnel Construction Project	
Phase 1	Assemble drill machine
Phase 2	⁶²Drill through rock
Phase 3	Install support columns
Phase 4	Lay down electrical cables

기차 터널 공사 프로젝트	
1단계	굴착용 기계 조립
2단계	**암석 굴착**
3단계	지지 기둥 설치
4단계	전기 케이블 부설

62 Look at the graphic. Which project phase was just completed?
(A) Phase 1
(B) Phase 2
(C) Phase 3
(D) Phase 4

시각 정보에 의하면, 어느 프로젝트 단계가 막 완료되었는가?
(A) 1단계
(B) 2단계
(C) 3단계
(D) 4단계

해설 **시각 정보 연계 - 막 완료된 단계**
남자가 첫 대사에서 이제 굴착 작업이 끝났다(The drilling is done now)고 했는데, 프로젝트 계획표에서 굴착 작업(Drill through rock)은 2단계(Phase 2)에 해당하므로 정답은 (B)이다.

63 What does the woman ask the man to do?
(A) Request an earlier delivery date
(B) Consult with a safety inspector
(C) Post some construction plans
(D) Forward an invoice

여자는 남자에게 무엇을 해 달라고 요청하는가?
(A) 더 빠른 배송일 요청하기
(B) 안전 조사관과 상의하기
(C) 공사 계획 게시하기
(D) 거래 내역서 전송하기

어휘 request 요청하다, 요구하다 consult 상의하다, 상담하다 post 게시하다 forward 전송하다 invoice 거래 내역서

해설 **세부 사항 관련 - 여자의 요청 사항**
여자가 세 번째 대사에서 배송이 더 신속히 될 수 있는지 확인해 보자며, 그렇게 해 줄 수 있는지(Let's see if the shipment can be expedited. Can you do that?) 묻고 있으므로 정답은 (A)이다.

Paraphrasing
대화의 the shipment can be expedited
→ 정답의 an earlier delivery date

64 What does the woman intend to do next?
(A) Review some data
(B) Move a vehicle
(C) Increase the size of a crew
(D) Contact the management team

여자는 다음에 무엇을 할 생각인가?
(A) 데이터 검토하기
(B) 차량 옮기기
(C) 작업팀 규모 늘리기
(D) 경영진에 연락하기

어휘 crew 작업팀, 조

해설 세부 사항 관련 – 여자가 다음에 할 일
여자가 마지막 대사에서 경영진에 이메일을 쓰겠다(I'm going to write an e-mail to management ~)고 했으므로 정답은 (D)이다.

Paraphrasing
대화의 write an e-mail → 정답의 Contact

65-67 대화 + 안내도 M-Au / W-Am

M The city just posted its new parking rates, and we need to talk about how they'll affect ⁶⁵ **our restaurant**'s food delivery service. I'm worried we'll lose money because we'll need to pay more for parking while the delivery driver takes the food to customers.

W Wow. ⁶⁶ **Parking in our main delivery area is up to fifteen dollars an hour**? That is a problem. But offering free delivery attracts a lot of business. ⁶⁷ **What else can we do to lower expenses?**

M ⁶⁷ **We could start using bicycle delivery whenever possible. That should help.**

W Good idea. I'll talk to our drivers to see who's willing to switch to bicycle deliveries for customers nearby. Some people really like the exercise.

남 시에서 방금 새 주차 요금을 공시했는데, 그게 **우리 레스토랑**의 음식 배달 서비스에 어떤 영향을 미칠지 이야기해 봐야 합니다. 배달 기사가 고객에게 음식을 가져다주는 동안 주차비를 더 내야 해서 손해를 볼까 봐 걱정입니다.

여 와우. **우리 주요 배달 구역에 주차하는 데 1시간에 최대 15달러인 건가요?** 이건 문제네요. 하지만 무료 배달 서비스를 제공하는 게 많은 거래를 유치해요. **비용을 낮추기 위해 또 무엇을 할 수 있죠?**

남 **가능할 때는 자전거 배달 서비스를 이용할 수 있을 겁니다. 도움이 될 거예요.**

여 좋은 생각입니다. 제가 기사들과 이야기해서 누가 근처에 있는 고객들을 대상으로 자전거 배달 서비스로 바꿀 의향이 있는지 알아볼게요. 어떤 사람들은 운동을 정말 좋아하거든요.

어휘 post 공시하다, 게시하다　rate 요금　affect 영향을 미치다　up to ~까지　attract 유치하다, 끌어들이다　switch 바꾸다　exercise 운동　district 구역, 지역　residential 주거의

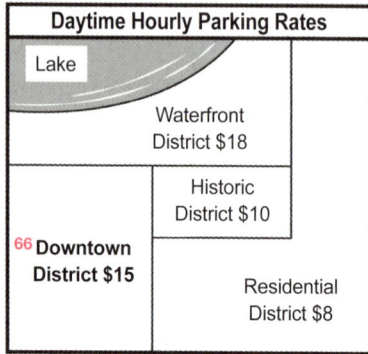

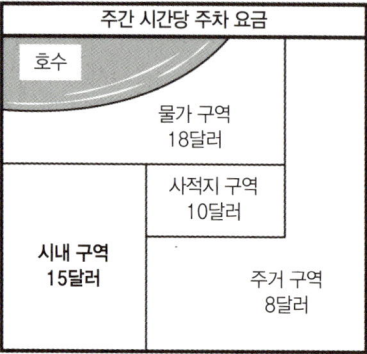

65 What type of business do the speakers work for?
(A) A restaurant
(B) A law firm
(C) An office-supply store
(D) A flower shop

화자들은 어떤 종류의 업체에서 일하는가?
(A) 레스토랑
(B) 법률 회사
(C) 사무용품 매장
(D) 꽃집

해설 전체 내용 관련 – 화자들의 근무 업체
남자가 첫 대사에서 우리 레스토랑(our restaurant)이라고 했으므로 정답은 (A)이다.

66 Look at the graphic. In which area of the city does the business make most of its deliveries?
(A) The waterfront district
(B) The historic district
(C) The residential district
(D) The downtown district

시각 정보에 의하면, 업체는 도시의 어느 구역에서 대부분의 배달을 하고 있는가?
(A) 물가 구역
(B) 사적지 구역
(C) 주거 구역
(D) 시내 구역

해설 **시각 정보 연계 – 대부분의 배달이 이뤄지는 구역**
여자가 첫 대사에서 주요 배달 구역에 주차하는 데 1시간에 최대 15달러(Parking in our main delivery area is up to fifteen dollars an hour?)라며 놀라움을 표현하고 있는데, 안내도에서 15달러로 표기된 곳은 시내 구역(Downtown District)이므로 정답은 (D)이다.

67 How does the man propose lowering business expenses?
(A) By reducing packaging waste
(B) By introducing bicycle delivery
(C) By switching to a new supplier
(D) By moving to a smaller building

남자는 사업상 지출을 어떻게 낮추도록 제안하는가?
(A) 포장 쓰레기를 감소시킴으로써
(B) 자전거 배달 서비스를 도입함으로써
(C) 새 공급 업체로 바꿈으로써
(D) 더 작은 건물로 이전함으로써

어휘 packaging 포장(재)   introduce 도입하다, 소개하다

해설 **세부 사항 관련 – 남자가 제안하는 지출 감소 방법**
여자가 첫 대사에서 비용을 낮추기 위해 또 무엇을 할 수 있는지(What else can we do to lower expenses?) 묻자, 남자가 자전거 배달 서비스를 언급하면서 도움이 될 것(We could start using bicycle delivery whenever possible. That should help)이라고 했으므로 정답은 (B)이다.

Paraphrasing
대화의 start using → 정답의 introducing

68-70 대화 + 제안서   M-Au / W-Br

M When customers walk into Southern Regional Bank, I want them to feel confident about entrusting their money to us. As I mentioned the last time we met, I'm hoping **68 your interior design firm** can give our lobby a more polished, professional look.

W Our proposal does just that. Here—take a look. The cover page includes a summary of the renovations.

M Hmm. **69 Do you really think we need skylights?** That would be a big expense.

W There aren't many windows in your lobby, so it's the best way to bring more natural light into the room. Besides, our proposed renovations would actually come in under budget. **70 If you turn to page four, you'll see the cost breakdown.**

남 고객들이 서던 리저널 은행으로 들어올 때, 우리에게 돈을 맡기는 것에 확신이 들게 하고 싶습니다. 지난번에 만났을 때 언급했던 것처럼, 귀하의 인테리어 디자인 회사에서 로비를 더 세련되고 전문적인 모습으로 만들어 주셨으면 해요.

여 저희 제안서가 바로 그렇습니다. 여기, 보시죠. 표지에 개조 공사 요약이 있습니다.

남 흠. 정말 천장 채광창이 필요하다고 생각하시나요? 이건 많은 비용이 들 텐데요.

여 로비에 창문이 많지 않아서, 자연광을 로비로 들어오게 하기 위한 최선의 방법입니다. 게다가, 저희가 제안한 개조 공사는 실제로 예산 범위 안에 있습니다. 4페이지로 넘기면, 세부 비용 내역이 보일 겁니다.

어휘 entrust 맡기다   mention 언급하다   polished 세련된   cover 표지   summary 요약(본)   renovation 개조, 보수   skylight 천장 채광창   besides 게다가   turn to ~로 넘기다   breakdown 세부 내역(서)   refinish 표면을 다시 손질하다   trim 다듬다, 마무리 손질하다   replace 교체하다

Proposal Summary
69 Step 1: Install skylights
Step 2: Refinish stone floors
Step 3: Paint walls and trim
Step 4: Replace furniture

제안서 요약
1단계: 천장 채광창 설치
2단계: 석재 바닥 표면 재손질
3단계: 벽면 도장 및 다듬기
4단계: 가구 교체

68 Who most likely is the woman?
(A) A hotel manager
(B) An interior designer
(C) A construction worker
(D) A real estate agent

여자는 누구인 것 같은가?
(A) 호텔 지배인
(B) 인테리어 디자이너
(C) 공사 인부
(D) 부동산 중개업자

해설   전체 내용 관련 – 여자의 직업
남자가 첫 대사에서 여자의 소속 업체를 인테리어 디자인 회사(your interior design firm)라고 했으므로 정답은 (B)이다.

69 Look at the graphic. Which step does the man ask about?
(A) Step 1
(B) Step 2
(C) Step 3
(D) Step 4

시각 정보에 의하면, 남자는 어느 단계에 대해 묻는가?
(A) 1단계
(B) 2단계
(C) 3단계
(D) 4단계

해설   시각 정보 연계 – 남자가 묻는 단계
남자가 두 번째 대사에서 정말 천장 채광창이 필요하다고 생각하는지(Do you really think we need skylights?) 물었는데, 제안서에서 천장 채광창 설치(Install skylights)는 1단계(Step 1)이므로 정답은 (A)이다.

70 What will the man most likely do next?
(A) Send a contract
(B) Go to the lobby
(C) Look at some photographs
(D) Review a cost estimate

남자는 다음에 무엇을 할 것 같은가?
(A) 계약서 보내기
(B) 로비로 가기
(C) 사진 보기
(D) 비용 견적서 검토하기

해설   세부 사항 관련 – 남자가 다음에 할 일
여자가 마지막 대사에서 4페이지로 넘기면 세부 비용 내역이 보일 것(If you turn to page four, you'll see the cost breakdown)이라고 했으므로 정답은 (D)이다.

> **Paraphrasing**
> 대화의 see the cost breakdown
> → 정답의 Review a cost estimate

PART 4

71-73 회의 발췌

> W-Am ⁷¹Welcome to the monthly company staff meeting. Before I begin my report on last month's sales figures, ⁷²I want to congratulate our fantastic IT team! The sales tracking system they built allows us to easily share results with colleagues from other branches. ⁷³All employees are required to attend a training session on how to use it. A registration link will be sent out this afternoon. Now, let's look at last month's figures. We need to decide if we're ready to expand into more markets.

> 월간 회사 직원회의에 오신 것을 환영합니다. 지난달 매출 수치에 관한 보고를 시작하기에 앞서, 환상적인 IT팀에 축하를 전하고 싶습니다! 그들이 만든 판매 추적 시스템은 다른 지점의 동료들과 결과를 쉽게 공유할 수 있게 해 줍니다. 모든 직원은 이용 방법에 관한 교육에 참석해야 합니다. 등록용 링크가 오늘 오후에 발송될 겁니다. 이제, 지난달 수치를 보시겠습니다. 우리는 더 많은 시장으로 사업을 확대할 준비가 되어 있는지 결정해야 합니다.

> 어휘   figure 수치, 숫자   tracking 추적   allow 할 수 있게 해 주다   share 공유하다   colleague 동료 (직원)   branch 지점, 지사   be required to ~해야 하다   session (특정 활동을 하는) 시간   registration 등록   expand 확대하다, 확장하다

71 Who most likely is the speaker?
(A) A department manager
(B) A news reporter
(C) A marketing consultant
(D) A computer programmer

화자는 누구인 것 같은가?
(A) 부서장
(B) 뉴스 기자
(C) 마케팅 컨설턴트
(D) 컴퓨터 프로그래머

해설   전체 내용 관련 – 화자의 직업
화자가 초반부에 회사 월간 회의에 온 것을 환영한다고 했고, 매출 수치에 관한 보고를 언급하고, IT팀에 축하를 전하는(Welcome to the monthly company staff meeting. Before I begin my report ~ I want to congratulate our fantastic IT team!) 등 회의를 진행하고 있다. 이는 부서의 책임자가 할 수 있는 일에 해당하므로 정답은 (A)이다.

138

72 Why does the speaker congratulate a team?
(A) For keeping expenses low
(B) For creating a useful tool
(C) For meeting a tight deadline
(D) For achieving the most sales

화자는 왜 한 팀을 축하하는가?
(A) 지출을 낮게 유지했기 때문에
(B) 유용한 도구를 만들어 냈기 때문에
(C) 빠듯한 마감 기한을 맞췄기 때문에
(D) 가장 많은 매출을 달성했기 때문에

어휘 tight 빠듯한, 빡빡한 achieve 달성하다, 성취하다

해설 세부 사항 관련 – 화자가 한 팀을 축하하는 이유
화자가 중반부에 IT팀을 축하하면서 그들이 만든 판매 추적 시스템은 다른 지점의 동료들과 결과를 쉽게 공유할 수 있게 해 준다(~ I want to congratulate our fantastic IT team! The sales tracking system they built allows us to easily share results ~)고 했으므로 정답은 (B)이다.

Paraphrasing
담화의 The sales tracking system they built allows us to easily share results → 정답의 creating a useful tool

73 What are the listeners required to do?
(A) Register for some training
(B) Review a floor plan
(C) Participate in a mentoring program
(D) Provide copies of certifications

청자들은 무엇을 해야 하는가?
(A) 교육에 등록하기
(B) 평면도 검토하기
(C) 멘토 프로그램에 참여하기
(D) 자격증 사본 제공하기

어휘 register for ~에 등록하다 floor plan (건물의) 평면도 participate in ~에 참여하다 certification 자격증, 증명서

해설 세부 사항 관련 – 청자들이 해야 하는 일
화자가 중반부에 모든 직원이 참석해야 하는 교육을 언급하며, 등록용 링크가 오후에 발송될 것(All employees are required to attend a training session ~ A registration link will be sent out this afternoon)이라고 했으므로 정답은 (A)이다.

74-76 녹음 메시지

M-Au Hello. You've reached the communications team of *Business As Usual*, the talk show about starting a new business. **⁷⁴If you are calling because you'd like to appear on our show, we'd love to hear your story! To record your story idea, please press one.** **⁷⁵Please note: it is necessary to keep your message under 60 seconds.** Submissions that are more than a minute long will not be reviewed. The typical timeline for the review process is two weeks, **⁷⁶with longer wait times expected around holidays.**

안녕하세요. 새로운 사업을 시작하는 것에 관한 토크쇼, 〈비즈니스 애즈 유주얼〉의 커뮤니케이션 팀입니다. 쇼에 출연하고 싶어서 전화하셨다면, 귀하의 이야기를 듣고 싶습니다! 귀하의 이야기를 녹음하시려면, 1번을 눌러 주세요. 유의해 주시기 바랍니다. 메시지는 60초 이내로 남겨 주셔야 합니다. 1분이 넘는 제출물은 검토되지 않을 것입니다. 검토 과정의 일반적인 일정은 2주이며, 휴일 전후로는 대기 시간이 더 길어질 것으로 예상됩니다.

어휘 reach 연락하다 appear 출연하다 note 유의하다 submission 제출(물) review 검토, 후기 process 과정 timeline 진행 일정

74 What are the listeners invited to do?
(A) Download a calendar
(B) Reserve tickets
(C) Submit a picture
(D) Share a story

청자들은 무엇을 하도록 요청받는가?
(A) 일정표 다운로드하기
(B) 티켓 예매하기
(C) 사진 제출하기
(D) 이야기 공유하기

어휘 be invited to ~하도록 요청받다 share 공유하다

해설 세부 사항 관련 – 청자들이 요청받는 일
화자가 초반부에 출연을 원해서 전화했다면 이야기를 들어 보고 싶다며, 이야기 녹음을 위해 1번을 눌러 달라(If you are calling because you'd like to appear on our show, we'd love to hear your story! To record your story idea, please press one)고 했으므로 정답은 (D)이다.

75 What guideline does the speaker emphasize?
(A) Recordings must be kept short.
(B) Electronic devices must be turned off.
(C) Professional references must be provided.
(D) Vehicles must be parked in a designated area.

화자는 어떤 가이드라인을 강조하는가?
(A) 녹음을 짧게 남겨야 한다.
(B) 전자 기기는 꺼야 한다.
(C) 전문가 추천서가 제출되어야 한다.
(D) 차량이 지정 구역에 주차되어야 한다.

어휘 emphasize 강조하다 device 기기, 장치 reference 추천서, 추천인 designated 지정된

TEST 5

해설 　세부 사항 관련 – 화자가 강조하는 가이드라인
　　　화자가 중반부에 유의해 달라며, 메시지는 60초 이내로 남겨
　　　야 한다(Please note: it is necessary to keep your
　　　message under 60 seconds)고 했으므로 정답은 (A)이다.

> **Paraphrasing**
> 담화의 note → 질문의 emphasize
> 담화의 keep your message under 60 seconds
> → 정답의 Recordings must be kept short

76. According to the speaker, what may cause a delay?
(A) Bad weather
(B) Holidays
(C) A construction project
(D) Staff changes

화자에 따르면, 무엇이 지연을 초래할 수 있는가?
(A) 악천후
(B) 휴일
(C) 건설 공사 프로젝트
(D) 직원 변경

해설 　세부 사항 관련 – 지연을 초래할 수 있는 것
　　　화자가 후반부에 휴일 전후로는 대기 시간이 더 길어질 것으로 예
　　　상된다(~ with longer wait times expected around
　　　holidays)고 했으므로 정답은 (B)이다.

> **Paraphrasing**
> 담화의 longer wait times → 질문의 a delay

77-79 투어 정보

> W-Am ⁷⁷**Welcome to the culinary tour of downtown Springfield.** Today, you'll taste a variety of local foods. ⁷⁸**Normally I'd start by taking you inside Zelda's Bakery to try one of their famous corn muffins**, but we have such a large group today. ⁷⁸**Instead, we're going to head directly to the open-air market**. There you'll find a wide selection of the homemade breads, jams, and pastries that we're noted for. After that, we'll head to the original Springfield cornmill, which is still in use today. And ⁷⁹**remember to keep your tour ticket. It's good for one free entry at the local museum.**

> 스프링필드 시내 요리 투어에 오신 것을 환영합니다. 오늘, 여러분께서는 다양한 지역 음식을 맛보실 것입니다. 평소라면 제가 젤다스 베이커리 내부로 모시고 가서 유명한 옥수수 머핀을 시식하는 것으로 시작하겠지만, 오늘은 단체 규모가 아주 큽니다. 대신, 노천 시장으로 곧장 향하겠습니다. 그곳에서 유명한 집에서 만든 빵과 잼, 그리고 패스트리 등 다양한 종류의 제품을 만날 수 있습니다. 그 후에는, 최초의 스프링필드 옥수수 제분소로 향할 텐데요. 이곳은 지금도 여전히 이용되고 있습니다. 그리고 투어 티켓을 보관하는 것을 기억하세요. 지역 박물관에 1회 무료로 입장할 수 있습니다.

어휘 　culinary 요리의　taste 맛보다　a variety of 다양한
　　　head to ~로 향하다　a selection of 다양한
　　　be noted for ~로 유명하다　original 최초의, 원래의
　　　cornmill 옥수수 제분소　in use 이용되는, 쓰이는　good 유효한

77 What is the focus of a tour?
(A) Food
(B) Architecture
(C) Nature
(D) Art

투어의 초점은 무엇인가?
(A) 음식
(B) 건축
(C) 자연
(D) 예술

어휘 　focus 초점, 중점

해설 　전체 내용 관련 – 투어의 초점
　　　화자가 초반부에 스프링필드 시내 요리 투어에 온 것을 환영
　　　한다(Welcome to the culinary tour of downtown
　　　Springfield)고 했으므로 정답은 (A)이다.

78 What does the speaker imply when she says, "we have such a large group today"?
(A) She is happy about the popularity of a tour.
(B) She will need to use a microphone.
(C) An additional tour guide is needed.
(D) A shop is not big enough for everyone.

화자가 "오늘은 단체 규모가 아주 큽니다"라고 말할 때 무엇을 암시하는가?
(A) 투어의 인기에 기뻐하고 있다.
(B) 마이크를 이용해야 할 것이다.
(C) 추가 투어 가이드가 필요하다.
(D) 매장이 모두가 들어갈 정도로 충분히 크지 않다.

어휘 　popularity 인기　additional 추가적인

해설 　화자의 의도 파악 – 단체 규모가 아주 크다는 말의 의도
　　　화자가 중반부에 평소라면 젤다스 베이커리 내부로 데리고 가
　　　서 유명한 옥수수 머핀을 시식하는 것으로 시작한다(Normally
　　　I'd start by taking you inside Zelda's Bakery ~)
　　　고 말한 뒤로 인용문을 언급하면서 대신 노천 시장으로 곧장 향
　　　하겠다(Instead, we're going to head directly to the
　　　open-air market)고 했다. 이는 단체 규모가 너무 커서 평소대
　　　로 베이커리에 갈 수 없다는 뜻이므로 정답은 (D)이다.

79 What will a ticket allow the listeners to do?
(A) Attend a performance
(B) Visit a museum
(C) Participate in a class
(D) Enter a contest

티켓으로 청자들은 무엇을 할 수 있는가?
(A) 공연 참석하기
(B) 박물관 방문하기
(C) 강좌 참가하기
(D) 콘테스트 참가하기

해설 세부 사항 관련 – 티켓으로 할 수 있는 것
화자가 후반부에 투어 티켓을 보관하라며, 지역 박물관에 1회 무료로 입장할 수 있다(~ remember to keep your tour ticket. It's good for one free entry at the local museum)고 했으므로 정답은 (B)이다.

Paraphrasing
담화의 It's good for → 질문의 allow
담화의 entry at the local museum → 정답의 Visit a museum

80-82 담화

W-Br The Novikov Award is named after Maksim Novikov, the founder of Novikov Aviation. **⁸⁰It is given each year to a company that has made outstanding contributions to the aviation industry.** The company chosen for the award this year was frustrated by the lack of qualified job applicants and decided to do something about it. **⁸¹Zenith Aviation's apprenticeship program has trained hundreds of workers for careers in aircraft maintenance and repair.** Dozens of firms nationwide have copied the program. Before I present the award, **⁸²please direct your attention to the screen for a video highlighting the program's effectiveness.**

노비코브 상은 노비코브 항공의 설립자, 막심 노비코브의 이름을 땄습니다. 이 상은 매년 항공 산업에 뛰어난 공헌을 한 회사에 주어집니다. 올해 수상 업체로 선정된 회사는 자격을 갖춘 구직자들의 부족에 좌절감을 겪었고, 뭔가 해 보기로 결정했습니다. 제니스 항공의 수습 프로그램은 항공기 정비 및 수리 분야에서 일할 수백 명의 근로자를 교육해 왔습니다. 전국적으로 수십 곳의 업체들이 이 프로그램을 모방했습니다. 시상하기에 앞서, 이 프로그램의 효과를 집중 조명하는 영상을 보실 수 있도록 스크린을 주목해 주시기 바랍니다.

어휘 be named after ~의 이름에서 따오다 founder 설립자 outstanding 뛰어난, 우수한 contribution 공헌, 기여 aviation 항공(술) frustrated 좌절한, 불만스러운 lack 부족 qualified 자격을 갖춘, 적격인 applicant 지원자, 신청자 apprenticeship 수습직, 수습 기간 maintenance 정비 dozens of 수십의 present 제공하다, 제시하다 direct one's attention to ~을 주목하다, ~로 시선을 돌리다 highlight 집중 조명하다, 강조하다 effectiveness 효과(성)

80 What industry was the Novikov Award created for?
(A) Aviation
(B) Chemical engineering
(C) Medical research
(D) Television production

노비코브 상은 어떤 업계를 위해 만들어졌는가?
(A) 항공
(B) 화학 공학
(C) 의학 연구
(D) 텔레비전 프로그램 제작

해설 세부 사항 관련 – 노비코브 상이 주어지는 업계
화자가 초반부에 노비코브 상을 소개하면서 매년 항공 산업에 뛰어난 공헌을 한 회사에 주어진다(It is given each year to a company that has made outstanding contributions to the aviation industry)고 했으므로 정답은 (A)이다.

81 Why was this year's award recipient selected?
(A) For launching a unique advertising campaign
(B) For developing a successful training program
(C) For maintaining a perfect safety record
(D) For making a scientific discovery

올해의 수상 업체는 왜 선정되었는가?
(A) 특별한 광고 캠페인을 시작했기 때문에
(B) 성공적인 교육 프로그램을 개발했기 때문에
(C) 완벽한 안전 기록을 유지했기 때문에
(D) 과학적 발견을 이뤘기 때문에

어휘 recipient 받는 사람, 수령인 select 선정하다 unique 특별한, 독특한 discovery 발견(된 것)

해설 세부 사항 관련 – 올해의 수상 업체가 선정된 이유
화자가 중반부에 제니스 항공의 수습 프로그램은 항공기 정비 및 수리 분야에서 일할 수백 명의 근로자를 교육해 왔다(Zenith Aviation's apprenticeship program has trained hundreds of workers ~)며, 많은 업체들이 이 프로그램을 모방했다고 했으므로 정답은 (B)이다.

Paraphrasing
담화의 apprenticeship program has trained hundreds of workers → 정답의 a successful training program

82 What does the speaker ask the listeners to do?
(A) Get ready to watch a video
(B) Applaud the winner
(C) Share copies of a handout
(D) Read a set of directions

화자는 청자들에게 무엇을 하라고 요청하는가?
(A) 영상을 시청할 준비하기
(B) 수상자에게 박수 쳐 주기
(C) 유인물 사본 공유하기
(D) 일련의 안내 사항 읽기

어휘 applaud 박수 치다 handout 유인물 directions 안내, 지시
해설 세부 사항 관련 – 화자의 요청 사항
화자가 후반부에 프로그램의 효과를 집중 조명하는 영상을 볼 수 있도록 스크린을 주목하라(~ please direct your attention to the screen for a video highlighting the program's effectiveness)고 했으므로 정답은 (A)이다.

Paraphrasing
담화의 direct your attention to the screen for a video
→ 정답의 Get ready to watch a video

83-85 회의 발췌

> M-Cn 83 **Thank you for allowing me the opportunity to speak at this city council meeting.** On behalf of the transportation department, I'd like to present a proposal to fund the replacement of all 350 bus-stop shelters in our city. We feel this is a worthwhile investment because 84 **the current shelters aren't in good shape. Many of them have cracked glass and broken benches.** We want to go with Urban Retreat because its shelters are made of durable materials. 85 While less expensive options are available, its models include a display for advertisements. 85 **These shelters could provide the city with a new source of income.**

이번 시 의회 회의에서 발언할 수 있는 기회를 주셔서 감사합니다. 교통국을 대표해, 저는 우리 시에 있는 버스 정류장 쉼터 350곳 모두를 교체하기 위한 자금을 제공하자는 제안을 발표하고자 합니다. 이것이 가치 있는 투자라고 생각하는데, **현재 쉼터들은 상태가 좋지 않기 때문입니다. 유리에 금이 가거나 벤치가 부서진 곳이 많습니다.** 저희는 어번 리트리트를 이용하고자 하는데, 이곳의 쉼터는 내구성이 좋은 자재로 만들어지기 때문입니다. 비용이 덜 드는 옵션도 있지만, 이곳의 모델에는 광고 디스플레이가 포함되어 있습니다. 이 쉼터들은 우리 시에 새로운 수입원을 제공해 줄 수 있을 것입니다.

어휘 council 의회 on behalf of ~을 대표해, ~을 대신해
present 발표하다, 제시하다 fund 자금을 제공하다; 자금, 기금
replacement 교체(품) shelter 쉼터, 보호소, 대피소
worthwhile 가치 있는 investment 투자(금)
in good shape 상태가 좋은 cracked 금이 간
broken 망가진, 고장 난 be made of ~로 만들어지다
durable 내구성이 좋은 source 원천, 근원 income 수입, 소득

83 Who is the speaker presenting to?
(A) Loan officers
(B) Construction workers
(C) City council members
(D) Bus drivers

화자는 누구에게 발표하고 있는가?
(A) 대출 담당 직원들
(B) 공사 인부들
(C) 시 의회 구성원들
(D) 버스 기사들

해설 전체 내용 관련 – 청자의 직업
화자가 초반부에 이번 시 의회 회의에서 발언할 수 있는 기회를 줘서 감사하다(Thank you for allowing me the opportunity to speak at this city council meeting)고 했으므로 정답은 (C)이다.

84 What does the speaker say about some existing structures?
(A) They are in disrepair.
(B) They are very small.
(C) They were not assembled correctly.
(D) They were installed last year.

화자는 기존 구조물에 대해 무엇이라고 말하는가?
(A) 파손되어 있다.
(B) 아주 작다.
(C) 제대로 조립되지 않았다.
(D) 작년에 설치되었다.

어휘 existing 기존의 structure 구조(물) disrepair 파손, 황폐
correctly 제대로, 정확히

해설 세부 사항 관련 – 화자가 기존 구조물에 대해 하는 말
화자가 중반부에 현재 쉼터들은 상태가 좋지 않다며, 유리에 금이 가거나 벤치가 부서진 곳이 많다(~ the current shelters aren't in good shape. Many of them have cracked glass and broken benches)고 했으므로 정답은 (A)이다.

Paraphrasing
담화의 cracked glass and broken benches
→ 정답의 in disrepair

85 Why does the speaker say, "its models include a display for advertisements"?
(A) To respond to a request for information
(B) To justify a cost
(C) To express surprise
(D) To suggest adding to a product line

화자는 왜 "이곳의 모델에는 광고 디스플레이가 포함되어 있습니다"라고 말하는가?
(A) 정보 요청에 답변하기 위해
(B) 비용을 정당화하기 위해
(C) 놀라움을 표현하기 위해
(D) 제품 라인에 추가하는 것을 권하기 위해

어휘 respond to ~에 답변하다, ~에 대응하다 justify 정당화하다
express (생각 등을) 표현하다

해설 　화자의 의도 파악 – 모델에 광고 디스플레이가 포함되어 있다는 말의 의도

화자가 후반부에 비용이 덜 드는 옵션도 있지만(While less expensive options are available)이라는 말과 함께 인용문을 언급했고, 이어서 이 쉼터들은 새로운 수입원을 제공해 줄 수 있을 것(These shelters could provide the city with a new source of income)이라고 했다. 이는 가장 저렴한 것은 아니지만 그만한 가치가 있음을 나타내는 말이므로 정답은 (B)이다.

86-88 전화 메시지 ▶동영상 강의

W-Br   Hi. It's Sarai. **86 I'm calling about the new wallpaper patterns that your team submitted.** We all really like the geometric prints. **86 I'm almost certain that all of those will be approved for production in several different color schemes.** And the wallpaper patterns for children's rooms are all so imaginative. **87 You have some truly creative people on your design team.** However, **88 the animal-themed prints you sent**—the thing is, we have a full supply of those in stock. Call me back so we can discuss it.

안녕하세요. 서라이입니다. **귀하의 팀에서 제출하신 새 벽지 패턴과 관련해 전화했습니다.** 저희는 모두 기하학적인 프린트가 정말 마음에 들어요. **모두 여러 가지 다양한 색상 조합으로 제작 승인이 될 거라고 거의 확신합니다.** 그리고 아이들 방을 위한 벽지 패턴들 모두 아주 상상력이 풍부해 보입니다. **귀하의 디자인 팀에 정말 창의적인 분들이 계시네요.** 하지만 보내 주신 동물 주제의 프린트들 말인데요. 문제는, 그런 제품들은 재고가 가득 있습니다. 이 부분을 논할 수 있도록 제게 다시 전화해 주시기 바랍니다.

어휘 　geometric 기하학적인   approve 승인하다
scheme 조합, 구성   imaginative 상상력이 풍부한
creative 창의적인   themed 주제로 하는   supply 재고품, 공급(량)

86 What does the speaker's company sell?
(A) Clothing
(B) Flowers
(C) Toys
(D) Wallpaper

화자의 회사는 무엇을 판매하는가?
(A) 의류
(B) 꽃
(C) 장난감
(D) 벽지

해설 　전체 내용 관련 – 화자의 회사가 판매하는 제품

화자가 초반부에 새 벽지 패턴과 관련해 전화했다(I'm calling about the new wallpaper patterns ~)고 했고, 벽지들이 모두 제작 승인이 될 거라고 거의 확신한다(I'm almost certain that all of those will be approved for production ~)고 했으므로 정답은 (D)이다.

87 Why does the speaker praise the listener's team?
(A) They stayed under budget.
(B) They won an award.
(C) They showed creativity.
(D) They completed some work on schedule.

화자는 왜 청자의 팀을 칭찬하는가?
(A) 예산보다 비용이 적게 들었다.
(B) 상을 받았다.
(C) 창의성을 보여 주었다.
(D) 일정대로 작업을 완료했다.

어휘 　praise 칭찬하다

해설 　세부 사항 관련 – 화자가 청자의 팀을 칭찬하는 이유

화자가 중반부에 청자의 디자인 팀에 정말 창의적인 사람들이 있다(You have some truly creative people on your design team)고 했으므로 정답은 (C)이다.

88 Why does the speaker say, "we have a full supply of those in stock"?
(A) To report that inventory has been completed
(B) To offer to share some supplies with another store
(C) To explain that some designs are not needed
(D) To confirm that a customer's order can be filled

화자는 왜 "그런 제품들은 재고가 가득 있습니다"라고 말하는가?
(A) 재고 조사가 완료되었음을 알리기 위해
(B) 다른 매장과 물품을 공유하자고 제안하기 위해
(C) 일부 디자인이 필요하지 않다는 점을 설명하기 위해
(D) 고객의 주문이 충족될 수 있음을 확인해 주기 위해

어휘 　confirm 확인해 주다, 확정하다

해설 　화자의 의도 파악 – 그런 제품들은 재고가 가득 있다는 말의 의도

화자가 후반부에 청자가 보낸 동물 주제의 프린트(the animal-themed prints you sent)를 언급하면서 인용문을 말하고 있다. 이는 이미 재고가 많기 때문에 동물 주제의 프린트는 필요치 않다는 뜻이므로 정답은 (C)이다.

89-91 방송

M-Cn In local news, **89the opening of the Stewart Performing Arts Center tomorrow night has attracted widespread attention.** This state-of-the-art center holds three different theaters. **90The designer won an award for the building's insulated walls. They have rubber material that absorbs sound from the other theaters and nearby trains.** On top of this, the interior decoration is magnificent. If you'd like to see some photos, browse upcoming shows, and plan your visit, go to the theater's Web site. **91We warn you, though— many shows are already sold out!**

지역 소식입니다. **내일 밤에 있을 스튜어트 공연 예술 센터의 개장이 폭넓은 관심을 끌고 있습니다.** 이 최신식 센터는 세 개의 극장을 보유하고 있습니다. **디자이너는 건물의 방음벽으로 상을 받았습니다. 이 벽은 다른 극장과 근처의 기차에서 나는 소리를 흡수하는 고무 소재로 되어 있습니다.** 그뿐만 아니라, 실내 장식도 훌륭합니다. 사진을 보고, 곧 있을 공연도 둘러보시면서, 방문 계획을 세우기를 원하시면, 극장 웹사이트를 방문하세요. **하지만 주의하세요. 많은 공연이 이미 매진되었습니다!**

어휘 widespread 폭넓은, 광범위한 attention 관심, 주의
state-of-the-art 최신식의, 최첨단의 win an award 상을 받다
insulated 방음 처리된, 단열 처리된 absorb 흡수하다
on top of ~뿐만 아니라, ~ 외에도 decoration 장식(물)
magnificent 훌륭한, 장엄한 browse 둘러보다
upcoming 곧 있을, 다가오는 sold out 매진된

89 According to the speaker, what will be opening soon?
(A) A restaurant
(B) A sports arena
(C) A performing arts center
(D) A train station

화자에 따르면, 무엇이 곧 개장할 것인가?
(A) 레스토랑
(B) 스포츠 경기장
(C) 공연 예술 센터
(D) 기차역

해설 세부 사항 관련 – 곧 개장할 것
화자가 초반부에 내일 밤에 있을 스튜어트 공연 예술 센터의 개장이 폭넓은 관심을 끌고 있다(~ the opening of the Stewart Performing Arts Center tomorrow night has attracted widespread attention)고 했으므로 정답은 (C)이다.

Paraphrasing
담화의 tomorrow night → 질문의 soon

90 Why did the building's designer win an award?
(A) For using solar power
(B) For creating a rooftop garden
(C) For installing a moving light display
(D) For employing sound-absorbing walls

건물 디자이너는 왜 상을 받았는가?
(A) 태양열 에너지를 이용했기 때문에
(B) 옥상 정원을 만들었기 때문에
(C) 움직이는 조명 디스플레이를 설치했기 때문에
(D) 소리를 흡수하는 벽을 이용했기 때문에

어휘 solar power 태양열 에너지 employ 이용하다

해설 세부 사항 관련 – 건물 디자이너가 상을 받은 이유
화자가 중반부에 디자이너가 건물의 방음벽으로 상을 받았다며, 이 벽이 소리를 흡수하는 고무 소재로 되어 있다(The designer won an award for the building's insulated walls. They have rubber material that absorbs sound ~)고 했으므로 정답은 (D)이다.

91 What does the speaker emphasize about upcoming events?
(A) Many of them are sold out.
(B) Some of them will be affected by the weather.
(C) Public transportation will be free.
(D) Discounts are available for large groups.

화자는 곧 있을 행사들과 관련해 무엇을 강조하는가?
(A) 그중 많은 것이 매진되었다.
(B) 일부는 날씨의 영향을 받을 것이다.
(C) 대중교통이 무료일 것이다.
(D) 대규모 단체는 할인을 받을 것이다.

해설 세부 사항 관련 – 곧 있을 행사들과 관련해 강조하는 것
화자가 후반부에 주의하라며, 많은 공연이 이미 매진되었다(We warn you, though—many shows are already sold out!)고 했으므로 정답은 (A)이다.

Paraphrasing
담화의 warn → 질문의 emphasize

92-94 팟캐스트

W-Am Regular listeners of the *Going Electric* podcast may be familiar with today's guest because she was on the podcast last year. **92Dr. Mona Alamri is a leading transportation engineer. 93In today's episode, she'll be talking about electric ships that can operate with zero emissions.** These high-speed ships may completely change the way people and goods are moved along the world's coastlines. But, before I welcome Dr. Alamri, **94please note there is a change to next month's schedule**—most notably, I'll be on vacation for three weeks.

〈고잉 일렉트릭〉의 애청자들은 오늘 초대 손님이 익숙하실 수도 있는데, 작년에 우리 팟캐스트에 나오셨기 때문입니다. **모나 알라미 박사님은 손꼽히는 교통 공학자입니다. 오늘 방송에서는 배출물이 전혀 없이 운행할 수 있는 전기 선박에 관해 이야기해 주실 예정입니다.** 이 고속 선박은 사람과 상품이 세계의 해안선을 따라 수송되는 방식을 완전히 바꿀 수 있습니다. 하지만 알라미 박사님을 환영하기 전에, **다음 달 일정에 변동이 있다는 점에 유의하시기 바랍니다.** 가장 주목할 만한 것은, 제가 3주 동안 휴가를 간다는 점입니다.

어휘 regular 단골의, 주기적인 be familiar with ~에 익숙하다 leading 손꼽히는, 선도적인 episode 1회 방송분, 에피소드 operate 운행하다, 가동되다 emission 배출(물) completely 완전히 notably 주목할 만하게, 현저히, 특히

92 Who is Mona Alamri?
(A) A local official
(B) A ship captain
(C) A marine scientist
(D) An engineer

모나 알라미는 누구인가?
(A) 지역 공무원
(B) 선장
(C) 해양 과학자
(D) 공학자

해설 세부 사항 관련 - 모나 알라미의 직업
화자가 초반부에 모나 알라미 박사가 손꼽히는 교통 공학자(Dr. Mona Alamri is a leading transportation engineer)라고 했으므로 정답은 (D)이다.

93 What is the focus of today's podcast episode?
(A) Coastal mapping
(B) Offshore wind farms
(C) Electric ships
(D) Bridge construction

오늘 팟캐스트 방송의 초점은 무엇인가?
(A) 해안 지도 제작
(B) 연안 지역 풍력 발전소
(C) 전기 선박
(D) 다리 건설

어휘 mapping 지도 제작 offshore 연안 지역의 wind farm 풍력 발전소

해설 전체 내용 관련 - 팟캐스트 방송의 초점
화자가 중반부에 오늘 방송에서는 모나 알라미 박사가 전기 선박에 관해 이야기해 줄 것(In today's episode, she'll be talking about electric ships ~)이라고 했으므로 정답은 (C)이다.

94 What does the speaker alert the listeners to?
(A) A schedule change
(B) A volunteer opportunity
(C) An updated Web site
(D) A project start date

화자는 청자들에게 무엇에 대해 주의를 주는가?
(A) 일정 변경
(B) 자원봉사 기회
(C) 업데이트된 웹사이트
(D) 프로젝트 시작 날짜

어휘 alert 주의를 주다 volunteer 자원봉사(자)

해설 세부 사항 관련 - 화자가 주의를 주는 것
화자가 후반부에 다음 달 일정에 변동이 있다는 점에 유의하라(~ please note there is a change to next month's schedule ~)고 했으므로 정답은 (A)이다.

Paraphrasing
담화의 note → 질문의 alert

95-97 공지 + 지도

M-Cn Good morning, everyone, and **95welcome to the fifteenth annual Summerhaven Bicycle Race.** **96The profits from this year's race will help our town fix the Grant Park footbridge,** which is in serious need of maintenance. Please take a look at the map to familiarize yourselves with the route the cyclists will be taking. Remember, **97there's a beverage stand located between city hall and the art museum,** so you can stay hydrated while you watch the race.

안녕하세요, 여러분. **제15회 연례 서머헤이븐 자전거 경주 대회에 오신 것을 환영합니다.** 올해 경주 대회의 수익금은 우리 시가 그랜트 파크 보행자 전용 다리를 수리하는 데 도움을 줄 예정인데요. 이곳은 관리를 심각하게 필요로 하는 상태입니다. 자전거 선수들이 이용할 경로를 숙지할 수 있도록 지도를 보시기 바랍니다. 기억하세요. **시청과 미술관 사이에 음료 스탠드가 있으므로,** 경주를 관람하는 동안 수분을 섭취하실 수 있습니다.

어휘 annual 연례적인, 해마다의 profit 수익(금) fix 수리하다 footbridge 보행자 전용 다리 in need of ~을 필요로 하는 familiarize oneself with ~을 숙지하다, ~에 익숙해지다 route 경로, 노선 beverage 음료 located 위치해 있는 stay hydrated 수분을 섭취하다

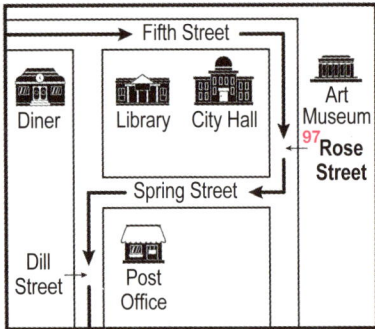

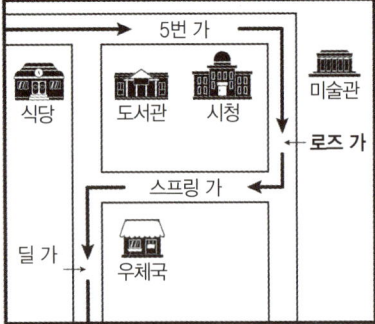

95 Where are the listeners?
(A) At a bicycle race
(B) At a marathon
(C) At a parade
(D) At a festival

청자들은 어디에 있는가?
(A) 자전거 경주 대회
(B) 마라톤 경주
(C) 퍼레이드
(D) 축제

해설 전체 내용 관련 – 청자들이 있는 곳
화자가 초반부에 제15회 연례 서머헤이븐 자전거 경주 대회에 온 것을 환영한다(~ welcome to the fifteenth annual Summerhaven Bicycle Race)고 했으므로 정답은 (A)이다.

96 What will proceeds from the event support?
(A) Creating an athletic field
(B) Renovating a city library
(C) Repairing a bridge
(D) Building a new playground

행사 수익금은 무엇을 지원할 것인가?
(A) 경기장 만들기
(B) 시립 도서관 개조하기
(C) 다리 수리하기
(D) 새 운동장 짓기

어휘 proceeds 수익금 athletic 경기의, 운동의

해설 세부 사항 관련 – 행사 수익금으로 지원하는 일
화자가 초반부에 올해 경주 대회의 수익금은 그랜트 파크 보행자 전용 다리를 수리하는 데 도움을 줄 것(The profits from this year's race will help our town fix the Grant Park footbridge ~)이라고 했으므로 정답은 (C)이다.

Paraphrasing
담화의 fix the Grant Park footbridge
→ 정답의 Repairing a bridge

97 Look at the graphic. On which street does the speaker say the listeners can find a beverage stand?
(A) Fifth Street
(B) Rose Street
(C) Spring Street
(D) Dill Street

시각 정보에 의하면, 화자는 청자들이 어느 거리에서 음료 스탠드를 찾을 수 있다고 말하는가?
(A) 5번 가
(B) 로즈 가
(C) 스프링 가
(D) 딜 가

해설 시각 정보 연계 – 음료 스탠드를 찾을 수 있는 거리
화자가 후반부에 시청과 미술관 사이에 음료 스탠드가 있다(~ there's a beverage stand located between city hall and the art museum ~)고 했는데, 지도에서 미술관과 시청 사이에 있는 거리는 로즈 가(Rose Street)이므로 정답은 (B)이다.

98-100 회의 발췌 + 차트

M-Au In today's meeting, we'll discuss where we are in our software development process for Universal Banking. In-depth user research will help us create **98 a better online banking application. 99 Sarai will start by telling us about her research into Universal Banking's target customers.** What features do they need in a banking app, and how comfortable are they with technology? But before Sarai begins her presentation, **100 let me remind you that as summer begins next week, so do summer hours. You'll be able to stop working at 2:00 o'clock on Friday afternoons,** so we'll be moving our regular meeting to Friday mornings.

오늘 회의에서는 유니버설 뱅킹을 위한 소프트웨어 개발 과정에서 우리가 어느 단계에 있는지 논의하겠습니다. 심층적인 이용자 조사는 **더 나은 온라인 뱅킹 애플리케이션**을 만드는 데 도움이 될 것입니다. **서라이가 유니버설 뱅킹의 목표 고객들에 대해 조사한 것을 이야기하며 시작할 예정입니다.** 고객들은 뱅킹 앱에서 어떤 기능을 필요로 하고, 기술 사용에 얼마나 익숙할까요? 하지만 서라이가 발표를 시작하기 전에, **다음 주부터 여름이 시작되면서 서머 타임도 시작된다는 것을 상기시켜 드립니다. 금요일 오후 2시에 업무를 중단할 수 있으므로,** 정기 회의를 금요일 오전으로 옮길 것입니다.

어휘 development 개발, 발전 in-depth 심층적인, 깊이 있는 target customer 목표 고객 feature 특징, 기능 be comfortable with ~에 대해 편하게 느끼다 remind 상기시키다 analyze 분석하다 population 인구(층) pilot 시험용의, 예비의

Market Research Stage Chart

99 Stage 1	Analyze Target Population
Stage 2	Design Application
Stage 3	Develop Application
Stage 4	Launch Pilot Software

시장 조사 단계 차트

1단계	목표 인구 분석
2단계	애플리케이션 디자인
3단계	애플리케이션 개발
4단계	시험용 소프트웨어 출시

98 What industry is the mobile app intended for?
(A) Entertainment
(B) Travel
(C) Education
(D) Finance

모바일 앱은 어떤 업계를 대상으로 하는가?
(A) 연예
(B) 여행
(C) 교육
(D) 금융

어휘 be intended for ~을 대상으로 하다 finance 금융, 재무

해설 세부 사항 관련 - 모바일 앱이 대상으로 하는 업계

화자가 초반부에 더 나은 온라인 뱅킹 애플리케이션(a better online banking application)을 만드는 일을 언급하고 있으므로 정답은 (D)이다.

Paraphrasing
담화의 online banking → 정답의 Finance

99 Look at the graphic. Which stage of market research will Sarai talk about?
(A) Stage 1
(B) Stage 2
(C) Stage 3
(D) Stage 4

시각 정보에 의하면, 사라이는 시장 조사의 어느 단계에 관해 이야기할 것인가?
(A) 1단계
(B) 2단계
(C) 3단계
(D) 4단계

해설 시각 정보 연계 - 사라이가 이야기할 단계

화자가 중반부에 사라이가 유니버설 뱅킹의 목표 고객들에 대해 조사한 것을 이야기하며 시작하겠다(Sarai will start by telling us about her research into Universal Banking's target customers)고 했는데, 차트에서 목표 인구 분석(Analyze Target Population)은 1단계(Stage 1)이므로 정답은 (A)이다.

Paraphrasing
담화의 research into ~ target customers
→ 시각 자료의 Analyze Target Population

100 What will begin next Friday?
(A) A seasonal work schedule
(B) A business conference
(C) A construction project
(D) A contract negotiation

다음 주 금요일에 무엇이 시작될 것인가?
(A) 계절성 근무 일정
(B) 비즈니스 콘퍼런스
(C) 건설 공사 프로젝트
(D) 계약 협상

어휘 seasonal 계절적인 negotiation 협상, 협의

해설 세부 사항 관련 - 다음 주 금요일에 시작될 것

화자가 후반부에 다음 주부터 여름이 시작되면서 서머 타임도 시작된다며, 금요일 오후 2시에 업무를 중단할 수 있다(~ as summer begins next week, so do summer hours. You'll be able to stop working at 2:00 o'clock on Friday afternoons ~)고 했으므로 정답은 (A)이다.

Paraphrasing
담화의 summer hours → 정답의 A seasonal work schedule

기출 TEST 6

동영상 강의

1 (C)	2 (A)	3 (D)	4 (B)	5 (D)
6 (C)	7 (A)	8 (A)	9 (C)	10 (C)
11 (B)	12 (C)	13 (B)	14 (B)	15 (A)
16 (B)	17 (A)	18 (C)	19 (C)	20 (C)
21 (B)	22 (A)	23 (C)	24 (C)	25 (B)
26 (B)	27 (A)	28 (C)	29 (C)	30 (B)
31 (B)	32 (C)	33 (D)	34 (C)	35 (A)
36 (B)	37 (C)	38 (D)	39 (A)	40 (C)
41 (C)	42 (B)	43 (B)	44 (B)	45 (A)
46 (C)	47 (B)	48 (A)	49 (C)	50 (A)
51 (D)	52 (C)	53 (A)	54 (B)	55 (B)
56 (C)	57 (B)	58 (C)	59 (A)	60 (C)
61 (C)	62 (B)	63 (D)	64 (B)	65 (A)
66 (C)	67 (D)	68 (D)	69 (C)	70 (A)
71 (B)	72 (B)	73 (C)	74 (A)	75 (A)
76 (C)	77 (D)	78 (A)	79 (B)	80 (B)
81 (A)	82 (C)	83 (C)	84 (D)	85 (B)
86 (C)	87 (A)	88 (C)	89 (B)	90 (D)
91 (C)	92 (B)	93 (A)	94 (B)	95 (B)
96 (D)	97 (B)	98 (A)	99 (C)	100 (B)

PART 1

1

M-Cn

(A) A restaurant buffet is filled with food.
(B) Cups are sitting in a sink.
(C) A dining area is empty.
(D) Some candles have been lit.

(A) 레스토랑 뷔페가 음식으로 가득 차 있다.
(B) 컵들이 싱크대에 놓여 있다.
(C) **식사 공간이 비어 있다.**
(D) 양초에 불이 붙여져 있다.

어휘 sit (사물) 놓여 있다   sink 싱크대   lit 불이 붙여진, 불이 켜진

해설 사물/풍경 사진 – 사물 묘사
(A) 사진에 없는 명사를 이용한 오답. 사진에 뷔페(buffet)와 음식(food)의 모습이 보이지 않으므로 오답.
(B) 사진에 없는 명사를 이용한 오답. 사진에 싱크대(a sink)의 모습이 보이지 않으므로 오답.
(C) 정답. 식사 공간(A dining area)이 비어 있는(is empty) 모습이므로 정답.
(D) 사진에 없는 명사를 이용한 오답. 사진에 양초들(Some candles)의 모습이 보이지 않으므로 오답.

2

W-Br

(A) He's facing a machine.
(B) He's lifting up a machine.
(C) He's wiping down a machine.
(D) He's repairing a machine with a tool.

(A) **남자가 기계를 향해 서 있다.**
(B) 남자가 기계를 들어 올리고 있다.
(C) 남자가 기계를 깨끗이 닦고 있다.
(D) 남자가 공구로 기계를 수리하고 있다.

어휘 face 향하다, 마주보다   lift up 들어 올리다
wipe down 깨끗이 닦다   repair 수리하다

해설 1인 등장 사진 – 사람의 동작/상태 묘사
(A) 정답. 남자가 기계를 향해 서 있는(is facing a machine) 모습이므로 정답.
(B) 동사 오답. 남자가 기계를 들어 올리고 있는(is lifting up a machine) 모습이 아니므로 오답.
(C) 동사 오답. 남자가 기계를 깨끗이 닦고 있는(is wiping down a machine) 모습이 아니므로 오답.
(D) 동사 오답. 남자가 공구로 기계를 수리하고 있는(is repairing a machine with a tool) 모습이 아니므로 오답.

3

W-Am

(A) A man is tying his shoe.
(B) A woman is looking through her purse.
(C) They're boarding a bus.
(D) They're walking past a bench.

(A) 남자가 신발끈을 묶고 있다.
(B) 여자가 지갑 속을 살펴보고 있다.
(C) 사람들이 버스에 탑승하고 있다.
(D) **사람들이 벤치를 지나 걸어가고 있다.**

어휘 tie 묶다, 매다   board 탑승하다

해설 2인 이상 등장 사진 – 사람의 동작/상태 묘사
(A) 동사 오답. 남자가 신발끈을 묶고 있는(is tying his shoe) 모습이 아니므로 오답.
(B) 동사 오답. 여자가 지갑 속을 살펴보고 있는(is looking through her purse) 모습이 아니므로 오답.
(C) 동사 오답. 사람들이 버스에 탑승하고 있는(are boarding a bus) 모습이 아니므로 오답.
(D) 정답. 사람들이 벤치를 지나 걸어가고 있는(are walking past a bench) 모습이므로 정답.

4

M-Cn

(A) She's organizing a workstation.
(B) She's holding a water bottle.
(C) She's removing a book from a shelf.
(D) She's reaching for a pen.

(A) 여자가 업무 공간을 정리하고 있다.
(B) 여자가 물병을 들고 있다.
(C) 여자가 선반에서 책을 꺼내고 있다.
(D) 여자가 펜을 향해 손을 뻗고 있다.

어휘 organize 정리하다 workstation 업무 공간, 작업대
remove 꺼내다, 벗다 reach for ~을 향해 손을 뻗다

해설 1인 등장 사진 – 사람의 동작/상태 묘사
(A) 동사 오답. 여자가 업무 공간을 정리하고 있는(is organizing a workstation) 모습이 아니므로 오답.
(B) 정답. 여자가 물병을 들고 있는(is holding a water bottle) 모습이므로 정답.
(C) 동사 오답. 여자가 선반에서 책을 꺼내고 있는(is removing a book from a shelf) 모습이 아니므로 오답.
(D) 동사 오답. 여자가 펜을 향해 손을 뻗고 있는(is reaching for a pen) 모습이 아니므로 오답.

5

W-Am

(A) A woman is lifting a suitcase onto a counter.
(B) A woman is writing on a piece of paper.
(C) A woman is leaning against a glass door.
(D) A woman is talking to a worker at a desk.

(A) 여자가 여행 가방을 카운터 위로 들어 올리고 있다.
(B) 여자가 종이에 글을 쓰고 있다.
(C) 여자가 유리문에 기대고 있다.
(D) 여자가 데스크에 있는 직원에게 말하고 있다.

어휘 suitcase 여행 가방 lean against ~에 기대다

해설 2인 이상 등장 사진 – 사람의 동작/상태 묘사
(A) 동사 오답. 여자가 여행 가방을 카운터 위로 들어 올리고 있는(is lifting a suitcase onto a counter) 모습이 아니므로 오답.
(B) 동사 오답. 여자가 종이에 글을 쓰고 있는(is writing on a piece of paper) 모습이 아니므로 오답.
(C) 동사 오답. 여자가 유리문에 기대고 있는(is leaning against a glass door) 모습이 아니므로 오답.
(D) 정답. 여자가 데스크에 있는 직원에게 말하고 있는(is talking to a worker at a desk) 모습이므로 정답.

6

▶동영상 강의

M-Au

(A) Some paintings have been hung above a sofa.
(B) Some wooden chairs are stacked in a corner.
(C) There are lamps lighting some seating areas.
(D) There are curtains framing a doorway.

(A) 그림들이 소파 위쪽에 걸려 있다.
(B) 목재 의자들이 구석에 쌓여 있다.
(C) 앉는 자리를 비추는 전등들이 있다.
(D) 출입구를 두르고 있는 커튼이 있다.

어휘 stack 쌓다 frame 테를 두르다 doorway 출입구

해설 사물/풍경 사진 – 사물 묘사
(A) 위치 오답. 그림들(Some paintings)이 소파 위쪽에 걸려 있는(have been hung above a sofa) 모습이 아니므로 오답.
(B) 동사 오답. 목재 의자들(Some wooden chairs)이 구석에 쌓여 있는(are stacked in a corner) 모습이 아니므로 오답.
(C) 정답. 앉는 자리를 비추는 전등들(lamps lighting some seating areas)의 모습이 보이므로 정답.
(D) 사진에 없는 명사를 이용한 오답. 사진에 출입구를 두르고 있는 커튼(curtains framing a doorway)의 모습이 보이지 않으므로 오답.

PART 2

7

M-Au / W-Br

How long will the renovations take?

(A) About a month.
(B) Mostly the roof.
(C) I finished that book.

개조 공사가 얼마나 걸릴까요?
(A) 한 달 정도요.
(B) 대체로 지붕이에요.
(C) 저는 그 책을 다 읽었어요.

어휘 renovation 개조, 보수 mostly 대체로, 대부분

해설 개조 공사 기간을 묻는 How long 의문문
(A) 정답. 개조 공사 기간을 묻는 질문에 한 달 정도라고 알려 주고 있으므로 정답.
(B) 연상 단어 오답. 질문의 renovations에서 연상 가능한 roof를 이용한 오답.
(C) 연상 단어 오답. 질문의 renovations에서 연상 가능한 finished를 이용한 오답.

8 W-Am / W-Br

▶ 동영상 강의

What is the factory's inspection process like?
(A) It's quite thorough.
(B) I didn't bring any.
(C) He likes working nights.

그 공장의 점검 과정은 어떤가요?
(A) 상당히 철저합니다.
(B) 저는 아무것도 가져오지 않았어요.
(C) 그는 야간에 근무하는 것을 좋아해요.

어휘 inspection 점검, 검사 process 과정, 절차
thorough 철저한, 꼼꼼한

해설 공장의 점검 과정이 어떤지 묻는 What 의문문
(A) 정답. 공장의 점검 과정이 어떤지 묻는 질문에 상당히 철저하다며 점검 수준이 어느 정도인지 알려 주고 있으므로 정답.
(B) 질문과 상관없는 오답.
(C) 질문과 상관없는 오답. 질문에 3인칭 대명사 He로 지칭할 인물이 언급된 적이 없으므로 오답.

9 W-Am / M-Au

Hasn't our merchandise arrived yet?
(A) Handmade clothing.
(B) I can drive you there.
(C) No, it was just shipped yesterday.

우리 상품이 아직 도착하지 않았나요?
(A) 수제 의류요.
(B) 제가 그곳에 차로 태워다 드릴 수 있어요.
(C) 아니요, 그건 어제 막 발송되었어요.

어휘 merchandise 상품, 물품 clothing 의류, 옷
ship 발송하다, 운송하다

해설 상품의 도착 여부를 확인하는 부정 의문문
(A) 연상 단어 오답. 질문의 merchandise에서 연상 가능한 clothing을 이용한 오답.
(B) 연상 단어 오답. 질문의 arrived에서 연상 가능한 drive를 이용한 오답.
(C) 정답. 상품의 도착 여부를 확인하는 질문에 아니요(No)라고 대답한 뒤, 어제 막 발송되었다며 부정 답변과 일관된 내용을 덧붙이고 있으므로 정답.

10 W-Br / M-Cn

Who's buying beverages for the retreat?
(A) At the café.
(B) I parked the car by the tree.
(C) Carlos and I are.

누가 야유회에 필요한 음료를 구입하나요?
(A) 그 카페에서요.
(B) 저는 그 나무 옆에 자동차를 주차했어요.
(C) 카를로스와 제가요.

어휘 beverage 음료 retreat 야유회, 짧은 여행

해설 음료를 구입할 사람을 묻는 Who 의문문
(A) 질문과 상관없는 오답. Where 의문문에 대한 응답이므로 오답.
(B) 유사 발음 오답. 질문의 retreat과 부분적으로 발음이 유사한 tree를 이용한 오답.
(C) 정답. 음료를 구입할 사람을 묻는 질문에 카를로스와 본인이라고 구체적으로 알려 주고 있으므로 정답.

11 M-Cn / M-Au

Why is the reception at a different location?
(A) Sure, let's go greet the guests.
(B) Because the conference room wasn't big enough.
(C) Yes, I can hear you very well—thank you.

축하 연회는 왜 다른 장소에서 열리는 건가요?
(A) 물론이죠, 가서 손님들을 맞이합시다.
(B) 대회의실이 충분히 크지 않았기 때문에요.
(C) 네, 아주 잘 들려요, 감사합니다.

어휘 reception 축하 연회, 환영회 location 장소, 위치
greet 맞이하다, 환영하다

해설 축하 연회가 다른 장소에서 열리는 이유를 묻는 Why 의문문
(A) Yes/No 불가 오답. Why 의문문에는 Yes/No 응답이 불가능한데, Sure도 일종의 Yes 응답이라고 볼 수 있으므로 오답.
(B) 정답. 축하 연회가 다른 장소에서 열리는 이유를 묻는 질문에 대회의실이 충분히 크지 않았기 때문이라는 이유를 제시하고 있으므로 정답.
(C) Yes/No 불가 오답. Why 의문문에는 Yes/No 응답이 불가능하므로 오답.

12 W-Am / W-Br

Would you like me to process your travel voucher?
(A) I didn't know that.
(B) A much larger convention center.
(C) Yes, if you have time.

여행 상품권을 처리해 드릴까요?
(A) 저는 몰랐어요.
(B) 훨씬 더 큰 컨벤션 센터요.
(C) 네, 시간이 있으시면요.

어휘 process 처리하다 voucher 상품권, 쿠폰

해설 제안/권유 의문문
(A) 질문과 상관없는 오답.
(B) 질문과 상관없는 오답.
(C) 정답. 여행 상품권을 처리해 줄지 묻는 질문에 네(Yes)라고 대답한 뒤, '시간이 있다면'이라는 조건을 덧붙이며 제안을 수락하는 의사를 표현하고 있으므로 정답.

13 M-Au / M-Cn

How far away is Azuma's Dry Cleaning Company?

(A) No, not until I've seen it.
(B) Oh, it's only a few minutes' walk from here.
(C) Five dollars per shirt.

아주마스 드라이 클리닝 회사가 얼마나 멀리 떨어져 있나요?
(A) 아니요, 제가 보기 전까지는요.
(B) 아, 여기서 단 몇 분만 걸어가면 됩니다.
(C) 셔츠당 5달러입니다.

해설 특정 회사와의 거리를 묻는 How far 의문문
(A) Yes/No 불가 오답. How 의문문에는 Yes/No 응답이 불가능하므로 오답.
(B) 정답. 아주마스 드라이 클리닝 회사와의 거리를 묻는 질문에 단 몇 분만 걸으면 된다며 대략적인 이동 시간으로 응답하고 있으므로 정답.
(C) 연상 단어 오답. 질문의 Dry Cleaning에서 연상 가능한 shirt를 이용한 오답.

14 W-Am / M-Au

Do we have the registration forms ready for the students?

(A) The manager's signature.
(B) Yes, I printed them.
(C) We require uniforms.

수강생들에게 필요한 등록 양식이 준비되어 있나요?
(A) 관리자의 서명이요.
(B) 네, 제가 출력했어요.
(C) 우리는 유니폼이 필요해요.

어휘 registration 등록 signature 서명
해설 수강생 등록 양식의 준비 여부를 묻는 조동사(Do) 의문문
(A) 연상 단어 오답. 질문의 registration forms에서 연상 가능한 signature를 이용한 오답.
(B) 정답. 수강생 등록 양식의 준비 여부를 묻는 질문에 네(Yes)라고 대답한 뒤, 자신이 출력했다며 긍정 답변과 일관된 내용을 덧붙이고 있으므로 정답.
(C) 유사 발음 오답. 질문의 forms와 부분적으로 발음이 유사한 uniforms를 이용한 오답.

15 M-Au / W-Am

I could provide you with a copy of the lease.

(A) Great—I need it for my records.
(B) At least another week.
(C) Why don't we offer a discount?

임대차 계약서 사본을 한 부 제공해 드릴 수 있어요.
(A) 잘됐네요, 기록용으로 필요하거든요.
(B) 최소한 일주일 더요.
(C) 할인을 제공하면 어떨까요?

어휘 lease 임대차 계약(서) at least 최소한, 적어도

해설 정보 전달의 평서문
(A) 정답. 임대차 계약서 사본을 한 부 제공해 줄 수 있다는 평서문에 잘됐다(Great)고 대답한 뒤, 기록용으로 필요하다는 이유를 덧붙이고 있으므로 정답.
(B) 유사 발음 오답. 평서문의 lease와 부분적으로 발음이 유사한 least를 이용한 오답.
(C) 평서문과 상관없는 오답.

16 M-Cn / M-Au

How many oil changes are scheduled for this afternoon?

(A) A few replacement pieces.
(B) Right now, there are five.
(C) Can you change the channel?

오늘 오후에 예정된 오일 교체 작업이 몇 건인가요?
(A) 교체 부품 몇 개요.
(B) 지금으로서는, 다섯 건이요.
(C) 채널 좀 바꿔 주시겠어요?

어휘 be scheduled for ~로 예정되다 replacement 교체(품)
해설 오후에 예정된 오일 교체 작업 건수를 묻는 How many 의문문
(A) 연상 단어 오답. 질문의 changes에서 연상 가능한 replacement pieces를 이용한 오답.
(B) 정답. 오후에 예정된 오일 교체 작업 건수를 묻는 질문에 다섯 건이라고 알려 주고 있으므로 정답.
(C) 파생어 오답. 질문의 changes와 파생어 관계인 change를 이용한 오답.

17 M-Cn / W-Br

When was the last time you traveled for business?

(A) About three years ago.
(B) It's the black briefcase.
(C) I have some stamps.

마지막으로 출장을 떠나신 게 언제였죠?
(A) 약 3년 전이요.
(B) 검은색 서류 가방이에요.
(C) 저에게 우표가 좀 있어요.

어휘 briefcase 서류 가방
해설 마지막으로 출장을 떠난 시점을 묻는 When 의문문
(A) 정답. 마지막으로 출장을 떠난 시점을 묻는 질문에 약 3년 전이라고 대략적인 시점으로 응답하고 있으므로 정답.
(B) 연상 단어 오답. 질문의 business에서 연상 가능한 briefcase를 이용한 오답.
(C) 질문과 상관없는 오답.

18 W-Br / M-Au

Should I order the parts online or over the phone?

(A) Just half—thank you.
(B) No, I've never been there.
(C) By phone is best.

부품들을 온라인으로 주문할까요, 아니면 전화로 할까요?
(A) 절반만이요, 감사합니다.
(B) 아니요, 저는 그곳에 가 본 적이 없어요.
(C) 전화로 하는 게 가장 좋아요.

어휘 part 부품   over the phone 전화상으로

해설 부품 주문 방식을 묻는 선택 의문문
(A) 질문과 상관없는 오답. How many 또는 How much 의문문에 대한 응답이므로 오답.
(B) Yes/No 불가 오답. 문장과 문장을 연결하는 경우를 제외하고는 선택 의문문에는 Yes/No 응답이 불가능하므로 오답.
(C) 정답. 부품들을 온라인으로 주문할지 아니면 전화로 할지 묻는 질문에 전화로 하는 게 가장 좋다며 둘 중 하나를 선택해 응답하고 있으므로 정답.

19 W-Am / M-Cn

Where should I pick up my conference badge?

(A) We signed the lease.
(B) About 10,000 units per week.
(C) There are three tables in the lobby.

콘퍼런스 출입증은 어디에서 수령해야 하나요?
(A) 우리는 그 임대차 계약에 서명했어요.
(B) 일주일마다 약 1만 개요.
(C) 로비에 테이블 세 개가 있어요.

어휘 lease 임대차 계약(서)   unit 한 개, 구성 단위

해설 콘퍼런스 출입증 수령 위치를 묻는 Where 의문문
(A) 질문과 상관없는 오답.
(B) 질문과 상관없는 오답. How many 의문문에 대한 응답이므로 오답.
(C) 정답. 콘퍼런스 출입증 수령 위치를 묻는 질문에 로비에 테이블이 세 개 있다며 그곳에서 수령할 수 있음을 우회적으로 알려주고 있으므로 정답.

20 M-Au / W-Am

Isn't the computer network running a bit slow?

(A) To an upgraded service.
(B) Actually, I prefer to walk.
(C) A technician's on the way.

컴퓨터 네트워크가 약간 느리게 작동하고 있지 않나요?
(A) 업그레이드된 서비스로요.
(B) 사실, 저는 걷는 걸 선호해요.
(C) 기술자가 오는 중이에요.

어휘 run 작동하다, 운영하다   technician 기술자

해설 컴퓨터 네트워크가 느리게 작동하고 있는지 확인하는 부정 의문문
(A) 연상 단어 오답. 질문의 computer network에서 연상 가능한 upgraded를 이용한 오답.
(B) 연상 단어 오답. 질문의 running을 달리기로 잘못 이해했을 경우 연상 가능한 walk를 이용한 오답.
(C) 정답. 컴퓨터 네트워크가 느리게 작동하고 있는지 확인하는 질문에 기술자가 오는 중이라며 우회적으로 동의를 표현하고 있으므로 정답.

21 M-Cn / W-Br

How do you like this office space?

(A) An afternoon appointment.
(B) I'd rather have a window.
(C) On page five of the contract.

이 사무 공간 어떠세요?
(A) 오후 예약이요.
(B) 창문이 하나 있으면 좋겠어요.
(C) 계약서 5페이지에요.

어휘 appointment 예약, 약속   contract 계약(서)

해설 사무 공간에 대한 의견을 묻는 How 의문문
(A) 질문과 상관없는 오답.
(B) 정답. 사무 공간에 대한 의견을 묻는 질문에 창문이 하나 있으면 좋겠다는 의견을 제시하고 있으므로 정답.
(C) 질문과 상관없는 오답. Where 의문문에 대한 응답이므로 오답.

22 M-Cn / W-Br

You can use the company van to make your deliveries.

(A) OK, I'll go get the key.
(B) A clothing manufacturer.
(C) It's on Market Street.

회사 밴을 이용해서 배달하시면 됩니다.
(A) 네, 가서 열쇠를 가져올게요.
(B) 의류 제조사요.
(C) 마켓 가에 있어요.

어휘 van 밴, 승합차   manufacturer 제조사

해설 정보 전달의 평서문
(A) 정답. 회사 밴을 이용해서 배달하면 된다는 평서문에 네(OK)라고 대답한 뒤, 가서 열쇠를 가져오겠다며 긍정 답변과 일관된 내용을 덧붙이고 있으므로 정답.
(B) 평서문과 상관없는 오답.
(C) 평서문과 상관없는 오답. Where 의문문에 대한 응답이므로 오답.

23 W-Br / M-Au

Isn't the city council meeting tonight?

(A) Thanks—that would be great.
(B) He's the recently elected mayor.
(C) Did you check their Web site?

시 의회 회의가 오늘 밤에 있지 않나요?
(A) 감사합니다, 그래 주시면 좋겠어요.
(B) 그는 최근에 선출된 시장이에요.
(C) 웹사이트를 확인해 보셨나요?

어휘 council 의회 recently 최근에 elect 선출하다 mayor 시장

해설 시 의회 회의가 오늘 밤에 있는지 확인하는 부정 의문문
(A) 질문과 상관없는 오답. 제안 의문문에 대한 응답이므로 오답.
(B) 질문과 상관없는 오답. 질문에 3인칭 대명사 He로 지칭할 인물이 언급된 적이 없으므로 오답.
(C) 정답. 시 의회 회의가 오늘 밤에 있는지 확인하는 질문에 웹사이트를 확인해 봤는지 되물으며 해당 정보를 확인할 방법을 알려 주고 있으므로 정답.

24 W-Am / M-Au ▶동영상 강의

Could you look at the revised logo tomorrow?
(A) A color printer.
(B) The score was tied.
(C) I have time now.

수정된 로고를 내일 봐 주시겠어요?
(A) 컬러 프린터요.
(B) 점수가 동점이었어요.
(C) 제가 지금 시간이 있어요.

어휘 revise 수정하다, 변경하다 tied 동점인, 무승부인

해설 부탁/요청의 의문문
(A) 연상 단어 오답. 질문의 logo에서 연상 가능한 color를 이용한 오답.
(B) 질문과 상관없는 오답.
(C) 정답. 수정된 로고를 내일 봐 줄 수 있는지 요청하는 질문에 지금 시간이 있다며 지금 바로 봐 주겠다는 뜻을 우회적으로 표현하고 있으므로 정답.

25 W-Am / W-Br

Is the business local or national?
(A) At the community center nearby.
(B) We have stores in every province.
(C) The flight's in two hours.

회사는 지역 업체인가요, 아니면 전국 규모인가요?
(A) 근처 지역 문화 센터에서요.
(B) 저희는 모든 주에 매장을 보유하고 있어요.
(C) 그 항공편은 두 시간 후에 있어요.

어휘 local 지역의, 현지의 nearby 근처에 province (행정 구역) 주

해설 사업의 규모를 묻는 선택 의문문
(A) 연상 단어 오답. 질문의 local에서 연상 가능한 community를 이용한 오답.
(B) 정답. 회사가 지역 업체인지 아니면 전국 규모인지 묻는 질문에 모든 주에 매장을 보유하고 있다며 전국적인 규모임을 우회적으로 알려 주고 있으므로 정답.
(C) 질문과 상관없는 오답. When 의문문에 대한 응답이므로 오답.

26 W-Br / M-Au

How do you make sure your products will sell well?
(A) No, I bought it last month.
(B) I conduct market research.
(C) OK, I'll bring it.

제품이 잘 팔리게 하기 위해 어떻게 하시나요?
(A) 아니요, 지난달에 구입했어요.
(B) 시장 조사를 실시합니다.
(C) 좋아요, 제가 가져갈게요.

어휘 make sure 반드시 ~하도록 하다 conduct 실시하다, 수행하다 research 조사, 연구

해설 제품이 잘 팔리게 할 방법을 묻는 How 의문문
(A) Yes/No 불가 오답. How 의문문에는 Yes/No 응답이 불가능하므로 오답.
(B) 정답. 제품이 잘 팔리게 할 방법을 묻는 질문에 시장 조사를 실시한다며 제품 판매를 위한 전략을 제시하고 있으므로 정답.
(C) Yes/No 불가 오답. How 의문문에는 Yes/No 응답이 불가능한데, OK도 일종의 Yes 응답이라고 볼 수 있으므로 오답.

27 M-Cn / W-Br

Who will fill the open manager position?
(A) Interviews will take place next week.
(B) I'd like a refill on my coffee, please.
(C) The desk should be in the corner.

공석인 관리자 직책은 누가 채우게 되나요?
(A) 다음 주에 면접이 진행될 거예요.
(B) 커피 리필 부탁드려요.
(C) 책상이 구석에 있어야 해요.

어휘 fill 채우다, 충원하다 open position 공석 take place 진행되다, 개최되다

해설 공석인 관리자 직책을 맡게 될 사람을 묻는 Who 의문문
(A) 정답. 공석인 관리자 직책을 맡게 될 사람을 묻는 질문에 다음 주에 면접이 진행될 것이라며 아직 정해지지 않았음을 우회적으로 알려 주고 있으므로 정답.
(B) 파생어 오답. 질문의 fill과 파생어 관계인 refill을 이용한 오답.
(C) 연상 단어 오답. 질문의 position을 위치로 잘못 이해했을 경우 연상 가능한 in the corner를 이용한 오답.

28 W-Am / W-Br ▶동영상 강의

Where do you want to store the extra brochures?
(A) The price lists for new products.
(B) I think that's right.
(C) There are none left.

여분의 안내 책자를 어디에 보관하고 싶으세요?
(A) 신제품 가격 목록이요.
(B) 그게 맞는 것 같아요.
(C) 남아 있는 게 없어요.

어휘 store 보관하다, 저장하다   extra 추가의, 여분의
brochure 안내 책자

해설 여분의 안내 책자를 보관할 장소를 묻는 Where 의문문
(A) 연상 단어 오답. 질문의 store를 매장으로 잘못 이해했을 경우 연상 가능한 price와 products를 이용한 오답.
(B) 질문과 상관없는 오답.
(C) 정답. 여분의 안내 책자를 보관할 장소를 묻는 질문에 남은 것이 없다며 보관할 게 없음을 우회적으로 알려 주고 있으므로 정답.

29 M-Au / W-Am

The new bottling machine's been installed, hasn't it?
(A) We'll have two packs, please.
(B) No, I didn't drive here.
(C) We're expecting delivery this afternoon.

새로운 병입 기계가 설치되었죠, 그렇지 않나요?
(A) 두 팩 주세요.
(B) 아니요, 저는 운전해서 오지 않았어요.
(C) 오늘 오후에 배송될 것으로 예상하고 있어요.

어휘 bottling 병에 담기   install 설치하다

해설 새 기계의 설치 여부를 확인하는 부가 의문문
(A) 질문과 상관없는 오답. How many 의문문에 대한 응답이므로 오답.
(B) 질문과 상관없는 오답.
(C) 정답. 새 기계의 설치 여부를 확인하는 질문에 오늘 오후에 배송될 것으로 예상하고 있다며 아직 설치되지 않았음을 우회적으로 알려 주고 있으므로 정답.

30 W-Am / M-Cn

Shouldn't we update our security protocol?
(A) About an hour.
(B) We have a good plan in place.
(C) No, it wasn't.

우리 보안 규정을 업데이트해야 하지 않나요?
(A) 약 한 시간이요.
(B) 좋은 계획이 준비되어 있어요.
(C) 아니요, 그렇지 않았어요.

어휘 protocol 규정, 규약   in place 준비가 되어 있는

해설 보안 규정 업데이트 필요 여부를 확인하는 부정 의문문
(A) 질문과 상관없는 오답. How long 의문문에 대한 응답이므로 오답.
(B) 정답. 보안 규정 업데이트 필요 여부를 확인하는 질문에 좋은 계획이 준비되어 있다며 이미 관련 논의가 진행되고 있음을 우회적으로 나타내고 있으므로 정답.
(C) 질문과 상관없는 오답. Should와 같은 조동사로 묻는 질문에 be동사인 was로 대답할 수 없으므로 오답.

31 M-Au / M-Cn

The engineering team would like to meet sometime today.
(A) Yes, Mr. Tamura is from Kyoto.
(B) Before or after the company-wide meeting?
(C) That was a long baseball game.

엔지니어링 팀이 오늘 중으로 만나고 싶어 해요.
(A) 네, 타무라 씨는 교토 출신이에요.
(B) 전 직원 회의 전에요, 아니면 그 후에요?
(C) 긴 야구 경기였어요.

어휘 company-wide 전 직원을 대상으로 하는, 회사 전체의

해설 정보 전달의 평서문
(A) 평서문과 상관없는 오답.
(B) 정답. 엔지니어링 팀이 오늘 중으로 만나고 싶어 한다는 평서문에 전체 직원 회의 전인지 아니면 그 후인지 관련된 내용을 묻고 있으므로 정답.
(C) 연상 단어 오답. 평서문의 team에서 연상 가능한 baseball game을 이용한 오답.

PART 3

32-34 W-Br / M-Cn

W ³²I saw one of the new commercials about our business on television last week. I guess the advertising campaign has already launched.

M This ad campaign's coming out at a great time for us. It's our busy season—³³people are starting to book our tours for their vacations.

W There's still some money in the budget. We should use it to advertise our most recent package—a guided exploration of the theater district, including tickets to a performance.

M That's a good idea. ³⁴Let me check how much it would cost to add that information to our current commercials.

여 지난주에 우리 회사 새 광고들 중 하나를 텔레비전에서 봤어요. 광고 캠페인이 이미 시작된 것 같아요.

남 광고 캠페인이 우리에게 아주 좋은 시기에 나오고 있어요. 지금은 바쁜 시즌이잖아요. **사람들이 휴가를 위해 우리 투어를 예약하기 시작하고 있거든요.**

여 아직 예산에 돈이 좀 있어요. 이 예산을 사용해서 우리 최신 여행 패키지를 광고해야 겠어요. 공연 티켓을 포함한 가이드 동반 극장가 탐방 말이에요.

남 좋은 아이디어예요. **현재 광고에 그 정보를 추가하는 데 비용이 얼마나 들지 확인해 볼게요.**

어휘 commercial 광고 방송 advertising 광고 (= ad) launch 시작하다, 출시하다 budget 예산 recent 최근의 guided 가이드를 동반한, 가이드가 안내하는 exploration 탐방 district 구역, 지역 performance 공연 current 현재의

32 According to the woman, what happened last week?
(A) A new product was launched.
(B) A new location opened.
(C) An advertising campaign started.
(D) A budget was approved.

여자에 따르면, 지난주에 무슨 일이 있었는가?
(A) 신제품이 출시되었다.
(B) 신규 지점이 개장했다.
(C) 광고 캠페인이 시작되었다.
(D) 예산이 승인되었다.

어휘 location 지점, 위치 approve 승인하다

해설 세부 사항 관련 - 지난주에 있었던 일
여자가 첫 대사에서 지난주에 회사의 새 광고들 중 하나를 텔레비전에서 봤다(I saw one of the new commercials about our business on television last week)며 광고 캠페인이 이미 시작된 것 같다(I guess the advertising campaign has already launched)고 말하고 있으므로 정답은 (C)이다.

Paraphrasing
대화의 has already launched → 정답의 started

33 What industry do the speakers work in?
(A) Finance
(B) Retail
(C) Energy
(D) Tourism

화자들은 어떤 업계에서 일하는가?
(A) 금융
(B) 소매
(C) 에너지
(D) 관광

해설 전체 내용 관련 - 화자들의 근무 업계
남자가 첫 대사에서 사람들이 휴가를 위해 우리 투어를 예약하기 시작하고 있다(~ people are starting to book our tours for their vacations)고 말하는 것으로 보아 화자들은 관광업계에서 일한다는 것을 알 수 있다. 따라서 정답은 (D)이다.

34 What does the man say he will check on?
(A) Transportation
(B) Tickets
(C) Some prices
(D) Some contracts

남자는 무엇을 확인할 것이라고 말하는가?
(A) 교통편
(B) 티켓
(C) 가격
(D) 계약

어휘 transportation 교통(편) contract 계약(서)

해설 세부 사항 관련 - 남자가 확인할 것
남자가 마지막 대사에서 현재 광고에 여자가 말한 정보를 추가하는 데 비용이 얼마나 들지 확인해 보겠다(Let me check how much it would cost to add that information to our current commercials)고 했으므로 정답은 (C)이다.

Paraphrasing
대화의 how much it would cost → 정답의 prices

35-37 W-Am / M-Cn

W Marcel, **35 we've been getting some complaints from our guests when they check out.** Some people think the parking garage fee is included in the room reservation. They don't know they have to pay when they exit.

M Oh. Well, it's written on the confirmation they receive. But **36 I'll start reminding our guests at check-in as well.**

W Great, thank you. Also, **37 remember the landscaping crew is coming by next week to plant some spring flowers by the entrance of the lobby.** It's starting to feel a bit warmer outside.

여 마르셀, **손님들이 체크아웃할 때 불만이 좀 들어오고 있어요.** 몇몇 분들이 주차장 요금이 객실 예약에 포함된다고 생각해요. 출차할 때 결제해야 한다는 점을 모르시네요.

남 아. 그게, 그분들께서 받으시는 확인서에 쓰여 있는데요. 하지만 **체크인할 때도 손님들에게 상기시켜 드리도록 할게요.**

여 좋아요, 고마워요. 그리고, **조경 작업팀이 다음 주에 로비 출입구에 봄꽃을 심으러 올 예정이라는 것을 기억해 주세요.** 밖이 조금씩 따뜻해지기 시작하는 것 같아요.

어휘 complaint 불만, 불평 parking garage 주차장 reservation 예약 exit 나가다 confirmation 확인(서) landscaping 조경 come by 들르다

35 Where do the speakers most likely work?
(A) At a hotel
(B) At a beauty salon
(C) At a gym
(D) At a shopping mall

화자들은 어디에서 일하는 것 같은가?
(A) 호텔
(B) 미용실
(C) 체육관
(D) 쇼핑몰

해설 전체 내용 관련 – 화자들의 근무 장소

여자가 첫 대사에서 손님들이 체크아웃할 때 불만이 좀 들어오고 있다(~ we've been getting some complaints from our guests when they check out)고 했고, 이어 객실 예약을 언급하는 것으로 보아 화자들은 호텔에서 근무한다는 것을 알 수 있다. 따라서 정답은 (A)이다.

36 How does the man plan to address a problem?
(A) By resending a confirmation e-mail
(B) By giving a verbal reminder
(C) By extending hours of operation
(D) By discounting the price of a service

남자는 어떻게 문제를 해결할 계획인가?
(A) 확인 이메일을 재발송함으로써
(B) 구두로 상기시킴으로써
(C) 운영 시간을 연장함으로써
(D) 서비스 가격을 할인함으로써

어휘 address 해결하다, 다루다 verbal 구두의, 말로 된
reminder 상기시키는 것 extend 연장하다, 확장하다

해설 세부 사항 관련 – 남자의 문제 해결 방법

남자가 첫 대사에서 체크인할 때도 손님들에게 상기시켜 주겠다(~ I'll start reminding our guests at check-in as well)고 했으므로 정답은 (B)이다.

> **Paraphrasing**
> 대화의 reminding our guests at check-in
> → 정답의 giving a verbal reminder

37 Why will landscapers come next week?
(A) To install a water fountain
(B) To cut down some tree branches
(C) To plant some flowers
(D) To cut the grass

조경 작업자들은 다음 주에 왜 오는가?
(A) 분수대를 설치하려고
(B) 나뭇가지를 자르려고
(C) 꽃을 심으려고
(D) 잔디를 깎으려고

어휘 install 설치하다 water fountain 분수대, 식수대

해설 세부 사항 관련 – 조경 작업자들이 오는 이유

여자가 두 번째 대사에서 조경 작업팀이 다음 주에 로비 출입구에 봄꽃을 심으러 올 예정이라는 것을 기억하라(~ remember the landscaping crew is coming by next week to plant some spring flowers by the entrance of the lobby)고 했으므로 정답은 (C)이다.

38-40 M-Au / W-Am

M **38 Polina, congratulations on being voted Nurse of the Year for our hospital.** You really deserve the honor!

W Thanks! I'm a little embarrassed by all the attention, though.

M Well, you shouldn't be. After all, your patients and colleagues all felt you should be recognized for your outstanding efforts. Actually, **39 I'm hoping you'll help me update the training materials for new nurses.**

W I'd be happy to help! And by the way, will you be at **40 the awards ceremony next week?** All the hospital's winners will be celebrated.

M Of course! I'm looking forward to it.

남 폴리나, 우리 병원의 올해의 간호사로 선정된 것을 축하해요. 당신은 정말로 이 상을 받을 자격이 있어요!

여 감사합니다! 이 모든 관심이 좀 쑥스럽긴 하네요.

남 글쎄요, 그러지 않으셔도 됩니다. 어쨌든, 환자들과 동료 직원들이 모두 당신이 뛰어난 노력에 대해 인정받아야 한다고 느낀 거잖아요. 실은, 신입 간호사들을 위한 교육 자료 업데이트를 도와주셨으면 해요.

여 기꺼이 도와드릴게요! 그건 그렇고, 다음 주에 있을 시상식에 오실 건가요? 병원의 모든 수상자가 축하받을 거예요.

남 물론이죠! 무척 기대하고 있어요.

어휘 vote 선정하다, 투표하다 deserve 받을 만하다
honor 상, 명예 embarrassed 쑥스러운 attention 관심
patient 환자 recognize 인정하다 outstanding 뛰어난
material 자료, 재료 celebrate 축하하다, 기념하다
look forward to ~을 고대하다

38 What is the woman's job?
(A) School administrator
(B) Reporter
(C) Laboratory technician
(D) Nurse

여자의 직업은 무엇인가?
(A) 학교 행정 직원
(B) 기자
(C) 실험실 기술자
(D) 간호사

해설 전체 내용 관련 – 여자의 직업

남자가 첫 대사에서 여자에게 우리 병원의 올해의 간호사로 선정된 것을 축하한다(Polina, congratulations on being voted Nurse of the Year for our hospital)고 했으므로 정답은 (D)이다.

39 What does the man ask the woman to help with?
(A) Updating training materials
(B) Recording an interview
(C) Ordering some supplies
(D) Designing a Web page

남자는 여자에게 무엇을 도와달라고 요청하는가?
(A) 교육 자료 업데이트하기
(B) 인터뷰 녹화하기
(C) 물품 주문하기
(D) 웹페이지 디자인하기

해설 세부 사항 관련 – 남자의 요청 사항
남자가 두 번째 대사에서 신입 간호사들을 위한 교육 자료 업데이트를 도와주었으면 한다(~ I'm hoping you'll help me update the training materials for new nurses)고 말하고 있으므로 정답은 (A)이다.

40 What will take place next week?
(A) A press conference
(B) An awards ceremony
(C) A facility inspection
(D) A board meeting

다음 주에 무슨 일이 있을 것인가?
(A) 기자 회견
(B) 시상식
(C) 시설 점검
(D) 이사회 회의

어휘 facility 시설　inspection 점검, 검사　board 이사회

해설 세부 사항 관련 – 다음 주에 있을 일
여자가 두 번째 대사에서 다음 주에 있을 시상식(~ the awards ceremony next week)을 언급하고 있으므로 정답은 (B)이다.

41-43 3인 대화　M-Cn / W-Am / M-Au

M1　Hello. **41 I'm looking for a book that's listed in your library's catalog**, but I can't find it on the shelves. Could you help me?

W　**42 Sorry, I'm helping another patron on the phone right now.** Let me get one of my coworkers for you.

M2　Hi. How can I help you?

M1　I'm looking for a book about abstract art called *Night Canvases*.

M2　Oh! We just received several copies of that, but **43 they're still packed in the box.** If you come back tomorrow, they'll be ready to borrow.

남1　안녕하세요. **도서관 카탈로그에 기재되어 있는 책을 한 권 찾고 있는데**, 책꽂이에서 찾을 수 없네요. 좀 도와주시겠어요?

여　**죄송하지만, 제가 지금 전화로 다른 고객님을 도와드리고 있어요**. 제 동료 중 한 명을 불러 드리겠습니다.

남2　안녕하세요. 무엇을 도와드릴까요?

남1　〈나이트 캔버스〉라는 추상 미술에 관한 책을 찾고 있어요.

남2　아! 저희가 막 그 책 여러 권을 받았는데, **아직 상자에 포장되어 있어요**. 내일 다시 오시면, 빌려 가실 준비가 되어 있을 겁니다.

어휘 list 기재하다, 목록에 올리다　patron 고객, 손님　coworker 동료　abstract 추상적인, 관념적인　pack 포장하다, 꾸리다　borrow 빌리다

41 Where most likely are the speakers?
(A) At a café
(B) At a museum
(C) At a public library
(D) At a community center

화자들은 어디에 있는 것 같은가?
(A) 카페
(B) 박물관
(C) 공공 도서관
(D) 지역 문화 센터

해설 전체 내용 관련 – 대화의 장소
첫 번째 남자가 첫 대사에서 여자에게 도서관 카탈로그에 기재되어 있는 책을 찾고 있다(I'm looking for a book that's listed in your library's catalog ~)고 말하고 있으므로 정답은 (C)이다.

42 Why is the woman unable to help?
(A) She is new to the job.
(B) She is busy with another task.
(C) She needs to attend a workshop.
(D) She will be leaving for the day.

여자는 왜 도울 수 없는가?
(A) 그 일은 처음이다.
(B) 다른 업무로 바쁘다.
(C) 워크숍에 참석해야 한다.
(D) 퇴근할 예정이다.

어휘 task 업무, 일　leave for the day 퇴근하다

해설 세부 사항 관련 – 여자가 도울 수 없는 이유
여자가 첫 대사에서 사과의 말과 함께 지금 전화로 다른 고객을 돕고 있다(Sorry, I'm helping another patron on the phone right now)고 했으므로 정답은 (B)이다.

Paraphrasing
대화의 helping another patron on the phone right now
→ 정답의 is busy with another task

43 Why is an item unavailable?
(A) It is sold out.
(B) It has not been unpacked yet.
(C) A shipment has been lost.
(D) A repair has not been made yet.

물품은 왜 이용할 수 없는가?
(A) 품절된 상태이다.
(B) 아직 개봉되지 않았다.
(C) 배송품이 분실되었다.
(D) 아직 수리가 완료되지 않았다.

어휘 unavailable 이용할 수 없는 sold out 품절된, 매진된 unpack 꺼내다, 풀다 shipment 배송(품) repair 수리

해설 세부 사항 관련 – 물품을 이용할 수 없는 이유
두 번째 남자가 마지막 대사에서 첫 번째 남자가 언급하는 책과 관련해 아직 상자에 포장되어 있다(~ they're still packed in the box)고 했으므로 정답은 (B)이다.

Paraphrasing
대화의 are still packed in the box
→ 정답의 has not been unpacked yet

44-46 M-Au / W-Br

M Silvia, I just heard the city mayor will hold a press conference this afternoon. **44 Can you cover it?** I'll be at the opening of the new train station.

W **44 OK, I'll get a camera crew together right away.** I hope the mayor will provide details about **45 the proposal to build an offshore wind farm.**

M Yes, that's what I heard he'll discuss. There's a lot of interest in wind energy, so this will likely be the lead story on tonight's news.

W Perfect. **46 I'm going to ask the mayor about funding for the project.** The city residents will want to know where the finances will come from.

남 실비아, 시장님께서 오늘 오후에 기자 회견을 개최할 거라는 얘기를 방금 들었어요. **취재해 주실 수 있을까요?** 저는 새 기차역 개장식에 가 있을 거예요.

여 **네, 지금 바로 카메라팀을 소집하겠습니다.** 시장님께서 **해상 풍력 발전소 건설 제안**에 대해 자세히 설명해 주시면 좋겠네요.

남 네, 그 얘기를 하실 거라고 들었어요. 풍력 에너지에 대한 관심이 많다 보니, 아마도 이 내용이 오늘 밤 뉴스의 톱뉴스가 될 것 같아요.

여 좋아요. **시장님께 프로젝트에 필요한 자금 조달에 관련해서 질문하려고요.** 주민들도 그 자금이 어디에서 나올지 알고 싶어할 거예요.

어휘 mayor 시장 cover 취재하다, 다루다 proposal 제안 offshore wind farm 해상 풍력 발전소 lead story 톱뉴스 funding 자금 (조달) resident 주민 finance 자금, 재원

44 Who most likely are the speakers?
(A) Repair technicians
(B) News reporters
(C) Business owners
(D) Construction engineers

화자들은 누구인 것 같은가?
(A) 수리 기사
(B) 뉴스 기자
(C) 업체 소유주
(D) 건설 기술자

해설 전체 내용 관련 – 화자들의 직업
남자가 첫 대사에서 여자에게 취재해 줄 수 있는지(Can you cover it?) 요청하자 여자가 카메라팀을 소집하겠다(OK, I'll get a camera crew together right away)며 수락했으므로 정답은 (B)이다.

45 What project is being proposed?
(A) A wind farm
(B) A road expansion
(C) A tourism initiative
(D) A building expansion

어떤 프로젝트가 제안되고 있는가?
(A) 풍력 발전소
(B) 도로 확장
(C) 관광 산업 계획
(D) 건물 확장

어휘 expansion 확장, 확대 initiative 계획, 주도권

해설 세부 사항 관련 – 제안되고 있는 프로젝트
여자가 첫 대사에서 해상 풍력 발전소 건설 제안(the proposal to build an offshore wind farm)을 언급했으므로 정답은 (A)이다.

46 What does the woman plan to inquire about?
(A) Architectural specifications
(B) Staffing arrangements
(C) A funding source
(D) A project timeline

여자는 무엇에 대해 물어볼 계획인가?
(A) 건축 사양
(B) 인력 운용 방식
(C) 자금 출처
(D) 프로젝트 진행 일정

어휘 inquire 물어보다, 알아보다 architectural 건축학적인 specifications 사양 staffing 직원 구성, 직원 채용 arrangement (처리) 방식, 배치 source 출처, 공급원

해설 세부 사항 관련 – 여자가 물어보려는 것
여자가 마지막 대사에서 시장님께 프로젝트에 필요한 자금 조달에 관련해 질문할 것(I'm going to ask the mayor about funding for the project)이라고 했으므로 정답은 (C)이다.

Paraphrasing
대화의 where the finances will come from
→ 정답의 A funding source

47-49 W-Br / M-Cn

W ⁴⁷**Koji, you weren't at the team meeting this morning. Is everything OK?**

M ⁴⁷**I had to take my car to the mechanic for repairs.** What did I miss?

W Well, ⁴⁸**we received some good news. Our firm is planning to hire more accountants!**

M That's great! We've been busier than ever since we started working with True Valley Industries.

W Yes. By the way, ⁴⁹**there's an article on our Web site about the founder of True Valley. I'd suggest reading it.**

M ⁴⁹**I'll be sure to check it out.**

여 코지, 오늘 아침 팀 회의에 오지 않으셨던데요. 괜찮으신 건가요?

남 수리를 위해 정비소에 차를 맡겨야 했어요. 제가 뭘 놓쳤나요?

여 그게, 좋은 소식을 좀 들었어요. 우리 회사가 회계사를 더 고용할 계획을 세우고 있어요!

남 잘됐네요! 트루 밸리 인더스트리 사와 협업하기 시작한 이후로 그 어느 때보다 더 바빴잖아요.

여 맞아요. 그건 그렇고, 우리 웹사이트에 트루 밸리 사 설립자에 관한 기사가 하나 있어요. 읽어 보시기를 추천해요.

남 꼭 확인해 볼게요.

어휘 mechanic 정비사 accountant 회계사 founder 설립자, 창립자

47 Why did the man miss a meeting?
(A) His train was late.
(B) His car was being repaired.
(C) He had a medical appointment.
(D) He was meeting with some clients.

남자는 왜 회의를 놓쳤는가?
(A) 기차가 늦었다.
(B) 자동차가 수리되고 있었다.
(C) 병원 예약이 있었다.
(D) 고객들을 만나고 있었다.

어휘 appointment 예약, 약속

해설 세부 사항 관련 – 남자가 회의를 놓친 이유
여자가 첫 대사에서 남자에게 오늘 아침 팀 회의에 오지 않는데 괜찮은지(Koji, you weren't at the team meeting this morning. Is everything OK?) 묻자, 남자가 수리를 위해 정비소에 차를 맡겨야 했다(I had to take my car to the mechanic for repairs)고 했으므로 정답은 (B)이다.

Paraphrasing
대화의 weren't at the team meeting
→ 질문의 miss a meeting
대화의 had to take my car to the mechanic for repairs
→ 정답의 His car was being repaired

48 What good news does the woman mention?
(A) More employees will be hired.
(B) A facility will be remodeled.
(C) Some equipment will be upgraded.
(D) A permit has been approved.

여자는 어떤 좋은 소식을 언급하는가?
(A) 직원이 더 고용될 것이다.
(B) 시설이 개조될 것이다.
(C) 장비가 업그레이드될 것이다.
(D) 허가증이 승인되었다.

어휘 remodel 개조하다 equipment 장비 permit 허가증 approve 승인하다

해설 세부 사항 관련 – 여자가 언급하는 좋은 소식
여자가 두 번째 대사에서 좋은 소식을 들었다(we received some good news)며 회사가 회계사를 더 고용할 계획을 세우고 있다(Our firm is planning to hire more accountants!)고 말하고 있으므로 정답은 (A)이다.

Paraphrasing
대화의 is planning to hire more accountants
→ 정답의 More employees will be hired

49 What does the man say he will do?
(A) Speak to a manager
(B) Present at a conference
(C) Read an article
(D) Sign up for a training course

남자는 무엇을 할 것이라고 말하는가?
(A) 매니저와 이야기하기
(B) 콘퍼런스에서 발표하기
(C) 기사 읽어 보기
(D) 교육 과정에 등록하기

어휘 present 발표하다 sign up for ~에 등록하다, ~을 신청하다

해설 세부 사항 관련 – 남자가 할 일
여자가 세 번째 대사에서 웹사이트에 있는 기사를 언급하며 읽어 보기를 추천한다(there's an article on our Web site about the founder of True Valley. I'd suggest reading it)고 하자, 남자가 꼭 확인해 보겠다(I'll be sure to check it out)고 했으므로 정답은 (C)이다.

50-52 3인 대화 W-Am / M-Cn / W-Br

W1 **⁵⁰Let's discuss the upcoming retreat for the architects at our firm.** How's the planning going, Hongtai and Raya?

M Well, the Evans Nature Reserve said they can organize a two-day expedition for us.

W2 Yes, ⁵¹**they're even offering a wildlife photography workshop on the second day. I'm excited about that.**

W1 ⁵¹**Oh, that is exciting!** Do you know if we'll be able to camp in the reserve overnight?

M Yes, that's an option. But ⁵²**I don't know if all our staff have tents and camping equipment. I'm sure we can rent enough for everybody, though. Let me look into it.**

여1 곧 있을 우리 회사 건축가들을 위한 야유회 얘기를 해 봅시다. 준비가 어떻게 되어 가고 있나요, 홍타이, 그리고 라야?

남 음, 에반스 자연 보호 구역에서 이틀 일정의 탐사를 준비해 줄 수 있다고 했어요.

여2 네, 심지어 둘째 날에는 야생 동물 사진 촬영 워크숍도 제공한대요. 저는 그게 기대돼요.

여1 아, 흥미롭겠네요! 우리가 보호 구역에서 야간에 캠핑을 할 수 있을지도 아시나요?

남 네, 그건 선택 사항이에요. 그런데 전 직원이 텐트와 캠핑용 장비를 갖고 있는지는 잘 모르겠어요. 그래도 모두가 사용할 만큼 충분히 대여할 수 있을 거예요. 제가 알아볼게요.

어휘 upcoming 곧 있을, 다가오는 retreat 야유회, 수련회 architect 건축가 nature reserve 자연 보호 구역 organize 준비하다, 조직하다 expedition 탐사, 탐험 wildlife 야생 동물 photography 사진 촬영, 사진술 overnight 야간에 rent 대여하다

50 What are the speakers planning?
(A) A company retreat
(B) An industry conference
(C) A retirement party
(D) A grand opening celebration

화자들은 무엇을 계획하고 있는가?
(A) 회사 야유회
(B) 업계 컨퍼런스
(C) 은퇴 기념 파티
(D) 개업식 행사

어휘 retirement 은퇴, 퇴직 celebration 기념 행사

해설 전체 내용 관련 – 화자들이 계획하고 있는 것
첫 번째 여자가 첫 대사에서 곧 있을 우리 회사 건축가들을 위한 야유회 얘기를 해 보자(Let's discuss the upcoming retreat for the architects at our firm)고 제안한 후, 야유회 준비에 관한 대화를 이어 나가고 있으므로 정답은 (A)이다.

51 What are the women excited about?
(A) Traveling to a new city
(B) Giving a product demonstration
(C) Meeting a guest speaker
(D) Attending a workshop

여자들은 무엇을 기대하고 있는가?
(A) 새로운 도시로 여행가기
(B) 제품 시연하기
(C) 초청 연사 만나기
(D) 워크숍 참석하기

어휘 demonstration 시연, 시범

해설 세부 사항 관련 – 여자들이 기대하는 것
두 번째 여자가 첫 대사에서 야생 동물 촬영 워크숍(~ a wildlife photography workshop ~)을 언급하며 기대된다(I'm excited about that)고 하자, 첫 번째 여자가 흥미롭겠다(Oh, that is exciting!)고 동조했으므로 정답은 (D)이다.

52 What will the man research?
(A) Driving directions
(B) Weather conditions
(C) Equipment rentals
(D) Dining options

남자는 무엇을 조사할 것인가?
(A) 운전 경로
(B) 기상 조건
(C) 장비 대여
(D) 식사 옵션

어휘 directions 경로 정보, 길 안내 정보 rental 대여 dining 식사

해설 세부 사항 관련 – 남자가 조사할 것
남자가 마지막 대사에서 전 직원이 텐트와 캠핑용 장비를 갖고 있는지는 모르겠다(I don't know if all our staff have tents and camping equipment)고 말한 뒤, 그래도 모두가 사용할 만큼 충분히 대여할 수 있을 것이라며 알아보겠다(I'm sure we can rent enough for everybody, though. Let me look into it)고 했으므로 정답은 (C)이다.

53-55 M-Au / W-Am ▶ 동영상 강의

M Hi, Ms. Espinoza. This is Malik calling from ACC Internet Providers. ⁵³**I'm here at your residence at 88 Glassbury Avenue to set up your Internet.**

W Oh! I'm sorry, but ⁵⁴**I'm still on my way home from work.** There's a lot of traffic right now.

M I see. Well, ⁵⁵**my next client's house isn't too far away. I could be back in about an hour. Does that sound OK?**

W ⁵⁵**Yes, that'd be great.** Thank you so much.

남 안녕하세요, 에스피노자 씨. ACC 인터넷 공급회사의 말릭입니다. 인터넷 설치를 위해 글래스버리 애비뉴 88번지에 있는 댁에 와 있습니다.
여 아! 죄송하지만, 제가 아직 퇴근해서 집으로 가는 중이에요. 지금 교통량이 많네요.
남 알겠습니다. 음, 제 다음 고객님 댁이 그렇게 많이 멀지 않은데요. 약 1시간 후에 돌아올 수 있을 거예요. 그렇게 해도 괜찮을까요?
여 네, 그렇게 해 주시면 좋겠네요. 정말 감사합니다.

어휘 residence 거주지, 주택 set up 설치하다, 준비하다
traffic 교통(량), 차량들

53 Who most likely is the man?
(A) A service technician
(B) A salesperson
(C) A delivery driver
(D) A real estate agent

남자는 누구인 것 같은가?
(A) 서비스 기사
(B) 영업 직원
(C) 배송 기사
(D) 부동산 중개업자

해설 전체 내용 관련 – 남자의 직업
남자가 첫 번째 대사에서 인터넷을 설치하기 위해 여자의 집에 와 있다(I'm here at your residence at ~ to set up your Internet)고 했으므로 정답은 (A)이다.

54 Why does the woman say, "There's a lot of traffic right now"?
(A) To request time off work
(B) To explain a delay
(C) To disagree with a plan
(D) To recommend another route

여자는 왜 "지금 교통량이 많네요"라고 말하는가?
(A) 휴무를 요청하려고
(B) 지연에 대해 설명하려고
(C) 계획에 반대하려고
(D) 다른 경로를 추천하려고

어휘 time off work 휴무, 휴가 delay 지연, 지체
disagree 반대하다 route 경로, 노선

해설 화자의 의도 파악 – 지금 교통량이 많다는 말의 의도
여자가 첫 대사에서 아직 퇴근해서 집으로 가는 중(~ I'm still on my way home from work)이라고 말한 뒤 인용문을 언급하고 있으므로, 늦게 도착하는 이유를 설명하려는 의도임을 알 수 있다. 따라서 정답은 (B)이다.

55 What will the man most likely do next?
(A) Listen to a news report
(B) Go to another client's home
(C) Cancel an Internet subscription
(D) Consult a handbook

남자는 다음에 무엇을 할 것 같은가?
(A) 뉴스 보도 청취하기
(B) 다른 고객의 집으로 가기
(C) 인터넷 서비스 가입 취소하기
(D) 안내서 참고하기

어휘 subscription 가입, 구독 consult 참고하다, 상의하다
handbook 안내서

해설 세부 사항 관련 – 남자가 다음에 할 일
남자가 두 번째 대사에서 다음 고객의 집이 많이 멀지 않아서 약 1시간 후에 돌아올 수 있을 거라며 그렇게 해도 괜찮을지(~ my next client's house isn't too far away. I could be back in about an hour. Does that sound OK?) 묻자 여자도 동의하고(Yes, that'd be great) 있으므로 정답은 (B)이다.

Paraphrasing
대화의 my next client's house
→ 정답의 another client's home

56-58 W-Am / M-Cn

W **56 Klaus, you were on the research team that went to the Arctic last month, right?** For the new project?
M **56 Yes.** I'll be going again next month. Are you joining?
W Yeah— **57 Sabine can't make it, so the project coordinator asked me to take her place.**
M Great, but prepare for the freezing temperatures! I'd recommend getting a heated jacket. The one I have is battery-operated, and there are heating elements inside the fabric. **58 I'll send you a link to the online store.** The jacket didn't cost too much.

여 클라우스, 지난달에 북극에 갔던 연구팀에 계셨죠, 그렇죠? 새로운 프로젝트 때문에요?
남 네. 다음 달에 다시 갈 예정이에요. 합류하시는 건가요?
여 네, 사빈이 갈 수 없게 돼서, 그 프로젝트 담당자가 저에게 대신해 달라고 요청했어요.
남 잘됐네요, 하지만 아주 추운 날씨에 대비하셔야 합니다! 저는 발열 재킷을 추천해요. 제가 갖고 있는 건 배터리로 작동하고, 옷 안에 발열체가 들어 있거든요. **온라인 매장으로 연결되는 링크를 보내 드릴게요.** 그 자켓이 아주 비싸지는 않았어요.

어휘 the Arctic 북극 coordinator 담당자, 조정자
freezing 아주 추운, 영하의 temperature 기온, 온도
heated 발열 처리된 battery-operated 배터리로 작동하는
heating elements 발열체 fabric 직물, 천

56 What did the man do last month?
(A) He managed a trade show booth.
(B) He attended a company picnic.
(C) He participated in a research project.
(D) He met with overseas clients.

남자는 지난달에 무엇을 했는가?
(A) 무역 박람회 부스를 관리했다.
(B) 회사 야유회에 참석했다.
(C) 연구 프로젝트에 참여했다.
(D) 해외 고객들과 만났다.

어휘 overseas 해외의

해설 세부 사항 관련 – 남자가 지난달에 한 일
여자가 첫 대사에서 남자에게 지난달에 북극에 갔던 연구팀에 속해 있었던 게 맞는지(Klaus, you were on the research team that went to the Arctic last month, right?) 묻자, 남자가 그렇다(Yes)고 대답했으므로 정답은 (C)이다.

Paraphrasing
대화의 were on the research team
→ 정답의 participated in a research project

57 Why will the woman be joining the man next month?
(A) Her job title has changed.
(B) Her colleague is unavailable.
(C) She has more experience than the man.
(D) She will be needed to translate documents.

여자는 왜 다음 달에 남자와 합류하는가?
(A) 직책이 변경되었다.
(B) 동료 직원이 참여할 수 없다.
(C) 남자보다 더 많은 경험을 보유하고 있다.
(D) 문서를 번역할 필요가 있을 것이다.

어휘 colleague 동료 (직원) unavailable 시간이 안 되는
translate 번역하다

해설 세부 사항 관련 – 여자가 다음 달에 합류하는 이유
여자가 두 번째 대사에서 사빈이 갈 수 없게 되어 그 프로젝트 담당자가 자신에게 대신해 달라고 요청했다(Sabine can't make it, so the project coordinator asked me to take her place)고 말하는 것으로 보아 동료 직원이 가지 못해 대신 참여하게 되었음을 알 수 있으므로 정답은 (B)이다.

Paraphrasing
대화의 Sabine can't make it
→ 정답의 Her colleague is unavailable.

58 What will the man send the woman a link to?
(A) An itinerary
(B) A magazine article
(C) An online store
(D) A list of hotels

남자는 여자에게 무엇으로 연결되는 링크를 보낼 것인가?
(A) 일정표
(B) 잡지 기사
(C) 온라인 매장
(D) 호텔 목록

해설 세부 사항 관련 – 남자가 보내는 링크가 연결되는 것
남자가 마지막 대사에서 온라인 매장으로 연결되는 링크를 보내 주겠다(I'll send you a link to the online store)고 했으므로 정답은 (C)이다.

59-61 W-Br / M-Cn

W We just got a rush order from Great Fitness. **59 They need T-shirts with their business name and logo printed on the front—1,000, to be exact.**

M That's an unusually large order.

W We're definitely going to need some employees to work overtime on it.

M Hmm, I don't know how easy that's going to be. It's the summer, and a lot of employees were hoping to take time off.

W Well, OK. **60 We could offer them an additional day off next month.**

M **61 I'm still worried about the three other orders we need to complete this week.**

W I know, but Great Fitness orders from us all the time.

여 방금 그레이트 피트니스로부터 급한 주문을 받았어요. **업체명과 로고가 전면에 인쇄된 티셔츠가 필요하대요. 정확히 1,000 장이요.**

남 평소와 달리 많은 주문량이네요.

여 이 건으로 초과 근무할 직원들이 반드시 필요하겠어요.

남 흠, 그게 얼마나 쉬울지는 모르겠어요. 여름이라, 많은 직원들이 휴가를 가고 싶어 해요.

여 음, 알겠어요. **다음 달에 추가 휴무를 제공할 수 있을 것 같아요.**

남 **저는 우리가 이번 주에 완료해야 하는 나머지 세 건의 주문도 여전히 걱정이에요.**

여 알아요, 하지만 그레이트 피트니스는 항상 우리에게 주문하는 곳이잖아요.

> **어휘** rush 급한 to be exact 정확히 unusually 평소와 달리 definitely 꼭, 분명히 additional 추가의 day off 휴무일 complete 완료하다 all the time 항상

59 What type of product are the speakers discussing?
(A) T-shirts
(B) Stickers
(C) Water bottles
(D) Tote bags

화자들은 어떤 종류의 제품에 대해 이야기하는가?
(A) 티셔츠
(B) 스티커
(C) 물병
(D) 토트백

해설 전체 내용 관련 – 화자들이 논의 중인 제품
여자가 첫 대사에서 업체명과 로고가 전면에 인쇄된 티셔츠가 필요하다(They need T-shirts with their business name and logo printed on the front ~)고 했으므로 정답은 (A)이다.

60 What does the woman propose offering to some employees?
(A) A gym membership
(B) A restaurant voucher
(C) A salary bonus
(D) An extra vacation day

여자는 직원들에게 무엇을 제공하자고 제안하는가?
(A) 체육관 회원권
(B) 레스토랑 쿠폰
(C) 보너스 급여
(D) 추가 휴무일

어휘 voucher 쿠폰, 상품권

해설 세부 사항 관련 – 여자가 제공하자고 제안하는 것
여자가 세 번째 대사에서 다음 달에 추가 휴무를 제공할 수 있을 것(We could offer them an additional day off next month)이라고 말하고 있으므로 정답은 (D)이다.

Paraphrasing
대화의 an additional day off
→ 정답의 An extra vacation day

61 What does the woman mean when she says, "Great Fitness orders from us all the time"?
(A) An invoice contains an error.
(B) More staff should be hired.
(C) Great Fitness's order is the priority.
(D) Great Fitness has complained about a delivery.

여자가 "그레이트 피트니스는 항상 우리에게 주문하는 곳이잖아요"라고 말할 때 무엇을 의미하는가?
(A) 거래 내역서에 오류가 있다.
(B) 직원이 더 고용되어야 한다.
(C) 그레이트 피트니스의 주문이 우선이다.
(D) 그레이트 피트니스가 배송과 관련해 불만을 제기했다.

어휘 invoice 거래 내역서 contain 포함하다, 담고 있다 priority 우선 (사항) complain 불만을 제기하다

해설 화자의 의도 파악 – 그레이트 피트니스는 항상 우리에게 주문하는 곳이라는 말의 의도
남자가 마지막 대사에서 이번 주에 완료해야 하는 나머지 세 건의 주문도 여전히 걱정(I'm still worried about the three other orders we need to complete this week)이라고 말하자 여자가 인용문을 언급하고 있다. 이는 그레이트 피트니스가 중요한 거래처이기 때문에 그들의 주문을 우선적으로 처리해야 한다는 것을 강조하려는 말이므로 정답은 (C)이다.

62-64 대화 + 배치도 M-Cn / W-Am

M **62 I'm looking forward to our anniversary banquet**, Shreya. It's hard to believe we've been in business for ten years!

W I know. **63 I was looking through old company photos last night. I found some** from when we had just started and were a team of only three people.

M Wow. **63 Those would be great to use for our slideshow during the welcome speech.**

W I agree. And by the way, since I'll be getting up a few times to make announcements, **64 I'd like to sit at the table closest to the stage.**

M **64 I'll make sure to reserve a seat for you there.**

남 우리 기념일 연회가 무척 기대돼요, 쉬레야. 우리가 10년 동안 영업해 왔다는 게 믿기지가 않네요!

여 맞아요. 어젯밤에 예전 회사 사진들을 훑어보고 있었어요. 우리가 막 시작해서 겨우 세 명짜리 팀이었을 때 찍은 사진들도 몇 장 발견했어요.

남 와우. 그걸 환영사 중에 슬라이드쇼에 사용하면 아주 좋을 것 같아요.

여 동의해요. 그나저나, 제가 발표하러 몇 차례 일어날 예정이라, 무대와 가장 가까운 테이블에 앉았으면 해요.

남 꼭 그쪽에 좌석을 지정해 두겠습니다.

어휘 anniversary 기념일 banquet 연회, 만찬 announcement 발표, 공지 reserve 지정하다, 예약하다

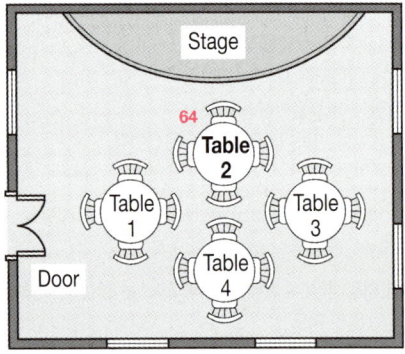

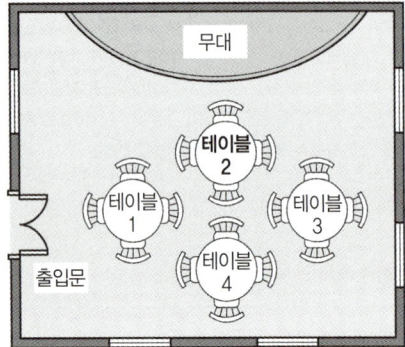

62 Why is the company hosting a banquet?
(A) To open a new facility
(B) To celebrate an anniversary
(C) To announce a merger
(D) To honor a retiring colleague

회사는 왜 연회를 주최하는가?
(A) 새로운 시설을 개장하기 위해
(B) 기념일을 축하하기 위해
(C) 합병을 발표하기 위해
(D) 은퇴하는 동료 직원을 기리기 위해

어휘 host 주최하다 merger 합병, 통합 honor 기리다, 영예를 주다 retire 은퇴하다

해설 전체 내용 관련 – 연회를 주최하는 목적
남자가 첫 대사에서 회사의 기념일 연회가 무척 기대된다(I'm looking forward to our anniversary banquet ~)고 말하는 것으로 보아 연회는 기념일을 축하하기 위한 행사임을 알 수 있으므로 정답은 (B)이다.

63 What does the man say should be included in a presentation?
(A) A summary of a company's profits
(B) A preview of a company's new product
(C) Some survey results
(D) Some photographs

남자는 발표에 무엇이 포함되어야 한다고 말하는가?
(A) 회사 수익 요약본
(B) 회사 신제품 미리보기
(C) 설문 조사 결과
(D) 사진

어휘 summary 요약 profit 수익, 수입 preview 미리보기 survey 설문 조사(지)

해설 세부 사항 관련 – 남자가 발표에 포함되어야 한다고 말하는 것
여자가 첫 대사에서 어젯밤에 예전 회사 사진들을 훑어보다가 몇 장을 발견했다(I was looking through old company photos last night. I found some ~)고 말하자 남자가 그것들을 환영사 중에 슬라이드쇼에 사용하면 아주 좋을 것 같다(Those would be great to use for our slideshow during the welcome speech)고 제안하고 있으므로 정답은 (D)이다.

Paraphrasing
대화의 our slideshow during the welcome speech
→ 질문의 a presentation

64 Look at the graphic. Where will the woman be seated?
(A) Table 1
(B) Table 2
(C) Table 3
(D) Table 4

시각 정보에 의하면, 여자는 어디에 앉을 것인가?
(A) 테이블 1
(B) 테이블 2
(C) 테이블 3
(D) 테이블 4

해설 시각 정보 연계 – 여자가 앉을 곳
여자가 두 번째 대사에서 무대와 가장 가까운 테이블에 앉았으면 한다(~ I'd like to sit at the table closest to the stage)고 말하자 남자가 꼭 그쪽에 좌석을 지정해 두겠다(I'll make sure to reserve a seat for you there)고 답하고 있고, 배치도에서 무대와 가장 가까운 좌석은 테이블 2이므로 정답은 (B)이다.

65-67 대화 + 일정표 W-Br / M-Cn

W Thank you for holding. This is Bianca. How can I help you?

M Hi. **65** I have a ticket for the bus to Springdale this morning, but my plans have changed and I need to switch my destination.

W Sure. I can help you with that.

M Thanks very much. **66** I need the bus to Centerton instead.

W No problem. **67** If you purchased your bus ticket electronically, I just need your confirmation number.

M OK, let me just find the e-mail that has it.

여	기다려 주셔서 감사합니다. 비앙카입니다. 무엇을 도와드릴까요?
남	안녕하세요. **제가 오늘 아침에 스프링데일로 가는 버스 티켓을 가지고 있는데, 계획이 변경되어 목적지를 바꿔야 합니다.**
여	알겠습니다. 제가 도와드릴 수 있어요.
남	정말 감사합니다. **대신 센터튼행 버스가 필요해요.**
여	별말씀을요. **온라인으로 티켓을 구입하신 경우, 확인 번호만 알려 주시면 됩니다.**
남	아, 그 번호가 적힌 이메일을 좀 찾아볼게요.

어휘 hold (전화를 끊지 않고) 기다리다 switch 바꾸다, 변경하다 destination 목적지 electronically 온라인으로, 컴퓨터로 confirmation 확인 departure 출발

DESTINATION	DEPARTURE TIME
• Springdale	10:34 A.M.
• Johnsonville	10:57 A.M.
[66] • Centerton	11:15 A.M.
• Belton City	11:41 A.M.

목적지	출발 시간
• 스프링데일	오전 10:34
• 존슨빌	오전 10:57
• 센터튼	오전 11:15
• 벨튼 시티	오전 11:41

65 Where does the woman most likely work?
(A) At a bus station
(B) At a train station
(C) At a ferry terminal
(D) At an airport

여자는 어디에서 일하는 것 같은가?
(A) 버스 터미널
(B) 기차역
(C) 여객선 터미널
(D) 공항

해설 전체 내용 관련 – 여자의 근무 장소
남자가 첫 대사에서 여자에게 오늘 아침에 스프링데일로 가는 버스 티켓을 가지고 있는데, 목적지를 바꿔야 한다(I have a ticket for the bus to Springdale this morning, ~ and I need to switch my destination)며 도움을 청하고 있는 것으로 보아 정답은 (A)이다.

66 Look at the graphic. What is the man's new departure time?
(A) 10:34 A.M.
(B) 10:57 A.M.
(C) 11:15 A.M.
(D) 11:41 A.M.

시각 정보에 의하면, 남자의 새로운 출발 시간은 몇 시인가?
(A) 오전 10:34
(B) 오전 10:57
(C) 오전 11:15
(D) 오전 11:41

해설 시각 정보 연계 – 남자의 새로운 출발 시간
남자가 두 번째 대사에서 대신 센터튼행 버스가 필요하다(I need the bus to Centerton instead)고 말하고 있고, 일정표에서 센터튼으로 가는 버스의 출발 시간은 오전 11시 15분이므로 정답은 (C)이다.

67 What does the woman ask the man for?
(A) His date of travel
(B) His seat preference
(C) A form of payment
(D) A confirmation number

여자는 남자에게 무엇을 요청하는가?
(A) 여행 날짜
(B) 선호 좌석
(C) 결제 수단
(D) 확인 번호

어휘 preference 선호(하는 것) payment 결제, 지불

해설 세부 사항 관련 – 여자의 요청 사항
여자가 세 번째 대사에서 온라인으로 티켓을 구입한 경우 확인 번호만 알려 주면 된다(If you purchased your bus ticket electronically, I just need your confirmation number)고 했으므로 정답은 (D)이다.

68-70 대화 + 도표 M-Au / W-Am

M	Henderson's Electricians. How can I help you?
W	Hello. I'm calling because [68] **I purchased a clothes dryer a few days ago.** But I have a problem. I'm not sure if my home's electric system can support it.
M	Well, let's see. [69] **Could you take a look at your electric panel?** There should be a series of switches on it.
W	Sure. Hold on. OK. I'm looking at it.
M	OK. Do you see any unused spaces where additional switches could be installed?
W	Just one.
M	I see. Well, a clothes dryer requires two spaces. So most likely, we'd need to install something called a subpanel. The good news is that [70] **you'd only need a 60-amp electrical switch to fix the problem.**

TEST 6 **165**

남	헨더슨즈 일렉트리션스입니다. 무엇을 도와드릴까요?
여	안녕하세요. **며칠 전에 의류 건조기를 한 대 구입해서** 전화했어요. 그런데 한 가지 문제가 있습니다. 저희 집 전기 시스템이 이 제품을 지원할 수 있는지 잘 모르겠네요.
남	네, 확인해 보죠. **댁의 전기 패널을 한번 봐 주시겠어요?** 일련의 스위치들이 있을 겁니다.
여	물론이죠. 잠시만요. 네, 보고 있어요.
남	좋아요. 스위치를 추가로 설치할 수 있는 사용되지 않는 공간이 있나요?
여	딱 하나요.
남	알겠습니다. 그게, 의류 건조기는 그 공간이 두 개 필요해요. 그래서 아마도 보조 패널이라는 것을 설치해야 할 것 같습니다. 좋은 소식은 **이 문제를 해결하는 데 60암페어짜리 전기 스위치만 필요하시다는 점이에요.**

어휘 a series of 일련의, 죽 늘어선   unused 사용하지 않은
additional 추가의   subpanel 보조 패널

Electrical Switch Type	Cost
70 60 amp	$25
80 amp	$30
100 amp	$38
125 amp	$46

전기 스위치 종류	비용
60암페어	**25달러**
80암페어	30달러
100암페어	38달러
125암페어	46달러

68 What has the woman recently purchased?
(A) A dishwasher
(B) A toaster oven
(C) A refrigerator
(D) A clothes dryer

여자는 최근에 무엇을 구입했는가?
(A) 식기세척기
(B) 오븐 겸용 토스터
(C) 냉장고
(D) 의류 건조기

해설 세부 사항 관련 – 여자가 최근에 구입한 것

여자가 첫 대사에서 며칠 전에 의류 건조기를 한 대 구입했다(~ I purchased a clothes dryer a few days ago)고 했으므로 정답은 (D)이다.

Paraphrasing
대화의 a few days ago → 질문의 recently

69 What does the man ask the woman to do?
(A) Check a warranty
(B) Visit a Web site
(C) Examine some equipment
(D) Take some photographs

남자는 여자에게 무엇을 해 달라고 요청하는가?
(A) 품질 보증서 확인하기
(B) 웹사이트 방문하기
(C) 장비 살펴보기
(D) 사진 촬영하기

어휘 warranty 품질 보증서   examine 살펴보다, 검사하다
equipment 장비

해설 세부 사항 관련 – 남자의 요청 사항

남자가 두 번째 대사에서 여자에게 집에 있는 전기 패널을 한번 봐 달라(Could you take a look at your electric panel?)고 요청하고 있으므로 정답은 (C)이다.

Paraphrasing
대화의 take a look at your electric panel
→ 정답의 Examine some equipment

70 Look at the graphic. How much will the woman probably pay for an electrical switch?
(A) $25
(B) $30
(C) $38
(D) $46

시각 정보에 의하면, 여자는 전기 스위치에 얼마를 지불할 것 같은가?
(A) 25달러
(B) 30달러
(C) 38달러
(D) 46달러

해설 시각 정보 연계 – 여자가 지불할 전기 스위치 비용

남자가 마지막 대사에서 문제를 해결하는 데 60암페어짜리 전기 스위치만 필요할 것(~ you'd only need a 60-amp electrical switch to fix the problem)이라고 말하고 있고, 도표에서 60암페어짜리 전기 스위치는 25달러이므로 정답은 (A)이다.

PART 4

71-73 공지

> M-Cn Good morning, and ⁷¹**welcome to the Third Annual Robotics Trade Show.** Please note that in order to accommodate the large number of guests who signed up for the afternoon panel discussion, ⁷²**that event has been moved to Exhibit Hall B.** That's on the lower level, to the left of the elevators. And ⁷³**will the person who left a backpack at the information desk please return to the desk to claim your item?** It's a silver Rugged Hiker model with a blue strap.
>
> 안녕하세요. 제3회 연례 로봇 공학 무역 박람회에 오신 것을 환영합니다. 오후 패널 토론회에 등록하신 많은 참가자를 수용하기 위해, **해당 행사는 전시 홀 B로 변경되었음**을 알려드립니다. 전시 홀 B는 아래층, 엘리베이터 좌측에 있습니다. 그리고 **안내 데스크에 배낭을 두고 가신 분께서는 데스크로 오셔서 물건을 찾아가시겠습니까?** 파란색 끈이 달린 은색 러기드 하이커 모델입니다.
>
> 어휘 annual 연례적인, 해마다의 accommodate 수용하다 exhibit 전시(회) claim 요구하다, 요청하다 strap 끈, 줄

71 Where most likely is the announcement being made?
 (A) At an art gallery
 (B) At a trade show
 (C) At a shopping mall
 (D) At a sporting event

공지는 어디에서 이루어지는 것 같은가?
 (A) 미술관
 (B) 무역 박람회
 (C) 쇼핑몰
 (D) 스포츠 행사

해설 전체 내용 관련 - 공지 장소
 화자가 초반부에 제3회 연례 로봇 공학 무역 박람회에 온 것을 환영한다(~ welcome to the Third Annual Robotics Trade Show)고 했으므로 정답은 (B)이다.

72 What does the speaker say has changed?
 (A) Opening hours
 (B) A location
 (C) An entry fee
 (D) A policy

화자는 무엇이 변경되었다고 말하는가?
 (A) 운영 시간
 (B) 장소
 (C) 입장료
 (D) 정책

해설 세부 사항 관련 - 변경 사항
 화자가 중반부에 행사가 전시 홀 B로 변경되었다(~ that event has been moved to Exhibit Hall B)며 이곳의 정확한 위치를 공유하고 있으므로 정답은 (B)이다.

Paraphrasing
 담화의 Exhibit Hall B → 정답의 A location

73 What does the speaker say is available at the information desk?
 (A) A discount coupon
 (B) A parking pass
 (C) A lost item
 (D) A map

화자는 안내 데스크에서 무엇을 가져갈 수 있다고 말하는가?
 (A) 할인 쿠폰
 (B) 주차권
 (C) 분실물
 (D) 안내도

해설 세부 사항 관련 - 안내 데스크에서 가져갈 수 있는 것
 화자가 후반부에 안내 데스크에 배낭을 두고 간 사람은 데스크로 와서 물건을 찾아가라(~ will the person who left a backpack at the information desk please return to the desk to claim your item?)고 요청하고 있으므로 정답은 (C)이다.

Paraphrasing
 담화의 left a backpack → 정답의 A lost item

74-76 담화

> W-Am ⁷⁴**Welcome to this course about computer programming.** I'm Jin-Ah Jeong. Unfortunately, the regular instructor, Mr. Ramirez, is sick today, so I'll be filling in. ⁷⁵**Although I've never taught this course before**, **I've been a computer programmer for seven years**. Now, to begin, let's go over some terms that are often used in the field of computer programming. ⁷⁶**I'll write them on the board—if you know any of their meanings, please raise your hand and I'll call on you.**
>
> 컴퓨터 프로그래밍에 관한 강좌에 오신 것을 환영합니다. 저는 정진아입니다. 안타깝게도, 원래 담당 강사이신 라미레즈 씨가 오늘 몸이 좋지 않으셔서, 제가 대신하게 되었어요. **저는 이 강좌를 가르쳐 본 적은 없지만, 7년 동안 컴퓨터 프로그래머로 일해 왔습니다.** 자, 우선, 컴퓨터 프로그래밍 분야에서 흔히 쓰이는 용어들을 살펴보도록 하죠. 칠판에 적을 테니, 어떤 것이든 그 의미를 알고 계신다면 손을 들어 주세요. 제가 호명하겠습니다.

> 어휘 unfortunately 안타깝게도 regular 평상시의, 보통의
> fill in 대신하다 to begin 우선 go over 살펴보다, 검토하다
> term 용어 meaning 의미 call on ~의 이름을 불러 시키다

74 Who most likely are the listeners?
(A) Students
(B) Professional athletes
(C) Business investors
(D) News reporters

청자들은 누구인 것 같은가?
(A) 수강생
(B) 프로 운동선수
(C) 사업 투자자
(D) 뉴스 기자

어휘 professional 전문적인, 직업의   athlete 운동선수
investor 투자자

해설 전체 내용 관련 – 청자들의 직업
화자가 초반부에 컴퓨터 프로그래밍에 관한 강좌에 온 것을 환영한다(Welcome to this course about computer programming)고 했으므로 정답은 (A)이다.

75 Why does the speaker say, "I've been a computer programmer for seven years"?
(A) To indicate that she is well qualified for a role
(B) To express appreciation for her employer
(C) To correct some inaccurate information
(D) To give a reason for a change in profession

화자는 왜 "7년 동안 컴퓨터 프로그래머로 일해 왔습니다"라고 말하는가?
(A) 자신이 역할에 적합하다는 것을 나타내기 위해
(B) 고용주에게 감사를 표현하기 위해
(C) 부정확한 정보를 바로잡기 위해
(D) 직업 변경 이유를 설명하기 위해

어휘 indicate 나타내다, 가리키다 qualified 적격인, 자격이 있는
express appreciation 감사를 표현하다 correct 바로잡다
inaccurate 부정확한 profession 직업, 직종

해설 화자의 의도 파악 – 7년 동안 컴퓨터 프로그래머로 일해 왔다는 말의 의도
화자가 중반부에 이 강좌를 가르쳐 본 적은 없지만(Although I've never taught this course before ~)이라고 말하면서 인용문을 언급한 것으로 보아, 자신이 오랫동안 컴퓨터 프로그래머로 일해 왔으므로 충분히 수업을 이끌만한 자격이 있다는 의미로 한 말임을 알 수 있다. 따라서 정답은 (A)이다.

76 According to the speaker, why should the listeners raise their hands?
(A) To make a suggestion
(B) To request a booklet
(C) To provide a definition
(D) To ask a question

화자에 따르면, 청자들은 왜 손을 들어야 하는가?
(A) 제안하기 위해
(B) 소책자를 요청하기 위해
(C) 정의를 제시하기 위해
(D) 질문하기 위해

어휘 suggestion 제안, 의견 booklet 소책자 definition 정의

해설 세부 사항 관련 – 청자들이 손을 들어야 하는 이유
화자가 후반부에 칠판에 용어들을 적을 테니, 어떤 것이든 그 의미를 알고 있다면 손을 들어 달라(I'll write them on the board—if you know any of their meanings, please raise your hand and I'll call on you)고 요청하고 있으므로 정답은 (C)이다.

> **Paraphrasing**
> 담화의 any of their meanings → 정답의 a definition

77-79 메시지

> M-Au Hi, Min-Jee. **77This is Anil Gupta from Jeremy's Family Restaurants** calling about the application you sent in. I was very impressed with your résumé and your successful completion of the managerial training program when you worked at Harry's Bistros. **78I understand the program included training in using bookkeeping software. That would be useful in our company.** Also, your supervisor at Harry's spoke very highly of your performance as a manager. So, I hope you haven't accepted any offers yet! **79Please call me at your earliest convenience at 555-0187.**

> 안녕하세요, 민지. 제출해 주신 지원서와 관련해 전화를 드리는 제레미스 패밀리 레스토랑의 아닐 굽타입니다. 당신의 이력서와 해리스 비스트로 재직 시 관리직 연수 과정을 성공적으로 수료하신 점에 깊은 인상을 받았어요. 해당 프로그램에 회계 소프트웨어 사용에 대한 교육이 포함되어 있는 것으로 알고 있거든요. 그게 저희 회사에서 유용할 겁니다. 또, 해리스에 계신 상사분께서 당신의 관리자로서의 업무 수행 능력을 매우 높이 평가하셨어요. 그러니, 아직 어떤 제안도 수락하지 않으셨길 바랍니다! 555-0187번으로 가급적 빨리 전화해 주세요.

어휘 application 지원서 send in 제출하다, 발송하다
résumé 이력서 completion 수료 managerial 관리직의
bookkeeping 회계, 부기 supervisor 상사, 관리자
performance 수행, 성과 speak highly of ~을 높이 평가하다
at your earliest convenience 가급적 빨리

77 What industry does the speaker work in?
(A) Technology
(B) Travel
(C) Agriculture
(D) Food service

화자는 어떤 업계에서 일하는가?
(A) 기술
(B) 여행
(C) 농업
(D) 음식 서비스

해설 전체 내용 관련 – 화자의 근무 업계
화자가 초반부에 자신을 제레미스 패밀리 레스토랑의 아닐 굽타(This is Anil Gupta from Jeremy's Family Restaurants ~)라고 소개했으므로 정답은 (D)이다.

78 According to the speaker, what would be useful?
(A) Knowledge of specialized software
(B) An understanding of consumer trends
(C) Customer-service training
(D) Team-building skills

화자에 따르면, 무엇이 유용할 것인가?
(A) 전문 소프트웨어에 대한 지식
(B) 소비자 경향에 대한 이해
(C) 고객 서비스 교육
(D) 팀워크 향상 능력

어휘 specialized 전문화된, 특수화된 consumer 소비자 trend 경향, 유행 team-building 팀워크 향상, 팀 단합

해설 세부 사항 관련 – 화자가 유용할 것이라고 말하는 것
화자가 중반부에 청자가 수료한 관리직 연수 과정에 회계 소프트웨어 사용에 대한 교육이 포함되어 있는 것으로 안다(I understand the program included training in using bookkeeping software)며 그게 자신의 회사에서 유용할 것(That would be useful in our company)이라고 말하는 것으로 보아 특정 소프트웨어에 대한 지식이 도움이 된다고 생각한다는 것을 알 수 있다. 따라서 정답은 (A)이다.

Paraphrasing
담화의 training in using bookkeeping software
→ 정답의 Knowledge of specialized software

79 What does the speaker imply when he says, "I hope you haven't accepted any offers yet"?
(A) He thinks the listener deserves a promotion.
(B) He would like to hire the listener.
(C) A company would not be good to work for.
(D) A salary offer is too low.

화자가 "아직 어떤 제안도 수락하지 않으셨길 바랍니다"라고 말할 때 무엇을 의미하는가?
(A) 청자가 승진할 자격이 있다고 생각한다.
(B) 청자를 고용하고 싶어 한다.
(C) 회사가 근무하기에 좋지는 않을 것이다.
(D) 급여 제안이 너무 낮다.

어휘 deserve ~할 자격이 충분하다, ~을 받을 만하다

해설 화자의 의도 파악 – 아직 어떤 제안도 수락하지 않았길 바란다는 말의 의도
화자가 앞에서 청자의 이력과 경험, 평판 전반에 대해 긍정적으로 평가한 뒤 인용문을 언급하고, 가급적 빨리 전화해 달라(Please call me at your earliest convenience ~)고 요청하고 있는 것으로 보아, 청자를 고용하고자 하는 의도로 한 말임을 알 수 있다. 따라서 정답은 (B)이다.

80-82 방송

M-Cn Welcome to another segment of *Belmack City Business News*. Belmack City has one of the biggest seaports in the country. **80 The port receives and distributes thousands of containers full of cargo each day.** Goods from the ships are usually distributed throughout the region by train or by truck. However, sometimes the goods need to wait for days before they are transported, **81 which can cause problems due to lack of affordable storage space.** Unfortunately, lease costs for storage space in the area are too high for many shipping companies to afford. After the break, we'll hear from **82 Pablo Alvarez, owner of Alva Shipping**, about this issue. So stay tuned!

〈벨맥 시티 비즈니스 뉴스〉의 또 다른 코너에 오신 것을 환영합니다. 벨맥 시티는 전국에서 가장 큰 항구들 중 하나를 보유하고 있습니다. **이 항구는 매일 화물로 가득한 수천 개의 컨테이너를 받아 유통시킵니다.** 선박에 실려 오는 상품들은 일반적으로 기차 또는 트럭을 통해 전역에 배송되죠. 그러나 때로 어떤 상품들은 운송되기까지 며칠을 기다려야 하며, **저렴한 보관 공간 부족으로 인해 문제가 발생할 수도 있습니다.** 안타깝게도, 지역 내 보관 공간 임대 비용은 많은 해상 운송 회사들이 감당하기에 너무 높습니다. 광고 후에, 이 문제에 대해 **알바 운송 회사의 소유주인 파블로 알바레즈**의 이야기를 들어 보도록 하겠습니다. 채널 고정해 주세요!

어휘 segment 부분, 조각 seaport(= port) 항구 (도시) distribute 유통시키다, 나누어 주다 cargo 화물 goods 상품 transport 운송하다 lack 부족 affordable 저렴한, 적당한 lease 임대 (계약) storage (창고) 보관, 저장 afford 감당하다 break (방송의) 광고 stay tuned 채널을 고정하다

80 What is the news segment about?
(A) The restoration of historic ships
(B) The distribution of goods
(C) A shortage of city housing
(D) The construction of a new port

뉴스 코너는 무엇에 관한 것인가?
(A) 역사적인 선박의 복원
(B) 상품의 유통
(C) 도시 주택 부족
(D) 새 항구의 건설

어휘 restoration 복원, 복구 historic 역사적인 shortage 부족
housing 주택 (공급)

해설 전체 내용 관련 – 방송 코너의 주제
화자가 초반부에 벨맥 시티의 항구를 언급하면서 그 항구는 매일 화물로 가득한 수천 개의 컨테이너를 받아 유통시킨다(The port receives and distributes thousands of containers full of cargo each day)고 설명한 뒤, 그 과정에서 발생하는 문제에 대한 이야기를 이어 가고 있으므로 정답은 (B)이다.

Paraphrasing
담화의 distributes thousands of containers full of cargo
→ 정답의 distribution of goods

81 What problem does the speaker mention?
(A) Storage space is not affordable.
(B) Trained workers are difficult to find.
(C) There is a shortage of supplies.
(D) Poor road conditions are causing delays.

화자는 어떤 문제를 언급하는가?
(A) 보관 공간이 저렴하지 않다.
(B) 훈련된 직원을 찾기 어렵다.
(C) 물량이 부족하다.
(D) 좋지 않은 도로 상태가 지연을 초래하고 있다.

어휘 trained 훈련된, 교육받은 supply 공급품, 공급량
condition 상태, 조건 delay 지연, 지체

해설 세부 사항 관련 – 화자가 언급하는 문제
화자가 중반부에 저렴한 보관 공간 부족으로 인해 문제가 발생할 수도 있다(~ which can cause problems due to lack of affordable storage space)고 했으므로 정답은 (A)이다.

82 Who is Pablo Alvarez?
(A) A real estate agent
(B) A city official
(C) A business owner
(D) An accountant

파블로 알바레즈는 누구인가?
(A) 부동산 중개업자
(B) 시 공무원
(C) 업체 소유주
(D) 회계사

어휘 agent 중개인, 대리인 official 공무원

해설 세부 사항 관련 – 파블로 알바레즈의 직업
화자가 후반부에 파블로 알바레즈를 알바 운송 회사의 소유주(Pablo Alvarez, owner of Alva Shipping)라고 소개했으므로 정답은 (C)이다.

Paraphrasing
담화의 owner of Alva Shipping → 정답의 A business owner

83-85 담화

M-Au Welcome. I'm delighted to be leading another outdoor workshop here in the botanical gardens. **83 The paintings that participants produced last time were extraordinary**—there's nothing like being surrounded by flowers to inspire creativity. Now, **84 remember that your participation fee does include a light lunch.** I see you've all found spots to set up your easels and you all have your own canvas and paints. That's perfect, since we don't provide painting supplies. Before we get started, **85 let's take a moment to have everyone tell us their names and why they signed up.**

환영합니다. 이곳 식물원에서 또 한 번 야외 워크숍을 진행하게 되어 기쁩니다. **참가자들께서 지난번에 그린 그림들은 대단히 훌륭했는데요.** 창의성을 북돋우는 데 꽃들에 둘러싸여 있는 것만 한 게 없죠. 자, **참가비에 가벼운 점심 식사가 포함되어 있다는 점을 기억하세요.** 여러분 모두 이젤을 설치하실 자리를 찾으셨고, 각자의 캔버스와 물감을 갖고 계시네요. 완벽합니다, 저희가 그림 용품을 제공해 드리지는 않거든요. 시작하기 전에, **잠시 시간을 내서 모두 각자의 이름과 등록하신 이유를 말해 봅시다.**

어휘 delighted 아주 기뻐하는 botanical garden 식물원
participant 참가자 extraordinary 대단히 훌륭한, 특별한
be surrounded by ~에 둘러싸여 있다 inspire 북돋우다
creativity 창의성 set up 설치하다

83 What is the focus of the workshop?
(A) Flower arranging
(B) Photography
(C) Painting
(D) Creative writing

워크숍의 초점은 무엇인가?
(A) 꽃꽂이
(B) 사진 촬영
(C) 그림 그리기
(D) 창의적 글쓰기

해설 　전체 내용 관련 - 워크숍의 초점

화자가 초반부에 참가자들이 지난번에 그린 그림들이 대단히 훌륭했다(The paintings that participants produced last time were extraordinary ~)고 했고, 그림 그리는 것에 관한 이야기를 이어 가고 있으므로 정답은 (C)이다.

84 What does the speaker say is included in a workshop fee?
(A) A museum membership
(B) A potted plant
(C) Some supplies
(D) A meal

화자는 워크숍 비용에 무엇이 포함되어 있다고 말하는가?
(A) 박물관 회원권
(B) 화분에 심은 식물
(C) 용품
(D) 식사

해설 　세부 사항 관련 - 워크숍 비용에 포함된 것

화자가 중반부에 참가비에 가벼운 점심 식사가 포함되어 있다는 점을 기억하라(~ remember that your participation fee does include a light lunch)고 했으므로 정답은 (D)이다.

Paraphrasing
담화의 a light lunch → 정답의 A meal

85 What will most likely happen next?
(A) The listeners will sign some forms.
(B) The listeners will introduce themselves.
(C) The speaker will give a demonstration.
(D) The speaker will lead a tour.

다음에 무슨 일이 일어날 것 같은가?
(A) 청자들이 양식에 서명할 것이다.
(B) 청자들이 자신을 소개할 것이다.
(C) 화자가 시범을 보일 것이다.
(D) 화자가 투어를 진행할 것이다.

어휘 　form 양식, 서식　demonstration 시범, 시연

해설 　세부 사항 관련 - 다음에 일어날 일

화자가 후반부에 잠시 시간을 내서 모두 각자의 이름과 등록한 이유를 말해 보자(~ let's take a moment to have everyone tell us their names and why they signed up)고 했으므로 정답은 (B)이다.

Paraphrasing
담화의 tell us their names and why they signed up
→ 정답의 introduce themselves

86-88 담화

W-Br　Currently, **86 you're all working on our design project** for Takahashi Systems. They like the suggestions you've made so far, such as how to update their logo to make it more modern. That's welcome news because they have high standards. **87 They mentioned they'll be in the area this Friday and expressed interest in visiting our office, so I've invited them.** But **88 as I was walking by the workstation area, I noticed a lot of clutter.** Please remember that making a good impression is important.

현재, 여러분 모두 타카하시 시스템 사를 위한 디자인 프로젝트 작업을 하고 계시죠. 그곳에서 여러분이 지금까지 제안해 주신 것들을 마음에 들어 합니다. 로고를 좀 더 현대적으로 업데이트하는 방법 같은 것들이요. 높은 기준을 갖고 있는 업체라 반가운 소식이네요. 그분들이 이번 주 금요일에 우리 지역으로 오실 거라면서, 우리 사무실을 방문하고 싶어 하셔서, 제가 초대를 했어요. 그런데 업무 구역을 지나면서 보니, 물건들이 너무 어수선하게 놓여 있더라고요. 좋은 인상을 주는 것이 중요하다는 점을 기억해 주세요.

어휘 　currently 현재, 지금　standard 기준, 표준　workstation 업무 공간　clutter 어수선하게 놓인 것, 잡동사니　impression 인상

86 What service does the company provide?
(A) Legal
(B) Architectural
(C) Graphic design
(D) Artificial intelligence

회사는 어떤 서비스를 제공하는가?
(A) 법률
(B) 건축
(C) 그래픽 디자인
(D) 인공 지능

해설 　전체 내용 관련 - 회사가 제공하는 서비스

화자가 초반부에 청자들이 모두 디자인 프로젝트 작업을 하고 있다(~ you're all working on our design project ~)고 했으므로 정답은 (C)이다.

87 What does the speaker say about Friday?
(A) A client will visit.
(B) Interviews will be conducted.
(C) An office will close early.
(D) Bonuses will be announced.

화자는 금요일에 대해 무엇이라고 말하는가?
(A) 고객이 방문할 것이다.
(B) 면접이 실시될 것이다.
(C) 사무실이 일찍 문을 닫을 것이다.
(D) 보너스가 공지될 것이다.

해설 세부 사항 관련 – 화자가 금요일에 대해 하는 말
화자가 중반부에 타카하시 시스템 사의 직원들이 이번 주 금요일에 우리 사무실을 방문하고 싶어 해서 초대했다(~ this Friday and expressed interest in visiting our office, so I've invited them)고 했으므로 정답은 (A)이다.

88 What does the speaker imply when she says, "making a good impression is important"?
(A) She will be providing her business card.
(B) She does not want employees to be late.
(C) She expects workstations to be clean.
(D) She is unsatisfied with some potential job candidates.

화자가 "좋은 인상을 주는 것이 중요하다"라고 말할 때 무엇을 의미하는가?
(A) 자신의 명함을 제공할 것이다.
(B) 직원들이 늦지 않기를 바라고 있다.
(C) 업무 공간이 깨끗하기를 기대하고 있다.
(D) 일부 잠재적 채용 후보자들에게 만족하지 못하고 있다.

어휘 unsatisfied 만족하지 못하는 potential 잠재적인 candidate 지원자, 후보자

해설 화자의 의도 파악 – 좋은 인상을 주는 것이 중요하다는 말의 의도
화자가 후반부에 업무 구역을 지나면서 보니 물건들이 너무 어수선하게 놓여 있었다(~ as I was walking by the workstation area, I noticed a lot of clutter)고 말한 뒤 인용문을 언급한 것으로 보아, 업무 공간을 깨끗하게 정리했으면 한다는 의도로 한 말임을 알 수 있다. 따라서 정답은 (C)이다.

89-91 회의 발췌 ▶동영상 강의

M-Au Good morning, everyone. **89 I appreciate you all getting here early before your assembly-line shift starts.** I have a major announcement to make. Remember our new injection mold machine was acting up yesterday? **90 A technician came at the end of the day**, and it turns out the hydraulic safety switch is turning itself off randomly. A part needs to be replaced, but that won't happen until later this week. In the meantime, **91 please use our older machine only, which, as you know, is not as fast as the new one. I'll need you to start working as soon as possible.**

안녕하세요, 여러분. **모두들 조립 라인 교대 근무가 시작되기 전에 일찍 와 주셔서 감사드립니다.** 전해 드릴 중요한 공지가 있습니다. 어제 새 사출 금형 기계가 말썽을 부렸던 것 기억하시죠? **일과가 마무리될 때쯤 기술자가 왔었는데**, 유압 안전 스위치가 무작위로 꺼지고 있는 것으로 드러난 상태입니다. 부품 하나가 교체되어야 하는데, 이번 주 후반이나 되어야 할 것 같아요. 그동안에는 예전 기계만 이용하셔야 하는데, 아시다피, 새것만큼 빠르지가 않아요. 여러분께서 작업을 가능한 한 빨리 시작해 주실 필요가 있습니다.

어휘 assembly 조립 shift 교대 근무 major 주요한, 큰 announcement 공지, 발표 injection mold 사출 금형 act up 말썽을 부리다, 제 기능을 못하다 technician 기술자 it turns out (that) ~하는 것으로 드러나다 hydraulic 유압의 randomly 무작위로 in the meantime 그동안

89 Where do the listeners most likely work?
(A) At a hospital
(B) At a factory
(C) At a bank
(D) At an auto repair shop

청자들은 어디에서 일하는 것 같은가?
(A) 병원
(B) 공장
(C) 은행
(D) 자동차 수리점

해설 전체 내용 관련 – 청자들의 근무 장소
화자가 초반부에 청자들에게 조립 라인 교대 근무가 시작되기 전에 일찍 온 것에 대해 감사하다(I appreciate you all getting here early before your assembly-line shift starts)고 인사하고 있으므로 정답은 (B)이다.

90 Who visited the business yesterday?
(A) A journalist
(B) A safety inspector
(C) A politician
(D) A repair person

어제 누가 업체를 방문했는가?
(A) 기자
(B) 안전 감독관
(C) 정치인
(D) 수리 기사

해설 세부 사항 관련 – 어제 업체를 방문한 사람
화자가 중반부에 어제 새 기계가 말썽을 부렸던 것을 언급하며, 일과가 마무리될 때쯤 기술자가 왔었다(A technician came at the end of the day, ~)고 했으므로 정답은 (D)이다.

Paraphrasing
담화의 A technician → 정답의 A repair person

91 Why are the listeners asked to start working right away?
(A) A large order was placed.
(B) Several employees are on vacation.
(C) A task will take longer than usual.
(D) An inspection will be conducted in the afternoon.

청자들은 왜 지금 바로 작업을 시작하도록 요청받는가?
(A) 대규모 주문이 접수되었다.
(B) 여러 직원들이 휴가 중이다.
(C) 업무가 평소보다 더 오래 걸릴 것이다.
(D) 오후에 점검이 실시될 것이다.

어휘 place an order 주문하다 on vacation 휴가 중인 inspection 점검, 조사

해설 세부 사항 관련 – 지금 바로 작업을 시작해야 하는 이유
화자가 후반부에 예전 기계만 이용해야 하는데 알다시피 새것만큼 빠르지 않다(~ please use our older machine only, which, as you know, is not as fast as the new one)며 가능한 한 빨리 작업을 시작할 필요가 있다(I'll need you to start working as soon as possible)고 당부하고 있다. 이는 느린 기계로 인해 작업 시간이 오래 걸릴 가능성을 염두에 둔 조치이므로 정답은 (C)이다.

> **Paraphrasing**
> 담화의 as soon as possible → 질문의 right away
> 담화의 not as fast as the new one
> → 정답의 A task will take longer than usual

92-94 전화 메시지

> **W-Br** Hi, Mr. Rossi. I work at Cullom Studios, and I'm a production assistant for a new film that'll be set in seventeenth-century France. **92 I'm calling because we'd like to hire you as a consultant for our film.** **93 I recently came across the book you wrote on the history of French fashion** and found it fascinating. Since you're an expert on French clothing and lifestyle trends of that time, your knowledge would be valuable as we develop costume and set designs. We'd be thrilled to work with you, and we're offering a generous compensation package. **94 I can send you the details**—I'll use the e-mail address that you have on your Web site.

안녕하세요, 로시 씨. 저는 컬럼 스튜디오에 근무하고 있고, 17세기 프랑스를 배경으로 할 새 영화의 제작 보조입니다. **귀하를 저희 영화의 자문으로 모시고자 전화를 드려요.** 최근에 프랑스 패션의 역사에 관해 쓰신 책을 우연히 발견했는데, 정말 흥미로웠습니다. 그 시대의 프랑스 의복 및 생활 방식 트렌드의 전문가이시니, 저희가 의상과 세트 디자인을 개발하는 데 귀하의 지식이 큰 도움이 되리라 생각합니다. 함께 일하게 된다면 정말 기쁠 것이며, 넉넉한 보수도 제공해 드릴 예정입니다. **자세한 내용을 보내 드릴게요.** 웹사이트에 있는 이메일 주소를 사용하겠습니다.

> **어휘** be set in ~을 배경으로 하다 consultant 자문
> come across ~을 우연히 발견하다 fascinating 매력적인
> expert 전문가 valuable 소중한 costume 의상
> thrilled 매우 기쁜, 신나는 generous 넉넉한, 후한
> compensation package (급여와 복리후생을 포함한) 보수

92 Why is the speaker calling?
(A) To ask the listener to donate to a charity
(B) To offer the listener a job
(C) To explain a publishing delay
(D) To request an interview for an article

화자는 왜 전화하는가?
(A) 청자에게 자선 단체에 기부하도록 요청하려고
(B) 청자에게 일자리를 제안하려고
(C) 출판 지연 문제를 설명하려고
(D) 기사에 필요한 인터뷰를 요청하려고

어휘 donate 기부하다 charity 자선 단체 publishing 출판

해설 전체 내용 관련 – 화자의 전화 목적
화자가 초반부에 청자를 영화의 자문으로 고용하고 싶어서 전화한다(I'm calling because we'd like to hire you as a consultant for our film)고 했으므로 정답은 (B)이다.

> **Paraphrasing**
> 담화의 hire you as a consultant
> → 정답의 offer the listener a job

93 How did the speaker first learn about the listener?
(A) She read one of his books.
(B) She attended a workshop he led.
(C) She saw his comment on a social media post.
(D) She watched a documentary about his work.

화자는 처음에 어떻게 청자에 대해 알게 되었는가?
(A) 청자의 책들 중 하나를 읽었다.
(B) 청자가 진행한 워크숍에 참석했다.
(C) 소셜 미디어 게시물에서 청자의 댓글을 보았다.
(D) 청자의 작품에 관한 다큐멘터리를 시청했다.

어휘 comment 댓글, 의견 post 게시물

해설 세부 사항 관련 – 화자가 청자를 알게 된 계기
화자가 중반부에 최근에 청자가 프랑스 패션의 역사에 관해 쓴 책을 우연히 발견했다(I recently came across the book you wrote on the history of French fashion ~)며 청자를 알게 된 배경을 설명하고 있으므로 정답은 (A)이다.

Paraphrasing
담화의 came across the book you wrote
→ 정답의 read one of his books

94 What will the speaker most likely do next?
(A) Print and sign a contract
(B) Send some information
(C) Reserve a meeting room
(D) Contact a talent agent

화자는 다음에 무엇을 할 것 같은가?
(A) 계약서 출력해 서명하기
(B) 정보 보내기
(C) 회의실 예약하기
(D) 소속사 담당자에게 연락하기

어휘 contract 계약(서) reserve 예약하다, 지정하다
talent agent (연예 기획사 등과 같은) 소속사 담당자

해설 세부 사항 관련 – 화자가 다음에 할 일
화자가 후반부에 자세한 내용을 보내 주겠다(I can send you the details ~)고 했으므로 정답은 (B)이다.

Paraphrasing
담화의 send you the details
→ 정답의 Send some information

95-97 광고 + 지도

W-Am Are you looking for a convenient way to get around the city? ⁹⁵**The city of Lakepoint offers on-demand transportation in several of our neighborhoods.** ⁹⁶**Just download the Lakepoint City application onto your mobile phone.** Once you make an appointment on the app, a shuttle will arrive within fifteen minutes. This easy-to-use service will take you to any destination within the service area, like your doctor's office or the library! And ⁹⁷**we've recently expanded service to Westbrook, so residents can take the shuttle to the soccer stadium.**

도시를 돌아다닐 편리한 방법을 찾고 계신가요? 레이크포인트 시는 여러 지역에서 수요응답형 교통편을 제공하고 있습니다. 휴대폰에 레이크포인트 시 애플리케이션을 다운로드하기만 하면 됩니다. 앱에서 예약하시면, 15분 이내에 셔틀이 도착합니다. 사용하기 쉬운 이 서비스가 병원이나 도서관 등 서비스 지역 내 원하는 곳 어디든 데려다 드릴 겁니다! 최근 웨스트브룩까지 서비스를 확대하여, 주민들은 축구 경기장에 셔틀을 타고 갈 수 있습니다.

어휘 convenient 편리한 on-demand transportation 수요응답형 교통(정해진 노선 없이 승객의 요청에 따라 차량이 운행되는 교통 시스템) destination 목적지 expand 확대하다, 확장하다 resident 주민

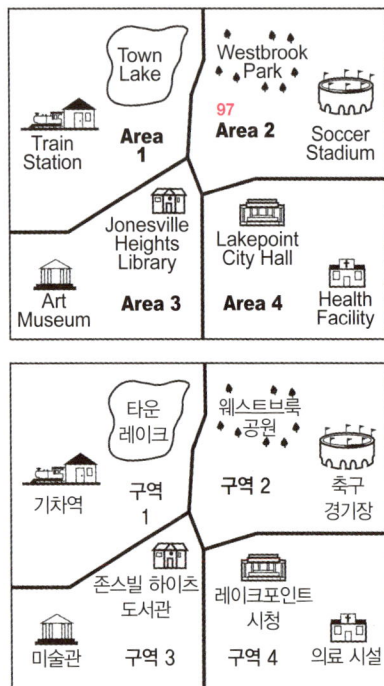

95 What type of service is being advertised?
(A) Recycling
(B) Transportation
(C) Grocery delivery
(D) Exercise classes

어떤 종류의 서비스가 광고되고 있는가?
(A) 재활용
(B) 교통
(C) 식료품 배달
(D) 운동 수업

해설 전체 내용 관련 – 광고되고 있는 서비스
화자가 초반부에 레이크포인트 시가 여러 지역에서 수요응답형 교통편을 제공하고 있다(The city of Lakepoint offers on-demand transportation in several of our neighborhoods)고 말한 뒤 셔틀 이용 방법과 특징에 대한 설명을 이어 가고 있으므로 정답은 (B)이다.

96 According to the speaker, how can the listeners use a new service?
(A) By entering payment information
(B) By placing a phone call
(C) By visiting a community center
(D) By using a mobile application

화자에 따르면, 청자들은 어떻게 새로운 서비스를 이용할 수 있는가?
(A) 결제 정보를 입력해서
(B) 전화를 걸어서
(C) 커뮤니티 센터를 방문해서
(D) 모바일 애플리케이션을 이용해서

해설 세부 사항 관련 – 새로운 서비스의 이용 방법
화자가 중반부에 휴대폰에 레이크포인트 시 애플리케이션을 다운 로드하기만 하면 된다(Just download the Lakepoint City application onto your mobile phone)며 서비스 이용 방법을 소개하고 있으므로 정답은 (D)이다.

Paraphrasing
담화의 download the Lakepoint City application onto your mobile phone
→ 정답의 By using a mobile application

97 Look at the graphic. Which area was recently added?
(A) Area 1
(B) Area 2
(C) Area 3
(D) Area 4

시각 정보에 의하면, 최근에 어떤 구역이 추가되었는가?
(A) 구역 1
(B) 구역 2
(C) 구역 3
(D) 구역 4

해설 시각 정보 연계 – 최근에 추가된 구역
화자가 후반부에 최근에 웨스트브룩으로 서비스를 확대하여 주민들이 축구 경기장에 셔틀을 타고 갈 수 있다(~ we've recently expanded service to Westbrook, so residents can take the shuttle to the soccer stadium)고 했고, 지도에서 축구 경기장은 구역 2에 있으므로 정답은 (B)이다.

Paraphrasing
담화의 expanded → 질문의 added

98-100 방송 + 시내 지도

M-Cn And ⁹⁸our last news item today is the Greenchester Archaeological Festival taking place this weekend. Greenchester is home to some rich prehistoric findings. If you've ever wondered what goes into excavating a site, here's your chance to find out. There'll be a special workshop where you can get hands-on experience practicing excavation skills. ⁹⁹The workshop will be held on the grounds in front of the historical society building. As for getting here, ¹⁰⁰I recommend that you simply walk over—many streets will be blocked off for the festival, and it will take longer to drive.

그리고 **오늘의 마지막 소식은 이번 주말에 열리는 그린체스터 고고학 축제입니다.** 그린체스터는 풍부한 선사 시대 유물의 중심지죠. 유적지를 발굴하는 데 어떤 노력이 필요한지 궁금하신 적이 있다면, 확인해 보실 수 있는 기회입니다. 발굴 기술을 연습하며 실무를 경험해 볼 수 있는 특별 워크숍이 있을 예정입니다. **워크숍은 역사 학회 건물 앞 부지에서 열립니다.** 이곳으로 가는 방법에 대해서는 **그냥 걸어가시는 것을 추천해 드립니다.** 축제를 위해 많은 도로가 통제될 예정이라 차로 이동하면 시간이 더 오래 걸릴 겁니다.

어휘 archaeological 고고학의 prehistoric 선사 시대의 findings 유물, 발견물 go into (노력, 시간 등이) 투입되다, 쓰이다 excavate 발굴하다, 굴착하다 hands-on 현장의, 실무의 grounds 부지, 구내 historical society 역사 학회 block off 폐쇄하다, 차단하다 nature preserve 자연 보호 구역

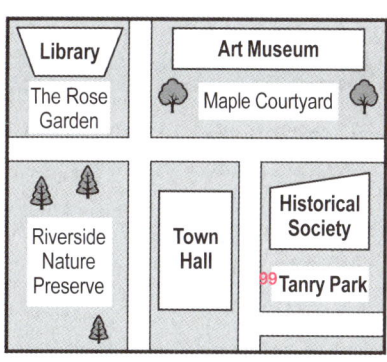

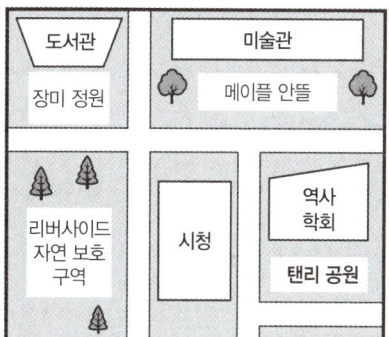

98 What event is the speaker mainly discussing?
(A) An archaeology festival
(B) A museum opening
(C) A gardening fair
(D) An outdoor concert

화자는 주로 어떤 행사에 대해 이야기하는가?
(A) 고고학 축제
(B) 박물관 개장
(C) 원예 박람회
(D) 야외 콘서트

어휘 archaeology 고고학   fair 박람회, 축제

해설 전체 내용 관련 – 방송의 주제
화자가 초반부에 오늘의 마지막 소식은 이번 주말에 열리는 그린 체스터 고고학 축제(~ our last news item today is the Greenchester Archaeological Festival taking place this weekend)라고 말한 뒤 해당 축제의 특징 및 방문 방법 등에 대한 소개를 이어 가고 있으므로 정답은 (A)이다.

99 Look at the graphic. Where will a workshop take place?
(A) In The Rose Garden
(B) In Maple Courtyard
(C) In Tanry Park
(D) In Riverside Nature Preserve

시각 정보에 의하면, 워크숍은 어디에서 개최될 것인가?
(A) 장미 정원
(B) 메이플 안뜰
(C) 탠리 공원
(D) 리버사이드 자연 보호 구역

해설 시각 정보 연계 – 워크숍 개최 장소
화자가 중반부에 워크숍은 역사 학회 건물 앞 부지에서 열린다(The workshop will be held on the grounds in front of the historical society building)고 말하고 있고, 지도에서 역사 학회 건물 앞 부지는 탠리 공원이므로 정답은 (C)이다.

100 What does the speaker recommend?
(A) Arriving early
(B) Walking
(C) Volunteering
(D) Bringing a jacket

화자는 무엇을 추천하는가?
(A) 일찍 도착하기
(B) 걸어가기
(C) 자원봉사 하기
(D) 재킷 챙겨가기

해설 세부 사항 관련 – 화자의 추천 사항
화자가 후반부에 방문하는 방법과 관련해 그냥 걸어가는 것을 추천한다(~ I recommend that you simply walk over ~)고 했으므로 정답은 (B)이다.

기출 TEST 7

동영상 강의

1 (B)	2 (A)	3 (A)	4 (C)	5 (A)
6 (D)	7 (B)	8 (B)	9 (A)	10 (B)
11 (C)	12 (B)	13 (B)	14 (C)	15 (A)
16 (B)	17 (A)	18 (B)	19 (C)	20 (B)
21 (C)	22 (C)	23 (B)	24 (B)	25 (B)
26 (C)	27 (B)	28 (C)	29 (B)	30 (A)
31 (B)	32 (C)	33 (A)	34 (A)	35 (B)
36 (C)	37 (D)	38 (A)	39 (A)	40 (C)
41 (A)	42 (B)	43 (D)	44 (C)	45 (C)
46 (D)	47 (C)	48 (B)	49 (A)	50 (D)
51 (B)	52 (C)	53 (C)	54 (D)	55 (B)
56 (C)	57 (D)	58 (B)	59 (A)	60 (C)
61 (D)	62 (A)	63 (B)	64 (D)	65 (A)
66 (D)	67 (B)	68 (A)	69 (B)	70 (C)
71 (B)	72 (C)	73 (A)	74 (B)	75 (A)
76 (D)	77 (C)	78 (D)	79 (D)	80 (A)
81 (B)	82 (A)	83 (C)	84 (B)	85 (A)
86 (A)	87 (A)	88 (C)	89 (B)	90 (D)
91 (A)	92 (C)	93 (B)	94 (D)	95 (D)
96 (B)	97 (B)	98 (A)	99 (B)	100 (C)

PART 1

1

M-Au

(A) She's holding a water bottle.
(B) She's looking at a newspaper.
(C) She's reaching for a book.
(D) She's standing next to a copier.

(A) 여자가 물병을 들고 있다.
(B) 여자가 신문을 보고 있다.
(C) 여자가 책을 향해 손을 뻗고 있다.
(D) 여자가 복사기 옆에 서 있다.

해설 1인 등장 사진 – 사람의 동작/상태 묘사
(A) 동사 오답. 여자가 물병을 들고 있는(is holding a water bottle) 모습이 아니므로 오답.
(B) 정답. 여자가 신문을 보고 있는(is looking at a newspaper) 모습이므로 정답.
(C) 동사 오답. 여자가 책을 향해 손을 뻗고 있는(is reaching for a book) 모습이 아니므로 오답.
(D) 사진에 없는 명사를 이용한 오답. 사진에 복사기(a copier)의 모습이 보이지 않으므로 오답.

2

W-Br

(A) A tire is leaning against a car.
(B) A chain has been left on the ground.
(C) A car is backing out of a garage.
(D) A box of tools has been set on top of a car.

(A) 타이어가 자동차에 기대어져 있다.
(B) 체인이 바닥에 놓여 있다.
(C) 자동차가 차고에서 후진으로 나오고 있다.
(D) 공구 상자가 자동차 위에 놓여 있다.

어휘 lean against ~에 기대어져 있다 garage 차고, 주차장

해설 사물/풍경 사진 – 사물 묘사
(A) 정답. 타이어(A tire)가 자동차에 기대어져 있는(is leaning against a car) 모습이므로 정답.
(B) 동사 오답. 체인(A chain)이 바닥에 놓여 있는(has been left on the ground) 모습이 아니므로 오답.
(C) 동사 오답. 자동차(A car)가 차고에서 후진으로 나오고 있는(is backing out of a garage) 모습이 아니므로 오답.
(D) 사진에 없는 명사를 이용한 오답. 사진에 공구 상자(A box of tools)의 모습이 보이지 않으므로 오답.

3

M-Cn

(A) He's pushing a cart toward a doorway.
(B) He's spraying cleaning liquid onto a glass door.
(C) He's mopping up a tiled floor.
(D) He's setting up a bulletin board.

(A) 남자가 출입구 쪽으로 카트를 밀고 있다.
(B) 남자가 유리문에 세척액을 분사하고 있다.
(C) 남자가 타일 바닥을 대걸레로 청소하고 있다.
(D) 남자가 게시판을 설치하고 있다.

어휘 liquid 액체 mop up ~을 대걸레로 청소하다, ~을 닦아 내다 bulletin board 게시판

해설 1인 등장 사진 – 사람의 동작/상태 묘사
(A) 정답. 남자가 출입구 쪽으로 카트를 밀고 있는(is pushing a cart toward a doorway) 모습이므로 정답.
(B) 동사 오답. 남자가 세척액을 분사하고 있는(is spraying cleaning liquid) 모습이 아니므로 오답.
(C) 동사 오답. 남자가 대걸레로 청소하고 있는(is mopping up) 모습이 아니므로 오답.
(D) 동사 오답. 남자가 게시판을 설치하고 있는(is setting up a bulletin board) 모습이 아니므로 오답.

4
W-Am

(A) The woman is walking across the street.
(B) The woman is repairing a bicycle.
(C) The woman is wearing a helmet.
(D) The woman is getting into a vehicle.

(A) 여자가 거리를 가로질러 걷고 있다.
(B) 여자가 자전거를 수리하고 있다.
(C) **여자가 헬멧을 착용한 상태이다.**
(D) 여자가 차량에 탑승하고 있다.

어휘 repair 수리하다 vehicle 차량

해설 1인 등장 사진 – 사람의 동작/상태 묘사
(A) 동사 오답. 여자가 거리를 가로질러 걷고 있는(is walking across the street) 모습이 아니므로 오답.
(B) 동사 오답. 여자가 자전거를 수리하고 있는(is repairing a bicycle) 모습이 아니므로 오답.
(C) 정답. 여자가 헬멧을 착용한(is wearing a helmet) 모습이므로 정답.
(D) 동사 오답. 여자가 차량에 탑승하는(is getting into a vehicle) 모습이 아니므로 오답.

5
M-Au

(A) Some umbrellas have been opened in an outdoor dining area.
(B) All the tables are occupied by diners.
(C) A worker is sweeping a dining area.
(D) Flowers have been placed on the tables.

(A) **파라솔들이 야외 식사 구역에 펼쳐져 있다.**
(B) 모든 테이블이 손님들로 차 있다.
(C) 직원이 식사 구역을 빗자루로 쓸고 있다.
(D) 꽃들이 테이블에 놓여 있다.

어휘 occupied (사람이 공간을) 사용 중인 diner 식사 손님
sweep 빗자루로 쓸다

해설 사물/풍경 사진 – 사람/사물/풍경 혼합 묘사
(A) 정답. 파라솔들(Some umbrellas)이 야외 식사 구역에 펼쳐져 있는(have been opened in an outdoor dining area) 모습이므로 정답.
(B) 동사 오답. 모든 테이블(All the tables)이 손님들로 차 있는(are occupied by diners) 모습이 아니므로 오답.
(C) 사진에 없는 명사를 이용한 오답. 사진에 직원(A worker)의 모습이 보이지 않으므로 오답.
(D) 위치 오답. 꽃들(Flowers)이 테이블에 놓여 있는(have been placed on the tables) 모습이 아니므로 오답.

---

6  ▶동영상 강의
W-Br

(A) File folders have been arranged on a shelf.
(B) Some window blinds have been raised.
(C) Some waste baskets have been turned upside down.
(D) An office chair has been pushed under a desk.

(A) 파일 폴더들이 선반에 정리되어 있다.
(B) 창문 블라인드들이 올려져 있다.
(C) 쓰레기통들이 거꾸로 뒤집혀 있다.
(D) **사무용 의자가 책상 아래로 밀려 들어가 있다.**

어휘 arrange 정리하다, 배치하다 raise 올리다, 높이다
upside down 거꾸로

해설 사물/풍경 사진 – 사물 묘사
(A) 사진에 없는 명사를 이용한 오답. 사진에 파일 폴더들(File folders)의 모습이 보이지 않으므로 오답.
(B) 동사 오답. 창문 블라인드들(Some window blinds)이 올려져 있는(have been raised) 모습이 아니므로 오답.
(C) 동사 오답. 쓰레기통들(Some waste baskets)이 거꾸로 뒤집혀 있는(have been turned upside down) 모습이 아니므로 오답.
(D) 정답. 사무용 의자(An office chair)가 책상 아래에 밀려 들어가 있는(has been pushed under a desk) 모습이므로 정답.

PART 2

7 M-Au / W-Am

Where do I sign this contract?
(A) A large account.
(B) Here at the bottom.
(C) Hang it on the wall.

계약서 어디에 서명하죠?
(A) 대형 거래처요.
(B) **여기 하단에요.**
(C) 벽에 걸어 주세요.

어휘 contract 계약(서) account 거래처, 계좌

해설 서명 위치를 묻는 Where 의문문
(A) 질문과 상관없는 오답.
(B) 정답. 서명 위치를 묻는 질문에 하단이라며 특정 위치를 알려 주고 있으므로 정답.
(C) 질문과 상관없는 오답.

8 M-Cn / W-Am

How about planting a vegetable garden?

(A) There's parking available on the next street.
(B) I think that's a good idea.
(C) A new hardware store.

채소밭을 가꿔 보는 게 어때요?
(A) 다음 거리에 이용 가능한 주차장이 있어요.
(B) 좋은 생각인 것 같아요.
(C) 새로운 철물점이요.

어휘 plant 가꾸다, 심다 hardware 철물, 장비

해설 제안/권유의 의문문
(A) 질문과 상관없는 오답.
(B) 정답. 채소밭을 가꿔 보는 게 어떤지 묻는 질문에 좋은 생각인 것 같다며 동의하고 있으므로 정답.
(C) 연상 단어 오답. 질문의 garden에서 연상 가능한 hardware store를 이용한 오답.

9 W-Br / M-Cn

When did the conference committee meeting get canceled?

(A) Yesterday morning.
(B) A new member.
(C) At the hotel on Main Street.

콘퍼런스 위원회 회의가 언제 취소된 거죠?
(A) 어제 아침이에요.
(B) 신입 회원이요.
(C) 메인 가에 있는 호텔에서요.

어휘 committee 위원회

해설 회의가 취소된 시점을 묻는 When 의문문
(A) 정답. 회의가 취소된 시점을 묻는 질문에 어제 아침이라고 알려 주고 있으므로 정답.
(B) 연상 단어 오답. 질문의 committee에서 연상 가능한 new member를 이용한 오답.
(C) 질문과 상관없는 오답. Where 의문문에 대한 응답이므로 오답.

10 W-Am / W-Br

Does the company pay for our hotel rooms?

(A) I have a layover in Dubai.
(B) No, we have to pay for them ourselves.
(C) That's my favorite airline.

회사에서 우리 호텔 객실 요금을 지불해 주나요?
(A) 저는 두바이에서 경유합니다.
(B) 아니요, 우리가 직접 지불해야 해요.
(C) 그게 제가 가장 좋아하는 항공사입니다.

어휘 layover 경유(지)

해설 회사가 호텔 객실 요금을 지불하는지 묻는 조동사(Does) 의문문
(A) 질문과 상관없는 오답.
(B) 정답. 회사가 호텔 객실 요금을 지불하는지 묻는 질문에 아니요(No)라고 대답한 뒤, 우리가 직접 지불해야 한다며 부정 답변과 일관된 내용을 덧붙이고 있으므로 정답.
(C) 연상 단어 오답. 질문의 hotel에서 연상 가능한 airline을 이용한 오답.

11 W-Br / M-Au

Our team's going to inspect the construction site tomorrow.

(A) His name is Alberto.
(B) The office down the hall.
(C) That's the first I've heard of it.

저희 팀이 내일 그 공사 현장을 점검합니다.
(A) 그의 이름은 알베르토입니다.
(B) 복도 저쪽에 있는 사무실이요.
(C) 그런 얘기는 처음 들어 봐요.

어휘 inspect 점검하다 site 부지, 현장

해설 정보 전달의 평서문
(A) 평서문과 상관없는 오답. 평서문에 3인칭 대명사 His로 지칭할 인물이 언급된 적이 없으므로 오답.
(B) 평서문과 상관없는 오답. Where 의문문에 대한 응답이므로 오답.
(C) 정답. 소속 팀이 내일 공사 현장을 점검한다는 평서문에 그런 얘기는 처음 듣는다는 말로 자신은 알지 못했던 정보라는 것을 우회적으로 표현하고 있으므로 정답.

12 M-Cn / W-Am

Why does the Moon look so close in this photograph?

(A) Are there seats available for the astronomy presentation?
(B) Because I used a special camera lens.
(C) She's always wanted to be an astronaut.

이 사진에서 달이 왜 이렇게 가까워 보이는 거죠?
(A) 그 천문학 발표회에 이용 가능한 자리가 있나요?
(B) 제가 특수 카메라 렌즈를 사용했기 때문입니다.
(C) 그녀는 항상 우주 비행사가 되고 싶어 했어요.

어휘 astronomy 천문학 astronaut 우주 비행사

해설 사진에서 달이 가까워 보이는 이유를 묻는 Why 의문문
(A) 연상 단어 오답. 질문의 Moon에서 연상 가능한 astronomy를 이용한 오답.
(B) 정답. 사진에서 달이 가까워 보이는 이유를 묻는 질문에 특수 카메라 렌즈를 사용했기 때문이라고 이유를 알려 주고 있으므로 정답.
(C) 질문과 상관없는 오답. 질문에 3인칭 대명사 She로 지칭할 인물이 언급된 적이 없으므로 오답.

13 W-Am / M-Au

How do I log on to this computer?
(A) Some printer ink and paper.
(B) I'll send you a temporary password.
(C) No, he was late.

이 컴퓨터에 어떻게 로그인할 수 있죠?
(A) 프린터 잉크와 용지요.
(B) 제가 임시 비밀번호를 보내 드릴게요.
(C) 아니요, 그는 늦었어요.

어휘 log on to ~에 로그인하다　temporary 임시의, 일시적인

해설 컴퓨터에 로그인하는 방법을 묻는 How 의문문
(A) 연상 단어 오답. 질문의 computer에서 연상 가능한 printer ink를 이용한 오답.
(B) 정답. 컴퓨터에 로그인하는 방법을 묻는 질문에 임시 비밀번호를 보내 주겠다며 방법을 제시하고 있으므로 정답.
(C) Yes/No 불가 오답. How 의문문에는 Yes/No 응답이 불가능하므로 오답.

14 M-Cn / M-Au

When does the property manager arrive?
(A) On Whitmer Boulevard.
(B) You're right, it doesn't fit.
(C) At ten o'clock.

건물 관리자는 언제 도착하나요?
(A) 위트머 대로예요.
(B) 당신 말이 옳아요, 그게 맞지 않아요.
(C) 10시에요.

어휘 property 건물, 부동산　fit 적합하다, 알맞다

해설 건물 관리자가 도착하는 시간을 묻는 When 의문문
(A) 질문과 상관없는 오답. Where 의문문에 대한 응답이므로 오답.
(B) 질문과 상관없는 오답.
(C) 정답. 건물 관리자가 도착하는 시간을 묻는 질문에 10시라고 구체적인 시간을 알려 주고 있으므로 정답.

15 M-Cn / W-Am

Let's have dinner at the French restaurant tonight.
(A) OK, I'll see you there.
(B) I'd like to buy some new cookware.
(C) Here's a copy of the agreement.

오늘 밤 그 프랑스 레스토랑에서 저녁 식사를 합시다.
(A) 좋아요, 그곳에서 뵙죠.
(B) 새 조리 도구를 좀 구입하고 싶어요.
(C) 여기 계약서 한 부입니다.

어휘 cookware 조리 도구　agreement 계약서

해설 제안/권유의 평서문
(A) 정답. 오늘 밤에 프랑스 레스토랑에서 저녁 식사를 하자고 제안하는 평서문에 좋다(OK)고 대답한 뒤, 그곳에서 보자며 긍정 답변과 일관된 내용을 덧붙이고 있으므로 정답.
(B) 연상 단어 오답. 평서문의 dinner에서 연상 가능한 cookware를 이용한 오답.
(C) 평서문과 상관없는 오답.

16 M-Au / W-Br

Who's supervising the production line?
(A) Please sign on the line.
(B) Luca's doing it.
(C) A 45-minute lunch break.

누가 생산 라인을 감독하고 있죠?
(A) 선 위에 서명해 주세요.
(B) 루카가 하고 있습니다.
(C) 45분간의 점심 식사 시간이요.

어휘 supervise 감독하다, 관리하다

해설 생산 라인을 감독하는 사람을 묻는 Who 의문문
(A) 단어 반복 오답. 질문의 line을 반복 이용한 오답.
(B) 정답. 생산 라인을 감독하는 사람을 묻는 질문에 루카라고 알려 주고 있으므로 정답.
(C) 질문과 상관없는 오답.

17 W-Br / W-Am

When will the reception for the artists start?
(A) After the lecture.
(B) Asian art.
(C) At the conference center.

미술가들을 위한 환영 연회는 언제 시작하나요?
(A) 강연 후에요.
(B) 아시아 미술이요.
(C) 콘퍼런스 센터에서요.

어휘 reception 환영 연회, 축하 연회

해설 환영 연회가 열리는 시간을 묻는 When 의문문
(A) 정답. 환영 연회가 열리는 시간을 묻는 질문에 강연 후라고 알려 주고 있으므로 정답.
(B) 연상 단어 오답. 질문의 artists에서 연상 가능한 art를 이용한 오답.
(C) 질문과 상관없는 오답. Where 의문문에 대한 응답이므로 오답.

18 W-Am / M-Au

How often should I submit my travel expenses?
(A) Sure, I'll trim the branches a little.
(B) Once a month.
(C) An updated owner's manual.

출장비는 얼마나 자주 제출해야 하나요?
(A) 물론이죠, 제가 가지들을 좀 다듬을게요.
(B) 한 달에 한 번씩이요.
(C) 업데이트된 사용자 설명서요.

| 어휘 | travel expense 출장비   trim 다듬다, 손질하다
branch (나뭇)가지   manual 설명서 |
|---|---|

해설 출장비 제출 빈도를 묻는 How often 의문문
(A) Yes/No 불가 오답. How often 의문문에는 Yes/No 응답이 불가능한데, Sure도 일종의 Yes 응답이라고 볼 수 있으므로 오답.
(B) 정답. 출장비 제출 빈도를 묻는 질문에 한 달에 한 번이라며 구체적인 빈도를 알려 주고 있으므로 정답.
(C) 질문과 상관없는 오답.

19 W-Br / W-Am ▶동영상 강의

Our print shop is going to have a sale on shirts.
(A) I'm afraid I have no more change.
(B) It's his favorite television show.
(C) OK—when will it start?

저희 인쇄소가 셔츠에 대해 할인 행사를 할 겁니다.
(A) 잔돈이 더 이상 없는 것 같아요.
(B) 그게 그가 가장 좋아하는 텔레비전 프로그램이에요.
(C) 좋아요, 언제 시작하나요?

어휘 change 잔돈, 거스름돈

해설 정보 전달의 평서문
(A) 평서문과 상관없는 오답.
(B) 평서문과 상관없는 오답. 평서문에 3인칭 대명사 his로 지칭할 인물이 언급된 적이 없으므로 오답.
(C) 정답. 인쇄소가 셔츠에 대해 할인 행사를 할 것이라는 평서문에 좋다(OK)고 대답한 뒤, 언제 시작하는지 물으며 관심을 표현하고 있으므로 정답.

20 M-Cn / W-Br

You already bought a new part for the sprinkler system, right?
(A) Check the weather forecast.
(B) Yes, I did that last week.
(C) That flight departs soon.

스프링클러 시스템에 필요한 새 부품을 이미 구입하셨죠, 맞죠?
(A) 일기 예보를 확인해 보세요.
(B) 네, 지난주에 그렇게 했습니다.
(C) 그 항공편은 곧 출발합니다.

어휘 part 부품 sprinkler 스프링클러 forecast 예보, 예측
depart 출발하다, 떠나다

해설 스프링클러 시스템에 필요한 새 부품을 구입했는지 확인하는 부가 의문문
(A) 질문과 상관없는 오답.
(B) 정답. 스프링클러 시스템에 필요한 새 부품을 구입했는지 확인하는 질문에 네(Yes)라고 대답한 뒤, 지난주에 그렇게 했다며 긍정 답변과 일관된 내용을 덧붙이고 있으므로 정답.
(C) 유사 발음 오답. 질문의 part와 부분적으로 발음이 유사한 departs를 이용한 오답.

21 M-Cn / W-Am

How many lamps are made at the factory every day?
(A) Some new machinery.
(B) A new line of men's clothing.
(C) About 500.

공장에서는 매일 몇 개의 전등이 만들어지나요?
(A) 새 기계들이요.
(B) 새로운 남성복 라인이요.
(C) 500개 정도요.

어휘 machinery 기계 clothing 의류, 옷

해설 공장에서 매일 만드는 전등의 수량을 묻는 How many 의문문
(A) 연상 단어 오답. 질문의 factory에서 연상 가능한 machinery를 이용한 오답.
(B) 질문과 상관없는 오답.
(C) 정답. 공장에서 매일 만드는 전등의 수량을 묻는 질문에 500개 정도라고 대략적인 수량으로 응답하고 있으므로 정답.

22 M-Cn / W-Br

Are you going out to eat, or did you bring your lunch from home?
(A) Right next to my office.
(B) That'll be five dollars, please.
(C) It's in the microwave.

나가서 식사하실 건가요, 아니면 댁에서 점심 도시락을 가져오셨나요?
(A) 제 사무실 바로 옆이에요.
(B) 전부 5달러입니다.
(C) 전자레인지에 있습니다.

어휘 microwave 전자레인지

해설 점심 식사 방식을 묻는 선택 의문문
(A) 질문과 상관없는 오답. Where 의문문에 대한 응답이므로 오답.
(B) 질문과 상관없는 오답. How much 의문문에 대한 응답이므로 오답.
(C) 정답. 나가서 먹을 건지, 아니면 집에서 점심 도시락을 가져왔는지 묻는 질문에 전자레인지에 있다는 말로 도시락을 가져왔다는 뜻을 나타내고 있으므로 정답.

23 W-Br / M-Cn

Can I place an order online?
(A) The post office on Main Street.
(B) Our Web site is currently down for maintenance.
(C) No, he put it in the filing cabinet.

온라인으로 주문할 수 있나요?
(A) 메인 가에 있는 우체국이요.
(B) 저희 웹사이트가 현재 점검으로 다운된 상태예요.
(C) 아니요, 그가 그걸 문서 보관함에 넣었어요.

어휘 place an order 주문하다   currently 현재
maintenance 점검, 유지 보수   filing cabinet 문서 보관함

해설 온라인 주문이 가능한지 묻는 조동사(Can) 의문문
(A) 질문과 상관없는 오답. Where 의문문에 대한 응답이므로 오답.
(B) 정답. 온라인 주문이 가능한지 묻는 질문에 웹사이트가 현재 점검으로 다운된 상태라며 불가능하다는 것을 우회적으로 알려 주고 있으므로 정답.
(C) 질문과 상관없는 오답. 질문에 3인칭 대명사 he로 지칭할 인물이 언급된 적이 없으므로 오답.

24 M-Au / W-Br

Shouldn't the new floor plan be finished today?
(A) I enjoyed the movie.
(B) My team is short-staffed right now.
(C) We met in the cafeteria.

새로운 평면도가 오늘 완료되어야 하지 않나요?
(A) 저는 그 영화가 즐거웠어요.
(B) 지금 저희 팀에 인원이 부족해요.
(C) 저희는 구내식당에서 만났어요.

어휘 floor plan (건물의) 평면도   short-staffed 인원[직원]이 부족한
cafeteria 구내식당

해설 새로운 평면도가 오늘 완료되어야 하는지 확인하는 부정 의문문
(A) 질문과 상관없는 오답.
(B) 정답. 새로운 평면도가 오늘 완료되어야 하는지 확인하는 질문에 지금 팀에 인원이 부족하다며 오늘 완료할 수 없음을 우회적으로 표현하고 있으므로 정답.
(C) 질문과 상관없는 오답.

25 M-Cn / M-Au

Who's the new head of the legal department?
(A) No, I think it's on the second floor.
(B) It hasn't been announced yet.
(C) Thanks, that'll help.

누가 신임 법무팀장인가요?
(A) 아니요, 2층에 있는 것 같아요.
(B) 아직 발표되지 않았어요.
(C) 감사합니다, 도움이 될 거예요.

어휘 legal department 법무팀, 법률 부서

해설 신임 법무팀장을 묻는 Who 의문문
(A) Yes/No 불가 오답. Who 의문문에는 Yes/No 응답이 불가능하므로 오답.
(B) 정답. 신임 법무팀장을 묻는 질문에 아직 발표되지 않았다며 현재로서는 알 수 없음을 우회적으로 알려 주고 있으므로 정답.
(C) 질문과 상관없는 오답.

26 M-Au / W-Am

Who's scheduled to repair the water heater in building two?
(A) There's a bottle of water in the refrigerator.
(B) Twenty dollars each.
(C) That job was completed yesterday.

누가 2동 건물의 온수기를 수리할 예정인가요?
(A) 냉장고에 물이 한 병 있어요.
(B) 각각 20달러입니다.
(C) 그 일은 어제 완료되었어요.

어휘 be scheduled to ~할 예정이다   refrigerator 냉장고
complete 완료하다

해설 2동 건물의 온수기를 수리할 사람을 묻는 Who 의문문
(A) 단어 반복 오답. 질문의 water를 반복 이용한 오답.
(B) 질문과 상관없는 오답. How much 의문문에 대한 응답이므로 오답.
(C) 정답. 2동 건물의 온수기를 수리할 사람을 묻는 질문에 그 일은 어제 이미 완료되었음을 알려 주고 있으므로 정답.

27 M-Au / W-Br   ▶동영상 강의

Why were the sales figures so high last quarter?
(A) I think that storefront is vacant.
(B) Koji is in charge of analyzing market trends.
(C) Let me unlock the door first.

지난 분기에 매출액이 왜 그렇게 높았던 거죠?
(A) 매장 앞 공간이 비어 있는 것 같아요.
(B) 코지가 시장 동향 분석을 담당하고 있습니다.
(C) 제가 먼저 그 문을 열어 드리겠습니다.

어휘 quarter 분기   storefront 매장 앞에 있는 공간
vacant 비어 있는   in charge of ~을 담당하고 있는
analyze 분석하다   unlock 열다, 잠금 해제하다

해설 지난 분기 매출액이 높았던 이유를 묻는 Why 의문문
(A) 연상 단어 오답. 질문의 sales에서 연상 가능한 storefront를 이용한 오답.
(B) 정답. 지난 분기 매출액이 높았던 이유를 묻는 질문에 코지가 시장 동향 분석을 담당하고 있다며 정보를 확인할 수 있는 방법을 알려 주고 있으므로 정답.
(C) 질문과 상관없는 오답.

28 M-Cn / W-Am

Ms. Martin is demonstrating the new software at the conference.
(A) I live on Vine Street.
(B) No, they catered food last year.
(C) I thought she was on vacation.

마틴 씨가 컨퍼런스에서 새 소프트웨어를 시연합니다.
(A) 저는 바인 가에 살아요.
(B) 아니요, 작년에는 출장 요리를 제공했어요.
(C) 저는 그분이 휴가 중이라고 생각했어요.

어휘 **demonstrate** 시연하다 **cater** 출장 요리를 제공하다

해설 정보 전달의 평서문
(A) 평서문과 상관없는 오답.
(B) 연상 단어 오답. 평서문의 conference에서 연상 가능한 catered food를 이용한 오답.
(C) 정답. 마틴 씨가 콘퍼런스에서 새 소프트웨어를 시연한다는 평서문에 그 사람이 휴가 중이라고 생각했다며 다른 사람이 하는 것으로 알고 있었다는 사실을 우회적으로 표현하고 있으므로 정답.

29 W-Br / M-Au

Let's hire Johnson Construction to fix this roof.
(A) They don't seem to be.
(B) They can't start until next month.
(C) I think it's on the bottom shelf.

이 지붕을 고치기 위해 존슨 컨스트럭션을 고용합시다.
(A) 그들은 그런 것 같지 않아요.
(B) 그곳은 다음 달이나 되어야 시작할 수 있어요.
(C) 맨 아래 선반에 있는 것 같아요.

어휘 **not ~ until …** …가 되어서야 ~ 하다 **shelf** 선반

해설 제안/권유의 평서문
(A) 평서문과 상관없는 오답.
(B) 정답. 지붕을 고치기 위해 존슨 컨스트럭션을 고용하자는 평서문에 그곳이 다음 달이나 되어야 시작할 수 있다며 다른 방법을 찾아야 할 것이라는 의견을 우회적으로 표현하고 있으므로 정답.
(C) 평서문과 상관없는 오답. Where 의문문에 대한 응답이므로 오답.

30 W-Am / M-Cn ▶동영상 강의

Your travel itinerary says you're going to Seattle, right?
(A) But I'm going to London.
(B) Turn left at the light, please.
(C) An e-mail update.

당신의 여행 일정표에 시애틀로 간다고 되어 있네요, 맞나요?
(A) 하지만 저는 런던으로 갑니다.
(B) 신호등에서 좌회전해 주세요.
(C) 이메일 업데이트요.

어휘 **itinerary** 일정(표) **say** (책자 등에) 나와 있다, 쓰여 있다

해설 여행 일정표에 시애틀로 간다고 되어 있는지 확인하는 부가 의문문
(A) 정답. 여행 일정표에 시애틀로 간다고 되어 있는지 확인하는 질문에 런던으로 간다며 자신의 실제 목적지를 밝히고 있으므로 정답.
(B) 유사 발음 오답. 질문의 right과 부분적으로 발음이 유사한 light를 이용한 오답.
(C) 질문과 상관없는 오답.

31 W-Br / W-Am

Won't theater tickets become available later today?
(A) A new pair of work boots.
(B) It should say on their Web site.
(C) Yes, I saw him at the convention.

극장 입장권이 오늘 이따가 구매 가능하게 되지 않을까요?
(A) 새 작업용 부츠 한 켤레요.
(B) 그곳 웹사이트에 나와 있을 겁니다.
(C) 네, 컨벤션에서 그를 봤어요.

어휘 **available** 구매 가능한, 이용 가능한 **pair** 쌍, 짝

해설 극장 입장권이 오늘 구매 가능하게 될지 확인하는 부정 의문문
(A) 질문과 상관없는 오답.
(B) 정답. 극장 입장권이 오늘 구매 가능하게 될지 확인하는 질문에 그곳 웹사이트에 나와 있을 것이라며 정보를 확인할 수 있는 방법을 알려 주고 있으므로 정답.
(C) 질문과 상관없는 오답. 질문에 3인칭 대명사 him으로 지칭할 인물이 언급된 적이 없으므로 오답.

PART 3

32-34 M-Cn / W-Am

M Carmen, I don't know if you realize it, but ³²**your office chair makes a squeaking sound every time you move. It's a little distracting when the office is so quiet.**

W Oh! I had my headset on, so I didn't realize that. ³³**I'll go swap this chair with one from the conference room.**

M Thanks for understanding. And ³⁴**don't forget that our team is ordering takeout from a Thai restaurant for lunch.** Do you want anything?

W Sure. I'd love some spring rolls!

남 카르멘, 알고 있는지 모르겠지만, **당신이 움직일 때마다 사무실 의자에서 삐걱거리는 소리가 나요. 사무실이 아주 조용할 땐 좀 방해가 되네요.**
여 아! 제가 헤드폰을 끼고 있어서, 그런 줄 몰랐어요. **가서 이 의자를 대회의실에 있는 것과 바꿀게요.**
남 이해해 주셔서 감사해요. 그리고 **우리 팀이 점심으로 태국 레스토랑에서 포장 주문하기로 한 거 잊지 마세요.** 원하시는 게 있을까요?
여 물론이죠. 저는 스프링 롤이 먹고 싶어요!

어휘 **realize** 알아차리다, 깨닫다 **squeaking** 삐걱거리는 **distracting** 방해가 되는 **swap** 바꾸다, 교체하다

32 What complaint does the man make?
(A) A room is too small.
(B) A noise is distracting.
(C) Some software is slow.
(D) A printer is broken.

남자는 어떤 불만을 제기하는가?
(A) 방이 너무 작다.
(B) 소음이 지장을 준다.
(C) 소프트웨어가 느리다.
(D) 프린터가 고장 났다.

어휘 complaint 불만, 불평 broken 고장 난, 망가진

해설 세부 사항 관련 – 남자가 제기하는 불만
남자가 첫 대사에서 여자의 사무실 의자에서 삐걱거리는 소리가 난다며 그것이 사무실이 아주 조용할 때는 좀 방해가 된다(~ your office chair makes a squeaking sound every time you move. It's a little distracting when the office is so quiet)고 말하고 있으므로 정답은 (B)이다.

Paraphrasing
대화의 a squeaking sound → 정답의 A noise

33 What does the woman say she will do?
(A) Change her chair
(B) Borrow a computer laptop
(C) Contact the help desk
(D) Work from home

여자는 무엇을 할 것이라고 말하는가?
(A) 자신의 의자 바꾸기
(B) 노트북 컴퓨터 빌리기
(C) 안내 데스크에 연락하기
(D) 재택 근무하기

어휘 work from home 재택 근무하다

해설 세부 사항 관련 – 여자가 할 일
여자가 첫 대사에서 자신의 의자를 대회의실에 있는 것과 바꾸겠다(I'll go swap this chair with one from the conference room)고 했으므로 정답은 (A)이다.

Paraphrasing
대화의 swap this chair with one from the conference room → 정답의 Change her chair

34 What does the man remind the woman about?
(A) A team lunch
(B) A training session
(C) A project deadline
(D) A policy change

남자는 여자에게 무엇에 대해 상기시키는가?
(A) 팀 점심 식사
(B) 교육
(C) 프로젝트 마감 기한
(D) 정책 변경

어휘 deadline 마감 기한 policy 정책, 방침

해설 세부 사항 관련 – 남자가 여자에게 상기시키는 것
남자가 두 번째 대사에서 우리 팀이 점심으로 태국 레스토랑에서 포장 주문하기로 한 것 잊지 말라(~ don't forget that our team is ordering takeout from a Thai restaurant for lunch)고 했으므로 정답은 (A)이다.

Paraphrasing
대화의 our team is ordering takeout ~ for lunch → 정답의 A team lunch

35-37 M-Cn / W-Br

M Amina, do you have a few minutes? **35 I finished preparing the sample dish that you asked for.** You can try it now if you'd like.

W Sure, I have time now. **36 I think the pasta is delicious. I like the hint of fresh lemon flavor.** It'll make a great addition to our summer menu.

M I agree. But we don't use lemons in any other dish. **37 Should I get in touch with our fruit and vegetable supplier?**

W Thanks. **37 Just ask him what the cost difference would be** if we added five kilograms of lemons to our regular delivery.

남 아미나, 잠깐 시간 있어요? **요청하셨던 샘플 요리 준비를 마쳤습니다.** 괜찮으시면 지금 한번 드셔 보세요.

여 네, 지금 시간이 있어요. **파스타가 맛있는 것 같아요. 약간의 상큼한 레몬 풍미가 마음에 들어요.** 우리 여름 메뉴에 훌륭한 추가가 될 거예요.

남 맞아요. 그런데 우리가 다른 요리에는 레몬을 사용하지 않잖아요. **우리 과일 및 채소 공급업체에 연락해야 할까요?**

여 고마워요. 정기 배송에 레몬 5킬로그램을 추가하면 **비용 차이가 얼마나 될지 그분께 물어봐 주세요.**

어휘 hint 약간 flavor 풍미, 맛 addition 추가, 보탬
get in touch with ~에게 연락하다 supplier 공급업체
regular 정기적인

35 What most likely is the man's occupation?
(A) Server
(B) Chef
(C) Farmer
(D) Food critic

남자의 직업은 무엇일 것 같은가?
(A) 종업원
(B) 요리사
(C) 농부
(D) 음식 평론가

해설 전체 내용 관련 – 남자의 직업

남자가 첫 대사에서 여자가 요청한 샘플 요리 준비를 마쳤다(I finished preparing the sample dish that you asked for)고 말하는 것으로 보아 남자는 요리사임을 알 수 있다. 따라서 정답은 (B)이다.

36 What does the woman say she likes?
(A) The design of a menu
(B) The business hours of a restaurant
(C) The flavor of a dish
(D) The color of some tablecloths

여자는 무엇이 마음에 든다고 말하는가?
(A) 메뉴 디자인
(B) 레스토랑 영업시간
(C) 요리의 풍미
(D) 일부 식탁보의 색상

해설 세부 사항 관련 – 여자가 마음에 들어 하는 것

여자가 첫 대사에서 파스타가 맛있는 것 같다(I think the pasta is delicious)며 약간의 상큼한 레몬 풍미가 마음에 든다(I like the hint of fresh lemon flavor)고 했으므로 정답은 (C)이다.

Paraphrasing
대화의 the hint of fresh lemon flavor
→ 정답의 The flavor of a dish

37 Why is the man going to make a phone call?
(A) To inquire about a job
(B) To consult a colleague
(C) To change a delivery date
(D) To ask about a cost

남자는 왜 전화를 걸 예정인가?
(A) 일자리에 관해 문의하기 위해
(B) 동료와 상의하기 위해
(C) 배송일을 변경하기 위해
(D) 가격에 관해 묻기 위해

어휘 inquire 문의하다 consult 상의하다, 참고하다
colleague 동료

해설 세부 사항 관련 – 남자가 전화하는 이유

남자가 두 번째 대사에서 과일 및 채소 공급업체에 연락해야 할지(Should I get in touch with our fruit and vegetable supplier?) 묻자 여자가 비용 차이가 얼마나 될지만 물어봐 달라(Just ask him what the cost difference would be ~)고 대답하고 있으므로 정답은 (D)이다.

Paraphrasing
대화의 ask him what the cost difference would be
→ 정답의 ask about a cost

38-40 M-Au / W-Am

M **38 Dr. Ruiz**, do you have a minute?
W Sure.
M **38 It looks like the hospital has a little money left over in our staff development budget.** Can you think of anything we could spend it on? I'm just looking for ideas.
W Well, **39 I'd love it if we could get a subscription to Prescriber Med's newsletter.** A lot of the expert summaries in it are useful for my clinical practice work.
M Sounds good. I'm going to ask other doctors, too, and see how best to use these funds.
W Great. **40 I'd suggest maybe sending out a survey, though.** That'd be more convenient.
M Good idea! I'll do that.

남 **루이즈 선생님**, 잠깐 시간 있으세요?
여 네.
남 **병원 직원 능력 개발 예산에 남아 있는 돈이 좀 있는 것 같아서요.** 어디에 쓰면 좋을지 생각나는 거 있으세요? 아이디어를 찾아보는 중이에요.
여 음, **프리스크라이버 메드의 소식지를 구독할 수 있으면 좋겠어요.** 그 안에 있는 많은 전문가 요약들이 제 임상 실무에 유용하거든요.
남 좋은 것 같아요. 다른 의사 선생님들께도 여쭤보고 이 자금을 가장 잘 사용할 방법을 알아보겠습니다.
여 훌륭해요. **그래도 설문지를 돌려보는 걸 제안하고 싶어요.** 그게 더 편리할 거예요.
남 좋은 생각이네요! 그렇게 해 보겠습니다.

어휘 budget 예산 spend 쓰다 subscription 구독
expert 전문가; 전문가의 summary 요약(본) useful 유용한
clinical practice work 임상 실무 convenient 편리한

38 Where do the speakers most likely work?
(A) At a hospital
(B) At a law firm
(C) At an accounting company
(D) At a publishing headquarters

화자들은 어디에서 일하는 것 같은가?
(A) 병원
(B) 법률 회사
(C) 회계 회사
(D) 출판사 본사

어휘 firm 회사, 업체 accounting 회계 headquarters 본사

TEST 7   185

해설 전체 내용 관련 – 화자들의 근무 장소

남자가 첫 대사에서 여자를 루이즈 선생님(Dr. Ruiz)이라고 부른 뒤, 병원 직원 능력 개발 예산에 남아 있는 돈이 좀 있는 것 같다(It looks like the hospital has a little money left over in our staff development budget)며 이야기를 이어 가고 있는 것으로 보아 화자들은 병원에서 근무하는 사람들임을 알 수 있다. 따라서 정답은 (A)이다.

39 What does the woman request?
(A) A newsletter subscription
(B) A parking pass
(C) Budget data
(D) Staff biographies

여자는 무엇을 요청하는가?
(A) 소식지 구독
(B) 주차권
(C) 예산 데이터
(D) 직원들 이력

어휘 biography 이력, 전기

해설 세부 사항 관련 – 여자의 요청 사항

여자가 두 번째 대사에서 프리스크라이버 메드의 소식지를 구독할 수 있으면 좋겠다(I'd love it if we could get a subscription to Prescriber Med's newsletter)고 했으므로 정답은 (A)이다.

40 What does the woman suggest the man do?
(A) Call a coworker
(B) Ask for an extension
(C) Send out a survey
(D) Request overtime hours

여자는 남자에게 무엇을 하라고 제안하는가?
(A) 동료에게 전화하기
(B) 기간 연장 요청하기
(C) 설문지 돌리기
(D) 초과 근무 시간 요청하기

어휘 coworker 동료 extension 연장, 확대
overtime 초과 근무의

해설 세부 사항 관련 – 여자의 제안 사항

여자가 세 번째 대사에서 그래도 설문지를 돌려 보는 것을 제안하고 싶다(I'd suggest maybe sending out a survey, though)고 했으므로 정답은 (C)이다.

41-43 M-Cn / W-Br

M Hello. **41 I just received a pair of shoes I ordered from your online store.** They're nice, but they don't fit. Can I ship them back to you for a refund?

W Yes. But for a refund, I'm afraid you'll have to ship the shoes back at your own expense. On the other hand, if you'd like to exchange them, we'll send you a return label for free.

M In that case, **42 I'll exchange them for another size.** How do I do that?

W **43 I'll e-mail you a link.** Just click on it, and you'll be redirected to the instructions for exchanges on our Web site.

남 안녕하세요. **제가 귀사의 온라인 매장에서 주문한 신발을 막 받았습니다.** 멋지긴 한데, 사이즈가 안 맞네요. 환불을 위해 반송해도 될까요?

여 네. 하지만 환불의 경우, 죄송하지만 신발을 고객님 부담으로 반송해 주셔야 해요. 반면, 교환하기를 원하신다면, 저희가 무료로 반품 라벨을 보내 드립니다.

남 그런 경우라면, **다른 사이즈로 교환할게요.** 어떻게 하면 되죠?

여 **제가 이메일로 링크를 보내 드리겠습니다.** 클릭하기만 하면, 저희 웹사이트의 제품 교환 안내 페이지로 연결되실 겁니다.

어휘 fit 맞다, 적합하다 ship 배송하다 refund 환불; 환불하다
expense 비용, 경비 exchange 교환; 교환하다
redirect (컴퓨터, 웹사이트 등에서) 자동으로 다른 페이지로 연결시키다
instructions 설명, 안내

41 What type of business is the man calling?
(A) A shoe company
(B) A marketing agency
(C) A shipping company
(D) A tailor shop

남자는 어떤 종류의 업체에 전화하고 있는가?
(A) 신발 회사
(B) 마케팅 대행사
(C) 배송 회사
(D) 양복점

해설 전체 내용 관련 – 남자가 전화하는 업체

남자가 첫 대사에서 귀사의 온라인 매장에서 주문한 신발을 막 받았다(I just received a pair of shoes I ordered from your online store)고 했으므로 정답은 (A)이다.

42 What does the man decide to do?
(A) Contact a different business
(B) Exchange some merchandise
(C) Write an online review
(D) Download a catalog

남자는 무엇을 하기로 결정하는가?
(A) 다른 업체에 연락하기
(B) 상품 교환하기
(C) 온라인 후기 작성하기
(D) 카탈로그 다운로드하기

어휘 merchandise 상품

해설 세부 사항 관련 - 남자의 결정 사항
남자가 두 번째 대사에서 그런 경우라면 다른 사이즈로 교환하겠다 (~ I'll exchange them for another size)고 했으므로 정답은 (B)이다.

Paraphrasing
대화의 exchange them for another size
→ 정답의 exchange some merchandise

43 What will the woman send by e-mail?
(A) Some design images
(B) A sales receipt
(C) Some delivery options
(D) A Web site link

여자는 이메일로 무엇을 보낼 것인가?
(A) 디자인 이미지
(B) 판매 영수증
(C) 배송 옵션
(D) 웹사이트 링크

어휘 receipt 영수증

해설 세부 사항 관련 - 여자가 이메일로 보낼 것
여자가 마지막 대사에서 이메일로 링크를 보내겠다(I'll e-mail you a link)고 했으므로 정답은 (D)이다.

44-46 M-Cn / W-Am

M On today's podcast, we have **44Gabriela Espinoza, a former history professor who focuses on ancient civilizations.** Recently, however, she left the university for another position—tell us about that.

W Well, last year, a film company was producing a movie about the famous pyramids at Giza. They needed an expert in ancient Egypt, and they found me. **45Now I work full-time as a consultant for the film industry.**

M Do you actually work on set?

W Yes. When there are last-minute changes, I make sure the changes are historically accurate. In fact, **46I'll be in Egypt next week**, sailing down the Nile River.

남 오늘 팟캐스트에서는, **고대 문명을 주로 연구하시는 전직 역사 교수 가브리엘라 에스피노자**를 모셨습니다. 그런데, 최근에, 다른 일을 위해 대학을 떠나셨는데요, 이 부분에 대해 말씀해 주세요.

여 음, 작년에, 한 영화사에서 기자에 있는 유명 피라미드들에 관한 영화를 제작하고 있었어요. 그쪽에서 고대 이집트 분야의 전문가를 필요로 했는데, 저를 찾은 거죠. **지금은 영화 업계에서 컨설턴트로서 정식으로 일하고 있습니다.**

남 실제로 세트장에서 일하시나요?

여 네. 막판에 변동이 있는 경우, 제가 그 내용이 역사적으로 정확한지 확인합니다. 사실, **다음 주에는 이집트에 있을 거예요**, 나일강을 따라 항해하면서요.

어휘 former 이전의 ancient 고대의 civilization 문명 consultant 컨설턴트, 상담 전문가 last-minute 마지막 순간의 historically 역사적으로 accurate 정확한 sail 항해하다

44 What is the woman's area of expertise?
(A) Music
(B) Biology
(C) History
(D) Mathematics

여자의 전문 분야는 무엇인가?
(A) 음악
(B) 생물학
(C) 역사학
(D) 수학

어휘 expertise 전문 지식, 전문 기술

해설 전체 내용 관련 - 여자의 전문 분야
남자가 첫 대사에서 여자의 이름과 함께 고대 문명을 주로 연구하는 전직 역사 교수(~ Gabriela Espinoza, a former history professor who focuses on ancient civilizations)라고 소개하고 있으므로 정답은 (C)이다.

45 What is the woman's current job?
(A) A recruiter for universities
(B) A curator for museums
(C) A consultant for film studios
(D) An editor for publishing companies

여자의 현재 직업은 무엇인가?
(A) 대학교 입학 담당자
(B) 박물관 큐레이터
(C) 영화사 컨설턴트
(D) 출판사 편집자

어휘 current 현재의 recruiter 모집 담당자 curator 큐레이터

해설 세부 사항 관련 - 여자의 현재 직업
여자가 첫 대사에서 지금은 영화 업계에서 컨설턴트로서 정식으로 일하고 있다(Now I work full-time as a consultant for the film industry)고 했으므로 정답은 (C)이다.

TEST 7 **187**

46 What will the woman do next week?
(A) Promote her new book
(B) Audition for a movie
(C) Teach a seminar
(D) Visit another country

여자는 다음 주에 무엇을 할 것인가?
(A) 자신의 신간 도서 홍보하기
(B) 영화 오디션 보기
(C) 세미나 진행하기
(D) 다른 국가 방문하기

어휘 promote 홍보하다 audition 오디션을 보다

해설 세부 사항 관련 – 여자가 다음 주에 할 일
여자가 마지막 대사에서 다음 주에는 이집트에 있을 것(~ I'll be in Egypt next week ~)이라고 했으므로 정답은 (D)이다.

Paraphrasing
대화의 will be in Egypt → 정답의 Visit another country

47-49 W-Br / M-Cn

W Pedro, **47 I just registered for the national marketing convention in June.**

M Me, too. And I printed out the program with all the talks and workshops.

W Oh, can I take a look? **48 This is great! It looks like there are plenty of breaks in the schedule for networking with potential clients.**

M Right. So **49 don't forget to bring your business cards with you.** You'll need a lot of them.

W Thanks for the reminder. I'd better order more.

여 페드로, 저 방금 6월에 있을 전국 마케팅 컨벤션에 등록했어요.
남 저도요. 그리고 모든 강연과 워크숍이 기재된 행사 일정표를 출력했어요.
여 아, 한번 봐도 될까요? 아주 좋네요! 스케줄상 잠재 고객들과 네트워킹할 수 있는 휴식 시간이 충분한 것 같아요.
남 맞습니다. 그러니 잊지 말고 명함을 가져오세요. 많이 필요하실 거예요.
여 알려 주셔서 감사합니다. 더 주문하는 게 좋겠네요.

어휘 register for ~에 등록하다 program 행사 일정표 break 휴식 시간 potential 잠재적인 reminder 상기시키는 것

47 What are the speakers preparing for in June?
(A) A company merger
(B) A fund-raising event
(C) An industry convention
(D) A product launch

화자들은 6월에 있을 무엇을 준비하고 있는가?
(A) 회사 합병
(B) 모금 행사
(C) 업계 컨벤션
(D) 제품 출시

어휘 merger 합병 fund-raising 모금 launch 출시, 공개

해설 전체 내용 관련 – 화자들이 6월에 준비하고 있는 것
여자가 첫 대사에서 방금 6월에 있을 전국 마케팅 컨벤션에 등록했다(I just registered for the national marketing convention in June)고 말한 뒤, 일정과 준비해야 할 사항 등에 대한 대화를 이어 가고 있으므로 정답은 (C)이다.

Paraphrasing
대화의 the national marketing convention
→ 정답의 An industry convention

---

48 Why is the woman pleased?
(A) She has been promoted to manager.
(B) She will have networking opportunities.
(C) An advertising campaign was successful.
(D) An article about the company is positive.

여자는 왜 기뻐하는가?
(A) 관리자로 승진되었다.
(B) 네트워킹 기회가 있을 것이다.
(C) 광고 캠페인이 성공적이었다.
(D) 회사에 관한 기사가 긍정적이다.

어휘 promote 승진시키다, 홍보하다 opportunity 기회 advertising 광고 positive 긍정적인

해설 세부 사항 관련 – 여자가 기뻐하는 이유
여자가 두 번째 대사에서 아주 좋다(That's great!)며 잠재 고객들과 네트워킹할 수 있는 휴식 시간이 충분한 것 같다(It looks like there are plenty of breaks ~ for networking with potential clients)고 했으므로 정답은 (B)이다.

Paraphrasing
대화의 breaks ~ for networking with potential clients
→ 정답의 networking opportunities

---

49 What does the man remind the woman about?
(A) Bringing business cards
(B) Compiling a guest list
(C) Reviewing a contract
(D) Submitting receipts

남자는 여자에게 무엇에 대해 상기시키는가?
(A) 명함 가져오기
(B) 손님 명단 정리하기
(C) 계약서 검토하기
(D) 영수증 제출하기

어휘 compile (자료 등을 모아) 정리하다 submit 제출하다

해설	세부 사항 관련 – 남자가 상기시키는 것

남자가 두 번째 대사에서 잊지 말고 명함을 가져오라(~ don't forget to bring your business cards with you)고 했으므로 정답은 (A)이다.

50-52 3인 대화 M-Cn / M-Au / W-Br ▶동영상 강의

> M1 **50 We need to come up with a new menu design for our seaside restaurant.** Something memorable. Do you two have any suggestions?
>
> M2 Maybe we could use a dolphin jumping out of the water. Junko, what do you think?
>
> W Oh, I really like that idea! And it's fitting, since our restaurant is at the beach. **51 Minoru, can you put together a graphic for the rest of us to look at?**
>
> M2 I'll start working on it immediately.
>
> M1 Great. Hopefully, we can finalize something before **52 next month's community fair.**

남1 우리 해변 레스토랑의 새로운 메뉴 디자인을 만들어야 해요. 뭔가 기억에 남을 만한 것으로요. 두 분 의견 있으신가요?
남2 물 밖으로 뛰어오르는 돌고래를 이용할 수 있지 않을까 해요. 준코, 어떻게 생각하세요?
여 오, 그 아이디어가 정말 마음에 들어요! 그리고 우리 레스토랑이 해변에 있으니, 딱이에요. **미노루, 다른 사람들도 볼 수 있게 그래픽을 하나 만들어 줄 수 있나요?**
남2 바로 시작할게요.
남1 좋아요. **다음 달에 있을 지역 축제** 전까지 뭔가 확정할 수 있으면 해요.

> 어휘 come up with ~을 만들어 내다, ~을 제안하다 memorable 기억할 만한 suggestion 의견, 제안 fitting 적합한, 어울리는 put together 만들다, 조립하다 immediately 즉시 finalize 확정하다, 마무리하다 fair 축제, 박람회

50 Who most likely are the speakers?
(A) Tour guides
(B) Hotel managers
(C) Marine biologists
(D) Business owners

화자들은 누구인 것 같은가?
(A) 여행 가이드
(B) 호텔 매니저
(C) 해양 생물학자
(D) 업체 소유주

해설	전체 내용 관련 – 화자들의 직업

첫 번째 남자가 첫 대사에서 해변 레스토랑의 새로운 메뉴 디자인을 만들어야 한다(We need to come up with a new menu design for our seaside restaurant)고 한 뒤, 컨셉과 일정에 대한 논의를 이어 가고 있는 것으로 보아 화자들은 해당 업체의 소유주임을 알 수 있다. 따라서 정답은 (D)이다.

---

51 What is Minoru asked to do?
(A) Confirm a reservation
(B) Create a logo
(C) Print some documents
(D) Review some résumés

미노루는 무엇을 하도록 요청받는가?
(A) 예약 확인하기
(B) 로고 만들기
(C) 문서 출력하기
(D) 이력서 검토하기

어휘 reservation 예약

해설	세부 사항 관련 – 미노루가 요청받는 일

여자가 첫 대사에서 미노루에게 다른 사람들도 볼 수 있게 그래픽을 하나 만들어 달라(Minoru, can you put together a graphic for the rest of us to look at?)고 요청하고 있다. 이는 앞서 두 번째 남자가 언급한 물 밖으로 뛰어오르는 돌고래 로고를 다른 사람들도 볼 수 있게 만들어 달라는 의미이므로 정답은 (B)이다.

> **Paraphrasing**
> 대화의 put together a graphic → 정답의 Create a logo

---

52 What event is taking place next month?
(A) A seasonal sale
(B) A trade show
(C) A community fair
(D) A company picnic

다음 달에 어떤 행사가 열리는가?
(A) 계절 할인
(B) 무역 박람회
(C) 지역 축제
(D) 회사 야유회

해설	세부 사항 관련 – 다음 달에 열리는 행사

첫 번째 남자가 마지막 대사에서 다음 달에 있을 지역 축제(next month's community fair)에 대해 언급하고 있으므로 정답은 (C)이다.

53-55 M-Au / W-Am

M Hello. ⁵³**Welcome to Henderson State Park.** Parking is free this weekend.

W That's great! I'm visiting here for the first time. Do you have a map of the park trails?

M I'm sorry. I just ran out of maps. It's been a very busy weekend.

W Well, ⁵⁴,⁵⁵ **I'm just a little concerned since I don't know the trails.**

M I understand. The visitor center is about 400 meters up the road.

W Oh, that's good to know. Thanks.

남 안녕하세요. **헨더슨 주립 공원에 오신 것을 환영합니다.** 이번 주말은 주차가 무료입니다.

여 잘됐네요! 제가 여기를 처음 방문했어요. 공원 산책로 지도가 있나요?

남 죄송합니다. 방금 지도가 다 떨어졌어요. 아주 바쁜 주말이었거든요.

여 음, **산책로를 몰라서 좀 걱정이 되네요.**

남 이해합니다. 방문자 센터는 도로를 따라 약 400미터 올라가면 있어요.

여 아, 좋은 정보네요. 감사합니다.

어휘 trail 산책로, 코스   run out of ~이 다 떨어지다, ~을 다 쓰다   concerned 걱정하는

53 Where is the conversation taking place?
(A) At a bus station
(B) At a city museum
(C) At a state park
(D) At a sports stadium

대화는 어디에서 진행되고 있는가?
(A) 버스 정류장
(B) 시립 박물관
(C) 주립 공원
(D) 스포츠 경기장

해설 전체 내용 관련 – 대화의 장소
남자가 첫 대사에서 헨더슨 주립 공원에 온 것을 환영한다(Welcome to Henderson State Park)고 했으므로 정답은 (C)이다.

54 Why does the woman say she is concerned?
(A) She is late for an appointment.
(B) She does not have a credit card.
(C) She did not reserve tickets.
(D) She is unfamiliar with a location.

여자는 왜 걱정된다고 말하는가?
(A) 예약 시간에 늦었다.
(B) 신용카드를 갖고 있지 않다.
(C) 티켓을 예매하지 않았다.
(D) 장소에 익숙하지 않다.

어휘 appointment 예약, 약속   reserve 예약하다   unfamiliar with ~에 익숙하지 않은   location 장소, 위치

해설 세부 사항 관련 – 여자가 걱정하는 이유
여자가 두 번째 대사에서 산책로를 몰라서 좀 걱정이 된다(I'm just a little concerned since I don't know the trails)고 말하는 것으로 보아 이 장소에 익숙하지 않아 걱정하는 상황임을 알 수 있다. 따라서 정답은 (D)이다.

Paraphrasing
대화의 don't know the trails
→ 정답의 is unfamiliar with a location

55 Why does the man say, "The visitor center is about 400 meters up the road"?
(A) To correct some information
(B) To offer a possible solution
(C) To suggest a payment option
(D) To point out a place to park

남자는 왜 "방문자 센터는 도로를 따라 약 400미터 올라가면 있어요"라고 말하는가?
(A) 정보를 바로잡기 위해
(B) 가능성 있는 해결책을 제시하기 위해
(C) 지불 옵션을 제안하기 위해
(D) 주차할 곳을 가리키기 위해

어휘 correct 바로잡다, 정정하다   solution 해결책   point out 가리키다, 지적하다

해설 화자의 의도 파악 – 방문자 센터는 도로를 따라 약 400미터 올라가면 있다는 말의 의도
여자가 두 번째 대사에서 산책로를 몰라서 좀 걱정이 된다(I'm just a little concerned since I don't know the trails)고 말한 뒤 남자가 인용문을 언급한 것으로 보아, 여자에게 해결책을 제시하려는 의도로 한 말임을 알 수 있다. 따라서 정답은 (B)이다.

56-58 3인 대화 M-Au / M-Cn / W-Br

> M1 Good morning, Mayor Ishikawa. ⁵⁶**I'm glad you could join Ms. Schneider and me for the ceremony as we begin this important first step—the building demolition.**
>
> M2 Happy to be here. The city appreciates your company's involvement in this project.
>
> W Our pleasure. ⁵⁷**TJO Property is excited to be investing in this community in such a substantial way.**
>
> M1 Right. And tearing down this old shopping center will give us the space to create a new mixed-use project of apartments, shops, and offices.
>
> M2 Community residents are looking forward to the new development.
>
> W Absolutely. Since the press is here, ⁵⁸**should we pose for a photograph in front of the wrecking ball before the work begins?**

남1 안녕하세요, 이시카와 시장님. **슈나이더 씨와 저와 함께, 이 중요한 첫 단계인 건물 철거를 시작하는 기념식에 참석해 주셔서 기쁩니다.**
남2 오게 되어 기쁩니다. 우리 시에서는 이 프로젝트에 대한 귀사의 참여를 감사하게 생각하고 있어요.
여 별말씀요. **저희 TJO 부동산도 지역 사회에 이렇게 큰 규모로 투자하게 되어 기쁩니다.**
남1 맞아요. 그리고 이 오래된 쇼핑센터를 허물면 아파트, 상점, 사무실이 함께 들어서는 새로운 복합 개발 단지를 조성할 공간이 생깁니다.
남2 지역 주민들이 새로운 개발을 아주 기대하고 있어요.
여 물론이죠. 취재진이 이곳에 와 있으니, **작업이 시작되기 전에 해체용 철구 앞에서 사진 촬영을 위해 포즈를 취할까요?**

어휘 demolition 철거 appreciate 고마워하다, 인정하다 involvement 참여 invest 투자하다 substantial 상당한 tear down ~을 허물다 mixed-use project 복합 개발 단지 (주거, 상업, 업무 공간이 함께 있는 복합 용도의 개발 형태) press 취재진, 언론 wrecking ball (건물) 해체용 철구

56 What are the speakers attending?
(A) A property inspection
(B) A contract signing
(C) **A building demolition**
(D) A grand opening

화자들은 무엇에 참석하고 있는가?
(A) 건물 점검
(B) 계약서 서명
(C) **건물 철거**
(D) 개장식

어휘 property 건물, 부동산 inspection 점검, 조사

해설 전체 내용 관련 – 화자들이 참석하고 있는 것
첫 번째 남자가 첫 대사에서 두 번째 남자에게 이 중요한 첫 단계인 건물 철거를 시작하는 기념식에 참석해 줘서 기쁘다(I'm glad you could join ~ for the ceremony as we begin this important first step—the building demolition)고 했으므로 정답은 (C)이다.

57 What does the woman say she is pleased about?
(A) Using the latest technology
(B) Improving safety policies
(C) Keeping expenses within budget
(D) **Investing in a community**

여자는 무엇에 대해 기쁘다고 말하는가?
(A) 최신 기술 이용
(B) 안전 정책 개선
(C) 예산 내 지출 유지
(D) **지역 사회 투자**

어휘 latest 최신의 improve 개선하다 policy 정책, 방침 expense 지출, 경비

해설 세부 사항 관련 – 여자가 기쁘다고 말하는 것
여자가 첫 대사에서 TJO 부동산도 지역 사회에 이렇게 큰 규모로 투자하게 되어 기쁘다(TJO Property is excited to be investing in this community in such a substantial way)고 했으므로 정답은 (D)이다.

58 What does the woman suggest doing?
(A) Distributing some handouts
(B) **Posing for a photograph**
(C) Enlarging some drawings
(D) Scheduling an interview with a reporter

여자는 무엇을 하자고 제안하는가?
(A) 유인물 배부하기
(B) **사진 촬영을 위해 포즈 취하기**
(C) 그림 확대하기
(D) 기자와 인터뷰 일정 잡기

어휘 distribute 배부하다, 나눠 주다 handout 유인물 enlarge 확대하다, 확장하다 drawing 그림

해설 세부 사항 관련 – 여자의 제안 사항
여자가 마지막 대사에서 작업이 시작되기 전에 해체용 철구 앞에서 사진 촬영을 위해 포즈를 취하자(~ should we pose for a photograph in front of the wrecking ball before the work begins?)고 제안하고 있으므로 정답은 (B)이다.

59-61 M-Cn / W-Am

M: Welcome to Schmidt's. **⁵⁹Are you interested in our hanging plants?** I'm happy to help you choose.

W: Please! **⁶⁰I got this coupon in the mail for fifteen percent off any outdoor plants. So, I thought I'd see if you have some flower baskets I could hang in my back patio area.**

M: **⁶¹These plants here bloom beautifully and do best in direct sunlight.**

W: Well, it's a covered patio.

M: OK. Just follow me. We have plenty of plants that do well in shade or partial sun.

남: 슈미츠에 오신 것을 환영합니다. 저희 행잉 플랜트에 관심이 있으신가요? 제가 선택하시는 걸 도와드릴게요.

여: 부탁드려요! 모든 야외 식물에 쓸 수 있는 15퍼센트 할인 쿠폰을 우편으로 받았거든요. 그래서 저희 집 뒤쪽 테라스 공간에 걸어 놓을 수 있는 꽃바구니가 좀 있는지 알아볼까 했어요.

남: 여기 있는 이 식물들이 꽃이 아름답게 피고, 직사광선에서도 잘 자랍니다.

여: 음, 지붕으로 덮여 있는 테라스예요.

남: 알겠습니다. 저만 따라오세요. 그늘이나 반그늘에서 잘 자라는 식물들도 많이 있어요.

어휘 hanging plant 행잉 플랜트(걸이식 화분) patio 테라스
bloom 꽃을 피우다 shade 그늘 partial 부분적인

59 Where does the man most likely work?
(A) At a garden center
(B) At a restaurant
(C) At a furniture store
(D) At a hardware store

남자는 어디에서 일하는 것 같은가?
(A) 원예 용품점
(B) 레스토랑
(C) 가구 매장
(D) 철물점

해설 전체 내용 관련 – 남자의 근무 장소
남자가 첫 대사에서 행잉 플랜트에 관심이 있는지(Are you interested in our hanging plants?) 물으며 도움을 제안하고 있는 것으로 보아 남자는 원예와 관련된 매장의 직원임을 알 수 있다. 따라서 정답은 (A)이다.

60 What motivated the woman to visit the business?
(A) She read about it in the newspaper.
(B) She heard an announcement on the radio.
(C) She received a coupon in the mail.
(D) She saw an advertisement on TV.

여자가 해당 업체를 방문한 동기는 무엇이었는가?
(A) 신문에서 그곳에 관한 글을 읽었다.
(B) 라디오에서 안내 방송을 들었다.
(C) 우편으로 쿠폰을 받았다.
(D) TV에서 광고를 봤다.

어휘 motivate 동기를 부여하다 announcement 안내, 공지
advertisement 광고

해설 세부 사항 관련 – 여자가 업체를 방문한 동기
여자가 첫 대사에서 모든 야외 식물에 쓸 수 있는 15퍼센트 할인 쿠폰을 우편으로 받았다(I got this coupon in the mail for fifteen percent off any outdoor plants)며 그래서 꽃 바구니를 좀 알아볼까 했다(So, I thought I'd see if you have some flower baskets ~)고 말하고 있으므로 정답은 (C)이다.

61 Why does the woman say, "it's a covered patio"?
(A) To offer reassurance
(B) To make a complaint
(C) To explain a decision
(D) To correct a misunderstanding

여자는 왜 "지붕으로 덮여 있는 테라스예요"라고 말하는가?
(A) 안심시키려고
(B) 불만을 제기하려고
(C) 결정에 대해 설명하려고
(D) 오해를 바로잡으려고

어휘 reassurance 안심시키기 complaint 불평, 불만
correct 바로잡다, 정정하다 misunderstanding 오해

해설 화자의 의도 파악 – 지붕으로 덮여 있는 테라스라는 말의 의도
남자가 두 번째 대사에서 여기 있는 이 식물들이 꽃이 아름답게 피고, 직사광선에서도 잘 자란다(These plants here bloom beautifully and do best in direct sunlight)고 하자, 여자가 인용문을 언급한 것으로 보아, 자신의 집 테라스가 직사광선이 드는 곳이 아님을 설명하기 위해 한 말임을 알 수 있다. 따라서 정답은 (D)이다.

62-64 대화 + 일정표 W-Br / M-Cn

W: Hey, Pablo. **⁶²I missed the intern team morning update. ⁶³Was there information about cleaning acrylic test tubes?** I wonder whether there are specific guidelines for these as opposed to glass tubes.

M: **⁶³You should check the intern lab manual**—I think it was updated this week with step-by-step instructions.

W: Good idea! You know, what I'm enjoying most so far is learning about the practical side of the work. But I wish we could start working alongside the researchers here.

M: **⁶⁴Professor Kwon is showing us how to analyze data later today.** She usually asks the interns to participate.

192

여	안녕하세요, 파블로. **제가 인턴 팀 오전 업데이트를 놓쳤어요. 아크릴 시험관 세척에 관한 정보가 있었나요?** 유리 시험관과는 다른 이것들에 대한 구체적인 지침이 있는지 궁금해서요.
남	**인턴 실험실 매뉴얼을 확인해 보세요.** 이번 주에 단계별 설명이 업데이트된 것 같아요.
여	좋은 생각이에요! 저, 지금까지 제일 재미있는 건 업무의 실무적인 부분들을 배우는 거예요. 그래도 이곳에 계신 연구원들과 함께 일해볼 수도 있으면 좋겠어요.
남	**권 교수님께서 오늘 이따가 우리에게 데이터 분석 방법을 알려 주실 거예요.** 그분께서는 보통 인턴들에게 참여하도록 요청하세요.

어휘 miss 놓치다 acrylic 아크릴로 만든 test tube 시험관
specific 특정한, 구체적인 guideline 지침, 기준
as opposed to ~와 달리, ~와 대비하여 lab 실험실
step-by-step 단계적으로 practical 실무의 analyze 분석하다

Professor Kwon's Schedule

Monday	Order equipment
Tuesday	Collect sample
Wednesday	Treat samples
64 Thursday	**Analyze data**

권 교수 일정

월요일	장비 주문
화요일	샘플 수집
수요일	샘플 처리
목요일	**데이터 분석**

62 Who are the speakers?
(A) Interns
(B) Researchers
(C) Maintenance staff
(D) Inspectors

화자들은 누구인가?
(A) 인턴
(B) 연구원
(C) 시설 관리 직원
(D) 검사관

해설 전체 내용 관련 – 화자들의 직업

여자가 첫 대사에서 인턴 팀 오전 업데이트를 놓쳤다(I missed the intern team morning update)며 남자에게 아크릴 시험관 세척에 관한 정보가 있었는지(Was there information about cleaning acrylic test tubes?) 묻고 있는 것으로 보아 화자들은 함께 일하는 인턴임을 알 수 있다. 따라서 정답은 (A)이다.

63 Why should the woman check a manual?
(A) To review waste disposal instructions
(B) To learn how to clean some equipment
(C) To check which chemicals to use
(D) To determine which protective clothing to wear

여자는 왜 매뉴얼을 확인해야 하는가?
(A) 폐기물 처리 설명을 살펴보기 위해
(B) 장비를 세척하는 방법을 배우기 위해
(C) 어떤 화학 물질을 사용할지 확인하기 위해
(D) 어떤 보호용 의류를 착용할지 정하기 위해

어휘 review 살펴보다, 검토하다 disposal 처리, 처분
chemical 화학 물질 determine 결정하다, 알아내다
protective 보호용의

해설 세부 사항 관련 – 여자가 매뉴얼을 확인해야 하는 이유

여자가 첫 대사에서 아크릴 시험관 세척에 관한 정보가 있었는지(Was there information about cleaning acrylic test tubes?) 묻자, 남자가 인턴 실험실 매뉴얼을 확인해 보라(You should check the intern lab manual)고 했으므로 정답은 (B)이다.

Paraphrasing
대화의 cleaning acrylic test tubes
→ 정답의 clean some equipment

64 Look at the graphic. What day does the conversation take place?
(A) On Monday
(B) On Tuesday
(C) On Wednesday
(D) On Thursday

시각 정보에 의하면, 대화는 무슨 요일에 이루어지는가?
(A) 월요일
(B) 화요일
(C) 수요일
(D) 목요일

해설 시각 정보 연계 – 대화의 시점

남자가 마지막 대사에서 권 교수님이 오늘 이따가 데이터 분석 방법을 알려 주실 것(Professor Kwon is showing us how to analyze data later today)이라고 했고, 일정표에서 데이터 분석은 목요일이므로 정답은 (D)이다.

65-67 대화 + 로고 디자인 M-Au / W-Br

M Hi, Farida. I'm excited to see the designs you created. People spend a lot of time outside during the summer, so ⁶⁵**we want to get our sunscreen on store shelves before the summer rush. We need to pick a logo design quickly.**

W Take a look at these logo designs. All of them will grab the attention of shoppers.

M ⁶⁶**I like this one with the palm tree in a circle.**

W I agree. The single palm tree's a simple, clean logo.

M Before we make our decision, ⁶⁷**I'd like to show it to a focus group that represents our target audience. We have a large group coming in next week.**

남 안녕하세요, 파리다. 당신이 만든 디자인을 보게 되어 기뻐요. 사람들이 여름철에 밖에서 많은 시간을 보내니, **여름 대목 전에 우리 자외선 차단제를 매장에 선보이고 싶어요. 빨리 로고 디자인을 골라야 합니다.**

여 이 로고 디자인들을 한번 보세요. 전부 쇼핑객들의 눈길을 끌 거예요.

남 **동그라미 안에 야자수가 있는 이 디자인이 마음에 드네요.**

여 동의해요. 야자수 하나가 단순하고 깔끔한 로고죠.

남 결정을 내리기 전에, **우리 목표 고객들을 대표하는 포커스 그룹에게 보여 주었으면 해요. 다음 주에 대규모 그룹이 오거든요.**

어휘 sunscreen 자외선 차단제 rush 대목, 수요 급증 grab (관심, 마음 등을) 사로잡다 attention 관심, 주의 focus group 포커스 그룹(시장 조사 등을 위해 선정된 그룹) represent 대표하다 target audience 목표 고객

65 Why does the man want to make a decision quickly?
(A) A busy season is approaching.
(B) A team is starting another project.
(C) A client has changed a deadline.
(D) A permit must be renewed.

남자는 왜 빨리 결정을 내리고 싶어 하는가?
(A) 성수기가 다가오고 있다.
(B) 팀이 다른 프로젝트를 시작한다.
(C) 고객이 마감 기한을 변경했다.
(D) 허가증이 갱신되어야 한다.

어휘 approach 다가오다 permit 허가증 renew 갱신하다

해설 세부 사항 관련 – 남자가 빨리 결정을 내리려는 이유

남자가 첫 대사에서 여름 대목 전에 우리 자외선 차단제를 매장에 선보이고 싶다며 빨리 로고 디자인을 골라야 한다(~ we want to get our sunscreen on store shelves before the summer rush. We need to pick a logo design quickly)고 했으므로 정답은 (A)이다.

> **Paraphrasing**
> 대화의 pick a logo design quickly
> → 질문의 make a decision quickly
> 대화의 before the summer rush
> → 정답의 A busy season is approaching

66 Look at the graphic. Which logo design does the man prefer?
(A) Design 1
(B) Design 2
(C) Design 3
(D) Design 4

시각 정보에 의하면, 남자는 어떤 로고 디자인을 선호하는가?
(A) 1번 디자인
(B) 2번 디자인
(C) 3번 디자인
(D) 4번 디자인

해설 시각 정보 연계 – 남자가 선호하는 로고 디자인

남자가 두 번째 대사에서 동그라미 안에 야자수가 있는 이 디자인이 마음에 든다(I like this one with the palm tree in a circle)고 했으므로 정답은 (D)이다.

67 What is scheduled for next week?
(A) A trade show
(B) A focus group
(C) A store opening
(D) A safety inspection

다음 주에 무엇이 예정되어 있는가?
(A) 무역 박람회
(B) 포커스 그룹
(C) 매장 개장
(D) 안전 점검

해설 세부 사항 관련 – 다음 주에 예정된 일

남자가 마지막 대사에서 우리 목표 고객들을 대표하는 포커스 그룹에게 보여 주고 싶다(~ I'd like to show it to a focus group that represents our target audience)며 다음 주에 대규모 그룹이 온다(We have a large group coming in next week)고 했으므로 정답은 (B)이다.

68-70 대화 + 일정표 W-Am / M-Cn

W Stefan, **68 have you given any more thought to that parcel of land that's available for lease?** If we leased it, we'd have space for a lot more crops this spring and summer.

M Yes, with the extra growing space, we'd definitely increase our yield. What crops do you think would be best?

W Well, **69 we could plant more celery, which is our most popular crop.** And we could even add cabbage as a new crop in the spring.

M That makes sense. We'll need to extend our irrigation system to the new parcel, though, and that could be expensive. **70 I can call Lynden Ag Supply for an estimate on that**.

W Sure, that would be great.

여 스테판, **임대 가능한 그 토지 구획에 대해 좀 더 생각해 보셨나요?** 우리가 임대하게 되면, 올봄과 여름에 훨씬 더 많은 작물을 위한 공간이 생길 거예요.

남 네, 추가 재배 공간이 생기면 수확량이 확실히 늘어날 겁니다. 어떤 작물이 가장 좋을 것 같으세요?

여 음, **셀러리를 더 심을 수 있어요, 우리의 가장 인기 있는 작물이잖아요.** 그리고 봄에는 양배추를 새 작물로 추가하는 것도 가능하죠.

남 일리가 있네요. 하지만, 관개 시스템을 새로운 구획까지 확대해야 할 텐데, 그게 많은 비용이 들 수 있어요. **제가 이 부분에 대한 견적서를 받을 수 있게 린덴 농업 용품점에 전화해 볼게요.**

여 네, 그래 주시면 좋죠.

어휘 give thought to ~에 대해 (신중히) 생각해 보다
parcel (토지의) 한 구획, 일정한 면적의 땅 lease 임대 crop 작물
growing 재배 definitely 분명히, 확실히 yield 수확량, 생산량
extend 확대하다 irrigation 관개, 급수 estimate 견적서

Planting Calendar

	Spring	Early Summer	Late Summer	Fall
Beets			✓	
Cabbage	✓			
69 Celery		✓		
Garlic				✓

재배 일정표

	봄	초여름	늦여름	가을
비트			✓	
양배추	✓			
셀러리		✓		
마늘				✓

---

68 What does the woman ask about?
(A) Leasing some land
(B) Offering workshops
(C) Opening a farm stand
(D) Replacing some equipment

여자는 무엇에 대해 물어보는가?
(A) 토지 임대
(B) 워크숍 제공
(C) 농산물 판매대 개설
(D) 장비 교체

어휘 farm stand 농산물 판매대 replace 교체하다, 대체하다

해설 전체 내용 관련 – 여자가 질문하는 것
여자가 첫 대사에서 남자에게 임대 가능한 그 토지 구획에 대해 좀 더 생각해 봤는지(~ have you given any more thought to that parcel of land that's available for lease?) 묻고 있으므로 정답은 (A)이다.

69 Look at the graphic. When is the most popular crop planted?
(A) Spring
(B) Early summer
(C) Late summer
(D) Fall

시각 정보에 의하면, 가장 인기 있는 작물은 언제 심는가?
(A) 봄
(B) 초여름
(C) 늦여름
(D) 가을

해설 시각 정보 연계 – 가장 인기 있는 작물을 심는 시기
여자가 두 번째 대사에서 셀러리를 더 심을 수 있다며 그것이 가장 인기있는 작물(~ we could plant more celery, which is our most popular crop)이라고 덧붙이고 있고, 일정표에서 셀러리는 초여름에 해당하므로 정답은 (B)이다.

70 What does the man offer to do?
(A) Check an inventory
(B) Select some seeds
(C) Get an estimate
(D) Reach out to customers

남자는 무엇을 하겠다고 제안하는가?
(A) 재고 확인하기
(B) 씨앗 선택하기
(C) 견적서 받아 보기
(D) 고객들에게 연락하기

어휘 inventory 재고, 재고 목록 seed 씨앗 reach out 연락하다

해설 세부 사항 관련 – 남자가 제안하는 것
남자가 마지막 대사에서 견적서를 받을 수 있게 린덴 농업 용품점에 전화해 보겠다(I can call Lynden Ag Supply for an estimate on that)고 했으므로 정답은 (C)이다.

PART 4

71-73 회의 발췌

W-Am Good morning, everyone. **71 Thank you for coming in a little bit early for your shift today.** **72 While production was closed down for the holiday, management took the opportunity to install a new type of safety equipment on all the machines on the assembly lines.** A special sensor called a light curtain automatically turns off the machines if an object gets too close during operation. **73 I'd like to show you how it works.** Let's go look at a machine now.

안녕하세요, 여러분. 오늘 여러분의 교대 근무에 조금 일찍 와 주셔서 감사합니다. 휴일로 생산이 중단된 사이, 경영진은 조립 라인의 모든 기계에 새로운 종류의 안전 장비를 설치할 기회를 가졌습니다. 작동 중에 물체가 너무 가까이 다가오는 경우, 라이트 커튼이라고 부르는 특수 센서가 자동으로 기계를 끕니다. 제가 어떻게 작동하는지 보여 드리려고 합니다. 지금 가서 기계를 한 대 보시죠.

어휘 shift 교대 근무   close down 중단하다, 폐쇄하다
management 경영진   equipment 장비   assembly 조립
automatically 자동으로   operation 작동, 가동

71 Why does the speaker thank the listeners?
(A) For responding to an employee survey
(B) For arriving early for a shift
(C) For agreeing to work overtime
(D) For planning a holiday party

화자는 왜 청자들에게 감사하는가?
(A) 직원 설문 조사에 답변해서
(B) 교대 근무에 일찍 도착해서
(C) 초과 근무하는 데 동의해서
(D) 휴일 파티를 계획해서

어휘 respond to ~에 답변하다   survey 설문 조사
work overtime 초과 근무하다, 야근하다

해설 세부 사항 관련 - 화자가 감사하는 이유
화자가 초반부에 청자들에게 교대 근무에 조금 일찍 와 주어 감사하다(Thank you for coming in a little bit early for your shift today)고 했으므로 정답은 (B)이다.

Paraphrasing
담화의 coming in a little bit early for your shift
→ 정답의 arriving early for a shift

72 Where do the listeners most likely work?
(A) At an appliance store
(B) At a hotel
(C) At a factory
(D) At a hospital

청자들은 어디에서 일하는 것 같은가?
(A) 가전 기기 매장
(B) 호텔
(C) 공장
(D) 병원

해설 전체 내용 관련 - 청자들의 근무 장소
화자가 중반부에 휴일로 생산이 중단된 사이 경영진이 조립 라인의 모든 기계에 새로운 안전 장비를 설치했다(While production was closed down for the holiday, ~ the machines on the assembly lines)고 말하는 것으로 보아 청자들은 공장에서 근무한다는 것을 알 수 있다. 따라서 정답은 (C)이다.

73 What will the speaker do next?
(A) Give a demonstration
(B) Distribute some documents
(C) Authorize a purchase
(D) Conduct some interviews

화자는 다음에 무엇을 할 것인가?
(A) 시연하기
(B) 문서 배부하기
(C) 구매 승인하기
(D) 인터뷰 실시하기

어휘 demonstration 시연, 시범   distribute 배부하다, 나눠 주다
authorize 승인하다, 권한을 부여하다   conduct 실시하다

해설 세부 사항 관련 - 화자가 다음에 할 일
화자가 후반부에 특수 센서가 어떻게 작동하는지 보여 주겠다(I'd like to show you how it works)고 했으므로 정답은 (A)이다.

Paraphrasing
담화의 show you how it works
→ 정답의 Give a demonstration

74-76 담화

W-Br Good job at all the rehearsals this week as we prepare for our upcoming performance, dancers. **74 You did great at quickly learning the newly choreographed steps to our main piece. 75 I recommend that you rest a lot over the weekend.** Please give your muscles time to recover after working so hard. When we return on Monday for our final rehearsal, **76 Erina will be here. She's in charge of the costumes** and will be making last-minute alterations to your outfits. Then we'll be ready for our first show on Tuesday night!

다가오는 공연을 준비하는 가운데 이번 주 모든 리허설에서 수고하셨어요, 댄서 여러분. **우리 메인 작품의 새 안무 동작들을 빠르게 잘 익혀 주셨어요. 주말 동안은 푹 쉬시기를 추천합니다.** 이렇게 열심히 연습하신 후에는 여러분의 근육에 회복할 시간을 주세요. 월요일에 마지막 리허설을 위해 다시 모일 때는, **에리나가 함께할 예정이에요. 의상을 담당하는 분**이고, 여러분의 의상에 최종 수선 작업을 해 주실 겁니다. 그리고 나면 화요일 밤에 있을 우리의 첫 공연 준비는 완료입니다!

어휘 rehearsal 리허설, 예행연습 upcoming 다가오는, 곧 있을 performance 공연 choreograph 안무를 짜다 piece 작품 recover 회복하다 in charge of ~을 담당하는 costume 의상 last-minute 최후의, 막바지의 alteration 수정, 변경

74 What does the speaker compliment the listeners on?
(A) Decorating an auditorium
(B) Learning new dance steps
(C) Selling tickets for a performance
(D) Winning a competition

화자는 무엇에 대해 청자들을 칭찬하는가?
(A) 강당을 장식한 것
(B) 새 댄스 스텝을 습득한 것
(C) 공연 티켓을 판매한 것
(D) 경연 대회에서 우승한 것

어휘 compliment ~ on ... …에 대해 ~을 칭찬하다 decorate 장식하다 competition 경연 대회, 경쟁

해설 세부 사항 관련 – 화자가 청자들을 칭찬하는 것
화자가 초반부에 청자들에게 우리 메인 작품의 새 안무 동작들을 빠르게 잘 익혔다(You did great at quickly learning the newly choreographed steps to our main piece)고 했으므로 정답은 (B)이다.

Paraphrasing
담화의 did great → 질문의 compliment
담화의 newly choreographed steps
→ 정답의 new dance steps

75 What does the speaker recommend doing?
(A) Getting some rest
(B) Drinking lots of water
(C) Opening a window
(D) Scheduling an additional performance

화자는 무엇을 하라고 권하는가?
(A) 휴식 취하기
(B) 물 많이 마시기
(C) 창문 열어 두기
(D) 추가 공연 일정 잡기

해설 세부 사항 관련 – 화자의 추천 사항
화자가 중반부에 주말 동안은 푹 쉬기를 추천한다(I recommend that you rest a lot over the weekend)고 했으므로 정답은 (A)이다.

Paraphrasing
담화의 rest a lot → 정답의 Getting some rest

76 What is Erina responsible for?
(A) Payroll
(B) Marketing
(C) Lighting
(D) Costumes

에리나는 무엇을 책임지고 있는가?
(A) 급여
(B) 마케팅
(C) 조명
(D) 의상

해설 세부 사항 관련 – 에리나가 책임지고 있는 것
화자가 후반부에 에리나가 함께할 예정(~ Erina will be here)이라며 의상을 담당하는 분(She's in charge of the costumes ~)이라고 덧붙이고 있으므로 정답은 (D)이다.

Paraphrasing
담화의 in charge of → 질문의 responsible for

77-79 담화

M-Au Attention, everyone. **77 Tonight we're filming a live performance of the Edmunsen Symphony Orchestra**, so the margin for error is zero. I know we've had a lot of adjustments to make **78 since we just upgraded our cameras to newer models last week**, but we've tested everything, and we know what we're doing. Remember, it's an important night because **77 this is a high-profile event that will be broadcast live to viewers.** If we do a great job, our services are bound to be in demand. **79 It's noon now, so let's break for lunch.** When we come back, we'll get set up.

여러분께 알립니다. **오늘 밤 우리는 에드문센 심포니 오케스트라의 라이브 공연을 촬영할 예정이라**, 실수할 여유가 전혀 없습니다. **지난주에 카메라를 새로운 모델로 업그레이드한 이후** 조정해야 할 사항들이 많았다는 것을 압니다만, 우리는 모든 테스트를 마쳤고, 또 우리는 우리 일을 잘 알고 있어요. 오늘 밤은 **시청자들에게 생중계되는 주목받는 행사이므로**, 중요하다는 것을 명심하세요. 우리가 잘 해낸다면, 틀림없이 우리 서비스의 수요가 늘어날 겁니다. **이제 정오이니, 점심 식사를 위해 잠시 휴식하겠습니다.** 돌아와서 준비를 시작하시죠.

어휘 film 촬영하다 margin 여유, 여지 adjustment 조정 high-profile 세간의 이목을 끄는 broadcast 방송하다 be bound to 틀림없이 ~하게 될 것이다, ~할 가능성이 크다 in demand 수요가 많은

77 Who most likely are the listeners?
(A) Musicians
(B) Actors
(C) A television production team
(D) Software technicians

청자들은 누구인 것 같은가?
(A) 음악가
(B) 배우
(C) 텔레비전 제작팀
(D) 소프트웨어 기술자

해설 전체 내용 관련 – 청자들의 직업
화자가 초반부에 오늘 밤 우리가 에드문센 심포니 오케스트라의 라이브 공연을 촬영한다(Tonight we're filming a live performance of the Edmunsen Symphony Orchestra ~)고 했고, 후반부에서는 그 공연이 시청자들에게 생중계되는 주목받는 행사(~ this is a high-profile event that will be broadcast live to viewers)라고 말하는 것으로 보아 청자들은 방송 프로그램을 만드는 텔레비전 제작팀임을 알 수 있다. 따라서 정답은 (C)이다.

78 What does the speaker say happened last week?
(A) An article was published.
(B) A renovation was completed.
(C) A budget was approved.
(D) Some equipment was replaced.

화자는 지난주에 무슨 일이 있었다고 말하는가?
(A) 기사가 실렸다.
(B) 개조 공사가 완료되었다.
(C) 예산이 승인되었다.
(D) 장비가 교체되었다.

어휘 renovation 개조, 보수 complete 완료하다 budget 예산 approve 승인하다 equipment 장비 replace 교체하다

해설 세부 사항 관련 – 지난주에 있었던 일
화자가 중반부에 지난주에 카메라를 새로운 모델로 업그레이드했다(~ since we just upgraded our cameras to newer models last week ~)고 했으므로 정답은 (D)이다.

Paraphrasing
담화의 upgraded our cameras to newer models
→ 정답의 Some equipment was replaced

79 What will the listeners do next?
(A) Pose for photographs
(B) Tune some instruments
(C) Interview a celebrity
(D) Take a break

청자들은 다음에 무엇을 할 것인가?
(A) 사진 촬영을 위해 포즈 취하기
(B) 악기 조율하기
(C) 유명 인사 인터뷰하기
(D) 휴식 시간 갖기

어휘 pose 포즈를 취하다, 자세를 잡다 tune 조율하다 instrument 악기, 기구 celebrity 유명 인사

해설 세부 사항 관련 – 청자들이 다음에 할 일
화자가 후반부에 이제 정오이니 점심 식사를 위해 잠시 휴식하자(It's noon now, so let's break for lunch)고 했으므로 정답은 (D)이다.

Paraphrasing
담화의 break for lunch → 정답의 Take a break

80-82 담화

W-Br Hi. I'm your supervisor, Maria Gonzales. **80 I'd like to extend a warm welcome to everyone here. I'm excited that you'll all be joining the customer service department.** I hope that the onboarding process has been going well so far. **81 After lunch, I'll share a video about our company's history, from its founding in 1971 to the present day.** Let's move on now to introductions. I'd like all of you to tell us something about yourselves. For example, **82 I just found out that Astrid plays saxophone in a jazz ensemble.** That certainly wasn't on her résumé. Klaus, would you go first?

안녕하세요, 저는 여러분의 상사 마리아 곤잘레스입니다. 이 자리에 계신 모든 분께 따뜻한 환영의 인사를 전하고 싶습니다. 여러분께서 모두 고객 서비스부에 합류하시게 되어 기뻐요. 신규 입사자 교육 과정이 지금까지 잘 진행되고 있기를 바랍니다. 점심 식사 후에는, 1971년 설립에서부터 현재에 이르기까지, 우리 회사의 역사에 대한 동영상을 공유해 드릴게요. 이제 소개 시간으로 넘어가 보겠습니다. 여러분 각자 자신에 대해 이야기해 주셨으면 해요. 예를 들면, 저는 애스트리드가 재즈 앙상블에서 색소폰을 연주한다는 걸 방금 알게 됐거든요. 그건 분명 이분의 이력서에는 없었습니다. 클라우스, 먼저 해 보시겠어요?

어휘 supervisor 상사, 책임자 extend (환영, 감사 등을) 전하다 onboarding 신규 입사자 교육 founding 설립, 창립 present 현재의 introduction 소개 certainly 분명히 résumé 이력서

80 What is the purpose of the talk?
(A) To welcome new employees
(B) To explain a new policy
(C) To celebrate a team's achievements
(D) To share customer feedback

담화의 목적은 무엇인가?
(A) 신입 직원 환영
(B) 새로운 정책 설명
(C) 팀의 업적 축하
(D) 고객 의견 공유

어휘 policy 정책, 방침   celebrate 축하하다, 기념하다
achievement 업적, 성취, 달성   feedback 의견

해설 전체 내용 관련 – 담화의 목적
화자가 초반부에 따뜻한 환영의 인사를 전하고 싶다(I'd like to extend a warm welcome ~)며 모두 고객 서비스부에 합류하게 되어 기쁘다(I'm excited that you'll all be joining the customer service department)고 했으므로 정답은 (A)이다.

Paraphrasing
담화의 extend a warm welcome → 정답의 welcome

81 What will the listeners do after lunch?
(A) Sign a document
(B) Watch a video
(C) Meet with some customers
(D) Plan an event

청자들은 점심 식사 후에 무엇을 할 것인가?
(A) 문서에 서명하기
(B) 동영상 시청하기
(C) 고객들과 만나기
(D) 행사 계획하기

해설 세부 사항 관련 – 청자들이 점심 식사 후에 할 것
화자가 중반부에 점심 식사 후에 1971년 설립에서부터 현재에 이르기까지, 우리 회사의 역사에 대한 동영상을 공유하겠다(After lunch, I'll share a video about our company's history, from its founding in 1971 to the present day)고 했으므로 정답은 (B)이다.

Paraphrasing
담화의 share a video → 정답의 Watch a video

82 Why does the speaker say, "That certainly wasn't on her résumé"?
(A) To express surprise
(B) To offer a recommendation
(C) To make an excuse
(D) To show disappointment

화자는 왜 "그건 분명 이분의 이력서에는 없었습니다"라고 말하는가?
(A) 놀라움을 표현하기 위해
(B) 추천을 제공하기 위해
(C) 핑계를 대기 위해
(D) 실망감을 나타내기 위해

어휘 excuse 핑계, 변명   disappointment 실망

해설 화자의 의도 파악 – 이력서에는 없었다는 말의 의도
화자가 후반부에 애스트리드가 재즈 앙상블에서 색소폰을 연주한다는 걸 방금 알게 되었다(I just found out that Astrid plays saxophone in a jazz ensemble)고 말한 뒤 인용문을 언급한 것으로 보아, 이력서에서는 확인하지 못했던 새로운 사실을 알게 되어 놀랍다는 의미로 한 말임을 알 수 있다. 따라서 정답은 (A)이다.

83-85 공지

M-Au Good afternoon and welcome aboard this train to Ashedale. 83 **Our next stop is Bruxton, famous for being the birthplace of renowned painter Oliver Murray.** As you may know, several of Mr. Murray's paintings hang in museums around the world. Please be advised that due to the short platform length, 84 **the doors of the last train car will not open. If you are in that car, you'll need to walk forward to exit the train.** 85 **There will also be a short delay at this station while our new train crew comes on and gets situated.** We apologize for any inconvenience.

안녕하세요, 애쉬데일행 열차에 탑승하신 것을 환영합니다. **다음 역은 브럭스턴이며, 명성 있는 화가 올리버 머레이의 출생지로 유명한 곳입니다.** 아시다시피, 머레이 씨의 그림 여러 점이 세계 곳곳의 미술관에 전시되어 있습니다. 승강장의 길이가 짧아, **마지막 칸의 출입문이 열리지 않는다는 점을 알려 드립니다. 그 칸에 계신 승객께서는 열차에서 내리시려면 앞쪽으로 이동해 주셔야 합니다.** 이 역에서는 또한 **새 승무원이 탑승하고 준비하는 동안 잠시 지연이 있을 예정입니다.** 불편을 드려 죄송합니다.

어휘 aboard 탑승한, 승선한   renowned 명성 있는, 유명한   car (열차의) 칸, 객차   delay 지연, 지체   crew 승무원   get situated 준비하다, 자리를 잡다   inconvenience 불편함

83 What does the speaker say Bruxton is known for?
(A) Its architectural landmarks
(B) Its archaeological significance
(C) Its connections to a renowned artist
(D) Its collection of botanical gardens

화자는 브럭스턴이 무엇으로 알려져 있다고 말하는가?
(A) 건축학적 명소들
(B) 고고학적 의의
(C) 명성 있는 화가와의 연관성
(D) 그곳에 모여 있는 식물원들

어휘 architectural 건축학의   landmark 명소, 인기 장소   archaeological 고고학의   significance 의의, 중요성   connection 연관성, 연결   collection 모음, 수집품   botanical 식물의

해설 세부 사항 관련 – 브럭스턴에서 유명한 것
화자가 초반부에 다음 역이 브럭스턴임을 알리면서 명성 있는 화가 올리버 머레이의 출생지로 유명한 곳(Our next stop is Bruxton, famous for being the birthplace of renowned painter Oliver Murray)이라고 했으므로 정답은 (C)이다.

TEST 7   **199**

Paraphrasing
담화의 being the birthplace of renowned painter
→ 정답의 connections to a renowned artist

84 According to the speaker, what should some passengers in the last car do?
(A) Present their tickets to the conductor
(B) Move to a car ahead of theirs
(C) Store heavy luggage in another car
(D) Refrain from talking on mobile phones

화자에 따르면, 마지막 칸에 있는 승객들은 무엇을 해야 하는가?
(A) 승무원에게 티켓 제시
(B) 앞쪽 칸으로 이동
(C) 다른 칸에 무거운 짐 보관
(D) 핸드폰 통화 자제

어휘 present 제시하다, 제공하다   conductor (버스, 기차의) 승무원
store 보관하다, 저장하다   luggage 짐, 수하물
refrain from -ing ~하는 것을 삼가다

해설 세부 사항 관련 – 마지막 칸의 승객들이 할 일
화자가 중반부에 마지막 칸의 출입문이 열리지 않는다(~ the doors of the last train car will not open)며 그 칸에 있는 승객들은 열차에서 내리려면 앞쪽으로 이동해야 한다(If you are in that car, you'll need to walk forward to exit the train)고 말하고 있으므로 정답은 (B)이다.

Paraphrasing
담화의 walk forward
→ 정답의 Move to a car ahead of theirs

85 According to the speaker, why will there be a delay?
(A) A staff change will take place.
(B) An express train needs to pass.
(C) Maintenance work is being done.
(D) Weather conditions require caution.

화자에 따르면, 왜 지연이 있을 것인가?
(A) 직원 교체가 있을 것이다.
(B) 급행 열차가 지나가야 한다.
(C) 정비 작업이 진행되고 있다.
(D) 기상 상태가 주의를 필요로 한다.

어휘 express 급행의, 특급의   maintenance 정비, 시설 관리
caution 주의, 경고

해설 세부 사항 관련 – 지연이 발생하는 이유
화자가 후반부에 새 승무원이 탑승하고 준비하는 동안 잠시 지연이 있을 예정(There will also be a short delay at this station while our new train crew comes on and gets situated)이라고 했으므로 정답은 (A)이다.

Paraphrasing
담화의 our new train crew comes on and gets situated
→ 정답의 A staff change will take place

86-88 회의 발췌

W-Am I have good news! **86 We've signed a contract with Lammert Technologies to plan the gardens and landscaping around their new office building.** I met with them last week to present our design proposals, and they agreed on a design plan. **87 They've decided to cover a lot of the open space with creeping thyme plantings instead of grass. Resource conservation is a priority for all of us.** And I must say, grass does require a lot of water. The project will start in August. I'll need to make the work schedule soon. **88 If you're planning to take any time off for vacation, send me those dates today, please.**

좋은 소식이 있습니다! 우리가 램머트 테크놀로지 사의 새 사무실 건물 주변의 정원과 조경을 설계하는 계약을 체결했어요. 우리 디자인 제안서를 발표하기 위해 지난주에 이 회사 분들과 만났고, 디자인 계획에 합의하셨습니다. 이분들께서는 개방된 공간의 많은 부분을 잔디 대신 크리핑 타임 식재로 덮기로 결정했어요. 자원 보존은 우리 모두에게 우선 과제죠. 그리고 솔직히 말해서, 잔디는 물을 정말 많이 필요로 합니다. 이 프로젝트는 8월에 시작될 예정입니다. 제가 곧 작업 일정표를 만들 거고요. 휴가를 낼 계획이시면, 오늘 중으로 제게 그 일정을 보내 주시기 바랍니다.

어휘 landscaping 조경   present 발표하다, 제시하다
proposal 제안(서)   creeping thyme 크리핑 타임(허브의 일종)
plantings 식재(심어진 식물들)   resource 자원, 자산
conservation 보존, 보호   priority 우선 순위

86 What industry does the speaker most likely work in?
(A) Landscape design
(B) Architecture
(C) Agriculture
(D) Corporate catering

화자는 어떤 업계에서 일하는 것 같은가?
(A) 조경 디자인
(B) 건축
(C) 농업
(D) 기업 출장 요리

어휘 catering 출장 요리, 음식 공급(업)

해설 전체 내용 관련 – 화자의 근무 업계
화자가 초반부에 램머트 테크놀로지 사의 새 사무실 건물 주변의 정원과 조경을 설계하는 계약을 체결했다(We've signed a contract with Lammert Technologies to plan the gardens and landscaping around their new office building)고 했으므로 정답은 (A)이다.

87 What does the speaker mean when she says, "grass does require a lot of water"?
(A) She agrees with a choice.
(B) She needs volunteers to help.
(C) Water costs have increased.
(D) A design plan should be changed.

화자가 "잔디는 물을 정말 많이 필요로 합니다"라고 말할 때 무엇을 의미하는가?
(A) 선택에 동의하고 있다.
(B) 도와줄 자원봉사자들이 필요하다.
(C) 수도 요금이 인상되었다.
(D) 디자인 계획이 변경되어야 한다.

어휘 volunteer 자원봉사자

해설 화자의 의도 파악 – 잔디는 물을 정말 많이 필요로 한다는 말의 의도
화자가 중반부에 그 회사가 개방된 공간의 많은 부분을 잔디 대신 크리핑 타임 식재로 덮기로 결정했다(They've decided to cover a lot of the open space with creeping thyme plantings instead of grass)면서 자원 보존은 우리 모두에게 우선 과제(Resource conservation is a priority for all of us)라고 말한 뒤 인용문을 언급한 것으로 보아, 많은 물이 필요한 잔디 대신 다른 것을 선택한 것이 자원 보존 측면에서 좋은 결정이라는 의미로 한 말임을 알 수 있다. 따라서 정답은 (A)이다.

88 What does the speaker ask the listeners to send her?
(A) Supply lists
(B) Photographs
(C) Vacation dates
(D) Travel recommendations

화자는 청자들에게 무엇을 자신에게 보내라고 요청하는가?
(A) 물품 목록
(B) 사진
(C) 휴가 날짜
(D) 추천 여행지

해설 세부 사항 관련 – 화자의 요청 사항
화자가 후반부에 휴가를 낼 계획이면, 오늘 중으로 그 일정을 보내 달라(If you're planning to take any time off for vacation, send me those dates today, please)고 요청하고 있으므로 정답은 (C)이다.

89-91 방송

M-Cn A market research firm has reported that **89 the department store chain Willoughby is partnering with the beauty retailer Rossi.** By the end of the year, Rossi stores will be in place at 500 Willoughby locations. Currently, most of the beauty retailer's sales come from small shops in urban areas. By joining forces with Willoughby, **90 Rossi hopes to meet its goal of expanding its customer base by entering suburban markets.** To accommodate the new retail spaces for Rossi, **91 participating Willoughby stores will start renovations in July.**

한 시장 조사 기관에서 **백화점 체인 윌러비가 뷰티 소매업체 로시와 제휴를 맺는다**는 사실을 발표했습니다. 올 연말까지, 로시 매장이 500곳의 윌러비 지점에 입점할 예정입니다. 현재, 이 뷰티 소매업체의 매출 대부분은 도심 지역의 소규모 매장에서 발생하고 있습니다. 윌러비와 제휴함으로써, **로시는 교외 시장에 진출해 자사의 고객 기반을 확대하겠다는 목표를 달성하기를 기대하고 있습니다.** 로시의 새로운 소매 공간을 확보하기 위해, **참여하는 윌러비 지점들은 7월에 개조를 시작할 예정입니다.**

어휘 partner 제휴하다, 협력하다 retailer 소매업체, 소매업자 currently 현재 urban 도시의 join forces 제휴하다, 협력하다 expand 확대하다, 확장하다 customer base 고객층 suburban 교외의 accommodate 수용하다, 공간을 제공하다 renovation 개조, 보수

89 What is the broadcast mainly about?
(A) A new company owner
(B) A business partnership
(C) Some store closings
(D) A product rebranding

방송은 주로 무엇에 관한 것인가?
(A) 새로운 회사 소유주
(B) 사업 제휴
(C) 매장 폐업
(D) 제품 리브랜딩

해설 전체 내용 관련 – 방송의 주제
화자가 초반부에 백화점 체인 윌러비가 뷰티 소매업체 로시와 제휴를 맺는다(~ the department store chain Willoughby is partnering with the beauty retailer Rossi)는 소식을 소개한 뒤 두 회사의 사업 제휴에 관련된 설명을 이어 가고 있으므로 정답은 (B)이다.

Paraphrasing
담화의 the department store chain Willoughby is partnering with the beauty retailer Rossi
→ 정답의 A business partnership

90 What goal does the speaker mention?
(A) Introducing a new product line
(B) Becoming more environmentally friendly
(C) Launching a social media campaign
(D) Expanding a customer base

화자는 어떤 목표를 언급하는가?
(A) 신제품 라인 도입
(B) 친환경성 증대
(C) 소셜 미디어 캠페인 개시
(D) 고객 기반 확대

어휘 environmentally friendly 친환경적인 launch 시작하다

해설 세부 사항 관련 – 화자가 언급하는 목표
화자가 중반부에 로시가 교외 시장에 진출해 자사의 고객 기반을 확대하겠다는 목표를 달성하기를 기대하고 있다(~ Rossi hopes to meet its goal of expanding its customer base by entering suburban markets)고 했으므로 정답은 (D)이다.

---

91 What does the Willoughby store chain plan to do in July?
(A) Renovate some of its stores
(B) Display beachwear
(C) Host a grand opening event
(D) Distribute a customer survey

윌러비 체인은 7월에 무엇을 할 계획인가?
(A) 매장 개조하기
(B) 비치웨어 진열하기
(C) 개장 기념 행사 열기
(D) 고객 설문 조사지 배부하기

어휘 renovate 개조하다, 보수하다 host 주최하다

해설 세부 사항 관련 – 윌러비 체인이 7월에 할 일
화자가 후반부에 참여하는 윌러비 지점들은 7월에 개조를 시작할 예정(~ participating Willoughby stores will start renovations in July)이라고 했으므로 정답은 (A)이다.

> **Paraphrasing**
> 담화의 participating Willoughby stores will start renovations → 정답의 Renovate some of its stores

---

92-94 회의 발췌  ▶동영상 강의

M-Au **92** Today I want to discuss some ways we can improve our solar panel installation business. **93** I'd like to pay for national certification for all of our installation techs, which will greatly improve our quality. Let's not forget that the Business Council's yearly ratings will be published soon. In addition, **94** we can attract new customers by offering 25 percent off the installation charge. I suggest we begin the promotion next month.

오늘 저는 우리 태양열 전지판 설치 사업을 개선할 수 있는 몇 가지 방법을 논의하려고 합니다. 저는 저희 설치 기술자 전원에게 국가 자격증 비용을 지원하고자 하며, 이는 우리의 품질을 크게 향상시켜 줄 것입니다. 기업 협의회의 연간 순위가 곧 발표될 것이라는 사실을 잊지 맙시다. 추가로, 설치 요금에 25퍼센트 할인을 제공하여 신규 고객을 끌어들일 수 있습니다. 다음 달에 이 판촉 행사를 시작할 것을 제안합니다.

어휘 solar panel 태양열 전지판 certification 자격증 installation 설치 tech 기술자(technician의 구어체 줄임말) rating 순위, 등급 publish 발표하다, 출판하다 attract 끌어들이다 charge 요금 promotion 판촉 (행사), 홍보

---

92 What is the purpose of the meeting?
(A) To propose increasing an advertising budget
(B) To announce a company merger
(C) To discuss ways to improve a business
(D) To recommend developing new products

회의의 목적은 무엇인가?
(A) 광고 예산 증액을 제안하는 것
(B) 회사 합병을 발표하는 것
(C) 사업 개선 방안을 논의하는 것
(D) 신제품 개발을 추천하는 것

어휘 propose 제안하다 merger 합병, 통합

해설 전체 내용 관련 – 회의의 목적
화자가 초반부에 태양열 전지판 설치 사업을 개선할 수 있는 몇 가지 방법을 논의하려고 한다(Today I want to discuss some ways we can improve our solar panel installation business)고 했으므로 정답은 (C)이다.

---

93 Why does the speaker say, "Let's not forget that the Business Council's yearly ratings will be published soon"?
(A) To offer to form a committee
(B) To support a proposal
(C) To congratulate award winners
(D) To suggest joining an organization

202

화자는 왜 "기업 협의회의 연간 순위가 곧 발표될 것이라는 사실을 잊지 맙시다"라고 말하는가?
(A) 위원회를 구성할 것을 제안하기 위해
(B) 제안을 뒷받침하기 위해
(C) 수상자들을 축하하기 위해
(D) 단체에 가입하도록 제안하기 위해

어휘 form 구성하다, 형성하다   committee 위원회
congratulate 축하하다   award winner 수상자
organization 단체, 기관

해설 화자의 의도 파악 – 기업 협의회의 연간 순위가 곧 발표된다는 사실을 잊지 말자는 말의 의도

화자가 중반부에 설치 기술자 전원에게 국가 자격증 비용을 지원하고자 한다며 그것이 품질을 크게 향상시켜 줄 것(I'd like to pay for national certification for all of our installation techs, which will greatly improve our quality)이라고 말한 뒤 인용문을 언급한 것으로 보아, 곧 있을 회사 평가를 상기시킴으로써 자신의 제안을 받아들이도록 설득하려는 의도로 한 말임을 알 수 있다. 따라서 정답은 (B)이다.

94 What does the speaker suggest doing next month?
(A) Advertising on social media
(B) Hiring additional employees
(C) Finalizing a production schedule
(D) Offering a discount to new customers

화자는 다음 달에 무엇을 하자고 제안하는가?
(A) 소셜 미디어 광고
(B) 추가 직원 고용
(C) 생산 일정 확정
(D) 신규 고객에게 할인 제공

어휘 advertise 광고하다

해설 세부 사항 관련 – 화자가 다음 달에 하자고 제안하는 것

화자가 후반부에 설치 요금에 25퍼센트 할인을 제공하여 신규 고객을 끌어들일 수 있다며 다음 달에 그 판촉 행사를 시작할 것을 제안한다(~ we can attract new customers by offering 25 percent off the installation charge. I suggest we begin the promotion next month)고 했으므로 정답은 (D)이다.

Paraphrasing
담화의 offering 25 percent off the installation charge
→ 정답의 Offering a discount

95-97 담화 + 지도

M-Cn Thank you for attending. ⁹⁵**Last fall, the city approved more funding for transportation projects.** ⁹⁶**Today my department is happy to announce that we'll use some of those funds to install covered benches at city bus stops.** They will give riders a place to rest and keep out of the sun, rain, or snow while they wait. This map shows the neighborhoods where we'll construct new bus shelters. ⁹⁷**We'll start with the neighborhood around the university** since students make up a large portion of the overall ridership.

참석해 주셔서 감사합니다. 작년 가을, 시에서 교통 프로젝트들에 대한 추가 자금 제공을 승인했습니다. 오늘 저희 부서는 시내버스 정류장에 지붕이 있는 벤치를 설치하는 데 그 자금 중 일부를 사용할 것이라는 점을 알려 드리게 되어 기쁩니다. 이 시설들은 승객들에게 기다리는 동안 휴식을 취하고 햇빛과 비, 또는 눈을 피할 장소를 제공해 줄 것입니다. 이 지도가 저희가 새 버스 정류장을 지을 지역들을 보여 줍니다. 학생들이 전체 이용자 수의 많은 부분을 차지하는 만큼, **대학교 주변 지역부터 시작할 예정입니다.**

어휘 approve 승인하다   funding 자금 (제공)   install 설치하다
bus shelter (지붕이 달린) 버스 정류소   make up ~을 차지하다
portion 부분, 몫   overall 전반적인   ridership 이용자 수, 승객 수

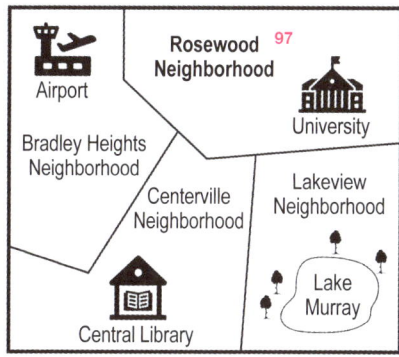

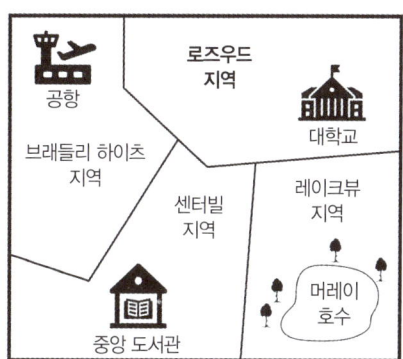

95 What happened last fall?
(A) An electric train line was added.
(B) A construction project was interrupted.
(C) Some computer systems were upgraded.
(D) Some city funding was approved.

작년 가을에 무슨 일이 있었는가?
(A) 전동 열차 노선이 추가되었다.
(B) 건설 프로젝트가 중단되었다.
(C) 컴퓨터 시스템이 업그레이드되었다.
(D) 시 자금이 승인되었다.

어휘 interrupt 중단하다, 방해하다

해설 세부 사항 관련 – 작년 가을에 있었던 일
화자가 초반부에 작년 가을에 시에서 교통 프로젝트들에 대한 추가 자금 제공을 승인했다(Last fall, the city approved more funding for transportation projects)고 했으므로 정답은 (D)이다.

> **Paraphrasing**
> 담화의 the city approved more funding
> → 정답의 Some city funding was approved

96 What department does the speaker most likely work in?
(A) Permits
(B) Transportation
(C) Parks
(D) Housing

화자는 어느 부서에서 일할 것 같은가?
(A) 인가
(B) 교통
(C) 공원
(D) 주택

어휘 permit 인가, 허가 housing 주택 (공급)

해설 전체 내용 관련 – 화자의 근무 부서
화자가 중반부에 자신의 부서가 시내버스 정류장에 지붕이 있는 벤치를 설치하는 데 그 자금 중 일부를 사용할 것이라는 점을 알리게 되어 기쁘다(Today my department is happy to announce that we'll use some of those funds to install covered benches at city bus stops)고 말하는 것으로 보아 화자는 교통 관련 부서에서 근무한다는 것을 알 수 있다. 따라서 정답은 (B)이다.

97 Look at the graphic. Which neighborhood will be served first?
(A) Bradley Heights
(B) Rosewood
(C) Centerville
(D) Lakeview

시각 정보에 의하면, 어느 지역에 먼저 서비스가 제공될 것인가?
(A) 브래들리 하이츠
(B) 로즈우드
(C) 센터빌
(D) 레이크뷰

어휘 serve (서비스를) 제공하다

해설 시각 정보 연계 – 먼저 서비스가 제공되는 지역
화자가 후반부에 대학교 주변 지역부터 시작할 예정(We'll start with the neighborhood around the university ~)이라고 했고, 지도에서 대학교가 포함된 구역은 로즈우드이므로 정답은 (B)이다.

98-100 전화 메시지 + 가격 목록

> **W-Br** Hi, Andrew. This is Samantha Evans. It was great running into you at the flower trade show in Boston. And thanks for recommending that I visit the art museum while I was in town. **98 I really enjoyed seeing the modern art exhibit.** I'm calling because I wanted to follow up with you right away about the tulips you're getting shipped from the Netherlands next week. **99 I'd like to buy ten dozen tulips from you for my flower shop.** However, **100 my budget is tight and I can't spend more than $250.00**, so I'd like to order tulips in that price range.

안녕하세요, 앤드류. 저는 사만다 에반스입니다. 보스턴 꽃 무역 박람회에서 우연히 뵙게 되어 정말 반가웠습니다. 그리고 시내에 있는 동안 미술관을 방문하라고 추천해 주셔서 감사해요. **현대 미술 전시회를 정말 재미있게 봤어요.** 귀하께서 다음 주에 네덜란드에서 배송받으실 튤립과 관련해 바로 더 알아보고자 전화를 드렸습니다. **제 꽃집에서 판매할 튤립 12송이짜리 10묶음을 구입하려고 합니다.** 하지만, **제 예산이 빠듯해서 250달러 넘게 쓰기는 어려워서**, 이 가격대에 맞는 튤립을 주문하고 싶어요.

어휘 run into ~와 우연히 만나다 trade show 무역 박람회 exhibit 전시회 follow up 더 알아보다, 후속 조치를 취하다 dozen 12개짜리 한 묶음 tight 빠듯한 range 범위 variety 품종, 종류

Variety	Price ($)
Tulips	10 dozen
Fringed tulips	295.00
Triumph tulips	280.00
100 **Double early tulips**	**240.00**
Parrot tulips	275.00

품종	가격 ($)
튤립	12송이짜리 10묶음
프린지드 튤립	295.00
트라이엄프 튤립	280.00
더블 얼리 튤립	**240.00**
패럿 튤립	275.00

98 What does the speaker say she enjoyed seeing while she was in Boston?
(A) An art exhibit
(B) A sports event
(C) A holiday parade
(D) A rock concert

화자는 보스턴에 있는 동안 무엇을 재미있게 봤다고 말하는가?
(A) 미술 전시회
(B) 스포츠 행사
(C) 휴일 퍼레이드
(D) 록 콘서트

해설 세부 사항 관련 – 화자가 보스턴에서 재미있게 본 것
화자가 중반부에 현대 미술 전시회를 정말 재미있게 봤다(I really enjoyed seeing the modern art exhibit)고 했으므로 정답은 (A)이다.

99 Who most likely is the speaker?
(A) An interior decorator
(B) A shop owner
(C) A journalist
(D) A painter

화자는 누구인 것 같은가?
(A) 실내 장식 전문가
(B) 매장 소유주
(C) 기자
(D) 화가

해설 전체 내용 관련 – 화자의 직업
화자가 중반부에 상대방으로부터 자신의 꽃집에서 판매할 튤립 12송이짜리 10묶음을 구입하고 싶다(I'd like to buy ten dozen tulips from you for my flower shop)고 말하는 것으로 보아 화자는 꽃집을 운영하고 있다는 것을 알 수 있다. 따라서 정답은 (B)이다.

100 Look at the graphic. What type of tulips will the speaker most likely order?
(A) Fringed tulips
(B) Triumph tulips
(C) Double early tulips
(D) Parrot tulips

시각 정보에 의하면, 화자는 어떤 종류의 튤립을 주문할 것 같은가?
(A) 프린지드 튤립
(B) 트라이엄프 튤립
(C) 더블 얼리 튤립
(D) 패럿 튤립

해설 시각 정보 연계 – 화자가 주문할 튤립의 종류
화자가 후반부에 예산이 빠듯해서 250달러 넘게 쓰지는 못한다(~ my budget is tight and I can't spend more than $250.00 ~)고 말하고 있고, 가격 목록에서 250달러 미만에 해당하는 품종은 더블 얼리 튤립이므로 정답은 (C)이다.

기출 TEST 8

1 (D)	2 (B)	3 (A)	4 (D)	5 (C)
6 (A)	7 (C)	8 (B)	9 (C)	10 (A)
11 (C)	12 (B)	13 (C)	14 (A)	15 (A)
16 (B)	17 (A)	18 (A)	19 (C)	20 (B)
21 (A)	22 (A)	23 (A)	24 (C)	25 (B)
26 (A)	27 (B)	28 (B)	29 (C)	30 (C)
31 (C)	32 (A)	33 (B)	34 (A)	35 (A)
36 (D)	37 (A)	38 (B)	39 (D)	40 (A)
41 (C)	42 (A)	43 (B)	44 (B)	45 (D)
46 (C)	47 (B)	48 (A)	49 (D)	50 (D)
51 (B)	52 (A)	53 (A)	54 (A)	55 (C)
56 (A)	57 (D)	58 (C)	59 (D)	60 (C)
61 (D)	62 (B)	63 (B)	64 (C)	65 (D)
66 (C)	67 (D)	68 (B)	69 (D)	70 (C)
71 (D)	72 (B)	73 (C)	74 (D)	75 (A)
76 (B)	77 (B)	78 (B)	79 (D)	80 (B)
81 (B)	82 (D)	83 (A)	84 (D)	85 (D)
86 (C)	87 (A)	88 (B)	89 (B)	90 (A)
91 (C)	92 (A)	93 (B)	94 (C)	95 (D)
96 (C)	97 (A)	98 (C)	99 (C)	100 (A)

PART 1

1

M-Cn

(A) A wooden post is being painted.
(B) Flowerpots have been placed under some chairs.
(C) A rug has been spread out on the ground.
(D) Some furniture has been placed on a covered patio.

(A) 나무 기둥이 페인트칠되고 있다.
(B) 화분들이 의자 밑에 놓여 있다.
(C) 양탄자가 바닥에 펼쳐져 있다.
(D) 가구가 지붕이 있는 테라스에 놓여 있다.

어휘 post 기둥 flowerpot 화분 place 놓다, 두다 rug 양탄자 spread out 펼쳐 놓다 covered 지붕으로 덮인 patio 테라스

해설 사물/풍경 사진 – 사물 묘사
(A) 동사 오답. 나무 기둥(A wooden post)이 페인트칠되고 있는(is being painted) 모습이 아니므로 오답.
(B) 위치 오답. 화분들(Flowerpots)이 의자 밑에 놓여 있는 (have been placed under some chairs) 모습이 아니 므로 오답.
(C) 동사 오답. 양탄자(A rug)가 바닥에 펼쳐져 있는(has been spread out on the ground) 모습이 아니므로 오답.
(D) 정답. 가구(Some furniture)가 지붕이 있는 테라스에 놓여 있는(has been placed on a covered patio) 모습이므 로 정답.

2

M-Au

(A) Some people are exiting a parked vehicle.
(B) A woman is walking past a pedestrian crosswalk.
(C) Some cars are crossing an intersection.
(D) A woman is taping a flyer to a light pole.

(A) 사람들이 주차된 차량에서 내리고 있다.
(B) 여자가 횡단보도를 지나쳐 걸어가고 있다.
(C) 자동차들이 교차로를 건너가고 있다.
(D) 여자가 가로등 기둥에 전단을 테이프로 붙이고 있다.

어휘 exit 나가다 vehicle 차량 past ~을 지나(쳐)
pedestrian crosswalk 횡단보도 cross 건너다, 가로지르다
intersection 교차로 tape 테이프로 붙이다 flyer 전단
light pole 가로등 기둥

해설 2인 이상 등장 사진 – 사람/사물/풍경 혼합 묘사
(A) 동사 오답. 주차된 차량에서 내리고 있는(are exiting a parked vehicle) 사람들의 모습이 보이지 않으므로 오답.
(B) 정답. 여자가 횡단보도를 지나쳐 걸어가고 있는(is walking past a pedestrian crosswalk) 모습이므로 정답.
(C) 동사 오답. 교차로를 건너가고 있는(are crossing an intersection) 자동차들(Some cars)의 모습이 보이지 않 으므로 오답.
(D) 동사 오답. 여자가 가로등 기둥에 전단을 테이프로 붙이고 있는 (is taping a flyer to a light pole) 모습이 아니므로 오답.

3

W-Br

(A) A man is standing behind a counter.
(B) A man is setting up a display of items.
(C) Some floor tiles are being repaired.
(D) Customers are lined up at a cash register.

(A) 남자가 카운터 뒤에 서 있다.
(B) 남자가 진열품들을 설치하고 있다.
(C) 바닥 타일들이 수리되고 있다.
(D) 고객들이 계산대 앞에 줄지어 서 있다.

어휘 set up 설치하다, 마련하다 display 진열(품), 전시(품)
be lined up 줄지어 있다 cash register 계산대, 금전 등록기

해설 1인 등장 사진 – 사람/사물/풍경 혼합 묘사
(A) 정답. 남자가 카운터 뒤에 서 있는(is standing behind a counter) 모습이므로 정답.
(B) 동사 오답. 남자가 진열품들을 설치하고 있는(is setting up a display of items) 모습이 아니므로 오답.
(C) 동사 오답. 바닥 타일들(Some floor tiles)이 수리되고 있는(are being repaired) 모습이 아니므로 오답.
(D) 사진에 없는 명사를 이용한 오답. 사진에 고객들(Customers)의 모습이 보이지 않으므로 오답.

4

W-Am

(A) Some desks are pushed up against a window.
(B) A light fixture is hanging from the ceiling.
(C) Some armchairs have been stacked in a corner.
(D) A fence is visible through the window.

(A) 책상들이 창문 쪽으로 밀려 있다.
(B) 조명이 천장에 매달려 있다.
(C) 팔걸이 의자들이 구석에 쌓여 있다.
(D) 창문을 통해 울타리가 보인다.

어휘 light fixture 조명 hang from ~에 매달려 있다
ceiling 천장 stack 쌓다 visible 보이는

해설 사물/풍경 사진 – 사물 묘사
(A) 사진에 없는 명사를 이용한 오답. 사진에 책상들(Some desks)의 모습이 보이지 않으므로 오답.
(B) 사진에 없는 명사를 이용한 오답. 사진에 조명(A light fixture)의 모습이 보이지 않으므로 오답.
(C) 동사 오답. 팔걸이 의자들(Some armchairs)이 구석에 쌓여 있는(have been stacked in a corner) 모습이 아니므로 오답.
(D) 정답. 울타리(A fence)가 창문을 통해 보이는(is visible through the window) 모습이므로 정답.

5

W-Br

(A) The women are assembling a shelving unit.
(B) One of the women is packing some store decorations.
(C) One of the women is holding up a book.
(D) The women are unloading a shipment of books.

(A) 여자들이 선반을 조립하고 있다.
(B) 여자들 중 한 명이 매장 장식물을 포장하고 있다.
(C) 여자들 중 한 명이 책을 들고 있다.
(D) 여자들이 도서 배송품을 내리고 있다.

어휘 assemble 조립하다 shelving unit 선반 pack 포장하다
decoration 장식(물) hold up 들다 unload 내리다
shipment 배송(품)

해설 2인 이상 등장 사진 – 사람의 동작/상태 묘사
(A) 동사 오답. 여자들이 선반을 조립하고 있는(are assembling a shelving unit) 모습이 아니므로 오답.
(B) 동사 오답. 여자들 중 한 명이 매장 장식물을 포장하고 있는(is packing some store decorations) 모습이 아니므로 오답.
(C) 정답. 여자들 중 한 명이 책을 들고 있는(is holding up a book) 모습이므로 정답.
(D) 동사 오답. 여자들이 도서 배송품을 내리고 있는(are unloading a shipment of books) 모습이 아니므로 오답.

6

M-Cn

(A) They're climbing some stairs.
(B) They're sitting in a park.
(C) They're raking some leaves.
(D) They're planting some trees.

(A) 사람들이 계단을 올라가고 있다.
(B) 사람들이 공원에 앉아 있다.
(C) 사람들이 나뭇잎을 갈퀴로 긁어모으고 있다.
(D) 사람들이 나무를 심고 있다.

어휘 climb 올라가다 rake 갈퀴로 긁어모으다 plant 심다, 가꾸다

해설 2인 이상 등장 사진 – 사람의 동작/상태 묘사
(A) 정답. 사람들이 계단을 올라가고 있는(are climbing some stairs) 모습이므로 정답.
(B) 동사 오답. 사람들이 공원에 앉아 있는(are sitting in a park) 모습이 아니므로 오답.
(C) 동사 오답. 사람들이 나뭇잎을 갈퀴로 긁어모으고 있는(are raking some leaves) 모습이 아니므로 오답.
(D) 동사 오답. 사람들이 나무를 심고 있는(are planting some trees) 모습이 아니므로 오답.

PART 2

7 M-Cn / W-Br

Can I pick up my prescription glasses here?
(A) It's a new magazine subscription.
(B) The window glass needs to be repaired.
(C) Yes, they'll be ready soon.

제 처방 안경을 이곳에서 가져갈 수 있나요?
(A) 새 잡지 구독입니다.
(B) 창문 유리가 수리되어야 해요.
(C) 네, 곧 준비될 겁니다.

어휘 pick up 가져가다, 가져오다 prescription 처방(전), 처방약
subscription 구독, 가입

해설 처방 안경을 가져갈 수 있는지 묻는 조동사(Can) 의문문
(A) 유사 발음 오답. 질문의 prescription과 부분적으로 발음이 유사한 subscription을 이용한 오답.
(B) 유사 발음 오답. 질문의 glasses와 부분적으로 발음이 유사한 glass를 이용한 오답.
(C) 정답. 자신의 처방 안경을 가져갈 수 있는지 묻는 질문에 네(Yes)라고 대답한 뒤, 곧 준비될 것이라며 긍정 답변과 일관된 내용을 덧붙이고 있으므로 정답.

8 M-Cn / W-Am

Have you signed up for delivery updates?
(A) I'm sorry—you can't park here.
(B) Yes, I get alerts on my phone.
(C) Where's the security desk?

배송 알림을 신청하셨나요?
(A) 죄송하지만, 이곳에 주차하실 수 없습니다.
(B) 네, 제 전화기로 알림을 받아요.
(C) 보안 창구가 어디 있죠?

어휘 sign up for ~을 신청하다, ~에 등록하다 alert 알림, 경보

해설 배송 알림을 신청했는지 묻는 조동사(Have) 의문문
(A) 질문과 상관없는 오답.
(B) 정답. 배송 알림을 신청했는지 묻는 질문에 네(Yes)라고 대답한 뒤, 자신의 전화기로 알림을 받는다며 긍정 답변과 일관된 내용을 덧붙이고 있으므로 정답.
(C) 질문과 상관없는 오답.

9 W-Br / M-Cn

Where are the notes from the client meeting?
(A) No, I already have plans.
(B) Yes, eight o'clock is fine.
(C) I saved them on my laptop.

고객 회의 기록은 어디 있나요?
(A) 아니요, 저는 이미 계획이 있어요.
(B) 네, 8시 좋습니다.
(C) 제 노트북 컴퓨터에 저장해 두었습니다.

어휘 note 기록, 메모

해설 고객 회의 기록이 있는 곳을 묻는 Where 의문문
(A) Yes/No 불가 오답. Where 의문문에는 Yes/No 응답이 불가능하므로 오답.
(B) Yes/No 불가 오답. Where 의문문에는 Yes/No 응답이 불가능하므로 오답.
(C) 정답. 고객 회의 기록이 있는 곳을 묻는 질문에 자신의 노트북 컴퓨터에 저장해 두었다는 말로 기록이 있는 곳을 알려 주고 있으므로 정답.

10 M-Cn / W-Am

Does Dr. Cao schedule appointments in the morning or in the afternoon?
(A) She leaves at noon.
(B) I agree, that's a good point.
(C) Flight number 223.

카오 의사 선생님은 오전에 진료 예약을 잡나요, 아니면 오후에 잡나요?
(A) 그분은 정오에 퇴근합니다.
(B) 동의해요, 좋은 지적입니다.
(C) 223번 항공편이요.

어휘 appointment 예약, 약속 agree 동의하다

해설 카오 의사 선생님이 진료 예약을 잡는 시간을 묻는 선택 의문문
(A) 정답. 카오 의사 선생님이 오전과 오후 중 언제 진료 예약을 잡는지 묻는 질문에 정오에 퇴근한다는 말로 오전에 진료 예약을 잡는다는 뜻을 나타내고 있으므로 정답.
(B) 유사 발음 오답. 질문의 appointments와 부분적으로 발음이 유사한 point를 이용한 오답.
(C) 질문과 상관없는 오답.

11 M-Au / W-Br

Can you bring these agendas to the staff meeting?
(A) The new travel agency.
(B) I'd prefer blue paint for the walls.
(C) Sure, I'll take them with me.

이 안건 자료들을 직원회의에 가져와 주실 수 있으신가요?
(A) 새 여행사요.
(B) 그 벽은 파란색 페인트가 좋을 것 같아요.
(C) 물론이죠, 제가 가져가겠습니다.

어휘 agenda 안건, 의제

해설 부탁/요청의 의문문
(A) 질문과 상관없는 오답.
(B) 질문과 상관없는 오답.
(C) 정답. 안건 자료들을 직원회의에 가져와 달라고 요청하는 말에 물론이죠(Sure)라고 수락한 뒤, 가져가겠다고 긍정 답변과 일관된 내용을 덧붙이고 있으므로 정답.

12 W-Am / W-Br

It'll be nice to get a bonus this month.

(A) My office wasn't cleaned last night.
(B) The money will be deposited tomorrow.
(C) The weather has been very nice.

이번 달에 보너스를 받으면 좋을 거예요.
(A) 제 사무실은 어젯밤에 청소되지 않았어요.
(B) 그 돈은 내일 입금될 예정이에요.
(C) 날씨가 아주 좋네요.

어휘 deposit 입금하다, 예금하다

해설 의사 전달의 평서문
(A) 평서문과 상관없는 오답.
(B) 정답. 이번 달에 보너스를 받으면 좋겠다는 평서문에 그 돈이 내일 입금된다는 말로 곧 받게 된다는 뜻을 나타내고 있으므로 정답.
(C) 단어 반복 오답. 평서문의 nice를 반복 이용한 오답.

13 W-Br / M-Au

When is the city council going to vote on the new housing development?

(A) Yes, I'm going.
(B) It's near the library.
(C) At the next meeting.

시 의회는 신규 주택 개발에 대한 투표를 언제 하나요?
(A) 네, 저는 갑니다.
(B) 그곳은 도서관 근처에 있어요.
(C) 다음 회의에서요.

어휘 council 의회 vote 투표하다 development 개발, 발전

해설 시 의회가 신규 주택 개발에 대한 투표를 하는 시기를 묻는 When 의문문
(A) Yes/No 불가 오답. When 의문문에는 Yes/No 응답이 불가능하므로 오답.
(B) 질문과 상관없는 오답. Where 의문문에 대한 응답이므로 오답.
(C) 정답. 시 의회가 신규 주택 개발에 대한 투표를 하는 시기를 묻는 질문에 다음 회의 때 한다고 구체적인 시기를 알려 주고 있으므로 정답.

14 W-Am / W-Br ▶ 동영상 강의

Why can't we keep the factory open for an overnight shift?

(A) Management might be changing that policy.
(B) No, production costs haven't increased.
(C) Only a thirty-minute commute.

왜 야간 근무를 위해 공장을 계속 열어 둘 수 없는 건가요?
(A) 경영진이 그 정책을 변경할 수도 있어요.
(B) 아니요, 생산비가 오르지 않았습니다.
(C) 단 30분 통근이요.

어휘 overnight 야간의, 하룻밤 사이의 shift 교대 근무(조) management 경영(진), 관리(진) policy 정책, 방침 increase 오르다, 증가되다 commute 통근, 통학

해설 야간 근무를 위해 공장을 열어 둘 수 없는 이유를 묻는 Why 의문문
(A) 정답. 야간 근무를 위해 공장을 열어 둘 수 없는 이유를 묻는 질문에 경영진이 그 정책을 변경할 수도 있다며 앞으로는 그렇게 될 가능성이 있음을 알려 주고 있으므로 정답.
(B) Yes/No 불가 오답. 이유를 묻는 Why 의문문에는 Yes/No 응답이 불가능하므로 오답.
(C) 질문과 상관없는 오답.

15 W-Am / M-Cn

I put out more of our informational brochures in the waiting room.

(A) Thanks for doing that.
(B) No, he's still waiting.
(C) About eight pages, I think.

제가 대기실에 우리 안내 책자를 더 꺼내 놓았습니다.
(A) 그렇게 해 주셔서 감사합니다.
(B) 아니요, 그는 여전히 기다리고 있어요.
(C) 약 여덟 페이지인 것 같아요.

어휘 put out 꺼내 놓다 informational 정보를 담은 brochure 안내 책자, 소책자

해설 정보 전달의 평서문
(A) 정답. 대기실에 안내 책자를 더 꺼내 놓았다고 알리는 평서문에 그렇게 한 것에 대한 감사 인사를 전하고 있으므로 정답.
(B) 평서문과 상관없는 오답. 평서문에 3인칭 대명사 he로 지칭할 인물이 언급된 적이 없으므로 오답.
(C) 연상 단어 오답. 평서문의 brochures에서 연상 가능한 eight pages를 이용한 오답.

16 W-Am / M-Au

What's the starting pay rate for a software engineer at your firm?

(A) Shifts are from nine to five.
(B) Around 50 dollars an hour.
(C) Our customer satisfaction rates are high.

귀사의 소프트웨어 엔지니어 초임은 얼마인가요?
(A) 근무 시간은 9시부터 5시까지입니다.
(B) 시간당 약 50달러입니다.
(C) 우리 고객 만족도는 높습니다

어휘 pay rate 급여 firm 회사, 업체 satisfaction 만족(도) rate 정도, 비율

해설 소프트웨어 엔지니어 초임을 묻는 What 의문문
(A) 질문과 상관없는 오답.
(B) 정답. 소프트웨어 엔지니어 초임을 묻는 질문에 구체적인 금액으로 응답하고 있으므로 정답.
(C) 파생어 오답. 질문의 rate과 파생어 관계인 rates를 이용한 오답.

17 M-Au / W-Br

That flight is scheduled to take off at seven P.M., right?

(A) Stormy weather is predicted.
(B) A seat on the aisle.
(C) In the lower right corner.

그 항공편은 오후 7시에 이륙할 예정이죠, 그렇죠?
(A) 폭풍우가 예상됩니다.
(B) 통로 쪽 좌석이요.
(C) 오른쪽 하단 구석이에요.

어휘 take off 이륙하다   stormy 폭풍우가 치는   predict 예측하다

해설 항공편이 오후 7시에 이륙할 예정인지 확인하는 부가 의문문
(A) 정답. 항공편이 오후 7시에 이륙할 예정인지 확인하는 질문에 폭풍우가 예상된다며 예정대로 이륙하지 못할 수 있음을 우회적으로 나타내고 있으므로 정답.
(B) 연상 단어 오답. 질문의 flight에서 연상 가능한 seat on the aisle을 이용한 오답.
(C) 질문과 상관없는 오답. Where 의문문에 대한 응답이므로 오답.

18 M-Cn / W-Br

Should we take the client to Asako's Steakhouse?

(A) He's a vegetarian.
(B) I don't have any extra copies.
(C) It was a very interesting report.

고객을 아사코스 스테이크하우스로 모시고 갈까요?
(A) 그분은 채식주의자예요.
(B) 저는 복사본 여분이 없어요.
(C) 아주 흥미로운 보고서였어요.

어휘 extra 여분의, 추가의

해설 고객을 스테이크하우스로 모시고 갈지 묻는 조동사(Should) 의문문
(A) 정답. 고객을 스테이크하우스로 모시고 갈지 묻는 질문에 그 사람이 채식주의자라는 말로 다른 식당으로 가야 한다는 뜻을 우회적으로 나타내고 있으므로 정답.
(B) 질문과 상관없는 오답.
(C) 질문과 상관없는 오답.

19 W-Br / M-Au

How often do you travel abroad?

(A) An overseas assignment.
(B) I love Italian food.
(C) Twice a year.

해외여행을 얼마나 자주 가시나요?
(A) 해외 근무요.
(B) 이탈리아 음식을 아주 좋아합니다.
(C) 일 년에 두 번이요.

어휘 abroad 해외로, 해외에   overseas 해외의
assignment 배정, 할당

해설 해외여행을 가는 빈도를 묻는 How often 의문문
(A) 연상 단어 오답. 질문의 abroad에서 연상 가능한 overseas를 이용한 오답.
(B) 연상 단어 오답. 질문의 travel에서 연상 가능한 Italian을 이용한 오답.
(C) 정답. 해외여행을 가는 빈도를 묻는 질문에 일 년에 두 번이라고 구체적인 빈도로 응답하고 있으므로 정답.

20 W-Am / M-Cn

The product launch was a success, wasn't it?

(A) No, I haven't eaten yet.
(B) Yes, we already have a lot of orders.
(C) He'll meet you next week.

제품 출시가 성공적이었어요, 그렇지 않나요?
(A) 아니요, 아직 안 먹었어요.
(B) 네, 벌써 주문을 많이 받았어요.
(C) 그가 다음 주에 당신을 만날 거예요.

해설 제품 출시가 성공적이었음을 확인하는 부가 의문문
(A) 연상 단어 오답. 질문의 launch를 lunch로 잘못 이해했을 경우 연상 가능한 eaten을 이용한 오답.
(B) 정답. 제품 출시가 성공적이었음을 확인하는 질문에 네(Yes)라고 대답한 뒤, 벌써 주문을 많이 받았다며 긍정 답변과 일관된 내용을 덧붙이고 있으므로 정답.
(C) 질문과 상관없는 오답. 질문에 3인칭 대명사 He로 지칭할 인물이 언급된 적이 없으므로 오답.

21 W-Am / W-Br

How many books are in this mystery series?

(A) There are seven.
(B) You can book an appointment online.
(C) A serious topic.

이 미스터리 시리즈는 책이 몇 권이죠?
(A) 일곱 권입니다.
(B) 온라인으로 예약하실 수 있습니다.
(C) 진지한 주제요.

어휘 book an appointment 예약하다

해설 미스터리 시리즈 책 권 수를 묻는 How many 의문문
(A) 정답. 미스터리 시리즈 책 권 수를 묻는 질문에 일곱 권이라고 구체적인 수량으로 대답하고 있으므로 정답.
(B) 유사 발음 오답. 질문의 books와 부분적으로 발음이 유사한 book을 이용한 오답.
(C) 유사 발음 오답. 질문의 series와 부분적으로 발음이 유사한 serious를 이용한 오답.

22 W-Am / M-Cn

Can we finalize the budget today?

(A) We haven't received the report from Marketing.
(B) No, I don't need anything from the store.
(C) A representative from the bank.

오늘 예산을 최종 확정할 수 있을까요?
(A) 마케팅부의 보고서를 받지 못했어요.
(B) 아니요, 저는 그 매장에서 어떤 것도 필요치 않습니다.
(C) 그 은행의 직원이요.

어휘 finalize 최종 확정하다, 마무리하다 budget 예산
representative 직원, 대표자

해설 오늘 예산을 최종 확정할 수 있을지 묻는 조동사(Can) 의문문
(A) 정답. 오늘 예산을 최종 확정할 수 있을지 묻는 질문에 마케팅부의 보고서를 받지 못했다는 말로 오늘 최종 확정할 수 없을 것임을 우회적으로 나타내고 있으므로 정답.
(B) 질문과 상관없는 오답.
(C) 질문과 상관없는 오답.

23 M-Cn / W-Br

Who should I talk to about moving some bookshelves?
(A) Mr. Kim can help you.
(B) Yes, I moved to Chicago a few years ago.
(C) To the new office.

책장을 옮기는 일과 관련해 누구에게 이야기해야 하나요?
(A) 김 씨가 도와드릴 수 있어요.
(B) 네, 저는 몇 년 전에 시카고로 이사했어요.
(C) 새 사무실로요.

해설 책장을 옮기는 일과 관련해 이야기할 사람을 묻는 Who 의문문
(A) 정답. 책장을 옮기는 일과 관련해 이야기할 사람을 묻는 질문에 김 씨가 도와줄 수 있다고 구체적인 사람 이름으로 응답하고 있으므로 정답.
(B) Yes/No 불가 오답. Who 의문문에는 Yes/No 응답이 불가능하므로 오답.
(C) 질문과 상관없는 오답. Where 의문문에 대한 응답이므로 오답.

24 M-Au / M-Cn   ▶동영상 강의

Wouldn't you rather lead the workshop next week?
(A) Twenty dollars per person.
(B) That meeting was productive.
(C) Abidemi is a better teacher.

당신이 다음 주에 있을 워크숍을 진행하는 게 좋지 않을까요?
(A) 1인당 20달러요.
(B) 회의는 생산적이었어요.
(C) 애비데미가 더 나은 강사입니다.

어휘 lead 진행하다, 이끌다 productive 생산적인

해설 다음 주에 있을 워크숍을 진행하는 게 어떨지 묻는 부정 의문문
(A) 질문과 상관없는 오답. How much 의문문에 대한 응답이므로 오답.
(B) 연상 단어 오답. 질문의 workshop에서 연상 가능한 productive를 이용한 오답.
(C) 정답. 다음 주에 있을 워크숍을 진행하는 게 어떨지 묻는 질문에 애비데미가 더 나은 강사라며 다른 사람을 추천하고 있으므로 정답.

25 W-Am / M-Au

When does the bookstore open?
(A) A new travel guide.
(B) At eight o'clock.
(C) On the shelf.

서점은 언제 문을 여나요?
(A) 새로운 여행 안내서요.
(B) 8시에요.
(C) 선반에요.

해설 서점이 문을 여는 시간을 묻는 When 의문문
(A) 연상 단어 오답. 질문의 bookstore에서 연상 가능한 travel guide를 이용한 오답.
(B) 정답. 서점이 문을 여는 시간을 묻는 질문에 구체적인 시간으로 응답하고 있으므로 정답.
(C) 질문과 상관없는 오답. Where 의문문에 대한 응답이므로 오답.

26 M-Au / M-Cn

Can't you help me install this furniture?
(A) Sure, if you can wait a minute.
(B) It's not very comfortable.
(C) That's a good sofa.

이 가구를 설치하는 걸 도와주실 수 있으실까요?
(A) 그럼요, 잠시 기다리실 수 있으시면요.
(B) 아주 편하지는 않습니다.
(C) 좋은 소파네요.

어휘 install 설치하다 comfortable 편한, 편안한

해설 부탁/요청의 의문문
(A) 정답. 가구 설치를 도와달라는 요청에 그럼요(Sure)라고 대답한 뒤, 잠시만 기다리라며 긍정 답변과 일관된 내용을 덧붙이고 있으므로 정답.
(B) 연상 단어 오답. 질문의 furniture에서 연상 가능한 comfortable을 이용한 오답.
(C) 연상 단어 오답. 질문의 furniture에서 연상 가능한 sofa를 이용한 오답.

27 W-Am / M-Cn

Where can I find the eating utensils?
(A) The meal was delicious.
(B) In the drawer next to the sink.
(C) That's very kind.

어디에서 식기를 찾을 수 있죠?
(A) 식사가 맛있었습니다.
(B) 싱크대 옆에 있는 서랍에서요.
(C) 아주 친절하시네요.

어휘 eating utensils 식기 drawer 서랍

해설 식기를 찾을 수 있는 곳을 묻는 Where 의문문
(A) 연상 단어 오답. 질문의 eating에서 연상 가능한 meal을 이용한 오답.
(B) 정답. 식기를 찾을 수 있는 곳을 묻는 질문에 싱크대 옆에 있는 서랍이라고 장소를 알려 주고 있으므로 정답.

(C) 유사 발음 오답. 질문의 find와 발음이 일부 유사한 kind를 이용한 오답.

28 M-Au / W-Br

What can I do for you, ma'am?
(A) Tomorrow would be fine.
(B) My key card doesn't work.
(C) Thanks, I will.

무엇을 도와드릴까요, 고객님?
(A) 내일이 좋을 것 같아요.
(B) 제 카드키가 작동하지 않아요.
(C) 감사합니다, 그럴게요.

어휘 work 작동하다, 기능하다

해설 무엇을 도와줄지 묻는 What 의문문
(A) 질문과 상관없는 오답. When 의문문에 대한 응답이므로 오답.
(B) 정답. 무엇을 도와줄지 묻는 질문에 자신의 카드키가 작동하지 않는다는 말로 도움이 필요한 문제를 언급하고 있으므로 정답.
(C) 질문과 상관없는 오답.

29 W-Am / M-Au

Why is the conference in London this year?
(A) Yes, they're coming too.
(B) Just last week.
(C) Because it's convenient to travel there.

그 콘퍼런스가 왜 올해는 런던에서 열리죠?
(A) 네, 그들도 옵니다.
(B) 바로 지난주에요.
(C) 이동이 편하기 때문입니다.

어휘 convenient 편리한

해설 콘퍼런스가 올해 런던에서 열리는 이유를 묻는 Why 의문문
(A) Yes/No 불가 오답. Why 의문문에는 Yes/No 응답이 불가능하므로 오답.
(B) 질문과 상관없는 오답. When 의문문에 대한 응답이므로 오답.
(C) 정답. 콘퍼런스가 올해 런던에서 열리는 이유를 묻는 질문에 이동이 편해서라고 구체적인 이유를 제시하고 있으므로 정답.

30 M-Cn / W-Br ▶동영상 강의

Dr. Tong's arriving at the laboratory tomorrow.
(A) No, an extra microscope.
(B) Fifty dollars a day.
(C) I saw him this morning.

통 박사님은 실험실에 내일 도착하실 거예요.
(A) 아니요, 추가 현미경이요.
(B) 하루에 50달러요.
(C) 제가 오늘 아침에 그분을 봤어요.

어휘 laboratory 실험실 extra 추가의, 별도의 microscope 현미경

해설 정보 전달의 평서문
(A) 연상 단어 오답. 평서문의 laboratory에서 연상 가능한 microscope을 이용한 오답.
(B) 평서문과 상관없는 오답. How much 의문문에 대한 응답이므로 오답.
(C) 정답. 통 박사님이 실험실에 내일 도착한다고 알리는 평서문에 오늘 아침에 봤다는 말로 이미 도착했음을 알리고 있으므로 정답.

31 M-Cn / W-Br

The restaurant is finally getting a new stove.
(A) The recipe requires a saucepan.
(B) Can I have a salad for lunch?
(C) I hope it arrives soon.

레스토랑에 드디어 새 스토브가 생깁니다.
(A) 그 조리법은 소스 냄비가 필요합니다.
(B) 점심 식사로 샐러드를 먹을 수 있나요?
(C) 곧 도착하기를 바랍니다.

어휘 stove 스토브, 레인지 saucepan 소스 냄비

해설 정보 전달의 평서문
(A) 연상 단어 오답. 평서문의 restaurant에서 연상 가능한 recipe와 saucepan을 이용한 오답.
(B) 연상 단어 오답. 평서문의 restaurant에서 연상 가능한 salad for lunch를 이용한 오답.
(C) 정답. 레스토랑에 드디어 새 스토브가 생긴다고 알리는 평서문에 곧 도착하기를 바란다는 말로 새 스토브에 대한 기대감을 나타내고 있으므로 정답.

PART 3

32-34 W-Am / M-Cn

W Luca, **32 after we finish rewiring the electricity in this room, the client asked if we could also fix the ceiling light in the kitchen.** It flickers off and on sometimes.

M Hmm. I know which light you're talking about, and that fixture's really old. **33 It'd be better to replace it.**

W **33 I agree**—it wouldn't be worth repairing. **34 I have a catalog of fixtures in my truck. Let me go get it so we can show the client.**

여 루카, **우리가 이 방의 전기 배선을 변경하는 일을 마친 후에, 주방 천장 전등도 고칠 수 있는지 고객님께서 물어보셨어요.** 가끔 깜박거립니다.

남 흠. 어느 전등을 말씀하시는지 아는데, 그 조명은 정말 오래되었어요. **교체하는 편이 더 나을 겁니다.**

여 **동의해요**, 수리할 만한 가치가 없을 겁니다. **제 트럭에 조명 카탈로그가 있어요. 고객님께 보여 드릴 수 있도록 제가 가져올게요.**

어휘 rewire 배선을 변경하다, 전선을 교체하다 fix 고치다
ceiling 천장 flicker off and on 깜박거리다 fixture 설비
replace 교체하다, 대체하다 worth 가치가 있는

어휘 calculate 계산하다 bill 청구서, 계산서 revise 수정하다
해설 세부 사항 관련 – 여자가 다음에 할 일
여자가 마지막 대사에서 트럭에 있는 카탈로그를 언급하면서 고객에게 보여 줄 수 있도록 가져오겠다(I have a catalog of fixtures in my truck. Let me go get it so we can show the client)고 했으므로 정답은 (A)이다.

32 Who most likely are the speakers?
(A) Electricians
(B) Real estate agents
(C) House painters
(D) Decorators

화자들은 누구인 것 같은가?
(A) 전기 기사
(B) 부동산 중개업자
(C) 주택 도색업자
(D) 장식 전문가

해설 전체 내용 관련 – 화자들의 직업
여자가 첫 대사에서 자신들이 하는 일과 관련해 전기 배선을 변경하는 일(rewiring the electricity)과 천장 전등을 고치는 일(fix the ceiling light)을 언급하고 있으므로 정답은 (A)이다.

35-37 M-Au / W-Am

M Hey, Silvia. **35 Did you leave the refrigerator door in the laboratory open this morning?**

W No, I just arrived at the lab. I haven't opened the refrigerator yet. Why?

M Well, **36 the temperature is off by a few degrees.** We just purchased that refrigerator last month, so it should be in perfect working order.

W Oh, I see. I'll be working late tonight. Would you like me to check the temperature every few hours?

M That's OK. **37 I can monitor it from home with my smartphone.** Thanks, anyway.

남 안녕하세요, 실비아. **오늘 아침에 실험실에 있는 냉장고 문을 열어 놓았나요?**
여 아니요, 저는 방금 실험실에 도착했어요. 냉장고는 아직 열지 않았어요. 왜요?
남 음, 온도가 몇 도 내려가 있어요. 그 냉장고는 지난달에 구입한 거라서, 완벽하게 작동해야 하거든요.
여 아, 그렇군요. 저는 오늘 밤에 늦게까지 일할 예정이에요. 몇 시간마다 온도를 확인해 볼까요?
남 괜찮습니다. 제가 집에서 스마트폰으로 관찰할 수 있어요. 어쨌든 감사합니다.

어휘 laboratory 실험실(= lab) temperature 온도
degree (온도 단위인) 도, 정도 monitor 관찰하다, 감시하다

33 What do the speakers agree to do?
(A) Come back on another day
(B) Replace an item
(C) Apply a discount
(D) Try a new technique

화자들은 무엇을 하는 것에 동의하는가?
(A) 다른 날 다시 오기
(B) 제품 교체하기
(C) 할인 적용하기
(D) 새 기술 시도해 보기

어휘 apply 적용하다
해설 세부 사항 관련 – 화자들이 동의하는 것
남자가 첫 대사에서 전등을 교체하는 편이 더 나을 것(It'd be better to replace it)이라고 하자, 여자가 동의한다(I agree)고 했으므로 정답은 (B)이다.

34 What will the woman do next?
(A) Go to her truck
(B) Call her manager
(C) Calculate a bill
(D) Revise a schedule

여자는 다음에 무엇을 할 것인가?
(A) 트럭으로 가기
(B) 상사에게 전화하기
(C) 청구서 계산하기
(D) 일정표 수정하기

35 Where do the speakers work?
(A) At a laboratory
(B) At a cafeteria
(C) At a grocery store
(D) At a hotel

화자들은 어디에서 일하는가?
(A) 실험실
(B) 구내식당
(C) 식료품점
(D) 호텔

해설 　전체 내용 관련 – 화자들의 근무 장소
남자가 첫 대사에서 여자에게 오늘 아침에 실험실에 있는 냉장고 문을 열어 놓았는지(Did you leave the refrigerator door in the laboratory open this morning?) 묻고 있으므로 정답은 (A)이다.

36 What problem does the man mention?
(A) Some data are incomplete.
(B) A deadline was missed.
(C) Funding may be insufficient.
(D) Equipment might be faulty.

남자는 어떤 문제를 언급하는가?
(A) 일부 데이터가 불완전하다.
(B) 마감 기한을 놓쳤다.
(C) 자금이 부족할 수도 있다.
(D) 장비에 결함이 있을 수도 있다.

어휘 　incomplete 미비한, 미완성의　deadline 마감 기한
miss 놓치다　funding 자금 (제공)　insufficient 불충분한
equipment 장비　faulty 결함이 있는

해설 　세부 사항 관련 – 남자가 언급하는 문제
남자가 두 번째 대사에서 온도가 몇 도 내려가 있다는 문제와 함께 그 냉장고는 지난달에 구입한 거라서, 완벽하게 작동해야 한다(the temperature is off by a few degrees. We just purchased that refrigerator last month, so it should be in perfect working order)고 했다. 이는 냉장고에 문제가 있을 수 있다는 말이므로 정답은 (D)이다.

37 What does the man say he will do?
(A) Monitor a situation
(B) Place an order
(C) Make a phone call
(D) Compile test results

남자는 무엇을 할 것이라고 말하는가?
(A) 상황 관찰하기
(B) 주문하기
(C) 전화하기
(D) 테스트 결과 정리하기

어휘 　place an order 주문하다　compile 정리하다
result 결과(물)

해설 　세부 사항 관련 – 남자가 할 일
남자가 마지막 대사에서 집에서 스마트폰으로 관찰할 수 있다(I can monitor it from home with my smartphone)고 했으므로 정답은 (A)이다.

38-40 W-Br / M-Au

W　Hiroki, good news! ³⁸**We've received the grant money we requested to digitize our rare book collection.**

M　Excellent! ³⁹**I'm glad we'll finally be able to expand access to our collections.** Right now, only local residents can see those books.

W　True. You know, I'm not sure how the digitization process works.

M　Well, ⁴⁰**Archester Library is running a workshop next month on digitization practices. I think we should attend.**

W　Great idea. Let's register right away.

여　히로키, 좋은 소식입니다! **우리가 희귀 도서 소장품을 디지털화하기 위해 요청한 보조금을 받았습니다.**

남　잘됐네요! **드디어 우리 소장품의 접근성을 높일 수 있게 되어서 기쁩니다.** 지금은 지역 주민들만 그 도서들을 볼 수 있잖아요.

여　맞아요. 있잖아요, 저는 디지털화 과정이 어떻게 진행되는지 잘 몰라요.

남　음, **아체스터 도서관에서 다음 달에 디지털화 실무에 관한 워크숍을 진행할 거예요. 우리가 참석하면 좋을 것 같아요.**

여　좋은 생각이에요. 지금 바로 등록합시다.

어휘 　grant money 보조금　digitize 디지털화하다
rare 희귀한, 드문　collection 소장(품), 수집(품)
expand 확대하다, 확장하다　access 접근(성), 이용 (권한)
local 지역의, 현지의　resident 주민　process (처리) 과정
practice 실행, 실습　register 등록하다

38 What are the speakers mainly discussing?
(A) Starting a book club
(B) Digitizing some books
(C) Partnering with another business
(D) Opening a new library location

화자들은 주로 무엇을 이야기하고 있는가?
(A) 독서 동호회 시작하기
(B) 도서 디지털화하기
(C) 다른 업체와 제휴 맺기
(D) 새 도서관 지점 개관하기

어휘 　partner with ~와 제휴를 맺다　location 지점, 위치

해설 　전체 내용 관련 – 대화 주제
여자가 첫 대사에서 희귀 도서 소장품을 디지털화하기 위해 요청한 보조금을 받았다(We've received the grant money we requested to digitize our rare book collection)고 말한 뒤로, 디지털화 과정에 관해 이야기하고 있으므로 정답은 (B)이다.

39 What does the man like about a project?
(A) Costs will be reduced.
(B) A process will be faster.
(C) An organization will receive publicity.
(D) Access to some materials will be expanded.

남자는 프로젝트에 대해 무엇을 마음에 들어 하는가?
(A) 비용이 줄어들 것이다.
(B) 과정이 더 빨라질 것이다.
(C) 단체가 홍보 효과를 얻을 것이다.
(D) 자료의 접근성이 높아질 것이다.

어휘 reduce 줄이다, 감소시키다   organization 단체, 기관   publicity 홍보 (효과), 광고   material 자료, 재료

해설 세부 사항 관련 – 남자가 마음에 들어 하는 점
남자가 첫 대사에서 소장품의 접근성을 높일 수 있게 되어서 기쁘다(I'm glad we'll finally be able to expand access to our collections)고 했으므로 정답은 (D)이다.

Paraphrasing
대화의 our collections → 정답의 some materials

40 What does the man suggest doing?
(A) Attending a workshop
(B) Hiring additional employees
(C) Investing in new equipment
(D) Changing a program design

남자는 무엇을 하자고 제안하는가?
(A) 워크숍 참석하기
(B) 추가 직원 고용하기
(C) 새 장비에 투자하기
(D) 프로그램 디자인 변경하기

어휘 additional 추가적인   invest 투자하다

해설 세부 사항 관련 – 남자의 제안 사항
남자가 두 번째 대사에서 아체스터 도서관에서 다음 달에 디지털화 실무에 관한 워크숍을 진행할 것이라며, 참석하면 좋을 것 같다(Archester Library is running a workshop next month on digitization practices. I think we should attend)고 제안하고 있으므로 정답은 (A)이다.

41-43 W-Am / M-Cn

W Jong-Gyu, I have some amazing news. Our proposal was approved!

M You mean **41 our design for the new wing of the city hall building?** That's fantastic.

W Yes! I just spoke with a representative from the mayor's office. **42 The mayor wants to meet with us next week.**

M It's a good thing we took those aerial photographs of the site. **43 We should use those to create a 3-D model of the building.**

W You're right. Then we can bring that to the meeting.

여 종규, 놀라운 소식이 있어요. 우리 제안서가 승인됐어요!
남 시청의 새 부속 건물을 위한 설계도 말인가요? 아주 잘됐네요.
여 네! 제가 방금 시장 집무실 직원과 이야기를 했어요. 시장님께서 다음 주에 우리를 만나고 싶어 하신대요.
남 우리가 그곳의 항공 사진을 촬영한 게 잘한 것 같아요. 그걸 이용해서 건물의 3D 모형을 만드는 게 좋겠어요.
여 맞아요. 그럼, 그것을 회의에 가져갈 수 있을 거예요.

어휘 proposal 제안(서)   approve 승인하다   wing 부속 건물   city hall 시청   representative 직원, 대리인   mayor 시장   aerial photograph 항공 사진   site 부지, 현장   create 만들다

41 Who most likely are the speakers?
(A) Information technology specialists
(B) Artists
(C) Architects
(D) Newspaper journalists

화자들은 누구인 것 같은가?
(A) 정보 기술 전문가
(B) 예술가
(C) 건축가
(D) 신문 기자

해설 전체 내용 관련 – 화자들의 직업
남자가 첫 대사에서 시청의 새 부속 건물을 위한 자신들의 설계도(our design for the new wing of the city hall building)를 언급하고 있으므로 정답은 (C)이다.

42 What will take place next week?
(A) A meeting with a government official
(B) A tour of a construction site
(C) A community celebration
(D) A trade show

다음 주에 무슨 일이 있을 것인가?
(A) 정부 관계자와의 회의
(B) 건축 현장 견학
(C) 지역 사회 기념행사
(D) 무역 박람회

어휘 official 관계자, 당국자   construction 공사, 건설   community 지역 사회   celebration 기념행사, 축하 행사

해설 세부 사항 관련 – 다음 주에 있을 일
여자가 두 번째 대사에서 시장이 다음 주에 자신들을 만나고 싶어 한다(The mayor wants to meet with us next week)고 했으므로 정답은 (A)이다.

Paraphrasing
대화의 The mayor → 정답의 a government official

TEST 8 215

43 What does the man want to do?
(A) Review a contract
(B) Create a model
(C) Reserve a meeting room
(D) Update a Web site

남자는 무엇을 하고 싶어 하는가?
(A) 계약서 검토하기
(B) 모형 만들기
(C) 회의실 예약하기
(D) 웹사이트 업데이트하기

해설 세부 사항 관련 – 남자가 하고 싶은 것
남자가 두 번째 대사에서 항공 사진을 언급하면서 그것을 이용해 건물의 3D 모형을 만드는 게 좋겠다(We should use those to create a 3-D model of the building)고 했으므로 정답은 (B)이다.

44-46 W-Br / M-Cn

W Hi. ⁴⁴I heard the county is sponsoring a program for residents to have their garden soil analyzed here at the county agriculture building.

M That's right. Interested residents get a free soil analysis.

W Great. How long will it take to get the results? ⁴⁵I want to plant a vegetable garden this spring, and I'm very curious about my soil quality.

M It only takes two to three days. Do you have your sample with you?

W Yes. I have it right here.

M OK. Here's a label. ⁴⁶Please write your name and phone number on it. Then I'll submit your sample.

여 안녕하세요. 주에서 주민들을 위해 이곳 주립 농업 건물에서 주민들의 정원 토양을 분석해 주는 프로그램을 주관한다고 들었습니다.
남 그렇습니다. 관심 있는 주민들이 무료로 토양 분석을 받을 수 있습니다.
여 좋네요. 결과를 받는 데 얼마나 걸릴까요? 제가 올봄에 채소밭을 가꾸고 싶은데, 토질이 아주 궁금합니다.
남 2~3일밖에 걸리지 않습니다. 샘플을 갖고 계신가요?
여 네. 바로 여기 있습니다.
남 좋습니다. 여기 라벨이 있습니다. 여기에 성함과 전화번호를 써 주시기 바랍니다. 그 후에 그 샘플을 제출해 드리겠습니다.

어휘 county 주, 카운티 sponsor 주관하다, 후원하다
resident 주민, 거주자 soil 흙, 토양 analyze 분석하다
agriculture 농업 interested 관심이 있는 analysis 분석
curious 궁금한, 호기심이 있는

44 Where does the man most likely work?
(A) At a university library
(B) At a government facility
(C) At a home improvement store
(D) At a county park

남자는 어디에서 일하는 것 같은가?
(A) 대학 도서관
(B) 정부 시설
(C) 주택 개조용품 매장
(D) 주립 공원

어휘 facility 시설(물) improvement 개조, 개선
해설 전체 내용 관련 – 남자의 근무 장소
여자가 첫 대사에서 주에서 주민들을 위해 이곳 주립 농업 건물에서 주민들의 정원 토양을 분석해 주는 프로그램을 주관한다고 들었다(I heard the county is sponsoring a program for residents to have their garden soil analyzed here at the county agriculture building)고 했고, 남자가 해당 프로그램에 대해 안내해 주고 있는 것으로 보아 남자는 주립 농업 건물에서 일하는 사람임을 알 수 있다. 따라서 정답은 (B)이다.

45 What does the woman want to do in the spring?
(A) Write a book
(B) Apply for a job
(C) Take a course
(D) Plant a garden

여자는 봄에 무엇을 하고 싶어 하는가?
(A) 책 집필하기
(B) 일자리에 지원하기
(C) 수강하기
(D) 정원 가꾸기

어휘 apply for ~에 지원하다, ~을 신청하다
해설 세부 사항 관련 – 여자가 봄에 하고 싶은 것
여자가 두 번째 대사에서 올봄에 채소밭을 가꾸고 싶다(I want to plant a vegetable garden this spring ~)고 했으므로 정답은 (D)이다.

46 What does the man ask the woman to do?
(A) Make a payment
(B) Visit a Web site
(C) Provide contact information
(D) Wait for a supervisor

남자는 여자에게 무엇을 하도록 요청하는가?
(A) 비용 지불하기
(B) 웹사이트 방문하기
(C) 연락처 제공하기
(D) 책임자 기다리기

어휘 payment 지불(액) supervisor 책임자, 상사

해설 세부 사항 관련 – 남자의 요청 사항
남자가 마지막 대사에서 여자에게 이름과 전화번호를 써 달라(Please write your name and phone number on it)고 요청하고 있으므로 정답은 (C)이다.

Paraphrasing
대화의 write your name and phone number
→ 정답의 Provide contact information

47-49 M-Cn / W-Br

> M Hi, Liliana. **47 Here's the current script for the cartoon episode to be televised in three months.** The animation department wants us to complete the episode's storyboards in five weeks.
>
> W **48 I'll go grab some lunch for us** before we get started. Do you like Danny's Café on the corner?
>
> M Sounds good. Thank you. After you get back, **49 we can read through the script** so we can check the timing of each scene.

남 안녕하세요, 릴리아나. **3개월 후에 텔레비전으로 방송될 만화 에피소드의 현재 대본이에요.** 애니메이션부는 우리가 5주 안에 이 에피소드의 스토리보드를 완료하기를 원해요.

여 시작하기 전에 제가 얼른 가서 우리가 먹을 점심을 좀 사 올게요. 모퉁이에 있는 대니스 카페 좋아하세요?

남 좋아요. 감사합니다. 돌아오시면, 각 장면의 타이밍을 확인해 볼 수 있도록 **대본을 함께 읽어 봅시다.**

어휘 current 현재의 script 대본, 원고 cartoon 만화 episode 1회 방송분 televise 텔레비전으로 방송하다 complete 완료하다 storyboard 스토리보드 grab 급히 ~하다

47 What are the speakers working on?
(A) A piece of music
(B) A television cartoon
(C) A theater production
(D) An advertisement

화자들은 어떤 작업을 하고 있는가?
(A) 음악
(B) 텔레비전 만화
(C) 연극 제작
(D) 광고

어휘 piece 작품 theater 연극, 극장 production 제작
해설 전체 내용 관련 – 화자들이 작업하는 것
남자가 첫 대사에서 대본을 주면서 3개월 후에 텔레비전으로 방송될 만화 에피소드의 현재 대본(Here's the current script for the cartoon episode to be televised in three months)이라고 했으므로 정답은 (B)이다.

48 What does the woman say she will do?
(A) Pick up some lunch
(B) Set up an interview
(C) Buy some art supplies
(D) Turn on some equipment

여자는 무엇을 할 것이라고 말하는가?
(A) 점심 사 오기
(B) 인터뷰 잡기
(C) 미술용품 구입하기
(D) 장비 켜기

어휘 pick up 사다, 가져오다 set up 마련하다, 설정하다 supplies 용품, 물품 turn on ~을 켜다 equipment 장비
해설 세부 사항 관련 – 여자가 할 일
여자가 첫 대사에서 자신들이 먹을 점심을 사 오겠다(I'll go grab some lunch for us ~)고 했으므로 정답은 (A)이다.

Paraphrasing
대화의 go grab some lunch → 정답의 Pick up some lunch

49 What does the man suggest that they do later?
(A) Download some software
(B) Review some expenses
(C) Contact a performer
(D) Read a script

남자는 이따가 무엇을 하자고 제안하는가?
(A) 소프트웨어 다운로드하기
(B) 지출 검토하기
(C) 연기자에게 연락하기
(D) 대본 읽기

어휘 expense 지출 (비용), 경비 performer 연기자, 연주자
해설 세부 사항 관련 – 남자의 제안 사항
남자가 마지막 대사에서 각 장면의 타이밍을 확인해 볼 수 있게 대본을 함께 읽어 보자(~ we can read through the script ~)고 제안하고 있으므로 정답은 (D)이다.

50-52 3인 대화 W-Br / W-Am / M-Au

> W1 Hi, my name is Kelly Stewart. **50 I really love your restaurant's outdoor dining area.** I was hoping to reserve it next Thursday evening for a group of 25.
>
> W2 Hello, Ms. Stewart. **51 I'm Sakura. Unfortunately, I believe another large group reserved the patio for Thursday**, but let me quickly check with my manager. Mr. Gomez? Do we have a large group on the patio this Thursday evening?
>
> M Actually, that group changed their reservation to Wednesday.

W1 Great! Is there a special menu for large groups?

M **52 We offer a special menu for large groups that charges a flat rate per person. Let me go get that for you.** Sakura, can you take down the customer's reservation details?

여1 안녕하세요, 제 이름은 켈리 스튜어트입니다. **저는 여기 레스토랑의 야외 식사 공간을 정말 좋아해요.** 다음 목요일 저녁에 그 자리로 25명 단체를 예약하고 싶어요.

여2 안녕하세요, 스튜어트 씨. **저는 사쿠라입니다. 안타깝게도, 다른 단체 손님들께서 목요일에 그 테라스를 예약하신 것 같은데,** 점장님께 빨리 확인해 보겠습니다. 고메즈 점장님? 이번 목요일 저녁에 테라스에 단체 손님들이 예약되어 있나요?

남 실은, 그 단체 손님들께서 예약을 수요일로 바꾸셨어요.

여1 잘됐네요! 단체 손님들을 위한 특별 메뉴가 있나요?

남 **저희는 인당 동일 요금이 부과되는 단체 손님용 특별 메뉴를 제공합니다. 제가 가서 가져다드리겠습니다.** 사쿠라, 고객님의 예약 상세 내역을 적어 주시겠어요?

어휘 outdoor 야외의 dining 식사 reserve 예약하다 unfortunately 유감스럽게도, 안타깝게도 patio 테라스 reservation 예약 charge 부과하다 flat rate 고정 요금 take down 받아 적다, 기록하다 details 상세 정보, 세부 사항

50 What does Ms. Stewart like about a restaurant?
(A) Its varied menu
(B) Its positive reviews
(C) Its convenient location
(D) Its outdoor seating

스튜어트 씨는 레스토랑에 대해 무엇을 마음에 들어 하는가?
(A) 다양한 메뉴
(B) 긍정적인 평가
(C) 편리한 위치
(D) 야외 좌석

어휘 varied 다양한, 다채로운 positive 긍정적인 review 평가, 후기 convenient 편리한

해설 세부 사항 관련 – 스튜어트 씨가 마음에 들어 하는 것
첫 번째 여자가 첫 대사에서 여기 레스토랑의 야외 식사 공간을 정말 좋아한다(I really love your restaurant's outdoor dining area)고 했으므로 정답은 (D)이다.

Paraphrasing
대화의 outdoor dining area → 정답의 outdoor seating

51 What problem does Sakura mention?
(A) A kitchen appliance is broken.
(B) A space may not be available.
(C) A daily special is no longer offered.
(D) A delivery may be delayed.

사쿠라는 어떤 문제를 언급하는가?
(A) 주방 기기가 고장 났다.
(B) 공간을 이용하지 못할 수도 있다.
(C) 오늘의 특별 요리가 더 이상 제공되지 않는다.
(D) 배달이 지연될 수도 있다.

어휘 appliance (가전) 기기 broken 고장 난, 망가진 available 이용 가능한, 구할 수 있는 delay 지연시키다

해설 세부 사항 관련 – 사쿠라가 언급하는 문제
두 번째 여자가 첫 대사에서 자신의 이름을 사쿠라라고 밝히면서, 다른 단체 손님들이 목요일에 그 테라스를 예약한 것 같다(I'm Sakura. Unfortunately, I believe another large group reserved the patio for Thursday, ~)고 했으므로 정답은 (B)이다.

Paraphrasing
대화의 another large group reserved the patio
→ 정답의 A space may not be available.

52 What will the man do next?
(A) Provide a menu
(B) Speak to a chef
(C) Prepare a dining area
(D) Order restaurant supplies

남자는 다음에 무엇을 할 것인가?
(A) 메뉴 제공하기
(B) 요리사와 이야기하기
(C) 식사 공간 준비하기
(D) 레스토랑 용품 주문하기

어휘 supplies 용품, 물품

해설 세부 사항 관련 – 남자가 다음에 할 일
남자가 마지막 대사에서 인당 동일 요금이 부과되는 단체 손님용 특별 메뉴를 제공한다며, 자신이 갖다주겠다(We offer a special menu for large groups that charges a flat rate per person. Let me go get that for you)고 했으므로 정답은 (A)이다.

53-55 W-Am / M-Au

W Hi! **53 How are you enjoying the agricultural trade show?**

M I've seen some great demonstrations. That being said, one of the reasons I came to this show was to visit your booth. I've been watching some promotional videos online about the machinery that you sell.

W Is this our new line of automated farming technology?

M That's right. **54 I watched a video about a machine that can transplant seedlings from** small pots to bigger pots. It handles 10,000 plants in an hour?

W It sure does! And we have several payment options. ⁵⁵**Let me give you some details about our financing plans.**

여 안녕하세요! **농업 무역 박람회를 어떻게 즐기고 계신가요?**
남 훌륭한 시연회를 몇 개 봤어요. 그렇지만, 제가 이 박람회에 온 이유 중 하나가 귀사의 부스를 방문하는 것이었어요. 귀사에서 판매하는 기계에 관한 홍보 영상을 온라인에서 봤거든요.
여 이거 저희 농업 자동화 기계 신제품 라인인가요?
남 맞습니다. **작은 화분에서 큰 화분으로 묘목을 옮겨 심을 수 있는 기계에 관한 영상을 봤어요. 1시간 만에 1만 개의 식물을 처리하는 거죠?**
여 그렇습니다! 그리고 여러 가지 비용 지불 선택지가 있습니다. **저희 금융 지원 제도에 대해 자세히 말씀드릴게요.**

어휘 agricultural 농업의 trade show 무역 박람회 demonstration 시연(회), 시범 promotional 홍보의, 판촉의 machinery 기계(류) automated 자동화된, 자동의 transplant 옮겨 심다, 이식하다 seedling 묘목 handle 처리하다, 다루다 financing plans 금융 지원 제도

53 Where are the speakers?
 (A) At a trade show
 (B) At a press conference
 (C) At a job fair
 (D) At a factory opening

화자들은 어디에 있는가?
(A) 무역 박람회
(B) 기자 회견
(C) 취업 박람회
(D) 공장 개장식

해설 전체 내용 관련 – 화자들이 있는 곳
여자가 첫 대사에서 농업 무역 박람회를 어떻게 즐기고 있는지(How are you enjoying the agricultural trade show?) 물었으므로 정답은 (A)이다.

54 Why does the man say, "It handles 10,000 plants in an hour"?
 (A) To express amazement
 (B) To justify an expense
 (C) To correct an error
 (D) To recommend caution

화자는 왜 "1시간 만에 1만 개의 식물을 처리하는 거죠?"라고 말하는가?
(A) 놀라움을 표현하기 위해
(B) 지출을 정당화하기 위해
(C) 오류를 바로잡기 위해
(D) 주의하도록 권하기 위해

어휘 express 표현하다 amazement 놀라움 justify 정당화하다 correct 바로잡다, 정정하다 caution 주의, 경고

해설 화자의 의도 파악 – 1시간 만에 1만 개의 식물을 처리한다는 말의 의도
남자가 두 번째 대사에서 자신이 작은 화분에서 큰 화분으로 묘목을 옮겨 심을 수 있는 기계에 관한 영상을 봤다(I watched a video about a machine that can transplant seedlings from small pots to bigger pots)고 말하면서 인용문을 언급하고 있다. 이는 그 기계의 뛰어난 성능을 구체적으로 언급함으로써 놀라움을 표현하는 말에 해당하므로 정답은 (A)이다.

55 What will the speakers do next?
 (A) Exchange business cards
 (B) Watch a product demonstration
 (C) Review financing options
 (D) Contact an event organizer

화자들은 다음에 무엇을 할 것인가?
(A) 명함 교환하기
(B) 제품 시연회 보기
(C) 금융 지원 선택지 살펴보기
(D) 행사 주최자에게 연락하기

어휘 exchange 교환하다 organizer 주최자, 조직자

해설 세부 사항 관련 – 화자들이 다음에 할 일
여자가 마지막 대사에서 금융 지원 제도에 대해 자세히 말해 주겠다(Let me give you some details about our financing plans)고 했으므로 정답은 (C)이다.

> **Paraphrasing**
> 대화의 give you some details about our financing plans
> → 정답의 Review financing options

56-58 3인 대화 W-Br / M-Cn / M-Au

W OK. ⁵⁶**You're all set to board flight 1216 to Toronto.** Thank you for flying with us. Unfortunately, I've just learned that the flight is delayed because of inclement weather in Canada.

M1 Oh, no! ⁵⁷**My colleague here and I are presenting at a conference in Toronto this evening.** Do you have any idea how long the delay might be?

W We'll be hearing from Toronto regularly. I'm sorry, but that's all we know at this point.

M2 It's all right, Jinyu. I doubt we'll get there in time. Maybe the organizers can reschedule us for tomorrow. I'll call them.

W In the meantime, ⁵⁸**I can offer you meal vouchers if you like.**

여	좋습니다. **토론토행 1216 항공편 탑승 준비가 완료되었습니다.** 저희 항공기를 이용해 주셔서 감사합니다. 안타깝게도 캐나다의 악천후로 인해 항공편이 지연되고 있다는 소식을 방금 들었습니다.
남1	아, 이런! **여기 제 동료와 저는 오늘 저녁에 토론토에서 열리는 콘퍼런스에서 발표를 해요.** 혹시 얼마나 지연될지 아시나요?
여	주기적으로 토론토로부터 소식을 들을 겁니다. 죄송하지만, 현재 저희가 알고 있는 건 그게 전부입니다.
남2	괜찮아요, 진유. 우리가 제때 도착할 것 같지 않네요. 아마 주최 측에서 우리 일정을 내일로 재조정해 줄 수 있을 거예요. 제가 전화해 볼게요.
여	그 사이에, **원하시면 식권을 제공해 드릴 수 있습니다.**

어휘 be set to ~할 준비가 되다, ~할 예정이다 board 탑승하다 delay 지연시키다; 지연 inclement weather 악천후 colleague 동료 (직원) present 발표하다 regularly 주기적으로 at this point 현재 doubt ~할 것 같지 않다, 의심하다 in time 제때, 늦지 않게 organizer 주최자, 조직자, 설립자 reschedule 일정을 재조정하다 in the meantime 그 사이에 voucher 상품권, 쿠폰

56 Where is the conversation taking place?
(A) At an airport
(B) At a travel agency
(C) At a bus station
(D) At a train station

대화는 어디에서 이루어지고 있는가?
(A) 공항
(B) 여행사
(C) 버스 정류장
(D) 기차역

어휘 take place 진행되다, 개최되다

해설 전체 내용 관련 – 대화 장소
여자가 첫 대사에서 토론토행 1216 항공편 탑승 준비가 완료되었다(You're all set to board flight 1216 to Toronto)고 했으므로 정답은 (A)이다.

57 Why are the men traveling to Toronto?
(A) To attend a sports event
(B) To meet with a client
(C) To tour a factory
(D) To present at a conference

남자들은 왜 토론토로 가고 있는가?
(A) 스포츠 행사에 참석하기 위해
(B) 고객과 만나기 위해
(C) 공장을 견학하기 위해
(D) 콘퍼런스에서 발표하기 위해

어휘 attend 참석하다 tour 견학하다, 둘러보다

해설 세부 사항 관련 – 남자들이 토론토로 가는 이유
첫 번째 남자가 첫 대사에서 자신의 동료와 자신이 오늘 저녁에 토론토에서 열리는 콘퍼런스에서 발표한다(My colleague here and I are presenting at a conference in Toronto this evening)고 했으므로 정답은 (D)이다.

58 What does the woman offer to do?
(A) Rebook a trip
(B) Restart a computer system
(C) Provide some vouchers
(D) Call a hotel

여자는 무엇을 하겠다고 제안하는가?
(A) 여행을 다시 예약하기
(B) 컴퓨터 시스템 다시 시작하기
(C) 쿠폰 제공하기
(D) 호텔에 전화하기

어휘 rebook 다시 예약하다

해설 세부 사항 관련 – 여자의 제안 사항
여자가 마지막 대사에서 남자들에게 원하면 식권을 제공해 줄 수 있다(I can offer you meal vouchers if you like)고 했으므로 정답은 (C)이다.

Paraphrasing
대화의 offer you meal vouchers
→ 정답의 Provide some vouchers

59-61 M-Au / W-Am ▶ 동영상 강의

M	So, Raquel, **59 I've been working on repairing this tractor**, but I'm not having much luck. I think it's the hydraulic system. I cleaned the pump, but it's not running any better. I've done this before, and it usually fixes it.
W	I see. Maybe it's a problem with a piston in the hydraulic cylinder. **60 But a repair that big should be under warranty. It was Hamdy Equipment that sold it to us.**
M	Good point. I'll give them a call later. I've spent too much time on this tractor. **61 I need to go over to the fields to check on the peppers and cucumbers**—it may be time to pick them.

남 그래서, 라켈, **제가 이 트랙터를 수리하는 작업을 하고 있는데**, 운이 별로 따르지 않네요. 유압 시스템이 문제인 것 같아요. 펌프를 세척했는데, 작동이 더 좋아지진 않네요. 전에 이렇게 해 본 적이 있는데, 보통은 고쳐지거든요.

여 알겠습니다. 아마 유압 실린더에 있는 피스톤 문제일 수도 있어요. **하지만 그 정도로 큰 수리라면 품질 보증이 적용될 거예요. 그걸 우리에게 판매한 곳은 햄디 이큅먼트였어요.**

남 좋은 지적입니다. 제가 나중에 그곳에 전화해 볼게요. 이 트랙터에 너무 많은 시간을 소비했어요. **고추와 오이를 확인하러 밭에 나가 봐야 해요.** 수확할 때가 됐을 수도 있거든요.

어휘 hydraulic 유압의, 수압의 run 작동하다, 기능하다
usually 보통 under warranty 품질 보증이 적용되는
pick 수확하다, 따다

59 What has the man been doing?
(A) Repairing a vehicle
(B) Painting a fence
(C) Training an assistant
(D) Cleaning out a shed

남자는 무엇을 하고 있는가?
(A) 차량 수리하기
(B) 울타리 도색하기
(C) 보조 직원 교육하기
(D) 헛간 청소하기

어휘 vehicle 차량 assistant 보조, 조수 shed 헛간, 창고

해설 전체 내용 관련 – 남자가 하고 있는 일
남자가 첫 대사에서 트랙터를 수리하는 작업을 하고 있다(I've been working on repairing this tractor ~)고 했으므로 정답은 (A)이다.

Paraphrasing
대화의 this tractor → 정답의 a vehicle

60 Why does the woman say, "It was Hamdy Equipment that sold it to us"?
(A) To complain about a decision
(B) To correct some misinformation
(C) To make a suggestion
(D) To give a compliment

여자는 왜 "그걸 우리에게 판매한 곳은 햄디 이큅먼트였어요"라고 말하는가?
(A) 결정에 대해 불만을 제기하기 위해
(B) 잘못된 정보를 정정하기 위해
(C) 제안하기 위해
(D) 칭찬하기 위해

어휘 complain 불만을 제기하다 decision 결정
misinformation 잘못된 정보 compliment 칭찬(의 말)

해설 화자의 의도 파악 – 그걸 판매한 곳은 햄디 이큅먼트였다는 말의 의도
여자가 첫 대사에서 그 정도로 큰 수리라면 품질 보증이 적용될 것(But a repair that big should be under warranty)이라며 인용문을 언급하고 있다. 이는 판매처에서 수리를 받을 것을 제안하는 말이므로 정답은 (C)이다.

61 What will the man check next?
(A) An invoice
(B) A manual
(C) Some cattle
(D) Some vegetables

남자는 다음에 무엇을 확인할 것인가?
(A) 거래 내역서
(B) 설명서
(C) 가축
(D) 채소

해설 세부 사항 관련 – 남자가 다음에 확인할 것
남자가 마지막 대사에서 고추와 오이를 확인하러 밭에 나가 봐야 한다(I need to go over to the fields to check on the peppers and cucumbers ~)고 했으므로 정답은 (D)이다.

Paraphrasing
대화의 the peppers and cucumbers
→ 정답의 Some vegetables

62-64 대화 + 가격표 W-Br / M-Cn ▶동영상 강의

W Hi. **62 I'm here to pick up my car.** My name's Olga Popova. **62 You replaced one of my tires.**

M Yes, Ms. Popova. Your car is ready. Your bill is $133.

W That's quite a bit more than listed on your Web site. **63 I thought the cost would be $98.**

M Let me look at the work order. It looks like I billed you for the wrong tire. Apologies—let me fix that. Also, **64 if you'd like to share your e-mail**, I can sign you up for our rewards program.

여 안녕하세요. **제 차를 가져가려고 왔어요.** 제 이름은 올가 포포바입니다. **여기서 타이어를 하나 교체했어요.**

남 네, 포포바 씨. 차가 준비되어 있습니다. 요금은 133달러입니다.

여 웹사이트에 기재된 것보다 훨씬 비싸네요. **비용이 98달러일 거라고 생각했어요.**

남 작업 지시서를 확인해 보겠습니다. 제가 엉뚱한 타이어 비용을 청구한 것 같습니다. 죄송합니다. 수정해 드리겠습니다. 그리고 **이메일을 공유해 주시면**, 저희 고객 보상 프로그램에 등록해 드리겠습니다.

어휘 bill 청구서, 계산서; 청구하다 work order 작업 지시(서)
apologies 죄송합니다 fix 수정하다, 고치다 share 공유하다
sign ~ up for ... ~을 …에 등록시키다, ~을 …에 가입시키다
rewards program 고객 보상 프로그램

Tire Model	Price per Tire
City Cruiser	$75
63 Snow King	**$98**
High Summit	$120
Sport Plus	$133

타이어 모델	개당 가격
시티 크루저	75달러
스노우 킹	**98달러**
하이 써밋	120달러
스포트 플러스	133달러

62 Who most likely is the woman?
(A) A mechanic
(B) A customer
(C) An auto parts supplier
(D) A social media coordinator

여자는 누구인 것 같은가?
(A) 정비사
(B) 고객
(C) 자동차 부품 공급업자
(D) 소셜 미디어 운영자

해설 전체 내용 관련 – 여자의 직업
여자가 첫 대사에서 자신의 차를 가져가려고 왔다며, 타이어 하나를 교체했다(I'm here to pick up my car. ~ You replaced one of my tires)고 했다. 따라서 차량 수리를 맡긴 고객인 것으로 볼 수 있으므로 정답은 (B)이다.

63 Look at the graphic. Which tire model should have been listed on an invoice?
(A) City Cruiser
(B) Snow King
(C) High Summit
(D) Sport Plus

시각 정보에 의하면, 어느 타이어 모델이 거래 내역서에 기재되었어야 하는가?
(A) 시티 크루저
(B) 스노우 킹
(C) 하이 써밋
(D) 스포트 플러스

해설 시각 정보 연계 – 거래 내역서에 기재되었어야 하는 타이어 모델
여자가 두 번째 대사에서 비용이 98달러일 거라고 생각했다(I thought the cost would be $98)고 하자, 남자가 사과의 말과 함께 수정하겠다고 했다. 가격표에서 비용이 $98로 표기된 제품은 Snow King이므로 정답은 (B)이다.

64 What does the man invite the woman to share?
(A) Some consultant names
(B) Some feedback
(C) An e-mail address
(D) A collection of photographs

남자는 여자에게 무엇을 공유하도록 요청하는가?
(A) 컨설턴트 이름
(B) 의견
(C) 이메일 주소
(D) 사진집

어휘 feedback 의견

해설 세부 사항 관련 – 남자의 요청 사항
남자는 마지막 대사에서 여자에게 이메일을 공유해 주면(~ if you'd like to share your e-mail, ~) 고객 보상 프로그램에 등록해 주겠다고 했으므로 정답은 (C)이다.

65-67 대화 + 안내 책자 W-Am / M-Au

W Hi. I want to buy a new pillow. **65 I recently started waking up with a stiff neck, so I want something that will help me sleep better.**

M I can assist you with that. The first thing you should consider is the position you sleep in. Do you sleep on your back, your stomach, or your side?

W On my side.

M OK. For side sleepers, **66 we recommend the Star Pillow**. It's a firm pillow that will give you good support.

W Sounds great. One question, though. **67 What's inside the pillow? I have an allergy to feathers.**

M This particular model is made with only nonallergenic materials.

여 안녕하세요. 새 베개를 사고 싶어요. **최근에 목이 뻣뻣한 상태로 잠에서 깨기 시작해서, 숙면에 도움이 되는 것을 원해요.**

남 제가 도와드릴게요. 처음으로 고려하셔야 하는 것은 자는 자세입니다. 반듯이 누워서 주무시나요, 아니면 엎드리거나 옆으로 주무시나요?

여 옆으로요.

남 알겠습니다. 옆으로 주무시는 분들께는 **스타 필로우를 추천합니다.** 지지력이 좋은 단단한 베개입니다.

여 좋은 것 같네요. 하지만 질문이 하나 있는데요. **베개 안에 뭐가 있죠? 제가 깃털에 알레르기가 있어요.**

남 이 모델은 비알레르기성 소재로만 만들어집니다.

어휘 pillow 베개 stiff 뻣뻣한 assist 돕다 consider 고려하다
position 자세, 자리 on one's back 반듯이 누워서
on one's stomach 엎드려서 firm 단단한 support 지지(력)
allergy 알레르기 feather 깃털 particular 특정한
be made with ~로 만들어지다 nonallergenic 비알레르기성의

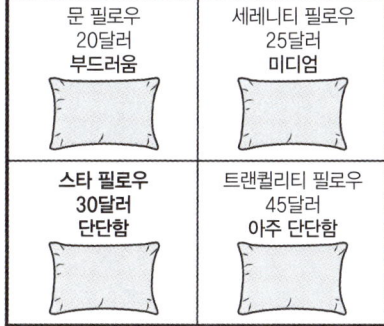

65 Why does the woman want to buy a new pillow?
(A) Her pillow is old.
(B) Her pillow is too small.
(C) She heard about a new model.
(D) She developed a pain in her neck.

여자는 왜 새로운 베개를 구입하고 싶어 하는가?
(A) 베개가 낡았다.
(B) 베개가 너무 작다.
(C) 새로운 모델에 관한 얘기를 들었다.
(D) 목에 통증이 생겼다.

어휘 develop (질병, 문제 등이) 생기다 pain 통증

해설 세부 사항 관련 – 여자가 베개를 구입하려는 이유
여자가 첫 대사에서 최근에 목이 뻣뻣한 상태로 잠에서 깨기 시작해서, 숙면에 도움이 되는 것을 원한다(I recently started waking up with a stiff neck, so I want something that will help me sleep better)고 했으므로 (D)가 정답이다.

Paraphrasing
대화의 started waking up with a stiff neck
→ 정답의 developed a pain in her neck

66 Look at the graphic. How much is the pillow that the man recommends?
(A) $20
(B) $25
(C) $30
(D) $45

시각 정보에 의하면, 남자가 추천하는 베개는 얼마인가?
(A) 20달러
(B) 25달러
(C) 30달러
(D) 45달러

해설 시각 정보 연계 – 남자가 추천하는 베개의 가격
남자가 두 번째 대사에서 스타 필로우를 추천한다(~ we recommend the Star Pillow)고 했는데, 안내 책자에서 Star Pillow로 표기된 제품의 가격은 $30로 쓰여 있으므로 정답은 (C)이다.

67 What does the woman ask about?
(A) A product warranty
(B) A promotional discount
(C) The store's business hours
(D) The materials used in a product

여자가 무엇에 관해 묻는가?
(A) 제품 품질 보증
(B) 판촉용 할인
(C) 매장 영업시간
(D) 제품에 사용된 소재

어휘 warranty 품질 보증(서) promotional 판촉의, 홍보의

해설 세부 사항 관련 – 여자가 묻는 것
여자가 세 번째 대사에서 베개 안에 뭐가 있는지 물으며, 깃털에 알레르기가 있다(What's inside the pillow? I have an allergy to feathers)고 했다. 이는 베개에 사용된 소재가 무엇인지 묻는 것이므로 정답은 (D)이다.

Paraphrasing
대화의 What's inside the pillow?
→ 정답의 The materials used in a product

68-70 대화 + 영업 과정 W-Br / M-Au

W Welcome to the team. **68 I hear you have a lot of experience designing software.** We need some new ideas for our business software package we're developing.

M Thanks. I also help set up for the sales presentations. **69 I just fixed a problem with the sound equipment in the conference room.** By the way, you're in sales, right? Aren't you presenting to a new client next week?

W Yes, I love sales. **70 But I especially like the step where we're getting a lot of questions from clients.** I can address doubts or objections and show them how the software really meets their needs.

여 팀에 오신 걸 환영해요. **소프트웨어 설계 경험이 많다고 들었어요.** 저희가 지금 비즈니스 소프트웨어 패키지를 개발 중인데, 새로운 아이디어가 좀 필요하거든요.

남 감사합니다. 저는 세일즈 프레젠테이션 준비도 돕고 있어요. **방금 회의실 음향 장비 문제를 해결했죠.** 그건 그렇고, 영업팀이시죠? 다음 주 새로운 고객에게 프레젠테이션 하지 않나요?

여 맞아요, 저는 영업 일을 정말 좋아하는데, **특히 고객들로부터 여러 질문을 받는 단계를 좋아해요.** 의문이나 반론에 대응하면서, 저희 소프트웨어가 고객의 요구를 실제로 어떻게 충족하는지 보여줄 수 있거든요.

어휘 develop 개발하다, 발전시키다 fix 고치다, 바로잡다
equipment 장비 present 발표하다, 제시하다 step 단계
address 해결하다, 처리하다 doubt 의구심 objection 반대
meet 충족하다 draft a contact 계약서 초안을 작성하다

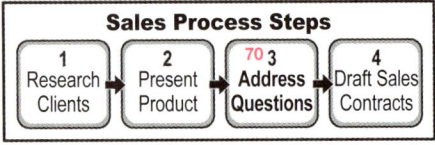

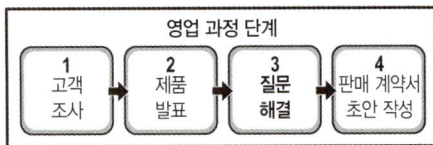

68 What is the man's area of expertise?
(A) Packaging new products
(B) Developing software
(C) Designing fitness equipment
(D) Training employees

남자의 전문 분야는 무엇인가?
(A) 신제품 포장
(B) 소프트웨어 개발
(C) 운동 장비 설계
(D) 직원 교육

어휘 expertise 전문 지식, 전문 기술 package 포장하다

해설 세부 사항 관련 – 남자의 전문 분야
여자가 첫 대사에서 남자가 소프트웨어 설계 경험이 많다고 들었다(I hear you have a lot of experience designing software)고 했으므로 정답은 (B)이다.

Paraphrasing
대화의 designing software → 정답의 Developing software

69 According to the man, what did he recently do?
(A) Reserve a conference room
(B) Complete some paperwork
(C) Meet with a supervisor
(D) Fix some equipment

남자에 따르면, 그는 최근에 무엇을 했는가?
(A) 회의실 예약하기
(B) 서류 작업 완료하기
(C) 책임자 만나기
(D) 장비 고치기

어휘 paperwork 서류 작업

해설 세부 사항 관련 – 남자가 최근에 한 일
남자가 첫 대사에서 방금 회의실 음향 장비 문제를 해결했다(I just fixed a problem with the sound equipment in the conference room)고 했으므로 정답은 (D)이다.

Paraphrasing
대화의 just → 질문의 recently

70 Look at the graphic. Which step of the sales process does the woman especially enjoy?
(A) Step 1
(B) Step 2
(C) Step 3
(D) Step 4

시각 정보에 의하면, 여자는 영업 과정의 어느 단계를 특히 즐거워하는가?
(A) 1단계
(B) 2단계
(C) 3단계
(D) 4단계

해설 시각 정보 연계 – 여자가 특히 즐거워하는 단계
여자가 마지막 대사에서 특히 고객들로부터 여러 질문을 받는 단계를 좋아한다(But I especially like the step where we're getting a lot of questions from clients)고 했다. 영업 과정에서 질문을 받고 이를 답변하는 일은 Address Questions에 해당하고, 이는 3단계이므로 정답은 (C)이다.

Paraphrasing
대화의 like → 질문의 enjoy

PART 4

71-73 회의 발췌

> W-Am **71 Thank you for attending Port Jefferson's city council meeting.** We have a lot on our agenda today. The first topic up for discussion is **72 a request from the head of the city's water system. He wants to buy two UAVs—or underwater autonomous vehicles.** These remotely operated vehicles can be used to inspect, maintain, and repair equipment underwater. Now, each UAV costs 30,000 dollars, so this is a big decision for us. But for perspective, the city spends more than that every year to hire divers to repair broken equipment. **73 Let's hear more about it from the chief engineer. He's going to give us some details about the vehicles.**
>
> 포트 제퍼슨 시 의회 회의에 참석해 주셔서 감사합니다. 오늘 안건이 많습니다. 첫 번째 논의 주제는 **시 수도 시스템 책임자의 요청입니다. 이분께서 두 대의 UAV, 즉 자율 무인 잠수정을 구입하기를 원합니다.** 이 원격으로 가동되는 잠수정은 수중에 있는 장비를 점검, 유지 관리 및 수리하는 데 이용될 수 있습니다. 현재, UAV 한 대당 3만 달러의 비용이 들기 때문에, 이는 우리에게 큰 결정입니다. 하지만 참고로, 시에서는 고장 난 장비를 수리할 다이버들을 고용하기 위해 매년 이보다 더 많은 돈을 쓰고 있습니다. **이와 관련해 수석 엔지니어로부터 더 많은 얘기를 들어 봅시다. 이분께서 이 잠수정에 관해 자세한 정보를 제공해 주실 것입니다.**

어휘 council 의회 agenda 안건, 의제 topic 주제
autonomous 자율적인, 자치의 vehicle 운송 수단, 차량
remotely 원격으로, 멀리 떨어져 operate 가동하다, 운영하다
inspect 점검하다, 검사하다 maintain 유지 관리하다
equipment 장비 for perspective 참고로, 비교해 보면

71 Who most likely is the speaker?
(A) A geologist
(B) A boat captain
(C) A maintenance supervisor
(D) A city official

화자는 누구인 것 같은가?
(A) 지질학자
(B) 보트 선장
(C) 유지 관리 책임자
(D) 시 관계자

해설 전체 내용 관련 – 화자의 직업

화자가 초반부에 포트 제퍼슨 시 의회 회의에 참석해 줘서 감사하다(Thank you for attending Port Jefferson's city council meeting)고 했으므로 시 의회 구성원인 것으로 볼 수 있다. 따라서 정답은 (D)이다.

72 What is the speaker mainly discussing?
(A) Conducting a safety inspection
(B) Buying some new equipment
(C) Building a new facility
(D) Recruiting qualified staff

화자는 주로 무엇에 대해 이야기하고 있는가?
(A) 안전 점검 실시하기
(B) 새로운 장비 구입하기
(C) 새로운 시설 건설하기
(D) 자격을 갖춘 직원 모집하기

어휘 conduct 실시하다, 수행하다 inspection 점검
recruit 모집하다 qualified 자격을 갖춘, 적격인

해설 전체 내용 관련 – 담화 주제

화자가 중반부에 시 수도 시스템 책임자의 요청을 언급하면서 두 대의 UAV, 즉 자율 무인 잠수정을 구입하기를 원한다(~ a request from the head of the city's water system. He wants to buy two UAVs—or underwater autonomous vehicles)고 밝힌 후, 그와 관련해 이야기하고 있으므로 정답은 (B)이다.

Paraphrasing
담화의 two UAVs—or underwater autonomous vehicles
→ 정답의 some new equipment

73 What will happen next?
(A) A survey will be administered.
(B) A video will be shown.
(C) An expert will speak.
(D) A process will be demonstrated.

다음에 무슨 일이 있을 것인가?
(A) 설문 조사가 실시될 것이다.
(B) 동영상이 상영될 것이다.
(C) 전문가가 이야기할 것이다.
(D) 과정을 시범 보일 것이다.

어휘 survey 설문 조사(지) administer 실시하다, 집행하다
expert 전문가 demonstrate 시범 보이다, 시연하다

해설 세부 사항 관련 – 다음에 있을 일

화자가 후반부에 수석 엔지니어로부터 더 많은 얘기를 들어 보자며, 잠수정에 관해 자세한 정보를 제공해 줄 것(Let's hear more about it from the chief engineer. He's going to give us some details about the vehicles)이라고 했으므로 정답은 (C)이다.

Paraphrasing
담화의 hear more about it from the chief engineer
→ 정답의 An expert will speak.

74-76 소개

> M-Cn Team, I'd like you to meet Alka Raj. **74She is the new safety and compliance officer for our pharmaceutical lab. 75Alka will primarily review our safety practices and ensure they meet or exceed all current pharmaceutical industry standards. 76I'm thrilled that she's here just in time to finish inspections before the due date to file our workplace safety paperwork.** This will ensure that all the paperwork is submitted on time.

> 팀원 여러분, 알카 라지를 소개해 드리고 싶습니다. 이분은 우리 제약 실험실의 신임 안전 및 준법 감독관이십니다. 알카는 주로 안전과 관련된 업무를 검토하여, 현재의 모든 제약 업계 기준을 충족하거나 초과하도록 해줄 것입니다. 직장 안전 서류를 제출하는 마감일 전에 점검을 마칠 수 있도록 그녀가 제때 합류해 주셔서 대단히 기쁩니다. 모든 서류가 제시간에 제출될 수 있을 것입니다.

> 어휘 compliance 준법, 준수 pharmaceutical 제약의 lab 실험실 primarily 주로 practice 업무, 실행 ensure 보장하다, 반드시 ~하도록 하다 exceed 초과하다 standard 기준, 표준 thrilled 대단히 기쁜 due date 마감일 file 제출하다 submit 제출하다 on time 제시간에, 정시에

74 What type of industry does the speaker most likely work in?
(A) Transportation
(B) Hospitality
(C) Construction
(D) Pharmaceutical

화자는 어떤 종류의 업계에서 일하고 있는 것 같은가?
(A) 교통
(B) 접객
(C) 건설
(D) 제약

해설 전체 내용 관련 – 화자의 근무 업계

화자가 초반부에 알카 라지를 소개하면서 우리 제약 실험실의 신임 안전 및 준법 감독관(She is the new safety and compliance officer for our pharmaceutical lab)이라고 했으므로 정답은 (D)이다.

75 What will be Alka Raj's job responsibility?
(A) Ensuring compliance with safety practices
(B) Creating product development schedules
(C) Ordering new equipment
(D) Hiring and training staff

알카 라지의 직무는 무엇이 될 것인가?
(A) 안전 관련 규정 준수하게 하기
(B) 제품 개발 일정 만들기
(C) 새로운 장비 주문하기
(D) 직원 고용 및 교육하기

어휘 responsibility 책임, 책무

해설 세부 사항 관련 – 알카 라지의 직무

화자가 중반부에 알카가 주로 안전과 관련된 업무를 검토하여, 현재의 모든 제약 업계 기준을 충족하거나 초과하도록 해줄 것(Alka will primarily review our safety practices and ensure they meet or exceed all current pharmaceutical industry standards)이라고 했으므로 정답은 (A)이다.

> **Paraphrasing**
> 담화의 review our safety practices and ensure they meet or exceed ~ industry standards
> → 정답의 Ensuring compliance with safety practices

76 Why does the speaker say he is thrilled?
(A) An employee will be promoted.
(B) Some deadlines will be met.
(C) Product sales have increased.
(D) A trip abroad has been approved.

화자는 왜 대단히 기쁘다고 말하는가?
(A) 직원이 승진될 것이다.
(B) 마감 기한을 맞출 것이다.
(C) 제품 판매량이 증가했다.
(D) 해외 출장이 승인되었다.

해설 세부 사항 관련 – 화자가 대단히 기쁘다고 말하는 이유

화자가 후반부에 직장 안전 서류를 제출하는 마감일 전에 점검을 마칠 수 있도록 알카가 제때 합류해 주어 대단히 기쁘다(I'm thrilled that she's here just in time to finish inspections before the due date to file our workplace safety paperwork)고 했으므로 정답은 (B)이다.

> **Paraphrasing**
> 담화의 finish inspections before the due date
> → 정답의 Some deadlines will be met.

77-79 회의 발췌

> M-Au Now, let's move on to another important topic. **77I know it's too cold in your offices right now to work comfortably. 78Even though we like to keep the conference room open for client meetings, you can work there until Marion adjusts the temperature.** I've e-mailed her twice, but she hasn't responded yet. It's frustrating that we can't control the temperature in our own offices. **79That's Marion's job.** In the meantime, let me know if any other building issues have come up, and I'll report them to her.

이제, 또 다른 중요한 주제로 넘어갑시다. **현재 여러분의 사무실이 너무 추워서 편안하게 근무할 수 없다는 것을 알고 있습니다.** 고객 회의 때문에 회의실을 열어 두는 것이 좋지만, **매리언이 온도를 조절하실 때까지 그곳에서 근무하셔도 됩니다.** 제가 매리언에게 두 번이나 이메일을 보냈는데, 아직 답장은 없네요. 우리 사무실의 온도를 우리가 제어할 수 없다는 게 답답합니다. **그건 매리언의 일입니다.** 그동안, **다른 건물 관련 문제가 생기면 제게 알려 주세요. 제가 그분께 전달하겠습니다.**

어휘 move on to ~로 넘어가다 comfortably 편안하게 adjust 조절하다 temperature 온도 respond 답장하다 frustrating 답답하게 하는, 실망스러운 control 제어하다 in the meantime 그동안, 그사이에 issue 문제, 사안 come up 발생하다, 생기다

77 What problem does the speaker mention?
(A) Some clients are unhappy.
(B) Some offices are too cold.
(C) Some construction is too noisy.
(D) Some colleagues are sick.

화자는 어떤 문제를 언급하는가?
(A) 고객들이 불만스러워한다.
(B) 사무실이 너무 춥다.
(C) 공사 소리가 너무 시끄럽다.
(D) 동료들이 아프다.

해설 전체 내용 관련 – 화자가 언급하는 문제
화자가 초반부에 사무실이 너무 추워서 편안하게 근무할 수 없다는 것을 알고 있다(I know it's too cold in your offices right now to work comfortably)고 했으므로 정답은 (B)이다.

78 What are the listeners temporarily allowed to do?
(A) Use their personal e-mail accounts
(B) Work from a conference room
(C) Go home early
(D) Close some windows

청자들은 임시로 무엇을 하는 것이 허용되는가?
(A) 개인 이메일 계정 이용하기
(B) 회의실에서 근무하기
(C) 일찍 집에 가기
(D) 창문 닫기

어휘 be allowed to ~하도록 허용되다 temporarily 임시로 account 계정, 계좌

해설 세부 사항 관련 – 청자들에게 임시로 허용된 것
화자가 중반부에 회의실을 언급하며 매리언이 온도를 조절할 때까지 그곳에서 근무해도 된다(~ we like to keep the conference room open for client meetings, you can work there ~)고 했으므로 정답은 (B)이다.

Paraphrasing
담화의 until Marion adjusts the temperature
→ 질문의 temporarily

79 Who most likely is Marion?
(A) A cafeteria employee
(B) A parking garage attendant
(C) A product supplier
(D) A building manager

매리언은 누구인 것 같은가?
(A) 구내식당 직원
(B) 주차장 안내원
(C) 제품 공급업자
(D) 건물 관리자

해설 세부 사항 관련 – 매리언의 직업
화자가 후반부에 사무실 온도 조절을 매리언의 일(That's Marion's job)이라고 언급했고, 건물 관련 문제가 생기면 그녀에게 전달하겠다(~ let me know if any other building issues have come up, and I'll report them to her)고 했으므로 매리언은 건물 관리자로 볼 수 있다. 따라서 정답은 (D)이다.

80-82 회의 발췌

W-Am I just want to have a quick meeting **80 while we have all the nurses from the night shift and day shift here at the same time.** First, **81 per our safety policy**, jewelry is not allowed when you're working with patients. This is because rings or bracelets could easily puncture gloves. Also, **82 remember that medical staff are not permitted to bring food or drinks into the clinical areas.** Of course, the break room is open 24 hours a day. Please talk to me if you have any questions.

야간 근무조 간호사들과 주간 근무조 간호사들 모두 동시에 이곳에 계실 때 간단히 회의를 하고자 합니다. 우선, **우리 안전 정책에 따라**, 환자 대면 업무를 할 때는 장신구가 허용되지 않습니다. 반지나 팔찌가 장갑에 쉽게 구멍을 낼 수 있기 때문입니다. 또한, **의료진은 임상 구역에 음식이나 음료를 반입할 수 없다는 점을 기억하시기 바랍니다.** 물론, 휴게실은 하루 24시간 열려 있습니다. 질문이 있으시면 제게 말씀해 주시기 바랍니다.

어휘 shift 교대 근무(조) per ~에 따라 allow 허용하다 patient 환자 bracelet 팔찌 puncture 구멍을 내다 permit 허용하다 clinical 임상의 break room 휴게실

80 Where is the meeting taking place?
(A) At a pharmacy
(B) At a hospital
(C) At a car dealership
(D) At a jewelry store

회의는 어디에서 진행되고 있는가?
(A) 약국
(B) 병원
(C) 자동차 대리점
(D) 장신구 매장

어휘 take place 진행되다, 개최되다   dealership 대리점, 영업소

해설 **전체 내용 관련 – 회의 장소**
화자가 초반부에 야간 근무조 간호사들과 주간 근무조 간호사들 모두 동시에 이곳에 있을 때(~ while we have all the nurses from the night shift and day shift here at the same time) 회의를 하고자 했다고 했으므로 정답은 (B)이다.

81 What is the speaker mainly discussing?
(A) Business travel
(B) Company policies
(C) Parking
(D) Vacation

화자는 주로 무엇을 이야기하고 있는가?
(A) 출장
(B) 회사 정책
(C) 주차
(D) 휴가

해설 **전체 내용 관련 – 담화 주제**
화자가 초반부에 안전 정책에 따라(per our safety policy) 허용되지 않는 것들을 상기시키고 있으므로 정답은 (B)이다.

82 Why does the speaker say, "the break room is open 24 hours a day"?
(A) To disagree with an idea
(B) To ask for assistance
(C) To explain a schedule
(D) To suggest an alternative

화자는 왜 "휴게실은 하루 24시간 열려 있습니다"라고 말하는가?
(A) 아이디어에 동의하지 않기 위해
(B) 도움을 요청하기 위해
(C) 일정을 설명하기 위해
(D) 대안을 제안하기 위해

어휘 disagree with ~에 동의하지 않다   ask for ~을 요청하다
assistance 도움, 지원   alternative 대안

해설 **화자의 의도 파악 – 휴게실이 하루 24시간 열려 있다는 말의 의도**
화자가 후반부에 임상 구역에 음식이나 음료를 반입할 수 없다는 점을 기억하라(~ remember that medical staff are not permitted to bring food or drinks into the clinical areas)고 요청하면서 인용문을 언급하고 있다. 이는 음식을 임상 구역이 아닌 휴게실에서 먹도록 대안을 제시하는 것이므로 정답은 (D)이다.

83-85 광고

M-Au Ready to get your customers' attention? **83 Postela makes high-quality posters that are easy to order and easy to display in your store.** Whether you need just one or 2,000 posters, Postela has you covered. As always, **84 Postela offers great discounts on bulk orders.** Order 100 or more posters for as low as 80 cents per poster. **85 And what's really unique, Postela has officially licensed images from your favorite movies, video games, and sports teams that can be easily added to your posters.** In your order, just make sure to indicate the images and message you'd like included. The crew at Postela will take care of the rest!

고객들의 관심을 받을 준비가 되셨나요? **포스텔라는 주문하기도 쉽고 여러분의 매장에 게시하기도 쉬운 고품질 포스터를 제작합니다.** 포스터가 단 한 장 필요하시든 2,000장 필요하시든 포스텔라가 모두 해결해 드립니다. 늘 그렇듯이, **포스텔라는 대량 주문에 큰 폭의 할인을 제공해 드립니다.** 100장 이상의 포스터는 포스터당 최저 80센트부터 주문하실 수 있습니다. **그리고 정말로 특별한 점은, 포스텔라가 여러분께서 좋아하시는 영화와 비디오 게임, 그리고 스포츠 팀들의 공식 사용 허가된 이미지들을 보유하고 있어 여러분의 포스터에 쉽게 추가할 수 있다는 것입니다.** 주문하실 때 포함하고 싶으신 이미지와 메시지를 반드시 표시해 주세요. 나머지는 포스텔라의 직원들이 처리해 드리겠습니다!

어휘 attention 관심, 주목   display 게시하다, 진열하다
cover 떠맡다, 책임을 지다   bulk 대량의   unique 특별한, 독특한
officially 공식적으로, 정식으로   licensed 사용 허가를 받은
add 추가하다   indicate 표시하다, 나타내다   crew 직원들, 작업팀
take care of ~을 처리하다, ~을 다루다

83 Who is the advertisement intended for?
(A) Store owners
(B) Tour guides
(C) Interior designers
(D) Paper manufacturers

광고는 누구를 대상으로 하는가?
(A) 매장 소유주들
(B) 여행 가이드들
(C) 실내 디자이너들
(D) 종이 제조사들

어휘 be intended for ~을 대상으로 하다, ~을 위한 것이다

해설 **전체 내용 관련 – 광고 대상**
화자가 초반부에 포스텔라는 청자들의 매장에 게시하기 쉬운 고품질 포스터를 제작한다(Postela makes high-quality posters that are easy to order and easy to display in your store)고 했으므로 매장 소유주들을 대상으로 포스터 제작을 광고하는 상황임을 알 수 있다. 따라서 정답은 (A)이다.

84 How can the listeners receive a discount?
(A) By entering a code
(B) By writing a review
(C) By using a special link
(D) By ordering large quantities

청자들은 어떻게 할인을 받을 수 있는가?
(A) 코드를 입력함으로써
(B) 후기를 작성함으로써
(C) 특별 링크를 이용함으로써
(D) 대량으로 주문함으로써

어휘 quantity 수량

해설 세부 사항 관련 – 청자들이 할인받는 방법
화자가 중반부에 대량 주문에 큰 폭의 할인을 제공한다(~ Postela offers great discounts on bulk orders)고 했으므로 정답은 (D)이다.

Paraphrasing
담화의 bulk orders → 정답의 ordering large quantities

85 What does the speaker emphasize about a product?
(A) Shipping costs are included.
(B) It is available in many sizes.
(C) There are several framing options.
(D) Licensed images are available.

화자는 제품에 대해 무엇을 강조하는가?
(A) 배송비가 포함되어 있다.
(B) 다양한 사이즈로 이용할 수 있다.
(C) 선택할 수 있는 액자가 여러 가지이다.
(D) 허가받은 이미지를 사용할 수 있다.

어휘 emphasize 강조하다 include 포함하다
framing 액자(에 넣기)

해설 세부 사항 관련 – 화자가 강조하는 것
화자가 중반부에 정말로 특별한 점으로 포스텔라가 공식 사용 허가된 이미지를 보유하고 있어서 포스터에 쉽게 추가할 수 있다(And what's really unique, Postela has officially licensed images ~ that can be easily added to your posters)고 했으므로 정답은 (D)이다.

Paraphrasing
담화의 what's really unique → 질문의 emphasize
담화의 can be easily added → 정답의 are available

86-88 공지

M-Cn Hello, and welcome to this West Peak Rail service to Archerville. **86On our train today, you should take advantage of all the services we have to offer**—including our café car, which is fully stocked with refreshments, and the observation car, with its floor-to-ceiling windows. Our wireless Internet service has also been upgraded! You can connect to our complimentary service 87**using the access code printed on your ticket.** Now, 88**we're operating on schedule right now, but** there's significant maintenance work on the track ahead. I'll continue to provide updates throughout our journey.

안녕하세요. 아처빌행 웨스트 피크 레일 열차에 탑승하신 것을 환영합니다. **오늘 저희 열차에서 제공하는 모든 서비스를 이용해 보시기 바라며**, 여기에는 간식으로 가득 채워진 카페 칸과 바닥에서 천장까지 창으로 이루어진 전망 칸이 포함됩니다. 무선 인터넷 서비스도 업그레이드되었습니다! **탑승권에 인쇄되어 있는 접속 코드를 이용하여** 무료로 연결하실 수 있습니다. 자, **저희가 현재 일정대로 운행되고 있기는 하지만, 앞쪽 철로에 중요한 정비 작업이 있습니다.** 여행 내내 지속적으로 새로운 소식을 제공해 드리겠습니다.

어휘 take advantage of ~을 이용하다, ~을 활용하다
including ~을 포함하여 car (열차의) 칸, 객차
be stocked with ~으로 채워져 있다 fully 가득, 완전히
refreshments 간식, 다과 observation 관찰, 관측
floor-to-ceiling 바닥에서 천장에 이르는 connect 연결하다
complimentary 무료의, 칭찬하는 access 접속, 이용
operate 운행하다, 운영되다 on schedule 일정대로
significant 중요한, 상당한 maintenance 유지 관리, 정비
ahead 앞쪽에, 앞서

86 What is the announcement mostly about?
(A) A renovated station
(B) A frequent-traveler program
(C) Services on a train
(D) Some new train destinations

공지는 주로 무엇에 대한 것인가?
(A) 보수된 역
(B) 단골 승객을 위한 프로그램
(C) 열차 내 서비스들
(D) 새로운 열차 목적지들

어휘 renovate 보수하다 frequent-traveler 자주 여행하는 사람
destination 목적지

해설 전체 내용 관련 – 공지 주제
화자가 초반부에 열차에서 제공하는 모든 서비스를 이용해 보기 바란다(On our train today, you should take advantage of all the services we have to offer ~)며, 어떤 서비스들이 있는지 소개하고 있으므로 정답은 (C)이다.

87 According to the speaker, what can be found on a ticket?
(A) An access code
(B) A discount coupon
(C) An assistance telephone number
(D) A layout of the train

화자에 따르면, 탑승권에서 무엇을 찾을 수 있는가?
(A) 접속 코드
(B) 할인 쿠폰
(C) 지원 전화번호
(D) 열차 배치도

어휘 layout 배치(도), 구획

해설 세부 사항 관련 – 탑승권에서 찾을 수 있는 것
화자가 중반부에 무선 인터넷 서비스를 언급하면서 탑승권에 인쇄되어 있는 접속 코드를 이용하여(~ using the access code printed on your ticket) 연결할 수 있다고 했으므로 정답은 (A)이다.

---

88 What does the speaker mean when he says, "there's significant maintenance work on the track ahead"?
(A) The listeners cannot visit a specific station.
(B) The listeners should anticipate some delays.
(C) The listeners may need to plan alternate routes.
(D) The listeners will receive a ticket refund.

화자가 "앞쪽 철로에 중요한 정비 작업이 있습니다"라고 말할 때 무엇을 의미하는가?
(A) 청자들이 특정 역을 방문할 수 없다.
(B) 청자들이 약간의 지연을 예상해야 한다.
(C) 청자들이 대체 경로를 계획해야 할 수도 있다.
(D) 청자들이 탑승권을 환불받을 것이다.

어휘 specific 특정한, 구체적인 anticipate 예상하다, 기대하다 delay 지연, 지체 alternate 대체의, 대안의 route 경로, 노선 refund 환불(액)

해설 화자의 의도 파악 – 앞쪽 철로에 중요한 정비 작업이 있다는 말의 의도
화자가 후반부에 현재는 열차가 일정대로 운행되고 있다(we're operating on schedule right now ~)고 알리면서 대조를 나타내는 but과 함께 인용문을 언급하고 있다. 이는 일정대로 운행되고 있는 현재의 상황과 대조적으로 정비 작업으로 인한 지연이 발생할 가능성을 알리는 것이므로 정답은 (B)이다.

89-91 전화 메시지

W-Br Hi. This is Marina Aljohani. **89 I'm the superintendent of the Trenton municipal water department.** I'm calling because we need to replace several maintenance hole covers on our city streets. These covers are essential for preventing too much debris from entering the water system. I noticed on your Web site that your company casts many different types of metal products, including maintenance hole covers. **90 I'd like to find out how much it would cost to make 30 new covers.** Please call our office at 555-0102. **91 While I'll be away most of next week, Lihong Hao, the assistant superintendent, will be in the office. She can take your call.** Thank you.

안녕하세요. 매리나 알조하니입니다. 저는 트렌턴 시립 수도 관리국장입니다. 우리 시 거리에 있는 맨홀 뚜껑 여러 개를 교체해야 해서 전화했습니다. 이 뚜껑은 너무 많은 쓰레기가 수도 시스템에 들어가는 것을 막는 데 필수적입니다. 귀사의 웹사이트에서 맨홀 뚜껑을 포함해 다양한 종류의 많은 금속 제품을 주조하신다는 것을 알았습니다. 새로운 뚜껑을 30개를 제작하는 비용이 얼마인지 알고 싶습니다. 555-0102번으로 저희 사무실에 전화해 주시기 바랍니다. 제가 다음 주에는 대부분 자리를 비우겠지만, 리홍 하오 부국장이 사무실에 있을 겁니다. 이분이 귀하의 전화를 받을 수 있습니다. 감사합니다.

어휘 superintendent 국장, 관리자 municipal 시의 maintenance hole 맨홀 essential 필수적인, 본질적인 prevent 막다, 방지하다 debris 쓰레기, 잔해 notice 알게 되다 cast 주조하다 find out 파악하다, 알아내다

---

89 Who is the speaker?
(A) A plumber
(B) A city employee
(C) A bank supervisor
(D) A swimming pool cleaner

화자는 누구인가?
(A) 배관공
(B) 시 공무원
(C) 은행 관리자
(D) 수영장 청소 담당자

해설 전체 내용 관련 – 화자의 직업
화자가 초반부에 자신을 트렌턴 시립 수도 관리국장(I'm the superintendent of the Trenton municipal water department)이라고 소개하고 있으므로 정답은 (B)이다.

Paraphrasing
담화의 the superintendent of the Trenton municipal water department → 정답의 A city employee

90 Why is the woman calling?
(A) To request a price quote
(B) To cancel an order
(C) To report a malfunction
(D) To respond to an inquiry

여자는 왜 전화하는가?
(A) 견적을 요청하기 위해
(B) 주문을 취소하기 위해
(C) 고장을 알리기 위해
(D) 문의에 대응하기 위해

어휘 quote 견적(서) malfunction 고장, 기능 불량 inquiry 문의

해설 전체 내용 관련 – 여자가 전화하는 목적
화자가 중반부에 새로운 뚜껑을 30개를 제작하는 비용이 얼마인지 알고 싶다(I'd like to find out how much it would cost to make 30 new covers)고 했으므로 정답은 (A)이다.

Paraphrasing
담화의 would like to find out how much it would cost to make 30 new covers → 정답의 request a price quote

91 What does the speaker say about Lihong Hao?
(A) She has a professional certification.
(B) She is an environmental expert.
(C) She will be available next week.
(D) She has recently been promoted.

화자는 리홍 하오에 대해 무엇이라고 말하는가?
(A) 전문 자격증이 있다.
(B) 환경 전문가이다.
(C) 다음 주에 시간이 있을 것이다.
(D) 최근에 승진되었다.

어휘 certification 자격증, 증명(서) available 시간이 있는

해설 세부 사항 관련 – 화자가 리홍 하오에 대해 하는 말
화자가 후반부에 자신이 다음 주에는 대부분 자리를 비우겠지만, 리홍 하오 부국장이 사무실에 있을 것이며, 그녀가 전화를 받을 것(While I'll be away most of next week, Lihong Hao, the assistant superintendent, will be in the office. She can take your call)이라고 했으므로 정답은 (C)이다.

Paraphrasing
담화의 can take your call → 정답의 will be available

92-94 전화 메시지 ▶동영상 강의

M-Cn Hi, Ms. Alvarez. **92 I'm calling to let you know I e-mailed the price estimate you requested for the replacement of your metal roof.** 93 I'm sure you've received lower estimates from other businesses. But you should know, I only use the highest-quality materials in my work. Please check out the reviews on my Web site if you have any doubts. I know you hoped that I'd complete the project before you go away on your vacation, but I'm completely booked for the month of March. 94 **I could start at the beginning of April, though.** I look forward to hearing back from you soon.

안녕하세요, 알바레즈 씨. 요청하신 금속 지붕 교체 견적서를 이메일로 보냈음을 알려 드리기 위해 전화했습니다. 분명 다른 업체에서 더 낮은 견적서를 받으셨을 겁니다. 하지만 알아 두셔야 하는 게 저는 작업할 때 최고 품질의 자재만 사용합니다. 의문이 있으시다면 웹사이트에 있는 후기를 확인해 보시기 바랍니다. 귀하께서 휴가를 떠나기 전에 제가 그 프로젝트를 완료하길 원하신 것은 알고 있지만, 제가 3월에는 예약이 꽉 차 있습니다. **하지만 4월 초에는 시작할 수 있을 것입니다.** 곧 연락 주시기를 고대합니다.

어휘 estimate 견적(서) replacement 교체(품), 대체(품) completely 완전히, 전적으로 booked 예약된 look forward to ~하기를 고대하다

92 What industry does the speaker most likely work in?
(A) Construction
(B) Transportation
(C) Marketing
(D) Shipping

화자는 어떤 업계에서 일하는 것 같은가?
(A) 건설
(B) 교통
(C) 마케팅
(D) 배송

해설 전체 내용 관련 – 화자의 근무 업계
화자가 초반부에 금속 지붕 교체 견적서를 이메일로 보냈음을 알리기 위해 전화한다(I'm calling to let you know I e-mailed the price estimate you requested for the replacement of your metal roof)고 했다. 이를 통해 화자가 주택 공사와 관련된 업계 종사자임을 알 수 있으므로 정답은 (A)이다.

Paraphrasing
담화의 replacement of your metal roof
→ 정답의 Construction

93 Why does the speaker say, "I only use the highest-quality materials in my work"?
(A) To recommend a product
(B) To justify a price
(C) To refuse an offer
(D) To request a promotion

화자는 왜 "저는 작업할 때 최고 품질의 자재만 사용합니다"라고 말하는가?
(A) 제품을 추천하기 위해
(B) 가격을 정당화하기 위해
(C) 제안을 거절하기 위해
(D) 홍보를 요청하기 위해

어휘 justify 정당화하다 refuse 거절하다, 거부하다
promotion 홍보, 판촉, 승진

해설 화자의 의도 파악 – 최고 품질의 자재만 사용한다는 말의 의도
화자가 중반부에 분명 다른 업체에서 더 낮은 견적서를 받았을 것(I'm sure you've received lower estimates from other businesses)이라고 말하면서 인용문을 언급하고 있다. 이는 타 업체보다 비싼 가격을 정당화하기 위해 한 말이므로 정답은 (B)이다.

94 What does the speaker say could happen in April?
(A) An employee could retire.
(B) An invoice could arrive.
(C) A project could begin.
(D) A price could increase.

화자는 4월에 무슨 일이 있을 수 있다고 말하는가?
(A) 직원이 은퇴할 수 있다.
(B) 거래 내역서가 도착할 수 있다.
(C) 프로젝트가 시작될 수 있다.
(D) 가격이 인상될 수 있다.

어휘 retire 은퇴하다, 퇴직하다 invoice 거래 내역서

해설 세부 사항 관련 – 4월에 있을 수 있는 일
화자가 후반부에 청자가 요청한 공사 프로젝트와 관련해 4월 초에는 시작할 수 있을 것(I could start at the beginning of April)이라고 했으므로 정답은 (C)이다.

95-97 담화 + 재고 보고서

M-Au **95 The time is right for Snowville Refrigeration to begin marketing our commercial refrigerators internationally.** Due to supply chain problems, many companies that manufacture refrigerators are low on inventory. Their customers are on long wait lists to receive their products. However, **96 our most popular model is in stock — we currently have 380 of them available.** Considering this, **97 I'm going to assemble a team** to come up with a viable marketing plan.

이제 스노우빌 냉장고가 상업용 냉장고를 국제적으로 판매할 때가 되었습니다. 공급망 문제로 인해, 냉장고를 제조하는 많은 회사들이 재고 수준이 낮습니다. 고객들은 제품을 받기 위해 오랫동안 대기자 명단에 올라와 있습니다. 하지만 **가장 인기 있는 우리 모델은 재고가 있으며, 현재 380대가 준비되어 있습니다.** 이를 고려해, 저는 실행 가능한 마케팅 계획을 제시할 **팀을 꾸릴 것입니다.**

어휘 market (시장에) 내놓다, 팔다 commercial 상업의
due to ~로 인해, ~ 때문에 supply chain 공급망
manufacture 제조하다 inventory 재고 (목록), 재고품
in stock 재고가 있는 currently 현재, 지금
considering ~을 고려해 (볼 때) assemble 모으다, 조립하다
come up with ~을 제시하다, ~을 생각해 내다 quantity 수량

Inventory Report	
Refrigerator Model	Quantity in Stock
JH-883	265
JK-966	400
96 LH-655	**380**
LK-303	410

재고 보고서	
냉장고 모델	재고 수량
JH-883	265
JK-966	400
LH-655	**380**
LK-303	410

95 What is the talk mainly about?
(A) Merging with another company
(B) Revising an inspection process
(C) Building a new manufacturing plant
(D) Selling products internationally

담화는 주로 무엇에 대한 것인가?
(A) 다른 회사와 합병하기
(B) 점검 과정 변경하기
(C) 새 제조 공장 짓기
(D) 국제적으로 제품 판매하기

어휘 merge with ~와 합병하다   revise 변경하다, 수정하다
inspection 점검, 검사   plant 공장

해설 **전체 내용 관련 – 담화 주제**
화자가 초반부에 이제 스노우빌 냉장고를 상업용 냉장고를 국제적으로 판매할 때가 되었다(The time is right for Snowville Refrigeration to begin marketing our commercial refrigerators internationally)고 했고, 그와 관련된 이야기를 이어 가고 있으므로 정답은 (D)이다.

Paraphrasing
담화의 marketing our commercial refrigerators
→ 정답의 Selling products

96 Look at the graphic. What is the company's top-selling refrigerator model?
(A) JH-883
(B) JK-966
(C) LH-655
(D) LK-303

시각 정보에 의하면, 회사에서 가장 잘 팔리는 냉장고 모델은 무엇인가?
(A) JH-883
(B) JK-966
(C) LH-655
(D) LK-303

어휘 top-selling 가장 많이 팔리는

해설 **시각 정보 연계 – 가장 잘 팔리는 냉장고 모델**
화자가 중반부에 가장 인기 있는 모델은 재고가 있으며, 현재 380대가 준비되어 있다(~ our most popular model is in stock—we currently have 380 of them available)고 했는데, 재고 보고서에서 수량이 380인 제품 모델은 LH-655이므로 정답은 (C)이다.

Paraphrasing
담화의 most popular → 질문의 top-selling

97 What does the speaker say he will do?
(A) Put together a team
(B) Visit a business partner
(C) Sign a contract
(D) Prepare a presentation

화자는 무엇을 할 것이라고 말하는가?
(A) 팀을 꾸리기
(B) 사업 파트너 방문하기
(C) 계약하기
(D) 발표 준비하기

어휘 put together 만들다, 조립하다   sign a contract 계약을 맺다

해설 **세부 사항 관련 – 화자가 할 일**
화자가 후반부에 실행 가능한 마케팅 계획을 제시할 팀을 꾸릴 것(I'm going to assemble a team ~)이라고 했으므로 정답은 (A)이다.

Paraphrasing
담화의 assemble a team → 정답의 Put together a team

98-100 녹음 메시지 + 투어 일정표

W-Br Thank you for calling the Wilson Park visitor center. Due to the high volume of visitors in the summer, as well as limited parking, **98we encourage everyone to take the city bus to the park.** Most of the tours are booked for today, but **99we still have spots open for the mountain bike tour**. And remember, there are plenty of things you can do around the park on your own. As you enter the park, **100brochures are available with maps of all the hiking trails located throughout the park.**

윌슨 공원 방문객 센터에 전화해 주셔서 감사합니다. 여름철 많은 방문객 수와 제한된 주차 공간으로 인해, **시내버스를 타고 공원에 오시기를 권합니다.** 오늘 투어의 대부분은 예약이 완료되었으나, **산악자전거 투어는 아직 남아 있는 자리가 있습니다.** 그리고 공원 곳곳에 혼자서도 하실 수 있는 것들이 많다는 것을 기억하세요. 공원에 입장하실 때, **공원 곳곳에 위치한 모든 하이킹 코스의 지도가 포함된 안내 책자를 가져가실 수 있습니다.**

어휘 volume 양   limited 제한적인   encourage 권하다
spot 자리, 장소   plenty of 많은   on one's own 혼자, 스스로
brochure 안내 책자   trail 코스, 산길   located 위치해 있는
cave 동굴   exploration 탐험, 탐사   ride 타고 가기

Wilson Park-Tuesday Tour Schedule	
10:00 A.M.	Cave Exploration
12:30 P.M.	Boat Tour
99 1:45 P.M.	**Mountain Bike Ride**
3:30 P.M.	Bird-Watching

윌슨 공원 – 화요일 투어 일정표	
오전 10:00	동굴 탐험
오후 12:30	보트 투어
오후 1:45	**산악자전거 타기**
오후 3:30	조류 관찰

98 What does the speaker encourage the listeners to do?
(A) Visit a gift shop
(B) Buy an annual membership
(C) Use public transportation
(D) Make a reservation online

화자는 청자들에게 무엇을 하도록 권하는가?
(A) 선물 매장 방문하기
(B) 연간 회원권 구입하기
(C) 대중교통 이용하기
(D) 온라인으로 예약하기

어휘 annual 연간의, 해마다의 public transportation 대중교통 make a reservation 예약하다

해설 세부 사항 관련 – 화자의 권장 사항
화자가 중반부에 시내버스를 타고 공원에 오기를 권한다(~ we encourage everyone to take the city bus to the park)고 했으므로 정답은 (C)이다.

Paraphrasing
담화의 take the city bus → 정답의 Use public transportation

99 Look at the graphic. When can the listeners book a tour today?
(A) At 10:00 A.M.
(B) At 12:30 P.M.
(C) At 1:45 P.M.
(D) At 3:30 P.M.

시각 정보에 의하면, 청자들이 오늘 예약할 수 있는 투어는 언제인가?
(A) 오전 10시
(B) 오후 12시 30분
(C) 오후 1시 45분
(D) 오후 3시 30분

해설 시각 정보 연계 – 예약할 수 있는 투어 시간
화자가 중반부에 산악자전거 투어는 아직 남아 있는 자리가 있다(~ we still have spots open for the mountain bike tour)고 했다. 투어 일정표에서 산악자전거 투어 시간은 오후 1시 45분인 것을 알 수 있으므로 정답은 (C)이다.

100 What does the speaker say about some brochures?
(A) They contain trail maps.
(B) They contain discount coupons.
(C) They list a schedule of holidays.
(D) They list volunteer opportunities.

화자는 안내 책자에 대해 무엇이라고 말하는가?
(A) 코스 지도가 들어 있다.
(B) 할인 쿠폰이 들어 있다.
(C) 휴일 일정이 기재되어 있다.
(D) 자원봉사 기회가 기재되어 있다.

어휘 contain 들어 있다, 포함하다 volunteer 자원봉사 opportunity 기회

해설 세부 사항 관련 – 화자가 안내 책자에 대해 하는 말
화자가 후반부에 공원에 입장할 때, 공원 곳곳에 위치한 모든 하이킹 코스의 지도가 포함된 안내 책자를 가져갈 수 있다(~ brochures are available with maps of all the hiking trails located throughout the park)고 했으므로 정답은 (A)이다.

기출 TEST 9

1 (D)	2 (A)	3 (C)	4 (B)	5 (C)
6 (C)	7 (C)	8 (A)	9 (B)	10 (B)
11 (B)	12 (C)	13 (A)	14 (B)	15 (B)
16 (A)	17 (A)	18 (B)	19 (C)	20 (A)
21 (C)	22 (C)	23 (B)	24 (B)	25 (C)
26 (B)	27 (B)	28 (A)	29 (C)	30 (A)
31 (A)	32 (C)	33 (A)	34 (B)	35 (D)
36 (C)	37 (B)	38 (A)	39 (D)	40 (A)
41 (C)	42 (C)	43 (B)	44 (A)	45 (C)
46 (D)	47 (B)	48 (A)	49 (C)	50 (A)
51 (B)	52 (D)	53 (C)	54 (A)	55 (C)
56 (D)	57 (C)	58 (A)	59 (A)	60 (B)
61 (B)	62 (A)	63 (D)	64 (C)	65 (C)
66 (A)	67 (D)	68 (B)	69 (B)	70 (D)
71 (D)	72 (B)	73 (A)	74 (A)	75 (C)
76 (B)	77 (C)	78 (A)	79 (B)	80 (B)
81 (C)	82 (D)	83 (B)	84 (A)	85 (D)
86 (C)	87 (D)	88 (B)	89 (A)	90 (B)
91 (C)	92 (C)	93 (C)	94 (B)	95 (D)
96 (C)	97 (B)	98 (B)	99 (A)	100 (D)

PART 1

1

M-Cn

(A) A man is placing books into a shelving unit.
(B) A man is hanging up some flyers.
(C) A man is picking up tools from the floor.
(D) A man is bending over some wires.

(A) 남자가 책을 선반에 넣고 있다.
(B) 남자가 전단을 걸고 있다.
(C) 남자가 바닥에서 도구를 집어 들고 있다.
(D) 남자가 전선 위로 몸을 숙이고 있다.

어휘 place 놓다, 두다 shelving unit 선반 hang up 걸다, 매달다
flyer 전단 bend over ~ 위로 몸을 숙이다

해설 1인 등장 사진 – 사람의 동작/상태 묘사
(A) 동사 오답. 남자가 책을 선반에 넣고 있는(is placing books into a shelving unit) 모습이 아니므로 오답.
(B) 동사 오답. 남자가 전단을 걸고 있는(is hanging up some flyers) 모습이 아니므로 오답.
(C) 동사 오답. 남자가 도구를 집어 들고 있는(is picking up tools) 모습이 아니므로 오답.
(D) 정답. 남자가 전선 위로 몸을 숙이고 있는(is bending over some wires) 모습이므로 정답.

2

W-Br

(A) A picnic area is covered by a roof.
(B) A bin is filled with flowers.
(C) A picnic area is shaded by trees.
(D) A road leads to a picnic area.

(A) 피크닉 구역이 지붕으로 덮여 있다.
(B) 통이 꽃들로 가득 차 있다.
(C) 피크닉 구역이 나무들로 인해 그늘져 있다.
(D) 도로가 피크닉 구역으로 이어져 있다.

어휘 cover 덮다 be filled with ~로 가득 차 있다
shade 그늘지게 하다 bin 통 lead to ~로 이어지다

해설 사물/풍경 사진 – 풍경 묘사
(A) 정답. 피크닉 구역(A picnic area)이 지붕으로 덮여 있는(is covered by a roof) 모습이므로 정답.
(B) 사진에 없는 명사를 이용한 오답. 사진에 꽃들(flowers)의 모습이 보이지 않으므로 오답.
(C) 사진에 없는 명사를 이용한 오답. 사진에 나무들(trees)의 모습이 보이지 않으므로 오답.
(D) 사진에 없는 명사를 이용한 오답. 사진에 도로(A road)의 모습이 보이지 않으므로 오답.

3

M-Cn

(A) She's dusting a counter.
(B) She's loading paper into a copy machine.
(C) She's distributing some envelopes.
(D) She's opening some cabinet doors.

(A) 여자가 카운터의 먼지를 털고 있다.
(B) 여자가 용지를 복사기에 넣고 있다.
(C) 여자가 봉투를 분류하고 있다.
(D) 여자가 캐비닛 문을 열고 있다.

어휘 dust 먼지를 털다 load 넣다, 싣다 distribute 분류하다

해설 1인 등장 사진 – 사람의 동작/상태 묘사
(A) 동사 오답. 여자가 먼지를 털고 있는(is dusting) 모습이 아니므로 오답.
(B) 동사 오답. 여자가 용지를 복사기에 넣고 있는(is loading paper into a copy machine) 모습이 아니므로 오답.

TEST 9 235

(C) 정답. 여자가 봉투를 분류하고 있는(is distributing some envelopes) 모습이므로 정답.
(D) 동사 오답. 여자가 캐비닛 문을 열고 있는(is opening some cabinet doors) 모습이 아니므로 오답.

4

W-Am

(A) Some people are waiting in line to order.
(B) A menu board has been hung on a wall.
(C) A server is placing some food on a tray.
(D) A server is taking an order from a customer.

(A) 사람들이 주문하기 위해 줄을 서서 대기하고 있다.
(B) 메뉴판이 벽에 걸려 있다.
(C) 종업원이 음식을 쟁반에 올려놓고 있다.
(D) 종업원이 고객으로부터 주문을 받고 있다.

어휘 server 종업원 tray 쟁반 take an order 주문을 받다

해설 2인 이상 등장 사진 – 사람/사물/풍경 혼합 묘사
(A) 동사 오답. 줄을 서서 대기하고 있는(are waiting in line) 사람들의 모습이 보이지 않으므로 오답.
(B) 정답. 메뉴판(A menu board)이 벽에 걸려 있는(has been hung on a wall) 모습이므로 정답.
(C) 사진에 없는 명사를 이용한 오답. 사진에 종업원(A server)의 모습이 보이지 않으므로 오답.
(D) 사진에 없는 명사를 이용한 오답. 사진에 종업원(A server)의 모습이 보이지 않으므로 오답.

5

M-Au

(A) One of the men is stacking vegetables in a basket.
(B) One of the men is selling merchandise in front of a tent.
(C) One of the men is riding a motorcycle down a street.
(D) One of the men is walking into a store.

(A) 남자들 중 한 명이 바구니에 채소를 쌓고 있다.
(B) 남자들 중 한 명이 천막 앞에서 상품을 판매하고 있다.
(C) 남자들 중 한 명이 거리를 따라 오토바이를 타고 있다.
(D) 남자들 중 한 명이 매장으로 걸어 들어가고 있다.

어휘 stack 쌓다, 쌓아 올리다 merchandise 상품

해설 2인 이상 등장 사진 – 사람의 동작/상태 묘사
(A) 동사 오답. 남자들 중 한 명이 채소를 쌓고 있는(is stacking vegetables) 모습이 아니므로 오답.

(B) 동사 오답. 남자들 중 한 명이 상품을 판매하고 있는(is selling merchandise) 모습이 아니므로 오답.
(C) 정답. 남자들 중 한 명이 거리를 따라 오토바이를 타고 있는(is riding a motorcycle down a street) 모습이므로 정답.
(D) 동사 오답. 남자들 중 한 명이 매장으로 걸어 들어가고 있는(is walking into a store) 모습이 아니므로 오답.

6

W-Am

(A) The woman is standing in front of a painting.
(B) The woman is carrying a painting through a doorway.
(C) One of the paintings is displayed in a round frame.
(D) Some paintings are leaning against a wooden bench.

(A) 여자가 그림 앞에 서 있다.
(B) 여자가 출입구를 통해 그림을 옮기고 있다.
(C) 그림들 중 하나가 둥근 액자 속에 진열되어 있다.
(D) 그림들이 나무 벤치에 기대어져 있다.

어휘 carry 옮기다 doorway 출입구 display 진열하다, 전시하다 frame 액자, 틀 lean against ~에 기대어져 있다

해설 1인 등장 사진 – 사람/사물/풍경 혼합 묘사
(A) 동사 오답. 여자가 그림 앞에 서 있는(is standing in front of a painting) 모습이 아니므로 오답.
(B) 동사 오답. 여자가 그림을 옮기고 있는(is carrying a painting) 모습이 아니므로 오답.
(C) 정답. 그림들 중 하나(One of the paintings)가 둥근 액자 속에 진열되어 있는(is displayed in a round frame) 모습이므로 정답.
(D) 동사 오답. 그림들(Some paintings)이 나무 벤치에 기대어져 있는(are leaning against a wooden bench) 모습이 아니므로 오답.

PART 2

7
W-Br / M-Au

Would you like me to check the price on that item?

(A) A couple of bowls.
(B) I hadn't noticed.
(C) Yes, thank you.

그 제품 가격을 확인해 드릴까요?
(A) 움푹한 그릇 두어 개요.
(B) 저는 눈치채지 못했어요.
(C) 네, 감사합니다.

어휘 bowl 움푹한 그릇　notice 알아차리다, 주목하다

해설 제안/권유의 의문문
(A) 질문과 상관없는 오답. How many 의문문에 대한 응답이므로 오답.
(B) 질문과 상관없는 오답.
(C) 정답. 제품 가격을 확인해 줄지 묻는 질문에 네(Yes)라고 대답한 뒤, 감사를 표현하고 있으므로 정답.

8 M-Au / W-Am

Shouldn't we have submitted the expense report by now?

(A) No, the deadline is tomorrow.
(B) Yes, it is very expensive.
(C) Did you check the batteries?

지금쯤 그 지출 보고서를 제출했어야 하지 않나요?
(A) 아니요, 마감 기한이 내일이에요.
(B) 네, 그건 아주 비싸요.
(C) 배터리를 확인해 보셨나요?

어휘 submit 제출하다　expense 지출, 경비

해설 지금쯤 지출 보고서를 제출했어야 하는지 확인하는 부정 의문문
(A) 정답. 지금쯤 지출 보고서를 제출했어야 하는지 확인하는 질문에 아니요(No)라고 대답한 뒤, 마감 기한이 내일이라며 부정 답변과 일관된 내용을 덧붙이고 있으므로 정답.
(B) 유사 발음 오답. 질문의 expense와 부분적으로 발음이 유사한 expensive를 이용한 오답.
(C) 질문과 상관없는 오답.

9 M-Cn / W-Br

How can we resolve the problem with our client?

(A) Please change the ink cartridge.
(B) By hiring a consulting firm.
(C) His office is on the third floor.

고객과의 문제를 어떻게 해결할 수 있을까요?
(A) 잉크 카트리지를 바꿔 주세요.
(B) 컨설팅 업체를 고용해서요.
(C) 그의 사무실은 3층에 있어요.

어휘 resolve 해결하다

해설 고객과의 문제 해결 방법을 묻는 How 의문문
(A) 질문과 상관없는 오답.
(B) 정답. 고객과의 문제 해결 방법을 묻는 질문에 컨설팅 업체를 고용하는 방법을 제시하고 있으므로 정답.
(C) 질문과 상관없는 오답. Where 의문문에 대한 응답이므로 오답.

10 W-Am / W-Br

Was the restaurant really expensive?

(A) I can pick up some today.
(B) Yes, it was a lot.
(C) OK, I'll close the door.

그 레스토랑이 정말로 비쌌나요?
(A) 제가 오늘 좀 가져올 수 있어요.
(B) 네, 꽤 비쌌어요.
(C) 네, 제가 문을 닫을게요.

해설 레스토랑이 정말로 비쌌는지 묻는 Be동사 의문문
(A) 질문과 상관없는 오답.
(B) 정답. 레스토랑이 정말로 비쌌는지 묻는 질문에 네(Yes)라고 대답한 뒤, 꽤 비쌌다며 긍정 답변과 일관된 내용을 덧붙이고 있으므로 정답.
(C) 질문과 상관없는 오답.

11 W-Am / M-Cn

When will the dishwasher prototype be ready?

(A) On Treetown Avenue.
(B) Next Tuesday.
(C) OK, thanks for the update.

식기세척기 시제품이 언제 준비될까요?
(A) 트리타운 가예요.
(B) 다음 주 화요일에요.
(C) 네, 업데이트해 주셔서 감사합니다.

어휘 prototype 시제품, 원형

해설 시제품이 준비되는 시점을 묻는 When 의문문
(A) 질문과 상관없는 오답. Where 의문문에 대한 응답이므로 오답.
(B) 정답. 시제품이 준비되는 시점을 묻는 질문에 다음 주 화요일이라고 알려 주고 있으므로 정답.
(C) Yes/No 불가 오답. When 의문문에는 Yes/No 응답이 불가능한데, OK도 일종의 Yes 응답이라고 볼 수 있으므로 오답.

12 M-Au / M-Cn

Let's cancel our appointment.

(A) The shipping and receiving department.
(B) My dentist has an office downtown.
(C) Sure, I'll do that now.

우리 예약을 취소합시다.
(A) 배송 및 수취 담당 부서요.
(B) 제 치과 의사 선생님은 병원이 시내에 있어요.
(C) 네, 제가 지금 할게요.

어휘 appointment 예약, 약속　shipping 배송
receiving 수취, 수령　dentist 치과 의사

해설 제안/권유의 평서문
(A) 평서문과 상관없는 오답.
(B) 연상 단어 오답. 평서문의 appointment에서 연상 가능한 dentist를 이용한 오답.
(C) 정답. 예약을 취소하자고 제안하는 평서문에 좋다(Sure)고 수락한 뒤, 지금 그렇게 하겠다며 긍정 답변과 일관된 내용을 덧붙이고 있으므로 정답.

13 W-Am / M-Cn

It's OK if we don't check these receipts until later.

(A) Good, because I'm busy at the moment.
(B) I haven't seen that show either.
(C) About 200 dollars.

이 영수증들은 나중에 확인해도 괜찮아요.
(A) 잘됐네요, 제가 지금 바쁘거든요.
(B) 저도 그 공연을 본 적이 없어요.
(C) 약 200달러요.

어휘 until later 나중까지 receipt 영수(증)

해설 정보 전달의 평서문
(A) 정답. 영수증들을 나중에 확인해도 괜찮다는 평서문에 잘됐다(Good)고 대답한 뒤, 지금 바쁘기 때문이라는 이유를 덧붙이고 있으므로 정답.
(B) 평서문과 상관없는 오답.
(C) 평서문과 상관없는 오답. How much 의문문에 대한 응답이므로 오답.

14 M-Cn / W-Br

Where can I find the shipping address?

(A) He doesn't mind.
(B) It's on my business card.
(C) No, I'm fine.

배송 주소를 어디에서 찾을 수 있나요?
(A) 그는 상관하지 않아요.
(B) 제 명함에 있습니다.
(C) 아니요, 저는 괜찮습니다.

어휘 business card 명함

해설 배송 주소를 찾을 수 있는 곳을 묻는 Where 의문문
(A) 질문과 상관없는 오답. 질문에 3인칭 대명사 He로 지칭할 인물이 언급된 적이 없으므로 오답.
(B) 정답. 배송 주소를 찾을 수 있는 곳을 묻는 질문에 자신의 명함에 있다고 응답하고 있으므로 정답.
(C) Yes/No 불가 오답. Where 의문문에는 Yes/No 응답이 불가능하므로 오답.

15 M-Au / W-Am

Which bus stop is closest to the apartment building?

(A) No, I don't have any coins.
(B) The one on Eighth Street.
(C) An extra bag for groceries.

어느 버스 정류장이 그 아파트 건물과 가장 가까운가요?
(A) 아니요, 저는 동전이 하나도 없어요.
(B) 8번 가에 있는 것이요.
(C) 식료품을 담을 별도의 가방이요.

어휘 extra 별도의, 추가의 groceries 식료품

해설 아파트 건물과 가장 가까운 버스 정류장을 묻는 Which 의문문
(A) Yes/No 불가 오답. Which 의문문에는 Yes/No 응답이 불가능하므로 오답.
(B) 정답. 아파트 건물과 가장 가까운 버스 정류장을 묻는 질문에 8번 가에 있는 것이라고 구체적으로 알려 주고 있으므로 정답.
(C) 질문과 상관없는 오답.

16 M-Cn / W-Br

Who's the main performer at the music festival next weekend?

(A) The famous singer Bradley Patel.
(B) Some seats near the stage.
(C) The corner of Main Street and First Avenue.

누가 다음 주말에 있을 음악 축제의 메인 공연자인가요?
(A) 유명 가수 브래들리 파텔이요.
(B) 무대 근처의 좌석이요.
(C) 메인 가와 1번 가가 만나는 모퉁이요.

어휘 performer 공연자, 연주자

해설 음악 축제의 메인 공연자를 묻는 Who 의문문
(A) 정답. 음악 축제의 메인 공연자를 묻는 질문에 유명 가수 브래들리 파텔이라고 구체적인 인물로 응답하고 있으므로 정답.
(B) 연상 단어 오답. 질문의 music festival에서 연상 가능한 stage를 이용한 오답.
(C) 질문과 상관없는 오답. Where 의문문에 대한 응답이므로 오답.

17 W-Am / M-Cn

When are we meeting again?

(A) Tomorrow after lunch.
(B) It was about two hours long.
(C) I prefer to use local suppliers.

우리는 언제 다시 만나나요?
(A) 내일 점심 이후에요.
(B) 약 2시간 길이였어요.
(C) 저는 지역 공급업체들을 이용하는 걸 선호해요.

어휘 local 지역의, 현지의 supplier 공급업체, 공급업자

해설 다시 만나는 시간을 묻는 When 의문문
(A) 정답. 다시 만나는 시간을 묻는 질문에 내일 점심 이후라고 구체적인 시점으로 응답하고 있으므로 정답.
(B) 질문과 상관없는 오답. How long 의문문에 대한 응답이므로 오답.
(C) 질문과 상관없는 오답.

18 M-Au / W-Br   ▶ 동영상 강의

That project's been approved, right?

(A) Dinner is at eight.
(B) We're waiting for the final cost estimate.
(C) There's a store nearby.

그 프로젝트가 승인되었죠, 그렇죠?
(A) 저녁 식사는 8시입니다.
(B) 최종 견적서를 기다리고 있어요.
(C) 근처에 매장이 하나 있습니다.

어휘 approve 승인하다　cost estimate (비용) 견적서
　　　nearby 근처에

해설 프로젝트의 승인 여부를 확인하는 부가 의문문
　　(A) 질문과 상관없는 오답. When 의문문에 대한 응답이므로 오답.
　　(B) 정답. 프로젝트의 승인 여부를 확인하는 질문에 최종 견적서를 기다리고 있다는 말로 아직 승인되지 않은 상태임을 우회적으로 나타내고 있으므로 정답.
　　(C) 질문과 상관없는 오답.

19　M-Cn / M-Au

Did you put the brochures in the lobby?
(A) The conference center is on Walnut Avenue.
(B) Do you have a reservation?
(C) Yes, I left them at the front desk.

안내 책자들을 로비에 두셨나요?
(A) 콘퍼런스 센터는 월넛 가에 있어요.
(B) 예약하셨나요?
(C) 네, 프런트 데스크에 두었어요.

어휘 brochure 안내 책자, 소책자　reservation 예약

해설 안내 책자들을 로비에 두었는지 묻는 조동사(Did) 의문문
　　(A) 질문과 상관없는 오답. Where 의문문에 대한 응답이므로 오답.
　　(B) 질문과 상관없는 오답.
　　(C) 정답. 안내 책자들을 로비에 두었는지 묻는 질문에 네(Yes)라고 대답한 뒤, 프런트 데스크에 두었다며 긍정 답변과 일관된 내용을 덧붙이고 있으므로 정답.

20　M-Au / W-Am

How soon will we be able to replace the furniture in the waiting room?
(A) We'll do that at the end of the summer.
(B) Agreed—that painting looks good in this room!
(C) Put all the old files upstairs.

대기실에 있는 가구를 얼마나 빨리 교체할 수 있을까요?
(A) 여름이 끝날 무렵 할 겁니다.
(B) 동의해요, 저 그림이 이 방에 잘 어울리네요!
(C) 오래된 파일은 모두 위층에 올려놓으세요.

어휘 replace 교체하다　agree 동의하다, 합의하다　upstairs 위층에

해설 대기실 가구 교체 가능 시점을 묻는 How soon 의문문
　　(A) 정답. 대기실 가구 교체 가능 시점을 묻는 질문에 여름이 끝날 무렵 할 것이라며 대략적인 시점으로 응답하고 있으므로 정답.
　　(B) 단어 반복 오답. 질문의 room을 반복 이용한 오답.
　　(C) 질문과 상관없는 오답. Where 의문문에 대한 응답이므로 오답.

21　W-Br / M-Au

Who is the keynote speaker on Friday?
(A) The keys are on my desk.
(B) Yes, she gave a nice speech.
(C) Here's the schedule.

누가 금요일 기조 연설자인가요?
(A) 열쇠들은 제 책상에 있어요.
(B) 네, 그녀가 훌륭한 연설을 했어요.
(C) 여기 일정표입니다.

해설 금요일 기조 연설자를 묻는 Who 의문문
　　(A) 유사 발음 오답. 질문의 keynote와 부분적으로 발음이 유사한 keys를 이용한 오답.
　　(B) Yes/No 불가 오답. Who 의문문에는 Yes/No 응답이 불가능하므로 오답.
　　(C) 정답. 금요일 기조 연설자를 묻는 질문에 관련 정보를 확인할 수 있는 일정표를 건네주고 있으므로 정답.

22　M-Au / M-Cn

When should we order the gift baskets?
(A) No, just me this time.
(B) From the florist down the street.
(C) Let's discuss that at our next meeting.

언제 선물 바구니를 주문해야 할까요?
(A) 아니요, 이번에는 저만요.
(B) 길 저쪽에 있는 꽃집에서요.
(C) 그건 다음 회의에서 논의해 봅시다.

해설 선물 바구니 주문 시점을 묻는 When 의문문
　　(A) Yes/No 불가 오답. When 의문문에는 Yes/No 응답이 불가능하므로 오답.
　　(B) 질문과 상관없는 오답. Where 의문문에 대한 응답이므로 오답.
　　(C) 정답. 선물 바구니 주문 시점을 묻는 질문에 다음 회의에서 논의하자는 말로 아직 결정되지 않았음을 우회적으로 표현하고 있으므로 정답.

23　M-Au / W-Br

Why was the seminar agenda changed?
(A) Try rebooting the computer.
(B) Because an additional speaker was added.
(C) That's a good idea.

세미나 일정표가 왜 변경됐나요?
(A) 컴퓨터를 재부팅해 보세요.
(B) 발표자가 한 명 더 추가되었기 때문입니다.
(C) 좋은 아이디어네요.

어휘 agenda (세미나 등의) 일정표, 안건 (목록)　reboot 재부팅하다

해설 세미나 일정표가 변경된 이유를 묻는 Why 의문문
　　(A) 질문과 상관없는 오답.
　　(B) 정답. 세미나 일정표가 변경된 이유를 묻는 질문에 발표자가 한 명 더 추가되었기 때문이라고 이유를 밝히고 있으므로 정답.
　　(C) 질문과 상관없는 오답.

24 W-Am / M-Cn

Are you taking the bus or a taxi to the client's office?

(A) To pick up some coffee.
(B) I brought my car today.
(C) They weren't too expensive.

고객의 사무실로 버스를 타고 가시나요, 아니면 택시를 타시나요?
(A) 커피를 좀 가져오려고요.
(B) 저는 오늘 차를 가져왔어요.
(C) 그렇게 비싸지는 않았어요.

해설 이용하려는 교통편을 묻는 선택 의문문
(A) 질문과 상관없는 오답. Why 의문문에 대한 응답이므로 오답.
(B) 정답. 고객의 사무실로 버스와 택시 중 무엇을 타고 갈지 묻는 질문에 자신의 차를 가져왔다며 두 선택지를 제외한 제3의 안을 제시하고 있으므로 정답.
(C) 질문과 상관없는 오답. 질문에 3인칭 대명사 They로 지칭할 사물이 언급된 적이 없으므로 오답.

25 W-Br / M-Cn ▶동영상 강의

Could you help me set up these chairs for the picnic?

(A) She moved to Singapore last year.
(B) The furniture store on Maple Street.
(C) I'm about to go pick up the cake.

야유회를 위해 이 의자들을 설치하는 일을 도와주실 수 있나요?
(A) 그녀는 작년에 싱가포르로 이사했어요.
(B) 메이플 가에 있는 가구 매장이요.
(C) 저는 막 케이크를 가지러 가려는 참인데요.

어휘 set up 설치하다, 마련하다 be about to 막 ~하려고 하다

해설 부탁/요청의 의문문
(A) 질문과 상관없는 오답. 질문에 3인칭 대명사 She로 지칭할 인물이 언급된 적이 없으므로 오답.
(B) 연상 단어 오답. 질문의 chairs에서 연상 가능한 furniture를 이용한 오답.
(C) 정답. 의자들을 설치하는 일을 도와달라고 요청하는 질문에 막 케이크를 가지러 가려는 참이라는 말로 거절의 뜻을 나타내고 있으므로 정답.

26 M-Au / W-Br

Who'll be selected to work on the prototype?

(A) No, it's not too heavy.
(B) Jacob's team has done some good work.
(C) I already have some.

시제품 작업을 할 사람으로 누가 선정될까요?
(A) 아니요, 그건 그렇게 무겁지 않아요.
(B) 제이콥의 팀이 좋은 성과를 내고 있어요.
(C) 저는 이미 몇 개 가지고 있어요.

어휘 select 선정하다

해설 시제품 작업을 하도록 선정될 사람을 묻는 Who 의문문
(A) Yes/No 불가 오답. Who 의문문에는 Yes/No 응답이 불가능하므로 오답.
(B) 정답. 시제품 작업을 하도록 선정될 사람을 묻는 질문에 제이콥의 팀이 좋은 성과를 내고 있다는 말로 그 팀이 선정될 가능성이 있음을 우회적으로 표현하고 있으므로 정답.
(C) 질문과 상관없는 오답.

27 M-Cn / W-Br

Ms. Lambert is responsible for the payroll.

(A) On the second floor.
(B) Yes, she's done it for years.
(C) No, it shouldn't be too difficult.

램버트 씨가 급여 관리 업무를 담당하고 계세요.
(A) 2층이에요.
(B) 네, 그분께서 몇 년간 그 일을 해 오셨죠.
(C) 아니요, 그렇게 어렵지 않을 겁니다.

어휘 responsible for ~을 담당하는 payroll 급여 (관리 업무)

해설 정보 전달의 평서문
(A) 평서문과 상관없는 오답. Where 의문문에 대한 응답이므로 오답.
(B) 정답. 램버트 씨가 급여 관리 업무를 담당하고 있다는 평서문에 네(Yes)라고 대답한 뒤, 그 사람이 그 일을 몇 년간 해왔다며 긍정 답변과 일관된 내용을 덧붙이고 있으므로 정답.
(C) 평서문과 상관없는 오답.

28 W-Br / M-Cn

Can't we extend the advertising campaign?

(A) We're already over budget.
(B) Yes, it's a new printer.
(C) A retirement bonus.

그 광고 캠페인을 연장할 수 없나요?
(A) 이미 예산을 초과한 상태예요.
(B) 네, 그건 새 프린터입니다.
(C) 퇴직 보너스요.

어휘 extend 연장하다, 확장하다 advertising 광고 budget 예산 retirement 퇴직, 은퇴

해설 광고 캠페인의 연장 가능 여부를 확인하는 부정 의문문
(A) 정답. 광고 캠페인의 연장 가능 여부를 확인하는 질문에 이미 예산을 초과한 상태라며 연장할 수 없음을 우회적으로 나타내고 있으므로 정답.
(B) 질문과 상관없는 오답.
(C) 질문과 상관없는 오답.

29 M-Au / W-Am

Please close the door so that the presentation can start.

(A) The car keys are on my desk.
(B) Our filing cabinets are full.
(C) We're waiting for a few more people.

발표가 시작될 수 있도록 문을 닫아 주세요.
(A) 자동차 열쇠는 제 책상에 있어요.
(B) 파일 캐비닛들이 가득 차 있습니다.
(C) 몇 명 더 기다리고 있어요.

해설 부탁/요청의 평서문
(A) 연상 단어 오답. 평서문의 door에서 연상 가능한 keys를 이용한 오답.
(B) 연상 단어 오답. 평서문의 door에서 연상 가능한 cabinets를 이용한 오답.
(C) 정답. 발표가 시작될 수 있도록 문을 닫아 달라는 평서문에 몇 명 더 기다리고 있다는 말로 아직은 닫을 수 없음을 우회적으로 나타내고 있으므로 정답.

30 W-Br / W-Am ▶ 동영상 강의

How often have our packages been damaged during delivery?

(A) We need to find a new shipping partner.
(B) Several customers are waiting to have their cars serviced.
(C) No, we don't need to eat.

우리 소포가 배송 중에 얼마나 자주 파손되었나요?
(A) 새로운 운송 업체를 찾아야 해요.
(B) 여러 고객이 차량 서비스를 받기 위해 기다리고 있어요.
(C) 아니요, 저희는 먹을 필요 없어요.

어휘 package 소포, 포장물 damaged 손상된, 피해를 입은 shipping 운송

해설 배송 중 소포 손상 빈도를 묻는 How often 의문문
(A) 정답. 배송 중 소포 손상 빈도를 묻는 질문에 새로운 운송 업체를 찾아야 한다는 말로 자주 손상되었음을 우회적으로 나타내고 있으므로 정답.
(B) 질문과 상관없는 오답.
(C) Yes/No 불가 오답. How 의문문에는 Yes/No 응답이 불가능하므로 오답.

31 M-Au / W-Am

They're bringing a piano into the café, aren't they?

(A) There's not enough space.
(B) The food is fantastic.
(C) Turn left at the light.

그들이 카페에 피아노를 들여오는 거죠, 그렇지 않나요?
(A) 공간이 충분하지 않아요.
(B) 음식이 환상적이네요.
(C) 신호등에서 좌회전하세요.

해설 카페에 피아노를 들여오는지 여부를 확인하는 부가 의문문
(A) 정답. 카페에 피아노를 들여오는지 여부를 확인하는 질문에 공간이 충분하지 않다는 말로 사실상 어렵다는 뜻을 우회적으로 나타내고 있으므로 정답.
(B) 연상 단어 오답. 질문의 café에서 연상 가능한 food를 이용한 오답.
(C) 질문과 상관없는 오답.

PART 3

32-34 M-Au / W-Br

M Hello. I'm calling because I'll be staying in the city next week for work, and ³²I'd like to purchase a temporary gym membership.

W Of course! Our standard day pass is twenty dollars. ³³We also offer rentals on athletic equipment like exercise mats and tennis rackets if you're interested.

M I'll just purchase the pass for now, thanks.

W Great. First, I'll need to set you up in our system. ³⁴Can I have your name and e-mail address?

남 안녕하세요. 제가 다음 주에 업무차 그 도시에 머무를 예정이라, 임시 체육관 회원권을 구입하고 싶어서 전화했습니다.
여 물론입니다! 저희 일반 1일 이용권은 20달러입니다. 관심이 있으시면 운동용 매트와 테니스 라켓 같은 운동 장비 대여 서비스도 제공해 드리고 있어요.
남 일단은 이용권만 구입할게요, 감사합니다.
여 좋습니다. 먼저 저희 시스템에 등록해 드릴게요. 성함과 이메일 주소를 알려 주시겠어요?

어휘 purchase 구입하다 temporary 임의의, 일시적인 pass 이용권, 출입증 rental 대여 athletic 운동의, 경기의 equipment 장비

32 What is the purpose of the man's call?
(A) To question a charge on a bill
(B) To inquire about a job opening
(C) To purchase a membership
(D) To cancel a reservation

남자가 전화하는 목적은 무엇인가?
(A) 청구서 요금에 이의를 제기하기 위해
(B) 공석과 관련해 문의하기 위해
(C) 회원권을 구입하기 위해
(D) 예약을 취소하기 위해

어휘 question 이의를 제기하다 charge 요금 bill 청구서, 계산서 inquire 문의하다 reservation 예약

해설 전체 내용 관련 – 남자가 전화하는 목적
남자가 첫 대사에서 임시 체육관 회원권을 구입하고 싶다(~ I'd like to purchase a temporary gym membership)고 했으므로 정답은 (C)이다.

33 According to the woman, what additional service does the business offer?
(A) Equipment rentals
(B) Spa treatments
(C) Personalized training sessions
(D) Nutrition consultations

여자에 따르면, 업체는 어떤 추가 서비스를 제공하는가?
(A) 장비 대여
(B) 스파 치료
(C) 개인 맞춤 훈련
(D) 영양 상담

어휘 treatment 치료, 처치 personalized 개인에게 맞춰진 nutrition 영양

해설 세부 사항 관련 – 업체가 제공하는 추가 서비스
여자가 첫 대사에서 운동용 매트와 테니스 라켓 같은 운동 장비 대여 서비스도 제공한다(We also offer rentals on athletic equipment like exercise mats and tennis rackets ~)고 했으므로 정답은 (A)이다.

34 What does the woman ask the man to provide?
(A) Some referral letters
(B) Some contact information
(C) A copy of a receipt
(D) A discount code

여자는 남자에게 무엇을 제공해 달라고 요청하는가?
(A) 의뢰서
(B) 연락 정보
(C) 영수증 사본
(D) 할인 코드

해설 세부 사항 관련 – 여자의 요청 사항
여자가 마지막 대사에서 성함과 이메일 주소를 알려 달라(Can I have your name and e-mail address?)고 요청하고 있으므로 정답은 (B)이다.

Paraphrasing
대화의 name and e-mail address
→ 정답의 contact information

35-37 W-Br / M-Au

W **35** Welcome to Reynold's Ice Cream Factory. I'm so glad that you'll be joining our quality assurance team.

M Thanks! I'm excited to work with the rest of the group.

W Great! I saw on your résumé that you previously did quality control at a similar factory.

M Yes. **36** I learned a lot about food manufacturing regulations there.

W Then you'll already be familiar with the testing we do. **37** We test at the beginning of each shift to make sure all the equipment has been cleaned and sanitized.

여 레이놀즈 아이스크림 공장에 오신 것을 환영합니다. 품질 보증팀에 합류하시게 된다니 정말 기뻐요.
남 감사합니다! 다른 팀원들과 함께 일하게 되어 기대가 됩니다.
여 좋습니다! 이력서를 보니 전에 유사한 공장에서 품질 관리 업무를 하셨던데요.
남 네. 그곳에서 식품 제조 규정에 관해 많은 것을 배웠습니다.
여 그럼 저희가 하는 점검 방식에도 이미 익숙하실 겁니다. 저희는 모든 장비가 세척되고 소독되었는지 확인하기 위해 각 교대 근무 시작 시점에 점검을 실시합니다.

어휘 quality assurance 품질 보증 résumé 이력서 previously 이전에, 과거에 quality control 품질 관리 manufacturing 제조 regulation 규정, 규제 shift 교대 근무 sanitize 위생 처리하다, 살균하다

35 Who most likely is the man?
(A) A business client
(B) A board member
(C) A potential investor
(D) A new employee

남자는 누구인 것 같은가?
(A) 비즈니스 고객
(B) 이사회 구성원
(C) 잠재 투자자
(D) 신입 직원

어휘 board 이사회 potential 잠재적인, 가능성 있는 investor 투자자

해설 전체 내용 관련 – 남자의 직업
여자가 첫 대사에서 남자에게 환영 인사와 함께 품질 보증팀에 합류하게 된다니 정말 기쁘다(Welcome to Reynold's Ice Cream Factory. I'm so glad that you'll be joining our quality assurance team)고 했으므로 정답은 (D)이다.

36 What does the man say he learned from another factory?
(A) Assembly-line schedules
(B) Budgeting strategies
(C) Manufacturing regulations
(D) Sourcing considerations

남자는 다른 공장에서 무엇을 배웠다고 말하는가?
(A) 조립 라인 일정
(B) 예산 책정 전략
(C) 제조 관련 규정
(D) 조달 관련 고려 사항

어휘 assembly 조립 budgeting 예산 책정 strategy 전략 sourcing 조달, 공급 consideration 고려 사항

해설 세부 사항 관련 – 남자가 다른 공장에서 배운 것
남자가 두 번째 대사에서 전에 근무한 공장에서 식품 제조 규정에 관해 많은 것을 배웠다(I learned a lot about food manufacturing regulations there)고 했으므로 정답은 (C)이다.

37 What is done at the start of each shift?
(A) A database review
(B) A cleanliness test
(C) An attendance check
(D) A uniform inspection

각 교대 근무 시작 시에 무엇이 이루어지는가?
(A) 데이터베이스 검토
(B) 청결도 점검
(C) 출근 확인
(D) 유니폼 점검

어휘 cleanliness 청결 attendance 출근, 출석 inspection 점검, 조사

해설 세부 사항 관련 – 교대 근무 시작 시에 이루어지는 일
여자가 마지막 대사에서 모든 장비가 세척되고 소독되었는지 확인하기 위해 각 교대 근무 시작 시점에 점검을 실시한다(We test at the beginning of each shift to make sure all the equipment has been cleaned and sanitized)고 했으므로 정답은 (B)이다.

Paraphrasing
대화의 test ~ to make sure all the equipment has been cleaned and sanitized → 정답의 A cleanliness test

38-40 M-Cn / W-Br

M So-Jin, do you have a minute? I've got an assignment for you.
W Sure. What is it?
M **38** The human resources department is concerned that employees aren't reading their weekly staff newsletter. **39** They asked if one of our graphic designers could redesign the newsletter to make it more attractive.
W **39** All right. I'll start working on it after I've finished with the Web site update.
M **40** I'll ask Hiroki to take care of that so you're free to work on the newsletter.

남 소진, 잠깐 시간 있어요? 제가 맡길 일이 있어요.
여 네, 뭔가요?
남 인사부에서 직원들이 주간 직원 뉴스레터를 읽지 않는다고 걱정하고 있어요. 그쪽에서 우리 그래픽 디자이너가 뉴스레터를 보기 좋게 다시 디자인해 줄 수 있는지 물어봤어요.
여 알겠습니다. 웹사이트 업데이트를 마친 후에 그 작업을 시작할게요.
남 제가 그 일은 히로키에게 처리해 달라고 할 테니, 뉴스레터 작업을 하시면 됩니다.

어휘 assignment 임무, 과제 concerned 걱정하는 redesign 다시 디자인하다 attractive 눈에 띄는, 매력적인

38 According to the man, what is the human resources department concerned about?
(A) Lack of interest in a newsletter
(B) Employee compliance with a policy
(C) A shortage of qualified applicants
(D) Inadequate training materials

남자에 따르면, 인사부는 무엇을 걱정하는가?
(A) 뉴스레터에 대한 관심 부족
(B) 직원들의 정책 준수
(C) 적격한 지원자의 부족
(D) 부적합한 교육 자료

어휘 lack 부족 compliance 준수 shortage 부족 qualified 적격인 applicant 지원자 inadequate 부적합한

해설 세부 사항 관련 – 인사부가 걱정하는 것
남자가 두 번째 대사에서 인사부에서 직원들이 주간 직원 뉴스레터를 읽지 않는다고 걱정하고 있다(The human resources department is concerned that employees aren't reading their weekly staff newsletter)고 했으므로 정답은 (A)이다.

Paraphrasing
대화의 aren't reading their weekly staff newsletter → 정답의 Lack of interest in a newsletter

TEST 9 243

39 Which department does the woman most likely work in?
(A) Sales
(B) Shipping
(C) Legal
(D) Graphic design

여자는 어느 부서에서 일하는 것 같은가?
(A) 영업
(B) 배송
(C) 법무
(D) 그래픽 디자인

해설 전체 내용 관련 – 여자의 근무 부서
남자가 두 번째 대사에서 인사부에서 우리 그래픽 디자이너가 뉴스레터를 보기 좋게 다시 디자인해 줄 수 있는지 물어봤다 (They asked if one of our graphic designers could redesign the newsletter ~)고 하자, 여자가 알겠다며 웹사이트 업데이트를 마친 후에 그 작업을 시작하겠다(All right. I'll start working on it ~)고 이야기하고 있으므로 여자는 그래픽 디자인 부서에서 근무하고 있다는 것을 알 수 있다. 따라서 정답은 (D)이다.

40 What does the man say he will do?
(A) Reassign a task
(B) Publish a news report
(C) Move a project deadline
(D) Repair a link on a Web site

남자는 무엇을 할 것이라고 말하는가?
(A) 업무 재배정하기
(B) 뉴스 기사 발표하기
(C) 프로젝트 마감 기한 옮기기
(D) 웹사이트상의 링크 수정하기

어휘 reassign 재배정하다 publish 발표하다, 출판하다
deadline 마감 기한 repair 수정하다, 수리하다

해설 세부 사항 관련 – 남자가 할 일
남자가 마지막 대사에서 여자에게 웹사이트 업데이트 작업을 히로키에게 처리해 달라고 할 테니 뉴스레터 작업을 하면 된다(I'll ask Hiroki to take care of that so you're free to work on the newsletter)고 말하는 것으로 보아, 여자의 기존 업무를 히로키에게 다시 배정하려는 것임을 알 수 있다. 따라서 정답은 (A)이다.

Paraphrasing
대화의 ask Hiroki to take care of that
→ 정답의 Reassign a task

41-43 3인 대화 M-Au / M-Cn / W-Am

M1 **41 Did you hear that Ms. Hamdy is retiring? There's going to be an opening for an accounts payable manager.** I think you'd be a perfect fit for the job, Amanda.

M2 I agree. When anyone in accounting has a question, you're the one they go to.

W Thanks. **42 The only thing I worry about is that I've never managed a team before.**

M2 That's not a problem. The company provides an intensive training program for new managers. You learn how to motivate employees, how to handle budgets—all that stuff.

W I appreciate your encouragement. **43 I'll talk to Ms. Hamdy** to learn more about what she does.

남1 햄디 씨께서 은퇴하신다는 얘기 들으셨어요? 매입 회계 관리자 자리가 공석이 될 거예요. 당신이 그 일에 완벽한 적임자일 거라고 생각해요, 아만다.
남2 저도 동의해요. 회계부에 있는 사람이 질문이 있을 때 찾아가는 사람이 바로 당신이잖아요.
여 감사합니다. 제가 걱정하는 유일한 문제는 팀을 관리해 본 적이 없다는 거예요.
남2 그건 문제가 되지 않아요. 회사에서 신임 관리자들을 위해 집중 교육 프로그램을 제공하잖아요. 직원들에게 동기를 부여하는 방법, 예산을 처리하는 방법, 그런 것들을 모두 배워요.
여 격려 감사합니다. 햄디 씨와 이야기해서 그분이 어떤 일을 하시는지 더 알아볼게요.

어휘 retire 은퇴하다, 퇴직하다 opening 공석, 빈자리
accounts payable 매입 회계, 지출 회계(회사가 거래처에 지급해야 하는 비용 관련 업무) fit 적임자, 적합한 것 accounting 회계부
intensive 집중적인 motivate 동기를 부여하다, 자극하다
handle 처리하다, 다루다 encouragement 격려

41 What are the speakers mainly discussing?
(A) A future business trip
(B) An upcoming workshop
(C) A job opportunity
(D) A new employee's progress

화자들은 주로 무엇에 대해 이야기하고 있는가?
(A) 앞으로 있을 출장
(B) 다가오는 워크숍
(C) 일자리 기회
(D) 신입 직원의 발전

어휘 upcoming 다가오는, 곧 있을 opportunity 기회
progress 발전, 진전

해설 전체 내용 관련 – 대화의 주제

첫 번째 남자가 햄디 씨의 은퇴를 언급하며 매입 회계 관리자 자리가 공석이 될 것(Did you hear that Ms. Hamdy is retiring? There's going to be an opening for an accounts payable manager)이라고 말하고 있다. 이는 일자리 기회가 생긴다는 말과 같으므로 정답은 (C)이다.

Paraphrasing
대화의 an opening for an accounts payable manager
→ 정답의 A job opportunity

42 What is the woman concerned about?
(A) Difficulty speaking in public
(B) Missing an appointment
(C) A lack of experience
(D) A negative performance review

여자는 무엇을 걱정하는가?
(A) 사람들 앞에서 말하기의 어려움
(B) 예약 시간을 놓치는 것
(C) 경험 부족
(D) 부정적인 성과 평가

어휘 negative 부정적인   performance 성과, 실적

해설 세부 사항 관련 – 여자가 걱정하는 것

여자가 첫 대사에서 자신이 걱정하는 유일한 문제가 팀을 관리해 본 적이 없다는 것(The only thing I worry about is that I've never managed a team before)이라고 했으므로 정답은 (C)이다.

Paraphrasing
대화의 have never managed a team before
→ 정답의 A lack of experience

43 What does the woman say she will do?
(A) Update her résumé
(B) Speak to a colleague
(C) Review a budget
(D) Register for a training program

여자는 무엇을 할 것이라고 말하는가?
(A) 이력서 업데이트하기
(B) 동료와 이야기하기
(C) 예산 검토하기
(D) 교육 프로그램에 등록하기

어휘 colleague 동료   review 검토하다, 살펴보다
register for ~에 등록하다

해설 세부 사항 관련 – 여자가 할 일

여자가 마지막 대사에서 햄디 씨와 이야기하겠다(I'll talk to Ms. Hamdy ~)고 했으므로 정답은 (B)이다.

Paraphrasing
대화의 talk to Ms. Hamdy → 정답의 Speak to a colleague

44-46 W-Br / M-Au

W Hi, Rodrigo. Would you like to join me and the team for lunch? We're going to Café Milano. **44 We've all been working hard to finish this advertising campaign for our client.**

M Sure! **45 I can drive if you'd like.**

W The café is just down the street.

M Oh, they must have opened a second location. I only know about the one across town.

W Yes, this one just opened. **46 Would you like to see the menu? I have a copy in my office.**

여 안녕하세요, 로드리고. 저랑 팀원들과 함께 점심 식사하러 가실래요? 카페 밀라노에 가려고요. **우리 모두 고객을 위해 광고 캠페인을 마무리하려고 열심히 일하고 있잖아요.**

남 물론이죠! **원하시면 제가 운전할게요.**

여 **카페는 길 바로 저쪽에 있어요.**

남 아, 그곳이 두 번째 지점을 열었나 봐요. 저는 시내 반대편에 있는 곳만 알거든요.

여 네, 여기는 막 문을 열었어요. **메뉴를 보시겠어요? 제 사무실에 한 부 있어요.**

어휘 advertising 광고   location 지점, 위치

44 What have the speakers been working on?
(A) An advertising campaign
(B) A software update
(C) An office renovation
(D) A training course

화자들은 무슨 작업을 하고 있는가?
(A) 광고 캠페인
(B) 소프트웨어 업데이트
(C) 사무실 보수 공사
(D) 교육 과정

어휘 renovation 개조, 보수

해설 세부 사항 관련 – 화자들이 하는 작업

여자가 첫 번째 대사에서 우리 모두 고객을 위해 광고 캠페인을 마무리하느라 열심히 일하고 있다(We've all been working hard to finish this advertising campaign for our client)고 했으므로 정답은 (A)이다.

45 Why does the woman say, "The café is just down the street"?
(A) To praise a planning decision
(B) To give directions
(C) To reject an offer
(D) To show concern about parking

여자는 왜 "카페는 길 바로 저쪽에 있어요"라고 말하는가?
(A) 계획 결정을 칭찬하려고
(B) 길을 알려 주려고
(C) 제안을 거절하려고
(D) 주차에 대한 걱정을 나타내려고

어휘 praise 칭찬하다 decision 결정 directions 길 안내
reject 거절하다

해설 화자의 의도 파악 – 카페는 길 바로 저쪽에 있다는 말의 의도
남자가 첫 대사에서 원하면 자신이 운전하겠다(I can drive if you'd like)고 하자 여자가 인용문을 언급하는 것으로 보아, 가까워서 운전할 필요가 없기 때문에 남자의 제안을 거절하려는 의도로 한 말임을 알 수 있다. 따라서 정답은 (C)이다.

46 What does the woman offer to show the man?
(A) A schedule
(B) A photograph
(C) A map
(D) A menu

여자는 남자에게 무엇을 보여 주겠다고 제안하는가?
(A) 일정표
(B) 사진
(C) 지도
(D) 메뉴

해설 세부 사항 관련 – 여자의 제안 사항
여자가 마지막 대사에서 남자에게 메뉴를 보겠며 자신의 사무실에 한 부 있다(Would you like to see the menu? I have a copy in my office)고 말하고 있으므로 정답은 (D)이다.

47-49 M-Au / W-Am

M **47Thanks for agreeing to be interviewed for *Textiles Quarterly*** about your company's recycling process. Our readers will be intrigued.

W Simply put, we shred discarded fabric, turn it into a watery mixture called slurry, and then dry it and press it into new sheets of fabric. That fabric is then available to create new products. **48Reducing unnecessary waste is our goal.**

M It sounds like a great way to use leftover materials.

W Unfortunately, our facility is currently able to process only cotton waste. But in the next few years, we should be able to recycle more types of textiles here. **49It's my hope that it could eventually become as common as recycling aluminum is now.**

남 귀사의 재활용 공정에 대한 〈텍스타일 쿼털리〉와의 인터뷰에 응해 주셔서 감사합니다. 저희 독자들이 흥미로워할 거예요.
여 간단히 말하자면, 저희는 폐기된 천을 분쇄해 슬러리라고 부르는 액체 혼합물로 바꾼 다음, 건조하고 압축해 여러 장의 새 천으로 만듭니다. 그 천은 이후 새로운 제품을 만드는 데 사용될 수 있어요. 불필요한 폐기물을 감소시키는 것이 저희의 목표입니다.
남 남은 재료를 활용하는 아주 좋은 방법인 것 같네요.
여 아쉽게도, 저희 시설은 현재 면 폐기물만 처리할 수 있습니다. 하지만 앞으로 몇 년 이내에 이곳에서 더 많은 종류의 섬유를 재활용할 수 있게 될 거예요. 제 바람은 이것이 언젠가는 지금 알루미늄을 재활용하는 것만큼 보편화되는 겁니다.

어휘 recycling 재활용 process 공정, 과정; 처리하다, 가공하다
intrigued 아주 흥미로워 하는 shred 분쇄하다, 찢다
discarded 폐기된 fabric 천, 직물 watery 물의, 물 같은
mixture 혼합물 slurry 슬러리(걸쭉한 물질) reduce 감소시키다
unnecessary 불필요한 leftover 남은, 나머지의 facility 시설
currently 현재 textile 섬유, 직물 eventually 언젠가는, 결국

47 Who most likely is the man?
(A) A salesperson
(B) A journalist
(C) A company intern
(D) A safety inspector

남자는 누구인 것 같은가?
(A) 영업사원
(B) 기자
(C) 회사 인턴
(D) 안전 감독관

해설 전체 내용 관련 – 남자의 직업
남자가 첫 대사에서 여자에게 〈텍스타일 쿼털리〉와의 인터뷰에 응해 주어 감사하다(Thanks for agreeing to be interviewed for *Textiles Quarterly* ~)고 말하는 것으로 보아 남자는 이 잡지의 기자임을 알 수 있다. 따라서 정답은 (B)이다.

48 What does the woman say her company's goal is?
(A) To decrease material waste
(B) To open additional facilities
(C) To improve employee morale
(D) To acquire international contracts

여자는 무엇이 자신의 회사의 목표라고 말하는가?
(A) 폐기물 줄이기
(B) 추가 시설 열기
(C) 직원 사기 높이기
(D) 해외 계약 따내기

어휘 decrease 줄이다, 감소시키다 improve 개선하다, 향상시키다
morale 사기, 의욕 acquire 얻다, 획득하다 contract 계약

해설 세부 사항 관련 – 여자의 회사의 목표

여자가 첫 대사에서 불필요한 폐기물을 감소시키는 것이 우리의 목표(Reducing unnecessary waste is our goal)라고 했으므로 정답은 (A)이다.

Paraphrasing
대화의 Reducing unnecessary waste
→ 정답의 decrease material waste

49 What does the woman hope will happen?
(A) Some funding will become available.
(B) A fashion line will be popular.
(C) A process will be widely adopted.
(D) Export fees will be reduced.

여자는 무슨 일이 있기를 바라는가?
(A) 일부 자금이 이용 가능하게 될 것이다.
(B) 패션 제품 라인이 인기를 얻을 것이다.
(C) 공정이 널리 채택될 것이다.
(D) 수출 수수료가 인하될 것이다.

어휘 funding 자금 widely 널리, 폭넓게 adopt 채택하다 export 수출

해설 세부 사항 관련 – 여자가 바라는 일

여자가 마지막 대사에서 자신의 바람은 이것이 언젠가는 지금 알루미늄을 재활용하는 것만큼 보편화되는 것(It's my hope that it could eventually become as common as recycling aluminum is now)이라고 말하고 있고, 이것은 앞서 논의한 천 폐기물 재활용 공정을 가리키는 것이므로 정답은 (C)이다.

Paraphrasing
대화의 become as common as
→ 정답의 be widely adopted

50-52 M-Au / W-Br ▶동영상 강의

M Well, I think we've found the right person for the job. Sergey has a confident presence when speaking with reporters, and he knows the travel industry well. ⁵⁰**He'll be a great spokesperson for our airline.**

W I liked the media clips he shared with us. He speaks clearly and naturally. However, ⁵¹**he also does some consulting as an extra source of income. Will he be available whenever we need him?**

M You bring up a good point. ⁵²**We should call him about that.**

W Well, ⁵²**we have his final interview scheduled for tomorrow. Let's wait until then.**

남 저, 우리가 그 일에 적합한 사람을 찾은 것 같아요. 세르게이가 기자들과 이야기할 때 자신감 있는 태도를 보이고, 여행 산업에 대해서도 잘 알고 있어요. **우리 항공사의 훌륭한 대변인이 될 겁니다.**

여 그가 우리에게 공유해 준 방송 영상들이 마음에 들었어요. 명확하고 자연스럽게 말하더라고요. 그런데 **그는 부수입원으로 자문도 하고 있잖아요. 우리가 필요할 때마다 시간이 될까요?**

남 좋은 지적이네요. **그 부분에 대해서 전화해 봐야겠어요.**

여 음, **그의 최종 면접이 내일로 예정되어 있어요. 그때까지 기다려 봅시다.**

어휘 confident 자신 있는, 확신하는 presence 태도, 존재감 spokesperson 대변인 clip 동영상 consulting 자문, 상담 source 원천, 공급원 income 수입, 소득 bring up 제기하다

50 Which department are the speakers most likely hiring for?
(A) Product Development
(B) Technical Support
(C) Public Relations
(D) Graphic Design

화자들은 어느 부서를 위해 채용 중인 것 같은가?
(A) 제품 개발
(B) 기술 지원
(C) 홍보
(D) 그래픽 디자인

해설 세부 사항 관련 – 화자들이 채용 중인 부서

남자가 첫 대사에서 세르게이의 장점을 언급하면서 우리 항공사의 훌륭한 대변인이 될 것(He'll be a great spokesperson for our airline)이라고 말하고 있다. 대변인은 회사의 홍보와 관련된 업무를 하는 사람이므로 정답은 (C)이다.

51 Why is the woman unsure about a candidate?
(A) He lives too far from headquarters.
(B) He might have limited availability.
(C) He cannot provide any references.
(D) He does not have relevant experience.

여자는 왜 지원자에 대해 확신하지 못하는가?
(A) 본사에서 너무 먼 곳에 살고 있다.
(B) 가능한 시간이 제한적일지도 모른다.
(C) 추천서를 전혀 제출할 수 없다.
(D) 관련 경력을 가지고 있지 않다.

어휘 candidate 지원자, 후보자 headquarters 본사 limited 제한적인, 한정된 availability 이용 가능성 reference 추천서 relevant 관련된

해설 세부 사항 관련 – 여자가 확신하지 못하는 이유

여자가 첫 대사에서 세르게이가 부수입원으로 자문도 하고 있다(~ he also does some consulting ~)며 자신들이 필요할 때마다 시간이 될지(Will he be available whenever we need him?) 의구심을 표하고 있으므로 정답은 (B)이다.

52 What does the woman suggest doing?
(A) Scheduling a press conference
(B) Canceling a training session
(C) Making a lunch reservation
(D) Postponing a phone call

여자는 무엇을 하자고 제안하는가?
(A) 기자 회견 일정 잡기
(B) 교육 취소하기
(C) 점심 식사 예약하기
(D) 전화 통화 미루기

어휘 press conference 기자 회견 reservation 예약
postpone 미루다, 연기하다

해설 세부 사항 관련 – 여자의 제안 사항
남자가 두 번째 대사에서 그 부분에 대해 세르게이에게 전화해 봐야겠다(We should call him about that)고 하자 여자가 최종 면접이 내일로 예정되어 있으니(we have his final interview scheduled for tomorrow) 그때까지 기다려 보자(Let's wait until then)고 했으므로 정답은 (D)이다.

Paraphrasing
대화의 Let's wait until then → 정답의 Postponing

53-55 W-Br / M-Au

W Good morning, Mr. Murray. ⁵³**I'm here to help you start planning the opening of your newest art gallery.**

M Great! As you know, this will be our third location. So ⁵⁴**I think I might like to try a different kind of approach this time.**

W I understand. **I have many options for you to consider.**

M ⁵⁴**Glad to hear it.**

W ⁵⁵**Let me grab the catering menu and the book of flower selections from my van.** It's parked just outside.

여 안녕하세요, 머레이 씨. **새 미술관 개관식 준비를 시작하시는 것을 도와드리러 왔습니다.**
남 잘됐네요! 아시겠지만, 이곳이 저희 세 번째 지점이 될 겁니다. 그래서 **이번에는 좀 색다른 방식을 시도해 보는 것도 좋을 것 같아요.**
여 알겠습니다. **고려하실 수 있는 옵션이 많이 있습니다.**
남 그 말씀을 들으니 기쁘네요.
여 제 밴에서 출장 요리 메뉴와 꽃 카탈로그를 가져올게요. 바로 밖에 주차되어 있어요.

어휘 approach 방식, 접근법 grab 잡다, 움켜쥐다
catering 출장 요리 selection 모음, 선택할 수 있는 것

---

53 What is the conversation mainly about?
(A) A holiday gathering
(B) A community festival
(C) An art gallery opening
(D) A fashion design show

대화는 주로 무엇에 대한 것인가?
(A) 휴일 모임
(B) 지역 축제
(C) 미술관 개관식
(D) 패션 디자인 쇼

해설 전체 내용 관련 – 대화의 주제
여자가 첫 대사에서 남자의 새 미술관 개관식 준비를 시작하는 것을 도와주러 왔다(I'm here to help you start planning the opening of your newest art gallery)고 말한 뒤, 준비 사항에 대한 대화를 이어 가고 있으므로 정답은 (C)이다.

---

54 Why does the woman say, "I have many options for you to consider"?
(A) To recommend budgeting carefully
(B) To offer reassurance
(C) To praise the work her team did
(D) To question a decision

여자는 왜 "고려하실 수 있는 옵션이 많이 있습니다"라고 말하는가?
(A) 예산을 신중히 세울 것을 권하기 위해
(B) 안심시키기 위해
(C) 자신의 팀이 한 일을 칭찬하기 위해
(D) 결정에 이의를 제기하기 위해

어휘 budget 예산을 세우다 reassurance 안심시키기

해설 화자의 의도 파악 – 고려할 수 있는 옵션이 많이 있다는 말의 의도
남자가 첫 대사에서 이번에는 좀 색다른 방식을 시도해 보는 것도 좋을 것 같다(I think I might like to try a different kind of approach this time)고 하자 여자가 인용문을 언급했고, 다시 남자가 그 말을 들으니 기쁘다(Glad to hear it)고 반응하고 있다. 따라서 남자가 여자의 말을 듣고 안심하고 있다는 것을 알 수 있으므로 정답은 (B)이다.

---

55 What will the woman do next?
(A) Contact a colleague
(B) Drive to a bank
(C) Retrieve items from a vehicle
(D) Take the man to an event venue

여자는 다음에 무엇을 할 것인가?
(A) 동료에게 연락하기
(B) 은행에 운전해서 가기
(C) 차에서 물건 가져오기
(D) 남자를 행사 장소로 데려가기

어휘 retrieve 가져오다, 되찾아오다 vehicle 차량 venue 행사 장소

해설　세부 사항 관련 – 여자가 다음에 할 일

여자가 마지막 대사에서 자신의 밴에서 출장 요리 메뉴와 꽃 카탈로그를 가져오겠다(Let me grab the catering menu and the book of flower selections from my van)고 말하고 있으므로 정답은 (C)이다.

Paraphrasing
대화의 grab the catering menu and the book of flower selections from my van
→ 정답의 Retrieve items from a vehicle

56-58 M-Cn / W-Br

M Thanks for joining my podcast, Bianca. I'm enjoying your unique cookbook, **56 which takes traditional dishes from around the world and adds unusual ingredients**—which gives them a contemporary flair. What's your inspiration?

W Well, **57 after finishing university, I was looking for a way to combine my knowledge of history that I learned there with cooking**. So I decided to attend culinary school.

M **58 I also noticed that you provide the recipes in a variety of other languages. That's a nice touch that many readers will appreciate.** Is it based on where the dish originated?

남 제 팟캐스트에 함께해 주셔서 감사합니다, 비앙카. 당신의 독특한 요리책을 즐겁게 보고 있어요. **전 세계의 전통 요리들을 다루면서 흔치 않은 재료들을 추가하시더라고요.** 그게 요리들에 현대적인 감각을 더해주고요. 무엇에서 영감을 얻으시나요?

여 음, **대학을 마친 후에, 그곳에서 배운 역사 지식을 요리와 결합할 방법을 찾고 있었어요.** 그래서 요리 학교에 다니기로 결정했죠.

남 **또한 레시피를 여러 다른 언어로 제공하시는 점도 눈에 띄었습니다. 그건 많은 독자들이 감사하게 여길 세심한 배려거든요.** 요리가 유래한 지역을 기준으로 한 건가요?

어휘　traditional 전통적인　unusual 흔치 않은, 드문　ingredient 재료　contemporary 현대적인　flair 감각, 솜씨　inspiration 영감　combine 결합하다　culinary 요리의　notice 발견하다, 알아채다　recipe 조리법　originate 유래하다

56 What is unique about the woman's cookbook recipes?
(A) They are inspired by the woman's university friends.
(B) They are intended for large holiday celebrations.
(C) They are collected from places the woman has traveled to.
(D) They add unusual ingredients to traditional dishes.

여자의 요리책 레시피에서 독특한 점은 무엇인가?
(A) 그녀의 대학 친구들을 통해 영감을 얻었다.
(B) 대규모 명절 행사를 위한 것이다.
(C) 여자가 여행했던 장소에서 수집되었다.
(D) 전통적인 요리에 흔치 않은 재료를 추가한다.

어휘　inspire 영감을 주다　intend 의도하다　celebration 기념 행사, 축하 행사　collect 수집하다, 모으다

해설　세부 사항 관련 – 여자의 요리책 레시피에서 독특한 점

남자가 첫 대사에서 여자의 요리책을 언급하면서 전 세계의 전통 요리들을 다루면서 흔치 않은 재료들을 추가한다(~ which takes traditional dishes from around the world and adds unusual ingredients)는 특징을 덧붙이고 있으므로 정답은 (D)이다.

57 What did the woman most likely study at university?
(A) Accounting
(B) Biology
(C) History
(D) Computer science

여자는 대학에서 무엇을 공부했을 것 같은가?
(A) 회계학
(B) 생물학
(C) 역사학
(D) 컴퓨터 공학

해설　세부 사항 관련 – 여자가 대학에서 공부한 것

여자가 첫 대사에서 대학을 마친 후에 그곳에서 배운 역사 지식을 요리와 결합할 방법을 찾고 있었다(~ after finishing university, I was looking for a way to combine my knowledge of history that I learned there with cooking)고 했으므로 정답은 (C)이다.

58 According to the man, what will some of the readers appreciate about the recipes?
(A) They appear in multiple languages.
(B) They explain how to measure ingredients.
(C) They list alternative cooking methods.
(D) They include color photographs.

남자에 따르면, 독자들은 레시피에 대해 무엇을 감사하게 여길 것인가?
(A) 다양한 언어로 제공된다.
(B) 재료를 계량하는 방법을 설명한다.
(C) 대체 요리 방법을 나열한다.
(D) 컬러 사진을 포함하고 있다.

어휘　multiple 다양한, 다수의　measure 계량하다, 재다　list 나열하다　alternative 대체의, 대안의　method 방법, 방식

해설 **세부 사항 관련 – 독자들이 레시피에 대해 감사하게 여길 점**
남자가 마지막 대사에서 레시피를 여러 다른 언어로 제공하는 점도 눈에 띄었다(I also noticed that you provide the recipes in a variety of other languages)며 그것이 많은 독자들이 감사하게 여길 세심한 배려(That's a nice touch that many readers will appreciate)라고 했으므로 정답은 (A)이다.

Paraphrasing
대화의 provide the recipes in a variety of other languages
→ 정답의 appear in multiple languages

59-61 3인 대화 W-Am / M-Au / M-Cn

W Hi, Ji-Soo and Alberto. ⁵⁹**Are you planning on attending the pharmaceutical conference next month?** I think it'll be a great opportunity for us to learn from and network with other industry professionals.

M1 Yes, we're going. In fact, ⁶⁰**Alberto and I will be leading a roundtable discussion on sustainable health care.**

W That's fantastic. When is it?

M1 I can't remember the time. Alberto, do you have the schedule?

M2 Yes, I actually just downloaded the conference's app. It should be listed there. Let's see. It looks like it's on Thursday at four.

W Great! ⁶¹**I'll download the app now and sign up.**

여 안녕하세요, 지수 그리고 알베르토. **다음 달에 있을 제약 콘퍼런스에 참석할 계획이신가요?** 우리가 다른 업계 전문가들로부터 배우고 그들과 교류도 할 수 있는 아주 좋은 기회가 될 거라고 생각해요.
남1 네, 갑니다. 실은, **알베르토와 제가 지속 가능한 의료 서비스에 관한 원탁 토론을 진행할 예정이에요.**
여 굉장하네요. 그게 언제인가요?
남1 시간은 기억이 나지 않네요. 알베르토, 일정표를 가지고 있나요?
남2 네, 사실 이 콘퍼런스의 앱을 방금 다운로드했어요. 거기에 나와 있을 거예요. 어디 보자. 목요일 4시에 있는 것 같네요.
여 좋네요! **저도 지금 그 앱을 다운로드하고 등록할게요.**

어휘 pharmaceutical 제약의, 약학의 network 교류하다 professional 전문가; 전문가의 sustainable 지속 가능한 sign up 신청하다, 등록하다

59 Which industry do the speakers work in?
  (A) Pharmaceuticals
  (B) Technology
  (C) Construction
  (D) Agriculture

화자들은 어느 업계에서 일하는가?
  (A) 제약
  (B) 기술
  (C) 건설
  (D) 농업

해설 **전체 내용 관련 – 화자들의 근무 업계**
여자가 첫 대사에서 남자들에게 다음 달에 있을 제약 콘퍼런스에 참석할 계획인지(Are you planning on attending the pharmaceutical conference next month?) 묻는 것으로 보아 화자들은 제약 업계 종사자임을 알 수 있다. 따라서 정답은 (A)이다.

60 What will the men be doing?
  (A) Planning a hiring process
  (B) Leading a discussion
  (C) Conducting a tour
  (D) Inspecting a renovation project

남자들은 무엇을 할 예정인가?
  (A) 채용 프로세스 기획
  (B) 토론회 진행
  (C) 견학 인솔
  (D) 보수 프로젝트 점검

어휘 hiring 채용 conduct 실시하다, 수행하다 inspect 점검하다

해설 **세부 사항 관련 – 남자들이 할 일**
첫 번째 남자가 첫 대사에서 알베르토와 자신이 지속 가능한 의료 서비스에 관한 원탁 토론을 진행할 예정(Alberto and I will be leading a roundtable discussion on sustainable health care)이라고 했으므로 정답은 (B)이다.

61 What will the woman most likely do next?
  (A) Write a review
  (B) Download a mobile application
  (C) Consult a manager
  (D) Print some documents

여자는 다음에 무엇을 할 것 같은가?
  (A) 후기 작성하기
  (B) 모바일 애플리케이션 다운로드하기
  (C) 관리자와 상담하기
  (D) 문서 출력하기

해설 **세부 사항 관련 – 여자가 다음에 할 일**
여자가 마지막 대사에서 지금 앱을 다운로드하고 등록하겠다(I'll download the app now and sign up)고 했으므로 정답은 (B)이다.

62-64 대화 + 일정표 W-Br / M-Cn

W Our water park will be reopening for the summer season soon, and **62 we're looking for ways to increase park attendance. This has been an ongoing problem.**

M I agree. It's mainly weekdays that have poor attendance. So I've come up with a plan with special offers on those days. What do you think?

W It's good. I like the free parking. In fact, I think we should offer it on another day too. **63 How about we replace the free arcade tickets with another day of free parking?**

M Sure. **64 But first I'm going to talk to the maintenance staff and make sure the repairs to the overflow parking area are done** before customers start arriving.

여 우리 워터 파크가 곧 여름 시즌을 맞아 재개장할 예정인데, **입장률을 높일 방법을 찾고 있어요. 이건 계속되어 온 문제예요.**

남 동의해요. 입장률이 저조한 건 주로 평일이에요. 그래서 이 요일들에 특별 혜택을 제공하는 계획을 생각해 봤습니다. 어떻게 생각하세요?

여 이거 좋네요. 저는 무료 주차가 마음에 들어요. 사실, 우리가 무료 주차를 다른 날에도 제공하면 좋겠어요. **오락실 무료 이용권을 또 다른 무료 주차의 날로 바꾸는 건 어때요?**

남 네. 하지만 손님들이 오기 시작하기 전에, **제가 먼저 시설 관리 직원들과 이야기해서 임시 주차장 수리 작업이 완료된 상태인지 확인할게요.**

어휘 attendance 입장률, 참석률 ongoing 지속되는, 진행 중인 come up with ~을 생각해 내다 replace 바꾸다, 대신하다 arcade 오락실, 게임장 maintenance 시설 관리, 정비 overflow parking area 임시 주차장 admission 입장(료)

Waterville Water Park Special Offers	
Day	Offer
Monday	Free parking
Tuesday	Discounted menu items
Wednesday	Discounted admission
63 Thursday	**Free arcade tickets**

워터빌 워터 파크 특별 혜택	
요일	제공 서비스
월요일	무료 주차
화요일	메뉴 품목 할인
수요일	입장료 할인
목요일	**오락실 무료 이용권**

---

62 What problem does the woman mention?
(A) Low attendance
(B) High maintenance costs
(C) Few trained staff
(D) Poor customer service

여자는 어떤 문제를 언급하는가?
(A) 저조한 입장률
(B) 높은 시설 관리 비용
(C) 훈련된 직원의 부족
(D) 열악한 고객 서비스

해설 전체 내용 관련 – 여자가 언급하는 문제점

여자가 첫 대사에서 워터 파크 입장률을 높일 방법을 찾고 있다는 말과 함께 그것이 계속되어 온 문제(~ we're looking for ways to increase park attendance. This has been an ongoing problem)라고 언급하고 있으므로 정답은 (A)이다.

63 Look at the graphic. Which day does the woman want to change the special offer for?
(A) Monday
(B) Tuesday
(C) Wednesday
(D) Thursday

시각 정보에 의하면, 여자는 어느 요일의 특별 혜택을 변경하고 싶어 하는가?
(A) 월요일
(B) 화요일
(C) 수요일
(D) 목요일

해설 시각 정보 연계 – 여자가 특별 혜택을 변경하려는 요일

여자가 두 번째 대사에서 오락실 무료 이용권을 무료 주차의 날로 바꾸는 것(How about we replace the free arcade tickets with another day of free parking?)을 제안했고, 일정표에서 오락실 무료 이용권은 목요일이므로 정답은 (D)이다.

64 What does the man say he wants to confirm?
(A) Some posters have been distributed.
(B) A schedule has been printed.
(C) Some repairs have been completed.
(D) A park map has been updated.

남자는 무엇을 확인하고 싶다고 말하는가?
(A) 포스터가 배부되었다.
(B) 일정표가 인쇄되었다.
(C) 수리 작업이 완료되었다.
(D) 공원 안내도가 업데이트되었다.

해설 세부 사항 관련 – 남자가 확인하고 싶어 하는 것

남자가 마지막 대사에서 시설 관리 직원들과 이야기해서 임시 주차장 수리 작업이 완료된 상태인지 확인하겠다(~ I'm going to talk to the maintenance staff and make sure the repairs to the overflow parking area are done ~)고 했으므로 정답은 (C)이다.

Paraphrasing
대화의 the repairs to the overflow parking area are done
→ 정답의 Some repairs have been completed

65-67 대화 + 매장 진열 상품 W-Am / M-Cn ▶동영상 강의

W I can't find this shirt in my size. Do you have any more in a size small?

M ⁶⁵**The exhibit of Narumi Azuma's drawings** is very popular. The gift shop has sold out of a lot of the merchandise. ⁶⁶**Do you want me to see if the display shirt is a small?**

W Sure. That print is one of my favorites.

M You're in luck. ⁶⁶**It's a small. I'll ring it up for you.** ⁶⁷**Are you a museum member?**

W No, I'm not.

M ⁶⁷**You might consider becoming one.** Members get a ten percent discount at the gift shop.

여 이 셔츠의 제 사이즈를 찾을 수가 없네요. 스몰 사이즈로 더 있나요?

남 **나루미 아주마의 드로잉 전시회**가 아주 인기가 많아요. 저희 기념품 매장에서 많은 상품들이 매진되었어요. **진열된 셔츠가 스몰인지 확인해 드릴까요?**

여 네, 저 프린트가 제가 가장 좋아하는 것 중 하나거든요.

남 운이 좋으시네요. **스몰입니다. 계산해 드릴게요.** 박물관 회원이신가요?

여 아니요, 아닙니다.

남 **회원이 되는 걸 고려해 보시는 것도 좋겠어요.** 회원은 기념품 매장에서 10퍼센트 할인을 받거든요.

어휘 exhibit 전시회 sell out of ~을 다 팔아버리다, 매진되다 merchandise 상품 display 진열(품) in luck 운이 좋은 ring up 계산하다

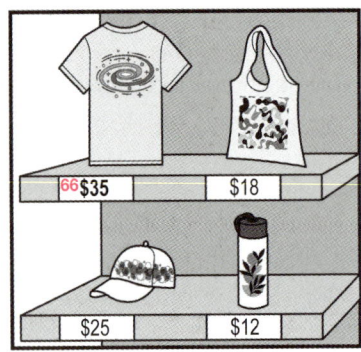

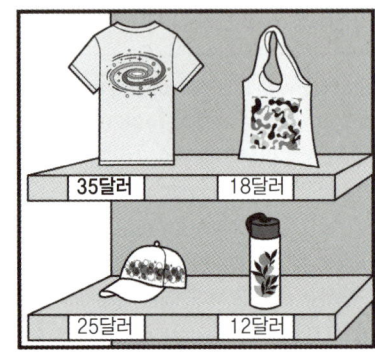

65 Where most likely is the gift shop?
(A) At an airport
(B) At a sports stadium
(C) At a museum
(D) At a concert hall

기념품 매장은 어디에 있는 것 같은가?
(A) 공항
(B) 스포츠 경기장
(C) 미술관
(D) 콘서트홀

해설 세부 사항 관련 – 기념품 매장의 위치

남자가 첫 번째 대사에서 나루미 아주마의 드로잉 전시회(The exhibit of Narumi Azuma's drawing ~)에 대해 언급하고 있는 것으로 보아 기념품 매장이 미술관에 있음을 알 수 있다. 따라서 정답은 (C)이다.

66 Look at the graphic. How much will the woman pay for an item?
(A) $35
(B) $18
(C) $25
(D) $12

시각 정보에 의하면, 여자는 제품에 대해 얼마를 지불할 것인가?
(A) 35달러
(B) 18달러
(C) 25달러
(D) 12달러

해설 시각 정보 연계 – 여자가 지불할 비용

남자가 첫 대사에서 진열된 셔츠가 스몰인지 확인해 주기를 원하는지(Do you want me to see if the display shirt is a small?) 물은 뒤, 두 번째 대사에서는 스몰이 맞다며 그 제품을 계산해 주겠다(It's a small. I'll ring it up for you)고 말하고 있다. 매장 진열 상품에서 티셔츠의 가격은 35달러로 표기되어 있으므로 정답은 (A)이다.

67 What does the man suggest doing?
(A) Visiting a Web site
(B) Registering for a class
(C) Printing some tickets
(D) Becoming a member

남자는 무엇을 하도록 제안하는가?
(A) 웹사이트 방문
(B) 강좌 등록
(C) 티켓 출력
(D) 회원 가입

해설 세부 사항 관련 – 남자의 제안 사항

남자가 두 번째 대사에서 미술관 회원인지(Are you a museum member?) 물은 뒤, 세 번째 대사에서 회원이 되는 걸 고려해 보는 것도 좋겠다(You might consider becoming one)고 제안하고 있으므로 정답은 (D)이다.

68-70 대화 + 조경도 W-Am / M-Cn

W Hi. I'm interested in installing a new fence on my property.

M You called the right place. What type of fence are you looking for?

W **68 Something sturdy to put around the garden** to keep animals from eating the vegetables.

M OK. A mesh fence might work well for you. In fact, right now, we have a promotion on fences. **69 If you pay half the cost in advance, you'll get twenty percent off the price.**

W Sounds great. Can you give me a cost estimate?

M **70 Not until I take measurements. I can do that on Saturday**, if you're available.

여 안녕하세요. 제 땅에 새 울타리를 설치하고 싶은데요.
남 제대로 전화하셨습니다. 어떤 종류의 울타리를 찾고 계신가요?
여 동물들이 채소를 먹지 못하게 **정원을 둘러쌀 튼튼한 것이요.**
남 알겠습니다. 철망 울타리가 잘 맞을 것 같네요. 실은 지금 저희가 울타리에 대한 특별 할인 행사를 하고 있어요. **비용의 절반을 미리 지불하시면, 전체 가격에서 20퍼센트를 할인받으실 수 있습니다.**
여 좋네요. 견적서를 주실 수 있나요?
남 **제가 측정을 먼저 해야 합니다.** 괜찮으시다면, **토요일에 해 드릴 수 있어요.**

어휘 install 설치하다 property 땅, 건물 sturdy 튼튼한, 견고한 mesh 철망 promotion 특별 할인 행사, 판촉 in advance 미리 take measurements 측정하다

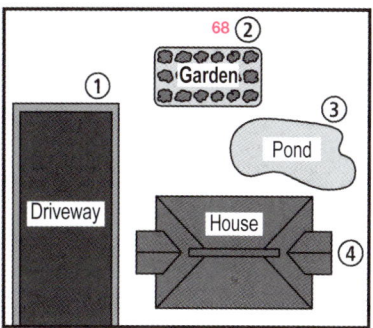

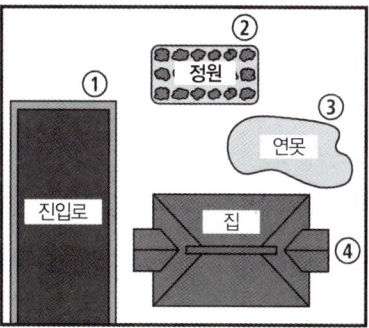

68 Look at the graphic. Where does the woman want to install a fence?
(A) In location 1
(B) In location 2
(C) In location 3
(D) In location 4

시각 정보에 의하면, 여자는 어디에 울타리를 설치하고 싶어 하는가?
(A) 1번 위치
(B) 2번 위치
(C) 3번 위치
(D) 4번 위치

해설 시각 정보 연계 – 여자가 울타리를 설치하려는 곳

여자가 두 번째 대사에서 정원을 둘러쌀 튼튼한 것(Something sturdy to put around the garden ~)을 찾고 있다고 했고, 조경도에서 정원은 2번 위치이므로 정답은 (B)이다.

69 How can the woman receive a discount?
(A) By posting a review on social media
(B) By paying half the cost in advance
(C) By enrolling in a loyalty program
(D) By referring a friend

여자는 어떻게 할인을 받을 수 있는가?
(A) 소셜 미디어에 후기를 게시해서
(B) 미리 비용의 절반을 지불해서
(C) 고객 보상 프로그램에 등록해서
(D) 친구를 소개해서

어휘 enroll in ~에 등록하다 refer 소개하다, 추천하다

해설 | 세부 사항 관련 – 여자가 할인을 받는 방법
남자가 두 번째 대사에서 비용의 절반을 미리 지불하면 전체 가격에서 20퍼센트를 할인받을 수 있다(If you pay half the cost in advance, you'll get twenty percent off the price)고 했으므로 정답은 (B)이다.

70 Why will the man visit the property on Saturday?
(A) To obtain a signature
(B) To deliver some materials
(C) To take some photographs
(D) To take some measurements

남자는 왜 토요일에 땅을 방문할 것인가?
(A) 서명을 받기 위해
(B) 자재를 전달하기 위해
(C) 사진을 촬영하기 위해
(D) 측정을 하기 위해

어휘 | obtain 얻다, 획득하다 signature 서명

해설 | 세부 사항 관련 – 남자가 토요일에 방문하는 목적
남자가 마지막 대사에서 측정을 먼저 해야 한다면서 토요일에 할 수 있다(Not until I take measurements. I can do that on Saturday ~)고 했으므로 정답은 (D)이다.

PART 4

71-73 여행 정보

W-Br Welcome aboard Sunshine Cruises. On today's tour, **71 you'll have the opportunity to see several of the city's most famous buildings directly from the Camille River.** Our route along the river provides a great view of the architecture. And **72 we also have a professional photographer on board the boat who is available to take your picture for a small fee.** OK, it's time for us to get going. **73 Please take your seats for departure.**

선샤인 크루즈에 탑승하신 것을 환영합니다. 오늘 투어에서는, 도시의 가장 유명한 건물 몇 곳을 카밀 강 위에서 직접 바라보는 기회를 갖게 되실 것입니다. 강을 따라 이어지는 우리의 경로는 그 건축물들의 훌륭한 전경을 제공합니다. 또한 약간의 비용으로 사진을 찍어 드릴 전문 사진작가 한 분도 보트에 승선해 계십니다. 좋아요, 이제 출발할 시간이네요. 출발을 위해 모두 착석해 주시기 바랍니다.

어휘 | aboard 승선한, 탑승한 route 경로, 노선 view 경관, 전망 architecture 건축 양식, 건축학 on board 승선한, 탑승한 fee 요금, 수수료 departure 출발, 떠남

71 What is the focus of the tour?
(A) Rock formations
(B) Wildlife species
(C) Bridges
(D) Buildings

투어의 초점은 무엇인가?
(A) 암석 지형
(B) 야생 동물 종
(C) 다리
(D) 건물

해설 | 전체 내용 관련 – 투어의 초점
화자가 초반부에 도시의 가장 유명한 건물 몇 곳을 카밀 강 위에서 직접 바라보는 기회를 갖게 된다(~ you'll have the opportunity to see several of the city's most famous buildings directly from the Camille River)고 했으므로 정답은 (D)이다.

72 What does the speaker say is available on board the boat?
(A) Personalized merchandise
(B) Professional photography
(C) Meals made to order
(D) Recorded audio guides

화자는 보트에서 무엇을 이용할 수 있다고 말하는가?
(A) 개인 맞춤형 상품
(B) 전문적인 사진 촬영
(C) 주문 즉시 조리되는 식사
(D) 녹음된 오디오 가이드

어휘 | personalized 개인 맞춤형의 photography 사진 촬영(술) made to order 주문 즉시 제작된

해설 | 세부 사항 관련 – 보트에서 이용 가능한 것
화자가 중반부에 약간의 비용으로 사진을 찍어 줄 전문 사진작가도 보트에 승선해 있다(~ we also have a professional photographer on board the boat who is available to take your picture for a small fee)고 했으므로 정답은 (B)이다.

Paraphrasing
담화의 professional photographer ~ to take your picture
→ 정답의 Professional photography

73 What will the listeners most likely do next?
(A) Go to their seats
(B) Present their tickets
(C) Put on their name tags
(D) Store their belongings

청자들은 다음에 무엇을 할 것 같은가?
(A) 좌석으로 이동하기
(B) 티켓 제시하기
(C) 명찰 착용하기
(D) 소지품 보관하기

| 어휘 | present 제시하다, 제출하다 store 보관하다, 저장하다
belongings 소지품 |
|---|---|
| 해설 | 세부 사항 관련 – 청자들이 다음에 할 일
화자가 후반부에 출발을 위해 모두 착석해 달라(Please take your seats for departure)고 요청하고 있으므로 정답은 (A)이다. |

Paraphrasing
담화의 take your seats → 정답의 Go to their seats

74-76 공지

> **M-Cn** Attention, customers of George's Grocery. **74 We are pleased to share the launch of our shopper's rewards program** and want you to be a part of it! This new program offers all members exclusive perks like personalized coupons and special discounts. Signing up is easy and can be done right at the register when you check out. **75 Just present your driver's license or other identification** and you'll be given a membership card. Also, **76 don't forget that we will be closed tomorrow in honor of the national holiday.**

조지스 그로서리 고객 여러분께 알립니다. **저희 쇼핑객 보상 프로그램의 시작을 알리게 되어 기쁘게 생각하며**, 여러분의 참여를 기다립니다! 이 새로운 프로그램은 모든 회원들께 개인 맞춤형 쿠폰과 특별 할인 등의 전용 혜택을 제공합니다. 가입은 간단하며, 계산하실 때 계산대에서 바로 신청하실 수 있습니다. **운전면허증이나 기타 신분증을 제시해 주시면**, 회원 카드를 발급해 드리겠습니다. 아울러, **내일은 국경일을 맞아 휴점하오니 이 점 유의해 주시기 바랍니다.**

| 어휘 | launch 개시, 출시 reward 보상 exclusive 독점적인
perk (특별) 혜택 register 계산대 check out 계산하다
identification 신분증 in honor of ~을 기념해, ~을 기리기 위해 |
|---|---|

74 According to the speaker, what is the business launching?
(A) A rewards program
(B) A recycling program
(C) A new logo
(D) A delivery service

화자에 따르면, 업체가 시작하는 것은 무엇인가?
(A) 보상 프로그램
(B) 재활용 프로그램
(C) 새로운 로고
(D) 배달 서비스

| 해설 | 전체 내용 관련 – 업체가 시작하는 것
화자가 초반부에 쇼핑객 보상 프로그램의 시작을 알리게 되어 기쁘게 생각한다(We are pleased to share the launch of our shopper's rewards program ~)고 말한 뒤 이 프로그램의 특징 및 가입 방법 등에 대한 이야기를 이어 가고 있으므로 정답은 (A)이다. |
|---|---|

75 What should the listeners be prepared to show?
(A) A coupon
(B) A receipt
(C) A piece of identification
(D) A signed enrollment form

청자들은 무엇을 보여 줄 준비가 되어 있어야 하는가?
(A) 쿠폰
(B) 영수증
(C) 신분증
(D) 서명한 등록 양식

어휘	enrollment 등록 form 양식, 서식
해설	세부 사항 관련 – 청자들이 준비해야 하는 것
화자가 중반부에 운전면허증이나 기타 신분증을 제시해 달라(Just present your driver's license or other identification ~)고 말하고 있으므로 정답은 (C)이다.

Paraphrasing
담화의 present → 질문의 show

76 Why will the business be closed tomorrow?
(A) For some floor repairs
(B) For a national holiday
(C) For a training exercise
(D) For an equipment installation

업체는 왜 내일 문을 닫을 것인가?
(A) 바닥 수리 작업 때문에
(B) 국경일이기 때문에
(C) 훈련 연습 때문에
(D) 장비 설치 작업 때문에

어휘	repair 수리 exercise 연습, 운동 installation 설치
해설	세부 사항 관련 – 업체가 내일 문을 닫는 이유
화자가 후반부에 내일은 국경일을 맞아 휴점하니 이 점 유의해 달라(~ don't forget that we will be closed tomorrow in honor of the national holiday)고 당부하고 있으므로 정답은 (B)이다.

77-79 뉴스 보도

W-Am This just in on News Channel Six: **77 there is a traffic delay on Highway 59** with expected delays of about fifteen minutes in the direction of the sports stadium. **78 Apparently, a tree has fallen into the easternmost lane of the road.** Many residents will recognize this tree—it's been featured in many publications about the area. Join me as I interview **79 Jingdao Wei, an area photographer** who has captured some of the most iconic images of this tree. Mr. Wei, thanks for talking with me.

저희 뉴스 채널 식스에 방금 들어온 소식입니다. **59번 고속도로에 교통 정체가 발생해** 스포츠 경기장 방면으로 약 15분 가량 지체가 예상되고 있습니다. **나무 한 그루가 이 도로의 가장 동쪽 차선에 쓰러진 것으로 보입니다.** 많은 주민들께서 이 나무를 알아보실 텐데요. 지역 관련 여러 매체에 특집으로 실린 바 있습니다. 이 나무의 가장 상징적인 사진들을 촬영한 **지역 사진작가, 징다오 웨이**와의 인터뷰를 함께 하시겠습니다. 웨이 씨, 말씀 나누어 주셔서 감사합니다.

어휘 traffic 교통 delay 지체, 지연 direction 방향 apparently 보아하니, 듣자 하니 easternmost 가장 동쪽의 lane 차선, 도로 resident 주민 recognize 알아보다, 인식하다 feature 특집으로 싣다, 특별히 포함하다 publication 출판(물) capture 담아내다, 포착하다 iconic 상징적인

77 What is the speaker reporting on?
(A) A store opening
(B) A celebrity visit
(C) A traffic delay
(D) A sports tournament

화자는 무엇에 대해 보도하고 있는가?
(A) 매장 개점
(B) 유명 인사 방문
(C) 교통 정체
(D) 스포츠 토너먼트

어휘 celebrity 유명 인사

해설 전체 내용 관련 – 보도의 주제
화자가 초반부에 59번 고속도로에 교통 정체가 발생했다(~ there is a traffic delay on Highway 59 ~)고 알린 뒤 그곳의 상황에 대한 설명을 이어 가고 있으므로 정답은 (C)이다.

78 What is causing a problem?
(A) A fallen tree
(B) A broken piece of equipment
(C) A permitting process
(D) A parking lot closure

무엇이 문제를 초래하고 있는가?
(A) 쓰러진 나무
(B) 고장 난 장비
(C) 허가 과정
(D) 주차장 폐쇄

해설 세부 사항 관련 – 문제의 원인
화자가 중반부에 정체의 원인과 관련해 나무 한 그루가 그 도로의 가장 동쪽 차선에 쓰러진 것으로 보인다(Apparently, a tree has fallen into the easternmost lane of the road)고 언급하고 있으므로 정답은 (A)이다.

79 Who is Mr. Wei?
(A) A landscaper
(B) A photographer
(C) An athlete
(D) A road maintenance worker

웨이 씨는 누구인가?
(A) 조경 전문가
(B) 사진작가
(C) 운동선수
(D) 도로 유지 관리 작업자

해설 세부 사항 관련 – 웨이 씨의 직업
화자가 후반부에 징다오 웨이의 이름과 함께 지역 사진작가(~ Jingdao Wei, an area photographer ~)라고 소개하고 있으므로 정답은 (B)이다.

80-82 전화 메시지 ▶동영상 강의

M-Cn Junko, I just read your e-mail about the photo-sharing app that **80 our social media company**'s launching tomorrow. You know, the e-mail about updating the language in the community guidelines for the app. **81 We've already spent a lot of time reviewing the guideline document**, and actually, I was just about to post it. **82 Since we'll both be at the all-staff meeting at one o'clock**, let's stay after it finishes to touch base on upcoming projects.

준코, **우리 소셜 미디어 회사**가 내일 출시하는 사진 공유 앱에 대한 이메일을 방금 읽었어요. 그러니까, 이 앱의 커뮤니티 가이드라인 문구를 업데이트하는 것에 관한 이메일이요. **저희가 이미 그 가이드라인 문서를 검토하는 데 많은 시간을 들였고**, 실은, 그걸 막 게시하려던 참이었어요. **1시에 있을 전체 직원회의에 저희 둘 다 참석하니**, 끝난 후에 남아서 다가오는 프로젝트들에 관해 잠깐 이야기합시다.

어휘 touch base 잠깐 이야기하다, 간단히 연락하다

80 Where does the speaker work?
(A) At a print shop
(B) At a social media company
(C) At an electronics store
(D) At a community center

화자는 어디에서 일하는가?
(A) 인쇄소
(B) 소셜 미디어 회사
(C) 전자제품 매장
(D) 커뮤니티 센터

해설 전체 내용 관련 – 화자의 근무 장소
화자가 초반부에 우리 소셜 미디어 회사(~ our social media company ~)라고 지칭하고 있으므로 정답은 (B)이다.

81 What does the speaker imply when he says, "I was just about to post it"?
(A) He misunderstood the timeline for a task.
(B) Some technical assistance is needed.
(C) It is too late to make a change.
(D) An immediate answer is required.

화자가 "그걸 막 게시하려던 참이었어요"라고 말할 때 무엇을 암시하는가?
(A) 업무 진행 일정을 오해했다.
(B) 기술 지원이 필요하다.
(C) 변경하기에는 너무 늦었다.
(D) 즉각적인 답변이 요구된다.

어휘 assistance 지원, 도움 immediate 즉각적인

해설 화자의 의도 파악 – 막 게시하려는 참이었다는 말의 의도
화자가 중반부에 이미 가이드라인 문서를 검토하는 데 많은 시간을 들였다(We've already spent a lot of time reviewing the guideline document)고 말한 뒤 인용문을 언급했다. 따라서 이미 충분히 검토한 후 게시하려는 시점이기 때문에 변경하기에는 늦었다는 의미로 한 말임을 알 수 있으므로 정답은 (C)이다.

82 What does the speaker say will happen at one o'clock?
(A) A client will visit.
(B) An interview will take place.
(C) A shipment will arrive.
(D) A staff meeting will be held.

화자는 1시에 무슨 일이 있을 것이라고 말하는가?
(A) 고객이 방문할 것이다.
(B) 면접이 진행될 것이다.
(C) 배송이 도착할 것이다.
(D) 직원회의가 개최될 것이다.

해설 세부 사항 관련 – 1시에 있을 일
화자가 후반부에 1시에 있을 전체 직원회의에 우리 둘 다 참석할 것(Since we'll both be at the all-staff meeting at one o'clock ~)이라고 말하고 있으므로 정답은 (D)이다.

83-85 안내

W-Am Thanks, again, for taking on this project. **83You'll be authoring a comprehensive handbook that describes all the standard operating procedures** to be used by **84our flight crew and airport staff.** The goal is to have a master document from which we can pull out different sections as needed. **85On your screens, you'll see a list of who will be responsible for drafting each chapter.** All chapters will be cowritten with one other author.

이 프로젝트를 맡아 주셔서 다시 한번 감사드립니다. 여러분께서는 우리 항공기 승무원들과 공항 직원들이 사용할 모든 표준 운영 절차를 설명하는 포괄적인 안내서를 집필하시게 됩니다. 목표는 우리가 필요에 따라 다양한 부분들을 뽑아 쓸 수 있는 기준 문서를 마련하는 것입니다. 여러분의 화면에 각 챕터의 초안 작성을 담당할 사람의 목록이 보이실 겁니다. 모든 챕터는 한 명의 다른 저자와 함께 공동으로 집필될 예정입니다.

어휘 take on ~을 맡다, 책임지다 author 집필하다; 집필자 comprehensive 포괄적인, 종합적인 handbook 안내서, 편람 operating 운영의, 가동하는 procedure 절차 crew 승무원 master document 기준 문서, 통합 문서 pull out 꺼내다 draft 초안을 작성하다 cowrite 공동 저술하다

83 What is the focus of a project?
(A) Analyzing survey results
(B) Documenting operating procedures
(C) Reducing technology expenses
(D) Recruiting qualified staff

프로젝트의 초점은 무엇인가?
(A) 설문 조사 결과 분석하기
(B) 운영 절차 문서화하기
(C) 기술 관련 지출 줄이기
(D) 자격을 갖춘 직원 채용하기

어휘 analyze 분석하다 survey 설문 조사 document 문서화하다 recruit 모집하다 qualified 자격을 갖춘

해설 전체 내용 관련 – 프로젝트의 초점
화자가 초반부에 청자들이 모든 표준 운영 절차를 설명하는 포괄적인 안내서를 집필하게 될 것(You'll be authoring a comprehensive handbook that describes all the standard operating procedures ~)이라고 말한 뒤, 그 목적 및 집필 방식 등과 관련한 설명을 이어 가고 있으므로 정답은 (B)이다.

Paraphrasing
담화의 authoring a comprehensive handbook that describes all the standard operating procedures
→ 정답의 Documenting operating procedures

84 Which industry does the speaker most likely work in?
(A) Aviation
(B) Forestry management
(C) Real estate
(D) Health care

화자는 어느 업계에서 일하는 것 같은가?
(A) 항공
(B) 산림 관리
(C) 부동산
(D) 의료 서비스

해설 전체 내용 관련 – 화자의 근무 업계
화자가 중반부에 소속 업체의 직원들을 우리 항공기 승무원들과 공항 직원들(~ our flight crew and airport staff)이라고 지칭하고 있으므로 정답은 (A)이다.

Paraphrasing
담화의 flight → 정답의 Aviation

85 What will the listeners see on their screens?
(A) Workplace policies
(B) Budget proposals
(C) Definitions of technical terms
(D) Work assignments

청자들은 자신들의 화면에서 무엇을 볼 것인가?
(A) 근무 규정
(B) 예산 제안서
(C) 기술 용어의 정의
(D) 업무 배정

어휘 proposal 제안(서)   definition 정의   term 용어
assignment 배정

해설 세부 사항 관련 – 화면에 보이는 것
화자가 후반부에 여러분의 화면에 각 챕터의 초안 작성을 담당할 사람의 목록이 보일 것(On your screens, you'll see a list of who will be responsible for drafting each chapter)이라고 했으므로 정답은 (D)이다.

Paraphrasing
담화의 a list of who will be responsible for drafting each chapter → 정답의 Work assignments

86-88 담화

M-Au One final thing before we close the team leaders' meeting. Some educators from various countries will be visiting our company next week. I will be giving a brief presentation to introduce ⁸⁶**all of the educational software products we make.** After that, ⁸⁷**I'd like some of you to give demonstrations of the software your team developed.** I'll have a final agenda ready soon and ⁸⁷**will meet with those of you who will be presenting that day to go over the details.** ⁸⁸**We wanted to go to lunch with the visitors afterward at the restaurant next door, but it's closed for renovations.** Luckily, a new restaurant has opened close by.

팀장 회의를 마치기 전에 마지막으로 한 가지 말씀드리겠습니다. 다음 주에 다양한 국가의 교육 전문가들이 우리 회사를 방문할 예정이에요. 저는 저희가 제작한 모든 교육 소프트웨어 제품을 소개하는 간단한 발표를 할 겁니다. 그 후에, 여러분 중 일부가 각 팀에서 개발한 소프트웨어를 시연해 주셨으면 합니다. 제가 곧 최종 안건을 준비할 것이고, 그날 발표를 하게 될 분들과 만나 세부 사항을 검토할 예정입니다. 일정이 끝난 뒤에 방문객들과 함께 옆 건물 레스토랑에서 점심을 하려고 했는데, 개조 공사로 문을 닫은 상태네요. 다행히, 근처에 새로운 레스토랑이 문을 열었습니다.

어휘 educator 교육 전문가, 교육자   brief 간단한, 짧은
demonstration 시연, 설명   agenda 안건, 의제, 일정(표)
go over ~을 검토하다, ~을 점검하다   afterward 나중에, 그 후에

86 What does the speaker's company develop?
(A) Recipes
(B) Medical devices
(C) Educational software
(D) Web sites

화자의 회사는 무엇을 개발하는가?
(A) 조리법
(B) 의료 기기
(C) 교육용 소프트웨어
(D) 웹사이트

해설 세부 사항 관련 – 화자의 회사가 개발하는 것
화자가 초반부에 우리가 제작한 모든 교육 소프트웨어 제품(~ all of the educational software products we make)을 언급하고 있으므로 정답은 (C)이다.

Paraphrasing
담화의 make → 질문의 develop

87 Why will the speaker meet with some of the listeners?
(A) To finalize some relocation plans
(B) To go over professional certifications
(C) To confirm project deadlines
(D) To prepare for some product demonstrations

화자는 왜 청자들과 만날 것인가?
(A) 이전 계획을 확정하기 위해
(B) 전문 자격증을 검토하기 위해
(C) 프로젝트 마감 기한을 확인하기 위해
(D) 제품 시연을 준비하기 위해

어휘 finalize 확정하다, 마무리하다 relocation 이전, 이사 certification 자격증, 수료증

해설 세부 사항 관련 – 청자들을 만나려는 이유
화자가 중반부에 청자들 중 일부가 각 팀에서 개발한 소프트웨어를 시연해 주었으면 한다(I'd like some of you to give demonstrations of the software your team developed)며 그날 발표를 하게 될 분들과 만나 세부 사항을 검토할 것(~ will meet with those of you who will be presenting that day to go over the details)이라고 말하는 것으로 보아 제품 시연을 준비하려는 것임을 알 수 있으므로 정답은 (D)이다.

Paraphrasing
담화의 demonstrations of the software
→ 정답의 some product demonstrations

88 Why does the speaker say, "a new restaurant has opened close by"?
(A) To complain about some noise
(B) To suggest an alternative
(C) To highlight an accomplishment
(D) To clarify a misunderstanding

화자는 왜 "근처에 새로운 레스토랑이 문을 열었습니다"라고 말하는가?
(A) 소음에 대해 항의하기 위해
(B) 대안을 제시하기 위해
(C) 성과를 강조하기 위해
(D) 오해를 바로잡기 위해

어휘 complain 항의하다, 불평하다 alternative 대안 highlight 강조하다 accomplishment 성과, 업적 clarify 명확하게 하다, 분명히 하다

해설 화자의 의도 파악 – 근처에 새로운 레스토랑이 문을 열었다는 말의 의도
화자가 후반부에 방문객들과 점심을 하려 했던 옆 건물 레스토랑이 개조 공사로 인해 문을 닫은 상태(We wanted to go to lunch with the visitors afterward at the restaurant next door, but it's closed for renovations)라고 말한 뒤 다행히(Luckily)라고 덧붙이며 인용문을 언급하고 있다. 이는 대신 갈 수 있는 레스토랑, 즉 대안을 제시하려는 의도로 한 말임을 알 수 있다. 따라서 정답은 (B)이다.

89-91 광고

M-Cn Are you ready to launch a new career in the technology industry? At Job Lift Enterprises, **89 we provide hands-on training to help you learn the skills and earn the certifications that tech professionals need.** **90 Unlike other job-training programs, our courses are tuition-free.** So students leave our school debt-free and ready to pursue their careers. Our schools are conveniently located throughout the Grand Lakes region. **91 Visit our Web site today to find the location closest to you!**

기술 업계에서 새로운 경력을 시작할 준비가 되셨나요? 저희 잡 리프트 엔터프라이즈 사에서는, **여러분이 기술을 배우고, 기술 전문가들이 필요로 하는 자격증을 취득할 수 있도록 실무 교육을 제공하고 있습니다. 다른 직업 교육 프로그램들과 달리, 저희 과정은 수강료가 없습니다.** 따라서 학생들은 빚 없이 경력을 시작할 준비가 된 상태로 졸업합니다. 저희 교육 기관은 그랜드 레이크스 전역에 걸쳐 편리하게 위치해 있습니다. **오늘 저희 웹사이트에 방문해서 가장 가까운 지점을 찾아보세요!**

어휘 hands-on 실무의, 현장의 earn 취득하다, 얻다, 벌다 certification 자격증, 수료증 tuition-free 수강료가 없는 debt-free 빚이 없는 pursue 추구하다 career 경력, 직업 conveniently 편리하게 region 지역, 지방

89 What kind of service is being advertised?
(A) Career training
(B) Financial planning
(C) Language translation
(D) Home inspection

어떤 종류의 서비스가 광고되고 있는가?
(A) 직업 교육
(B) 재무 설계
(C) 언어 번역
(D) 주택 점검

어휘 translation 번역

해설 전체 내용 관련 – 광고의 주제
화자가 초반부에 기술을 배우고, 기술 전문가들이 필요로 하는 자격증을 취득할 수 있도록 실무 교육을 제공한다(~ we provide hands-on training to help you learn the skills and earn the certifications that tech professionals need)고 했으므로 정답은 (A)이다.

Paraphrasing
담화의 hands-on training to help you learn the skills and earn the certifications → 정답의 Career training

90 According to the speaker, what is unique about the business?
(A) Its employees work remotely.
(B) Its services are free of charge.
(C) Its services are guaranteed.
(D) It operates worldwide.

화자에 따르면, 해당 업체에 대해 어떤 점이 특별한가?
(A) 직원들이 원격으로 근무한다.
(B) 서비스가 무료이다.
(C) 서비스가 보증된다.
(D) 전 세계적으로 운영된다.

어휘 remotely 원격으로, 멀리서 free of charge 무료의 guarantee 보증하다 operate 운영되다, 영업하다

해설 세부 사항 관련 – 업체의 특별한 점
화자가 중반부에 자사의 과정은 다른 직업 교육 프로그램들과 달리 수강료가 없다(Unlike other job-training programs, our courses are tuition-free)고 했으므로 정답은 (B)이다.

Paraphrasing
담화의 Unlike other → 질문의 unique
담화의 our courses are tuition-free
→ 정답의 Its services are free of charge

91 Why should the listeners visit a Web site?
(A) To download a brochure
(B) To complete a survey
(C) To find a nearby location
(D) To schedule an appointment

청자들은 왜 웹사이트를 방문해야 하는가?
(A) 안내 책자를 다운로드하기 위해
(B) 설문 조사를 완료하기 위해
(C) 가까운 지점을 찾기 위해
(D) 예약 일정을 잡기 위해

어휘 complete 완료하다, 작성하다 nearby 가까운, 근처의

해설 세부 사항 관련 – 웹사이트를 방문해야 하는 이유
화자가 후반부에 오늘 웹사이트에 방문해서 가장 가까운 지점을 찾아보라(Visit our Web site today to find the location closest to you!)고 했으므로 정답은 (C)이다.

Paraphrasing
담화의 find the location closest to you
→ 정답의 find a nearby location

92-94 회의 발췌

W-Br ⁹²I'd like to thank you all for attending Omnicon Department Store's staff meeting. As you'll recall, ⁹³six months ago we made a deal with Euphora sports clothing to sell their merchandise exclusively in our department stores. The hope is that we can attract new customers to our stores by selling this brand. ⁹⁴Data show that foot traffic in the department stores containing Euphora clothing is up twenty percent from last year. Keep in mind, however, that total sales revenues are still being calculated.

모두 옴니콘 백화점 직원회의에 참석해 주셔서 감사합니다. 기억하시겠지만, 6개월 전 저희는 스포츠 의류를 만드는 유포라와 우리 백화점에서 상품을 독점적으로 판매하는 계약을 체결했습니다. 바라는 것은, 이 브랜드를 판매해 신규 고객들을 매장으로 유치하는 겁니다. 데이터에 따르면 유포라 의류를 취급하는 백화점에서 고객 유입이 작년보다 20퍼센트 증가했습니다. 다만, 총매출액은 아직 집계 중이라는 점을 유의해 주시기 바랍니다.

어휘 recall 기억하다, 회상하다 make a deal 계약하다, 거래하다 merchandise 상품 exclusively 독점적으로, 전적으로 attract 끌어들이다, 유치하다 foot traffic 고객 유입, 유동 인구 contain 포함하다 keep in mind 명심하다 revenue 수익, 수입 calculate 산출하다, 계산하다

92 Who are the listeners?
(A) Shareholders
(B) Customers
(C) Employees
(D) Journalists

청자들은 누구인가?
(A) 주주
(B) 고객
(C) 직원
(D) 기자

해설 전체 내용 관련 – 청자들의 직업
화자가 초반부에 청자들에게 모두 옴니콘 백화점 직원회의에 참석해 주어 감사하다(I'd like to thank you all for attending Omnicon Department Store's staff meeting)고 인사하고 있으므로 정답은 (C)이다.

93 According to the speaker, what happened six months ago?
(A) A corporate office was relocated.
(B) An advertising campaign was launched.
(C) A business partnership was formed.
(D) A new executive director was hired.

화자에 따르면, 6개월 전에 무슨 일이 있었는가?
(A) 기업 사무실이 이전했다.
(B) 광고 캠페인이 시작되었다.
(C) 사업 제휴 관계가 형성되었다.
(D) 신임 총괄 책임자가 고용되었다.

어휘 corporate 기업의 relocate 이전하다 form 형성하다
executive director 총괄 책임자, 전무 이사

해설 세부 사항 관련 – 6개월 전에 있었던 일

화자가 초반부에 6개월 전 스포츠 의류를 만드는 유포라와 자사의 백화점에서 상품을 독점적으로 판매하는 계약을 체결했다(~ six months ago we made a deal with Euphora sports clothing to sell their merchandise exclusively in our department stores)고 했으므로 정답은 (C)이다.

Paraphrasing
담화의 made a deal ~ to sell their merchandise
→ 정답의 A business partnership was formed

94 Why does the speaker say, "total sales revenues are still being calculated"?
(A) To express disappointment
(B) To warn against reaching a conclusion too soon
(C) To offer an excuse for missing an important deadline
(D) To suggest that a budget be revised

화자는 왜 "총매출액은 아직 집계 중"이라고 말하는가?
(A) 실망감을 표현하려고
(B) 성급하게 결론을 내리지 말라고 경고하려고
(C) 중요한 마감일을 놓친 것을 변명하려고
(D) 예산을 수정하자고 제안하려고

어휘 disappointment 실망 warn 경고하다 excuse 변명
revise 조정하다, 수정하다

해설 화자의 의도 파악 – 총매출액은 아직 집계 중이라는 말의 의도

화자가 후반부에 데이터에 따르면 유포라 의류를 취급하는 백화점에서 고객 유입이 작년보다 20퍼센트 증가했다(Data show that foot traffic in the department stores containing Euphora clothing is up twenty percent from last year)고 말한 뒤 인용문을 언급하고 있는 것으로 보아, 아직 최종 데이터가 아니므로 긍정적인 효과에 대해 성급하게 결론을 내리지 말라는 의도로 한 말임을 알 수 있다. 따라서 정답은 (B)이다.

95-97 회의 발췌 + 도표

M-Au **95 Thanks for inviting me to represent the parking authority at this month's city council meeting.** As you know, **96 parking in city parking garages will no longer be free on Saturdays.** My office has updated the parking rate schedule and posted copies in all city garages. If you look at the screen, you'll see the new rates that went into effect this week. We're planning to use some of the additional revenue to cover the cost of new payment kiosks for the garages. **97 I will provide a revenue report at next month's meeting.**

이번 달 시 의회 회의에 주차 관리국 대표로 초대해 주셔서 감사합니다. 아시다시피, **토요일에 시립 주차장은 더 이상 무료가 아닙니다.** 저희 사무실에서 주차 요금표를 업데이트하여 모든 시립 주차장에 게시했습니다. 화면을 보시면, 이번 주부터 시행된 새로운 요금이 보이실 겁니다. 추가로 발생하는 수입 중 일부는 주차장에 설치될 새로운 결제 키오스크 비용을 충당하는 데 사용할 계획입니다. **다음 달 회의에서 수익 보고서를 제출하겠습니다.**

어휘 represent 대표하다 authority 당국, 권한 council 의회
rate 요금 go into effect 시행되다 revenue 수입, 수익
cover (비용 등을) 충당하다 payment 결제, 지불

City Parking Garage Rates	
Monday–Thursday	$22
Friday	$24
96 Saturday	**$10**
Sunday	Free

시립 주차장 요금	
월요일–목요일	22달러
금요일	24달러
토요일	**10달러**
일요일	무료

95 Who most likely is the speaker?
(A) A news reporter
(B) A garage attendant
(C) An engineer
(D) A city official

화자는 누구인 것 같은가?
(A) 뉴스 기자
(B) 주차장 안내원
(C) 엔지니어
(D) 시 공무원

어휘 attendant 안내원, 수행원 official 공무원

해설 전체 내용 관련 - 화자의 직업

화자가 초반부에 이번 달 시 의회 회의에 주차 관리국 대표로 초대해 주어 감사하다(Thanks for inviting me to represent the parking authority at this month's city council meeting)고 인사하고 있는 것으로 보아 화자는 시 공무원임을 알 수 있다. 따라서 정답은 (D)이다.

96 Look at the graphic. Which parking rate has been changed?
(A) $22
(B) $24
(C) $10
(D) Free

시각 정보에 의하면, 어느 주차 요금이 변경되었는가?
(A) 22달러
(B) 24달러
(C) 10달러
(D) 무료

해설 시각 정보 연계 - 변경된 주차 요금

화자가 중반부에 토요일에 시립 주차장은 더 이상 무료가 아니다 (~ parking in city parking garages will no longer be free on Saturdays)라고 했고, 도표에서 토요일 주차 요금은 10달러이므로 정답은 (C)이다.

Paraphrasing
담화의 will no longer be free → 질문의 has been changed

97 What will be presented next month?
(A) A marketing proposal
(B) A revenue report
(C) Survey results
(D) Some construction plans

다음 달에 무엇이 제출될 것인가?
(A) 마케팅 제안서
(B) 수익 보고서
(C) 설문 조사 결과
(D) 건설 계획

어휘 construction 건설, 공사

해설 세부 사항 관련 - 다음 달에 제출될 것

화자가 후반부에 다음 달 회의에서 수익 보고서를 제출하겠다(I will provide a revenue report at next month's meeting)고 했으므로 정답은 (B)이다.

98-100 공지 + 항공편 정보

W-Am Attention, passengers! **98 Flight AU354 will now be departing from a different gate.** The new gate will appear on screens throughout the terminal shortly. Your boarding time remains as scheduled and will begin in approximately 25 minutes. **99 If you do not yet have a seat assignment, please come up to the counter now so that Claudia can assist you.** **100 And one important reminder: all carry-on baggage must comply with our height and width restrictions.** Size-check templates are available throughout the terminal for your reference.

승객 여러분께 알립니다! AU354편 항공기가 다른 탑승구에서 출발할 예정입니다. 새로운 탑승구는 곧 터미널 곳곳의 스크린에 표시될 예정입니다. 탑승 시간은 예정대로이며, 약 25분 후에 시작됩니다. 아직 좌석 배정을 받지 않으신 경우, 클라우디아가 도와드릴 수 있도록 지금 카운터로 와 주시기 바랍니다. 그리고 한 가지 중요한 안내 말씀드립니다. 모든 기내 반입 수하물은 저희 항공사의 높이 및 너비 제한을 반드시 준수해야 합니다. 터미널 곳곳에 수하물 크기 확인용 샘플이 비치되어 있으니 참고 부탁드립니다.

어휘 depart 출발하다, 떠나다 shortly 곧 boarding 탑승
remain 계속 ~이다, 남다 approximately 약, 대략
assignment 배정 reminder (메시지 등의) 상기시키는 것
carry-on baggage 기내 휴대용 수하물
comply with ~을 준수하다 height 높이 width 너비
restriction 제한, 제약 template 샘플, 견본
reference 참고, 참조

Flight Number	Destination	Gate
BK107	Austin	A5
98 AU354	**Los Angeles**	**D8**
MX262	Detroit	C3
YT418	New Orleans	B2

항공편 번호	목적지	탑승구
BK107	오스틴	A5
AU354	**로스앤젤레스**	**D8**
MX262	디트로이트	C3
YT418	뉴올리언스	B2

98 Look at the graphic. What is the destination of the affected flight?
(A) Austin
(B) Los Angeles
(C) Detroit
(D) New Orleans

시각 정보에 의하면, 영향을 받은 항공편의 목적지는 어디인가?
(A) 오스틴
(B) 로스앤젤레스
(C) 디트로이트
(D) 뉴올리언스

해설 시각 정보 연계 – 영향을 받은 항공편의 목적지

화자가 초반부에 AU354편 항공기가 다른 탑승구에서 출발할 예정(Flight AU354 will now be departing from a different gate)이라고 말하고 있고, 항공편 정보에서 AU354편의 목적지는 로스앤젤레스이므로 정답은 (B)이다.

99 According to the announcement, what will Claudia provide at the counter?
(A) Seat assignments
(B) Airport maps
(C) Food vouchers
(D) Hotel recommendations

공지에 따르면, 클라우디아는 카운터에서 무엇을 제공할 것인가?
(A) 좌석 배정
(B) 공항 안내도
(C) 음식 쿠폰
(D) 호텔 추천

어휘 voucher 쿠폰, 상품권

해설 세부 사항 관련 – 클라우디아가 제공할 것

화자가 중반부에 아직 좌석 배정을 받지 않은 경우, 클라우디아가 도울 수 있도록 지금 카운터로 와 달라(If you do not yet have a seat assignment, please come up to the counter now so that Claudia can assist you)고 했으므로 정답은 (A)이다.

100 What does the speaker remind the listeners about?
(A) Complimentary Internet access
(B) Boarding procedures
(C) Automatic text notifications
(D) Luggage size restrictions

화자는 청자들에게 무엇에 대해 상기시키는가?
(A) 무료 인터넷 접속
(B) 탑승 절차
(C) 자동 문자 메시지 알림
(D) 수하물 크기 제한

어휘 complimentary 무료의 access 접속, 접근
notification 알림, 통보

해설 세부 사항 관련 – 화자가 상기시키는 것

화자가 후반부에 한 가지 중요한 안내 말씀드린다며 모든 기내 반입 수하물은 항공사의 높이 및 너비 제한을 반드시 준수해야 한다(And one important reminder: all carry-on baggage must comply with our height and width restrictions)고 했으므로 정답은 (D)이다.

Paraphrasing
담화의 height and width restrictions
→ 정답의 size restrictions

기출 TEST 10

1 (D)	2 (C)	3 (C)	4 (D)	5 (B)
6 (B)	7 (A)	8 (A)	9 (B)	10 (B)
11 (B)	12 (B)	13 (B)	14 (C)	15 (A)
16 (C)	17 (B)	18 (A)	19 (A)	20 (A)
21 (B)	22 (C)	23 (C)	24 (C)	25 (B)
26 (A)	27 (B)	28 (A)	29 (A)	30 (C)
31 (C)	32 (A)	33 (C)	34 (B)	35 (C)
36 (B)	37 (B)	38 (B)	39 (D)	40 (C)
41 (D)	42 (B)	43 (A)	44 (C)	45 (A)
46 (B)	47 (D)	48 (C)	49 (D)	50 (A)
51 (C)	52 (D)	53 (C)	54 (B)	55 (D)
56 (A)	57 (D)	58 (D)	59 (A)	60 (C)
61 (B)	62 (B)	63 (A)	64 (A)	65 (D)
66 (C)	67 (B)	68 (A)	69 (C)	70 (B)
71 (C)	72 (B)	73 (A)	74 (C)	75 (A)
76 (D)	77 (B)	78 (C)	79 (A)	80 (B)
81 (D)	82 (C)	83 (A)	84 (D)	85 (B)
86 (D)	87 (A)	88 (B)	89 (A)	90 (D)
91 (B)	92 (A)	93 (B)	94 (C)	95 (D)
96 (B)	97 (A)	98 (A)	99 (B)	100 (B)

PART 1

1

M-Cn

(A) He's reaching for the ceiling.
(B) He's carrying a bucket of paint.
(C) He's fixing a doorway.
(D) He's climbing down a ladder.

(A) 남자가 천장을 향해 손을 뻗고 있다.
(B) 남자가 페인트 통을 나르고 있다.
(C) 남자가 출입구를 고치고 있다.
(D) 남자가 사다리에서 내려오고 있다.

어휘 reach for ~을 향해 손을 뻗다 bucket 통, 양동이 fix 고치다
climb down ~에서 내려오다

해설 1인 등장 사진 – 사람의 동작/상태 묘사
(A) 동사 오답. 남자가 천장을 향해 손을 뻗고 있는(is reaching for the ceiling) 모습이 아니므로 오답.
(B) 동사 오답. 남자가 페인트 통을 나르고 있는(is carrying a bucket of paint) 모습이 아니므로 오답.
(C) 동사 오답. 남자가 출입구를 고치고 있는(is fixing a doorway) 모습이 아니므로 오답.
(D) 정답. 남자가 사다리에서 내려오고 있는(is climbing down a ladder) 모습이므로 정답.

2

W-Br

(A) She's reading a poster on the wall.
(B) A chair is propped against the door.
(C) A laptop has been left open.
(D) She's speaking into a microphone.

(A) 여자가 벽에 걸린 포스터를 읽고 있다.
(B) 의자가 문에 기대어져 있다.
(C) 노트북 컴퓨터가 열린 채로 놓여 있다.
(D) 여자가 마이크에 대고 말하고 있다.

어휘 be propped against ~에 기대어져 있다

해설 1인 등장 사진 – 사람/사물/풍경 혼합 묘사
(A) 사진에 없는 명사를 이용한 오답. 사진에 벽에 걸린 포스터(a poster on the wall)의 모습이 보이지 않으므로 오답.
(B) 동사 오답. 의자(A chair)가 문에 기대어져 있는(is propped against the door) 모습이 아니므로 오답.
(C) 정답. 노트북 컴퓨터(A laptop)가 열린 채로 놓여 있는(has been left open) 모습이므로 정답.
(D) 동사 오답. 여자가 마이크에 대고 말하고 있는(is speaking into a microphone) 모습이 아니므로 오답.

3

M-Au

(A) They're strolling in a park.
(B) They're shaking hands.
(C) He's holding up an umbrella.
(D) She's handing him a phone.

(A) 사람들이 공원에서 산책하고 있다.
(B) 사람들이 악수하고 있다.
(C) 남자가 우산을 들고 있다.
(D) 여자가 남자에게 전화기를 건네주고 있다.

어휘 stroll 산책하다, 거닐다 hold up (떠받치듯) 들다
hand 건네주다, 넘겨주다

해설 2인 이상 사진 – 사람의 동작/상태 묘사
(A) 동사 오답. 사람들이 공원에서 산책하고 있는(are strolling) 모습이 아니므로 오답.
(B) 동사 오답. 사람들이 악수하고 있는(are shaking hands)

모습이 아니므로 오답.
(C) 정답. 남자가 우산을 들고 있는(is holding up an umbrella) 모습이므로 정답.
(D) 동사 오답. 여자가 남자에게 전화기를 건네주고 있는(is handing him a phone) 모습이 아니므로 오답.

4 ▶동영상 강의

W-Br

(A) A car is being towed down a street.
(B) Some men are removing a tire from a truck.
(C) One of the men is unloading equipment from a truck.
(D) **A building has a clock tower on top of it.**

(A) 자동차가 길을 따라 견인되고 있다.
(B) 남자들이 트럭에서 타이어를 제거하고 있다.
(C) 남자들 중 한 명이 트럭에서 장비를 내리고 있다.
(D) 건물 꼭대기에 시계탑이 있다.

어휘 tow 견인하다   remove 제거하다, 없애다   unload 내리다   equipment 장비

해설 2인 이상 등장 사진 – 사람/사물/풍경 혼합 묘사
(A) 동사 오답. 자동차(A car)가 견인되고 있는(is being towed) 모습이 아니므로 오답.
(B) 동사 오답. 남자들이 트럭에서 타이어를 제거하고 있는(are removing a tire) 모습이 아니므로 오답.
(C) 동사 오답. 남자들 중 한 명이 트럭에서 장비를 내리고 있는(is unloading equipment) 모습이 아니므로 오답.
(D) 정답. 건물(A building)의 꼭대기에 시계탑이 있는(has a clock tower on top of it) 모습이므로 정답.

5

M-Cn

(A) Some of the bicycles are being repaired.
(B) **The bicycles are lined up in a row.**
(C) One of the bicycles is leaning against a traffic sign.
(D) A bicycle path is being painted.

(A) 자전거들 중 몇 대가 수리되고 있다.
(B) 자전거들이 일렬로 늘어서 있다.
(C) 자전거들 중 한 대가 교통 표지판에 기대어져 있다.
(D) 자전거 전용 도로가 페인트칠되고 있다.

어휘 repair 수리하다   be line up 줄지어 서 있다   in a row 일렬로   lean against ~에 기대어져 있다

해설 사물/풍경 사진 – 사물 묘사
(A) 동사 오답. 자전거들 중 몇 대(Some of the bicycles)가 수리되고 있는(are being repaired) 모습이 아니므로 오답.
(B) 정답. 자전거들(The bicycles)이 일렬로 늘어서 있는(are lined up in a row) 모습이므로 정답.
(C) 사진에 없는 명사를 이용한 오답. 사진에 교통 표지판(a traffic sign)의 모습이 보이지 않으므로 오답.
(D) 사진에 없는 명사를 이용한 오답. 사진에 자전거 전용 도로(A bicycle path)의 모습이 보이지 않으므로 오답.

6

W-Am

(A) Some ships are moving under a bridge.
(B) **Some boats are docked near a shore.**
(C) A ferryboat is traveling through a marina.
(D) There are buildings along the side of a street.

(A) 선박들이 다리 밑을 지나가고 있다.
(B) 보트들이 물가에 정박해 있다.
(C) 여객선이 정박지 사이를 지나가고 있다.
(D) 길가를 따라 건물들이 있다.

어휘 dock (배를) 정박시키다, 부두에 대다   shore 물가, 해안   marina 정박지

해설 사물/풍경 사진 – 풍경 묘사
(A) 사진에 없는 명사를 이용한 오답. 사진에 다리(a bridge)의 모습이 보이지 않으므로 오답.
(B) 정답. 보트들(Some boats)이 물가에 정박해 있는(are docked near a shore) 모습이므로 정답.
(C) 동사 오답. 여객선(A ferryboat)이 정박지 사이를 지나가고 있는(is traveling through a marina) 모습이 아니므로 오답.
(D) 사진에 없는 명사를 이용한 오답. 사진에 거리(a street)의 모습이 보이지 않으므로 오답.

PART 2

7 M-Au / W-Am

Would you like me to order some more business cards for you?
(A) Sure, that'd be great.
(B) They'll be busy at that time.
(C) No, it wasn't.

제가 명함을 좀 더 주문해 드릴까요?
(A) 네, 그래 주시면 좋겠어요.
(B) 그들은 그 시간에 바쁠 겁니다.
(C) 아니요, 그렇지 않았어요.

해설 제안/권유의 의문문
(A) 정답. 명함 추가 주문을 제안하는 질문에 네(Sure)라고 대답한 뒤, 그래 주면 좋겠다며 긍정 답변과 일관된 내용을 덧붙이고 있으므로 정답.
(B) 유사 발음 오답. 질문의 business와 부분적으로 발음이 유사한 busy를 이용한 오답.
(C) 질문과 상관없는 오답. 질문에 3인칭 단수 대명사 it으로 지칭할 사물이 언급된 적이 없으므로 오답.

8 W-Br / M-Au ▶동영상 강의

Why don't you ask Ms. Kim for help?
(A) Because she's on a conference call.
(B) There's no more paper in the cabinet.
(C) I've already seen that one.

왜 김 씨에게 도움을 요청하지 않으세요?
(A) 그분이 전화 회의 중이시라서요.
(B) 캐비닛에 더 이상 용지가 없어요.
(C) 저는 이미 그것을 봤어요.

어휘 conference call 전화 회의
해설 김 씨에게 도움을 요청하지 않는 이유를 묻는 Why 의문문
(A) 정답. 김 씨에게 도움을 요청하지 않는 이유를 묻는 질문에 그분이 전화 회의 중이기 때문이라고 구체적인 이유를 제시하고 있으므로 정답. 이와 같이 "Why don't you ~?"가 제안이 아닌 이유를 묻는 질문으로 출제되기도 하므로, 맥락을 파악하고 소거법을 활용해 정답을 추론하도록 한다.
(B) 질문과 상관없는 오답.
(C) 질문과 상관없는 오답.

9 M-Cn / W-Br

Do you want to review the report together, or on your own?
(A) No, I don't need any more copies.
(B) I'd prefer to look it over myself.
(C) A fifteen-page document.

보고서를 같이 검토하고 싶으세요, 아니면 혼자 하시겠어요?
(A) 아니요, 사본이 더 필요하지는 않습니다.
(B) 혼자 훑어보고 싶어요.
(C) 15페이지짜리 문서예요.

어휘 review 검토하다, 살펴보다   look over 훑어보다
해설 원하는 보고서 검토 방식을 묻는 선택 의문문
(A) 연상 단어 오답. 질문의 report에서 연상 가능한 copies를 이용한 오답.
(B) 정답. 보고서를 같이 검토하고 싶은지, 아니면 혼자 하고 싶은지 묻는 질문에 혼자 훑어보고 싶다며 둘 중 하나를 선택해 응답하고 있으므로 정답.
(C) 연상 단어 오답. 질문의 report에서 연상 가능한 document를 이용한 오답.

10 W-Am / M-Cn

When's the marketing conference?
(A) The convention center downtown.
(B) Sometime next month.
(C) I need a room with a projector.

마케팅 콘퍼런스는 언제인가요?
(A) 시내에 있는 컨벤션 센터요.
(B) 다음 달 중에요.
(C) 프로젝터가 있는 방이 필요해요.

어휘 downtown 시내에, 시내로
해설 마케팅 콘퍼런스 개최 시점을 묻는 When 의문문
(A) 질문과 상관없는 오답. Where 의문문에 대한 응답이므로 오답.
(B) 정답. 마케팅 콘퍼런스 개최 시점을 묻는 질문에 다음 달 중이라고 대략적인 시기를 알려 주고 있으므로 정답.
(C) 연상 단어 오답. 질문의 conference에서 연상 가능한 a room with a projector를 이용한 오답.

11 M-Au / W-Am

Where are the safety goggles kept?
(A) I'm visiting an eye doctor soon.
(B) They're in the first-floor supply closet.
(C) Sure, I'll try them on.

보안경은 어디에 보관되어 있나요?
(A) 곧 안과 진료를 받으러 가려고요.
(B) 1층 비품실에 있습니다.
(C) 네, 착용해 볼게요.

어휘 safety goggles 보안경
해설 보안경 보관 장소를 묻는 Where 의문문
(A) 연상 단어 오답. 질문의 goggles에서 연상 가능한 eye를 이용한 오답.
(B) 정답. 보안경 보관 장소를 묻는 질문에 1층 비품실에 있다고 구체적인 장소를 알려 주고 있으므로 정답.
(C) Yes/No 불가 오답. Where 의문문에는 Yes/No 응답이 불가능한데, Sure도 일종의 Yes 응답이라고 볼 수 있으므로 오답.

12 W-Br / M-Au

When did this restaurant change its name?
(A) Yes, it is well-known.
(B) I'm not sure.
(C) It's my favorite type of cuisine.

이 레스토랑이 언제 이름을 변경했죠?
(A) 네, 그곳은 잘 알려져 있어요.
(B) 잘 모르겠네요.
(C) 제가 가장 좋아하는 요리 종류예요.

어휘 well-known 잘 알려진   cuisine 요리

해설 레스토랑이 이름을 변경한 시점을 묻는 When 의문문
(A) Yes/No 불가 오답. When 의문문에는 Yes/No 응답이 불가능하므로 오답.
(B) 정답. 레스토랑이 이름을 변경한 시점을 묻는 질문에 잘 모르겠다며 자신은 알지 못한다는 뜻을 표현하고 있으므로 정답.
(C) 연상 단어 오답. 질문의 restaurant에서 연상 가능한 cuisine을 이용한 오답.

13 M-Au / W-Am

Did we complete the inventory, or is there more to do?
(A) OK, that'd be fine.
(B) We're not quite finished.
(C) About 1,000 dollars.

재고 조사를 완료한 건가요, 아니면 할 게 더 있나요?
(A) 네, 괜찮습니다.
(B) 완전히 끝난 건 아니에요.
(C) 약 1,000달러 정도요.

어휘 complete 완료하다   inventory 재고 조사, 재고 목록
not quite 완전히 ~한 것은 아닌

해설 재고 조사 완료 여부를 묻는 선택 의문문
(A) 질문과 상관없는 오답.
(B) 정답. 재고 조사를 완료했는지, 아니면 할 게 더 있는지 묻는 질문에 완전히 끝난 건 아니라며 아직 할 게 더 있음을 우회적으로 표현하고 있으므로 정답.
(C) 질문과 상관없는 오답. How much 의문문에 대한 응답이므로 오답.

14 M-Cn / M-Au

Can you get me a sandwich from the café down the street?
(A) He left an hour ago.
(B) The street signs will be replaced next week.
(C) I'm just about to start a meeting.

길 저쪽에 있는 카페에서 샌드위치 좀 사다 주시겠어요?
(A) 그는 한 시간 전에 갔어요.
(B) 거리 표지판이 다음 주에 교체될 거예요.
(C) 지금 막 회의를 시작하려던 참이에요.

어휘 replace 교체하다   be about to 막 ~하려고 하다

해설 부탁/요청의 의문문
(A) 질문과 상관없는 오답. 질문에 3인칭 대명사 He로 지칭할 인물이 언급된 적이 없으므로 오답.
(B) 단어 반복 오답. 질문의 street을 반복 이용한 오답.
(C) 정답. 카페에서 샌드위치를 좀 사다 달라고 요청하는 질문에 지금 막 회의를 시작하려던 참이라며 우회적으로 거절하고 있으므로 정답.

15 W-Am / M-Cn

How can we interest the client in our business?
(A) By sharing positive customer reviews.
(B) No, I didn't go this year.
(C) At the meeting last Wednesday.

어떻게 하면 고객이 우리 사업에 관심을 갖게 할 수 있을까요?
(A) 긍정적인 고객 후기를 공유해서요.
(B) 아니요, 저는 올해 가지 않았어요.
(C) 지난주 수요일 회의에서요.

어휘 interest 관심을 갖게 하다   positive 긍정적인

해설 고객의 관심을 끌 방법을 묻는 How 의문문
(A) 정답. 고객의 관심을 끌 방법을 묻는 질문에 긍정적인 고객 후기를 공유하는 방법을 제시하고 있으므로 정답.
(B) Yes/No 불가 오답. How 의문문에는 Yes/No 응답이 불가능하므로 오답.
(C) 질문과 상관없는 오답. Where 의문문 또는 When 의문문에 대한 응답이므로 오답.

16 M-Au / M-Cn

Are you planning to work at home tomorrow?
(A) Yes, in the city directory.
(B) Every day at three o'clock.
(C) No, I'll be going into the office.

내일 재택근무하실 계획이신가요?
(A) 네, 시 안내 책자예요.
(B) 매일 3시에요.
(C) 아니요, 사무실에 갈 예정입니다.

어휘 directory (이름, 주소, 연락처 등이 포함된) 안내 책자, 명부

해설 내일 재택근무할 계획인지 묻는 Be동사 의문문
(A) 질문과 상관없는 오답.
(B) 질문과 상관없는 오답. How often 의문문 또는 When 의문문에 대한 응답이므로 오답.
(C) 정답. 내일 재택근무할 계획인지 묻는 질문에 아니요(No)라고 대답한 뒤, 사무실에 갈 예정이라며 부정 답변과 일관된 내용을 덧붙이고 있으므로 정답.

17 M-Cn / W-Br

Don't you have the promotional materials with you?
(A) Thanks, that's great news.
(B) Yes, they're in my bag.
(C) It's lightweight but durable.

당신이 홍보 자료를 갖고 있지 않나요?
(A) 감사합니다, 아주 좋은 소식이네요.
(B) 네, 제 가방에 있어요.
(C) 가볍지만 내구성이 좋아요.

어휘 promotional 홍보의   material 자료, 재료
lightweight 가벼운, 경량의   durable 내구성이 좋은

해설 홍보 자료를 가지고 있는지 확인하는 부정 의문문
(A) 질문과 상관없는 오답.
(B) 정답. 홍보 자료를 가지고 있는지 확인하는 질문에 네(Yes)라고 대답한 뒤, 자신의 가방에 있다며 긍정 답변과 일관된 내용을 덧붙이고 있으므로 정답.
(C) 연상 단어 오답. 질문의 materials에서 연상 가능한 lightweight but durable을 이용한 오답.

18 M-Cn / W-Am

The projector needs to be fixed before our presentation.
(A) A technician has been notified.
(B) The quarterly sales figures.
(C) These pens have our logo on them.

우리 발표 전에 프로젝터가 수리되어야 해요.
(A) 기술자에게 연락해 두었어요.
(B) 분기별 판매 수치요.
(C) 이 펜들에 우리 로고가 있어요.

어휘 fix 수리하다, 고치다   notify 알리다   quarterly 분기의   sales 판매량, 매출   figure 수치, 숫자

해설 정보 전달의 평서문
(A) 정답. 발표 전에 프로젝터가 수리되어야 한다는 평서문에 기술자에게 연락해 두었다며 이미 조치가 이루어졌음을 알려 주고 있으므로 정답.
(B) 연상 단어 오답. 평서문의 presentation에서 연상 가능한 sales figures를 이용한 오답.
(C) 평서문과 상관없는 오답.

19 M-Cn / M-Au

What's the price of this printer?
(A) I don't work here.
(B) It's on Washington Avenue.
(C) Yes, I like it a lot.

이 프린터 가격이 얼마인가요?
(A) 저는 여기서 일하지 않아요.
(B) 워싱턴 가에 있어요.
(C) 네, 아주 마음에 드네요.

해설 프린터 가격을 묻는 What 의문문
(A) 정답. 프린터 가격을 묻는 질문에 자신은 여기서 일하지 않는다며 가격에 대해서는 알지 못한다는 뜻을 나타내고 있으므로 정답.
(B) 질문과 상관없는 오답. Where 의문문에 대한 응답이므로 오답.
(C) Yes/No 불가 오답. What 의문문에는 Yes/No 응답이 불가능하므로 오답.

20 W-Br / M-Au

How many people are attending the orientation session?
(A) There should be 21 people.
(B) Maybe next week.
(C) I can't see the screen.

오리엔테이션에 몇 명이나 참석하나요?
(A) 21명일 거예요.
(B) 아마도 다음 주요.
(C) 스크린이 안 보여요.

해설 오리엔테이션 참석 인원을 묻는 How many 의문문
(A) 정답. 오리엔테이션 참석 인원을 묻는 질문에 21명일 거라며 구체적인 숫자로 응답하고 있으므로 정답.
(B) 질문과 상관없는 오답. When 의문문에 대한 응답이므로 오답.
(C) 질문과 상관없는 오답.

21 W-Am / M-Au

There's a free shuttle bus to the airport, right?
(A) She has an overnight flight.
(B) Yes, it stops right outside.
(C) No, I don't have any.

공항으로 가는 무료 셔틀버스가 있죠, 그렇죠?
(A) 그녀는 야간 항공편을 타요.
(B) 네, 바로 바깥쪽에 정차해요.
(C) 아니요, 저는 가지고 있는 게 없어요.

해설 공항으로 가는 무료 셔틀버스가 있는지 확인하는 부가 의문문
(A) 질문과 상관없는 오답. 질문에 3인칭 대명사 She로 지칭할 인물이 언급된 적이 없으므로 오답.
(B) 정답. 공항으로 가는 무료 셔틀버스가 있는지 확인하는 질문에 네(Yes)라고 대답한 뒤, 바로 바깥쪽에 정차한다며 긍정 답변과 일관된 내용을 덧붙이고 있으므로 정답.
(C) 질문과 상관없는 오답.

22 W-Br / W-Am   ▶동영상 강의

Who has time to edit this article?
(A) The library is on Walton Street.
(B) To meet the client.
(C) It was checked this morning.

누가 이 기사를 편집할 시간이 있나요?
(A) 그 도서관은 월튼 가에 있어요.
(B) 고객과 만나기 위해서요.
(C) 그건 오늘 아침에 검토되었어요.

어휘 edit 편집하다, 수정하다

해설 기사를 편집할 시간이 있는 사람을 묻는 Who 의문문
(A) 질문과 상관없는 오답. Where 의문문에 대한 응답이므로 오답.
(B) 질문과 상관없는 오답. Why 의문문에 대한 응답이므로 오답.
(C) 정답. 기사를 편집할 시간이 있는 사람을 묻는 질문에 그건 오늘 아침에 검토되었다며 편집할 필요가 없음을 나타내고 있으므로 정답.

23 W-Br / M-Au

What time does the factory shift end?
(A) Because it's too far.
(B) I'm glad you like it.
(C) The schedule is posted in the break room.

공장 교대 근무는 몇 시에 끝나나요?
(A) 너무 멀기 때문에요.
(B) 마음에 드신다니 기쁘네요.
(C) 일정표가 휴게실에 게시되어 있어요.

어휘 shift 교대 근무(조) post 게시하다

해설 공장 교대 근무 종료 시간을 묻는 What 의문문
(A) 질문과 상관없는 오답. Why 의문문에 대한 응답이므로 오답.
(B) 질문과 상관없는 오답.
(C) 정답. 공장 교대 근무 종료 시간을 묻는 질문에 일정표가 휴게실에 게시되어 있다며 정보를 확인할 수 있는 방법을 알려 주고 있으므로 정답.

---

24 W-Am / W-Br

These train tickets are expensive.
(A) Just a one-way ticket, please.
(B) Did you complete the training?
(C) Yes, it's an express train.

이 기차표들은 비싸네요.
(A) 그냥 편도 티켓 한 장 주세요.
(B) 교육을 완료하셨나요?
(C) 네, 급행열차예요.

어휘 express 급행의, 신속한

해설 정보 전달의 평서문
(A) 단어 반복 오답. 평서문의 ticket을 반복 이용한 오답.
(B) 유사 발음 오답. 평서문의 train과 부분적으로 발음이 유사한 training을 이용한 오답.
(C) 정답. 기차표들이 비싸다는 평서문에 네(Yes)라고 대답한 뒤, 급행열차라며 가격이 비싼 이유를 덧붙이고 있으므로 정답.

---

25 M-Cn / W-Am

Isn't this television prototype supposed to have more advanced features?
(A) He has an advanced degree in economics.
(B) We're already over budget.
(C) I really enjoyed that television program.

이 텔레비전 시제품에는 더 발전된 기능들이 있어야 하는 거 아닌가요?
(A) 그는 경제학 고급 학위를 소지하고 있어요.
(B) 우리는 이미 예산을 초과했어요.
(C) 저는 그 텔레비전 프로그램을 정말 재밌게 봤어요.

어휘 be supposed to ~하기로 되어 있다 prototype 시제품, 원형
advanced 발전된, 고급의 feature 기능, 특징
degree 학위, 정도 economics 경제학 budget 예산

해설 시제품에 더 발전된 기능이 있어야 하는 게 아닌지 확인하는 부정의문문
(A) 단어 반복 오답. 질문의 advanced를 반복 이용한 오답.
(B) 정답. 시제품에 더 발전된 기능이 있어야 하는 게 아닌지 확인하는 질문에 이미 예산을 초과했다며 그렇게 하기는 어려운 상황임을 우회적으로 나타내고 있으므로 정답.
(C) 단어 반복 오답. 질문의 television을 반복 이용한 오답.

---

26 M-Cn / W-Br

What should we do to prepare for the sales meeting?
(A) Let's discuss it after lunch.
(B) With the sixteen summer interns.
(C) The conference center on Mill Street.

영업 회의를 준비하기 위해 무엇을 해야 하나요?
(A) 점심 식사 후에 논의해 봅시다.
(B) 여름 인턴 16명과 함께요.
(C) 밀 가에 위치한 콘퍼런스 센터요.

해설 영업 회의 준비를 위해 해야 할 일을 묻는 What 의문문
(A) 정답. 영업 회의 준비를 위해 해야 할 일을 묻는 질문에 점심 식사 후에 논의해 보자며 나중에 정하자는 의사를 우회적으로 표현하고 있으므로 정답.
(B) 질문과 상관없는 오답. Who 의문문에 대한 응답이므로 오답.
(C) 질문과 상관없는 오답. Where 의문문에 대한 응답이므로 오답.

---

27 W-Am / M-Cn

Do you think Ms. Wang would be interested in joining the event planning committee?
(A) Let's reserve the hotel ballroom.
(B) She'll be on vacation for the next month.
(C) I'd love a cup of tea.

왕 씨가 행사 기획 위원회에 참여하는 데 관심이 있을 것 같아요?
(A) 그 호텔 연회장을 예약하죠.
(B) 그분은 다음 한 달 동안 휴가 중일 거예요.
(C) 차 한 잔 마시면 정말 좋겠어요.

어휘 committee 위원회 reserve 예약하다

해설 행사 기획 위원회 참여에 대한 왕 씨의 관심 여부를 묻는 조동사(Do) 의문문
(A) 연상 단어 오답. 질문의 event에서 연상 가능한 hotel ballroom을 이용한 오답.
(B) 정답. 행사 기획 위원회 참여에 대한 왕 씨의 관심 여부를 묻는 질문에 그 사람이 다음 한 달 동안 휴가 중일 것이라며 참여 가능성이 낮음을 우회적으로 표현하고 있으므로 정답.
(C) 질문과 상관없는 오답.

---

28 M-Au / W-Am ▶동영상 강의

Dr. Marino has the survey results on his desk.
(A) His office door is locked.
(B) He passed his driving test.
(C) The pharmacy on Maple Street.

마리노 박사님 책상에 설문 조사 결과가 있어요.
(A) 그분의 사무실 문이 잠겨 있어요.
(B) 그분이 운전면허 시험에 합격했어요.
(C) 메이플 가에 있는 약국이요.

어휘 survey 설문 조사 result 결과 pharmacy 약국

해설 정보 전달의 평서문
(A) 정답. 마리노 박사의 책상에 설문 조사 결과가 있다는 평서문에 그 사람의 사무실 문이 잠겨 있다며 결과물을 확인할 수 없는 상황임을 우회적으로 나타내고 있으므로 정답.
(B) 평서문과 상관없는 오답.
(C) 평서문과 상관없는 오답. Where 의문문에 대한 응답이므로 오답.

29 M-Cn / W-Am

The keynote speech wasn't very inspiring, was it?
(A) It was too technical.
(B) No, the one on the right side.
(C) Some receipts for expenses.

기조 연설이 그렇게 고무적이지는 않았어요, 그렇죠?
(A) 너무 전문적이었어요.
(B) 아니요, 오른쪽에 있는 것이요.
(C) 지출 영수증 몇 장이에요.

어휘 keynote speech 기조 연설 inspiring 고무적인
technical 전문적인, 기술적인

해설 기조 연설에 대한 의견을 묻는 부가 의문문
(A) 정답. 기조 연설이 고무적이지 않았는지 묻는 질문에 너무 전문적이었다며 고무적이지 않았다는 데 동의하고 있으므로 정답.
(B) 질문과 상관없는 오답.
(C) 질문과 상관없는 오답.

30 W-Am / W-Br

Our company is upgrading its bookkeeping software.
(A) No, I took a different flight.
(B) How was your business trip to Shanghai?
(C) I signed up for a training session this morning.

우리 회사가 회계 소프트웨어를 업그레이드하고 있어요.
(A) 아니요, 저는 다른 항공편을 탔어요.
(B) 상하이 출장은 어떠셨어요?
(C) 저는 오늘 아침에 교육에 등록했어요.

어휘 bookkeeping 회계, 부기 sign up 등록하다, 신청하다

해설 정보 전달의 평서문
(A) 연상 단어 오답. 평서문에 쓰인 bookkeeping의 일부 발음인 book(예약하다)에서 연상 가능한 flight을 이용한 오답.
(B) 연상 단어 오답. 평서문에 쓰인 bookkeeping의 일부 발음인 book(예약하다)에서 연상 가능한 trip을 이용한 오답.
(C) 정답. 회사가 회계 소프트웨어를 업그레이드하고 있다는 평서문에 오늘 아침에 교육에 등록했다며 변화에 따른 자신의 조치를 알려 주고 있으므로 정답.

31 M-Cn / W-Am

Should we set up the buffet table for tomorrow's luncheon indoors or outdoors?
(A) I haven't seen her.
(B) We won't need any more copies.
(C) It's supposed to be a beautiful day.

내일 오찬을 위한 뷔페 테이블을 실내에 차릴까요, 아니면 실외에 차릴까요?
(A) 그녀를 본 적이 없어요.
(B) 사본이 더 필요하지는 않을 거예요.
(C) 화창한 날이 될 거예요.

어휘 luncheon 오찬 indoors 실내에 outdoors 실외에

해설 뷔페 테이블을 차릴 위치를 묻는 선택 의문문
(A) 질문과 상관없는 오답. 질문에 3인칭 대명사 her로 지칭할 인물이 언급된 적이 없으므로 오답.
(B) 질문과 상관없는 오답.
(C) 정답. 뷔페 테이블을 실내와 실외 중 어느 위치에 차릴지 묻는 질문에 화창한 날이 될 거라며 실외에 차렸으면 하는 의사를 우회적으로 표현하고 있으므로 정답.

PART 3

32-34 M-Au / W-Br

M Bianca, **32 the retail space next door to us will become available in June. That means we can begin the store expansion we've been planning.**

W That's great news! After we increase our space, **33 we can finally do more than just sell musical instruments.**

M I knew you'd be happy to hear the news. **34 We'll be able to add practice rooms so we can offer private music lessons by the end of the year.**

남 비앙카, **6월에 저희 옆에 있는 소매 공간을 이용할 수 있게 될 거예요. 우리가 계획해 온 매장 확장을 시작할 수 있다는 뜻이죠.**

여 좋은 소식이네요! 공간을 넓히고 나면, **드디어 단순히 악기를 판매하는 것 이상의 일을 할 수 있겠어요.**

남 이 소식을 들으면 기뻐하실 줄 알았어요. **연말까지 개인 음악 레슨을 제공할 수 있도록 연습실을 추가할 수 있을 겁니다.**

어휘 retail 소매의 available 이용 가능한, 구할 수 있는
expansion 확장, 확대 increase 커지다, 증가하다
musical instrument 악기 practice 연습 private 개인의

32 What is the speakers' business planning to do in June?
(A) Expand a space
(B) Take product inventory
(C) Plan an annual sale
(D) Change a window display

화자들의 업체는 6월에 무엇을 할 계획을 세우고 있는가?
(A) 공간 확장하기
(B) 재고 조사하기
(C) 연례 세일 행사 계획하기
(D) 창문 진열품 변경하기

어휘 expand 확장하다, 확대하다 annual 연례적인, 해마다의

해설 세부 사항 관련 – 6월에 계획하고 있는 일
남자가 첫 대사에서 6월에 옆에 있는 소매 공간을 이용할 수 있게 된다(~ the retail space next door to us will become available in June)며 이는 계획해 온 매장 확장을 시작할 수 있다는 뜻(That means we can begin the store expansion we've been planning)이라고 했으므로 정답은 (A)이다.

Paraphrasing
대화의 store expansion → 정답의 Expand a space

33 Where do the speakers most likely work?
(A) At a dance studio
(B) At a culinary school
(C) At a music shop
(D) At an arts and crafts store

화자들은 어디에서 일하는 것 같은가?
(A) 댄스 스튜디오
(B) 요리 학원
(C) 악기점
(D) 미술 및 공예 용품점

어휘 culinary 요리의 craft 공예(품)

해설 전체 내용 관련 – 화자들의 근무 장소
여자가 첫 대사에서 드디어 단순히 악기를 판매하는 것 이상의 일을 할 수 있을 것(we can finally do more than just sell musical instruments)이라고 했으므로 정답은 (C)이다.

34 What does the man say he would like to do by the end of the year?
(A) Advertise a contest
(B) Offer private lessons
(C) Increase operating hours
(D) Provide repair services

남자는 연말까지 무엇을 하고 싶다고 말하는가?
(A) 콘테스트 광고하기
(B) 개인 레슨 제공하기
(C) 운영 시간 늘리기
(D) 수리 서비스 제공하기

어휘 advertise 광고하다

해설 세부 사항 관련 – 남자가 연말까지 하고 싶어 하는 일
남자가 두 번째 대사에서 연말까지 개인 음악 레슨을 제공할 수 있도록 연습실을 추가할 수 있을 것(We'll be able to add practice rooms so we can offer private music lessons by the end of the year)이라고 했으므로 정답은 (B)이다.

35-37 M-Au / W-Am

M Hi. **35 I'm working on renovating the lobby of my office**, and I'd like to get some paint for the walls.
W Sure. What do you have in mind?
M Well, I want to paint the walls with one of the colors from our new logo, either green or red.
W Hmm... **36 I wouldn't choose red—it will fade too fast.**
M Oh, OK. Then let's go with green.
W Do you have a copy of the logo with you? If I have the image, I can mix a custom paint to match it.
M Actually, I don't.
W Well, **37 if you e-mail me a picture of the logo**, I can have the paint ready for you by Friday.

남 안녕하세요. **제가 사무실 로비를 보수하는 작업을 하고 있는데요**, 벽에 칠할 페인트를 구매하려고 합니다.
여 네. 생각하고 계신 게 있나요?
남 어, 저희 새 로고에 있는 색상들 중 하나로 벽을 칠하고 싶어요. 초록이나 빨강이요.
여 흠… **저라면 빨강은 선택하지 않을 것 같아요. 너무 빨리 바랠 거예요.**
남 아, 알겠습니다. 그럼 초록으로 하죠.
여 로고 사본을 가지고 계신가요? 이미지가 있으면, 그 색에 맞춰서 맞춤 페인트를 혼합할 수 있어요.
남 사실, 없어요.
여 그럼, **이메일로 로고 사진을 보내 주시면**, 금요일까지 페인트를 준비해 드릴 수 있습니다.

어휘 renovate 보수하다, 개조하다 fade 바래다, 희미해지다
custom 맞춤 제공의, 주문 제작의 match 일치하다, 어울리다

35 What type of project is the man working on?
(A) Restoring a piece of art
(B) Designing a logo
(C) Renovating a lobby
(D) Developing a hair dye

남자는 어떤 종류의 프로젝트를 진행하고 있는가?
(A) 미술품 복원
(B) 로고 디자인
(C) 로비 보수
(D) 헤어 염색제 개발

어휘 restore 복원하다, 복구하다 dye 염색(제)

해설 세부 사항 관련 – 남자가 진행하고 있는 프로젝트
남자가 첫 대사에서 사무실 로비를 보수하는 작업을 하고 있다(I'm working on renovating the lobby of my office ~)고 했으므로 정답은 (C)이다.

36 Why does the woman recommend avoiding the color red?
(A) It is expensive to produce.
(B) It fades quickly.
(C) It is too bright.
(D) It is very popular.

여자는 왜 빨간색을 피하라고 권하는가?
(A) 생산 비용이 많이 든다.
(B) 빨리 바랜다.
(C) 너무 밝다.
(D) 인기가 매우 많다.

해설 세부 사항 관련 – 여자가 빨간색을 피하라고 권하는 이유
여자가 두 번째 대사에서 자신이라면 빨강은 선택하지 않을 것 같다며 너무 빨리 바랠 것(I wouldn't choose red—it will fade too fast)이라는 이유를 덧붙이고 있으므로 정답은 (B)이다.

Paraphrasing
대화의 wouldn't choose → 질문의 avoiding
대화의 too fast → 정답의 quickly

37 What does the woman ask the man to do?
(A) Pay a deposit
(B) Send a picture
(C) Test a product
(D) Schedule a consultation

여자는 남자에게 무엇을 해 달라고 요청하는가?
(A) 선금 지불하기
(B) 사진 보내기
(C) 제품 테스트하기
(D) 상담 일정 잡기

어휘 deposit 선금, 보증금 consultation 상담, 상의

해설 세부 사항 관련 – 여자의 요청 사항
여자가 마지막 대사에서 이메일로 로고 사진을 보내 주면(if you e-mail me a picture of the logo ~) 페인트를 준비하겠다고 했으므로 정답은 (B)이다.

Paraphrasing
대화의 e-mail → 정답의 Send

38-40 W-Br / M-Au

W Welcome to the Western Airlines customer service desk. How can I assist you?
M Hi. I flew in yesterday from Canada and was told that my luggage was accidentally put on a flight arriving this morning.
W OK. ³⁹Do you have your boarding pass?
M Yes—here it is. ³⁸,⁴⁰Can I go to the unclaimed baggage area and pick up my luggage?
W That area is past security. ⁴⁰I can use information on the boarding pass to locate the luggage for you.

여 웨스턴 항공사 고객 서비스 데스크입니다. 무엇을 도와드릴까요?
남 안녕하세요. 어제 캐나다에서 비행기를 타고 왔는데, 제 수하물이 실수로 오늘 아침에 도착하는 항공편에 실렸다고 들었습니다.
여 알겠습니다. **탑승권을 가지고 계신가요?**
남 네, 여기 있습니다. **제가 미수령 수하물 보관 구역으로 가서 제 짐을 가져올 수 있을까요?**
여 그 구역은 보안 검색대를 지나서 있습니다. 제가 탑승권에 있는 정보를 이용해서 수하물을 찾아 드릴 수 있어요.

어휘 assist 돕다 fly in 비행기로 도착하다 luggage 수하물, 짐 accidentally 실수로, 우연히 boarding pass 탑승권 unclaimed baggage 미수령 수하물, 분실 수하물 locate (~의 위치를) 찾다, 확인하다

38 What is the man trying to do?
(A) Join a tour group
(B) Pick up some luggage
(C) Call a taxi
(D) Buy some gifts

남자는 무엇을 하려고 하는가?
(A) 투어 그룹 합류하기
(B) 수하물 가져오기
(C) 택시 부르기
(D) 선물 구입하기

해설 세부 사항 관련 – 남자가 하려는 것
남자가 두 번째 대사에서 미수령 수하물 보관 구역으로 가서 짐을 가져올 수 있을지(Can I go to the unclaimed baggage area and pick up my luggage?) 물었으므로 정답은 (B)이다.

39 What does the woman ask to see?
(A) Photo identification
(B) A valid visa
(C) A customs declaration
(D) A boarding pass

272

여자는 무엇을 보여 달라고 요청하는가?
(A) 사진이 부착된 신분증
(B) 유효한 비자
(C) 세관 신고서
(D) 탑승권

어휘 valid 유효한   customs declaration 세관 신고서

해설 세부 사항 관련 – 여자의 요청 사항
여자가 두 번째 대사에서 남자에게 탑승권을 갖고 있는지(Do you have your boarding pass?) 물었으므로 정답은 (D)이다.

40 Why does the woman say, "That area is past security"?
(A) To clarify a policy
(B) To express surprise
(C) To reject a request
(D) To describe a floor plan

여자는 왜 "그 구역은 보안 검색대를 지나서 있습니다"라고 말하는가?
(A) 정책을 분명히 하기 위해
(B) 놀라움을 표현하기 위해
(C) 요청을 거절하기 위해
(D) 평면도를 설명하기 위해

어휘 clarify 분명히 하다   policy 정책, 방침   reject 거절하다
describe 설명하다, 묘사하다   floor plan (건물) 평면도

해설 화자의 의도 파악 – 그 구역은 보안 검색대를 지나서 있다는 말의 의도
남자가 두 번째 대사에서 미수령 수하물 보관 구역으로 가서 짐을 가져올 수 있을지(Can I go to the unclaimed baggage area and pick up my luggage?) 묻자, 여자가 인용문을 언급한 뒤 본인이 수하물을 찾아 줄 수 있다(~ locate the luggage for you)고 했다. 이는 남자의 요청을 거절하고 다른 방법을 제안하는 것이므로 정답은 (C)이다.

41-43 M-Cn / W-Br

M **41 We're so happy to have you join our office as our new dental hygienist**, Maria. As you know, **41 you'll be cleaning our patients' teeth** before I come in to complete the exam.

W I'll also be responsible for updating the patients' files and scheduling their next appointments, right?

M Yes. We use a software program called DentalX for all our patient records. Have you used it before?

W Yes, **42 I'm familiar with that software.**

M Great. Also, **43 remember that our office closes every day from twelve to one thirty for lunch,** so please be mindful of that when scheduling patients.

남 우리 병원에 새로운 치위생사로 합류하시게 되어 기쁩니다, 마리아. 아시다시피, 제가 검사를 마무리하러 들어가기 전에 **환자들의 치아를 세정하시게 될 거예요.**

여 환자들의 파일을 업데이트하고, 다음 예약을 잡는 일도 제가 맡게 되는 거죠, 맞죠?

남 네, 저희는 모든 환자 기록에 덴탈엑스라는 소프트웨어 프로그램을 사용해요. 전에 사용해 본 적이 있으신가요?

여 네, **그 소프트웨어에 익숙합니다.**

남 잘됐네요. 그리고, **저희 병원은 매일 12시부터 1시 반까지 점심시간으로 문을 닫는다는 점 명심하시고,** 환자 예약을 잡을 때 유의해 주세요.

어휘 dental hygienist 치위생사   patient 환자   exam 검사
be responsible for ~을 담당하다, ~을 책임지다
appointment 예약, 약속   be mindful of ~에 유의하다

41 Where do the speakers most likely work?
(A) At a bookstore
(B) At a marketing firm
(C) At an electronics manufacturer
(D) At a dental office

화자들은 어디에서 일하는 것 같은가?
(A) 서점
(B) 마케팅 회사
(C) 전자제품 제조사
(D) 치과

해설 전체 내용 관련 – 화자들의 근무 장소
남자가 첫 대사에서 여자에게 우리 병원에 새로운 치위생사로 합류하게 되어 기쁘다(We're so happy to have you join our office as our new dental hygienist ~)며 환자들의 치아를 세정하게 될 것(~ you'll be cleaning our patients' teeth ~)이라고 설명하고 있는 것으로 보아 화자들은 치과에서 근무한다는 것을 알 수 있다. 따라서 정답은 (D)이다.

42 What does the woman say she is familiar with?
(A) A university course
(B) A software program
(C) An industry conference
(D) A safety procedure

여자는 무엇이 익숙하다고 말하는가?
(A) 대학 과정
(B) 소프트웨어 프로그램
(C) 업계 콘퍼런스
(D) 안전 절차

어휘 procedure 절차

해설 세부 사항 관련 – 여자가 익숙하다고 말하는 것
여자가 두 번째 대사에서 앞서 남자가 언급한 덴탈엑스를 가리켜 그 소프트웨어에 익숙하다(I'm familiar with that software)고 말하고 있으므로 정답은 (B)이다.

43 What does the man remind the woman about?
(A) A lunch break
(B) A dress code
(C) A parking policy
(D) A benefits program

남자는 여자에게 무엇에 대해 상기시키는가?
(A) 점심시간
(B) 복장 규정
(C) 주차 정책
(D) 복지 혜택 프로그램

어휘 benefits (급여 이외에 제공하는) 복지 혜택, 복리 후생

해설 세부 사항 관련 – 남자가 상기시키는 것
　　남자가 마지막 대사에서 우리 병원은 매일 12시부터 1시 반까지 점심시간으로 문을 닫는다는 점 명심하라(remember that our office closes every day from twelve to one thirty for lunch ~)고 말하고 있으므로 정답은 (A)이다.

Paraphrasing
대화의 every day from twelve to one thirty for lunch
→ 정답의 A lunch break

44-46 3인 대화 M-Au / W-Br / W-Am

M　Next, I wanted to check with the design team about our water-permeable bricks for walkways. I think the bricks will be popular in areas with water drainage problems. But **44 I'm concerned that the final design won't be ready in time for the trade show.**

W1　Right, **45 we still need to finish the durability testing. Camille, how's that going?**

W2　So far, they seem to be as durable as we anticipated. But we still have a few more tests to run.

M　Great. Please keep me posted on your progress. In the meantime, **46 we should start putting together a promotional video to show at our booth at the trade show. Who'd like to help me with that project?**

남　다음으로, 우리 회사의 보도용 투수성 벽돌과 관련해 디자인팀에 확인해 보고 싶습니다. 저는 이 벽돌이 배수 문제가 있는 지역에서 인기가 있을 거라고 생각해요. 하지만 **최종 디자인이 무역 박람회 일정에 맞춰 준비되지 못할까 봐 걱정됩니다.**
여1　맞습니다, **아직 내구성 테스트를 마쳐야 해요. 카밀, 어떻게 되어 가고 있나요?**
여2　지금까지는, 우리가 예상했던 것만큼의 내구성을 보이는 것 같아요. 하지만 아직 몇 가지 테스트를 더 해야 합니다.
남　좋아요. 진행 상황을 계속 알려 주세요. 그동안, **우리는 무역 박람회의 부스에서 상영할 홍보 영상을 만들기 시작해야겠군요. 이 프로젝트를 도와주실 분 계신가요?**

어휘 water-permeable 투수성의(물이 잘 빠지는)
brick 벽돌　walkway 보도, 통로　water drainage 배수
durability 내구성　anticipate 예상하다, 기대하다
keep ~ posted ~에게 계속 알려 주다　progress 진행, 진척
in the meantime 그동안　put together 만들다, 준비하다
promotional 홍보의

44 What is the man concerned about?
(A) A staff shortage
(B) A design budget
(C) A project timeline
(D) A weather forecast

남자는 무엇을 걱정하는가?
(A) 직원 부족
(B) 디자인 예산
(C) 프로젝트 진행 일정
(D) 일기 예보

어휘 shortage 부족　budget 예산　timeline 진행 일정

해설 세부 사항 관련 – 남자가 걱정하는 것
　　남자가 첫 대사에서 최종 디자인이 무역 박람회에 일정에 맞춰 준비되지 못할까 봐 걱정된다(~ I'm concerned that the final design won't be ready in time for the trade show)고 말하는 것으로 보아 남자는 해당 프로젝트의 진행 일정에 대해 걱정하고 있음을 알 수 있다. 따라서 정답은 (C)이다.

Paraphrasing
대화의 the final design won't be ready in time for the trade show → 정답의 A project timeline

45 What is Camille working on?
(A) Durability testing
(B) Contract negotiations
(C) A marketing presentation
(D) A product manual

카밀은 어떤 작업을 하고 있는가?
(A) 내구성 테스트
(B) 계약 협상
(C) 마케팅 발표
(D) 제품 사용 설명서

어휘 contract 계약, 계약서　negotiation 협상　manual 설명서

해설 세부 사항 관련 – 카밀이 작업하는 것
　　첫 번째 여자가 첫 대사에서 아직 내구성 테스트를 마쳐야 한다(~ we still need to finish the durability testing)며 카밀에게 그 일이 어떻게 되어 가고 있는지(Camille, how's that going?) 묻고 있으므로 정답은 (A)이다.

46 What would the man like assistance with?
(A) Interviewing a job candidate
(B) Making a video
(C) Booking a venue
(D) Packing some materials

남자는 무엇에 대해 도움을 받고 싶어 하는가?
(A) 입사 지원자 면접 보기
(B) 동영상 만들기
(C) 행사장 예약하기
(D) 물품 포장하기

어휘 candidate 지원자, 후보자   venue 행사장

해설 세부 사항 관련 – 남자가 도움을 원하는 일
남자가 마지막 대사에서 무역 박람회의 부스에서 상영할 홍보 영상을 만들기 시작해야겠다(~ we should start putting together a promotional video to show at our booth at the trade show)면서 이 프로젝트를 도와줄 사람이 있는지(Who'd like to help me with that project?) 묻고 있으므로 정답은 (B)이다.

Paraphrasing
대화의 putting together a promotional video
→ 정답의 Making a video

47-49 M-Cn / W-Am   ▶동영상 강의

M Excuse me—officer? **⁴⁷Do you happen to know where rideshare drivers park to wait for passengers? It's my first time at this airport.**

W Yes. Drive to the pickup area by terminal A. Look out for the orange sign that says "rideshare." I'm sure you'll see other drivers there. By the way, **⁴⁸I recommend taking the terminal bypass. That bridge will take you there faster.**

M Great. Thank you. **⁴⁹Oh—is there a fuel station near the airport?** My tank is almost empty.

W **⁴⁹You'll see one by the rental-car lot on your way out.**

남 실례지만, 직원이시죠? 혹시 승차 공유 운전자들이 승객들을 기다리기 위해 주차하는 곳이 어딘지 아시나요? 제가 이 공항은 처음이라서요.
여 네. 터미널 A 옆 픽업 구역으로 가시면 됩니다. "승차 공유"라고 쓰여 있는 주황색 표지판을 찾아보세요. 거기서 다른 운전자들을 보실 수 있을 거예요. 그런데, **터미널 우회로를 이용하는 걸 추천해요. 그 다리를 타면 더 빨리 갈 수 있습니다.**
남 잘됐네요. 감사합니다. 아, 공항 근처에 주유소가 있나요? 연료통이 거의 비어서요.
여 나가시는 길에 렌터카 주차장 옆에 한 군데 보이실 겁니다.

어휘 happen to 혹시 ~하다   rideshare 승차 공유   passenger 승객   bypass 우회로   empty 빈

---

47 What most likely is the man's job?
(A) Gift shop worker
(B) Flight attendant
(C) Security guard
(D) Rideshare driver

남자의 직업은 무엇인 것 같은가?
(A) 선물 매장 직원
(B) 항공 승무원
(C) 보안 직원
(D) 승차 공유 운전자

해설 전체 내용 관련 – 남자의 직업
남자가 첫 대사에서 혹시 승차 공유 운전자들이 승객을 기다리기 위해 주차하는 곳이 어디인지 아냐(Do you happen to know where rideshare drivers park to wait for passengers?)고 물으며 이 공항은 처음(It's my first time at this airport)이라고 말하는 것으로 보아 남자는 승차 공유 운전자임을 알 수 있다. 따라서 정답은 (D)이다.

---

48 How does the woman recommend getting to terminal A?
(A) By taking a shuttle bus
(B) By riding an escalator
(C) By using a bridge
(D) By crossing a street

여자는 어떻게 터미널 A로 가라고 권하는가?
(A) 셔틀버스를 이용해서
(B) 에스컬레이터를 타고
(C) 다리를 이용해서
(D) 길을 건너서

해설 세부 사항 관련 – 여자의 권유 사항
여자가 첫 대사에서 터미널 우회로를 이용하는 걸 추천하면서 그 다리를 타면 더 빨리 간다(~ I recommend taking the terminal bypass. That bridge will take you there faster)고 했으므로 정답은 (C)이다.

---

49 What does the woman say is by the rental-car lot?
(A) A department store
(B) A bank
(C) A restaurant
(D) A fuel station

여자는 렌터카 주차장 옆에 무엇이 있다고 말하는가?
(A) 백화점
(B) 은행
(C) 레스토랑
(D) 주유소

해설 세부 사항 관련 – 여자가 렌터카 주차장 옆에 있다고 말하는 것
남자가 두 번째 대사에서 공항 근처에 주유소가 있는지(Oh— is there a fuel station near the airport?) 묻자 여자가 렌터카 주차장 옆에 한 군데 보일 것(You'll see one by the rental-car lot on your way out)이라고 알려 주고 있으므로 정답은 (D)이다.

50-52 M-Au / W-Br

M This traffic is really terrible.

W I know. **50, 51 We've been stuck in this bus for hours now! It's frustrating. I wonder what's going on.**

M **I heard the Day Street Bridge is being worked on.**

W Oh, really? I didn't know that.

M Yes. I think it's down to just one lane for the next couple of weeks.

W That's good to know. **52 I'll take the train into the city tomorrow instead**, so I won't be late for my appointments.

남 이곳 교통량은 정말 끔찍하네요.
여 그러게요. 지금 몇 시간째 이 버스에 갇혀 있잖아요! 답답하네요. 무슨 일이 있는 건지 궁금해요.
남 데이 스트리트 다리가 공사 중이라는 얘기를 들었어요.
여 아, 그래요? 그런 줄 몰랐어요.
남 네. 제 생각에 앞으로 몇 주 동안은 차선이 하나로 좁혀질 것 같아요.
여 좋은 정보네요. 저는 내일 대신 기차를 타고 시내로 갈 거예요. 그래야 약속에 늦지 않겠어요.

어휘 traffic 교통(량) be stuck in ~에 갇혀 있다
frustrating 답답하게 하는, 불만스러운

50 Where are the speakers?
(A) On a bus
(B) On a boat
(C) At a car dealership
(D) At a train station

화자들은 어디에 있는가?
(A) 버스
(B) 보트
(C) 자동차 대리점
(D) 기차역

해설 전체 내용 관련 – 대화 장소
여자가 첫 대사에서 지금 몇 시간째 이 버스에 갇혀 있다(We've been stuck in this bus for hours now!)고 했으므로 (A)가 정답이다.

51 Why does the man say, "I heard the Day Street Bridge is being worked on"?
(A) To confirm some information
(B) To make a correction
(C) To explain a delay
(D) To recommend leaving early

남자는 왜 "데이 스트리트 다리가 공사 중이라는 얘기를 들었어요"라고 말하는가?
(A) 정보를 확인해 주려고
(B) 정정하려고
(C) 지연 이유를 설명하려고
(D) 일찍 나갈 것을 권하려고

어휘 confirm 확인해 주다, 승인하다   correction 정정, 수정

해설 화자의 의도 파악 – 데이 스트리트 다리가 공사 중이라는 말의 의도
여자가 첫 대사에서 몇 시간째 버스에 갇혀 있는 것에 대해 무슨 일인지 궁금하다(We've been stuck in this bus for hours now! ~ I wonder what's going on)고 말한 뒤 남자가 인용문을 언급하는 것으로 보아 차량 통행이 더딘 이유를 알려 주려는 의도로 한 말임을 알 수 있다. 따라서 정답은 (C)이다.

52 What does the woman say she will do tomorrow?
(A) Purchase a monthly pass
(B) Download a map
(C) Check a schedule
(D) Use alternate transportation

여자는 내일 무엇을 할 것이라고 말하는가?
(A) 월간 이용권 구입하기
(B) 지도 다운로드하기
(C) 일정표 확인하기
(D) 대체 교통편 이용하기

어휘 alternate 대체의, 대신의 transportation 교통(편)

해설 세부 사항 관련 – 여자가 내일 할 일
여자가 마지막 대사에서 내일 대신 기차를 타고 시내로 갈 것(I'll take the train into the city tomorrow instead ~)이라고 말하는 것으로 보아 버스가 아닌 다른 교통편을 이용하겠다는 것이므로 정답은 (D)이다.

Paraphrasing
대화의 take the train ~ instead
→ 정답의 Use alternate transportation

53-55 W-Br / M-Cn

W Girard Electronics. How can I help you?

M Hi. ⁵³**I bought a camera from your store last week**, but I'm having trouble with it now.

W What's the problem?

M Well, I changed the lens from the standard to a telephoto one today, and ⁵⁴**now an error message pops up on the LCD screen.**

W Hmm. I'm sorry, but ⁵⁴**I can't know for sure without looking at it**, as it could be caused by a few things.

M ⁵⁴**I could come by this afternoon.**

W OK. I won't be here, but ⁵⁵**one of the other employees can definitely help you. Let me just write a note down.**

M Thanks.

여 지라드 일렉트로닉스입니다. 무엇을 도와드릴까요?
남 안녕하세요. **제가 지난주에 그 매장에서 카메라를 하나 구입했는데**, 지금 문제가 있어서요.
여 무슨 문제인가요?
남 음, 제가 오늘 렌즈를 표준에서 망원 사진용으로 바꾸었는데, **LCD 화면에 오류 메시지가 뜹니다.**
여 흠. 죄송하지만, **제가 그걸 직접 보지 않고는 정확히 알 수 없어요.** 원인이 여러 가지일 수 있어서요.
남 **제가 오늘 오후에 들를 수 있습니다.**
여 알겠습니다. 저는 없겠지만, **다른 직원들 중 한 명이 분명 도와드릴 수 있을 겁니다. 제가 메모 하나 남겨 놓겠습니다.**
남 감사합니다.

어휘 have trouble with ~에 문제를 겪다　standard 표준(의)　telephoto 망원 사진의　pop up 불쑥 나타나다, 돌출하다　cause 초래하다, 일으키다　definitely 분명히, 명확히

53 What product is the man calling about?
(A) A portable game system
(B) A printer
(C) A camera
(D) A tablet computer

남자는 어떤 제품과 관련해 전화하는가?
(A) 휴대용 게임기
(B) 프린터
(C) 카메라
(D) 태블릿 컴퓨터

어휘 portable 휴대용의

해설 세부 사항 관련 – 남자가 문의하는 제품의 종류
남자가 첫 대사에서 지난주에 그 매장에서 카메라를 하나 구입했다(I bought a camera from your store last week ~)고 말한 뒤 해당 제품에 대해 문의하고 있으므로 정답은 (C)이다.

54 Why will the man go to a store?
(A) To purchase an extended warranty
(B) To resolve a problem
(C) To receive a refund
(D) To pick up some accessories

남자는 왜 매장에 갈 것인가?
(A) 연장된 품질 보증 서비스를 구입하기 위해
(B) 문제를 해결하기 위해
(C) 환불을 받기 위해
(D) 액세서리를 받아오기 위해

어휘 extend 연장하다, 확장하다　warranty 품질 보증서　resolve 해결하다　refund 환불

해설 세부 사항 관련 – 남자가 매장에 가는 이유
남자가 두 번째 대사에서 LCD 화면에 오류 메시지가 뜬다(~ now an error message pops up on the LCD screen)고 말한 뒤 여자가 직접 보지 않고는 정확히 알기 어렵다(~ I can't know for sure without looking at it, ~)고 하자 오늘 오후에 들를 수 있다(I could come by this afternoon)고 응답하고 있다. 따라서 남자는 자신이 언급한 문제를 해결하기 위해 매장을 방문하려는 것임을 알 수 있으므로 정답은 (B)이다.

55 Who will the woman most likely give a note to?
(A) A parking attendant
(B) A product designer
(C) A customer
(D) A colleague

여자는 누구에게 메모를 전해줄 것 같은가?
(A) 주차 안내원
(B) 제품 디자이너
(C) 고객
(D) 동료

어휘 attendant 안내원　colleague 동료

해설 세부 사항 관련 – 여자가 메모를 전해줄 사람
여자가 마지막 대사에서 다른 직원들 중 한 명이 분명 도와줄 수 있을 것(~ one of the other employees can definitely help you)이라며 메모를 하나 남겨 놓겠다(Let me just write a note down)고 말하는 것으로 보아 여자의 동료 직원이 메모를 받게 될 것임을 알 수 있다. 따라서 정답은 (D)이다.

Paraphrasing
대화의 one of the other employees → 정답의 colleague

56-58 3인 대화 M-Au / W-Am / W-Br

M   Hi. ⁵⁶**I have a delivery of medical supplies addressed to Eun-Mi Park.**
W1 That's Eun-Mi sitting at the desk over there.
W2 I'm Eun-Mi. I've been waiting for these sterile pads and bandages.
M   Great. ⁵⁷**I just need you to sign here to confirm the delivery.**
W2 OK, sure. Oh, ⁵⁸**Claudia, do you have time to help me carry these boxes to the storage closet?**
W1 ⁵⁸**Of course.** I have a patient at one o'clock, but I have a few minutes now.
W2 OK, thanks!

남   안녕하세요. **박은미 앞으로 배달된 의료용품이 있습니다.**
여1 저쪽 책상에 앉아 계신 분이 은미입니다.
여2 제가 은미입니다. 이 멸균 패드와 붕대를 기다리고 있었어요.
남   잘됐네요. **배송 확인을 위해 여기 서명만 해 주시면 됩니다.**
여2 네, 물론이죠. 아, **클라우디아, 시간 있으면 이 상자들을 보관실로 옮기는 것 좀 도와주실래요?**
여1 **그럼요.** 1시에 환자가 있긴 하지만, 지금은 잠깐 시간 있어요.
여2 좋아요, 감사합니다!

어휘 address (우편물 등을) ~ 앞으로 보내다, 주소를 쓰다 sterile 멸균의, 살균의 storage 보관, 저장

56 Where do the women most likely work?
(A) At a medical clinic
(B) At a department store
(C) At a hotel
(D) At a manufacturing plant

여자들은 어디에서 일하는 것 같은가?
(A) 병원
(B) 백화점
(C) 호텔
(D) 제조 공장

해설 전체 내용 관련 – 화자들의 근무 장소
남자가 첫 대사에서 여자들 중 한 명인 박은미 앞으로 배달된 의료용품이 있다(I have a delivery of medical supplies addressed to Eun-Mi Park)고 말하는 것으로 보아 여자들은 의료용품을 다루는 곳에서 근무한다는 사실을 알 수 있다. 따라서 정답은 (A)이다.

57 What does the man request?
(A) A schedule
(B) A list of employees
(C) A facility tour
(D) A signature

남자는 무엇을 요청하는가?
(A) 일정표
(B) 직원 명단
(C) 시설 견학
(D) 서명

해설 세부 사항 관련 – 남자의 요청 사항
남자가 두 번째 대사에서 배송 확인을 위해 여기 서명만 해 주면 된다(I just need you to sign here to confirm the delivery)고 요청하고 있으므로 정답은 (D)이다.

Paraphrasing
대화의 sign → 정답의 A signature

58 What will the women most likely do next?
(A) Attend a staff meeting
(B) Check some reports
(C) Take a lunch break
(D) Move some boxes

여자들은 다음에 무엇을 할 것 같은가?
(A) 직원회의 참석하기
(B) 보고서 확인하기
(C) 점심시간 갖기
(D) 상자 옮기기

해설 세부 사항 관련 – 여자들이 다음에 할 일
두 번째 여자가 두 번째 대사에서 첫 번째 여자에게 시간 있으면 이 상자들을 보관실로 옮기는 것 좀 도와달라(Claudia, do you have time to help me carry these boxes to the storage closet?)고 요청하자 첫 번째 여자가 알겠다(Of course)고 했으므로 정답은 (D)이다.

Paraphrasing
대화의 carry → 정답의 move

59-61 M-Cn / W-Br ▶동영상 강의

M Dola Commercial Cleaners. How can I help you?
W I manage a new bed-and-breakfast here in town, and ⁵⁹**I'm looking for a company to wash, dry, and fold our linens.** I have a few questions for you.
M Sure.
W How do you work in terms of scheduling?
M ⁶⁰**We work around the clock** to guarantee a 24-hour turnaround time. We run three separate shifts.
W That's good to hear.
M Could I ask where you're located?
W Oh, we're at 647 Pond Street.
M ⁶¹**In that case, pickup and delivery will not add to your service charge**, since you're within a fifteen-kilometer radius of us.

남 돌라 커머셜 클리너스입니다. 무엇을 도와드릴까요?
여 저는 시내에서 새 민박을 운영하고 있는데요. **저희 리넨 제품을 세탁 및 건조하고, 개서 정리해 줄 회사를 찾고 있어요.** 질문이 몇 가지 있습니다.
남 네.
여 일정 측면에서 어떻게 일하시나요?
남 저희는 24시간 내 처리를 보장해 드리기 위해 **밤낮없이 일하고 있습니다.** 삼교대로 운영하고 있죠.
여 반가운 얘기네요.
남 어디에 위치해 계신지 여쭤봐도 될까요?
여 아, 저희는 폰드 가 647번지에 있습니다.
남 **그러시면, 수거 및 배달은 추가 요금이 붙지 않을 겁니다.** 저희 회사에서 반경 15킬로미터 안에 계시니까요.

어휘 bed-and-breakfast 민박(아침 식사를 제공하는 숙박 시설) linens (침구류, 식탁보 등) 리넨 제품 in terms of ~의 측면에서 around the clock 밤낮없이, 24시간 내내 guarantee 보장하다 turnaround time 처리 소요 시간 separate 나뉜, 분리된 shift 교대 근무(조) charge 요금 radius 반경, 반지름

59 Why is the woman calling?
(A) To inquire about a service
(B) To arrange an interview
(C) To request a refund
(D) To make a reservation

여자는 왜 전화하는가?
(A) 서비스에 대해 문의하기 위해
(B) 인터뷰를 잡기 위해
(C) 환불을 요청하기 위해
(D) 예약하기 위해

어휘 inquire 문의하다 arrange 마련하다, 조치하다 refund 환불(액) reservation 예약

해설 전체 내용 관련 – 여자가 전화하는 이유
여자가 첫 대사에서 리넨 제품을 세탁 및 건조하고, 개서 정리해 줄 회사를 찾고 있다(I'm looking for a company to wash, dry, and fold our linens)고 말하는 것으로 보아 관련 서비스에 대해 문의하고 있음을 알 수 있다. 따라서 정답은 (A)이다.

Paraphrasing
대화의 to wash, dry, and fold our linens → 정답의 a service

60 What does the man say about his company?
(A) It ensures customer satisfaction.
(B) It has been in business for three years.
(C) It operates 24 hours a day.
(D) It is family owned.

남자는 그의 회사에 대해 무엇이라고 말하는가?
(A) 고객 만족을 보장한다.
(B) 3년 동안 영업해 왔다.
(C) 하루 24시간 운영된다.
(D) 가족이 소유하고 있다.

어휘 ensure 보장하다 satisfaction 만족, 충족 operate 운영되다, 영업하다 own 소유하다

해설 세부 사항 관련 – 남자가 소속 회사에 대해 하는 말
남자가 세 번째 대사에서 밤낮없이 일한다(We work around the clock ~)고 설명하고 있으므로 정답은 (C)이다.

Paraphrasing
대화의 work around the clock
→ 정답의 operates 24 hours a day

61 According to the man, what will his company provide?
(A) Directions to a facility
(B) Pickup and delivery
(C) A member discount
(D) An updated receipt

남자에 따르면, 그의 회사는 무엇을 제공할 것인가?
(A) 시설로 가는 길 안내
(B) 수거 및 배달
(C) 회원 할인
(D) 갱신된 영수증

어휘 directions 길 안내 facility 시설(물) receipt 영수증

해설 세부 사항 관련 – 남자의 회사가 제공할 것
남자가 마지막 대사에서 여자에게 그러면 수거 및 배달은 추가 요금이 붙지 않을 것(In that case, pickup and delivery will not add to your service charge ~)이라고 설명하는 것으로 보아 그의 회사가 수거 및 배달을 제공할 것임을 알 수 있다. 따라서 정답은 (B)이다.

62-64 대화 + 신청서 M-Au / W-Br

M **⁶²Welcome to Centerville Fitness Center.**
W Hi. I hear you're having a fund-raising campaign.
M Yes, today's the start of our annual fund-raiser. All proceeds go toward the purchase of new sports equipment for the center. You'll be entered into a raffle to win a prize based on your donation amount.
W Sounds great. **⁶³I'd like to donate $50.**
M Wonderful! Just fill out the donation form, and I'll get you your raffle ticket.
W How will I find out if I won?
M The drawing's on Friday, and **⁶⁴winners will receive a phone call from the organizers.**

남 센터빌 피트니스 센터에 오신 것을 환영합니다.
여 안녕하세요. 모금 캠페인을 진행하신다고 들었어요.
남 네, 오늘이 저희 연례 모금 행사가 시작되는 날입니다. 모든 수익금은 센터의 새 스포츠 장비 구입에 쓰이고요. 기부 금액에 따라 경품을 받을 수 있는 추첨에 참여하게 됩니다.
여 좋네요. **저는 50달러 기부할게요.**
남 훌륭합니다! 기부 신청서를 작성해 주시면, 추첨권을 드리겠습니다.
여 제가 당첨됐는지는 어떻게 알 수 있나요?
남 추첨은 금요일에 하고, **당첨자는 주최 측으로부터 전화를 받을 거예요.**

어휘 fund-raising 모금 fund-raiser 모금 행사 proceeds 수익금 go toward ~에 쓰이다, ~에 도움되다 raffle (경품) 추첨 donation 기부(금) drawing 추첨 getaway 여행, 휴가

DONATION FORM

Prize	Donation
63 Bicycle	**$50**
Theater Tickets	$75
Camera	$100
Weekend getaway	$150

Name _____

기부 신청서

경품	기부금
자전거	**50달러**
극장 입장권	75달러
카메라	100달러
주말 여행	150달러

성명 _____

62 Where is the conversation taking place?
(A) At a department store
(B) At a fitness center
(C) At a library
(D) At a restaurant

대화는 어디에서 이루어지는가?
(A) 백화점
(B) 피트니스 센터
(C) 도서관
(D) 레스토랑

해설 전체 내용 관련 – 대화의 장소
남자가 첫 대사에서 센터빌 피트니스 센터에 온 것을 환영한다(Welcome to Centerville Fitness Center)고 했으므로 정답은 (B)이다.

63 Look at the graphic. Which prize could the woman win?
(A) A bicycle
(B) Theater tickets
(C) A camera
(D) A weekend getaway

시각 정보에 의하면, 여자는 어떤 경품을 받을 수 있는가?
(A) 자전거
(B) 극장 입장권
(C) 카메라
(D) 주말 여행

해설 시각 정보 연계 – 여자가 받을 수 있는 경품
여자가 두 번째 대사에서 50달러를 기부하고 싶다(I'd like to donate $50)고 했고 신청서에서 기부금 50달러에 해당하는 경품은 자전거이므로 정답은 (A)이다.

64 How will winners be notified?
(A) By telephone
(B) By text message
(C) By e-mail
(D) By letter

당첨자는 어떻게 통보받는가?
(A) 전화로
(B) 문자 메시지로
(C) 이메일로
(D) 편지로

어휘 notify 통보하다, 알리다

해설 세부 사항 관련 – 당첨자가 통보받는 방법
남자가 마지막 대사에서 당첨자는 주최 측으로부터 전화를 받을 것(~ winners will receive a phone call from the organizers)이라고 했으므로 정답은 (A)이다.

Paraphrasing
대화의 receive a phone call → 정답의 By telephone

65-67 대화 + 가격 목록 W-Am / M-Cn

W Hi. Some of us at work decided to get together to **65 buy some flowers here. They're for a colleague who just received a promotion.**

M We have a nice selection of arrangements that are appropriate for an event like that. Here's a list of the most popular, in a range of prices.

W Oh, **66 I have enough money for the Harmony arrangement.** Can you make that while I wait?

M Sure, I'll have it made for you now. And **67 will you want a greeting card to go with that?**

W Actually, **no card is needed.** We already have one that we've all signed.

여 안녕하세요. 저희 직장 동료 몇 명이 여기에서 같이 꽃을 사기로 했어요. 막 승진을 한 동료에게 드리려고요.

남 그런 행사에 어울리는 멋진 꽃다발이 다양하게 있습니다. 여기 다양한 가격의 인기 제품 목록입니다.

여 아, 하모니 꽃다발을 살 수 있겠네요. 기다리는 동안 만들어 주실 수 있나요?

남 물론이죠, 바로 만들어 드리겠습니다. 그리고 함께 넣을 축하 카드도 원하세요?

여 실은, 카드는 필요 없어요. 이미 저희가 모두 사인한 것이 있거든요.

어휘 get together 모이다, 합치다 promotion 승진
a selection of 다양한 arrangement 배합, 배열, 배치
appropriate 적합한, 알맞은 a range of 다양한, 폭넓은

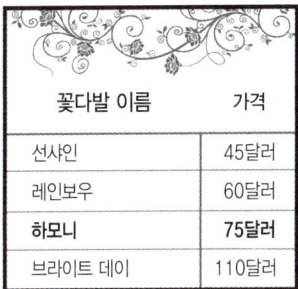

Name of Flower Arrangement	Price
Sunshine	$45
Rainbow	$60
66 Harmony	**$75**
Bright Day	$110

꽃다발 이름	가격
선샤인	45달러
레인보우	60달러
하모니	75달러
브라이트 데이	110달러

65 Why does the woman want to purchase flowers?
(A) To decorate a building lobby
(B) To observe a company anniversary
(C) To mark the completion of a work project
(D) To celebrate a coworker's promotion

여자는 왜 꽃을 구입하고 싶어 하는가?
(A) 건물 로비를 장식하려고
(B) 회사 기념일을 축하하려고
(C) 업무 프로젝트의 완료를 기념하려고
(D) 동료의 승진을 축하하려고

어휘 observe 축하하다 anniversary 기념일 mark 기념하다
completion 완료, 완성 celebrate 축하하다, 기념하다

해설 세부 사항 관련 – 여자가 꽃을 구입하는 이유

여자가 첫 대사에서 여기에서 꽃을 사기로 했다(~ buy some flowers here)며 막 승진을 한 동료에게 주려고 한다(They're for a colleague who just received a promotion)고 했으므로 정답은 (D)이다.

Paraphrasing
대화의 for a colleague who just received a promotion
→ 정답의 To celebrate a coworker's promotion

66 Look at the graphic. How much will the woman pay for the flower arrangement?
(A) $45
(B) $60
(C) $75
(D) $110

시각 정보에 의하면, 여자는 꽃다발 가격으로 얼마를 지불할 것인가?
(A) 45달러
(B) 60달러
(C) 75 달러
(D) 110달러

해설 시각 정보 연계 – 여자가 지불할 꽃다발 가격

여자가 두 번째 대사에서 하모니 꽃다발을 살 수 있겠다(I have enough money for the Harmony arrangement)고 했고 가격 목록에서 하모니 꽃다발의 가격은 75달러이므로 정답은 (C)이다.

67 What additional item do the speakers discuss?
(A) A chocolate bar
(B) A greeting card
(C) A bunch of balloons
(D) A decorative bow

화자들은 어떤 추가 항목에 대해 이야기하는가?
(A) 초콜릿 바
(B) 축하 카드
(C) 풍선 다발
(D) 장식용 리본

어휘 a bunch of ~의 한 다발 balloon 풍선
decorative 장식용의

해설 세부 사항 관련 – 화자들이 이야기하는 추가 항목

남자가 두 번째 대사에서 함께 넣을 축하 카드를 원하는지(~ will you want a greeting card to go with that?) 묻자 여자가 카드는 필요하지 않다(~ no cad is needed)고 대답하고 있으므로 정답은 (B)이다.

Paraphrasing
대화의 a greeting card to go with that
→ 질문의 additional item

68-70 대화 + 표 W-Am / M-Au

W Hi, Andrew. ⁶⁸**How have you enjoyed your first week here at Jebreen Farms?**

M It's been great. I'm definitely learning a lot about commercial agriculture.

W So glad to hear that. ⁶⁹**Let's go over to where we'll store the upcoming corn harvest.** As you know, we sell a lot of corn as feed for livestock farms in the area.

M Yes. I'm eager to get some hands-on experience with drying and storing the corn.

W Good. If the process is done right, it can be stored for long periods, but conditions inside the grain bin have to be just right.

M ⁷⁰**How long will the drying process take after the harvest?**

W About four to six weeks.

여 안녕하세요, 앤드류. **제브린 농장에서의 첫 주는 어떻게 보내셨나요?**

남 아주 좋았습니다. 상업 농업에 대해 확실히 많은 걸 배우고 있어요.

여 그 말씀을 들으니 기쁘네요. **우리가 곧 수확할 옥수수를 보관할 장소로 가 봅시다.** 아시다시피, 이 지역 내 축산 농장에 사료용 옥수수를 많이 판매하고 있어요.

남 네. 저는 옥수수 건조와 저장을 직접 경험해 보고 싶습니다.

여 좋습니다. 과정을 제대로 거치면 장기간 저장이 가능하지만, 곡물 보관통 내부의 상태가 적절해야 해요.

남 **수확 후 건조 과정은 얼마나 걸리나요?**

여 약 4~6주 정도입니다.

어휘 definitely 확실히, 분명히 commercial 상업의 agriculture 농업 store 보관하다, 저장하다 harvest 수확(물) feed 먹이 livestock 가축 be eager to ~하고 싶어 하다 hands-on 직접 해보는 grain 곡물 bin 통

Jebreen Farms Grain Bins	
Bin 1	Barley
Bin 2	Wheat
⁶⁹**Bin 3**	**Corn**
Bin 4	Oats

제브린 농장 곡물 보관통	
보관통 1	보리
보관통 2	밀
보관통 3	**옥수수**
보관통 4	귀리

68 Who most likely is the man?
(A) A new employee
(B) An investor
(C) A university professor
(D) A business owner

남자는 누구인 것 같은가?
(A) 신입 직원
(B) 투자자
(C) 대학 교수
(D) 사업체 소유주

해설 전체 내용 관련 – 남자의 직업

여자가 첫 대사에서 남자에게 제브린 농장에서의 첫 주는 어떻게 보냈는지(How have you enjoyed your first week here at Jebreen Farms?) 묻고 있는 것으로 보아 남자는 이제 막 첫 주를 보낸 신입 직원임을 알 수 있다. 따라서 정답은 (A)이다.

69 Look at the graphic. Where will the upcoming harvest be stored?
(A) Bin 1
(B) Bin 2
(C) Bin 3
(D) Bin 4

시각 정보에 의하면, 곧 수확할 작물은 어디에 보관될 것인가?
(A) 보관통 1
(B) 보관통 2
(C) 보관통 3
(D) 보관통 4

해설 시각 정보 연계 – 수확물이 보관될 장소

여자가 두 번째 대사에서 곧 수확할 옥수수를 보관할 장소로 가 보자(Let's go over to where we'll store the upcoming corn harvest)고 말하고 있고, 표에서 옥수수는 보관통 3으로 표기되어 있으므로 정답은 (C)이다.

70 What does the man ask about?
(A) When some work will begin
(B) How long a process will take
(C) Who will buy a product
(D) When a delivery will arrive

남자는 무엇에 대해 묻는가?
(A) 작업이 언제 시작할지
(B) 과정이 얼마나 걸릴지
(C) 누가 제품을 구입할지
(D) 배송이 언제 도착할지

해설 세부 사항 관련 – 남자가 묻는 것

남자가 마지막 대사에서 수확 후 건조 과정은 얼마나 걸리는지(How long will the drying process take after the harvest?) 묻고 있으므로 정답은 (B)이다.

PART 4

71-73 안내

M-Au Welcome to your first day of work at Schneider Technology. **71 Our navigation devices enable vehicles to direct drivers to their destination** by taking into consideration a variety of factors such as distance, weather, and traffic conditions. **72 Moritz Schneider, the president of the company, will be here in person at ten o'clock to welcome you** and tell you all about the company's history. **73 But first, I'll help you set up your computer accounts.** Cybersecurity is very important to us, so we've added extra steps to verify your identity.

슈나이더 테크놀로지에서의 첫 출근을 환영합니다. **우리 내비게이션 장치**는 거리와 날씨, 교통 상황과 같은 다양한 요소를 고려하여 차량이 운전자를 목적지로 안내할 수 있도록 합니다. **우리 회사의 모리츠 슈나이더 사장님께서 10시에 직접 오셔서 여러분을 환영하고** 회사의 역사에 대해 말씀해 주실 예정입니다. **하지만 먼저, 컴퓨터 계정을 설정하시는 것을 도와드리겠습니다.** 사이버 보안은 우리에게 아주 중요하므로, 여러분의 신원을 확인하기 위해 몇 가지 추가 절차를 마련해 두었습니다.

어휘 device 장치, 기기 enable 가능하게 하다 direct 안내하다 take ~ into consideration ~을 고려하다 a variety of 다양한 factor 요소, 요인 distance 거리 in person 직접 account 계정 verify 확인하다, 입증하다 identity 신분

71 What does Schneider Technology produce?
(A) Automobile engines
(B) Audio equipment
(C) Navigation devices
(D) Medical equipment

슈나이더 테크놀로지는 무엇을 생산하는가?
(A) 자동차 엔진
(B) 오디오 장비
(C) 내비게이션 장치
(D) 의료 장비

해설 세부 사항 관련 – 슈나이더 테크놀로지가 생산하는 것
화자가 초반부에 우리 내비게이션 장치(Our navigation devices)를 언급했으므로 정답은 (C)이다.

72 Who will the listeners meet with at ten o'clock?
(A) An important client
(B) The company president
(C) The head of security
(D) A government official

청자들은 10시에 누구와 만날 것인가?
(A) 중요한 고객
(B) 회사 사장
(C) 보안팀장
(D) 정부 관계자

해설 세부 사항 관련 – 청자들이 10시에 만날 사람
화자가 중반부에 회사의 모리츠 슈나이더 사장이 10시에 직접 와서 청자들을 환영할 것(Moritz Schneider, the president of the company, will be here in person at ten o'clock to welcome you ~)이라고 말하고 있으므로 정답은 (B)이다.

Paraphrasing
담화의 be here in person → 질문의 meet

73 What will the listeners do next?
(A) Set up their computer accounts
(B) Receive their security badges
(C) Tour a facility
(D) Watch a demonstration

청자들은 다음에 무엇을 할 것인가?
(A) 컴퓨터 계정 설정하기
(B) 보안 출입증 받기
(C) 시설 견학하기
(D) 시연회 참관하기

어휘 facility 시설 demonstration 시연(회)

해설 세부 사항 관련 – 청자들이 다음에 할 일
화자가 후반부에 먼저 청자들이 컴퓨터 계정을 설정하는 것을 도와주겠다(But first, I'll help you set up your computer accounts)고 했으므로 정답은 (A)이다.

74-76 공지

W-Br Good afternoon. **74 This is Captain Jeong giving you a heads-up on our plane's departure status.** As you can see, **75 there's a light dusting of snow on the ground.** Air traffic control is holding us here at the gate while the snowplows clear the runway. It should take just a few minutes, then we'll be cleared for takeoff. I apologize for the delay. **76 And a reminder: please ensure that children remain seated with their seat belts fastened throughout the flight.**

안녕하세요. **우리 비행기의 출발 현황을 안내해 드리는 정 기장입니다.** 보시다시피, **지상에 눈이 살짝 쌓여 있습니다.** 제설 차량이 활주로를 치우는 동안 항공 교통 관제소에서 저희를 게이트에 대기시키고 있습니다. 몇 분 정도면 끝날 것이고, 이후 이륙 허가를 받게 될 예정입니다. 지연에 대해 사과드립니다. **그리고 한 가지 당부드릴 말씀이 있습니다. 비행 내내 아이들이 반드시 좌석에 앉아 안전벨트를 착용하고 있도록 해 주시기 바랍니다.**

> 어휘 heads-up 안내, 미리 알려 줌 departure 출발
> status 현황, 상태 dusting (눈, 가루 등이) 얇게 뿌려진 것
> air traffic control 항공 교통 관제소 snowplow 제설 차량
> be cleared for ~에 대해 허가를 받다 takeoff 이륙, 출발
> apologize 사과하다 reminder (메시지 등의) 상기시키는 것
> ensure 보장하다 fasten 고정하다, 매다

74 Where does the announcement most likely take place?
(A) On a train
(B) On a ship
(C) On an airplane
(D) On a bus

공지는 어디에서 이루어지는 것 같은가?
(A) 기차
(B) 배
(C) 비행기
(D) 버스

해설 전체 내용 관련 – 공지 장소
화자가 초반부에 자신을 비행기의 출발 현황을 안내하는 기장(This is Captain Jeong giving you a heads-up on our plane's departure status)이라고 했으므로 정답은 (C)이다.

75 What is causing a delay?
(A) Weather conditions
(B) Heavy traffic
(C) Malfunctioning equipment
(D) A staff shortage

무엇이 지연을 초래하고 있는가?
(A) 기상 상태
(B) 극심한 교통량
(C) 장비 오작동
(D) 직원 부족

어휘 malfunction 오작동하다 shortage 부족

해설 세부 사항 관련 – 지연을 초래하는 원인
화자가 초반부에 지상에 눈이 살짝 쌓여 있다(~ there's a light dusting of snow on the ground)고 언급한 뒤, 관련 조치 사항에 대한 설명 및 사과의 말을 덧붙이고 있으므로 정답은 (A)이다.

Paraphrasing
담화의 a light dusting of snow
→ 정답의 Weather conditions

76 What does the speaker remind the listeners to do?
(A) Store luggage in overhead compartments
(B) Show tickets to an attendant
(C) Avoid eating and drinking
(D) Keep children in their seats

화자는 청자들에게 무엇을 하라고 상기시키는가?
(A) 짐을 머리 위 짐칸에 보관하기
(B) 승무원에게 표 보여 주기
(C) 먹거나 마시지 않기
(D) 아이들을 좌석에 앉아 있게 하기

어휘 overhead 머리 위쪽의 compartment 짐칸, 수납 공간

해설 세부 사항 관련 – 화자가 상기시키는 것
화자가 후반부에 한 가지 당부 말씀이 있다면서 비행 내내 아이들이 반드시 좌석에 앉아 안전벨트를 착용하고 있도록 해 달라(And a reminder: please ensure that children remain seated with their seat belts fastened throughout the flight)고 당부하고 있으므로 정답은 (D)이다.

Paraphrasing
담화의 ensure that children remain seated with their seat belts fastened → 정답의 Keep children in their seats

77-79 방송

M-Cn Good morning, and thanks for tuning in to *News at Four*. **77 We've just learned that the Natural Zoological Museum, one of Springfield's most popular museums, will soon close for a renovation project.** **78 To those who are planning to visit the exhibits in person**, be aware that the workers arrive in six weeks. But if you miss that window, don't worry. You can still visit the museum virtually during the renovation period. **79 Video tours will soon be available on the museum's Web site**, and videos showing the progress of the project will also be posted regularly.

안녕하세요, 〈뉴스 앳 포〉를 청취해 주셔서 감사합니다. 저희가 방금 입수한 소식에 따르면, 스프링필드에서 가장 인기 있는 박물관 중 하나인 자연 동물 박물관이 곧 보수 공사를 위해 문을 닫을 예정입니다. 직접 전시를 보러 갈 계획 중인 분들은, 작업자들이 6주 후에 도착한다는 점을 알아 두시기 바랍니다. 하지만 이 기회를 놓치더라도 걱정하지 마세요. 보수 공사 기간 중에도 박물관을 가상으로 방문할 수 있습니다. 박물관 웹사이트에서 곧 비디오 투어가 제공될 예정이며, 공사의 진행 상황을 보여 주는 영상들도 정기적으로 게시될 것입니다.

어휘 tune in to (방송을) 청취하다, (채널을) ~에 맞추다
renovation 개조, 보수 exhibit 전시(회) be aware 알다
window (잠깐의) 기회, (기회의) 창 virtually 가상으로
progress 진행 상황, 진척 regularly 정기적으로

77 What project does the speaker mention?
(A) The addition of traffic lights
(B) The renovation of a museum
(C) The expansion of a sports stadium
(D) The construction of a bridge

화자는 어떤 프로젝트를 언급하는가?
(A) 신호등 추가
(B) 박물관 보수
(C) 경기장 확장
(D) 다리 건설

어휘 expansion 확장, 확대 construction 건설

해설 전체 내용 관련 – 화자가 언급하는 프로젝트
화자가 초반부에 방금 입수한 소식에 따르면, 자연 동물 박물관이 곧 보수 공사를 위해 문을 닫을 예정(We've just learned that the Natural Zoological Museum ~ will soon close for a renovation project)이라고 말한 뒤 관련된 설명을 이어가고 있으므로 정답은 (B)이다.

78 What does the speaker imply when he says, "the workers arrive in six weeks"?
(A) The listeners should attend a welcome reception.
(B) Some training will be offered soon.
(C) The listeners have a limited amount of time.
(D) A hiring need has already been fulfilled.

화자가 "작업자들이 6주 후에 도착합니다"라고 말할 때 무엇을 의미하는가?
(A) 청자들은 환영회에 참석해야 한다.
(B) 곧 교육이 제공될 것이다.
(C) 청자들에게 제한된 시간이 있다.
(D) 채용 수요는 이미 충족되었다.

어휘 limited 제한적인 fulfill 충족하다, 이행하다

해설 화자의 의도 파악 – 작업자들이 6주 후에 도착한다는 말의 의도
화자가 중반부에 직접 전시를 보러 갈 계획 중인 사람들(To those who are planning to visit the exhibits in person ~)을 지칭하면서 인용문을 언급하고 있는 것으로 보아, 보수 공사가 시작되기 전까지 6주가 남아 있으므로 박물관을 방문할 수 있는 시간이 제한되어 있다는 의미로 한 말임을 알 수 있다. 따라서 정답은 (C)이다.

79 What does the speaker assure the listeners of?
(A) Videos will be available online.
(B) Prices will not increase.
(C) Roads will remain open.
(D) A schedule will not change.

화자는 청자들에게 무엇을 확신시켜 주는가?
(A) 영상이 온라인에서 이용 가능할 것이다.
(B) 가격이 인상되지 않을 것이다.
(C) 도로는 계속 개방되어 있을 것이다.
(D) 일정이 변경되지 않을 것이다.

어휘 assure 확신시키다, 보장하다 remain 유지되다

해설 세부 사항 관련 – 화자가 확신시켜 주는 것
화자가 후반부에 박물관 웹사이트에서 곧 비디오 투어가 제공될 예정(Video tours will soon be available on the museum's Web site ~)이라고 안내하고 있다. 이는 온라인 상에서 이용 가능한 영상 견학 서비스를 가리키는 것이므로 정답은 (A)이다.

Paraphrasing
담화의 Video tours will soon be available on the museum's Web site
→ 정답의 Videos will be available online

80-82 광고

W-Am At Jin-Ah's Jewelers, ⁸⁰**we create custom-made jewelry** that showcases your style and celebrates the most important moments in your life. Meet for a video consultation with one of our talented artists, who can design earrings, bracelets, and more, just for you. ⁸¹**And unlike our competitors, who only send you a sketch, we'll send you a simple metal prototype.** You can approve or request changes to the sample before your final piece is made. ⁸²**To get your order started, just enter your information on our Web site**, and one of our designers will contact you.

저희 진아스 주얼러스에서는, 여러분의 스타일을 표현하고, 인생에서 가장 중요한 순간들을 기념할 **주문 제작 주얼리를 만들어 드립니다**. 재능 있는 아티스트 중 한 명과 영상 상담을 진행해 보세요. 귀걸이, 팔찌 등 다양한 제품을 고객님만을 위해 디자인해 드릴 수 있습니다. **그리고 스케치만 보내는 경쟁사들과 달리, 저희는 간단한 금속 견본을 보내 드립니다**. 최종 제품이 제작되기 전에 샘플을 승인하거나 변경을 요청하실 수 있습니다. **주문을 시작하시려면, 저희 웹사이트에 정보를 입력해 주세요**. 저희 디자이너 중 한 명이 연락을 드릴 것입니다.

어휘 custom-made 주문 제작의, 맞춤 제작의 showcase 선보이다 consultation 상담, 상의 talented 재능이 있는 competitor 경쟁사, 경쟁자 prototype 견본, 원형 approve 승인하다, 찬성하다

80 What does the company make?
(A) Clothing
(B) Jewelry
(C) Eyeglass frames
(D) Ceramic vases

회사는 무엇을 만드는가?
(A) 의류
(B) 주얼리
(C) 안경테
(D) 도자기 꽃병

해설 　전체 내용 관련 – 회사가 만드는 것
　　　화자가 초반부에 자신의 회사를 소개하며 주문 제작 주얼리를 만든다(~ we create custom-made jewelry ~)고 했으므로 정답은 (B)이다.

81 How is the company different from its competitors?
(A) It uses eco-friendly materials.
(B) It offers online consultations.
(C) It promises one-week delivery.
(D) It provides product prototypes.

회사는 경쟁사들과 어떻게 다른가?
(A) 친환경적인 소재를 이용한다.
(B) 온라인 상담을 제공한다.
(C) 일주일 배송을 약속한다.
(D) 제품의 견본을 제공한다.

어휘 　eco-friendly 친환경적인
해설 　세부 사항 관련 – 경쟁사들과 다른 점
　　　화자가 중반부에 스케치만 보내는 경쟁사들과 달리 간단한 금속 견본을 보내 준다(And unlike our competitors, who only send you a sketch, we'll send you a simple metal prototype)고 언급하고 있으므로 정답은 (D)이다.

Paraphrasing
담화의 unlike our competitors
→ 질문의 different from its competitors
담화의 send you a simple metal prototype
→ 정답의 provides product prototypes

82 Why should the listeners visit a Web site?
(A) To enter a contest
(B) To receive a discount code
(C) To start an order
(D) To view some photographs

청자들은 왜 웹사이트를 방문해야 하는가?
(A) 콘테스트에 참가하기 위해
(B) 할인 코드를 받기 위해
(C) 주문을 시작하기 위해
(D) 사진을 보기 위해

어휘 　enter 참가하다, 들어가다
해설 　세부 사항 관련 – 청자들이 웹사이트를 방문해야 하는 이유
　　　화자가 후반부에 주문을 시작하려면 회사 웹사이트에서 정보를 입력하라(To get your order started, just enter your information on our Web site ~)고 말하고 있으므로 정답은 (C)이다.

Paraphrasing
담화의 get your order started → 정답의 start an order

83-85 팟캐스트

M-Cn On today's episode of our podcast, we'll be talking to Rebecca Taylor, the chair and founder of Real Estate Investments LLC. As we know, **83 the housing market has had its ups and downs in recent years. 84 Ms. Taylor is widely known for her ability to correctly predict trends in the real estate market.** Her opinion is highly valued. We are fortunate to be able to interview her today before **85 she travels to the National Real Estate Conference in Chicago, where she has been invited to deliver the keynote speech.**

저희 팟캐스트의 오늘 에피소드에서는 리얼 에스테이트 인베스트먼트 LLC의 의장이자 창립자인 레베카 테일러와 이야기를 나눌 예정입니다. 아시다시피, **주택 시장은 최근 몇 년 동안 오르내림을 겪어 왔습니다. 테일러 씨는 부동산 시장 동향을 정확히 예측하는 능력으로 널리 알려져 있습니다.** 이분의 의견은 매우 중요하게 여겨집니다. 우리는 운 좋게도 오늘 **그녀가 시카고에서 열리는 전국 부동산 콘퍼런스에 가기 전에** 인터뷰할 수 있게 되었습니다. **이 콘퍼런스에서 테일러 씨는 기조 연설을 맡도록 초청받으셨습니다.**

어휘 　ups and downs 오르내림, 우여곡절　recent 최근의
correctly 정확히　predict 예측하다　trend 동향, 추세
highly valued 높이 평가받는　fortunate 운이 좋은
keynote speech 기조 연설

83 What is the focus of the podcast?
(A) Real estate
(B) Food services
(C) Graphic design
(D) Tourism

팟캐스트의 초점은 무엇인가?
(A) 부동산
(B) 음식 서비스
(C) 그래픽 디자인
(D) 관광 산업

해설 　전체 내용 관련 – 팟캐스트 주제
　　　화자가 초반부에 주택 시장이 최근 몇 년 동안 오르내림을 겪어 왔다(~ the housing market has had its ups and downs in recent years)며 관련 분야의 전문가와 이야기를 나눌 예정임을 소개하고 있으므로 정답은 (A)이다.

84 What does the speaker say Rebecca Taylor is known for?
(A) Organizing workshops
(B) Providing technology support
(C) Promoting products
(D) Predicting market trends

화자는 레베카 테일러가 무엇으로 알려져 있다고 말하는가?
(A) 워크숍 주최
(B) 기술 지원 서비스 제공
(C) 제품 홍보
(D) 시장 동향 예측

어휘 organize 주최하다, 조직하다   promote 홍보하다, 촉진하다

해설 세부 사항 관련 – 테일러가 유명한 이유
화자가 중반부에 테일러 씨가 부동산 시장 동향을 정확히 예측하는 능력으로 널리 알려져 있다(Ms. Taylor is widely known for her ability to correctly predict trends in the real estate market)고 했으므로 정답은 (D)이다.

85 According to the speaker, what will Ms. Taylor do in Chicago?
(A) Release a book
(B) Speak at a conference
(C) Appear on television
(D) Announce an award winner

화자에 따르면, 테일러 씨는 시카고에서 무엇을 할 것인가?
(A) 도서 발매하기
(B) 콘퍼런스에서 연설하기
(C) 텔레비전에 출연하기
(D) 수상자 발표하기

어휘 release 발매하다, 출시하다   appear 출연하다, 나오다

해설 세부 사항 관련 – 테일러 씨가 시카고에서 할 일
화자가 후반부에 그녀가 시카고에서 열리는 전국 부동산 콘퍼런스에 가는데 이 콘퍼런스에서 테일러 씨가 기조 연설을 맡도록 초청되었다(~ she travels to the National Real Estate Conference in Chicago, where she has been invited to deliver the keynote speech)고 말하고 있으므로 정답은 (B)이다.

Paraphrasing
담화의 National Real Estate Conference in Chicago ~ deliver the keynote speech
→ 정답의 Speak at a conference

86-88 회의 발췌   ▶ 동영상 강의

W-Am **86 The topic for today's workshop is writing business correspondence.** Business correspondence has different guidelines than the informal type of writing you use when writing to a friend. For example, when writing to a friend you might address them by their first name or perhaps include emojis. You know—symbols like smiley faces that are commonly used to express feelings. However, **87 emojis are considered inappropriate in business writing. Also, business correspondence should always include the recipient's title and last name.** Remember, we don't want to offend our clients. Now, I will project some slides of informally worded e-mails. In your notebooks, **88 rewrite the e-mails using wording and style appropriate for business correspondence.**

오늘 워크숍의 주제는 비즈니스 서신 작성하기입니다. 비즈니스 서신은 친구에게 글을 쓰는 경우에 사용하는 일상적인 글쓰기와는 다른 가이드라인을 따릅니다. 예를 들어, 친구에게 글을 쓸 때는 이름을 부르거나 어쩌면 이모지를 포함할 수도 있습니다. 그러니까, 감정을 표현하는 데 흔히 쓰이는 웃는 얼굴 같은 기호들 말이죠. 하지만, 이모지는 비즈니스 글쓰기에서는 부적절하다고 여겨집니다. 또한, 비즈니스 서신은 항상 수신인의 직함과 성을 포함해야 합니다. 기억하세요. 우리는 고객들을 불쾌하게 만드는 것을 원하지 않습니다. 이제, 제가 격식 없는 문구로 작성된 이메일들이 담긴 슬라이드를 화면에 띄우겠습니다. 여러분의 노트에 이 이메일들을 비즈니스 서신에 알맞은 문구와 스타일로 다시 작성해 보세요.

어휘 correspondence 서신   informal 일상적인, 격식 없는   address (호칭으로) 부르다   commonly 흔히   inappropriate 부적절한, 부적합한   recipient 수신인, 수취인   title 직함   offend 불쾌하게 만들다   project 비추다

86 What is the main topic of the workshop?
(A) Creating new advertisements
(B) Designing Web sites
(C) Giving effective presentations
(D) Writing for business communication

워크숍의 주제는 무엇인가?
(A) 새로운 광고 만들기
(B) 웹사이트 디자인하기
(C) 효과적인 발표하기
(D) 비즈니스 커뮤니케이션용 글쓰기

어휘 advertisement 광고   effective 효과적인

해설 전체 내용 관련 – 워크숍의 주제

화자가 초반부에 오늘 워크숍의 주제는 비즈니스 서신 작성하기 (The topic for today's workshop is writing business correspondence)라고 했으므로 정답은 (D)이다.

Paraphrasing
담화의 writing business correspondence
→ 정답의 Writing for business communication

87 Why does the speaker say, "we don't want to offend our clients"?
(A) To stress the importance of some guidelines
(B) To announce a change
(C) To request feedback
(D) To propose that a meeting be rescheduled

화자는 왜 "우리는 고객들을 불쾌하게 만드는 것을 원하지 않습니다"라고 말하는가?
(A) 가이드라인의 중요성을 강조하기 위해
(B) 변경 사항을 발표하기 위해
(C) 피드백을 요청하기 위해
(D) 회의 일정이 재조정되어야 한다고 제안하기 위해

어휘 stress 강조하다 propose 제안하다, 제의하다
reschedule 일정을 재조정하다

해설 화자의 의도 파악 – 우리는 고객들을 불쾌하게 만드는 것을 원하지 않는다는 말의 의도

화자가 중반부에 이모지가 비즈니스 글쓰기에 부적절하다는 점과 비즈니스 서신은 항상 수신인의 직함과 성을 포함해야 한다는 점 (~ emojis are considered inappropriate in business writing. Also, business correspondence should always include the recipient's title and last name)을 설명한 뒤 인용문을 언급하는 것으로 보아, 비즈니스 서신 작성 시 지켜야 하는 규칙들, 즉 가이드라인이 그만큼 중요하다는 것을 강조하려는 의도임을 알 수 있다. 따라서 정답은 (A)이다.

88 What are the listeners asked to do?
(A) Update some contact information
(B) Rewrite some e-mails
(C) Do an online search
(D) Download some software

청자들은 무엇을 하도록 요청받는가?
(A) 연락 정보 업데이트하기
(B) 이메일 다시 작성하기
(C) 온라인에서 조사하기
(D) 소프트웨어 다운로드하기

해설 세부 사항 관련 – 청자들이 요청받는 일

화자가 후반부에 청자들에게 비즈니스 서신에 알맞은 문구와 스타일로 자신이 보여 주는 이메일들을 다시 작성하도록(~ rewrite the e-mails using wording and style appropriate for business correspondence) 요청하고 있으므로 정답은 (B)이다.

89-91 보도

W-Br In the world of business, 89 **athletic retailer Clementine Stores has filed a complaint against software firm Stephion.** 90 **Clementine claims that the Stephion logo, which is round and orange, is too similar to its own.** However, 91 **a Stephion public relations representative, Friedrich Weber**, responded by saying that the two company logos were similar but not similar enough to confuse consumers. Furthermore, Weber maintained that the Stephion design was not problematic because the two companies are in completely different markets. Our in-house legal analyst will join us next.

비즈니스 소식입니다. 운동용품 소매업체 클레멘타인 스토어스가 소프트웨어 회사 스테피온을 상대로 소송을 제기했습니다. 클레멘타인은 둥근 모양에 주황색인 스테피온 로고가 자사 로고와 너무 유사하다고 주장합니다. 그러나 스테피온 사의 홍보 담당 프리드리히 베버는 두 회사 로고가 비슷하기는 하지만 소비자들을 혼동시킬 정도로 비슷하지는 않다고 답했습니다. 게다가, 베버는 두 회사가 완전히 다른 시장에 속해 있기 때문에 스테피온 사의 디자인이 문제가 되지 않는다고 주장했습니다. 이어서 저희 내부 법률 분석가께서 함께 하시겠습니다.

어휘 athletic 운동의, 경기의 retailer 소매업체, 소매업자
file a complaint against ~을 상대로 소송을 제기하다
public relations 홍보 representative 직원, 대표자
respond 대답하다, 대응하다 confuse 혼동시키다
furthermore 더욱이, 게다가 maintain 주장하다, 내세우다
problematic 문제가 있는 completely 완전히
in-house (회사) 내부의 legal 법률의 analyst 분석가

89 Why is Clementine Stores in the news report?
(A) It filed a complaint.
(B) It closed some factories.
(C) It merged with another company.
(D) It started an internship program.

클레멘타인 스토어스는 왜 뉴스 보도에 등장하는가?
(A) 소송을 제기했다.
(B) 일부 공장을 폐쇄했다.
(C) 다른 회사와 합병했다.
(D) 인턴십 프로그램을 시작했다.

어휘 merge with ~와 합병하다

해설 전체 내용 관련 – 클레멘타인 스토어스가 뉴스 보도에 등장한 이유

화자가 초반부에 운동용품 소매업체 클레멘타인 스토어스가 스테피온을 상대로 소송을 제기했다(~ athletic retailer Clementine Stores has filed a complaint against software firm Stephion)고 했으므로 정답은 (A)이다.

90 According to the report, what do the companies have in common?
(A) They have international clients.
(B) They are family-owned businesses.
(C) They sell athletic clothing.
(D) They have similar logos.

보도에 따르면, 회사들은 어떤 공통점을 가지고 있는가?
(A) 해외 고객들을 보유하고 있다.
(B) 가족 소유의 업체들이다.
(C) 운동용 의류를 판매한다.
(D) 유사한 로고를 가지고 있다.

해설 세부 사항 관련 – 회사들의 공통점
화자가 초반부에 클레멘타인이 둥근 모양에 주황색인 스테피온 로고가 자사 로고와 너무 유사하다고 주장한다(Clementine claims that the Stephion logo, which is round and orange, is too similar to its own)고 했으므로 정답은 (D)이다.

91 Who is Friedrich Weber?
(A) A news reporter
(B) A public relations associate
(C) A corporate attorney
(D) A graphic designer

프리드리히 베버는 누구인가?
(A) 뉴스 기자
(B) 홍보 담당 직원
(C) 기업 변호사
(D) 그래픽 디자이너

어휘 associate 직원, 동료, 동업자 attorney 변호사

해설 세부 사항 관련 – 프리드리히 베버의 직업
화자가 중반부에 프리드리히 베버를 스테피온의 홍보 담당(a Stephion public relations representative, Friedrich Weber)이라고 언급하고 있으므로 정답은 (B)이다.

Paraphrasing
담화의 representative → 정답의 associate

92-94 회의 발췌

> M-Cn Thanks for coming in early this morning. I wanted to update you on ⁹²**the café refrigerators that our customers use.** We recently installed a new temperature monitoring system. ⁹³,⁹⁴**I've noticed that every increase in temperature can be traced to the refrigerator doors being left open for extended periods of time. This is alarming because it compromises the freshness and safety of our food.** We all know that customers often take a while to make their selection. I'll be meeting with the management team to discuss ways to address this.

오늘 아침 일찍 나와 주셔서 감사합니다. **우리 고객들이 이용하는 카페 냉장고**에 대해 업데이트해 드리고 싶었습니다. 우리가 최근 새로운 온도 모니터링 시스템을 설치했습니다. **저는 온도가 올라가는 모든 경우가 냉장고 문이 장시간 열려 있는 것과 관련이 있음을 확인했습니다. 이는 우리 음식의 신선도와 안전성을 해칠 수 있어 우려되는 부분입니다.** 우리는 모두 고객들이 선택을 하는 데 시간이 걸린다는 것을 알고 있습니다. 이 문제를 해결할 방법을 논의하기 위해 경영진과 회의를 가질 예정입니다.

어휘 refrigerator 냉장고 install 설치하다
temperature 온도 notice 알게 되다, 주목하다
be traced to ~와 관련이 있다, ~에 기인하다
extended 연장된, 장시간에 걸친 alarming 우려되는, 걱정스러운
compromise 해가 되다, 위태롭게 하다 freshness 신선도
selection 선택 address (문제 등을) 해결하다, 다루다

92 Where does the speaker most likely work?
(A) At a café
(B) At an appliance store
(C) At a food manufacturing plant
(D) At a repair shop

화자는 어디에서 일하는 것 같은가?
(A) 카페
(B) 가전기기 매장
(C) 식품 제조 공장
(D) 수리점

해설 전체 내용 관련 – 화자의 근무 장소
화자가 초반부에 우리 고객들이 이용하는 카페 냉장고(~ the café refrigerators that our customers use)에 대해 언급하고 있으므로 정답은 (A)이다.

93 What is the speaker concerned about?
(A) Package labeling
(B) Increased temperature readings
(C) Product costs
(D) Limited business hours

화자는 무엇을 걱정하는가?
(A) 포장지 라벨 작업
(B) 온도 측정값 상승
(C) 제품 비용
(D) 제한된 영업시간

어휘 reading (눈금 등의) 값, 수치 limited 제한적인

해설 세부 사항 관련 – 화자가 걱정하는 것
화자가 중반부에 냉장고 온도가 올라가는 것(I've noticed that every increase in temperature ~)에 관해 언급하며, 이것이 우려되는 부분(This is alarming ~)이라고 했으므로 정답은 (B)이다.

Paraphrasing
담화의 alarming → 질문의 concerned

94 Why does the speaker say, "customers often take a while to make their selection"?
(A) To recommend rearranging a display
(B) To encourage staff to be attentive
(C) To emphasize a problem
(D) To remind staff of a policy

화자는 왜 "고객들이 선택을 하는 데 시간이 걸린다"라고 말하는가?
(A) 진열대를 재배치하도록 권하려고
(B) 직원들에게 주의를 기울이도록 독려하려고
(C) 문제점을 강조하려고
(D) 직원들에게 정책을 상기시키려고

어휘 rearrange 재배치하다, 다시 배열하다 display 진열, 전시 attentive 주의를 기울이는, 조심성 있는 emphasize 강조하다

해설 화자의 의도 파악 – 고객들이 선택을 하는 데 시간이 걸린다는 말의 의도

화자가 중반부에 냉장고 문이 장시간 열려 있는 것(~ the refrigerator doors being left open for extended periods of time)과 관련해 우리 음식의 신선도와 안전성을 해칠 수 있어 우려된다(This is alarming because it compromises the freshness and safety of our food)고 말한 뒤 인용문을 언급하는 것으로 보아, 고객들이 냉장고 문을 열고 오랫동안 음식을 고르는 것이 문제임을 강조하려고 한 말임을 알 수 있다. 따라서 정답은 (C)이다.

95-97 회의 발췌 + 등록 양식

W-Am **95 First, I'd like to welcome our new employees.** Won-Sahng Kwon has joined the human resources department as a junior associate, and So-Jin Cho is our newest chief of building security. Welcome! Next, I want to inform everyone about an upcoming recommended safety workshop. Links to the registration form have been e-mailed. When filling out the registration form, **96 you do not need to fill in the street address. Leave that field blank.** Do enter your work e-mail in the appropriate place. Finally, don't forget that **97 the cafeteria will be closed next week**, so you'll need to bring your lunch.

먼저, 우리 신입 직원들을 환영하고 싶습니다. 권원상 씨는 인사부에 사원급으로 합류하셨고, 조조진 씨는 신임 건물 보안 책임자이십니다. 환영합니다! 다음으로 모두에게 곧 있을 권장 안전 워크숍에 대해 알려 드리고자 합니다. 등록 양식 링크가 이메일로 발송되었습니다. 등록 양식을 작성하실 때, **거리 주소란은 기재하지 않으셔도 됩니다. 그 항목은 빈칸으로 남겨 두세요.** 여러분의 회사 이메일은 해당 란에 반드시 입력해 주십시오. 마지막으로, **다음 주에 구내식당이 문을 닫으니**, 점심을 가져오셔야 한다는 것을 잊지 마시기 바랍니다.

어휘 chief 책임자, ~장 upcoming 곧 있을, 다가오는 inform 알리다 registration 등록 form 양식, 서식 fill out 작성하다 fill in 기입하다 blank 빈; 빈칸 appropriate 해당하는, 적합한 cafeteria 구내식당

Workshop Registration
1. Name
   [First]   [Last]
96 2. Street Address
3. Telephone Number
4. E-mail

워크숍 등록
1. 성명
   [이름]   [성]
2. 거리 주소
3. 전화번호
4. 이메일

95 How does the speaker begin the meeting?
(A) By announcing contest winners
(B) By reading a new policy
(C) By distributing a sign-up sheet
(D) By introducing new employees

화자는 어떻게 회의를 시작하는가?
(A) 콘테스트 수상자들을 발표하는 것으로
(B) 새로운 정책을 읽어 주는 것으로
(C) 가입 신청서를 나눠 주는 것으로
(D) 신입 직원들을 소개하는 것으로

어휘 distribute 나눠 주다, 배부하다 sign-up 가입, 등록

해설 세부 사항 관련 – 화자가 회의를 시작하는 방식

화자가 초반부에 먼저 신입 직원들을 환영하고 싶다(First, I'd like to welcome our new employees)고 언급하면서 두 사람을 소개하고 있으므로 정답은 (D)이다.

96 Look at the graphic. Which section does the speaker say the listeners should leave blank?
(A) Section 1
(B) **Section 2**
(C) Section 3
(D) Section 4

시각 정보에 의하면, 화자는 청자들에게 어느 항목을 빈칸으로 남겨 놓으라고 말하는가?
(A) 항목 1
(B) **항목 2**
(C) 항목 3
(D) 항목 4

해설 **시각 정보 연계 – 빈칸으로 남겨야 하는 항목**
화자가 중반부에 거리 주소란은 기재하지 않아도 된다(~ you do not need to fill in the street address)며 그 항목은 빈칸으로 남겨 두라(Leave that field blank)고 말하고 있고, 등록 양식에서 거리 주소란은 항목 2에 해당하므로 정답은 (B)이다.

97 What does the speaker say will happen next week?
(A) **A cafeteria will be closed.**
(B) Free snacks will be provided.
(C) Certificates will be distributed.
(D) New ID badges will be issued.

화자는 다음 주에 무슨 일이 있을 것이라고 말하는가?
(A) **구내식당이 문을 닫을 것이다.**
(B) 무료 간식이 제공될 것이다.
(C) 수료증이 배부될 것이다.
(D) 새 사원증이 발급될 것이다.

어휘 certificate 수료증, 자격증 issue 발급하다, 지급하다

해설 **세부 사항 관련 – 다음 주에 있을 일**
화자가 후반부에 다음 주에 구내식당이 문을 닫는다(~ the cafeteria will be closed next week ~)는 것을 잊지 말라고 했으므로 정답은 (A)이다.

98-100 전화 메시지 + 안내판

M-Au Hi, Marta. **⁹⁸This is Oleg from Sola Salon returning your call. You wanted to know about my availability for haircuts**—yes, I am accepting new clients. **⁹⁹This week, I can fit you in on Wednesday at four o'clock. Please let me know whether that day and time work for you.** And in case you didn't know, there's a parking garage with reasonable rates right under our building. ¹⁰⁰**A full styling session takes about one and a half hours, so you won't need to park for more than two hours in the garage.**

안녕하세요, 마타. 회신 전화를 드리는 솔라 미용실의 올렉입니다. 헤어컷 가능 여부를 문의하셨죠. 네, 신규 고객도 받고 있습니다. 이번 주에는 수요일 4시에 시간을 낼 수 있습니다. 그 날짜와 시간이 괜찮으신지 알려 주세요. 그리고 혹시 모르실까 봐 말씀드리면, 저희 건물 바로 아래에 합리적인 요금의 주차장이 있습니다. 전체 스타일링 시간이 약 한 시간 반 정도 걸리니, 주차장에 두 시간 이상 주차하실 필요는 없을 겁니다.

어휘 availability 이용 가능성, 가능 여부 accept 받다 fit ~ in ~을 만날 시간을 내다 in case ~할 경우에 (대비해) reasonable 합리적인, 알맞은 rate 요금 garage 주차장

PARKING RATES	
1 hour or less	$3.00
¹⁰⁰ 1–3 hours	**$5.00**
3–5 hours	$7.00
5–8 hours	$9.00

주차 요금	
1시간 이하	3달러
1–3시간	**5달러**
3–5시간	7달러
5–8시간	9달러

98 Where does the speaker work?
(A) **At a hair salon**
(B) At a doctor's office
(C) At a talent agency
(D) At a photographer's studio

화자는 어디에서 일하는가?
(A) **미용실**
(B) 병원
(C) 연예 기획사
(D) 사진작가의 작업실

해설 **전체 내용 관련 – 화자의 근무 장소**
화자가 초반부에 회신 전화하는 솔라 미용실의 올렉(This is Oleg from Sola Salon returning your call)이라고 자신을 소개하면서 청자가 헤어컷 서비스를 문의한 것(You wanted to know about my availability for haircuts ~)에 대해 언급하고 있으므로 정답은 (A)이다.

99 What does the speaker ask the listener to do?
(A) Write an online review
(B) Confirm an appointment
(C) Submit a form
(D) Download an application

화자는 청자에게 무엇을 해 달라고 요청하는가?
(A) 온라인 후기 작성하기
(B) 예약 확인하기
(C) 양식 제출하기
(D) 신청서 다운로드하기

어휘 submit 제출하다   application 신청서, 지원서

해설 세부 사항 관련 – 화자의 요청 사항

화자가 중반부에 이번 주에는 수요일 4시에 시간을 낼 수 있다(This week, I can fit you in on Wednesday at four o'clock)며 그 날짜와 시간이 괜찮은지 알려 달라(Please let me know whether that day and time work for you)고 요청하고 있다. 이는 해당 예약 일정을 확인해 달라는 뜻이므로 정답은 (B)이다.

> **Paraphrasing**
> 담화의 let me know whether that day and time work for you → 정답의 Confirm an appointment

100 Look at the graphic. How much will the listener most likely pay for parking?
(A) $3.00
(B) $5.00
(C) $7.00
(D) $9.00

시각 정보에 의하면, 청자는 주차하는 데 얼마를 지불할 것 같은가?
(A) 3달러
(B) 5달러
(C) 7달러
(D) 9달러

해설 시각 정보 연계 – 청자가 지불할 주차 요금

화자가 후반부에 주차장에 대해 안내하면서 전체 스타일링 시간이 약 한 시간 반 정도 걸리니, 주차장에 두 시간 이상 주차할 필요는 없을 것(A full styling session takes about one and a half hours, so you won't need to park for more than two hours in the garage)이라고 했다. 안내판에서 1~3시간 요금은 5달러이므로 정답은 (B)이다.